THE SINEWS OF INDEPENDENCE: monthly strength reports of the Continental Army, ed. by Charles H. Lesser. Chicago, 1976. 262p il tab bibl (Clements Library Bicentennial studies, v.2) 75-12227. 12.50. ISBN 0-226-47332-5. C.I.P.

This reference book should be in every library seeking to collect standard works on the American Revolution. It is a suitable companion to the same publisher's recent *The toll of independence,* edited by Howard H. Peckham (CHOICE, May 1975). As the earlier book gave us hitherto unavailable accurate statistics of American casualties in the Revolutionary War, so the present volume offers unprecedentedly complete statistics of American military strength, including officers, noncommissioned officers, staff officers, rank and file, sick present, sick absent, on command and extra service, confined, deaths in a given period, desertions, taken prisoner, discharged, and joined in a given period. The foundation of the volume is the "elephant folio" in the William L. Clements Library at the University of Michigan, the most complete available manuscript of Continental Army strength returns. Painstaking research has supplemented the folio — though our knowledge of strength of and regiments composing the Continental Army will never be as complete as our knowledge [illegible] later wars. A helpful introduction suggests uses for the statistics [illegible]nd the obvious use of enhancing understanding of battles and campaigns.

THE SINEWS OF INDEPENDENCE

CHARLES H. LESSER served as research editor of the American Revolution Bicentennial Project, William L. Clements Library. He is assistant director for archives and publication at the Department of Archives and History of the state of South Carolina.

Clements Library Bicentennial Studies

This series is made possible by a grant from
Lilly Endowment, Inc.

The Toll of Independence: Engagements & Battle Casualties of the American Revolution, edited by Howard H. Peckham

The Sinews of Independence: Monthly Strength Reports of the Continental Army, edited by Charles H. Lesser

THE SINEWS OF INDEPENDENCE

Monthly Strength Reports of the Continental Army

Edited by

CHARLES H. LESSER

★ ★ ★ ★ ★ ★ ★ ★ ★ ★ ★ ★ ★

THE UNIVERSITY OF CHICAGO PRESS

Chicago *London*

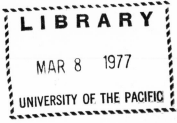

THE UNIVERSITY OF CHICAGO PRESS, CHICAGO 60637
THE UNIVERSITY OF CHICAGO PRESS, LTD., LONDON

Library of Congress Cataloging in Publication Data
Main entry under title:

The Sinews of independence.

(Clements Library bicentennial studies; v. 2)
Bibliography: p.
Includes index.
1. United States. Army. Continental Army—Registers. 2. United States—History—Revolution, 1775-1783—Registers, lists, etc. 3. United States—History—Revolution, 1775-1783—Sources. I. Lesser, Charles H. II. Series.
E259.S56 973.3'4 75-12227
ISBN 0-226-47332-5

CONTENTS

ILLUSTRATIONS

FOREWORD

Few books in the Clements Library have posed as much challenge to us as the "elephant folio," a manuscript volume of army strength returns kept under Adjutants General Alexander Scammell and Edward Hand during the American Revolution. Since the entries in this folio date back only to March 1778, we wondered if there were any earlier record books kept by other adjutants general. If not, could reports for the beginning of the war be compiled from the returns published in Peter Force's *American Archives* and from the papers of other generals? Where could the money be found to publish such data?

The approaching Bicentennial observance of the Revolution stirred us to action. We had other questions about the war which were unanswered. Formulation of those inquiries into an application to Lilly Endowment, Inc., produced a grant to the Clements Library to finance several statistical investigations. The first result was my book, *The Toll of Independence: Engagements & Battle Casualties of the American Revolution*. The present work is the second volume in the Clements Library Bicentennial Studies; others, emphasizing source materials, will follow.

Statistics may not be fun to read, but they are important. Here they are not just numbers; they represent real people identified by regimental units, commanders' names, locations each month, and the disposition of the men. Study of these neutral numbers provides a picture of the struggle to create an army; they give dimensions to an amorphous body. For the first time we have the best available figures, albeit not always complete, on the month-by-month strength of the American forces in the field. They show alarming variations of "effectives" (fit for duty) according to the fortunes of war. The great care with which the figures were assembled is apparent throughout the volume in the footnotes, the citing of sources, and the careful notation of variant readings. At every stage of the editorial work the numbers have been meticulously proofread.

It is safe to say that Dr. Lesser knows more about the size of the American forces which were available to General Washington than Washington himself knew. He has found returns that never reached headquarters; he has totaled unit reports; he has corrected numerous errors that were made on the original manuscripts; and he has created monthly reports from late submissions. The result is a solid reference work which should be useful in a variety of ways.

Howard H. Peckham, Director
William L. Clements Library
University of Michigan

INTRODUCTION

"Without those Returns," wrote George Washington in 1776, "it is impossible that the business of the Army can be conducted with any degree of regularity or propriety."[1] From the very beginning of his service as commander in chief until the end of the war, Washington considered regular reports of the army's strength to be "of the utmost importance"[2] and pondered them as the most basic data necessary for making decisions. Although the statistical material contained in the reports on the various regiments and brigades provides some of the most fundamental information about the rebel army, the documents have heretofore remained largely unpublished and little used, scattered in a number of manuscript repositories. The present volume makes these sources readily available.

The primary focus of the records, of course, is on the Continental Army, that often ragged body of men who provided the sinews of the revolutionary movement. Unfortunately, the term "Continental Army" is shrouded in ambiguities and requires definition. There were, in fact, three categories of soldiers who fought for the colonial cause: the Continental soldier, the militiaman, and the state soldier. The most regular of these was the Continental soldier, the man who had enlisted for a lengthy term of service (or for the duration of the war), who was paid by the Continental congress, and who served in a clearly defined Continental unit. If Washington's desires had come to fruition, his army would have consisted entirely of such men, and the calling out of militia would have been limited to extraordinary events. For most of the war, however, these Continental soldiers did not materialize in sufficient numbers; the colonies were often unable to meet their quotas of recruits. The result was that, at many times during the war, Continental troops were inadequate for carrying on what Washington regarded as a proper campaign.

Driven by necessity, the general frequently had to fill out his forces with the other two categories of warriors, the militiamen and the state soldiers.

1. George Washington, General Orders, Jan. 8, 1776, *The Writings of George Washington*, ed. John C. Fitzpatrick, 39 vols. (Washington: Government Printing Office, 1931-44), 4: 223.

2. Washington, New York, June 16, 1776, to Brigadier General John Sullivan, *Writings of Washington*, 5: 150.

Coopted into the Continental Army (and put into the pay of Continental Congress), these men thus form a substantial, if irregular, component of our statistical records. The revolutionary legislatures of the new states required most able-bodied males between certain ages to be members of the militia. Though the criteria for inclusion varied, at least by law the militia was virtually coextensive with the male population, except for children and the aged. Some of these militiamen were called into service, as needed, for periods ranging from a few days to several weeks or months and might even march outside their state; but at any given time the majority of them were at home pursuing their everyday civilian activities. The various states also needed more regular troops than the militia provided and therefore organized state regiments. These state soldiers served in units that were formed for a given number of months and for a particular purpose (perhaps to guard the state's frontiers). Normally the men were drafted or "levied" from the militia, with each militia regiment required to furnish a certain number of men. Thus the state troops were sometimes known as "levies." They also served occasionally in other states when special needs arose.

These then are the three categories of revolutionary soldiers, and they may be thought of as functioning in a hierarchy ranging from the regular Continental soldier, down through the man in the state regiments (or levies), to the all-encompassing militiaman. There were wide variations in the way that each state organized its regiments, so that what constituted a militia or state regiment in one situation acquired a different cast under other circumstances. Furthermore, from the viewpoint of the Continental officers, any unit other than a Continental regiment was sometimes considered simply militia; extant records occasionally reflect this confusion. Continental, state, and militia regiments all appeared at various times in the strength reports of the Continental Army, but state and militia units were not included unless they were in Continental service.[3]

The Creation of the Reports and Their Subsequent History

The history of these records points up their considerable importance. The first item in Continental Congress's initial instructions to Washington was "to make a return to us as soon as possible of all the forces which you shall have under your command." A resolution had already been passed providing for an adjutant general who would have charge of such records and who would

3. Although scattered strength reports do exist for militia and state regiments not serving in the Continental Army, it would be impossible to do anything systematic with them. We have kept to the criteria used by the adjutants that a regiment had to be serving with the Continental Army or be in Continental pay if it was to be included in the reports. The only exceptions are the state and militia units included on the same manuscript with two Continental regiments in March 1776 and the exception noted on the December 1775 report.

receive pay equal to that of a brigadier general.[4] Washington carried out his instructions. Immediately upon assuming command of the New England troops besieging Boston (July 2, 1775), he ordered that the commanding officer of each regiment "make two Returns of the Number of men in their respective Regiments, distinguishing such as are sick, wounded or absent on furlough, and also the quantity of ammunition each Regim. now has."[5]

A few days after Washington was chosen commander in chief, Horatio Gates was appointed by Continental Congress as the first adjutant general. Before the end of the war ten men had filled this office:[6]

Horatio Gates	June 17, 1775-June 5, 1776
Joseph Reed	June 5, 1776-Jan. 13, 1777
George Weedon (Acting)	Jan. 13, 1777-March 1, 1777
Arthur St. Clair Isaac Budd Dunn } (Acting)	March 1, 1777-April 9, 1777
Morgan Connor (Acting)	April 9, 1777-June 18, 1777
Timothy Pickering	June 18, 1777-Jan. 5, 1778
Alexander Scammell	Jan. 5, 1778-Jan. 1, 1781
Otho Holland Williams (Acting)	Dec. 25, 1779-April 11, 1780
Edward Hand	Jan. 8, 1781-Nov. 3, 1783

Under their direction the rebelling Continental Army kept surprisingly extensive records.

The form of those records, indeed much of the organization of the army, was but an adaptation of the British practices with which the colonists were familiar. Officers could turn to an American reprint of Thomas Simes's *Military Guide for Young Officers*[7] to find the basic format for strength

4. U.S. Continental Congress, *Journals of the Continental Congress, 1774-1789*, 34 vols. (Washington: Government Printing Office, 1904-37), 2: 93-4, 101 [instruction under date of June 20 and resolution of June 16].

5. Washington, General Orders, July 3, 1775, *Writings of Washington*, 3: 305-6.

6. The best list compiled by the army (Gordon R. Young, ed., *The Army Almanac: A Book of Facts Concerning the Army of the United States*, 2d ed. [Harrisburg, Pa.: The Stackpole Co., 1952], pp. 42-43) has a number of errors. As long ago as 1847 William B. Reed (*Life and Correspondence of Joseph Reed*, 2 vols. [Philadelphia: Lindsay and Blackiston, 1847], 1: 299) correctly noted that Weedon was Reed's acting successor, but the *Army Almanac* incorrectly lists St. Clair. St. Clair later supervised his aide-de-camp Isaac Budd Dunn, but Dunn was the one actually named acting adjutant general in Washington's general orders. Otho Holland Williams's term as acting adjutant general was during the time that Alexander Scammell was temporarily absent on leave. Williams later was deputy adjutant general for the Southern Department. See *Writings of Washington*, 7: 5, 190, 218, and 382; 8: 264; 17: 320; and 18: 249.

7. Two vols. (Philadelphia: J. Humphreys, R. Bell, and R. Aitken, 1776), 1: 271. The Clements Library has copies of a number of other guides that were reprinted, but

reports as well as instruction in all manner of things from tactics to funerals. Returns of strength, made out on both a weekly and a monthly basis, reported the number and condition of the soldiers and, by detailing both the additions and the deaths, desertions, and other subtractions that had occurred in the elapsed interval, accounted for the changes in strength since the last such return. Regular strength reports (or, to use the eighteenth-century term, "returns") were altered slightly in format during the war, but attention to them was constant.[8]

Washington laid particular stress on these reports. When he called his generals together for a council of war in order to make tactical decisions, one of his first items of business was always to give the best possible idea of the numbers of men who could be relied upon, based on the latest returns. Similarly, Washington used the same records to tell the various governors and legislatures the status of the regiments the states had supplied as well as the number of men needed to fill the states' quotas. He was always careful to include returns of strength in his official reports to Continental Congress and successively to its Board of War and Secretary of War.[9]

As befitted their importance in the management of the Continental Army, several copies were made of each strength return. Unfortunately, what may have been the best file of these reports is no longer extant. In a disastrous fire which struck the offices of the Secretary of War on November 8, 1800, the officially submitted copies of the strength reports were destroyed.[10] Two other extensive runs of these reports have survived. One of these, a huge, bound manuscript of ninety-eight leaves, is a prized holding of the William L. Clements Library at the University of Michigan. Generally referred to as the

---

only Simes, first published in London in 1772, actually prints the form for returns. Louis Clinton Hatch, *The Administration of the American Revolutionary Army* (New York: Longmans, Green, and Co., 1904) yields no information on the subject of returns.

8. The periodic strength return was not the only variety of numerical report compiled by the Revolutionary army. For an example of a different type of statistical record, see the abstracts of musters for the end of the war published in Friedrich Kapp, *The Life of Fredrick William Von Steuben* (New York: Mason Brothers, 1859), pp. 710–26. These tell nothing about the condition or status of the men, but only provide totals for each rank. Occasionally special returns were made out of the numbers of men whose term of service would expire at successive future dates. Of course, there were also returns of provisions, armaments, and other matériel.

9. Examples of these uses are sprinkled generously over the pages in the relevant volumes of Fitzpatrick's edition of the *Writings of Washington*.

10. Mabel E. Deutrich, *Struggle for Supremacy; the Career of General Fred C. Ainsworth* (Washington: Public Affairs Press, 1962), p. 53.

"elephant folio"[11] of Washington returns, this volume is the most important source for our monthly reports. Its unique value is that it contains the only known surviving copies of monthly strength reports compiled at the regimental level for the bulk of the war. The other extant run of strength returns, located in the National Archives, generally gives only brigade totals, not figures for individual regiments.[12] Since brigades were only temporary organizational units during the American Revolution, and because they often contained regiments from different states, brigade totals are not nearly as useful as are the figures for each individual regiment.

The precise origin of the elephant folio is unknown. In October 1924 the Michigan industrialist William L. Clements went to Ann Arbor for a meeting of the Committee of Management of the library of Americana which he had recently given to the University of Michigan. While at the meeting Clements told the library's young director about "two large folios pertaining to the Revolution"[13] sent to him on approval by the book company of the late George D. Smith. The next year the library acquired both the volume of returns and the other "large folio," a William Howe orderly book. "The Statistical Account of Washington's Army," which director Randolph G. Adams thought "of such enormous importance that I cannot but feel we should make every effort to secure it,"[14] became a central item in what was then emerging as a major repository of Revolutionary materials.

Although the provenance of the elephant folio cannot be traced any further than this appearance in 1924,[15] the manuscript must have originally been a part of the headquarters' files. With the exception of an additional return

11. Actually, "atlas folio" would be the more correct term in library terminology. The leaves of the manuscript measure 52.5 by 73.5 cm. and contain entries in several hands.

12. The National Archives file of these documents does, however, include returns for 1775 and 1776 that, although not the monthly reports, are to the regimental level. As explained below, we were able to use these manuscripts as substitutes for the monthly returns that are missing for the opening months of the war.

13. William L. Clements, Bay City, Mich., Oct. 27, 1924, to Randolph G. Adams, Randolph G. Adams Papers, Clements Library.

14. Randolph G. Adams, Oct. 31, 1924, to William L. Clements, Clements Papers, Clements Library.

15. Clements was negotiating to buy a collection of fine bindings for his personal library in Bay City. The purchase of the elephant folio and the Howe orderly book by the library in Ann Arbor became a part of the deal for the bindings, but nothing was mentioned about where Smith (the preeminent book dealer of his day) or Smith's company had acquired the two volumes. In the deflated book market of the period after Smith's death, a mere $500 purchased both of these important manuscripts. Although

mounted on the back fly-leaf (which appears to have been from a different source and added to the volume at a later date), the returns bear neither the marginal notes nor the signatures that would have appeared on officially submitted copies. Unfortunately, the present opening leaves of the manuscript have been damaged, and earlier pages of the volume have disappeared entirely. What are now the first leaves of the volume look as if they may have been chewed by mice at the corners. The first surviving leaf contains the last few lines of the February 1778 monthly return. Any earlier pages, probably more extensively damaged, may well have been removed when the original binding was repaired at some point in the past. Because the manuscript is not now complete, we had to look elsewhere for the statistics for the first part of the war.[16]

The second of the two major surviving files of strength reports provided most of those missing statistics. These returns, which are now in the Record Group 93 of the National Archives, also have gaps, but they do supply much that is not available in the Clements Library folio. This second body of returns consists of signed and annotated copies that were retained in George Washington's military papers. When the federal government (by acts of Congress of 1834 and 1849) purchased the Washington papers, these returns came into the custody of the State Department. In the 1890s Colonel Fred C. Ainsworth (head of the War Department's Record and Pension Office) secured congressional approval for the transfer of all the muster rolls, returns, orderly books, and other similar military materials in the Washington papers to the War Department. Thus these copies of strength reports that had been kept as part of Washington's own records became separated from his papers and were

---

Smith was involved with some fake Washington items shortly before his death, there can be no question of the elephant folio's authenticity. Its hundreds of thousands of figures match the other surviving run of these reports. What is known of the volume's origin can be traced in the files of correspondence between Clements and Adams in the Clements and Adams Papers in the Clements Library and also in the George D. Smith folder in the Clements Papers; in Accession No. 340, Clements Library Book Accession Records; and in Randolph G. Adams, Jan. 15, 1925, to George P. Winship, Clements Library Correspondence, Michigan Historical Collections / Bentley Historical Library. See also Charles F. Heartman, *George D. Smith: G.D.S., 1870-1920* (Beauvoir Community, Miss.: privately printed, 1945), and Margaret Maxwell, *Shaping a Library: William L. Clements as Collector* (Amsterdam: Nico Israel, 1973), pp. 190-92, 194-95.

16. The elephant folio contains no monthly returns for the months August 1781-January 1782 inclusive, but it would seem these reports never were a part of the volume. The opening pages of the Howe orderly book acquired in the same purchase are also damaged.

deposited in the National Archives as a part of the War Department Collection of Revolutionary War Records.[17]

This second run of strength reports has until now been the only set of these records to receive even minimal attention. In the early nineteenth century Peter Force had these "Continental Army Returns" completely transcribed for use in his projected *American Archives*. Force's gargantuan effort at printing the colonial and Revolutionary records of the United States never got beyond nine folio volumes covering the years 1774-76, but the volumes for 1775 and 1776 did accurately print strength reports for that period, and the transcripts (in the Force Papers in the Library of Congress) have seen use by scholars. The National Archives has recently made the original returns more accessible by including them in a microfilm publication.[18]

THE STRUGGLE TO OBTAIN COMPLETE AND TIMELY REPORTS

Washington's adjutants expected to receive regularly all the returns necessary to compile general strength reports for the whole Continental Army, including all departments, outposts, and independent commands. Submitting monthly returns was a requirement of the articles of war; a court martial was specified for officers accused of neglect or falsehood in this crucial matter.[19] Before Washington took command of the New England army, General Artemas

17. Mabel E. Deutrich and Howard H. Wehmann, *Preliminary Inventory of the War Department Collection of Revolutionary War Records* (Washington: The National Archives, 1970), pp. 1-2; John C. Fitzpatrick, Introduction, *Writings of Washington*, 1: xl-xlii, xlviii-li; and Deutrich, *Struggle for Supremacy*, pp. 52-56.

18. Peter Force, comp., *American Archives: Consisting of a Collection of Authentick Records, State Papers, Debates, and Letters and Other Notices of Publick Affairs. . .*, 9 vols. (Washington: Peter Force, 1837-53). The general strength returns in Record Group 93 are contained in reels 136-38 and reel 116 of Microcopy 246. The latter reel has artillery returns for 1775 and 1776 that were unfortunately separated from the main group of returns when the papers were rearranged in the War Department.

19. Articles 62 and 63 of the resolution of Congress of May 10, 1775 and Section V of the later resolves of Sept. 20, 1776. U.S. Continental Congress, *Rules and Articles for the Better Government of the Troops Raised, or to be raised, and kept in pay by and at the joint Expence of the Twelve United English Colonies of North America* (Philadephia: William and Thomas Bradford, 1775); U.S. Continental Congress, *Rules and Articles for the Better Government of the Troops Raised or to be Raised and kept in Pay by and at the Expense of the United States of America* (Philadelphia: John Dunlap, 1776) and later editions of the latter, (Boston: Benjamin Edes, 1777) and (Charlestown: John Wells, Jun., 1780), all in the Clements Library.

Ward's orders about returns had met with only "imperfect Obedience."[20] Washington's firm insistence on accurate records[21] secured a remarkable degree of compliance, at least from those officers in the proximity of both the main army and the feathered hats of the adjutant general and his assistants (a red-and-green feather was the distinguishing mark of their uniform).[22]

Such was not always the case with those portions of the Continental Army stationed at distant points. When Washington became commander in chief, the only detached command was the force in New York state, which Continental Congress had placed under Major General Philip Schuyler; Washington immediately ordered Schuyler "to make regular Returns to me, once a Month and to the Continental Congress, and oftener as Occurrences may require, of the forces under your Command, of your Provisions, Stores, &c."[23] Later, Washington persuaded Congress to pass a resolution to make "the Commanding Officers in the different Districts . . . more attentive than they otherwise would be" to the necessity of making "Monthly returns to the Commander in Chief of the Continental Army, of the State of their Troops in their department."[24] Deputy adjutants general were appointed for the larger detached commands.[25] Despite his frequent requests, Washington's hopes for monthly returns from distant points were seldom realized. More often than not, no reports were received from such places as the Southern Department and Fort Pitt.

"I could not get a return of the Army in Canada, all last year," Washington complained in the spring of 1776.[26] Later, the annotations on his copies of the strength reports echoed the same problem. Endlessly, the adjutants general were forced to note that they had received no returns for various military units at remote places. Only late in the war did they give up, change the heading on

20. Washington, Cambridge, July 10, 1775, to the President of Congress, *Writings of Washington*, 3: 323.

21. For just a few of a great many examples, see *Writings of Washington*, 4: 205, 223, 225; 6: 12-13; 16: 11-13.

22. At least this was their uniform late in the war. Washington, General Orders, July 14, 1780, *Writings of Washington*, 19: 172-73.

23. Washington, New York, June 25, 1775, to Philip Schuyler, *Writings of Washington*, 3: 303.

24. Washington, New York, May 5, 1776, to the President of Congress, *Writings of Washington*, 5: 16-17. The resolution was passed on May 10.

25. The Western Department was considered too small to need such an officer, although it was expected that returns would be received from Fort Pitt. Washington, Middle Brook, May 3, 1779, to Colonel Daniel Brodhead, *Writings of Washington*, 14: 482.

26. Washington, New York, May 5, 1776, to the President of Congress, *Writings of Washington*, 5: 17.

their monthly general returns, and cease pretending that their reports reflected anything other than that part of the Continental Army "under the immediate command of his excellency George Washington."[27] Considering the means of transportation then available, these difficulties should come as no surprise. When reports did arrive from distant colonies, often a month or more had passed since they had been made out.

This volume seeks to surmount the deficiencies in the general returns caused by data that were late in arriving and by returns that were not received at all. A massive search for manuscript returns was the first step in this remedial effort. The editor, together with the research team that sought battle reports for volume one of our Clements Library Bicentennial Studies, combed federal and state archives and historical societies in the eastern part of the United States. We sought to fill the gaps in the extant runs of general returns as well as to find strength reports for those detached commands whose data never reached Continental headquarters. Despite the fact that archivists have seldom differentiated these records from muster rolls and other similar lists of names, we have succeeded in uncovering a considerable body of statistical returns.[28] This material enabled us to supplement the data in the two surviving series of reports made out at Washington's headquarters. On each edited report in the text of this volume, a separate section lists the sources for that month; principal manuscripts (or, in some cases, printed transcriptions) and their locations are cited in capital letters. Variant manuscripts and any previous printings are listed in lower case immediately thereafter.[29] In those places where we have utilized these additional records in some way, our departure from the principal source has been carefully noted. The bibliography contains a consolidated list of manuscript collections which yielded usable material.

27. This admission first appeared on the July 1781 monthly return. Weekly returns had never attempted to report on more than Washington's "immediate command." As well, weekly returns were almost always made out only to the brigade level (even in the Clements folio). The exceptions (compiled regiment by regiment) are the returns for early in the war in the National Archives.

28. Returns were originally made out by individual regiments, then compiled for brigades, and finally for the whole department or area. Scattered regimental returns have survived, but generally we did not attempt the impossible task of reconstructing reports for whole commands from these manuscripts; instead, we searched for the major reports compiled from them at the time. Our most important debts are acknowledged at the end of this introduction. The editor would appreciate learning of any significant monthly general returns (not for single regiments or brigades) that may have been missed.

29. Except in the few cases where they were actually used, we have not listed the transcripts in the Peter Force Papers of the run of returns that is now in the National Archives.

Monthly returns were supposed to give the state of the Continental Army at the end of the month for which they were compiled, but the adjutants had to do the best they could with whatever data was available, even if it was occasionally several months old. Usually the adjutants general carefully noted which sections of the returns were based on late-arriving reports from distant places. As a result, we have been able to remove those sections of the returns and place them with the proper month's report. In each case, we have attached an explanatory note. If the figures for a distant place were not so annotated, we kept them with the month's report where they appeared in the manuscript. The reader is cautioned, therefore, that in those few instances where statistics for places like Fort Pitt appear without comment, they may actually represent conditions a month or more earlier.

To distinguish between the original manuscripts and our modern compilations, in the body of this volume we have always used the eighteenth-century term "return" to refer to our sources and the word "report" to indicate our edited data. Despite our numerous additions, the reports are usually incomplete; a footnote has been attached to the total figure whenever annotations on the manuscripts supply names of military units for which no returns were available.

EXPLANATION OF THE DATA AND EDITORIAL PROCEDURES

In order to make this volume more readily usable and of a size that was financially feasible to publish, a number of other editorial steps were taken which require explanation. In addition, some information about what the adjutants reported in the various columns is needed. For convenience, these items will be discussed in the order in which the columns appear on our finished reports, moving from left to right. An occasional glance at those reports may make this technical section of the introduction more intelligible.

The columns at the extreme left of the reports identify who is being reported. The names of military units and their commanders are often perplexingly brief on the original returns, especially early in the war. We have supplied complete identifications of the regiments or other military units, together with the full name and rank of the commanding officer. In this regard, Francis B. Heitman's *Historical Register of Officers of the Continental Army during the War of the Revolution, April, 1775 to December, 1783*[30] was useful, though many of the entries proved to be either inaccurate or inadequate. The wide variety of other resources used to track down regimental

30. (1893; reprint ed., with revisions and supplements of 1914 and 1932, Baltimore: Genealogical Publishing Co., 1973). Fred Anderson Berg, *Encyclopedia of Continental Army Units; Battalions, Regiments, and Independent Corps* (Harrisburg: Stackpole Books, 1972) is of some value, but, along with other limitations, it attempts thorough treatment of only the Continental units.

histories and officers' careers is presented in the bibliography. It was impossible to footnote each time we researched an officer's first name or filled out an incomplete regimental designation, but we have noted those cases in which we corrected actual errors on the manuscripts.

Since regiments are the units most commonly listed, the word "regiment" is understood unless a company, brigade, or some other type of unit is indicated. All officers are colonels unless otherwise specified. The person entered in the commanding officer column on the returns was not always physically present with his unit. Indeed, the manuscript (and consequently our report) often listed a man who was only nominally in command. "Late" before a name in the context of the strength returns meant only "formerly commanded by"; although the officer in question might have died, he also might have resigned or been promoted to a larger command. Capitalization has been minimized in the unit and officer columns, and abbreviations are used to conserve space. A table of abbreviations appears at the end of this introduction. These first two columns and their accompanying footnotes complete or correct a number of hitherto imperfectly understood points in the history of Revolutionary military organizations.

The statistical data that appear on the strength reports fall into several main divisions. The first of these, "Present Fit for Duty & on Duty," counts those men able and ready to fight who were present at the place where their regiment was stationed. Soldiers in a variety of other conditions swelled the total size of regiments, but it was only those "Present Fit for Duty" who were generally relied upon in case of battle. Some of the less robust and ready men might be pressed into action in dire need. For example, the manuscript of the April 1778 monthly return in the National Archives has calculations on its reverse showing "⅔ of the sick present that might act on an emergency." Similarly, Washington himself in a council of war a few months later referred to "such of the sick present as might be capable of acting on an emergency."[31] In normal circumstances, however, the figures for "Present Fit for Duty" provided the principal index of the effective strength of the army. All other soldiers were in varying degrees ineffective because they were sick, absent, or on some kind of special duty.

Four columns plus a total enumerate the "Present Fit for Duty" in the reports in this volume. Although the sections of the manuscript returns for commissioned, noncommissioned, and staff officers are further divided to give the numbers for each individual rank, considerations of space dictated that only totals for each type of officer be given here. During the Revolution the section for commissioned officers at various times included columns for colonels, lieutenant colonels, majors, captains, subalterns, captain lieutenants, first lieutenants, second lieutenants, and ensigns. Appearing in the noncom-

31. Council of War, Valley Forge, June 17, 1778, *Writings of Washington*, 12: 76.

misioned officers section were sergeant majors, drum majors, fife majors, trumpet majors, sergeants, quartermaster sergeants, bombardiers, gunners, foremen, farriers, saddlers, cadets, drums and fifes, and trumpeters. Chaplains, adjutants, quartermasters, surgeons, mates, conductors, commissaries, contractors, clerks, wagonmasters, riding masters, and paymasters were considered to be staff officers.[32] The "Rank & File" were, of course, the privates, or their equivalent in the artillery, the matrosses.[33] Corporals in the infantry were not counted separately on the manuscript general returns but were included in the figures for rank and file. In the artillery and cavalry, however, corporals were considered noncommissioned officers and are therefore counted in that way on our reports.[34]

As the war progressed, Washington occasionally ordered changes in the form of the returns so as to provide more detail on some subjects. One of these changes, set forth in his General Order of May 27, 1781,[35] affected the "Present Fit for Duty" area on the returns. Men in this category were now subdivided into those who were "Fit for Duty" and those actually "On Duty." Made late in the war, this distinction is not of sufficient importance to merit an extra column here, but it does affect our edited reports. For the artillery and the officers of the infantry, the adjutants unfortunately did not find a way to record those who were "On Duty" regiment by regiment. Because of this, beginning with our June 1781 report (see p. 204), a special "On Duty"line sometimes appears after all the individual regiments are listed. This line gives

32. All of the ranks listed here do not appear on each and every return, but each of them was used as a column heading at some time during the war. Early in the war, brigadier generals were counted differently from the way they were later, and, in this as in other matters, we have scrupulously followed our sources. For most of the war, brigadier generals were not included among commissioned officers "Present Fit for Duty," but were listed as "On the Staff" in the separate section at the foot of the returns for officers who were sick, absent, or doing special duty. With the June 1781 return, brigadier generals begin to appear in the "Present Fit for Duty" section. See footnote A on that report.

33. In the four cases in which the general return included members of the two artificer regiments (Aug. and Sept. 1776, Dec. 1778, and Jan. 1779), rank and file also included carpenters, wheelwrights, masons, blacksmiths, and armourers. General returns normally omitted the Artificer Corps, but we have included them in the few cases where they do appear.

34. In the Invalid Corps corporals were counted as noncommissioned officers until the change in reporting procedures for invalids in January 1782. After that change (explained in footnote A on our April 1779 report) they became like the infantry in this matter. The "Return of the Regiment of Foot in the service of the United States of America, under the command of Colonel Morris Graham, Camp White-Plains, October 31, 1776," in Force, *American Archives* (5th ser., 2: 1321-22), illustrates that corporals in the infantry were considered rank and file.

35. *Writings of Washington*, 22: 122-23.

the total number of these additional effective men. Where this separate "On Duty" line does appear, the figures listed under "Present Fit for Duty & on Duty" for the individual regiments underestimate their actual fighting strength, but it is not possible to know how many of the officers or artillerymen in the "On Duty" total belonged to any particular regiment.

The "Present Fit for Duty & on Duty" portion of the returns provided regular reports of the effective strength of the army. Moving further to the right on the forms (into the area that reported on men who were sick or otherwise ineffective), we find that the reports served the command in a different way. During the Revolution there was a constant fear that the army might melt away through desertion, and to deter any such occurrence deserters were executed when it was felt an example was needed. Given this concern, Washington felt it was necessary to keep close tabs on each and every soldier. The remaining columns on the returns helped to fill this need.

In the figures that make up this right-hand side of the returns, officers are largely ignored. Although the format which the rebels adopted from the British provided for listing the sick and absent officers by name, Washington's early returns did little to enumerate officers beyond those who were in camp and ready to fight (present fit for duty). Later, a section was appended to the bottom of the forms, giving totals for the officers who were infirm, on furlough, or on some special duty,[36] but the general returns never provided these statistics for officers on a regiment-by-regiment basis. On the other hand, a detailed accounting was kept of those rank and file who, for one reason or another, could not be relied on in case of battle. This data provides a fascinating index to the changing fortunes of the various regiments that composed the Continental Army.[37]

Most of the column headings used by the adjutants to report noneffective rank and file are self-explanatory. A few words are needed, however, about the "On Command & Extra Service" column. This column enumerates those soldiers who, because they had received special assignments, could not "be counted upon as part of the effective force of the army."[38] Some of these men were serving for a time in such capacities as servants to officers, waggoners, artificers, butchers, and bakers. Others had been sent on detached military duty and therefore were not available to fight at the place where their military

36. From the beginning, returns for the artillery gave these totals, but these figures for Washington's infantry do not start to be reported until December 1778. The artillery sections of the returns also differed in that they did not break the statistics for rank and file who were sick, absent, or on special duty down to the regimental level as did the other sections of the returns.

37. Judging from the figures for "Present Fit for Duty & on Duty," the rank and file comprised, on the average, about 80 percent of the Continental Army.

38. Washington, General Orders, Jan. 22, 1780, *Writings of Washington*, 17: 424.

unit was stationed. Before 1780 all the men in both of these categories were reported in one column headed "On Command." Washington then ordered that a further distinction be made, and the men performing the civilian tasks began to be listed in an additional column entitled "On Extra Service," while the military detachments remained under "On Command."[39] Although this distinction is of some interest, space considerations (and the nearly insuperable problem that the cavalry and detached commands did not immediately adopt this practice) dictated that our edited reports continue to give a combined figure, just as the manuscripts had for most of the war.

All other figures for "Rank & File Sick, on Furlough, etc." are entered just as they appear in our sources. Both in this division and elsewhere on our edited reports, any exceptions (i.e., places where we have entered figures under a column heading that is not the same as on the manuscript) are footnoted.[40]

The manuscript general returns had separate sections for the infantry, the artillery, the cavalry, the Invalid Corps, and the Sappers and Miners. (The section for the Invalid Corps presented special difficulties for part of the war; see Footnote A on our April 1779 report.) Sometimes one of these sections (e.g., the artillery) reported a category of noneffective men (e.g., "recruiting") that was not used as a separate column by the other sections of the return. Therefore, on our edited reports that extra column is blank except for that particular portion of the army which used this special category. This kind of entry should not necessarily be interpreted to mean that there were no men in that category elsewhere; the point is that men were not reported under that rubric in the other parts of the army.

Blank spaces in the reports merit a more general word of caution; their meaning can often be ambiguous. Unfortunately, the adjutants of the Continental Army did not use zeros to indicate the lack of any men in a particular category. Instead, the appropriate spaces were either simply left blank or marked with a tiny dot. This practice did not distinguish between those cases in which there were no men in a category and those in which there was no information available at all. Especially when no figures are given for a regiment throughout a main division such as "Rank & File Sick, on Furlough, etc.," one should suspect that the adjutants had not received that data, and therefore the statistics are probably incomplete. Footnotes to some of the more significant of these blank areas will remind the reader of this, but careful observation of the data with this problem in mind is strongly recommended.

39. Ibid.

40. With the exception of the problem with the Invalid Corps mentioned in the next paragraph, these departures from the sources are noted on every monthly report where they occur, not just at their first appearance. When a problem involved all the regiments in a brigade or a whole state line on a particular month's return, the footnote letter itself was often attached only to the first affected regiment.

Once one gets into the division of the reports for "Rank & File Sick, on Furlough, etc.," a larger dose of healthy skepticism should be taken. When the men being reported were not physically present, the figures were more likely to be inflated. "I very much suspect," wrote George Washington in 1777, "that a great deal of pay is drawn for Sick Absent who do not exist."[41] Conscious deceit in order to reap financial benefit did not necessarily have to be involved.[42] A more straightforward, frequent problem with this portion of the returns must have been that men who were at first justifiably absent simply never returned. It was difficult to know whether and when these men had deserted, and undoubtedly there was reluctance, as well, to admit large desertion figures. Even with the best of intentions, it must have been exceedingly difficult to be precise. The official strength reports give the best statistics we shall ever have about the Continental Army, but, as with other historical sources, their authors' limitations and potential motives for deception ought not to be overlooked.

Following the enumeration of the effective fighting force and of the sick and absent rank and file, the format for monthly returns provided for a "Wanting to Complete" division. This portion of the return gave officers and governmental officials concerned with recruiting ready access to the number of sergeants, drums and fifes, and rank and file required to bring a regiment up to its designated strength. "Wanting to Complete" figures were kept only for the infantry. Because it is the actual size and makeup of the regiments that are of most interest, not the number of soldiers needed to meet some legislated composition, we have omitted the "Wanting to Complete" columns from our edited reports. A measure of the deficiency of a regiment can be calculated, however, by subtracting the total of its rank and file from the legislated size of the regiment. Following the official organization of the Continental Army on January 1, 1776, the "Establishment" (i.e., the number that a regiment was supposed to have) for a continental infantry regiment was 640 rank and file.[43] A resolution of Congress of May 27, 1778, reduced this unrealized ideal to

41. Washington, Morristown, May 20, 1777, to Brigadier General William Maxwell, *Writings of Washington*, 8: 97. This same letter was sent to eight other brigadier generals.

42. Lieutenant Robert Nicholson of the first North Carolina regiment, for example, was found guilty on May 4, 1779, of "repeatedly signing false returns," but the cause was "neglect and inattention," not deception. In the case of Adjutant Robert Ralston of the first Pennsylvania brigade (Nov. 22, 1777), however, negligence was apparently not the primary factor in "Making a false return, and signing it"; Ralston was cashiered. Washington's approval or disapproval of the sentences of courts-martial were announced in general orders; these cases can be found in the general orders for May 14, 1779 and Dec. 18, 1777, *Writings of Washington*, 15: 70 and 10: 169.

43. Eight companies with seventy-six privates and four corporals each. Washington, General Orders, Nov. 12, 1775, *Writings of Washington*, 4: 86.

504.[44] Prior to 1776, however, it will be nearly impossible to calculate this measure, since the legislated size of the different New England regiments besieging Boston varied widely; [45] as a result, the adjutants themselves only partially attempted to calculate "Wanting to Complete" figures in 1775.

A final main division of the monthly returns, titled "Alterations," served to explain the monthly variations in the size of each regiment. This section reported decreases by death, desertion, discharge, and capture as well as increases by enlistment or other addition to the regiment. No alterations appear on our reports until December 1777; occasionally they are missing after that date. This is because no true monthly returns are available for those periods. When the monthly return did not survive, we were frequently able to substitute another variety of strength return. A weekly return dated near the end of a month supplied most of the same data, but it did not, of course, give us the full month's report on alterations. These other official strength returns are all that are extant for early in the war (and sometimes later), and we have used them to report most of the statistics for the month but have had to leave the alterations blank.[46]

As in other portions of the returns, there were slight changes in the way "Alterations" were reported during the war. A "Taken Prisoner" column was not used by the adjutants until July of 1779.[47] As early as July 1778, Washington ordered that the count of men discharged be subdivided into separate figures for those whose terms of service had expired and for those

44. Nine companies, one of which was light infantry, each with fifty-three privates and three corporals. Announced in Washington, General Orders, June 7, 1778, *Writings of Washington*, 12: 30.

45. Some Massachusetts regiments had ten companies and others had eleven. The official size of Connecticut regiments varied from 600 to 1,000; Rhode Island and New Hampshire had regiments with a uniform 590 (including officers). Washington, Cambridge, Aug. 4, 1775, to the President of Congress, *Writings of Washington*, 3: 391; Mark M. Boatner III, *Encyclopedia of the American Revolution* (New York: David McKay Co., 1966), 927. It should also be noted that the problem of widely varying "Establishments" affected militia and state units off and on throughout the rest of the war.

46. The official monthly returns were compiled in the last few days of the month on which they reported or in the early days of the following month. When they were not extant, we looked for a strength report dated as close as possible to that period and only occasionally included anything more than a few days away from that ideal. Titles and dates of returns used are given on each report. In a few cases the alterations are blank not because no monthly return survived, but because the alterations figures were too irregular or scattered to be of use.

47. Exceptions are the returns for the cavalry for August and October 1778 and the return for Huger's brigade for January 1779.

discharged "For Inability" by the Muster Master General and the surgeons.[48] This new distinction does not appear in the monthly returns until a year later. When this differentiation begins to appear on the July 1779 monthly return, we have supplied a footnote to the discharged column on our edited reports giving the proportion that were discharged "For Inability."[49] There was also some variance in the way additions to the regiments were reported. Generally, figures under the single heading "Joined" failed to distinguish whether the men were new recruits or transfers from another regiment. Although a few returns supplied detail as to how the men had joined, we have followed the bulk of the returns in providing only a combined figure. Footnotes will alert the reader to those cases where the editor feels certain that large additions to a regiment represent reorganization rather than new soldiers.

Although the alterations columns were supposed to account for the change in size of each regiment, it is not always clear exactly which elements the adjutants used in their calculations. We know that commissioned and staff officers were excluded. Therefore, at the maximum, the reports count deaths, desertions, etc., for only somewhat more than 90 percent of any regiment.[50] The situation in regard to noncommissioned officers is less clear. Sergeants and drums and fifes do appear in the figures for "Joined," but these noncommissioned officers may not have been included in the other alterations columns. We have made repeated attempts (using the figures from successive months) to determine precisely who were counted in the other alterations columns, but have not been able to obtain consistent results. To summarize, the monthly alterations figures report on the rank and file and, at least in the "Joined" column, some of the noncommissioned officers, but they do not represent full totals for the entire regiment.[51]

At the far right on our edited monthly reports we have supplied a column giving the location of the various regiments. For the period from November 1778 through October 1780 the manuscripts themselves provide this information for Washington's infantry; we have silently corrected spelling and

48. Washington, General Orders, July 29, 1778, *Writings of Washington*, 12: 247.

49. Until February 1781 this separate column was used only for Washington's infantry. After that date it began to be used elsewhere.

50. Judging from the figures for "Present Fit for Duty & on Duty," commissioned and staff officers formed, on the average, about 7 percent of the Continental Army.

51. Because of this problem in the definition of the alterations division of the return, we felt better justified in omitting (for lack of space) three columns ("Transferred," "Promoted," and "Reduced") which reported merely technical changes in the regiments.

added abbreviations for states.[52] Elsewhere (and for the artillery and cavalry in that period), the locations are a product of our editorial research. If we were not certain where a regiment was stationed at the end of any month, we left this column blank.

When the manuscripts did provide the whereabouts of an encamped regiment, it was often included on a line giving a subtotal for a brigade or for some larger portion of the army. Putting the locations in our right-hand column was but one of several ways in which we presented information that originally appeared on the subtotal lines of the manuscripts. Brigade indications have been moved to the extreme left of our form,[53] and subtotals themselves have been omitted, since, if needed, they can easily be calculated.[54] All totals that do appear are careful new computations. The adjutants or their assistants—without the benefit of modern adding machines—correctly added the very long columns of figures much of the time, but they made many mistakes as well. When stains on the manuscript coincided with notable numbers of errors, we sometimes jokingly conjectured that the problem might have been too much port!

SUGGESTIONS FOR USING THE STATISTICS

The Continental Army's strength reports provide more than just the basic data for writing histories of individual regiments, engagements, or campaigns. Information on the size and condition of military units may indeed enlighten future tales in the great tradition of "drum and bugle" military history, but these statistics should also provide opportunities for more analytic and far-ranging undertakings. Not only specialists in the American Revolution, but also persons interested in the history of medicine, historical demography, and comparative history may find these reports to be a valuable source.

Philip Cash, in his recent book *Medical Men at the Siege of Boston, April, 1775–April, 1776: Problems of the Massachusetts and Continental Armies,*[55] has used the few early returns that have been previously published to provide basic percentages of illness for his discussion of sickness and medical care in

52. Generally we did not research the correctness of those infantry locations which the manuscripts provided. Because the adjutants' notations may have occasionally been out of date or inaccurate, these locations should be used in conjunction with other sources.

53. Since brigades were temporary combinations of regiments which changed frequently, we did not attempt to supply them when they were not given in the returns.

54. Chaplains not connected with any particular regiment in a brigade who appear in the brigade total have been added into the total for staff officers for the last regiment of that brigade. These additions are all footnoted and can be removed when that particular regiment is the object of study.

55. American Philisophical Society Memoirs, vol. 98 (Philadelphia: American Philosophical Society, 1973), pp. 105, 109, 112–13, and Appendix 1.

the opening months of the struggle against Great Britain. We have followed up on Cash's work and, as a small case study in the use of the full series of adjutants' statistics, we offer a table and accompanying graph showing the percentage of the main army's total rank and file who fell sick during the war. The horror of Valley Forge is known to every schoolboy, but other alarming peaks of illness can also be seen. Especially vivid are the last part of 1776 and the smallpox epidemic that broke out when the troops returned north after Yorktown. From the peak of 35.5 percent sick at Valley Forge at the end of February 1778 to more minor variations, the table supplies mathematical measurements to use in conjunction with surviving verbal evidence.

The steps involved in the production of our table and graph illustrate several points about our data and its use. In calculating our percentages we ignored those military units for which there is no data other than those men present fit for duty. If we had included these regiments, it would have distorted the results by erroneously lowering the percentage who were sick. By the same token, we have excluded the figures for the Southern Department and the Canadian expedition. Despite our efforts, reports for these commands remain irregular. The Southern Department has especially poor representation in the extant strength returns; indeed, some of the "missing" reports may well never have been made out. Otho Holland Williams, deputy adjutant general for the Southern Department from the autumn of 1780 until the spring of 1782, insistently complained of a nearly total lack of paper and forms, of officers who could not or would not submit "suitable returns," and of a variety of other obstacles in the performance of his duties.[56] If our percentages had included the figures from the occasional reports for these distant places (with different climates), our measurements of illness would have been randomly distorted. What figures we do have consistently show that many more troops were sick on the Canadian expedition than within the main army; the partial data for the South sometimes also indicate more extensive illness.

In our graph, we have used a dotted line to bridge gaps in the data. The two major breaks in the series of general returns made out by Washington's adjutants general, one for much of 1777 and the other in late 1781, will necessitate similar adjustments in other uses of this volume's statistics. For each of these periods, neither the monthly returns nor a suitable substitute variety of official strength report could be located. In fact, some of these documents never existed. A newly reorganized Continental Army officially went into effect on January 1, 1777, but during the first four months of that year there was nearly total disarray. Officers tried in vain to fully recruit the new

56. Maryland Historical Records Survey, *Calendar of the General Otho Holland Williams Papers in the Maryland Historical Society* (Baltimore: Maryland Historical Records Survey Project, 1940), pp. 24, 31, 33-34, and 36. Among other things, the Southern Department had lost its past records at the battle of Camden.

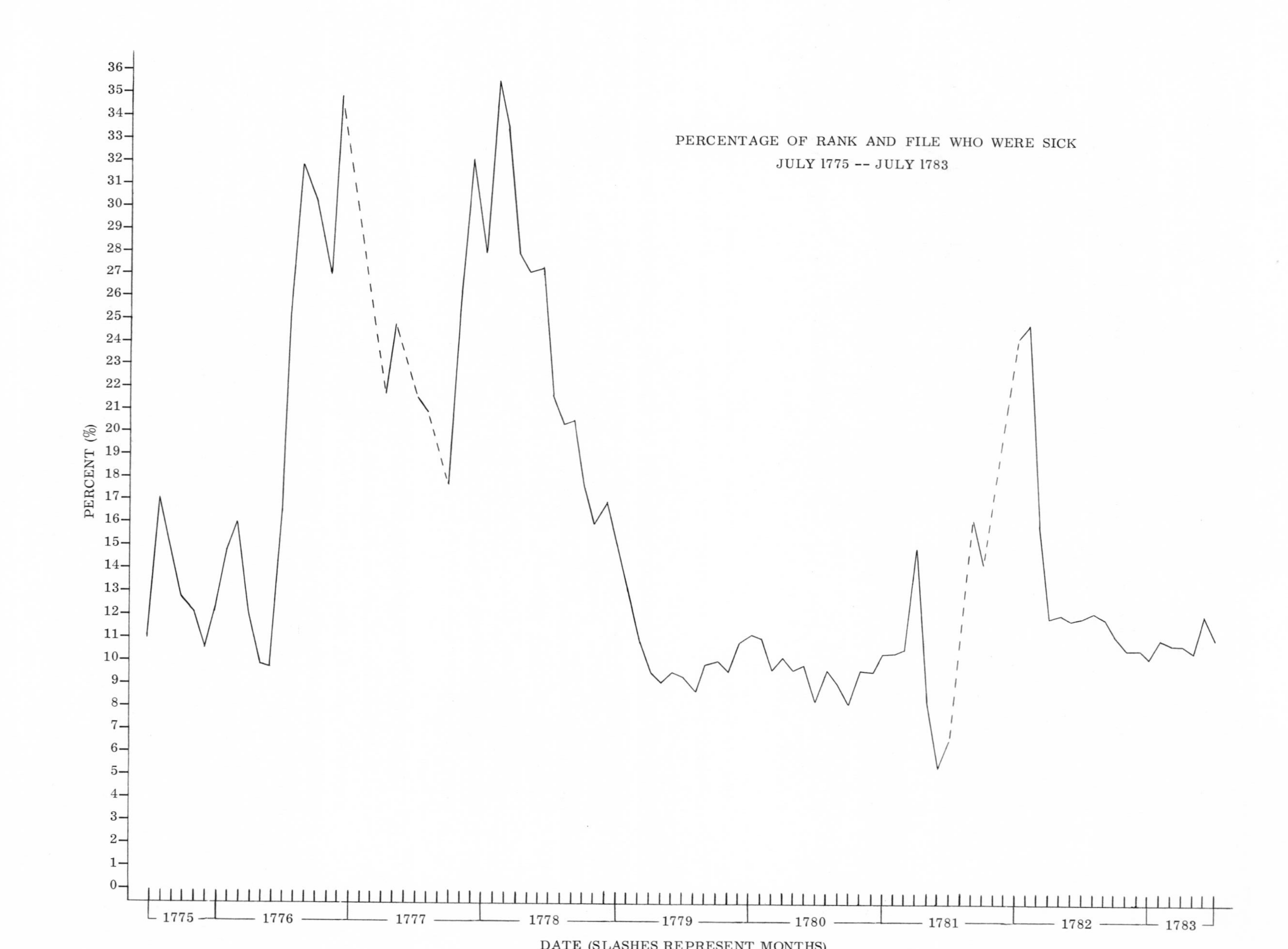
PERCENTAGE OF RANK AND FILE WHO WERE SICK
JULY 1775 -- JULY 1783
PERCENT (%)
36
35
34
33
32
31
30
29
28
27
26
25
24
23
22
21
20
19
18
17
16
15
14
13
12
11
10
9
8
7
6
5
4
3
2
1
0
1775
1776
1777
1778
1779
1780
1781
1782
1783
DATE (SLASHES REPRESENT MONTHS)

PERCENTAGE OF RANK AND FILE WHO WERE SICK

Year	Month	Sick Present	Sick Absent	Sick TOTAL	Rank & File TOTAL	Sick %
1775	July	1409	697	2106	19081	11.0
	August	2381	1176	3557	20823	17.1
	September	1908	946	2854	19253	14.8
	October	1476	952	2428	19048	12.8
	November	1490	812	2302	18831	12.2
	December	1216	552	1768	16668	10.6
1776	January	1422	245	1667	13564	12.3
	February	2417	376	2793	18887	14.8
	March	1071	172	1243	7720	16.1
	April	789	698	1487	12205	12.2
	May	588	308	896	9051	9.9
	June	875	217	1092	11227	9.7
	July	2313	259	2572	15529	16.6
	August	1878	998	2876	11389	25.3
	September	8403	4310	12713	39892	31.9
	October	6225	6190	12415	40962	30.3
	November	2825	3306	6131	22735	27.0
	December	600	2580	3180	9125	34.9
1777	January, February, March	Missing				
	April	199	275	474	2188	21.7
	May	1057	1020	2077	8378	24.8
	June	Missing				
	July	448	481	929	4306	21.6
	August	655	803	1458	6945	21.0
	September	Missing				
	October	1511	4339	5850	33021	17.7
	November	1821	4754	6575	25004	26.3
	December	2087	5008	7095	22047	32.2
1778	January	1455	3598	5053	18033	28.0
	February	3201	3680	6881	19402	35.5
	March	3285	2923	6208	18558	33.5
	April	3798	2311	6109	21848	28.0
	May	3766	1670	5436	20032	27.1
	June	951	5116	6067	22223	27.3
	July	1175	4079	5254	24300	21.6
	August	2270	2927	5197	25422	20.4
	September	2274	4062	6336	30695	20.6
	October	1911	3214	5125	29256	17.5
	November	1749	2979	4728	29483	16.0
	December	1660	3043	4703	28035	16.8
1779	January	1875	2310	4185	27485	15.2
	February	1349	1883	3232	24886	13.0
	March	1265	1283	2548	23288	10.9
	April	1143	993	2136	22279	9.6
	May	975	890	1865	20244	9.2
	June	788	968	1756	18962	9.6
	July	829	1210	2039	21793	9.4
	August	910	754	1664	19052	8.7
	September	1119	844	1963	20077	9.8
	October	1144	1327	2471	24593	10.0
	November	990	932	1922	20394	9.4
	December	931	760	1691	15604	10.8
1780	January	1244	794	2038	18334	11.1
	February	1043	762	1805	16349	11.0
	March	843	598	1441	14843	9.7
	April	660	431	1091	10673	10.2
	May	603	410	1013	10477	9.7
	June	357	572	929	9498	9.8
	July	529	527	1056	12746	8.3
	August	1051	909	1960	20353	9.6
	September	1016	853	1869	21043	8.9
	October	591	581	1172	14317	8.2
	November	465	914	1379	14294	9.7
	December	354	287	641	6723	9.5
1781	January	333	233	566	5468	10.4
	February	248	234	482	4618	10.4
	March	251	293	544	5115	10.6
	April	369	494	863	5804	14.9
	May	406	208	614	7392	8.3
	June	199	271	470	8661	5.4
	July	286	292	578	8737	6.6
	August	Missing				
	September	411	396	807	4995	16.2
	October	1233	805	2038	14240	14.3
	November, December	Missing				
1782	January	1676	620	2296	9469	24.3
	February	1752	503	2255	9080	24.8
	March	924	465	1389	8664	16.0
	April	736	320	1056	8853	11.9
	May	677	392	1069	8842	12.1
	June	756	422	1178	9969	11.8
	July	903	340	1243	10414	11.9
	August	792	503	1295	10603	12.2
	September	725	445	1170	9825	11.9
	October	722	411	1133	10165	11.2
	November	656	442	1098	10359	10.6
	December	715	404	1119	10575	10.6
1783	January	726	312	1038	10202	10.2
	February	787	323	1110	10134	11.0
	March	794	285	1079	10115	10.7
	April	813	238	1051	9807	10.7
	May	798	234	1032	9874	10.5
	June	181	131	312	2577	12.1
	July	203	54	257	2328	11.0

regiments and vaccinate them against smallpox. Repeatedly, Washington had to inform Congress and the Board of War that he could not supply the desired returns.[57] As the army attempted to get organized on its new basis, the turmoil was such that Washington reported, "a Regiment is scarcely the same a Week together."[58] In March he estimated that the present fit for duty figure was under three thousand, all but 981 of which were militia whose terms of service would expire at the end of the month.[59] Washington was not able to submit his first return of the year to Congress until May.[60] Although no general returns ever existed for the first four months of 1777, we did find one partial report that met our criteria for inclusion[61] and could be used for April 1777. Most of the other missing general returns also probably never existed.[62]

Applications considerably more sophisticated than our calculation of the percentage of sick should be forthcoming from the publication of this data. What, for example, was the relationship between the rate of desertion and where a regiment came from? Did soldiers of certain states desert more often than those of others? Was the relationship one of distance, with desertion most likely to occur when the army was encamped in a regiment's home state? Perhaps there was a seasonal change in the rate of desertion. Were the militia as unreliable as some of Washington's statements make them appear? Another line of enquiry might be to determine which states had the healthiest soldiers. One also wonders if regiments with many officers present fit for duty had significantly lower desertions and higher numbers of rank and file present and

57. Washington, Morristown, Feb. 20, 1777, to the President of Congress; Washington, Morristown, March 14, 1777, to the President of Congress; and Washington, Morristown, April 17, 1777, to Richard Peters, Secretary of the Board of War, *Writings of Washington*, 7: 168, 288, and 418.

58. Washington, Morristown, April 17, 1777, to Richard Peters, Secretary of the Board of War, *Writings of Washington*, 7: 418.

59. Washington, Morristown, March 14, 1777, to the President of Congress, *Writings of Washington*, 7: 288. About an additional one thousand men were under innoculation or caring for those who were in that state.

60. Washington, Morristown, May 10, 1777, to the President of Congress, *Writings of Washington*, 8: 34.

61. See footnote 46 above.

62. In October 1777, Washington, in response to a complaint from Continental Congress about a lack of general returns, pointed out that for quite some time the army had seldom been in one place two days in a row, and officers sometimes had no paper on which to write the returns; Washington, Headquarters near White Marsh, Oct. 22, 1777, to the Board of War, *Writings of Washington*, 9: 415. The missing returns in 1781 coincide with the movement to and from Yorktown; the way the returns are entered in the elephant folio suggest that those missing in 1781 were never a part of that manuscript.

healthy; or, were officers relatively unimportant and ineffective in a country with an emerging republican ideology? As these and countless other questions begin to be asked of this basic Revolutionary source, our understanding of both colonial society and the rebel army should be markedly enriched.

A final cautionary tale, however, is provided by the almost comic history of the most notable use of this data in the past. The story begins less than a decade after the close of the Revolutionary War with a request by the House of Representatives to Secretary of War Henry Knox for information about the numbers of soldiers that the various states had contributed to the War for Independence. Knox set about his computations in the one natural place to look, "the official returns, deposited in the War Office." Earlier, Knox had been Secretary of the Board of War under the Articles of Confederation; his predecessor in that position, Joseph Carlston, had attempted (in 1785) a similar "General Return of the Non-comd: officers and Privates of the late American Army, specifying the strength of the several Lines as they stand upon the general Returns, at the commencement of the several Campaigns during the War."[63] Rummaging through the War Department files, Knox was able to find some of the records Carlston had reported missing five years before, and, after a good deal of work, submitted his report to the House on May 10, 1790.

Knox's "A Statement of the number of Non-commissioned Officers and Privates of the Regular troops and Militia furnished by the several States from time to time, for the support of the late war" was compiled from much the same body of data as that contained in this volume. Knox used the officially submitted returns that were subsequently destroyed by fire in 1800, but, because it seems certain that many of the returns now missing never existed, he probably did not have much more extensive statistics than we have today. In his letter of submission, Knox himself particularly noted the gaps in hard data relating to militia and the Southern states. Doing the best he could to estimate the size of the state contributions for which he did not have records, the Secretary of War attempted to total the number of men each state had supplied for each year of the war. Whether Knox tried to average the size of a regiment from the different months' returns or simply took one months' figures for each year is not clear, but his report did represent a conscientious attempt to supply the data needed by Congress in their attempt to settle the relative Revolutionary contributions of the various states. Knox's figures first appeared in print in a government report on Revolutionary finances in 1791.[64]

63. Carlston's return, dated at the War Office, April 27, 1785, is in the James McHenry Papers (photostats), 2d ser., folio 327, Manuscript Division, Library of Congress. Knox succeeded Carlston a few days later on March 8, 1785.

64. U.S. Register of the Treasury, *Statements of the Receipts and Expenditures of Public Monies, During the Administration of the Finances by Robert Morris, Esquire, Late Superintendant of Finances; with Other Extracts and Accounts from the Public*

Historians, however, have often cited the report from an 1832 collected volume of government documents,[65] unaware that this printing left out a line from the 1779 figures (909 men from South Carolina).[66] Even though one modern historian has judged that Knox's results were "obviously not trustworthy,"[67] the report has remained, until the publication of this volume, the only widely available body of statistics relating to the strength of the rebel forces. Compressed into several different simplified tables, Knox's figures have been frequently reprinted since the early nineteenth century.[68]

The Knox report was based on one of the more dubious uses of the statistics in the strength reports (the attempt to derive totals from an incomplete body of data); it came to be used for all sorts of purposes alien to its original intent. Knox had prepared the report to aid Congress in its efforts to settle the hotly contested question of the Revolutionary War debts, but state partisanship about Revolutionary contributions did not die with the adoption of funding and assumption. In 1830 an article in *Niles Weekly Register* used Knox's figures to debunk the pretensions of South Carolina, where there was "a wonderful blustering" about Revolutionary services during arguments for nullification; as used in the article, Knox's data showed that Massachusetts (with some aid from other New England troops and God) all but fought the war alone.[69] At the turn of the century Edward McGrady could come to South Carolina's defense only by deprecating the value of Knox's efforts.[70] In one

---

Records. . . (Philadelphia: Francis Childs and John Swaine, 1791), pp. 25-34. This is available in the Early American Imprint microcards under Evans no. 23922.

65. Walter Lowrie and Matthew St. Clair Clarke, eds., *American State Papers: Military Affairs*, 7 vols. (Washington: Gales and Seaton, 1832-61), 1: 14-19.

66. I am indebted to Richard Buel, Jr. for helping me to discover this error. Professor Buel's unpublished paper for a National Archives conference, "Comparing State Mobilization in the Revolutionary War," correctly uses the Knox estimates as the best available figures.

67. John R. Alden, *The American Revolution, 1775-1783* (New York and Evanston, Ill.: Harper and Row, 1954), p. 208, note 18.

68. For example, New Hampshire Historical Society, *Collections* 1 (1824): 236; *American Almanac and Repository of Useful Knowledge* 1 (1830): 187; *Niles Weekly Register* 38 (1830): 398-99; New Jersey Historical Society, *Proceedings*, n.s. 7 (1922): 173-74. The full Knox report was reprinted from *American States Papers* [and thus the error in that printing perpetuated] in Thomas H. S. Hamersly, *Complete Regular Army Register of the United States: For One Hundred Years, [1779 to 1879]* (Washington: T. H. S. Hamersly, 1880), pt. 2, pp. 195-203.

69. *Niles Weekly Register* 38 (1830): 398-99.

70. Edward McGrady, *The History of South Carolina, 1775-1783*, 2 vols. (New York: Macmillan, 1901-2; reprint ed., New York: Russell & Russell, 1969), 1: 289-94.

form or another, the Knox estimates circulated very widely, often with no mention of their origin; sometimes they were even attributed to others.[71] As the debate continued over the preeminence of the Revolutionary efforts of various states, a New Jersey historian unwittingly used the figures for one year from the Knox report (misdated) to argue against the figures in a table that, unknown to the historian, actually contained Knox's totals for the entire war![72]

Our befuddled New Jersey apologist may stand as a warning of the inherent dangers in "cliometrics," but he should not discourage cautious use of this body of evidence. Statistics, like any other source, can easily be misused, but the monthly strength reports of the Continental Army offer a considerable challenge to the historical imagination. The continued existence of Washington's army allowed the Revolution to succeed; perhaps, as we begin to explore this data, we shall better understand these rebel soldiers, the sinews of independence.

ACKNOWLEDGMENTS

An undertaking of this size and complexity accumulates many debts. The institutions listed in the bibliography have not only given us permission to use statistics from their manuscript returns, but also, through their courteous staffs, enabled us to locate these sources in the first place. J. Todd White, George Wise, James E. Brady, John D. McBride, Randall Shrock, Joseph J. Casino, and John G. Fowler, Jr., were involved in the identification of materials that we ultimately used; the services of the other holders of our 1972 summer Lilly research fellowships are also appreciated. Richard K. Showman, editor of the Nathanael Greene papers, earmarked materials that might be of interest to the project. Howard H. Wehmann of the National Archives was of noteworthy assistance in the especially valuable search conducted by J. Todd White in the District of Columbia. The hospitable Naval History Division was the site for William C. Heimdahl's work on our unsuccessful attempt to compile annual estimates of the strength of the Continental and state navies. The institutions which supplied the illustrations are credited elsewhere; I am also grateful for assistance from the Frick Art Reference Library.

Processing the hundreds of thousands of figures required vast amounts of labor in Ann Arbor. David Whitesell, an exceptional undergraduate volunteer, spent many hours checking the transcription against the original sources. Also verifying figures and giving generously of his time was David Robbins. For helping to research and verify the accuracy of regimental designations and

71. This would seem to be the case in Heitman's *Historical Register*, p. 691, where Knox figures appear as Heitman's first column in his "Number of Troops Furnished During the War of the Revolution by the Several States," but are said to be "an approximate estimate by Colonel Pierce."

72. Cornelius C. Vermeule, "Number of Soldiers in the Revolution," New Jersey Historical Society, *Proceedings*, n.s. 7 (1922): 223-27.

officers' names and ranks, Jo Ann Staebler deserves much credit. Both Janice Holm and Barbara Mitchell spent many long hours meticulously typing the final edited reports and, with the editor, proofreading them. Their services, however, went beyond the mechanical: their alert eyes, inquiring minds, and skills in grammar have done much to improve this volume. Tim Donahue considerably lightened my ponderous prose. Without the thousands of painstaking hours of work performed by Joan Gittens this volume would have no existence. Month after month she endured the tedium of carefully transcribing figures and totalling them on an adding machine. Her insight, intelligence, and patience made this book possible; I cannot adequately thank her.

Professors John Shy and James Vann of the University of Michigan history department have served as advisors to this series. Their assistance is reflected on every page. In thanking them, however, I acknowledge that the ultimate responsibility for this volume, whatever its defects, must be my own.

Last, but by no means least, I wish to express my personal gratitude to each and every member of the staff of the William L. Clements Library. Howard H. Peckham, the library's director, was and is the moving force behind the entire American Revolution Bicentennial Project; he conceived the idea for this volume. John C. Dann, curator of manuscripts, did much to improve this introduction. During the three and a half years that I worked for the library's Revolution project, the entire staff went out of its way to be helpful in thousands of ways, both large and small. Although their names do not all appear here, their deeds and their friendship are in my thoughts.

ABBREVIATIONS

☆

bn.: battalion
brig.: brigade
Brig. Gen.: Brigadier General

Capt.: Captain
co., cos.: company, companies
Conn.: Connecticut
cont'l.: continental

Del.: Delaware
dept.: department
det.: detachment
div.: division

Ga.: Georgia
Gen.: General

Lt. Col.: Lieutenant Colonel

Maj.: Major
Mass.: Massachusetts
Md.: Maryland

N.C.: North Carolina
N.H.: New Hampshire
N.J.: New Jersey
N.Y.: New York

Pa.: Pennsylvania
Phila.: Philadelphia
pt.: part

regt.: regiment
R.I.: Rhode Island

S.C.: South Carolina

Va.: Virginia

MONTHLY REPORTS OF THE CONTINENTAL ARMY

☆

JULY 1775

BRIGADE

UNIT	COMMANDING OFFICER	PRESENT FIT FOR DUTY & ON DUTY: COMMISSIONED OFFICERS	NONCOMMISSIONED OFFICERS	STAFF OFFICERS	RANK & FILE	TOTAL	RANK & FILE SICK, ON FURLOUGH, ETC.: SICK PRESENT	SICK ABSENT	ON COMMAND & EXTRA SERVICE	ON FURLOUGH	GRAND TOTAL	ALTERATIONS: DEATHS	DESERTED	TAKEN PRISONER	DISCHARGED	JOINED, ENLISTED, RECRUITED	LOCATION
ARMY OF THE UNITED COLONIES UNDER COMMANDER-IN-CHIEF GENERAL GEORGE WASHINGTON																	
Ward's (Mass.) A	(late) Maj. Gen. Artemus Ward	30	57	4	353	444	37	49		3	533						vicinity of Boston, Mass.
Thomas' (Mass.)	(late) Maj. Gen. John Thomas	33	53	5	419	510	40	22	2		574						vicinity of Boston, Mass.
Walker's (Mass.)	Timothy Walker	26	48	4	336	414	18	14	103	10	559						vicinity of Boston, Mass.
Cotton's (Mass.)	Theophilus Cotton	31	57	5	374	467	23	13	94	7	604						vicinity of Boston, Mass.
Whitcomb's (Mass.)	Asa Whitcomb	36	58	4	415	513	46	34		15	608						vicinity of Boston, Mass.
Read's (Mass.)	Joseph Read	29	52	4	399	484	30	15	48		577						vicinity of Boston, Mass.
Mansfield's (Mass.)	John Mansfield	27	49	3	388	467	32	33	15	9	556						vicinity of Boston, Mass.
Danielson's (Mass.)	Timothy Danielson	33	61	3	391	488	53	8	13	14	576						vicinity of Boston, Mass.
Prescott's (Mass.)	William Prescott	24	51	3	295	373	58	58		8	497						vicinity of Boston, Mass.
Frye's (Mass.)	James Frye	25	34	4	314	377	42	36	13	19	487						vicinity of Boston, Mass.
Bridge's (Mass.)	Ebenezer Bridge	25	54	3	327	409	35	51	63	6	564						vicinity of Boston, Mass.
Paterson's (Mass.)	John Paterson	24	51	5	357	437	50	27	3	15	532						vicinity of Boston, Mass.
Scammon's (Mass.)	James Scammon	27	56	4	404	491	36	11		15	553						vicinity of Boston, Mass.
Learned's (Mass.)	Ebenezer Learned	32	60	5	430	527	37		2	5	571						vicinity of Boston, Mass.
Gardner's (Mass.)	(late) Thomas Gardner	20	52	4	376	452	8	27		14	501						vicinity of Boston, Mass.
Nixon's (Mass.)	John Nixon	24	57	4	353	438	35	23		8	504						vicinity of Boston, Mass.
Fellows' (Mass.)	John Fellows	27	52	5	389	473	44	20	11	4	552						vicinity of Boston, Mass.
Doolittle's (Mass.)	Ephraim Doolittle	25	47	4	207	283	64	44	4	11	406						vicinity of Boston, Mass.
J. Brewer's (Mass.)	Jonathan Brewer	19	67	4	238	328	30	15	15	5	393						vicinity of Boston, Mass.
D. Brewer's (Mass.)	David Brewer	30	52	4	383	469	16	3	4	2	494						vicinity of Boston, Mass.
Heath's (Mass.)	(late) Brig. Gen. William Heath	21	41	3	303	368	20	11	146	1	546						vicinity of Boston, Mass.
Woodbridge's (Mass.)	Benjamin Ruggles Woodbridge	16	34	5	265	320	43	12		12	387						vicinity of Boston, Mass.
Glover's (Mass.)	John Glover	32	50	4	440	526	12	15	17	20	590						vicinity of Boston, Mass.
Little's (Mass.)	Moses Little	25	42	5	392	464	45	45		16	570						vicinity of Boston, Mass.
Gerrish's (Mass.)	Samuel Gerrish	32	54	4	420	510	41	30		11	592						vicinity of Boston, Mass.
Phinney's (Mass.)	Edmund Phinney	33	60	3	422	518	10		16	3	547						vicinity of Boston, Mass.
Independent cos.					239	239					239						vicinity of Boston, Mass.
2nd Conn.	Samuel Wyllys																vicinity of Boston, Mass.
3rd Conn.	Experience Storrs	107	219	18	2169	2513	199	20	1	16	2749						vicinity of Boston, Mass.
6th Conn.	Samuel Holden Parsons																vicinity of Boston, Mass.
1st N. H.	John Stark																vicinity of Boston, Mass.
2nd N. H.	Enoch Poor	79	149	12	1118	1358	150	47	121	36	1712						vicinity of Boston, Mass.
3rd N. H.	James Reed																vicinity of Boston, Mass.
1st R.I.	James Mitchell Varnum																vicinity of Boston, Mass.
2nd R.I.	Daniel Hitchcock	77	106	13	983	1179	79	7	1	2	1268						vicinity of Boston, Mass.
3rd R.I.	Thomas Church																vicinity of Boston, Mass.
TOTAL OF INFANTRY		969	1823	148	13899	16839	1333	690	692	287	19841						
ARTILLERY																	
United Colonies artillery	Richard Gridley	41	164	7	241	453	9	7		5	474						vicinity of Boston, Mass.
R.I. artillery co.	Maj. John Crane	5	13	1	60	79	9		5		93						vicinity of Boston, Mass.
TOTAL OF ARTILLERY		46	177	8	301	532	18	7	5	5	567						
TOTAL OF WASHINGTON'S ARMY		1015	2000	156	14200	17371	1351	697	697	292	20408 C						

BRIGADE

JULY 1775
(continued)

UNIT	COMMANDING OFFICER	PRESENT FIT FOR DUTY & ON DUTY: COMMISSIONED OFFICERS	NONCOMMISSIONED OFFICERS	STAFF OFFICERS	RANK & FILE	TOTAL	RANK & FILE SICK, ON FURLOUGH, ETC.: SICK PRESENT	SICK ABSENT	ON COMMAND & EXTRA SERVICE	ON FURLOUGH				GRAND TOTAL	ALTERATIONS: DEATHS	DESERTED	TAKEN PRISONER	DISCHARGED	JOINED, ENLISTED, RECRUITED	LOCATION
ARMY IN NEW YORK UNDER MAJOR GENERAL PHILIP SCHUYLER																				
1st Conn.	Brig. Gen. David Wooster	24	47		481	552	9			15				576						New York City, N. Y.
5th Conn.	David Waterbury	39	77		789	905	24							929						New York City, N. Y.
Pt. 4th Conn.	Benjamin Hinman	19	38		406	463	15							478						Ticonderoga, N. Y.
Pt. 4th Conn.	Benjamin Hinman	12	23		254	289	4							293						Crown Point, N. Y.
Pt. 4th Conn.	Benjamin Hinman	4	8		80	92	6							98						"Landing," N. Y.
Pt. 4th Conn.	Benjamin Hinman	3	6		95	104								104						Fort George, N. Y.
Mass. Bay forces		2	2		36	40								40						Ticonderoga, N. Y.
Mass. Bay forces		8	12		89	109								109						Crown Point, N. Y.
Mass. Bay forces		1	1		23	25								25						Fort George, N. Y.
N. Y. forces		15	24	4[B]	166	209								209						Fort George, N. Y.
TOTAL OF ARMY IN NEW YORK		127	238	4[B]	2419	2788	58			15				2861						
GRAND TOTAL		1142	2238	160	16619	20159	1409	697	697	307				23269						

OFFICERS SICK, ON FURLOUGH, ETC.	WASHINGTON'S ARTILLERY (ONLY): COMMISSIONED	NONCOMMISSIONED	STAFF	TOTAL
Sick Present	4	4		8
Sick Absent	1	5		6
On Furlough	2	5		7
On Command		1		1
TOTAL	7	15		22

SOURCES OF THIS REPORT

1. GENERAL RETURN OF THE ARMY OF THE UNITED COLONIES COMMANDED BY HIS EXCELLENCY GEORGE WASHINGTON...JULY 29, 1775, RECORD GROUP 93, NATIONAL ARCHIVES.

2. RETURN OF THE REGIMENT OF ARTILLERY IN THE SERVICE OF THE UNITED COLONIES COMMANDED BY COL. RICHARD GRIDLEY, JULY 29, 1775, RECORD GROUP 93, NATIONAL ARCHIVES.

3. RETURN OF MAJOR CRANE'S COMPANY OF THE TRAIN OF ARTILLERY OF THE RHODE ISLAND FORCES, JULY 21, 1775, RECORD GROUP 93, NATIONAL ARCHIVES.

3a. Return of Major Crane's Company, printed in Peter Force, American Archives, ser. 4, 2: 1629.

4. A GENERAL MONTHLY RETURN OF THE ARMY OF THE ASSOCIATED COLONIES IN THE COLONY OF NEW YORK UNDER THE COMMAND OF MAJOR GENERAL PHILIP SCHUYLER, JULY 14, 1775, RECORD GROUP 360, NATIONAL ARCHIVES.

4a. A General Monthly Return of the Army...in...New York, printed in Peter Force, American Archives, ser. 4, 2: 1667. [The date of the return has been read incorrectly from the manuscript or misprinted.]

A. The twenty-seven battalions of the Massachusetts line organized after Lexington and later adopted by the Continental Congress as Continental units were generally known by the names of their respective commanders; although an overall set of numbers was developed for all the regiments in Washington's army of 1775, they were very seldom used. When any of these twenty-seven regiments had a new commander appointed, we have retained the original commander's name in the unit designation so as to indicate the continuity of the regiment.

B. This figure represents the one chaplain, one surgeon, and two surgeon's mates who were not attached to any particular regiment.

C. The manuscript notes that Colonel Sargent's regiment (Paul Dudley Sargent's Massachusetts regiment) is not included in the return.

AUGUST 1775

BRIGADE	UNIT	COMMANDING OFFICER	PRESENT FIT FOR DUTY & ON DUTY: COMMISSIONED OFFICERS	NONCOMMISSIONED OFFICERS	STAFF OFFICERS	RANK & FILE	TOTAL	RANK & FILE SICK, ON FURLOUGH, ETC.: SICK PRESENT	SICK ABSENT	ON COMMAND & EXTRA SERVICE	ON FURLOUGH	PRISONERS OF WAR			GRAND TOTAL	ALTERATIONS: DEATHS	DESERTED	TAKEN PRISONER	DISCHARGED	JOINED, ENLISTED, RECRUITED	LOCATION
	ARMY OF THE UNITED COLONIES UNDER COMMANDER-IN-CHIEF GENERAL GEORGE WASHINGTON																				
	Frye's (Mass.)	James Frye	24	42	4	305	375	61	35	41	11				523						vicinity of Boston, Mass.
	Pa. rifle regt.	William Thompson	51	60	5	808	924	19	21	1					965						vicinity of Boston, Mass.
	3rd N. H.	James Reed	24	43	4	290	361	109	39	62	3				574						vicinity of Boston, Mass.
	Learned's (Mass.)	Ebenezer Learned	29	60	5	408	502	48	12	4	4				570						vicinity of Boston, Mass.
	Nixon's (Mass.)	John Nixon	25	52	3	336	416	40	32	3	3				494						vicinity of Boston, Mass.
	J. Brewer's (Mass.)	Jonathan Brewer	23	47	4	257	331	40	40	16	5				432						vicinity of Boston, Mass.
	1st N. H.	John Stark	25	56	3	367	451	82	16	48	10				607						vicinity of Boston, Mass.
	Fellows' (Mass.)	John Fellows	33	56	5	375	469	77	9	8					563						vicinity of Boston, Mass.
	D. Brewer's (Mass.)	David Brewer	28	56	5	348	437	49	15	19	8				528						vicinity of Boston, Mass.
	Prescott's (Mass.)	William Prescott	24	60	3	333	420	53	50		3				526						vicinity of Boston, Mass.
	2nd N. H.	Enoch Poor	26	38	4	352	420	114	9	68	9				620						vicinity of Boston, Mass.
	1st R. I.	James Mitchell Varnum	23	51	5	303	382	44		57					483						vicinity of Boston, Mass.
	9 cos. 6th Conn.	Samuel Holden Parsons	34	71	5	539	649	123	16	19	10				817						vicinity of Boston, Mass.
	2nd R. I.	Daniel Hitchcock	24	39	4	333	400	56	13	40	1				510						vicinity of Boston, Mass.
	3rd R. I.	Thomas Church	25	34	4	368	431	30							461						vicinity of Boston, Mass.
	Cotton's (Mass.)	Theophilus Cotton	33	60	5	352	450	31	13	108	5				607						vicinity of Boston, Mass.
	Little's (Mass.)	Moses Little	31	43	5	363	442	44	67		3				556						vicinity of Boston, Mass.
	Danielson's (Mass.)	Timothy Danielson	33	61	4	354	452	62	9	52	9				584						vicinity of Boston, Mass.
	Mansfield's (Mass.)	John Mansfield	24	43	4	341	412	43	49	56	1				561						vicinity of Boston, Mass.
	Read's (Mass.)	Joseph Read	26	44	4	379	453	25	35	50	7				570						vicinity of Boston, Mass.
	Glover's (Mass.)	John Glover	25	47	3	395	470	9	14	64	20				577						vicinity of Boston, Mass.
	Walker's (Mass.)	Timothy Walker	22	46	4	277	349	93	60	7	5				514						vicinity of Boston, Mass.
	Whitcomb's (Mass.)	Asa Whitcomb	36	60	3	386	485	66	51	33					635						vicinity of Boston, Mass.
	Doolittle's (Mass.)	Ephraim Doolittle	27	50	4	260	341	75	50	14	1				481						vicinity of Boston, Mass.
	Woodbridge's (Mass.)	Benjamin Ruggles Woodbridge	23	35	4	213	275	52	12	79	5				423						vicinity of Boston, Mass.
	Paterson's (Mass.)	John Paterson	31	55	5	338	429	60	30	1	8				528						vicinity of Boston, Mass.
	Bridge's (Mass.)	Ebenezer Bridge	26	54	4	376	460	38	46	12	3				559						vicinity of Boston, Mass.
	Sargent's (Mass.)	Paul Dudley Sargent	28	54	5	337	424	51	14	7	8				504						vicinity of Boston, Mass.
	8th Conn.	Jedediah Huntington	24	55	6	286	371	101	13	29	1				515						vicinity of Boston, Mass.
	Scammon's (Mass.)	James Scammon	29	52	4	400	485	39	9		13				546						vicinity of Boston, Mass.
	Phinney's (Mass.)	Edmund Phinney	29	52	4	378	463	66	14		2				545						vicinity of Boston, Mass.
	Ward's (Mass.)	Jonathan Ward	27	57	3	351	438	40	57		3				538						vicinity of Boston, Mass.
	2nd Conn.	Samuel Wyllys	35	83	6	586	710	132	62	36	37				977						vicinity of Boston, Mass.
	3rd Conn.	Experience Storrs	30	72	6	682	790	80		81	19				970						vicinity of Boston, Mass.
	Thomas' (Mass.)	John Bailey	26	57	5	432	520	29	17		6				572						vicinity of Boston, Mass.
	Heath's (Mass.)	John Greaton	27	50	3	389	469	35	53		1				558						vicinity of Boston, Mass.
	Gardner's (Mass.)	(late) Thomas Gardner	19	31	4	261	315	23	60	112					510						vicinity of Boston, Mass.
	Gerrish's (Mass.)	(late) Samuel Gerrish	32	56	4	449	541	40	29		1				611						vicinity of Boston, Mass.
A	6 cos., 2 from 4th Conn.		19	36		394	449								449						vicinity of Boston, Mass.
	TOTAL OF INFANTRY		1080	2018	162	14701	17961	2179	1071	1127	225				22563						
	ARTILLERY																				
	United Colonies artillery	Richard Gridley	45	149	7	239	440	15	9		5				469						vicinity of Boston, Mass.
	R. I. artillery co.	Maj. John Crane	4	13	1	66	84	6	2		1				93						vicinity of Boston, Mass.
	TOTAL OF ARTILLERY		49	162	8	305	524	21	11		6				562						
	TOTAL OF WASHINGTON'S ARMY		1129	2180	170	15006	18485	2200	1082	1127	231				23125						

AUGUST 1775 (continued)

BRIGADE	UNIT	COMMANDING OFFICER	PRESENT FIT FOR DUTY & ON DUTY: COMMISSIONED OFFICERS	NONCOMMISSIONED OFFICERS	STAFF OFFICERS	RANK & FILE	TOTAL	RANK & FILE SICK, ON FURLOUGH, ETC.: SICK PRESENT	SICK ABSENT	ON COMMAND & EXTRA SERVICE	ON FURLOUGH	PRISONERS OF WAR		GRAND TOTAL	ALTERATIONS: DEATHS	DESERTED	TAKEN PRISONER	DISCHARGED	JOINED, ENLISTED, RECRUITED	LOCATION
ARMY IN NEW YORK UNDER MAJOR GENERAL PHILIP SCHUYLER																				
	Pt. 1st Conn.	Brig. Gen. David Wooster	2	6		56	64	27	2		1			94						Ticonderoga, N. Y.
	Pt. 4th Conn. B	Benjamin Hinman	12	28	4	250	294	68	16		4			382						Ticonderoga, N. Y.
	Pt. 5th Conn.	David Waterbury																		Ticonderoga, N. Y.
	1 co. 6th Conn.	Samuel Holden Parsons	3	6	1	58	68	11	15					94						Ticonderoga, N. Y.
	Pt. 4th Conn.	Benjamin Hinman	4	9		57	70	21			2			93						north end, Lake George, N.Y.
	Pt. 5th Conn.	David Waterbury	2	1		38	41	4						45						north end, Lake George, N.Y.
	Pt. 1st Conn.	Brig. Gen. David Wooster	29	54	6	504	593	8	37		21			659						New York City, N. Y.
	Pt. 4th Conn.	Benjamin Hinman	11	17		234	262	10	20			1		293						Crown Point, N. Y.
	Mass. regt.	James Easton	9	14	3	107	133	32	4 C		17	1		187						Crown Point, N. Y.
	TOTAL OF ARMY IN NEW YORK		72	135	14	1304	1525	181	94		45	2		1847						
	GRAND TOTAL		1201	2315	184	16310	20010	2381	1176	1127	276	2		24972						

OFFICERS SICK, ON FURLOUGH, ETC.	WASHINGTON'S ARTILLERY (ONLY): COMMISSIONED	NONCOMMISSIONED	STAFF	TOTAL	SCHUYLER'S NEW YORK ARMY: COMMISSIONED	NONCOMMISSIONED	STAFF	TOTAL	GRAND TOTAL
On Furlough	2	2		4	4	6	2	12	16
Sick Absent	1	15		16	1	1		2	18
Sick Present	1	10		11	4	12		16	27
On the Staff					6		2	8	8
TOTAL	4	27		31	15	19	4	38	69

SOURCES OF THIS REPORT

1. GENERAL RETURN OF THE ARMY OF THE UNITED COLONIES COMMANDED BY HIS EXCELLENCY GEORGE WASHINGTON. . . AUGUST 26, 1775, RECORD GROUP 93, NATIONAL ARCHIVES.

2. RETURN OF THE REGIMENT OF ARTILLERY. . . COMMANDED BY COLONEL RICHARD GRIDLEY, AUGUST 26, 1775, RECORD GROUP 93, NATIONAL ARCHIVES.

3. RETURN OF THE COMPANY OF THE TRAIN OF ARTILLERY, OF THE RHODE ISLAND FORCES, COMMANDED BY MAJOR JOHN CRANE, AUGUST 25, 1775, RECORD GROUP 93, NATIONAL ARCHIVES.

4. A GENERAL MONTHLY RETURN OF THE ARMY OF THE UNITED COLONIES IN THE COLONY OF NEW YORK UNDER THE COMMAND OF MAJOR GENERAL PHILIP SCHUYLER, AUGUST 19, 1775, SCHUYLER PAPERS, MANUSCRIPTS AND ARCHIVES DIVISION, THE NEW YORK PUBLIC LIBRARY; ASTOR, LENOX, AND TILDEN FOUNDATIONS.

A. Two companies from Colonel Benjamin Hinman's 4th Connecticut regiment (much of which was serving under Schuyler in New York) plus four independent companies. For some unknown reason, the figures for these six companies that appear on this manuscript return are copied unchanged on the manuscript returns for the rest of the year.

B. The manuscript is blank for the portion of this unit which was at Ticonderoga.

C. Of the ninety-four men in Schuyler's army included in "sick absent," eighty-nine actually are marked "sick in hospital" on the original return. A "sick in hospital" category appears only on a very few returns; in those few cases, we have always included the men in "sick absent" and noticed the matter in a footnote. Although there were some hospitals in camp areas during the war, it appears that, in those few cases in which a "sick in hospital" category appears on the returns used in this volume, the men really were "sick absent," not "sick present." A clear case of this can be seen by comparing the two different returns including forces of Nathanael Greene's division that were used in compiling our September 1776 report; a "sick in hospital" column on the return of Greene's division alone has been put into the "sick absent" column by the adjutant general in compiling the general return.

SEPTEMBER 1775

BRIGADE

UNIT	COMMANDING OFFICER	PRESENT FIT FOR DUTY & ON DUTY: COMMISSIONED OFFICERS	NONCOMMISSIONED OFFICERS	STAFF OFFICERS	RANK & FILE	TOTAL	RANK & FILE SICK, ON FURLOUGH, ETC.: SICK PRESENT	SICK ABSENT	ON COMMAND & EXTRA SERVICE	ON FURLOUGH			GRAND TOTAL	ALTERATIONS: DEATHS	DESERTED	TAKEN PRISONER	DISCHARGED	JOINED, ENLISTED, RECRUITED	LOCATION
ARMY OF THE UNITED COLONIES UNDER COMMANDER-IN-CHIEF GENERAL GEORGE WASHINGTON																			
Frye's (Mass.)	James Frye	20	55	3	372	450	36	31	21	14			552						vicinity of Boston, Mass.
Pa. rifle regt.	William Thompson	30	33	5	485	553	26	23	1				603						vicinity of Boston, Mass.
3rd N. H.	James Reed	24	44	5	330	403	56	36	64	10			569						vicinity of Boston, Mass.
Learned's (Mass.)	Ebenezer Learned	32	60	5	391	488	33	17	17	18			573						vicinity of Boston, Mass.
Nixon's (Mass.)	John Nixon	18	46	3	231	298	24	31	130	7			490						vicinity of Boston, Mass.
J. Brewer's (Mass.)	Jonathan Brewer	23	46	5	255	329	37	27	28	3			424						vicinity of Boston, Mass.
1st N. H.	John Stark	23	47	5	328	403	61	22	102	6			594						vicinity of Boston, Mass.
Fellows' (Mass.)	John Fellows	33	59	5	325	422	62	8	73	2			567						vicinity of Boston, Mass.
D. Brewer's (Mass.)	David Brewer	26	58	3	352	439	53	5	23	20			540						vicinity of Boston, Mass.
Prescott's (Mass.)	William Prescott	34	61	4	341	440	24	38	17	16			535						vicinity of Boston, Mass.
2nd N. H.	Enoch Poor	20	41	3	340	404	98	16	68	13			599						vicinity of Boston, Mass.
1st R. I.	James Mitchell Varnum	18	47	5	362	432	50		8	2			492						vicinity of Boston, Mass.
6th Conn.	Samuel Holden Parsons	33	68	6	518	625	110	10	105	26			876						vicinity of Boston, Mass.
2nd R. I.	Daniel Hitchcock	17	31	4	310	362	42	17	47	5			473						vicinity of Boston, Mass.
3rd R. I.	Thomas Church	20	31	2	247	300	26	31	78	9			444						vicinity of Boston, Mass.
Cotton's (Mass.)	Theophilus Cotton	32	60	4	409	505	55	25	5	17			607						vicinity of Boston, Mass.
Little's (Mass.)	Moses Little	29	50	5	390	474	35	37	13	3			562						vicinity of Boston, Mass.
Danielson's (Mass.)	Timothy Danielson	33	61	4	340	438	34	5	85	17			579						vicinity of Boston, Mass.
Mansfield's (Mass.)	(late) John Mansfield	24	42	5	364	435	38	38	42	1			554						vicinity of Boston, Mass.
Read's (Mass.)	Joseph Read	26	45	4	363	438	30	31	55	16			570						vicinity of Boston, Mass.
Glover's (Mass.)	John Glover	26	43	4	414	487	12	18	22	20			559						vicinity of Boston, Mass.
Walker's (Mass.)	Timothy Walker	24	43	4	300	371	61	33	10	28			503						vicinity of Boston, Mass.
Whitcomb's (Mass.)	Asa Whitcomb	36	58	4	393	491	39	31	45	10			616						vicinity of Boston, Mass.
Doolittle's (Mass.)	Ephraim Doolittle	31	58	4	288	381	79	38	49	4			551						vicinity of Boston, Mass.
Woodbridge's (Mass.)	Benjamin Ruggles Woodbridge	28	41	4	286	359	44	25	20	3			451						vicinity of Boston, Mass.
Paterson's (Mass.)	John Paterson	33	57	5	336	431	42	19	35	13			540						vicinity of Boston, Mass.
Bridge's (Mass.)	Ebenezer Bridge	26	55	4	358	443	46	49	15	4			557						vicinity of Boston, Mass.
Sargent's (Mass.)	Paul Dudley Sargent	27	51	5	319	402	46	27	28	14			517						vicinity of Boston, Mass.
8th Conn.	Jedediah Huntington	24	56	4	269	353	60	28	41	21			503						vicinity of Boston, Mass.
Scammon's (Mass.)	James Scammon	24	49	5	382	460	20	16	17	15			528						vicinity of Boston, Mass.
Phinney's (Mass.)	Edmund Phinney	33	60	4	381	478	39	5	7	10			539						vicinity of Boston, Mass.
Ward's (Mass.)	Jonathan Ward	22	56	5	348	431	24	46	32	4			537						vicinity of Boston, Mass.
2nd Conn.	Samuel Wyllys	28	71	6	487	592	174	11	118	57			952						vicinity of Boston, Mass.
3rd Conn.	Experience Storrs	31	77	5	612	725	102	8	155	25			1015						vicinity of Boston, Mass.
Thomas' (Mass.)	John Bailey	27	50	5	388	470	36	28	23	4			561						vicinity of Boston, Mass.
Heath's (Mass.)	John Greaton	33	60	4	363	460	37	40	19	16			572						vicinity of Boston, Mass.
Gardner's (Mass.)	(late) Thomas Gardner	24	47	4	315	390	23	40	47	5			505						vicinity of Boston, Mass.
Gerrish's (Mass.)	(late) Samuel Gerrish	32	57	4	431	524	47	21	4	10			606						vicinity of Boston, Mass.
4 cos. Va. & Md. riflemen		16	24	1	213	254	25		81				360						vicinity of Boston, Mass.
6 cos., 2 from 4th Conn. A		19	36		394	449							449						vicinity of Boston, Mass.
TOTAL OF INFANTRY		1059	2034	166	14330	17589	1886	931	1750	468			22624						
ARTILLERY																			
United Colonies artillery	Richard Gridley	39	150	7	224	420	17	11		10			458						vicinity of Boston, Mass.
R.I. artillery co.	Maj. John Crane	5	16	1	64	86	5	4		2			97						vicinity of Boston, Mass.
TOTAL OF ARTILLERY		44	166	8	288	506	22	15		12			555						
TOTAL OF WASHINGTON'S ARMY		1103	2200	174	14618	18095	1908	946	1750	480			23179						

OFFICERS SICK, ON FURLOUGH, ETC.	GRIDLEY'S ARTILLERY REGT. (ONLY)			
	COMMISSIONED	NONCOMMISSIONED	STAFF	TOTAL
Sick Present	3	18		21
Sick Absent	2	3		5
On Furlough	3	5		8
On Command	1			1
TOTAL	9	26		35

SOURCES OF THIS REPORT

1. GENERAL RETURN OF THE ARMY OF THE UNITED COLONIES COMMANDED BY HIS EXCELLENCY GEORGE WASHINGTON...SEPTEMBER 23, 1775, RECORD GROUP 93, NATIONAL ARCHIVES.

2. RETURN OF THE REGIMENT OF ARTILLERY IN THE SERVICE OF THE UNITED COLONIES, COMMANDED BY COL. RICHARD GRIDLEY, SEPTEMBER 23, 1775, RECORD GROUP 93, NATIONAL ARCHIVES.

3. RETURN OF MAJOR JOHN CRANE'S COMPANY OF THE TRAIN OF ARTILLERY OF THE RHODE ISLAND FORCES, OCTOBER 1, 1775, RECORD GROUP 93, NATIONAL ARCHIVES.

A. Two companies from Colonel Benjamin Hinman's 4th Connecticut regiment plus four independent companies. The figures for these six companies (only) are the same as on the August return. See footnote A on the August 1775 report.

BRIGADE

OCTOBER 1775

UNIT	COMMANDING OFFICER	PRESENT FIT FOR DUTY & ON DUTY: COMMISSIONED OFFICERS	NONCOMMISSIONED OFFICERS	STAFF OFFICERS	RANK & FILE	TOTAL	RANK & FILE SICK, ON FURLOUGH, ETC.: SICK PRESENT	SICK ABSENT	ON COMMAND & EXTRA SERVICE	ON FURLOUGH	GRAND TOTAL	ALTERATIONS: DEATHS	DESERTED	TAKEN PRISONER	DISCHARGED	JOINED, ENLISTED, RECRUITED	LOCATION
ARMY OF THE UNITED COLONIES UNDER COMMANDER-IN-CHIEF GENERAL GEORGE WASHINGTON																	
Frye's (Mass.)	James Frye	24	39	1	306	370	25	31	18	4	448						vicinity of Boston, Mass.
Pa. rifle regt.	William Thompson	30	34	4	471	539	30	32	1	1	603						vicinity of Boston, Mass.
3rd N. H.	James Reed	23	42	4	283	352	52	37	23	103	567						vicinity of Boston, Mass.
Learned's (Mass.)	Ebenezer Learned	32	61	5	371	469	27	5	23	28	552						vicinity of Boston, Mass.
Nixon's (Mass.)	John Nixon	18	42	4	208	272	19	28	19	141	479						vicinity of Boston, Mass.
1st N. H.	John Stark	20	41	3	276	340	40	27	21	128	556						vicinity of Boston, Mass.
J. Brewer's (Mass.)	Jonathan Brewer	24	42	4	236	306	41	30	19	38	434						vicinity of Boston, Mass.
Fellows' (Mass.)	John Fellows	33	59	5	312	409	36	11	11	98	565						vicinity of Boston, Mass.
D. Brewer's (Mass.)	David Brewer	27	58	3	358	446	32	8	17	30	533						vicinity of Boston, Mass.
Prescott's (Mass.)	William Prescott	28	61	4	350	443	19	37	6	14	519						vicinity of Boston, Mass.
2nd N. H.	Enoch Poor	20	37	5	294	356	77	20	23	117	593						vicinity of Boston, Mass.
1st R. I.	James Mitchell Varnum	20	33	5	241	299	53		11	88	451						vicinity of Boston, Mass.
6th Conn.	Samuel Holden Parsons	29	69	5	566	669	84	8	34	45	840						vicinity of Boston, Mass.
2nd R. I.	Daniel Hitchcock	17	31	3	293	344	29	18	26	49	466						vicinity of Boston, Mass.
3rd R. I.	Thomas Church	13	21	1	234	269	11	46	27	76	429						vicinity of Boston, Mass.
Cotton's (Mass.)	Theophilus Cotton	32	60	5	394	491	23	36	22	27	599						vicinity of Boston, Mass.
Little's (Mass.)	Moses Little	23	36	5	340	404	21	41	15	102	583						vicinity of Boston, Mass.
Danielson's (Mass.)	Timothy Danielson	33	59	4	316	412	36	3	26	85	562						vicinity of Boston, Mass.
Mansfield's (Mass.)	(late) John Mansfield	22	42	3	290	357	34	35	24	108	558						vicinity of Boston, Mass.
Read's (Mass.)	Joseph Read	24	43	4	370	441	19	17	9	55	541						vicinity of Boston, Mass.
Glover's (Mass.)	John Glover	19	35	3	320	377	7	22	18	121	545						vicinity of Boston, Mass.
Walker's (Mass.)	Timothy Walker	24	43	5	311	383	36	31	22	18	490						vicinity of Boston, Mass.
Whitcomb's (Mass.)	Asa Whitcomb	26	44	5	369	444	50	21	23	49	587						vicinity of Boston, Mass.
Doolittle's (Mass.)	Ephraim Doolittle	19	43	5	212	279	47	39	17	67	449						vicinity of Boston, Mass.
Woodbridge's (Mass.)	Benjamin Ruggles Woodbridge	27	37	4	280	348	37	21	15	45	466						vicinity of Boston, Mass.
Paterson's (Mass.)	John Paterson	25	48	5	309	387	14	25	16	43	485						vicinity of Boston, Mass.
Bridge's (Mass.)	Ebenezer Bridge	30	49	4	334	417	39	44	14	33	547						vicinity of Boston, Mass.
Sargent's (Mass.)	Paul Dudley Sargent	22	54	3	315	394	36	27	28	26	511						vicinity of Boston, Mass.
8th Conn.	Jedediah Huntington	31	83	5	406	525	60	13	22	68	688						vicinity of Boston, Mass.
Scammon's (Mass.)	James Scammon	22	50	4	377	453	25	5	18	29	530						vicinity of Boston, Mass.
Phinney's (Mass.)	Edmund Phinney	26	52	4	376	458	25	7	21	15	526						vicinity of Boston, Mass.
Ward's (Mass.)	Jonathan Ward	28	57	5	352	442	25	17	11	45	540						vicinity of Boston, Mass.
2nd Conn.	Samuel Wyllys	28	76	6	499	609	133	9	47	128	926						vicinity of Boston, Mass.
3rd Conn.	Experience Storrs	30	69	5	533	637	99		25	148	909						vicinity of Boston, Mass.
Thomas' (Mass.)	John Bailey	24	44	5	295	368	25	51	24	79	547						vicinity of Boston, Mass.
Heath's (Mass.)	John Greaton	33	60	4	338	435	15	47	18	52	567						vicinity of Boston, Mass.
Gardner's (Mass.)	(late) Thomas Gardner	21	48	4	298	371	13	39	13	47	483						vicinity of Boston, Mass.
Gerrish's (Mass.)	(late) Samuel Gerrish	31	58	4	436	529	29	28	17	6	609						vicinity of Boston, Mass.
7th Conn.	Charles Webb	39	73	5	445	562	19	35	2	43	661						vicinity of Boston, Mass.
4 cos. Va. & Md. riflemen		12	17		215	244	34	1		1	280						vicinity of Boston, Mass.
6 cos., 2 from 4th Conn.A		19	36		394	449					449						vicinity of Boston, Mass.
TOTAL OF WASHINGTON'S INFANTRY		1028	1986	162	13923	17099	1476	952	746	2400	22673						

SOURCE OF THIS REPORT

1. GENERAL RETURN OF THE ARMY OF THE UNITED COLONIES COMMANDED BY HIS EXCELLENCY GEORGE WASHINGTON... OCTOBER 17, 1775, RECORD GROUP 93, NATIONAL ARCHIVES.

A. Two companies from Colonel Benjamin Hinman's 4th Connecticut regiment plus four independent companies. The figures for these six companies (only) are the same as on the August return. See footnote A on the August 1775 report.

BRIGADE

NOVEMBER 1775

UNIT	COMMANDING OFFICER	PRESENT FIT FOR DUTY & ON DUTY: COMMISSIONED OFFICERS	NONCOMMISSIONED OFFICERS	STAFF OFFICERS	RANK & FILE	TOTAL	RANK & FILE SICK, ON FURLOUGH, ETC.: SICK PRESENT	SICK ABSENT	ON COMMAND & EXTRA SERVICE	ON FURLOUGH	GRAND TOTAL	ALTERATIONS: DEATHS	DESERTED	TAKEN PRISONER	DISCHARGED	JOINED, ENLISTED, RECRUITED	LOCATION
ARMY OF THE UNITED COLONIES UNDER COMMANDER-IN-CHIEF GENERAL GEORGE WASHINGTON																	
Frye's (Mass.)	James Frye	21	32	2	276	331	33	22	115	17	518						vicinity of Boston, Mass.
Pa. rifle regt.	William Thompson	25	29	4	303	361	47	42	42	4	496						vicinity of Boston, Mass.
3rd N. H.	James Reed	20	36	4	254	314	34	30	128	38	544						vicinity of Boston, Mass.
Learned's (Mass.)	Ebenezer Learned	32	60	5	336	433	18	6	30	56	543						vicinity of Boston, Mass.
Nixon's (Mass.)	John Nixon	16	37	4	210	267	37	37	101	18	460						vicinity of Boston, Mass.
1st N. H.	John Stark	21	44	4	265	334	32	29	130	50	575						vicinity of Boston, Mass.
J. Brewer's (Mass.)	Jonathan Brewer	19	32	3	152	206	55	21	88	39	409						vicinity of Boston, Mass.
Fellows' (Mass.)	John Fellows	31	59	5	293	388	37	13	87	35	560						vicinity of Boston, Mass.
D. Brewer's (Mass.)	(late) David Brewer	24	58	2	315	399	37	5	35	35	511						vicinity of Boston, Mass.
Prescott's (Mass.)	William Prescott	19	54	3	311	387	24	29	19	35	494						vicinity of Boston, Mass.
2nd N. H.	Enoch Poor	16	27	5	316	364	70	9	56	44	543						vicinity of Boston, Mass.
1st R. I.	James Mitchell Varnum	10	29	2	237	278	49	1	62	12	402						vicinity of Boston, Mass.
6th Conn.	Samuel Holden Parsons	22	69	3	428	522	74	11	82	113	802						vicinity of Boston, Mass.
2nd R. I.	Daniel Hitchcock	20	33	4	238	295	47	7	78	27	454						vicinity of Boston, Mass.
3rd R. I.	Thomas Church	16	19	2	234	271	46	4	69	25	415						vicinity of Boston, Mass.
Cotton's (Mass.)	Theophilus Cotton	31	60	5	364	460	14	31	25	68	598						vicinity of Boston, Mass.
Little's (Mass.)	Moses Little	22	26	5	280	333	27	43	105	65	573						vicinity of Boston, Mass.
Danielson's (Mass.)	Timothy Danielson	31	60	4	268	363	28	4	87	59	541						vicinity of Boston, Mass.
Mansfield's (Mass.)	(late) John Mansfield	15	37	5	247	304	31	26	120	41	522						vicinity of Boston, Mass.
Read's (Mass.)	Joseph Read	20	45	4	331	400	16	16	49	46	527						vicinity of Boston, Mass.
Glover's (Mass.)	John Glover	15	32	2	196	245	17	11	253	15	541						vicinity of Boston, Mass.
Walker's (Mass.)	Timothy Walker	23	43	5	315	386	15	23	31	22	477						vicinity of Boston, Mass.
Whitcomb's (Mass.)	Asa Whitcomb	36	59	5	298	398	42	30	70	59	599						vicinity of Boston, Mass.
Doolittle's (Mass.)	(late) Ephraim Doolittle	20	40	4	235	299	33	43	64	24	463						vicinity of Boston, Mass.
Woodbridge's (Mass.)	Benjamin Ruggles Woodbridge	24	37	4	279	344	28	27	61	11	471						vicinity of Boston, Mass.
Paterson's (Mass.)	John Paterson	23	53	3	265	344	28	27	58	32	489						vicinity of Boston, Mass.
Bridge's (Mass.)	Ebenezer Bridge	23	40	2	280	345	39	44	68	29	525						vicinity of Boston, Mass.
Sargent's (Mass.)	Paul Dudley Sargent	24	56	5	268	353	36	21	33	46	489						vicinity of Boston, Mass.
8th Conn.	Jedediah Huntington	26	73	5	310	414	55	5	78	69	621						vicinity of Boston, Mass.
Scammon's (Mass.)	James Scammon	26	52	5	347	430	18	8	41	31	528						vicinity of Boston, Mass.
Phinney's (Mass.)	Edmund Phinney	15	41	2	268	326	24	9	47	89	495						vicinity of Boston, Mass.
Ward's (Mass.)	Jonathan Ward	21	55	1	331	408	24	12	34	30	508						vicinity of Boston, Mass.
2nd Conn.	Samuel Wyllys	22	65	5	339	431	130	8	174	85	828						vicinity of Boston, Mass.
3rd Conn.	Experience Storrs	25	48	5	416	494	84		197	48	823						vicinity of Boston, Mass.
Thomas' (Mass.)	John Bailey	23	47	5	272	347	9	35	96	51	538						vicinity of Boston, Mass.
Heath's (Mass.)	John Greaton	33	60	4	290	387	14	37	63	57	558						vicinity of Boston, Mass.
Gardner's (Mass.)	(late) Thomas Gardner	17	40	4	256	317	15	56	53	27	468						vicinity of Boston, Mass.
Gerrish's (Mass.)	(late) Samuel Gerrish	26	58	3	441	528	15	13	4	34	594						vicinity of Boston, Mass.
7th Conn.	Charles Webb	35	68	5	392	500	48	9	57	39	653						vicinity of Boston, Mass.
4 cos. Md. & Va. riflemen		12	17		215	244	34	1		1	280						vicinity of Boston, Mass.
6 cos., 2 from 4th Conn.[A]		19	36		394	449					449						vicinity of Boston, Mass.
TOTAL OF INFANTRY		919	1866	149	12065	14999	1464	805	2990	1626	21884						
ARTILLERY																	
United Colonies artillery	(late) Richard Gridley	40	144	11	218	413	20	6		13	452						vicinity of Boston, Mass.
R. I. artillery co.	Maj. John Crane	4	14	1	64	83	6	1		2	92						vicinity of Boston, Mass.
TOTAL OF ARTILLERY		44	158	12	282	496	26	7		15	544						
TOTAL OF WASHINGTON'S ARMY		963	2024	161	12347	15495	1490	812	2990	1641	22428						

OFFICERS SICK, ON FURLOUGH, ETC.	WASHINGTON'S ARTILLERY (ONLY)			
	COMMISSIONED	NONCOMMISSIONED	STAFF	TOTAL
Sick Present	1	14		15
Sick Absent	2	6		8
On Furlough	3	9		12
TOTAL	6	29		35

SOURCES OF THIS REPORT

1. GENERAL RETURN OF THE ARMY OF THE UNITED COLONIES COMMANDED BY HIS EXCELLENCY GEORGE WASHINGTON...NOVEMBER 25, 1775, RECORD GROUP 93, NATIONAL ARCHIVES.

2. RETURN OF THE REGIMENT OF ARTILLERY IN THE SERVICE OF THE UNITED COLONIES, COMMANDED BY COLONEL RICHARD GRIDLEY, NOVEMBER 18, 1775, RECORD GROUP 93, NATIONAL ARCHIVES.

3. RETURN OF MAJOR JOHN CRANE'S COMPANY OF ARTILLERY, IN THE SERVICE OF THE UNITED STATES COLONIES, NOVEMBER 17, 1775, RECORD GROUP 93, NATIONAL ARCHIVES.

A. Two companies from Colonel Benjamin Hinman's 4th Connecticut regiment plus four independent companies. The figures for these six companies (only) are the same as on the August return. See footnote A on the August 1775 report.

DECEMBER 1775

BRIGADE	UNIT	COMMANDING OFFICER	PRESENT FIT FOR DUTY & ON DUTY: COMMISSIONED OFFICERS	NONCOMMISSIONED OFFICERS	STAFF OFFICERS	RANK & FILE	TOTAL	RANK & FILE SICK, ON FURLOUGH, ETC.: SICK PRESENT	SICK ABSENT	ON COMMAND & EXTRA SERVICE	ON FURLOUGH	CONFINED	BOWMEN	CAMP SIX MEN D	GRAND TOTAL	ALTERATIONS: DEATHS	DESERTED	TAKEN PRISONER	DISCHARGED	JOINED, ENLISTED, RECRUITED	LOCATION
	ARMY OF THE UNITED COLONIES UNDER COMMANDER-IN-CHIEF GENERAL GEORGE WASHINGTON																				
	Frye's (Mass.)	James Frye	24	43	4	313	384	39	21	63	28				535						vicinity of Boston, Mass.
	Pa. rifle regt.	William Thompson	26	29	4	313	372	45	40	42	5				504						vicinity of Boston, Mass.
	3rd N. H.	James Reed	22	42	4	321	389	33	12	72	22				528						vicinity of Boston, Mass.
	Learned's (Mass.)	Ebenezer Learned	31	55	5	300	391	20	1	24	23				459						vicinity of Boston, Mass.
	Nixon's (Mass.)	John Nixon	23	51	5	267	346	39	25	56	32				498						vicinity of Boston, Mass.
	1st N. H.	John Stark	26	47	4	264	341	32	28	136	50				587						vicinity of Boston, Mass.
	J. Brewer's (Mass.)	Jonathan Brewer	22	39	3	251	315	61	12	12	17				417						vicinity of Boston, Mass.
	Fellows' (Mass.)	John Fellows	31	59	5	323	418	47	8	56	19				548						vicinity of Boston, Mass.
	D. Brewer's (Mass.)	(late) David Brewer	27	56	3	265	351	25	2	54	28				460						vicinity of Boston, Mass.
	Prescott's (Mass.)	William Prescott	21	57	4	325	407	27	15	27	17				493						vicinity of Boston, Mass.
	2nd N. H.	Enoch Poor	24	37	5	301	367	75	7	37	48				534						vicinity of Boston, Mass.
	1st R. I.	James Mitchell Varnum	19	40	3	307	369	31	1	58	23				482						vicinity of Boston, Mass.
	6th Conn. A	Samuel Holden Parsons	10	12	3	152	177	1		4					182						vicinity of Boston, Mass.
	2nd R. I.	Daniel Hitchcock	24	34	4	255	317	39	1	70	18				445						vicinity of Boston, Mass.
	3rd R. I.	Thomas Church	16	20	2	247	285	38	1	58	24				406						vicinity of Boston, Mass.
	Cotton's (Mass.)	Theophilus Cotton	30	60	5	389	484	12	14	14	50				574						vicinity of Boston, Mass.
	Little's (Mass.)	Moses Little	25	36	4	284	349	27	40	106	42				564						vicinity of Boston, Mass.
	Danielson's (Mass.)	Timothy Danielson	27	57	2	331	417	26	3	72	21				539						vicinity of Boston, Mass.
	Mansfield's (Mass.)	(late) John Mansfield	21	36	4	277	338	29	17	192	33				609						vicinity of Boston, Mass.
	Read's (Mass.)	Joseph Read	23	38	2	351	414	21	11	48	35				529						vicinity of Boston, Mass.
	Glover's (Mass.)	John Glover	16	36	3	174	229	21	8	275	14				547						Beverly, Mass.
	Walker's (Mass.)	Timothy Walker	26	49	5	326	406	30	9	29	12				486						vicinity of Boston, Mass.
	Whitcomb's (Mass.)	Asa Whitcomb	35	60	5	311	411	59	12	81	24				587						vicinity of Boston, Mass.
	Doolittle's (Mass.)	(late) Ephraim Doolittle	26	40	4	257	327	29	19	58	15				448						vicinity of Boston, Mass.
	Woodbridge's (Mass.)	Benjamin Ruggles Woodbridge	24	40	4	234	302	31	11	152	10				506						vicinity of Boston, Mass.
	Paterson's (Mass.)	John Paterson	28	49	3	336	416	7	30	36	50				539						vicinity of Boston, Mass.
	Bridge's (Mass.)	Ebenezer Bridge	25	50	3	282	360	45	33	73	22				533						vicinity of Boston, Mass.
	Sargent's (Mass.)	Paul Dudley Sargent	17	37	4	300	358	59	13	32	21				483						vicinity of Boston, Mass.
	8th Conn.	Jedediah Huntington	11	11	3	115	140	1	1	4	18				164						vicinity of Boston, Mass.
	Scammon's (Mass.)	James Scammon	30	57	5	371	463	22	6	28	31				550						vicinity of Boston, Mass.
	Phinney's (Mass.)	Edmund Phinney	23	52	3	349	427	54	6	24	8				519						vicinity of Boston, Mass.
	Ward's (Mass.)	Jonathan Ward	26	56	4	322	408	43	6	43	12				512						vicinity of Boston, Mass.
	2nd Conn.	Samuel Wyllys	17	31	4	137	189	8	50	24	25				296						vicinity of Boston, Mass.
	3rd Conn.	Experience Storrs	7	9	4	62	82			15	57				154						vicinity of Boston, Mass.
	Thomas' (Mass.)	John Bailey	25	49	5	333	412	9	12	78	32				543						vicinity of Boston, Mass.
	Heath's (Mass.)	John Greaton	33	60	4	325	422	15	20	44	57				558						vicinity of Boston, Mass.
	Gardner's (Mass.)	(late) Thomas Gardner	20	47	4	238	309	24	32	73	38				476						vicinity of Boston, Mass.
	Gerrish's (Mass.)	(late) Samuel Gerrish	31	58	4	464	557	28	13	3	31				632						vicinity of Boston, Mass.
	7th Conn.	Charles Webb	27	44	2	371	444	20	1						465						vicinity of Boston, Mass.
	4 cos. Md. & Va. riflemen		12	17		215	244	34	1		1				280						vicinity of Boston, Mass.
	6 cos., 2 from 4th Conn. B		19	36		394	449								449						vicinity of Boston, Mass.
	TOTAL OF INFANTRY		950	1736	148	11752	14586	1206	542	2273	1013				19620						
	ARTILLERY																				
	United Colonies artillery	(late) Richard Gridley	40	149	11	235	435	7	8		8				458						vicinity of Boston, Mass.
	R. I. artillery	Maj. John Crane	4	15	1	64	84	3	2		4				93						vicinity of Boston, Mass.
	TOTAL OF ARTILLERY		44	164	12	299	519	10	10		12				551						
	TOTAL OF WASHINGTON'S ARMY		994	1900	160	12051	15105	1216	552	2273	1025				20171						

DECEMBER 1775 (continued)

BRIGADE

UNIT	COMMANDING OFFICER	PRESENT FIT FOR DUTY & ON DUTY: COMMISSIONED OFFICERS	NONCOMMISSIONED OFFICERS	STAFF OFFICERS	RANK & FILE	TOTAL	RANK & FILE SICK, ON FURLOUGH, ETC.: SICK PRESENT	SICK ABSENT	ON COMMAND & EXTRA SERVICE	ON FURLOUGH	CONFINED	BOWMEN	CAMP SIX MEN[D]	GRAND TOTAL	ALTERATIONS: DEATHS	DESERTED	TAKEN PRISONER	DISCHARGED	JOINED, ENLISTED, RECRUITED	LOCATION
TROOPS UNDER COLONEL ROBERT HOWE AT NORFOLK, VIRGINIA																				
2nd N. C.	Robert Howe	19	30	3	341	393	28							421						Norfolk, Va.
Det. 1st Va. state	Patrick Henry	11	12	1	138	162	15		25		1	1	2	206						Norfolk, Va.
2nd Va. state	William Woodford	23	21	5	224	273	50		2		29	7	15	376						Norfolk, Va.
Culpepper minute bn.[C]		10	8	1	118	137	10		6		2	5	4	164						Norfolk, Va.
Southern minute bn.[C]		13	9		175	197								197						Norfolk, Va.
TOTAL OF TROOPS UNDER HOWE		76	80	10	996	1162	103[E]		33		32	13	21	1364						
GRAND TOTAL		1070	1980	170	13047	16267	1871[F]	←	2306	1025	32	13	21	21535						

OFFICERS SICK, ON FURLOUGH, ETC.	WASHINGTON'S ARTILLERY (ONLY): COMMISSIONED	NONCOMMISSIONED	STAFF	TOTAL
Sick Present	2	7		9
Sick Absent	1	6		7
On Furlough	3	8		11
TOTAL	6	21		27

SOURCES OF THIS REPORT

1. GENERAL RETURN OF THE ARMY OF THE UNITED COLONIES COMMANDED BY HIS EXCELLENCY GEORGE WASHINGTON...DECEMBER 30, 1775, RECORD GROUP 93, NATIONAL ARCHIVES.
   1a. General Return of the Army...Commanded by...Washington, printed in Peter Force, American Archives, ser. 4, 4: 491-92.

2. RETURN OF THE REGIMENT OF ARTILLERY IN THE SERVICE OF THE UNITED COLONIES, COMMANDED BY COL. RICHARD GRIDLEY, DECEMBER 30, 1775, PRINTED IN PETER FORCE, AMERICAN ARCHIVES, ser. 4, 4: 491.

3. RETURN OF A COMPANY OF ARTILLERY OF THE RHODE ISLAND FORCES IN THE SERVICE OF THE UNITED COLONIES, COMMANDED BY MAJOR JOHN CRANE, DECEMBER 30, 1775, PRINTED IN PETER FORCE, AMERICAN ARCHIVES, ser. 4, 4: 492.

4. A MORNING RETURN OF THE FORCES NOW UNDER THE COMMAND OF COL. ROBT. HOWE, DECEMBER 29, 1775, MILITARY COLLECTION, TROOP RETURNS, NORTH CAROLINA DEPARTMENT OF ARCHIVES AND HISTORY.

A. The terms of service of the 2nd, 3rd, 4th, 6th, 7th, and 8th Connecticut regiments had ended in the middle of the month, but the regiments are still included on this return. Although the organization and enlistments for the new Continental regiments of 1776 had been in process for some time, the entire army was still kept in the form of the old regiments until the end of the month. The men listed for these Connecticut regiments were probably those men who had reenlisted for the new Continental regiments of 1776. The old regiments also had Massachusetts and New Hampshire militia incorporated in them temporarily; Washington called out 5,000 militia from those colonies to serve until January 15 until the new units could be set in being and enlisted to strength. The return does not indicate whether these temporary militia reinforcements are included in the figures for these old regiments. Later, Washington urged these militia to stay until the end of January, but with only partial success.

B. Two companies from Colonel Benjamin Hinman's 4th Connecticut regiment plus four independent companies. The figures for these six companies (only) are the same as on the August return. See footnote A on the August 1775 report.

C. In July 1775 the Virginia Convention dissolved the volunteer companies and grouped the counties of the state into sixteen districts, each of which was to have a battalion of minute men enlisted from its militia. Two of these minute battalions were with Robert Howe at Norfolk. These two units were not, strictly speaking, in Continental service, as were most of the units that have been included in this volume, but the return of the forces under Howe was thought to be of sufficient interest to justify its inclusion here. The first and second Virginia state regiments were not officially brought into Continental pay until February 13, 1776, but at that point this was made retroactive to November 1, 1775.

D. The meaning of "Bowmen" and "Camp 6 Men" is not clear. What appears to be a "6" on the manuscript might have been intended as a "C," and thus the "Camp 6 Men" could be camp color men. For camp color men see footnote I on our September 1779 report.

E. The return of the troops under Howe does not divide the sick into "sick present" and "sick absent." For convenience, they have been put in the sick present column, although they are designated only as "sick" on the manuscript.

F. Total of all sick (present and absent).

The manuscript folio of strength returns in the rare book room of the William L. Clements Library. A fifteen-inch-long Revolutionary fife played by John McLouth (1758–1820; private, fifer, and, later, sergeant) is laid across the manuscript to help establish the scale of this huge volume. The portrait is of Mr. Clements. (Photograph by George F. Feitel)

JANUARY 1776

BRIGADE	UNIT	COMMANDING OFFICER	PRESENT FIT FOR DUTY & ON DUTY: COMMISSIONED OFFICERS	NONCOMMISSIONED OFFICERS	STAFF OFFICERS	RANK & FILE	TOTAL	RANK & FILE SICK, ON FURLOUGH, ETC.: SICK PRESENT	SICK ABSENT	ON COMMAND & EXTRA SERVICE	ON FURLOUGH	ENLISTED BUT NOT YET JOINED			GRAND TOTAL	ALTERATIONS: DEATHS	DESERTED	TAKEN PRISONER	DISCHARGED	JOINED, ENLISTED, RECRUITED	LOCATION
	FORCES UNDER COMMANDER-IN-CHIEF GENERAL GEORGE WASHINGTON																				
	Pa. riflemen (1st cont'l.)	William Thompson	38	47	5	503	593	80	53	44	6				776						vicinity of Boston, Mass.
	2nd cont'l. (N. H.)	James Reed	7	48	3	448	506	67	3	4	1				581						vicinity of Boston, Mass.
	3rd cont'l. (Mass.)	Ebenezer Learned	48	70	5	545	668	78	12	37	13	31			839						vicinity of Boston, Mass.
	4th cont'l. (Mass.)	John Nixon	21	44	4	306	375	27	9	51	15				477						vicinity of Boston, Mass.
	5th cont'l. (N. H.)	John Stark	29	33	4	341	407	49	8	98	9				571						vicinity of Boston, Mass.
	6th cont'l. (Mass.)	Asa Whitcomb	22	34	4	264	324	28	11	18	11	52			444						vicinity of Boston, Mass.
	7th cont'l. (Mass.)	William Prescott	22	37	3	261	323	31	9	20	42				425						vicinity of Boston, Mass.
	8th cont'l. (N. H.)	Enoch Poor	34	46	4	398	482	49	7	33	29				600						vicinity of Boston, Mass.
	9th cont'l. (R. I.)	James Mitchell Varnum	15	34	4	230	283	38	2	39	12	21			395						vicinity of Boston, Mass.
	10th cont'l. (Conn.)	Samuel Holden Parsons	29	47	5	440	521	50	9	16	8	32			636						vicinity of Boston, Mass.
	11th cont'l. (R. I.)	Daniel Hitchcock	16	37	2	256	311	32	1	5	9	23			381						vicinity of Boston, Mass.
	12th cont'l. (Mass.)	Moses Little	17	28	4	280	329	51	8	81	18				487						vicinity of Boston, Mass.
	13th cont'l. (Mass.)	Joseph Read	36	66	4	493	599	82	9	65	17	50			822						vicinity of Boston, Mass.
	14th cont'l. (Mass.)	John Glover								188					188						Beverly, Mass.
	15th cont'l. (Mass.)	John Paterson	21	32	4	222	279	37	5	13	43				377						vicinity of Boston, Mass.
	16th cont'l. (Mass.)	Paul Dudley Sargent	24	43	4	257	328	46	11	67	22				474						vicinity of Boston, Mass.
	17th cont'l. (Conn.)	Jedediah Huntington	28	43	3	324	398	53		112	2	48			613						vicinity of Boston, Mass.
	18th cont'l. (Mass.)	Edmund Phinney	20	38	5	216	279	52	7	22	14				374						vicinity of Boston, Mass.
	19th cont'l. (Conn.)	Charles Webb	23	33	4	335	395	44	5	29	29				502						vicinity of Boston, Mass.
	20th cont'l. (Conn.)	(late) Benedict Arnold	71	80	5	614	770	180		116	11				1077						vicinity of Boston, Mass.
	21st cont'l. (Mass.)	Jonathan Ward	50	84	5	752	891	115	7	2	29	13			1057						vicinity of Boston, Mass.
	22nd cont'l. (Conn.)	Samuel Wyllys	26	44	4	340	414	41	3	45	16	51			570						vicinity of Boston, Mass.
	23rd cont'l. (Mass.)	John Bailey	46	61	4	502	613	50	17	52	7	16			755						vicinity of Boston, Mass.
	24th cont'l. (Mass.)	John Greaton	25	39	4	252	320	37	10	14	20				401						vicinity of Boston, Mass.
	25th cont'l. (Mass.)	William Bond	21	30	5	329	385	31	17	24	12	16			485						vicinity of Boston, Mass.
	26th cont'l. (Mass.)	Loammi Baldwin	32	54	3	437	526	42	4	7	22	30			631						vicinity of Boston, Mass.
	27th cont'l. (Mass.)	Israel Hutchinson	24	42	4	454	524	32	18	46	3	47			670						vicinity of Boston, Mass.
	TOTAL OF WASHINGTON'S INFANTRY		745	1194	105	9799	11843	1422	245	1248	420	430			15608						

SOURCE OF THIS REPORT

1. GENERAL RETURN OF THE ARMY OF THE UNITED COLONIES COMMANDED BY HIS EXCELLENCY GEORGE WASHINGTON. . . JANUARY 28, 1776, RECORD GROUP 93, NATIONAL ARCHIVES.

BRIGADE

FEBRUARY 1776

UNIT	COMMANDING OFFICER	PRESENT FIT FOR DUTY & ON DUTY: COMMISSIONED OFFICERS	NONCOMMISSIONED OFFICERS	STAFF OFFICERS	RANK & FILE	TOTAL	RANK & FILE SICK, ON FURLOUGH, ETC.: SICK PRESENT	SICK ABSENT	ON COMMAND & EXTRA SERVICE	ON FURLOUGH	UNFIT FOR DUTY[D]			GRAND TOTAL	ALTERATIONS: DEATHS	DESERTED	TAKEN PRISONER	DISCHARGED	JOINED, ENLISTED, RECRUITED	LOCATION
FORCES UNDER COMMANDER-IN-CHIEF GENERAL GEORGE WASHINGTON																				
Pa. riflemen (1st cont'l.)	William Thompson	38	50	4	591	683	80	25	48	6				842						vicinity of Boston, Mass.
2nd cont'l. (N. H.)	James Reed	24	37	4	321	386	70	5	11					472						vicinity of Boston, Mass.
3rd cont'l. (Mass.)	Ebenezer Learned	35	45	5	386	471	83	5	64	1				624						vicinity of Boston, Mass.
4th cont'l. (Mass.)	John Nixon	17	31	5	315	368	62	13	55	2				500						vicinity of Boston, Mass.
5th cont'l. (N. H.)	John Stark	19	34	3	312	368	42	8	13	4				435						vicinity of Boston, Mass.
6th cont'l. (Mass.)	Asa Whitcomb	22	35	4	260	321	74	4	21					420						vicinity of Boston, Mass.
7th cont'l. (Mass.)	William Prescott	26	34	4	313	377	54	15	16	4				466						vicinity of Boston, Mass.
8th cont'l. (N. H.)	Enoch Poor	30	39	4	354	427	106	3	46	3				585						vicinity of Boston, Mass.
9th cont'l. (R. I.)	James Mitchell Varnum	21	43	3	292	359	26	4	52	3				444						vicinity of Boston, Mass.
10th cont'l. (Conn.)	Samuel Holden Parsons	26	44	5	426	501	47	1	35					585						vicinity of Boston, Mass.
11th cont'l. (R. I.)	Daniel Hitchcock	22	43	4	295	364	40	1	10	2				417						vicinity of Boston, Mass.
12th cont'l. (Mass.)	Moses Little	22	38	5	354	419	47	9	65	1				541						vicinity of Boston, Mass.
13th cont'l. (Mass.)	Joseph Read	28	44	3	399	474	70	8	60					612						vicinity of Boston, Mass.
14th cont'l. (Mass.)	John Glover	35		4		39			273					312						Beverly, Mass.
15th cont'l. (Mass.)	John Paterson	23	46	4	288	361	80	22	23					486						vicinity of Boston, Mass.
16th cont'l. (Mass.)	Paul Dudley Sargent	20	28	4	209	261	70	10	136	3				480						vicinity of Boston, Mass.
17th cont'l. (Conn.)	Jedediah Huntington	28	46	4	356	434	93		49					576						vicinity of Boston, Mass.
18th cont'l. (Mass.)	Edmund Phinney	19	36	5	285	345	112	12	4					473						vicinity of Boston, Mass.
19th cont'l. (Conn.)	Charles Webb	27	44	4	399	474	66	5	42	1				588						vicinity of Boston, Mass.
20th cont'l. (Conn.)	(late) Benedict Arnold	23	45	5	325	398	57	17	42	3				517						vicinity of Boston, Mass.
21st cont'l. (Mass.)	Jonathan Ward	28	44	5	396	473	68	4	15	2				562						vicinity of Boston, Mass.
22nd cont'l. (Conn.)	Samuel Wyllys	27	42	5	336	410	84	5	68	2				569						vicinity of Boston, Mass.
23rd cont'l. (Mass.)	John Bailey	35	48	5	427	515	48	13	62					638						vicinity of Boston, Mass.
24th cont'l. (Mass.)	John Greaton	31	37	5	269	342	61	18	7	4				432						vicinity of Boston, Mass.
25th cont'l. (Mass.)	William Bond	29	40	5	393	467	49	17	15	1				549						vicinity of Boston, Mass.
26th cont'l. (Mass.)	Loammi Baldwin	25	43	5	417	490	61	12	7	1				571						vicinity of Boston, Mass.
27th cont'l. (Mass.)	Israel Hutchinson	30	43	5	452	530	73	40	59					702						vicinity of Boston, Mass.
TOTAL OF CONTINENTAL INFANTRY[A]		710	1059	118	9170	11057	1723	276	1298	43				14397						
NEW ENGLAND MILITIA IN CONTINENTAL SERVICE																				
N. H. militia	John Waldron	37	45	4	547	633	78	8	22					741						vicinity of Boston, Mass.
Mass. militia	Jacob French	38	51	5	555	649	68	7	64	1				789						vicinity of Boston, Mass.
Conn. militia	Erastus Wolcott	33	46	5	467	551	61	10	35					657						vicinity of Boston, Mass.
Conn. militia	James Wadsworth	34	47	4	448	533	37	8	55					633						vicinity of Boston, Mass.
Mass. militia	Josiah Whitney	35	42	3	503	583	101	3	7	3				697						vicinity of Boston, Mass.
Mass. militia	Lemuel Robinson	35	45	5	467	552	35	14	39					640						vicinity of Boston, Mass.
Mass. militia	Simeon Cary[B]	42	60	4	654	760	62	22	11					855						vicinity of Boston, Mass.
Mass. militia	Isaac Smith	29	34	4	463	530	49	1	3	1				584						vicinity of Boston, Mass.
Mass. militia	John Robinson	31	39	5	429	504	55	13	1	1				574						vicinity of Boston, Mass.
Conn. militia	John Douglass	31	53	5	437	526	129	5	39					699						vicinity of Boston, Mass.
TOTAL OF NEW ENGLAND MILITIA		345	462	44	4970	5821	675	91	276	6				6869						
ARTILLERY																				
United Colonies artillery	Henry Knox	57	184	4	318	563	19	9	13					604						vicinity of Boston, Mass.
TOTAL OF WASHINGTON'S ARMY		1112	1705	166	14458	17441	2417	376	1587	49				21870						

FEBRUARY 1776
(continued)

BRIGADE	UNIT	COMMANDING OFFICER	PRESENT FIT FOR DUTY & ON DUTY: COMMISSIONED OFFICERS	NONCOMMISSIONED OFFICERS	STAFF OFFICERS	RANK & FILE	TOTAL	RANK & FILE SICK, ON FURLOUGH, ETC.: SICK PRESENT	SICK ABSENT	ON COMMAND & EXTRA SERVICE	ON FURLOUGH	UNFIT FOR DUTY D			GRAND TOTAL	ALTERATIONS: DEATHS	DESERTED	TAKEN PRISONER	DISCHARGED	JOINED, ENLISTED, RECRUITED	LOCATION
	FORCES OF THE UNITED COLONIES IN CAMP BEFORE QUEBEC UNDER BRIGADIER GENERAL BENEDICT ARNOLD																				
	1st N. Y.	Alexander McDougall	10	15	2	98	125					75			200						vicinity of Quebec, Canada
	2nd N. Y.	Goose Van Schaick	9	14	3	98	124					41			165						vicinity of Quebec, Canada
	3rd N. Y.	James Clinton	17	19		151	187					54			241						vicinity of Quebec, Canada
	4th N. Y.	(late) James Holmes	4	10		68	82					32			114						vicinity of Quebec, Canada
	Arnold's det.	Brig. Gen. Benedict Arnold	6	13		95	114					64			178						vicinity of Quebec, Canada
	1st Canadian C	James Livingston	22	19		155	196					23			219						vicinity of Quebec, Canada
	Brown's det. C	Maj. John Brown	10	19		107	136					37			173						vicinity of Quebec, Canada
	TOTAL OF FORCES BEFORE QUEBEC		78	109	5	772	964					326			1290						
	GRAND TOTAL		1190	1814	171	15230	18405	2417	376	1587	49	326			23160						

OFFICERS SICK, ON FURLOUGH, ETC.	WASHINGTON'S ARTILLERY (ONLY): COMMISSIONED	NONCOMMISSIONED	STAFF	TOTAL	FORCES IN CANADA: COMMISSIONED	NONCOMMISSIONED	STAFF	TOTAL	GRAND TOTAL
Sick Present	6	17		23					23
Sick Absent		3		3					3
On Command D	1	4		5					5
Unfit for Duty D					25	31	3	59	59
TOTAL	7	24		31	25	31	3	59	90

SOURCES OF THIS REPORT

1. GENERAL RETURN OF THE ARMY OF THE UNITED COLONIES COMMANDED BY HIS EXCELLENCY GEORGE WASHINGTON. . . MARCH 2, 1776, RECORD GROUP 93, NATIONAL ARCHIVES.

1a. General Return of the Army. . . Commanded by. . . Washington, printed in Peter Force, American Archives, ser. 4, 5: 115-16.

2. GENERAL RETURN OF THE REGIMENTS OF MILITIA OF THE PROVINCE OF MASSACHUSETTS BAY [sic.; see footnote A below] IN THE SERVICE OF THE UNITED COLONIES, MARCH 3, 1776, PRINTED IN PETER FORCE, AMERICAN ARCHIVES, SER. 4, 5: 117-18.

3. RETURN OF THE REGIMENT OF ARTILLERY IN THE SERVICE OF THE UNITED COLONIES, COMMANDED BY HENRY KNOX, MARCH 3, 1776, PRINTED IN PETER FORCE, AMERICAN ARCHIVES, SER. 4, 5: 117.

4. A RETURN OF THE FORCES OF THE UNITED COLONIES IN CAMP BEFORE QUEBEC, FEBRUARY 10, 1776, RECORD GROUP 360, NATIONAL ARCHIVES.

A. On January 16, 1776, Washington was forced to call for thirteen regiments of militia to reinforce "the alarming and almost defenceless state of our lines" until April 1. Seven of these regiments came from Massachusetts, four from Connecticut, and two from New Hampshire. Later, one of these militia regiments from each of the three colonies was changed into a year-long regiment to go to Canada, leaving ten regiments (six Mass., three Conn., one N.H.) to reinforce Washington. The three extant returns of these ten militia regiments in the Continental service (the two used in this volume and a return of February 18 in the Massachusetts Archives) are headed "General Return of the Regiments of Militia of the Province of Massachusetts Bay in the Service of the United Colonies," but this is an error; the regiments came from three New England colonies, not just Massachusetts. Washington's letters calling forth the regiments, the names of the colonels, and Connecticut and New Hampshire records establish this beyond doubt. The erroneous heading on the returns has led to errors in Massachusetts Soldiers and Sailors of the Revolutionary War (16: 379, 420; 17: 876), where three of the non-Massachusetts colonels are listed although no first names could be established for them. The calling out of these militia regiments became necessary when many of the earlier New Hampshire and Massachusetts militia reinforcements left in the middle of January. Unlike the earlier militia draft, these men remained in militia regiments rather than being attached to deficient Continental units.

B. Although the return gives only the last name and Massachusetts Soldiers and Sailors of the Revolutionary War supplies over 250 pages of Smiths, Isaac Smith from Ipswich seems to fit the circumstances here (14: 415).

C. Men recruited from James Easton's and Timothy Bedel's disbanded corps.

D. The return of the forces before Quebec gives only combined figures for those men "who are either on Command, Sick in Camp or Hospital, Prisoners with the Enemy, deserted, dead, or on Furlough in some of the United Colonies." We have given these figures under "unfit for duty."

BRIGADE

MARCH 1776

UNIT	COMMANDING OFFICER	PRESENT FIT FOR DUTY & ON DUTY: COMMISSIONED OFFICERS	NONCOMMISSIONED OFFICERS	STAFF OFFICERS	RANK & FILE	TOTAL	RANK & FILE SICK, ON FURLOUGH, ETC.: SICK PRESENT	SICK ABSENT	ON COMMAND & EXTRA SERVICE	ON FURLOUGH	NOT JOINED			GRAND TOTAL	ALTERATIONS: DEATHS	DESERTED	TAKEN PRISONER	DISCHARGED	JOINED, ENLISTED, RECRUITED	LOCATION
FORCES UNDER COMMANDER-IN-CHIEF GENERAL GEORGE WASHINGTON (Moving and About to Move to New York)--NO RETURN AVAILABLE																				
FORCES REMAINING AT BOSTON																				
6th cont'l. (Mass.)	Asa Whitcomb	28	33	5	281	347	64	8	27					446						Boston, Mass. & vicinity
16th cont'l. (Mass.)	Paul Dudley Sargent	29	32	3	309	373	52	14	85	2				526						Boston, Mass. & vicinity
18th cont'l. (Mass.)	Edmund Phinney	29	46	5	328	408	72	16	6	1				503						Boston, Mass. & vicinity
27th cont'l. (Mass.)	Israel Hutchinson	34	44	4	461	543	55	24	73	1				696						Boston, Mass. & vicinity
TOTAL OF CONTINENTAL DIVISION AT BOSTON		120	155	17	1379	1671	243	62	191	4				2171						
NEW ENGLAND MILITIA IN CONTINENTAL SERVICE[A] (About to Be Discharged)																				
Conn. militia	John Douglass	34	53	4	424	515	132	4	10					661						Boston, Mass. & vicinity
N. H. militia	John Waldron	33	42	4	473	552	97	5						654						Boston, Mass. & vicinity
Mass. militia	Simeon Cary	42	60	5	588	695	92	44	16					847						Boston, Mass. & vicinity
Mass. militia	Lemuel Robinson	38	51	5	520	614	68	18	23					723						Boston, Mass. & vicinity
Mass. militia	Jacob French	37	49	5	493	584	102	14	49					749						Boston, Mass. & vicinity
Mass. militia	Josiah Whitney	35	46	3	518	602	69	5	9					685						Boston, Mass. & vicinity
Mass. militia	John Robinson	30	39	5	408	482	51	12	10	1				556						Boston, Mass. & vicinity
Conn. militia	James Wadsworth	34	46	4	421	505	91	2	21					619						Boston, Mass. & vicinity
Mass. militia	Isaac Smith	29	35	4	450	518	49	3						570						Boston, Mass. & vicinity
Conn. militia	Erastus Wolcott	32	48	5	422	507	77	3	33	14				634						Boston, Mass. & vicinity
TOTAL OF NEW ENGLAND MILITIA		344	469	44	4717	5574	828	110	171	15				6698						
TOTAL OF FORCES IN THE BOSTON AREA		464	624	61	6096	7245	1071	172	362	19				8869						
TROOPS BEFORE QUEBEC UNDER BRIGADIER GENERAL BENEDICT ARNOLD																				
Green Mountain boys	Seth Warner					102	271[D]							373						vicinity of Quebec, Canada
Maj. Cady's	Maj. Jeremiah Cady					82	50							132						vicinity of Quebec, Canada
1st Pa.	John Philip De Haas					225								225						vicinity of Quebec, Canada
Brown's det.	Maj. John Brown					38	132							170						vicinity of Quebec, Canada
Wooster's provisional	Brig. Gen. David Wooster					42	48							90						vicinity of Quebec, Canada
1st N. Y.[B]	Alexander McDougall					76	115							191						vicinity of Quebec, Canada
2nd N. Y.	Goose Van Schaick					81	77							158						vicinity of Quebec, Canada
3rd N. Y.	James Clinton					207	20							227						vicinity of Quebec, Canada
4th N. Y.	(late) James Holmes					91	23							114						vicinity of Quebec, Canada
1st Canadian	James Livingston					206								206						vicinity of Quebec, Canada
Arnold's[C]	Brig. Gen. Benedict Arnold					117	50							167						vicinity of Quebec, Canada
Canadians[C]	Jeremiah Dugan					123								123						vicinity of Quebec, Canada
2nd N. J.	William Maxwell					216								216						vicinity of Quebec, Canada
Mass. regt.	John Fellows					82								82						vicinity of Quebec, Canada
TOTAL OF INFANTRY						1688	786							2474						
ARTILLERY																				
Lamb's artillery	Capt. Isaiah Wool					31								31[G]						vicinity of Quebec, Canada
TOTAL OF ARNOLD'S TROOPS						1719	786							2505[G]						

MARCH 1776 (continued)

BRIGADE / UNIT	COMMANDING OFFICER	PRESENT FIT FOR DUTY & ON DUTY: COMMISSIONED OFFICERS	NONCOMMISSIONED OFFICERS	STAFF OFFICERS	RANK & FILE	TOTAL	RANK & FILE SICK, ON FURLOUGH, ETC.: SICK PRESENT	SICK ABSENT	ON COMMAND & EXTRA SERVICE	ON FURLOUGH	NOT JOINED		GRAND TOTAL	ALTERATIONS: DEATHS	DESERTED	TAKEN PRISONER	DISCHARGED	JOINED, ENLISTED, RECRUITED	LOCATION
NORTH CAROLINA CONTINENTAL REGIMENTS WITH STATE AND MILITIA FORCES AT WILMINGTON, NORTH CAROLINA																			
1st N. C.	James Moore	34	50	2 E	358	444	5 F		2	11	12		474						Wilmington, N. C.
2nd N. C.	Lt. Col. Alexander Martin	9	17		88	114	4			1			119						Wilmington, N. C.
Wilmington minute militia	Alexander Lillington												183						Wilmington, N. C.
Bladen Co. militia	Thomas Robeson												200						Wilmington, N. C.
Onslow Co. militia	William Cray												180						Wilmington, N. C.
New Hanover Co. militia	William Purviance												193						Wilmington, N. C.
Duplin Co. militia	James Kenan												357 H						Wilmington, N. C.
New Hanover volunteers	John Ashe												48						Wilmington, N. C.
Bladen independents	Griffith J. McRee												29						Wilmington, N. C.
TOTAL OF INFANTRY													1783						
CAVALRY																			
New Hanover light horse	Thomas Bloodworth												42						Wilmington, N. C.
New Hanover light horse	Patrick Stuart												20						Wilmington, N. C.
TOTAL OF CAVALRY													62 I						
TOTAL OF FORCES AT WILMINGTON													1845						
GRAND TOTAL													13219 J						

SOURCES OF THIS REPORT

1. RETURN OF THE REGIMENTS STATIONED IN BOSTON, MARCH 30, 1776, PETER FORCE PAPERS, CONTINENTAL ARMY TRANSCRIPTS, LIBRARY OF CONGRESS.

2. GENERAL RETURN OF TEN REGIMENTS OF MILITIA, OF THE PROVINCE OF MASSACHUSETTS BAY [sic.; see footnote A on the February 1776 report] IN THE SERVICE OF THE UNITED COLONIES, MARCH 30, 1776, PETER FORCE PAPERS, CONTINENTAL ARMY TRANSCRIPTS, LIBRARY OF CONGRESS.

3. A RETURN OF THE TROOPS BEFORE QUEBECK [sic.], IN THE SERVICE OF THE UNITED COLONIES, MARCH 30, 1776, PRINTED IN PETER FORCE, AMERICAN ARCHIVES, SER. 4, 5: 1100.

4. A GENERAL RETURN OF THE REGULAR TROOPS, MINUTE MEN, MILITIA, VOLUNTEERS & INDEPENDENTS AT WILMINGTON AND ON COMMAND, MARCH 29, 1776, MILITARY COLLECTION, TROOP RETURNS, NORTH CAROLINA DEPARTMENT OF ARCHIVES AND HISTORY.

A. See footnote A on the February report.
B. These New York units are the remnants of the original four New York Continental regiments. New regiments, also bearing these numbers, were being raised in New York State during March 1776.
C. Although commissioned as a colonel by Arnold and Wooster to raise Canadian troops, Dugan lost out to the efforts of Moses Hazen and Edward Antil, who got the commissions for the 2nd Canadian regiment from Continental Congress.
D. This return has only a "sick" category, not "sick present" and "sick absent." The return indicates that much of the illness was occasioned by "small pox by innoculation."
E. One adjutant and one surgeon for the entire force at Wilmington.
F. This return has only a "sick" category, not "sick present" and "sick absent."
G. The return notes that the term of service of 1,500 of these men would expire on April 15 and that probably one-half of those men would be retained in service. It is also noted that 350 men of various regiments had joined since the figures were collected.
H. This unit had contained twenty-six more men, but they were subtracted on the manuscript because they had "deserted from their Post at Old Town."
I. In addition to these men, the manuscript notes that "Col. Caswell with about 600 men is within ten miles of this town."
J. Because of the incompleteness of two of these returns, the grand total is the only combined figure that can be given here.

APRIL 1776

BRIGADE	UNIT	COMMANDING OFFICER	PRESENT FIT FOR DUTY & ON DUTY: COMMISSIONED OFFICERS	NONCOMMISSIONED OFFICERS	STAFF OFFICERS	RANK & FILE	TOTAL	RANK & FILE SICK, ON FURLOUGH, ETC.: SICK PRESENT	SICK ABSENT	ON COMMAND & EXTRA SERVICE	ON FURLOUGH	RECRUITING	PRISONERS OF WAR	GRAND TOTAL	ALTERATIONS: DEATHS	DESERTED	TAKEN PRISONER	DISCHARGED	JOINED, ENLISTED, RECRUITED	LOCATION
	FORCES UNDER COMMANDER-IN-CHIEF GENERAL GEORGE WASHINGTON																			
	Pa. riflemen (1st cont'l.)	Edward Hand	24	29	4	429	486	11	23	38	10			568						New York City & vicinity
	2nd cont'l. (N. H.)	James Reed	27	42	3	375	447	37	42	6				532						ordered to Canada
	3rd cont'l. (Mass.)	Ebenezer Learned	34	48	5	428	515	29	43	56				643						New York City & vicinity
	4th cont'l. (Mass.)	John Nixon	29	42	4	318	393	43	39	35	3			513						New York City & vicinity
	5th cont'l. (N. H.)	John Stark	31	43	3	363	440	32	30	18				520						ordered to Canada
	7th cont'l. (Mass.)	William Prescott	28	41	4	343	416	39	42	9				506						New York City & vicinity
	9th cont'l. (R. I.)	James Mitchell Varnum	26	40	3	275	344	9	13	88	1			455						New York City & vicinity
	4 cos. 10th cont'l. (Conn.)	Samuel Holden Parsons	13	12	2	141	168	5	3	2				178						New York City & vicinity
	11th cont'l. (R. I.)	Daniel Hitchcock	27	39	5	281	352	14	26	46				438						New York City & vicinity
	12 cont'l. (Mass.)	Moses Little	29	43	4	322	398	5	33	137				573						New York City & vicinity
	13th cont'l. (Mass.)	Joseph Read	34	42	3	446	525	36	49	15				625						New York City & vicinity
	6 cos. 17th cont'l. (Conn.)	Jedediah Huntington	19	30	5	277	331	26	52	20				429						New York City & vicinity
	19th cont'l. (Conn.)	Charles Webb	29	43	3	395	470	40	23	80	12			625						New York City & vicinity
	5 cos. 20th cont'l. (Conn.)	(late) Benedict Arnold	17	27	1	175	220	26	22	34	3			305						New York City & vicinity
	21st cont'l. (Mass.)	Jonathan Ward	29	45	5	440	519	23	19	9				570						New York City & vicinity
	22nd cont'l. (Conn.)	Samuel Wyllys	27	44	3	437	511	26	45	19	4			605						New York City & vicinity
	23rd cont'l. (Mass.)	John Bailey	29	45	4	442	520	15	42	52				629						New York City & vicinity
	26th cont'l. (Mass.)	Loammi Baldwin	22	28	5	282	337	32	63	125				557						New York City & vicinity
	3 cos. 4th Pa. bn.	Anthony Wayne	12	16	1	207	236	23	1	2	1			263						ordered to Canada
	1st N. J.	William Winds	19	43	4	391	457	64	5	30	17			573						ordered to Canada
	1st N. Y.	Alexander McDougall	28	41	4	212	285	38	1	25	1			350						New York City & vicinity
	5 cos. 3rd N. Y.	Rudolphus Ritzema	17	24	2	212	255	22		2				279						New York City & vicinity
	3rd N. J.	Elias Dayton	35	48	2	600	685							685						ordered to Canada
	6th Pa.	William Irvine	17	24	1	310	352	7	16					375						ordered to Canada
	TOTAL OF INFANTRY		602	879	80	8101	9662	602	632	848	52			11796						
	ARTILLERY																			
	United Colonies artillery	Henry Knox	38	132	5	183	358	11	7	45				421						New York City & vicinity
	TOTAL OF WASHINGTON'S ARMY AT NEW YORK		640	1011	85	8284	10020	613	639	893	52			12217						
	DIVISION IN MASSACHUSETTS UNDER MAJOR GENERAL ARTEMUS WARD																			
	6th cont'l. (Mass.)	Asa Whitcomb	30	42	5	348[A]	425	28	8	31				492						Boston, Mass. area
	14th cont'l. (Mass.)	John Glover	31	39	4	222	296	13	7	51	17			384						Beverly, Mass.
	16th cont'l. (Mass.)	Paul Dudley Sargent	27	40	4	331	402	25	14	126	20			587						Boston, Mass. area
	18th cont'l. (Mass.)	Edmund Phinney	17	43	3	307	370	68	9	48	3			498						Boston, Mass. area
	27th cont'l. (Mass.)	Israel Hutchinson	29	41	4	483	557	39	21	66				683						Boston, Mass. area
	TOTAL OF INFANTRY		134	205	20	1691	2050	173	59	322	40			2644						
	ARTILLERY																			
	United Colonies artillery co.	Capt. Edward Burbeck	5	16		20	41	3		16				60						Boston, Mass.
	TOTAL OF WARD'S DIVISION IN MASSACHUSETTS		139	221	20	1711	2091	176	59	338	40			2704						
	GEORGIA BATTALION (1st Ga.) IN SAVANNAH UNDER COLONEL LACHLAN McINTOSH																			
	Ga. bn.	Lachlan McIntosh	14[B]	40		196	250	10[C]		13	11	1	5	290[D]						Savannah, Ga.
	GRAND TOTAL		793	1272	105	10191	12361	799	698	1244	103	1	5	15211						

OFFICERS SICK, ON FURLOUGH, ETC.	WASHINGTON'S ARTILLERY (ONLY)				WARD'S DIVISION				GEORGIA BATTALION				GRAND TOTAL
	COMMISSIONED	NONCOMMISSIONED	STAFF	TOTAL	COMMISSIONED	NONCOMMISSIONED	STAFF	TOTAL	COMMISSIONED	NONCOMMISSIONED	STAFF	TOTAL	
Sick Present	1	3		4	10	8		18	1	2		3	46
Sick Absent	1	4		5	10	6		16					
On Command	4	23		27	7	16		23		1		1	51
On Furlough					3	4		7	2	1		3	10
Recruiting					9	2		11	11	4		15	26
Prisoners of War										2		2	2
TOTAL	6	30		36	39	36		75	14	10		24	135

SOURCES OF THIS REPORT

1. GENERAL RETURN OF THE ARMY OF THE UNITED COLONIES COMMANDED BY HIS EXCELLENCY GEORGE WASHINGTON... APRIL 28, 1776, RECORD GROUP 93, NATIONAL ARCHIVES.
   1a. General Return of the Army...Commanded by...Washington, printed in Peter Force, American Archives, ser. 4, 5: 1151-52.

2. RETURN OF THE REGIMENT OF ARTILLERY IN THE SERVICE OF THE UNITED COLONIES, COMMANDED BY HENRY KNOX, MAY 5, 1776, PRINTED IN PETER FORCE, AMERICAN ARCHIVES, SER. 4, 5: 1199.

3. RETURN OF THE DIVISION OF THE CONTINENTAL ARMY, COMMANDED BY MAJOR-GENERAL WARD, MAY 4, 1776, PRINTED IN PETER FORCE, AMERICAN ARCHIVES, SER. 4, 5: 1193-94.

4. A RETURN OF THE STRENGTH OF THE GEORGIA BATTALION, APRIL 28, 1776, PRINTED IN PETER FORCE, AMERICAN ARCHIVES, SER. 4, 5: 1107.

A. The figure 343 is printed in Force's American Archives; however, judging from the two totals, it is clear that the correct figure is 348. Apparently the number was copied incorrectly from the manuscript.
B. Including one captain who appears in the total but does not appear in any column in the return. Another part of this return makes it clear that this officer existed, though he may belong in the officers sick, on furlough, etc. section.
C. The return has only a "sick" category, not "sick present" and "sick absent."
D. The return notes, "By the information I have, I suppose our recruiting officers may have about seventy or eighty men more, who are not come in yet."

BRIGADE

MAY 1776

UNIT	COMMANDING OFFICER	PRESENT FIT FOR DUTY & ON DUTY: COMMISSIONED OFFICERS	NONCOMMISSIONED OFFICERS	STAFF OFFICERS	RANK & FILE	TOTAL	RANK & FILE SICK, ON FURLOUGH, ETC.: SICK PRESENT	SICK ABSENT	ON COMMAND & EXTRA SERVICE	ON FURLOUGH	GRAND TOTAL	ALTERATIONS: DEATHS	DESERTED	TAKEN PRISONER	DISCHARGED	JOINED, ENLISTED, RECRUITED	LOCATION
FORCES UNDER COMMANDER-IN-CHIEF GENERAL GEORGE WASHINGTON																	
Pa. riflemen (1st cont'l.)	Edward Hand	16	21	3	428	468	13	20	36	10	547						New York City & vicinity
3rd cont'l. (N. H.)	Ebenezer Learned	33	47	5	323	408	29	31	127		595						New York City & vicinity
4th cont'l. (Mass.)	John Nixon	30	46	5	340	421	22	37	41	3	524						New York City & vicinity
7th cont'l. (Mass.)	William Prescott	29	44	4	360	437	36	13	11		497						New York City & vicinity
9th cont'l. (R. I.)	James Mitchell Varnum	23	43	4	317	387	13	9	75		484						New York City & vicinity
10th cont'l. (Conn.)	Samuel Holden Parsons	34	48	4	466	552	44	32	25	1	654						New York City & vicinity
11th cont'l. (R. I.)	Daniel Hitchcock	31	45	5	328	409	14	12	49		484						New York City & vicinity
12th cont'l. (Mass.)	Moses Little	33	47	4	350	434	21	13	92		560						New York City & vicinity
13th cont'l. (Mass.)	Joseph Read	33	45	3	410	491	41	21	70	1	624						New York City & vicinity
17th cont'l. (Conn.)	Jedediah Huntington	33	41	5	437	516	37	25	44	8	630						New York City & vicinity
19th cont'l. (Conn.)	Charles Webb	29	41	3	422	495	44	17	58	11	625						New York City & vicinity
20th cont'l. (Conn.)	(late) Benedict Arnold	28	44	5	371	448	37	15	68	3	571						New York City & vicinity
21st cont'l. (Mass.)	Jonathan Ward	27	43	4	364	438	43	9	92		582						New York City & vicinity
22nd cont'l. (Conn.)	Samuel Wyllys	32	42	5	412	491	60	24	38	5	618						New York City & vicinity
23rd cont'l. (Mass.)	John Bailey	32	46	4	432	514	22	16	79		631						New York City & vicinity
26th cont'l. (Mass.)	Loammi Baldwin	23	30	5	314	372	34	7	143		556						New York City & vicinity
1st N. Y.	Alexander McDougall	22	39	4	244	309	29	1	53	1	393						New York City & vicinity
3rd N. Y.	Rudolphus Ritzema	29	45	3	399	476	38	1	8	18	541						New York City & vicinity
TOTAL OF INFANTRY		517	757	75	6717	8066	577	303	1109	61	10116						
ARTILLERY																	
United Colonies artillery	Henry Knox	38	128	4	175	345	11	5	91	2	454						New York City & vicinity
TOTAL OF WASHINGTON'S ARMY		555	885	79	6892	8411	588	308	1200	63	10570						
TROOPS OF THE UNITED COLONIES SERVING IN CANADA UNDER BRIGADIER GENERAL JOHN SULLIVAN (Dated May 11--Before the Defeat at the Cedars)[A]																	
2nd cont'l. (N. H.)	James Reed	23	44	3	350	420	36	45	10		511						Canada
5th cont'l. (N. H.)	John Stark	29	46	4	389	468	24	16	5		513						Canada
8th cont'l. (N. H.)	Enoch Poor	27	41	4	406	478	28	68	32	1	607						Canada
15th cont'l. (Mass.)	John Paterson	22	32	5	238	297	35	36	162	6	536						Canada
24th cont'l. (Mass.)	John Greaton	34	46	5	281	366	24	28	26		444						Canada
25th cont'l. (Mass.)	William Bond	14	23	4	230	271	18	25	42		356						Canada
Det. 4th Pa. bn.	Anthony Wayne	6	9		128	143	27	1			171						Canada
6th Pa. bn.	William Irvine	34	48	5	609	696	24	9	5	1	735						Canada
3rd N. J.	Elias Dayton	31	43	5	528	607	28		2	7	644						Canada
1st N. J.	William Winds	23	35	2	377	437	28		32	4	501						Canada
1st Pa. bn.	John Philip De Haas	34	40	4	471	549	44	24	46		663						Canada
5 cos. Bedel's N. H.	Timothy Bedel	7	11	1	106	125	38	15	13		191						Canada
2nd N. J.	William Maxwell	35	39	4	227	305	49	15	177		546						Canada
Burral's Conn.	Charles Burral	35	48	5	279	367	239	24	21	2	653						Canada
Mass. state	Elisha Porter	27	34	5	109	175	99	155	67		496						Canada
2nd Pa. bn.	Arthur St. Clair	28	34	4	312	378	39	12	52		481						Canada
TOTAL OF FORCES IN CANADA		409	573	60	5040	6082	780	473	692	21	8048						
GRAND TOTAL		964	1458	139	11932	14493	1368	781	1892	84	18618						

OFFICERS SICK, ON FURLOUGH, ETC.	WASHINGTON'S ARTILLERY (ONLY)			
	COMMISSIONED	NONCOMMISSIONED	STAFF	TOTAL
Sick Present		3		3
Sick Absent		3		3
On Command	13	54		67
TOTAL	13	60		73

SOURCES OF THIS REPORT

1. GENERAL RETURN OF THE ARMY OF THE UNITED COLONIES COMMANDED BY HIS EXCELLENCY GEORGE WASHINGTON...MAY 19, 1776, RECORD GROUP 93, NATIONAL ARCHIVES.

2. RETURN OF THE TROOPS OF THE UNITED COLONIES, SERVING IN CANADA, UNDER THE COMMAND OF BRIGADIER-GENERAL JOHN SULLIVAN, MAY 11, 1776, GATES PAPERS, NEW-YORK HISTORICAL SOCIETY.
2a. Return of the Troops...Serving in Canada, printed in Peter Force, American Archives, ser. 4, 6: 411-12.

A. For the difficulties in getting accurate returns of the forces in Canada during their retreat, see footnote C on our June 1776 report.

JUNE 1776

BRIGADE	UNIT	COMMANDING OFFICER	PRESENT FIT FOR DUTY & ON DUTY: COMMISSIONED OFFICERS	NONCOMMISSIONED OFFICERS	STAFF OFFICERS	RANK & FILE	TOTAL	RANK & FILE SICK, ON FURLOUGH, ETC.: SICK PRESENT	SICK ABSENT	ON COMMAND & EXTRA SERVICE	ON FURLOUGH	PRISONERS [B]	GRAND TOTAL	ALTERATIONS: DEATHS	DESERTED	TAKEN PRISONER	DISCHARGED	JOINED, ENLISTED, RECRUITED	LOCATION
	FORCES UNDER COMMANDER-IN-CHIEF GENERAL GEORGE WASHINGTON																		
	6 cos. Pa. riflemen (1st cont'l.)	Edward Hand	21	19	4	433	477	20	8	97	19		621						New York City & vicinity
	3rd cont'l. (Mass.)	Ebenezer Learned	29	41	5	264	339	29	16	239			623						New York City & vicinity
	4th cont'l. (Mass.)	John Nixon	26	43	5	303	377	23	21	88			509						New York City & vicinity
	7th cont'l. (Mass.)	William Prescott	29	44	5	320	398	25	16	55			494						New York City & vicinity
	9th cont'l. (R. I.)	James Mitchell Varnum	26	43	3	290	362	46	11	54			473						New York City & vicinity
	10th cont'l. (Conn.)	Samuel Holden Parsons	35	45	4	420	504	66	9	97	1		677						New York City & vicinity
	11th cont'l. (R. I.)	Daniel Hitchcock	26	39	3	249	317	26	9	108			460						New York City & vicinity
	12th cont'l. (Mass.)	Moses Little	28	39	4	289	360	45	10	125			540						New York City & vicinity
	13th cont'l. (Mass.)	Joseph Read	28	47	3	330	408	42	14	143	1		608						New York City & vicinity
	17th cont'l. (Conn.)	Jedediah Huntington	31	42	5	364	442	59	11	105	9		626						New York City & vicinity
	19th cont'l. (Conn.)	Charles Webb	27	37	4	335	403	67	13	142	4		629						New York City & vicinity
	20th cont'l. (Conn.)	(late) Benedict Arnold	33	45	4	373	455	42	4	122	1		624						New York City & vicinity
	21st cont'l. (Mass.)	Jonathan Ward	25	36	4	259	324	70	5	172			571						New York City & vicinity
	22nd cont'l. (Conn.)	Samuel Wyllys	30	41	5	334	410	63	8	147			628						New York City & vicinity
	23rd cont'l. (Mass.)	John Bailey	25	43	4	349	421	40	16	134			611						New York City & vicinity
	26th cont'l. (Mass.)	Loammi Baldwin	19	30	5	249	303	36	6	200	1		546						New York City & vicinity
	9 cos. 1st N. Y.	Alexander McDougall	28	51	4	293	376	41	10	114	3		544						New York City & vicinity
	3rd N. Y.	Rudolphus Ritzema	26	43	5	356	430	43	5	66	4		548						New York City & vicinity
	5th Pa. bn.	Robert Magaw	29	41	2	425	497	36	13	12	8		566						New York City & vicinity
	3rd Pa. bn.	John Shee A	33	44	3	461	541	14	10	22	10		597						New York City & vicinity
Scott	N. Y. militia	John Lasher	32	49	2	531	614						614						New York City & vicinity
Scott	N. Y. levies	William Malcolm	31	43	4	293	371	4		4			379						New York City & vicinity
Scott	N. Y. militia	Samuel Drake	30	45	2	487	564	12			1		577						New York City & vicinity
Scott	4 cos. N. Y. militia	Lt. Col. Johs. Hardenbergh, Jr.	13	20	1	221	255						255						New York City & vicinity
	TOTAL OF INFANTRY		660	970	90	8228	9948	849	215	2246	62		13320						
	ARTILLERY																		
	United Colonies artillery	Henry Knox	36	135	5	188	364	22	2	99	1		488						New York City & vicinity
	N. Y. artillery co.	Capt. Alexander Hamilton	5	16		61	82	4				2	88						New York City & vicinity
	TOTAL OF ARTILLERY		41	151	5	249	446	26	2	99	1	2	576						
	TOTAL OF WASHINGTON'S ARMY		701	1121	95	8477	10394	875	217	2345	63	2	13896						

OFFICERS SICK, ON FURLOUGH, ETC.	WASHINGTON'S ARTILLERY (ONLY): COMMISSIONED	NONCOMMISSIONED	STAFF	TOTAL
Sick Present	2	12		14
Sick Absent		2		2
On Command	16	70		86
TOTAL	18	84		102

[MAIN CHART CONTINUES ON FOLLOWING PAGE]

JUNE 1776 (continued)

BRIGADE	UNIT	COMMANDING OFFICER	PRESENT FIT FOR DUTY & ON DUTY					RANK & FILE SICK, ON FURLOUGH, ETC.							GRAND TOTAL	ALTERATIONS					LOCATION
			COMMISSIONED OFFICERS	NONCOMMISSIONED OFFICERS	STAFF OFFICERS	RANK & FILE	TOTAL	SICK PRESENT	SICK ABSENT	ON COMMAND & EXTRA SERVICE	ON FURLOUGH	PRISONERS [B]				DEATHS	DESERTED	TAKEN PRISONER	DISCHARGED	JOINED, ENLISTED, RECRUITED	
CONTINENTAL FORCES IN CANADA UNDER BRIGADIER GENERAL JOHN SULLIVAN (Dated June 12, 1776--By the End of the Month had Retreated to Ticonderoga) [C]																					
	2nd cont'l. (N. H.)	James Reed	24	44	3	230	301	100	59	50					510						Montreal, Canada
	5th cont'l. (N. H.)	John Stark	12	30	2	280	324	44	60	26	1				455						Sorel, Canada
	8th cont'l. (N. H.)	Enoch Poor	33	39	4	277	353	209	10	39					611						St. Johns, Canada
	15th cont'l. (Mass.)	John Paterson	11	47	5	200	263	35	156	80	6				540						Montreal, Canada
	24th cont'l. (Mass.)	John Greaton	11	48	5		64	305	28	26					423						St. Johns, Canada
	25th cont'l. (Mass.)	William Bond	25	26	4	230	285	18	25	42					370						Berthier & elsewhere
	1st Pa. bn.	John Philip De Haas	34	31	3	288	356	11	40	117					524						Sorel, Canada
	2nd N. J.	William Maxwell	30	32	4	324	390	42	44	73					549						Sorel, Canada
	1st N. J.	William Winds	28	37	3	357	425	26	23	15					489						Sorel, Canada
	2nd Pa. bn.	Arthur St. Clair	30	30	3	334	397	28	36	9					470						Sorel, Canada
	4th Pa. bn.	Anthony Wayne	11	14	2	146	173	16	1	56					246						Sorel, Canada
	Mass. state	Elisha Porter	14	16	2	108	140	11		67					218						Sorel, Chambly, etc.
	Burral's Conn.	Charles Burral	7	9	2	86	104	17	93	369					583						Sorel, Berthier, etc.
	6th Pa. bn.	William Irvine	31	41	4	493	569	31	3	93					696						Sorel, Canada
	Bedel's N. H.	Timothy Bedel	7	11	1	106	125	38	15	13					191						Berthier & unknown
	Independent co.	——— Stanton [D]	4	5		12	21	24	2						47						Berthier & unknown
	TOTAL OF FORCES IN CANADA		312	460	47	3471	4290	955	595	1075	7				6922						
	GRAND TOTAL		1013	1581	142	11948	14684	1830	812	3420	70	2			20818						

SOURCES OF THIS REPORT

1. GENERAL RETURN OF THE ARMY IN THE SERVICE OF THE UNITED COLONIES COMMANDED BY HIS EXCELLENCY GEORGE WASHINGTON... JUNE 29, 1776, RECORD GROUP 93, NATIONAL ARCHIVES.
   1a. Return of General Scott's Brigade, June 29, 1776 [this return included in the above], printed in Peter Force, American Archives, ser. 4, 6: 1119-20.
   1b. Return of the New York Company of Artillery... Commanded by Captain Hamilton, June 29, 1776 [this return included in the general return above], printed in Peter Force, American Archives, ser. 4, 6: 1122.

2. RETURN OF THE CONTINENTAL FORCES IN CANADA, JUNE 12, 1776, GATES PAPERS, NEW-YORK HISTORICAL SOCIETY.
   2a. Return of the... Forces in Canada, printed in Peter Force, American Archives, ser. 4, 6: 915-16.

A. The manuscript is creased badly at this entry, but it appears to be Shee's 3rd Pennsylvania battalion, which also follows Magaw in the July 1776 return and was present by this date.

B. It is not clear whether these prisoners are prisoners of war or confined by the Continental army.

C. The return notes, "The scattered and confused state of the troops when General Sullivan arrived in Canada has rendered it impossible to make an accurate Return. Even the Colonels of some Regiments cannot tell where some part of their Regiments are, they have been so harrassed and dispersed to different posts. I have as nearly ascertained the state of the Army as lay in my power; the totals are nearly right, but the distributions are somewhat erroneous. Some of those returned on command (Colonel De Haas, Colonel Maxwell, Colonel St. Clair, Colonel Wayne's and Colonel Irvine's) are either killed or taken prisoner at the Three Rivers--how many, are as yet unknown; and as some of them are daily returning, [I] hope [a] great part will recover our camp. Those of Colonel Paterson's, returned on command, and a greater part of Colonel Bedel's Regiment, not mentioned in the Return, were taken at the Cedars. Those returned sick are chiefly confined with the small-pox. As General Sullivan is using his utmost exertions to introduce order and regularity in the Army here, a true Return, with the casualties, will be forwarded very soon. Near two hundred Canadian volunteers this moment returned, but no return from Colonel Hazen."

D. We are unable to further identify this officer with certainty.

BRIGADE	UNIT	COMMANDING OFFICER	PRESENT FIT FOR DUTY & ON DUTY: COMMISSIONED OFFICERS	NONCOMMISSIONED OFFICERS	STAFF OFFICERS	RANK & FILE	TOTAL	RANK & FILE SICK, ON FURLOUGH, ETC.: SICK PRESENT	SICK ABSENT	ON COMMAND & EXTRA SERVICE	ON FURLOUGH	GRAND TOTAL	ALTERATIONS: DEATHS	DESERTED	TAKEN PRISONER	DISCHARGED	JOINED, ENLISTED, RECRUITED	LOCATION
	JULY 1776																	
	FORCES UNDER COMMANDER-IN-CHIEF GENERAL GEORGE WASHINGTON																	
	Pa. riflemen (1st cont'l.)	Edward Hand	24	29	4	243	300	26	9	11	16	362						New York City & vicinity
	3rd cont'l. (Mass.)	Ebenezer Learned	33	47	5	224	309	55	8	254		626						New York City & vicinity
	4th cont'l. (Mass.)	John Nixon	25	41	5	276	347	47	21	87		502						New York City & vicinity
	7th cont'l. (Mass.)	William Prescott	30	42	5	296	373	48	14	52		487						New York City & vicinity
	9th cont'l. (R. I.)	James Mitchell Varnum	26	42	3	282	353	64	10	41		468						New York City & vicinity
	10th cont'l. (Conn.)	Samuel Holden Parsons	32	45	4	307	388	137	5	136	6	672						New York City & vicinity
	11th cont'l. (R. I.)	Daniel Hitchcock	34	37	5	287	363	47	9	43		462						New York City & vicinity
	12th cont'l. (Mass.)	Moses Little	31	39	5	319	394	57	9	79		539						New York City & vicinity
	13th cont'l. (Mass.)	Joseph Read	28	45	3	245	321	108	11	161		601						New York City & vicinity
	17th cont'l. (Conn.)	Jedediah Huntington	32	45	5	226	308	134	25	151	2	620						New York City & vicinity
	19th cont'l. (Conn.)	Charles Webb	17	28	5	233	283	110	10	197	2	602						New York City & vicinity
	20th cont'l. (Conn.)	(late) Benedict Arnold	33	45	4	314	396	83	6	129		614						New York City & vicinity
	21st cont'l. (Mass.)	Jonathan Ward	26	38	4	218	286	115	1	179		581						New York City & vicinity
	22nd cont'l. (Conn.)	Samuel Wyllys	26	40	5	237	308	103	6	201		618						New York City & vicinity
	23rd cont'l. (Mass.)	John Bailey	25	32	4	227	288	141	9	161		599						New York City & vicinity
	26th cont'l. (Mass.)	Loammi Baldwin	16	20	5	187	228	98	5	196	1	528						New York City & vicinity
	7 cos. 1st N. Y.	Alexander McDougall	22	51	5	254	332	85	5	113		535						New York City & vicinity
	3rd N. Y.	Rudolphus Ritzema	17	33	5	253	308	122		81	3	514						New York City & vicinity
	5th Pa. bn.	Robert Magaw	33	43	4	401	481	53	28	10	3	575						New York City & vicinity
	3rd Pa. bn.	John Shee	34	43	4	435	516	49	10	2	4	581						New York City & vicinity
Scott	N. Y. militia	John Lasher	33	45	2	462	542	42	8	30	13	635						New York City & vicinity
Scott	N. Y. levies	William Malcolm	30	43	4	196	273	14	14	50	2	353						New York City & vicinity
Scott	N. Y. militia	Samuel Drake	32	46	3	359	440	57	12	40	12	561						New York City & vicinity
Scott	5 cos. N. Y. militia	Lt. Col. Johs. Hardenbergh, Jr.	16	24	3	222	265	22		7	3	297						New York City & vicinity
Heard	N. J. state	David Forman	32	44	5	370	451	42		13	7	513						New York City & vicinity
Heard	7 cos. N. J. militia	(late) Stephen Hunt	24	35	3	271	333	23		4	3	363						New York City & vicinity
Heard	7 cos. N. J. militia	Ephraim Martin	29	39	4	281	353	55	11	6	3	428						New York City & vicinity
Heard	3 cos. N. J. militia	Silas Newcomb	10	12	5	90	117	6		3		126						New York City & vicinity
Heard	5 cos. N. J. militia	Philip Van Cortlandt	17	24	4	176	221	14		4	6	245						New York City & vicinity
Wadsworth	1st Conn. state	Gold Selleck Silliman	31	43	5	245	324	36	2	92		454						New York City & vicinity
Wadsworth	2nd Conn. state	Fisher Gay	32	44	5	216	297	73		115		485						New York City & vicinity
Wadsworth	Conn. state	Philip Burr Bradley	32	44	4	398	478	43	2	28		551						New York City & vicinity
Wadsworth	3rd Conn. state	Comfort Sage	23	36	4	155	218	63	4	79		364						New York City & vicinity
Wadsworth	4th Conn. state	Samuel Selden	15	32	4	153	204	23		70		297						New York City & vicinity
Wadsworth	5th Conn. state	William Douglas	29	38	5	274	346	57		112		515						New York City & vicinity
Wadsworth	6th Conn. state	John Chester	26	40	4	184	254	44		126		424						New York City & vicinity
	TOTAL OF INFANTRY		955	1374	153	9516	11998	2296	254	3063	86	17697						
	ARTILLERY																	
	Cont'l. artillery	Henry Knox	29	123	5	178	335	17	5	114		471						New York City & vicinity
	TOTAL OF WASHINGTON'S ARMY		984	1497	158	9694	12333	2313	259	3177	86	18168						

JULY 1776 (continued)

BRIGADE

UNIT	COMMANDING OFFICER	PRESENT FIT FOR DUTY & ON DUTY: COMMISSIONED OFFICERS	NONCOMMISSIONED OFFICERS	STAFF OFFICERS	RANK & FILE	TOTAL	RANK & FILE SICK, ON FURLOUGH, ETC.: SICK PRESENT	SICK ABSENT	ON COMMAND & EXTRA SERVICE	ON FURLOUGH	GRAND TOTAL	ALTERATIONS: DEATHS	DESERTED	TAKEN PRISONER	DISCHARGED	JOINED, ENLISTED, RECRUITED	LOCATION
FLYING CAMP IN NEW JERSEY UNDER BRIGADIER GENERAL HUGH MERCER[E]																	
1st bn. Miles' rifle	Lt. Col. James Piper	27	30		409	466					466						New Jersey
2nd bn. Miles' rifle	Lt. Col. Daniel Brodhead	25	24		347	396					396						New Jersey
Pa. musketry	Samuel John Atlee	41	24		341	406					406						New Jersey
1st bn. Phila. associators	John Dickinson	32	36		360	428					428						New Jersey
2nd bn. Phila. associators	John Bayard	40	46		400	486					486						New Jersey
3rd bn. Phila. associators	John Cadwalader	34	42		310	386					386						New Jersey
4th bn. Phila. associators	Thomas McKean	33	39		285	357					357						New Jersey
5th bn. Phila. associators	Daniel Clymer	19	23		180	222					222						New Jersey
Chester Co. Pa. militia	William Montgomery	32	38		290	360					360						New Jersey
TOTAL OF INFANTRY		283	302		2922	3507					3507						
ARTILLERY																	
N. J. (6 pieces)					120	120					120						New Jersey
Philadelphia (2 pieces)	Samuel Mifflin				50	50					50						New Jersey
TOTAL OF ARTILLERY					170	170					170						
TOTAL OF FLYING CAMP		283	302		3092	3677					3677						
FORCES IN SOUTH CAROLINA[A]																	
1st N. C.	Francis Nash	34	42	3	278	357	88[B]				445						South Carolina
2nd N. C.	Alexander Martin	21	38	3	244	306	39			53	398						South Carolina
3rd N. C.	Jethro Sumner	34	34	2	272	342	55				397						South Carolina
8th Va.	Peter Muhlenberg	30	37	4	310	381	150			4	535						South Carolina
1st S. C.	Christopher Gadsden	24	42	3	257	326	94			2	422						South Carolina
2nd S. C.	William Moultrie	30	37	6	319	392	49			4	445						South Carolina
3rd S. C. (rangers)	William Thompson	27	18	3	366	414	18				432						South Carolina
5th S. C. (rifles)	Isaac Huger	15	16	4	262	297	13			4	314						South Carolina
6th S. C. (rifles)	Lt. Col. Thomas Sumter	24	26	2	247	303	26			7	336						South Carolina
TOTAL OF INFANTRY		239	290	30	2555	3118	532			74	3724						
CAVALRY																	
3rd co. N. C. horse	Capt. James Jones	3	2		36	41					41						South Carolina
ARTILLERY																	
4th S. C.[C]	Lt. Col. Owen Roberts																South Carolina
TOTAL OF FORCES IN SOUTH CAROLINA		242	292	30	2591	3155	532			74	3761						
GRAND TOTAL		1509	2091	188	15377	19165	3104	[D] ←	3177	160	25606						

JULY 1776
(continued)

OFFICERS SICK, ON FURLOUGH, ETC.	WASHINGTON'S ARTILLERY (ONLY)			
	COMMISSIONED	NONCOMMISSIONED	STAFF	TOTAL
Sick Present	2	7		9
Sick Absent		1		1
On Command	23	94		117
TOTAL	25	102		127

SOURCES OF THIS REPORT

1. RETURN OF THE ARMY IN THE SERVICE OF THE UNITED COLONIES...COMMANDED BY HIS EXCELLENCY GEORGE WASHINGTON...JULY 27, 1776, RECORD GROUP 93, NATIONAL ARCHIVES.
   1a. Return of the Army...Commanded by...Washington, printed in Peter Force, American Archives, ser. 5, 1: 639-40.

2. A GENERAL RETURN OF THE TROOPS IN NEW-JERSEY, UNDER THE COMMAND OF BRIG. GEN. MERCER, JULY 25, 1776, PRINTED IN PETER FORCE, AMERICAN ARCHIVES, SER. 5, 1: 574.

3. MONTHLY RETURN OF THE FORCES IN SOUTH CAROLINA, FOR JULY 1776, RECORD GROUP 93, NATIONAL ARCHIVES.
   3a. Monthly Return of the Forces in South Carolina, printed in Peter Force, American Archives, ser. 5, 1: 631-32.

A. This return notes, "These battalions were early hurried into a campaign, before several of them had time to form, therefore the Colonels cannot be so correct in their Returns as is necessary."
B. This return has only a "sick" category, not "sick present" and "sick absent."
C. No figures for this unit are given on the manuscript.
D. Total of all sick.
E. Although we have entered the figures for these troops in New Jersey under present fit for duty, the return itself gives only the numbers for the various ranks without specifying their condition. Doubtless, the figures represent a simple counting of those men who were present.

Engraved for Murray's History of the American War.
GENERAL LEE.

Major General Charles Lee as depicted in James Murray's *An Impartial History of the War in America* (Newcastle upon Tyne: T. Robson, 1780; from the copy in the Clements Library). At the time of this monthly report, Lee was supervising the defense of the Southern States. When the British left that area in the late summer, he rejoined the main army.

AUGUST 1776

BRIGADE	UNIT	COMMANDING OFFICER	PRESENT FIT FOR DUTY & ON DUTY: COMMISSIONED OFFICERS	NONCOMMISSIONED OFFICERS	STAFF OFFICERS	RANK & FILE	TOTAL	RANK & FILE SICK, ON FURLOUGH, ETC.: SICK PRESENT	SICK ABSENT	ON COMMAND & EXTRA SERVICE	ON FURLOUGH	GRAND TOTAL	ALTERATIONS: DEATHS	DESERTED	TAKEN PRISONER	DISCHARGED	JOINED, ENLISTED, RECRUITED	LOCATION
	FORCES UNDER COMMANDER-IN-CHIEF GENERAL GEORGE WASHINGTON (In Large Part Retreating from Long Island at the End of the Month)--NO RETURN AVAILABLE																	
	NORTHERN DEPARTMENT COMMANDED BY MAJOR GENERAL HORATIO GATES																	
1st brig.	24th cont'l. (Mass.)	John Greaton	15	20	3	115	153	69	20	125		367						Ticonderoga, N. Y.
1st brig.	25th cont'l. (Mass.)	William Bond	10	14	3	78	105	90	79	144		418						Ticonderoga, N. Y.
1st brig.	Cont'l regt. (Conn.)	Charles Burrall	10	26	2	121	159	83	61	143	7	453						Ticonderoga, N. Y.
1st brig.	Mass. militia	Elisha Porter	19	27	2	93	141	111	28	114	2	396						Ticonderoga, N. Y.
2nd brig.	2nd cont'l. (N. H.)	(late) James Reed	21	34	4	195	254	54	57	42		407						Ticonderoga, N. Y.
2nd brig.	15th cont'l. (Mass.)	John Paterson	18	28	3	150	199	74	65	79	14	431						Ticonderoga, N. Y.
2nd brig.	N. H. rangers	Lt. Col. Joseph Wait	18	26	3	138	185	49	19	52	160	465						Ticonderoga, N. Y.
3rd brig.	5th cont'l. (N. H.)	John Stark	28	33	5	188	254	79	57	29	1	420						Ticonderoga, N. Y.
3rd brig.	8th cont'l. (N. H.)	Enoch Poor	28	38	5	157	228	189	63	77	1	558						Ticonderoga, N. Y.
3rd brig.	2nd N. J.	William Maxwell	25	32	4	234	295	50	116	16		477						Ticonderoga, N. Y.
3rd brig.	Wingate's N. H.	Joshua Wingate	34	44	3	425	506	76	14	112		708						Ticonderoga, N. Y.
3rd brig.	Wyman's N. H.	Isaac Wyman	30	53	2	381	466	81	49	77		673						Ticonderoga, N. Y.
4th brig.	2nd Pa. bn.	(late) Arthur St. Clair	23	31	2	232	288	87	74	36		485						Ticonderoga, N. Y.
4th brig.	1st Pa. bn.	John Philip De Haas	31	31	4	274	340	74	83	24		521						Ticonderoga, N. Y.
4th brig.	1st N. J.	William Winds	28	44	2	225	299	97	55	31		482						Ticonderoga, N. Y.
4th brig.	4th Pa. bn.	Anthony Wayne	32	46	3	344	425	139	16	23		603						Ticonderoga, N. Y.
4th brig.	Independent rifle co.	Capt. John Nelson	4	4		49	57	9				66						Ticonderoga, N. Y.
5th brig.	Mass. militia	Jonathan Reed	35	48	4	474	561	39	20	95		715						Ticonderoga, N. Y.
5th brig.	Mass. militia	Edward Wigglesworth	34	39	4	291	368	12	21	118		519						Ticonderoga, N. Y.
5th brig.	Mass. militia	Ephraim Wheelock	18	27	3	224	272	15	5	291		583						Ticonderoga, N. Y.
5th brig.	Mass. militia	Benjamin Ruggles Woodbridge	29	46	2	511	588	39	11	18		656						Ticonderoga, N. Y.
	6th Pa.	William Irvine	27	42	4	297	370	97	40	68		575						Crown Point, N. Y.
	Pt. 5th N. Y.	Goose Van Schaick	17	33	3	183	236	45	2	51	7	341						Fort George, N. Y.
	Pt. N. Y. levies	Cornelius Van Dyck	10	14	3	93	120	23		26		169						Fort George, N. Y.
	Pt. Conn. state	Heman Swift	28	43	5	355	431	45	9	32	4	521						Skenesborough (Whitehall), N. Y.
	Pt. Conn. state	Samuel Mott	19	31		245	295	30	3	4		332						Skenesborough (Whitehall), N. Y.
	Pt. 4th N. Y.	Cornelius D. Wynkoop	13	14	3	78	108	35	12	16	4	175						Skenesborough (Whitehall), N. Y.
	Pt. N. Y. levies	Cornelius Van Dyck	6	8		55	69	10	6	7		92						Skenesborough (Whitehall), N. Y.
	Artificers		9	2		194	205	56			2	263						Skenesborough (Whitehall), N. Y.
	TOTAL OF INFANTRY		619	878	81	6399	7977	1857	985	1850	202	12871						
	ARTILLERY																	
	Cont'l. artillery co.	Maj. Stephen Badlam	8	35	3	48	94	21	13	14		142						Ticonderoga, N. Y.
	TOTAL OF NORTHERN DEPARTMENT		627	913	84	6447	8071	1878	998	1864	202	13013						

AUGUST 1776 (continued)

BRIGADE

UNIT	COMMANDING OFFICER	Present Fit for Duty & on Duty: Commissioned Officers	Noncommissioned Officers	Staff Officers	Rank & File	Total	Rank & File Sick, on Furlough, etc.: Sick Present	Sick Absent	On Command & Extra Service	On Furlough	GRAND TOTAL	Alterations: Deaths	Deserted	Taken Prisoner	Discharged	Joined, Enlisted, Recruited	LOCATION
FLYING CAMP IN NEW JERSEY UNDER BRIGADIER GENERAL HUGH MERCER (Dated August 20)																	
N. J. militia	Maj. Matthias Shipman	21	29	2	158	210	4 [C]				214						South Amboy, N. J.
Del. flying camp	Samuel Patterson	35	47	6	309	397	89				486						Perth Amboy, N. J.
N. J. militia	Lt. Col. Jonathan Deare	19	20	3	138	180	6			5	191						Perth Amboy, N. J.
N. J. militia	Richard Somers	12	27	3	74	116	6				122						Perth Amboy, N. J.
N. J. militia	David Chambers	15	23	3	207	248	4			3	255						Woodbridge, N. J.
N. J. militia	Samuel Dick	15	22	2	94	133	6				139						Woodbridge, N. J.
N. J. militia	Lt. Col. Enos Seeley [A]	23	26	3	145	197	12			2	211						Woodbridge, N. J.
Pa. flying camp	Lt. Col. Lawrence [A]	11	12		98	121					121						Elizabethtown, N. J.
N. J. militia	Edward Thomas	25	39	5	265	334					334						Elizabethtown, N. J.
N. J. militia	Jacob Ford, Jr.	24	37	4	278	343					343						Elizabethtown, N. J.
N. J. militia	Joseph Beavers	15	21	3	145	184					184						Elizabethtown, N. J.
Pa. flying camp	______ Moore [A]	25	26	4	157	212	26			4	242						Newark, N. J.
Pa. flying camp	Jacob Klotz	30	32		314	376	28			2	406						Fort Lee, N. J.
Pa. flying camp	Michael Swope	32	42	4	310	388	47			1	436						Fort Lee, N. J.
Pa. flying camp	Lt. Col. Frederick Watts	35	41	5	362	443	101			2	546						Fort Lee, N. J.
Pa. flying camp	William Montgomery	25	29	2	244	300	35				335						Fort Lee, N. J.
Pa. flying camp	Richard McAllister [B]	26	30	3	301	360	40			4	404						Fort Lee, N. J.
Pa. flying camp	Lt. Col. William Baxter [B]	23	30	4	289	346	36			8	390						Fort Lee, N. J.
TOTAL OF FLYING CAMP		411	533	56	3888	4888	440			31	5359 [F]						
GRAND TOTAL		1038	1446	140	10335	12959	3316 [D] ←		1864	233	18372						

SOURCES OF THIS REPORT

1. GENERAL RETURN OF THE FORCES OF THE UNITED STATES OF AMERICA SERVING IN THE NORTHERN DEPARTMENT, UNDER THE COMMAND OF THE HON. MAJOR-GENERAL GATES, AUGUST 24, 1776, PRINTED IN PETER FORCE, AMERICAN ARCHIVES, SER. 5, 1: 1199-1200.

2. A GENERAL RETURN OF THE ARMY IN NEW-JERSEY, UNDER THE COMMAND OF THE HON. HUGH MERCER, ESQ., BRIGADIER GENERAL, IN THE SERVICE OF THE UNITED STATES, AUGUST 20, 1776, PRINTED IN PETER FORCE, AMERICAN ARCHIVES, SER. 5, 1: 1079-80.

A. We have been unable to identify with certainty the first names of these officers.

B. Pennsylvania Archives, ser. 5, 5: 447, contains a roll that leaves no doubt of the identity of this commander of the Bucks County Flying Camp unit, although Heitman and Boatner were unable to get beyond his last name. See Mark M. Boatner, Encyclopedia of the American Revolution, pp. 371-73, 387.

C. This return has only a "sick" category, not "sick present" and "sick absent."

D. Total of all the sick.

E. The return notes, "All Dayton's, Elmore's, and Nicholson's Regiments, with most of Wynkoop's, and V. Dyck's and two Companies of V. Schaick's, are at Albany and upon the Mohawk River. As we never get Returns from these places, they are not included in the above General Return."

F. The return notes that four companies of Maryland enlisted militia had just joined the Flying Camp and were to stay until December 1 but are not on this return.

G. Actually, a large portion of the forces were on Mount Independence, across Lake Champlain (very narrow at this point) from Ticonderoga.

SEPTEMBER 1776

BRIGADE	UNIT	COMMANDING OFFICER	PRESENT FIT FOR DUTY & ON DUTY: COMMISSIONED OFFICERS	NONCOMMISSIONED OFFICERS	STAFF OFFICERS	RANK & FILE	TOTAL	RANK & FILE SICK, ON FURLOUGH, ETC.: SICK PRESENT	SICK ABSENT	ON COMMAND & EXTRA SERVICE	ON FURLOUGH				GRAND TOTAL	ALTERATIONS: DEATHS	DESERTED	TAKEN PRISONER	DISCHARGED	JOINED, ENLISTED, RECRUITED	LOCATION
FORCES UNDER COMMANDER-IN-CHIEF GENERAL GEORGE WASHINGTON																					
Parsons	7th cont'l. (Mass.)	William Prescott	14	30	4	186	234	57	75	71					437						Heights of Harlem & vicinity
Parsons	10th cont'l. (Conn.)	John Tyler	23	28	2	261	314	48	119	133	4				618						Heights of Harlem & vicinity
Parsons	17th cont'l. (Conn.)	Jedediah Huntington	9	28	3	97	137	33	105	93					368						Heights of Harlem & vicinity
Parsons	21st cont'l. (Mass.)	Jonathan Ward	16	27	5	142	190	35	101	206	2				534						Heights of Harlem & vicinity
Parsons	22nd cont'l. (Conn.)	Samuel Wyllys	20	25	2	197	244	24	138	145					551						Heights of Harlem & vicinity
G. Clinton	N. Y. militia	Thomas Thomas	20	42	3	236	301	45	43	24	1				414						Heights of Harlem & vicinity
G. Clinton	N. Y. militia	Morris Graham	24	37	3	136	200	39		47	4				290						Heights of Harlem & vicinity
G. Clinton	N. Y. militia	Jacobus Swartwout	20	36	5	250	311	66	8	17	3				405						Heights of Harlem & vicinity
G. Clinton	N. Y. militia	Isaac Nicoll	21	34	3	226	284	71	3	1	2				361						Heights of Harlem & vicinity
G. Clinton	N. Y. militia	Levi Pawling	26	36	3	282	347	51	6	15	4				423						Heights of Harlem & vicinity
Scott	N. Y. militia	John Lasher	27	31	5	165	228	48	13	11	2				302						Heights of Harlem & vicinity
Scott	N. Y. levies	William Malcolm	29	25	3	143	200	16	5	11	2				234						Heights of Harlem & vicinity
Scott	N. Y. militia	Samuel Drake	33	31	4	160	228	55	174	41					498						Heights of Harlem & vicinity
Scott	N. Y. militia	Cornelius Humphrey	15	22	2	140	179	49	24	17	3				272						Heights of Harlem & vicinity
Sargent	16th cont'l. (Mass.)	Paul Dudley Sargent	20	29	4	272	325	65	86	84					560						Heights of Harlem & vicinity
Sargent	Ward's Conn.	Andrew Ward	30	38	5	287	360	90	12	36					498						Heights of Harlem & vicinity
Hand	1st cont'l. (Pa.)	Edward Hand	27	39	5	229	300	32	26	23	7				388						Heights of Harlem & vicinity
Hand	Pa. bn. flying camp	Henry Haller	20	33	3	322	378	15			1				394						Heights of Harlem & vicinity
Hand	Pa. bn. flying camp	James Cunningham	30	24	3	364	431	55	28	4	7				525						Heights of Harlem & vicinity
	Conn. militia light horse	Maj. Ebenezer Backus	25	35	2	122	184	15	4	19					222						Heights of Harlem & vicinity
Nixon	4th cont'l. (Mass.)	Thomas Nixon	25	34	3	258	320	63	22	68					473						Heights of Harlem & vicinity
Nixon	9th cont'l. (R. I.)	James Mitchell Varnum	23	30	3	188	244	18	116	60					438						Fort Lee, N. J.
Nixon	11th cont'l. (R. I.)	Daniel Hitchcock	24	32	2	157	215	128	6	66					415						Fort Lee, N. J.
Nixon	12th cont'l. (Mass.)	Moses Little	24	40	3	250	317	36	58[D]	106					517						Fort Lee, N. J.
Nixon	23rd cont'l. (Mass.)	John Bailey	22	28	4	214	268	141	2	139					550						Fort Lee, N. J.
Wadsworth	2nd Conn. state	(late) Fisher Gay	29	46	5	184	264	65	133	48	1				511						Heights of Harlem & vicinity
Wadsworth	3rd Conn. state	Comfort Sage	31	45	4	175	255	120	135	60					570						Heights of Harlem & vicinity
Wadsworth	4th Conn. state	(late) Samuel Selden	30	43	4	255	332	62	105	75	1				575						Heights of Harlem & vicinity
Wadsworth	1st Conn. state	Gold Selleck Silliman	26	47	4	185	262	31	73	50					416						Heights of Harlem & vicinity
Wadsworth	Conn. state	Philip Burr Bradley	34	47	5	499	585	31	35	9	1				661						Bergen, N. J.
Wadsworth	5th Conn. state	William Douglas	33	49	3	171	256	147	148[E]	115					666						Heights of Harlem & vicinity
McDougall	19th cont'l. (Conn.)	Charles Webb	13	25	2	196	236	86	44	210	2				578						Heights of Harlem & vicinity
McDougall	1st N. Y.	Alexander McDougall	18	19	5	184	226	25	72	80					403						Heights of Harlem & vicinity
McDougall	3rd N. Y.	Rudolphus Ritzema	24	33	4	253	314	28	54	71	3				470						Heights of Harlem & vicinity
McDougall	Md. regt.	William Smallwood	34	54	3	419	510	110	237	80					937						Heights of Harlem & vicinity
Heard	N. J. militia	Philip Van Cortlandt	23	27	5	170	225	50	44	4	1				324						Heights of Harlem & vicinity
Heard	N. J. militia	Ephraim Martin	35	42	4	210	291	33	127		3				454						Heights of Harlem & vicinity
Heard	N. J. militia	Silas Newcomb	31	34	5	248	318	66	27	2					413						Heights of Harlem & vicinity
Heard	N. J. state	David Forman	22	30	5	195	252	25	131	16	2				426						Heights of Harlem & vicinity
Heard	N. J. militia	Joseph Phillips	21	28	4	160	213	21	13	10	2				259						Heights of Harlem & vicinity
Glover	3rd cont'l. (Mass.)	Ebenezer Learned	23	46	5	206	280	106	6	197	1				590						Bergen, N. J.
Glover	13th cont'l. (Mass.)	Joseph Read	25	38	3	226	292	138	8	128					566						Bergen, N. J.
Glover	14th cont'l. (Mass.)	John Glover	28	35	3	177	243	38	8	136					425						Fort Lee, N. J.
Glover	26th cont'l. (Mass.)	Loammi Baldwin	23	35	5	255	318	112	29	73					532						Fort Lee, N. J.
Fello	Mass. militia	Jonathan Holman	34	46	5	290	375	133	78	91					677						Heights of Harlem & vicinity
Fello	Mass. militia	Simeon Cary	38	54	4	271	367	159	62	66					654						Heights of Harlem & vicinity

SEPTEMBER 1776 (continued)

BRIGADE	UNIT	COMMANDING OFFICER	PRESENT FIT FOR DUTY & ON DUTY: COMMISSIONED OFFICERS	NONCOMMISSIONED OFFICERS	STAFF OFFICERS	RANK & FILE	TOTAL	RANK & FILE SICK, ON FURLOUGH, ETC.: SICK PRESENT	SICK ABSENT	ON COMMAND & EXTRA SERVICE	ON FURLOUGH	GRAND TOTAL	ALTERATIONS: DEATHS	DESERTED	TAKEN PRISONER	DISCHARGED	JOINED, ENLISTED, RECRUITED	LOCATION
	FORCES UNDER COMMANDER-IN-CHIEF GENERAL GEORGE WASHINGTON (continued)																	
Beall	2nd Md. bn. flying camp	Josias Carvil Hall	36	41	3	390	470	110				580						Heights of Harlem & vicinity
Beall	3rd Md. bn. flying camp	Thomas Ewing	24	31	3	336	394	97[E]	18			509						Heights of Harlem & vicinity
Beall	1st Md. bn. flying camp	Charles Greenberry Griffith	39	53	4	462	558	119	5	4	3	689						Heights of Harlem & vicinity
Beall	4th Md. bn. flying camp	William Richardson	26	35	3	385	449	140	34			623						Heights of Harlem & vicinity
Mifflin	27th cont'l. (Mass.)	Israel Hutchinson	26	31	3	253	313	69	12	175		569						Heights of Harlem & vicinity
Mifflin	3rd Pa. bn.	John Shee	33	41	4	332	410	65	80	6	1	562						Heights of Harlem & vicinity
Mifflin	5th Pa. bn.	Robert Magaw	29	42	4	291	366	67	103	8	5	549						Heights of Harlem & vicinity
Mifflin	Del.	John Haslet	32	47	5	429	513	39	92	8		652						Heights of Harlem & vicinity
Mifflin	Bn., Pa. regt. foot[A]	Lt. Col. Daniel Brodhead	17	14	3	87	121	33	44	13		211						Heights of Harlem & vicinity
Mifflin	Bn., Pa. regt. foot[A]	Lt. Col. Daniel Brodhead	16	15	4	158	193	48	30	24	1	296						Heights of Harlem & vicinity
Mifflin	Bn., Pa. regt. foot[A]	Lt. Col. Daniel Brodhead	6	11		81	98	13	37	3	2	153						Heights of Harlem & vicinity
	1st Va.	Isaac Read	35	46	4	321	406	130		6	48	590						Heights of Harlem & vicinity
	3rd Va.	George Weedon	36	57	6	398	497	139	56	18	1	711						Heights of Harlem & vicinity
	6th Conn. state	John Chester	31	43	4	292	370	125	20	107	2	624						Heights of Harlem & vicinity
	TOTAL OF WASHINGTON'S INFANTRY (includes light horse)		1563	2182	226	14759	18730	4161	3344	3384	122	29742						
	DIVISION UNDER MAJOR GENERAL NATHANAEL GREENE[B]																	
Greene's div.	Nixon's brig.	Brig. Gen. John Nixon																
Greene's div.	J. Clinton's brig.	Brig. Gen. James Clinton																
Greene's div.	Pa. militia brig.	Brig. Gen. James Ewing	107	119	9	993	1228	153	15	31	3	1430						Fort Lee, N. J.
Greene's div.	Conn. state	Philip Burr Bradley																
Greene's div.	N. J. militia	Theunis Dey	8	12	3	108	131					131						Fort Lee, N. J.
	TOTAL OF GREENE'S DIVISION NOT IN GENERAL RETURN		115	131	12	1101	1359	153	15	31	3	1561						
	ARTILLERY																	
	Cont'l. artillery	Henry Knox	31	139	3	172	345	17	35	46[F]	2	445						Mount Washington, N. Y.
	TOTAL OF WASHINGTON'S ARMY		1709	2452	242	16032	20435	4331	3394	3461	127	31748						

BRIGADE

SEPTEMBER 1776
(continued)

UNIT	COMMANDING OFFICER	PRESENT FIT FOR DUTY & ON DUTY: COMMISSIONED OFFICERS	NONCOMMISSIONED OFFICERS	STAFF OFFICERS	RANK & FILE	TOTAL	RANK & FILE SICK, ON FURLOUGH, ETC.: SICK PRESENT	SICK ABSENT	ON COMMAND & EXTRA SERVICE	ON FURLOUGH				GRAND TOTAL	ALTERATIONS: DEATHS	DESERTED	TAKEN PRISONER	DISCHARGED	JOINED, ENLISTED, RECRUITED	LOCATION
NORTHERN DEPARTMENT UNDER MAJOR GENERAL HORATIO GATES																				
24th cont'l. (Mass.)	John Greaton	17	28	3	91	139	81	14	127					361						Ticonderoga, N. Y.
25th cont'l. (Mass.)	(late) William Bond	15	24	3	40	82	194	29	77					382						Ticonderoga, N. Y.
Cont'l. regt. (Conn.)	Charles Burrall	15	27	3	75	120	83	38	125	25				391						Ticonderoga, N. Y.
Mass. militia	Elisha Porter	17	27	3	41	88	160	2	95	18				363						Ticonderoga, N. Y.
2nd cont'l. (N. H.)	(late) James Reed	22	39	4	88	153	176	12	43	9				393						Ticonderoga, N. Y.
15th cont'l. (Mass.)	John Paterson	23	26	3	159	211	81	57	44	33				426						Ticonderoga, N. Y.
N. H. rangers	(late) Timothy Bedel	16	31	4	123	174	102	22	59	97				454						Ticonderoga, N. Y.
Wyman's N. H.	Isaac Wyman	27	44	3	164	238	268	2	159					667						Ticonderoga, N. Y.
5th cont'l. (N. H.)	John Stark	30	34	3	153	220	124	28	28	1				401						Ticonderoga, N. Y.
8th cont'l. (N. H.)	Enoch Poor	28	39	4	117	188	205	39	87	2				521						Ticonderoga, N. Y.
2nd N. J.	William Maxwell	29	38	3	180	250	122	63	19					454						Ticonderoga, N. Y.
Wingate's N. H.	Joshua Wingate	31	38	4	159	232	246	6	198					682						Ticonderoga, N. Y.
2nd Pa. bn.	Joseph Wood	26	37	3	228	294	70	86	30					480						Ticonderoga, N. Y.
1st Pa. bn.	John Philip De Haas	33	28	4	220	285	39	147	26					497						Ticonderoga, N. Y.
Independent rifle co. (Pa.)	Capt. John Nelson	4	3		51	58	4	2						64						Ticonderoga, N. Y.
1st N. J.	William Winds	33	43	3	217	296	72	53	38					459						Ticonderoga, N. Y.
4th Pa. bn.	Anthony Wayne	30	46	5	342	423	123	17	21					584						Ticonderoga, N. Y.
6th cont'l. (Mass.)	Asa Whitcomb	22	28	4	187	241	110	51	96	2				500						Ticonderoga, N. Y.
Mass. militia	Jonathan Reed	31	48	4	219	302	271	9	120					702						Ticonderoga, N. Y.
Mass. militia	Ephraim Wheelock	34	18	4	147	203	234	4	244	2				687						Ticonderoga, N. Y.
Mass. militia	Edward Wigglesworth	28	25	5	160	218	145	10	156					529						Ticonderoga, N. Y.
Mass. militia	Benjamin Ruggles Woodbridge	33	46	4	285	368	192	9	84	1				654						Ticonderoga, N. Y.
Mass. regt.[C]	Samuel Brewer	41	58	5	386	490	137	16	116					759						Ticonderoga, N. Y.
Mass. regt.[C]	Aaron Willard	30	41	1	269	341	78	5	116					540						Ticonderoga, N. Y.
Conn. state	Heman Swift	11	25	3	130	169	201	111	66	2				549						Ticonderoga, N. Y.
Pt. Conn. state	Samuel Mott	9	16	2	111	138	65	19	38					260						Ticonderoga, N. Y.
6th Pa.	William Irvine	19	32	4	194	249	165	20	91	16				541						G
5th N. Y.	Goose Van Schaick	14	27	2	156	199	50	3	57	1				310						G
N. Y. levies	Cornelius Van Dyck	9	14	2	75	100	30	21	61					212						G
4th N. Y.	Cornelius D. Wynkoop	5	5	1	20	31	87	1	26					145						G
Pt. Conn. state	Samuel Mott	9	7	2	73	91	103	3	26	1				224						G
Artificers		6	7		57	70	28	3	15					116						Ticonderoga, N. Y.
TOTAL OF INFANTRY		697	949	98	4917	6661	4046	902	2488	210				14307						
ARTILLERY																				
Cont'l. artillery co.	Maj. Stephen Badlam	8	39	3	42	92	26	14	10					142						Ticonderoga, N. Y.
TOTAL OF NORTHERN DEPARTMENT		705	988	101	4959	6753	4072	916	2498	210				14449						
GRAND TOTAL		2414	3440	343	20991	27188	8403	4310	5959	337				46197						

OFFICERS SICK, ON FURLOUGH, ETC.	WASHINGTON'S ARTILLERY (ONLY)			
	COMMISSIONED	NONCOMMISSIONED	STAFF	TOTAL
Sick Present	7	12		19
Sick Absent	3	16	1	20
On Command	13	33	1	47
TOTAL	23	61	2	86

SOURCES OF THIS REPORT

1. GENERAL RETURN OF THE ARMY OF THE UNITED STATES OF AMERICA COMMANDED BY HIS EXCELLENCY GEORGE WASHINGTON...SEPTEMBER 28, 1776, RECORD GROUP 93, NATIONAL ARCHIVES.

1a. Return of Brigades under the more immediate command of His Excellency George Washington... September 30, 1776, printed in Peter Force, American Archives, ser. 5, 2: 607-8. [This is the same return, but to the brigade level only; the identical return of the artillery is attached to both returns.]

2. RETURN OF TROOPS IN GENERAL GREENE'S DIVISION, SEPTEMBER 29, 1776, RECORD GROUP 93, NATIONAL ARCHIVES.

2a. Return of Troops in General Greene's Division, printed in Peter Force, American Archives, ser. 5, 2: 607-8.

3. GENERAL RETURN OF THE FORCES OF THE UNITED STATES OF AMERICA SERVING IN THE NORTHERN DEPARTMENT UNDER THE COMMAND OF HON. MAJOR GENERAL GATES, SEPTEMBER 29, 1776, RECORD GROUP 360, NATIONAL ARCHIVES.

3a. General Return of...the Northern Department, printed in Peter Force, American Archives, ser. 5, 2: 617-18.

A. The two battalions of Miles' rifle regiment and Atlee's musketry battalion were ordered to be considered as one regiment under Brodhead after they were badly broken up at the battle of Long Island on August 27, 1776.

B. Nixon's brigade, Bradley's regiment, and Clinton's brigade (commanded by Glover) from Greene's division are included in the general return of Washington's army. The figures are the same on both returns for these units, and they have not been included twice. Figures are given for those units in Greene's division that are not included in the general return used above. Greene's division, with the exception of Thomas Nixon's 4th Continental regiment, was in New Jersey.

C. Two regiments raised during July and August to reinforce the American army at Ticonderoga.

D. The return of Greene's division included a separate "sick in hospital" category for Nixon's brigade, but those forty-six men were included in the "sick absent" column by the adjutant when compiling the general return.

E. Some figures for General Wadsworth's brigade and Colonel Griffith's regiment in General Beall's brigade are confused on the manuscript return; they are written over and in general are unclear. The figures have been read differently by the adjutant in computing the two sets of totals. We have taken the brigade totals, rather than the margin totals, to be correct, on the assumption that the brigade totals, being used more commonly, would have been checked with greater care.

F. The return of the artillery notes, "Those on command are in the Jerseys, at Fort Montgomery, and on the heights beyond King's Bridge."

G. The return notes that Dayton's regiment (not on the return), Van Schaick's, Van Dyck's, Wynkoop's, and half of Mott's regiments were upon the Mohawk and Hudson Rivers but were withdrawn on the approach of the enemy.

OCTOBER 1776

BRIGADE	UNIT	COMMANDING OFFICER	PRESENT FIT FOR DUTY & ON DUTY: COMMISSIONED OFFICERS	NONCOMMISSIONED OFFICERS	STAFF OFFICERS	RANK & FILE	TOTAL	RANK & FILE SICK, ON FURLOUGH, ETC.: SICK PRESENT	SICK ABSENT	ON COMMAND & EXTRA SERVICE	ON FURLOUGH				GRAND TOTAL	ALTERATIONS: DEATHS	DESERTED	TAKEN PRISONER	DISCHARGED	JOINED, ENLISTED, RECRUITED	LOCATION
	FORCES UNDER COMMANDER-IN-CHIEF GENERAL GEORGE WASHINGTON (Not Including the Forces Left at Ft. Washington & Vicinity)																				
Parsons	7th cont'l. (Mass.)	William Prescott	22	30	3	211	266	46	59	60					431						North of White Plains, N. Y.
	10th cont'l. (Conn.)	John Tyler	21	28	5	231	285	73	68	147	6				579						North of White Plains, N. Y.
	17th cont'l. (Conn.)	Jedediah Huntington	14	33	5	136	188	38	50	98					374						North of White Plains, N. Y.
	21st cont'l. (Mass.)	Jonathan Ward	19	28	2	176	225	26	72	207	1				531						North of White Plains, N. Y.
	Mass. militia	William McIntosh	24	41	5	259	329	20	23	1					373						North of White Plains, N. Y.
	Mass. militia	Thomas Carpenter	18	26	4	130	178	16	11	34					239						North of White Plains, N. Y.
	Mass. militia	Jonathan Cogswell	20	25	5	287	337	14	15	4	1				371						North of White Plains, N. Y.
	25th Conn. militia	Lt. Col. Dyar Throop	13	21	3	104	141	22	49	19					231						North of White Plains, N. Y.
	20th Conn. militia	Maj. Zabdiel Rogers	27	47	3	108	185	31	22	11					249						North of White Plains, N. Y.
	12th Conn. militia	Lt. Col. Obadiah Horsford	16	46	4	106	172		82	5					259						North of White Plains, N. Y.
	8th Conn. militia	Lt. Col. Oliver Smith	28	32	4	62	126	15	28	7					176						North of White Plains, N. Y.
Scott	N. Y. militia	John Lasher	24	30	4	104	162	25	24	74	5				290						North of White Plains, N. Y.
	N. Y. levies	William Malcolm	26	26	4	99	155	10	9	57					231						North of White Plains, N. Y.
	N. Y. militia	Samuel Drake	32	41	5	190	268	29	149	82					528						North of White Plains, N. Y.
	N. Y. militia	Cornelius Humphrey	16	20	3	123	162	20	6	57	2				247						North of White Plains, N. Y.
G. Clinton	N. Y. militia	Thomas Thomas	15	32	3	165	215	17	85	52	7				376						North of White Plains, N. Y.
	N. Y. militia	Morris Graham	22	33	3	102	160	22	53	67	4				306						North of White Plains, N. Y.
	N. Y. militia	Jacobus Swartwout	25	39	4	184	252	54	36	64	19				425						North of White Plains, N. Y.
	N. Y. militia	Isaac Nicoll	28	35	3	140	206	39	65	46	1				357						North of White Plains, N. Y.
	N. Y. militia	Levi Pawling	17	23	3	185	228	32	52	99	6				417						North of White Plains, N. Y.
Wadsworth	1st Conn. state	Gold Selleck Silliman	14	26	2	140	182	18	160	58					418						North of White Plains, N. Y.
	2nd Conn. state	(late) Fisher Gay	29	45	4	150	228	35	162	73	1				499						North of White Plains, N. Y.
	3rd Conn. state	Comfort Sage	15	46	2	170	233	72	185	51					541						North of White Plains, N. Y.
	4th Conn. state	Lt. Col. Jonathan Lattimer	15	27	2	224	268	42	142	69					521						North of White Plains, N. Y.
	5th Conn. state	William Douglas	19	37	4	228	288	36	128	72	1				525						North of White Plains, N. Y.
Nixon	4th cont'l. (Mass.)	Thomas Nixon	19	35	4	196	254	54	23	123					454						North of White Plains, N. Y.
	9th cont'l. (R. I.)	James Mitchell Varnum	23	29	3	161	216	21	108	79					424						North of White Plains, N. Y.
	11th cont'l. (R. I.)	Daniel Hitchcock	21	22	3	128	174	131	7	86					398						North of White Plains, N. Y.
	12th cont'l. (Mass.)	Moses Little	24	38	4	196	262	23	69	146					500						North of White Plains, N. Y.
	2nd R. I. militia	Christopher Lippitt	31	68	3	338	440	56	60	3					559						North of White Plains, N. Y.
J. Clinton	13th cont'l. (Mass.)	Joseph Read	17	34	2	232	285	123	7	125					540						North of White Plains, N. Y.
	14th cont'l. (Mass.)	John Glover	26	35	3	171	235	20	13	149					417						North of White Plains, N. Y.
	23rd cont'l. (Mass.)	John Bailey	17	29	3	175	224	158	2	147					531						North of White Plains, N. Y.
	3rd cont'l. (Mass.)	William Shepard	20	26	4	227	277	86	3	186	1				553						North of White Plains, N. Y.
	26th cont'l. (Mass.)	Loammi Baldwin	24	36	4	263	327	106	11	82					526						North of White Plains, N. Y.
McDougall	19th cont'l. (Conn.)	Charles Webb	16	27	3	191	237	73	46	208	9				573						North of White Plains, N. Y.
	1st N. Y.	Alexander McDougall	21	19	5	142	187	22	76	13	1				299						North of White Plains, N. Y.
	3rd N. Y.	Rudolphus Ritzema	21	27	4	198	250	12	61	61	10				394						North of White Plains, N. Y.
	Md. regt.	William Smallwood	30	37	8	298	373	84	354	57	1				869						North of White Plains, N. Y.
Fellows	Mass. militia	Jonathan Holman	22	29	4	306	361	102	84	80					627						North of White Plains, N. Y.
	Mass. militia	Simeon Cary	29	41	2	318	390	70	99	67					626						North of White Plains, N. Y.
	Mass. militia	Jonathan Smith	13	36	5	311	365	51	116	52					584						North of White Plains, N. Y.
Saltonstall	16th cont'l. (Mass.)	Paul Dudley Sargent	13	28	3	242	286	50	106	100					542						North of White Plains, N. Y.
	6th Conn. state	John Chester	9	25	4	234	272	107	41	135	3				558						North of White Plains, N. Y.
	5th Conn. militia	Lt. Col. Experience Storrs	5	23	3	62	93	48	78	42					261						North of White Plains, N. Y.
	21st Conn. militia	John Douglass	21	35	4	56	116	41	25	22	1				205						North of White Plains, N. Y.
	3rd Conn. militia	Lt. Col. John Ely	29	38	3	119	189	53	57	18					317						North of White Plains, N. Y.
	7th Conn. militia	Maj. Sylvanus Graves	5	16	2	57	80	47	122	15	2				266						North of White Plains, N. Y.
	10th Conn. militia	Lt. Col. Jonathan Baldwin	27	44	3	288	362	50	32	56					500						North of White Plains, N. Y.

OCTOBER 1776 (continued)

BRIGADE	UNIT	COMMANDING OFFICER	PRESENT FIT FOR DUTY & ON DUTY: COMMISSIONED OFFICERS	NONCOMMISSIONED OFFICERS	STAFF OFFICERS	RANK & FILE	TOTAL	RANK & FILE SICK, ON FURLOUGH, ETC.: SICK PRESENT	SICK ABSENT	ON COMMAND & EXTRA SERVICE	ON FURLOUGH	GRAND TOTAL	ALTERATIONS: DEATHS	DESERTED	TAKEN PRISONER	DISCHARGED	JOINED, ENLISTED, RECRUITED	LOCATION
	FORCES UNDER COMMANDER-IN-CHIEF GENERAL GEORGE WASHINGTON (continued)																	
Lincoln	Mass. militia	Eleazer Brooks	30	50	5	340	425	81	46		19	571						North of White Plains, N. Y.
Lincoln	Mass. militia	John Mosely	26	46	4	295	371	32	22			425						North of White Plains, N. Y.
Lincoln	Mass. militia	Benjamin Symonds	24	41	5	276	346	28	25		4	403						North of White Plains, N. Y.
Lincoln	Mass. militia	Samuel Howe	25	39	5	252	321	24	20		8	373						North of White Plains, N. Y.
Lord Stirling	1st Va.	Isaac Read	28	43	4	220	295	49	151	60	6	561						North of White Plains, N. Y.
Lord Stirling	3rd Va.	George Weedon	30	45	3	290	368	30	217	64	2	681						North of White Plains, N. Y.
Lord Stirling	Del.	John Haslet	13	21	3	273	310	26	228	21		585						North of White Plains, N. Y.
Lord Stirling	Pa. bn. flying camp	Henry Haller	19	28	4	260	311	6	27	7	1	352						North of White Plains, N. Y.
Lord Stirling	Pa. bn. flying camp	James Cunningham	32	38	3	318	391	57	47		7	502						North of White Plains, N. Y.
Lord Stirling	2nd bn. Miles' Pa. rifle	Maj. John Patton	13	13	1	196	223	15	59	13		310						North of White Plains, N. Y.
Lord Stirling	1st bn. Miles' Pa. rifle	Maj. Ennion Williams	12	11	2	132	157	9	41	26	5	238						North of White Plains, N. Y.
Heard	N. J. militia	Ephraim Martin	34	38	3	212	287	118	118			523						North of White Plains, N. Y.
Heard	N. J. militia	Silas Newcomb	29	32	4	184	249	48	41	45		383						North of White Plains, N. Y.
Heard	N. J. militia	Philip Van Cortlandt	19	26	5	173	223	35	38	6	10	312						North of White Plains, N. Y.
Heard	N. J. militia	Joseph Phillips	19	27	3	121	170	14	23	38	1	246						North of White Plains, N. Y.
Heard	N. J. state regt.	David Forman	34	21	5	193	253	20	115	22	4	414						North of White Plains, N. Y.
	1st cont'l. (Pa.)	Edward Hand	29	42	5	253	329	27	42	60	5	463						North of White Plains, N. Y.
	Ward's Conn.	Andrew Ward	16	19	3	208	246	61	116	63		486						North of White Plains, N. Y.
	TOTAL		1434	2174	242	13119	16969	3020	4711	3991	154	28845						
	TROOPS UNDER NATHANAEL GREENE IN NEW JERSEY																	
	Pa. militia	Brig. Gen. Daniel Roberdeau	81	118	7	802	1008	213	59	83	4	1367						Jersey shore
	Pa. militia	Brig. Gen. James Ewing[C]	94	116	12	837	1059	111	36	133	5	1344						Jersey shore
	Pa. bn. flying camp	Richard McAllister	23	28	3	218	272	21	16	1	1	311						Jersey shore
	Pa. bn. flying camp	Jacob Klotz	24	29	3	289	345	14	14	18	1	392						Jersey shore
	TOTAL OF TROOPS UNDER GREENE		222	291	25	2146	2684	359	125	235	11	3414						
	ARTILLERY																	
	9 cos. cont'l. artillery[A]	Henry Knox	39	144	4	182	369	13[F]	42	14	1	439						North of White Plains, N. Y.
	TOTAL OF WASHINGTON'S ARMY		1695	2609	271	15447	20022	3392	4878	4240	166	32698						

OCTOBER 1776 (continued)

BRIGADE	UNIT	COMMANDING OFFICER	PRESENT FIT FOR DUTY & ON DUTY: COMMISSIONED OFFICERS	NONCOMMISSIONED OFFICERS	STAFF OFFICERS	RANK & FILE	TOTAL	RANK & FILE SICK, ON FURLOUGH, ETC.: SICK PRESENT	SICK ABSENT	ON COMMAND & EXTRA SERVICE	ON FURLOUGH	GRAND TOTAL	ALTERATIONS: DEATHS	DESERTED	TAKEN PRISONER	DISCHARGED	JOINED, ENLISTED, RECRUITED	LOCATION
NORTHERN DEPARTMENT UNDER MAJOR GENERAL HORATIO GATES																		
1st brig.	24th cont'l. (Mass.)	John Greaton	17	27	4	131	179	52	3	97		331						Ticonderoga, N. Y.
	25th cont'l. (Mass.)	(late) William Bond	15	24	3	65	107	133	24	57		321						Ticonderoga, N. Y.
	Cont'l. regt. (Conn.)	Charles Burrall	22	31	2	81	136	66	36	51	28	317						Ticonderoga, N. Y.
	Mass. militia	Elisha Porter	17	19	3	89	128	68	28	66	19	309						Ticonderoga, N. Y.
	Conn. state	Heman Swift	23	40	5	135	203	130	89	30	2	454						Ticonderoga, N. Y.
	Conn. state	Samuel Mott	30	37	4	214	285	91	152	64		592						Ticonderoga, N. Y.
2nd brig.	2nd cont'l. (N. H.)	(late) James Reed	17	36	3	133	189	59	18	32	9	307						Ticonderoga, N. Y.
	15th cont'l. (Mass.)	John Paterson	26	32	3	168	229	64	46	20	33	392						Ticonderoga, N. Y.
	18th cont'l. (Mass.)	Edmund Phinney	29	39	5	184	257	110	17	44	1	429						Ticonderoga, N. Y.
	N. H. rangers	(late) Timothy Bedel	16	32	4	152	204	33	25	37	78	377						Ticonderoga, N. Y.
	Wyman's N. H.	Isaac Wyman	26	42	2	250	320	121	7	111		559						Ticonderoga, N. Y.
3rd brig.	5th cont'l. (N. H.)	John Stark	28	38	4	144	214	80	26	44	1	365						Ticonderoga, N. Y.
	8th cont'l. (N. H.)	Enoch Poor	24	41	4	133	202	157	43	72	2	476						Ticonderoga, N. Y.
	Wingate's N. H.	Joshua Wingate	29	39	4	237	309	175	4	115		603						Ticonderoga, N. Y.
4th brig.	1st Pa. bn.	John Philip De Haas	36	31	4	286	357	2	148	36		543						Ticonderoga, N. Y.
	2nd Pa. bn.	Joseph Wood	29	31	4	179	243	136	53	19	1	452						Ticonderoga, N. Y.
	4th Pa. bn.	Anthony Wayne	31	44	5	261	341	144	22	53		560						Ticonderoga, N. Y.
	6th Pa. bn.	William Irvine	21	27	4	199	251	182	62	26	1	522						Ticonderoga, N. Y.
	1st N. J.	William Winds	23	16	3	107	149	17	145	16		327						Ticonderoga, N. Y.
	2nd N. J.	William Maxwell	22	37	4	126	189	91	97	36		413						Ticonderoga, N. Y.
	3rd N. J.	Elias Dayton	33	48	3	445	529	24	49	11	2	615						Ticonderoga, N. Y.
	6th cont'l. (Mass.)	Asa Whitcomb	29	27	4	178	238	83	54	70		445						Ticonderoga, N. Y.
5th brig.	Mass. militia	Edward Wigglesworth	34	44	5	161	244	103	4	141	1	493						Ticonderoga, N. Y.
	Mass. militia	Benjamin Ruggles Woodbridge	32	47	4	336	419	115	2	88	1	625						Ticonderoga, N. Y.
	Mass. militia	Jonathan Reed	33	46	4	222	305	156	22	131		614						Ticonderoga, N. Y.
	Mass. militia	Ephraim Wheelock	30	26	4	180	240	130	25	217		612						Ticonderoga, N. Y.
	Mass. regt.[B]	Samuel Brewer	41	57	4	404	506	67	32	64	1	670						Ticonderoga, N. Y.
	Mass. regt.[B]	Aaron Willard	40	55	5	345	445	108	31	92		676						Ticonderoga, N. Y.
	5th N. Y.	Goose Van Schaick	15	21	3	132	171	48	1	60	4	284						Fort George, N. Y.
	N. Y. levies	Cornelius Van Dyck	6	13	1	39	59	10	15	87	1	172						Fort George, N. Y.
	4th N. Y.	Cornelius D. Wynkoop	11	12	1	52	76	52	16	38	6	188						Skenesborough (Whitehall), N. Y.
	TOTAL OF INFANTRY		785	1059	112	5768	7724	2807	1296	2025	191	14043[H]						
MILITIA WHICH JOINED THE NORTHERN DEPARTMENT TO DEFEND TICONDEROGA AFTER THE DEFEAT OF THE FLEET ON LAKE CHAMPLAIN (Dismissed Nov. 9)																		
	Mass. militia	Moses or B. Robinson[D]	24	28	3	93	148	1	3	9		161						Ticonderoga, N. Y.
	Mass. militia	Timothy Brownson	12	10	2	59	83			8		91						Ticonderoga, N. Y.
	14th N. H. militia	Enoch Hale	5	8	1	24	38					38						Ticonderoga, N. Y.
	13th N. H. militia	Samuel Ashley	20	12	3	100	135	3	1	3		142						Ticonderoga, N. Y.
	15th N. H. militia	Benjamin Bellows, Jr.	16	12	3	64	95					95						Ticonderoga, N. Y.
	17th N. H. militia	Jonathan Chase	21	19		54	94					94						Ticonderoga, N. Y.
	Mass. militia	Moses or B. Robinson[D]	19	18	3	93	133	6	2	30		171						Ticonderoga, N. Y.
	Mass. militia	Caleb Hyde	41	51		267	359		7			366						Ticonderoga, N. Y.
	TOTAL OF ADDITIONAL MILITIA		158	158	15	754	1085	10	13	50		1158						
ARTILLERY																		
	Cont'l. artillery co.	Maj. Stephen Badlam	11	37	3	40	91	16	3	8		118						Ticonderoga, N. Y.
	TOTAL OF NORTHERN DEPARTMENT		954	1254	130	6562	8900	2833	1312	2083	191	15319						
	GRAND TOTAL		2649	3863	401	22009	28922	6225	6190	6323	357	48017						

OFFICERS SICK, ON FURLOUGH, ETC.	WASHINGTON'S ARTILLERY (ONLY) COMMISSIONED	NONCOMMISSIONED	STAFF	TOTAL
Sick Present	1	8		9
Sick Absent	5	26		31
On Command	8	8	1	17
Wounded		1		1
TOTAL	14	43	1	58

SOURCES OF THIS REPORT

1. GENERAL RETURN OF THE ARMY IN THE SERVICE OF THE UNITED STATES, NOVEMBER 3, 1776, PRINTED IN PETER FORCE, AMERICAN ARCHIVES, SER. 5, 3: 499-502.

1a. Individual returns for the following regiments dated October 31, 1776 and containing the figures used in compiling the General Return, printed in Peter Force, American Archives, ser. 5, 3: 1319-22; 7th Cont'l. (William Prescott), N.Y. militia (Thomas Thomas), 8th Conn. militia (Oliver Smith), N.Y. militia (Jacobus Swartwout), and N.Y. militia (Morris Graham).

2. A RETURN OF THE FORCES ENCAMPED ON THE JERSEY SHORE UNDER THE COMMAND OF MAJOR GENERAL GREENE, OCTOBER 26, 1776, RECORD GROUP 93, NATIONAL ARCHIVES.

2a. Return of the forces...on the Jersey Shore, printed in Peter Force, American Archives, ser. 5, 2: 1250.

3. GENERAL RETURN OF THE FORCES OF THE UNITED STATES OF AMERICA SERVING IN THE NORTHERN DEPARTMENT, UNDER COMMAND OF THE HONOURABLE MAJOR-GENERAL GATES, NOVEMBER 9, 1776, PRINTED IN PETER FORCE, AMERICAN ARCHIVES, SER. 5, 3: 701-2.

A. Nine companies Continental artillery plus one colony company.

B. Two regiments raised in Massachusetts in July and August.

C. Force's printed version misreads the "Ewing" on the manuscript as "Ervin."

D. The return has only the name Robinson twice to identify two of these temporary reinforcement militia units. The letters of dismissal to Colonel B. Robinson and Colonel Moses Robinson from General Gates (dated November 9, 1776) are in Force's American Archives. Neither appears in Massachusetts Soldiers and Sailors of the Revolutionary War.

E. The individual regimental return of Colonel Thomas Thomas' regiment shows 165 rank and file fit for duty. However, the general monthly return gives the figure as 166. We have not been able to determine which of these printed returns is in error, and the problem is compounded by minor arithmetical errors on the totals of both these returns. We have given the figure from the individual regimental return, but it is possible that there was one more man in rank and file fit for duty.

F. Including four men who are listed in an unusual "wounded" category on this return.

G. As in the returns of Colonel Thomas' regiment (see footnote E), there is a disparity between the individual regimental return and the general monthly return on the number of men who were sick absent in Colonel Swartwout's regiment. We have used the figure 36 from the individual regimental return, rather than the 37 on the general return, but it is possible there was one more man sick absent in this regiment.

H. The return notes that "All Nicholson's and Elmore's Regiments, with part of Van Schaick's, Van Dyck's, and Wynkoop's Regiments" are not on this return since they were on the Mohawk and Hudson Rivers and made their returns to General Schuyler.

NOVEMBER 1776

BRIGADE	UNIT	COMMANDING OFFICER	PRESENT FIT FOR DUTY & ON DUTY: COMMISSIONED OFFICERS	NONCOMMISSIONED OFFICERS	STAFF OFFICERS	RANK & FILE	TOTAL	RANK & FILE SICK, ON FURLOUGH, ETC.: SICK PRESENT	SICK ABSENT	ON COMMAND & EXTRA SERVICE	ON FURLOUGH	GRAND TOTAL	ALTERATIONS: DEATHS	DESERTED	TAKEN PRISONER	DISCHARGED	JOINED, ENLISTED, RECRUITED	LOCATION
	FORCES UNDER COMMANDER-IN-CHIEF GENERAL GEORGE WASHINGTON																	
Mercer	27th cont'l. (Mass.)	Israel Hutchinson	21	29	3	179	232	74	15	95		416						New Jersey[C]
Mercer	20th cont'l. (Conn.)	John Durkee	28	42	6	343	419	52	28	55	4	558						New Jersey
Mercer	Md. regt.	(late) William Smallwood	21	24	7	210	262		534	23	2	821						New Jersey
Mercer	Conn. state	Philip Burr Bradley	7	13	2	86	108	1				109						New Jersey
Mercer	Md. & Va. rifle regt.	Lt. Col. Moses Rawlings	5	3		36	44					44						New Jersey
Stevens	4th Va.	Thomas Elliott	22	31	2	208	263	17				280						New Jersey
Stevens	5th Va.	Charles Scott	16	25	3	140	184	7				191						New Jersey
Stevens	6th Va.	Mordecai Buckner	31	38	5	224	298	50		15		363						New Jersey
Ewing	Pa. bn. flying camp	William Montgomery	22	31	3	177	233	13	39	45		330						New Jersey
Ewing	Pa. bn. flying camp	Lt. Col. Frederick Watts	20	23	5	134	182		28	63		273						New Jersey
Ewing	Pa. bn. flying camp	Richard McAllister	16	12	3	107	138	31				169						New Jersey
Ewing	Pa. bn. flying camp	Jacob Klotz	21	19	1	122	163	19	3	13		198						New Jersey
Ewing	Pa. bn. flying camp	——— Moore[A]	17	23	2	154	196	15	20	48	11	290						New Jersey
Hand	1st cont'l. (Pa.)	Edward Hand	27	39	6	246	318	40	52	22	4	436						New Jersey
Hand	Pa. bn. flying camp	Henry Haller	18	31	4	250	303	12				315						New Jersey
Hand	Pa. bn. flying camp	James Cunningham	35	37	3	347	422	50	27		8	507						New Jersey
	TOTAL UNDER WASHINGTON'S IMMEDIATE COMMAND		327	420	55	2963	3765	381	746	379	29	5300						
	DIVISION UNDER MAJOR GENERAL WILLIAM HEATH																	
	Parson's brig.	Brig. Gen. Samuel H. Parsons	72	95	11	569	747	95	249	399	4	1494						Peekskill, N. Y.
J. Clinton	Pt. 2nd N. Y.	(late) James Clinton	9	30	2	168	209	15		3	1	228						Fort Montgomery, N. Y.
J. Clinton	Pt. N. Y. militia	Cornelius Humphrey	10	33	4	178	225	15		6	2	248						Fort Montgomery, N. Y.
J. Clinton	Pt. N. Y. militia	Johannes Snyder	15	38	3	162	218	17		1	6	242						Fort Montgomery, N. Y.
J. Clinton	Pt. 2nd N. Y.	(late) James Clinton	8	16	3	102	129	17			4	150						Fort Constitution, N. Y.
J. Clinton	Pt. N. Y. militia	Cornelius Humphrey	3	8		44	55	11				66						Fort Constitution, N. Y.
J. Clinton	Pt. N. Y. militia	Johannes Snyder	9	24		103	136	10			2	148						Fort Constitution, N. Y.
G. Clinton	N. Y. militia	Thomas Thomas	14	28	3	168	213	23	64	53	5	358						Peekskill, N. Y.
G. Clinton	N. Y. militia	Morris Graham	18	33	2	108	161	26	37	84	9	317						Peekskill, N. Y.
G. Clinton	N. Y. militia	Jacobus Swartwout	23	28	4	210	265	22	85	20		392						Peekskill, N. Y.
G. Clinton	N. Y. militia	Isaac Nicoll	36	50	3	230	349	31	87	26	6	469						Peekskill, N. Y.
G. Clinton	N. Y. militia	Levi Pawling	26	33	3	248	310	32	48	71	20	481						Peekskill, N. Y.
G. Clinton	Det. N. H. militia	Thomas Tash	6	10		85	101	13		17		131						Peekskill, N. Y.
	Brig. N. Y. militia & levies	Brig. Gen. John Morin Scott	96	118	16	710	940	54	129	141	18	1282						Peekskill, N. Y.
	TOTAL OF HEATH'S INFANTRY		345	544	54	3085	4028	381	699	821	77	6006						
	ARTILLERY OF JAMES CLINTON'S BRIGADE																	
	Pt. Proctor's Pa. artillery	Maj. Thomas Proctor	2	5	1	35	43					43						Fort Montgomery, N. Y.
	Pt. cont'l. artillery	Henry Knox	1	1		8	10					10						Fort Montgomery, N. Y.
	Pt. cont'l. artillery	Henry Knox	1			7	8					8						Fort Constitution, N. Y.
	TOTAL OF ARTILLERY UNDER JAMES CLINTON		4	6	1	50	61					61						
	TOTAL OF FORCES UNDER HEATH		349	550	55	3135	4089	381	699	821	77	6067[B]						

NOVEMBER 1776
(continued)

BRIGADE	UNIT	COMMANDING OFFICER	PRESENT FIT FOR DUTY & ON DUTY: COMMISSIONED OFFICERS	NONCOMMISSIONED OFFICERS	STAFF OFFICERS	RANK & FILE	TOTAL	RANK & FILE SICK, ON FURLOUGH, ETC.: SICK PRESENT	SICK ABSENT	ON COMMAND & EXTRA SERVICE	ON FURLOUGH				GRAND TOTAL	ALTERATIONS: DEATHS	DESERTED	TAKEN PRISONER	DISCHARGED	JOINED, ENLISTED, RECRUITED	LOCATION
	FORCES UNDER MAJOR GENERAL CHARLES LEE (Dated November 24--Lee Finally Began His March to Join Washington Before the End of the Month)																				
Nixon	4th cont'l. (Mass.)	Thomas Nixon	15	32	4	172	223	57	13	135					428						North Castle, N. Y. area
	9th cont'l. (R. I.)	James Mitchell Varnum	15	37	3	178	233	21	83	80					417						North Castle, N. Y. area
	11th cont'l. (R. I.)	Daniel Hitchcock	17	15	1	132	165	30	80	91	2				368						North Castle, N. Y. area
	12th cont'l. (Mass.)	Moses Little	24	30	4	166	224	26	86	156	1				493						North Castle, N. Y. area
	2nd R. I. militia	Christopher Lippitt	27	51	3	296	377	61	68	24					530						North Castle, N. Y. area
Glover	3rd cont'l. (Mass.)	William Shepard	22	25	4	215	266	89	2	186	1				544						North Castle, N. Y. area
	14th cont'l. (Mass.)	John Glover	26	36	4	164	230	30	17	134					411						North Castle, N. Y. area
	19th cont'l. (Conn.)	Charles Webb	22	29	4	234	289	38	53	168	24				572						North Castle, N. Y. area
	23rd cont'l. (Mass.)	John Bailey	21	27	3	176	227	158	2	138					525						North Castle, N. Y. area
	26th cont'l. (Mass.)	Loammi Baldwin	25	33	4	259	321	116	10	69					516						North Castle, N. Y. area
McDougall	1st N. Y.	Alexander McDougall	20	14	3	97	134	67	74	72	1				348						North Castle, N. Y. area
	3rd N. Y.	Rudolphus Ritzema	17	25	2	215	259	28	71	27	4				389						North Castle, N. Y. area
	13th cont'l. (Mass.)	Joseph Read	26	32	3	236	297	126	5	106	1				535						North Castle, N. Y. area
Chester	16th cont'l. (Mass.)	Paul Dudley Sargent	9	17	4	169	199	41	139	100					479						North Castle, N. Y. area
	6th Conn. state	John Chester	19	25	4	258	306	65	66	94	2				533						North Castle, N. Y. area
	Ward's Conn.	Andrew Ward	18	16	2	214	250	31	116	63	6				466						North Castle, N. Y. area
	Conn. militia	Lt. Col. Jonathan Baldwin	23	41	3	327	394	27	53	16					490						North Castle, N. Y. area
Fellows	Mass. militia	Jonathan Holman	28	43	5	388	464	29	27	43					563						North Castle, N. Y. area
	Mass. militia	Simeon Cary	30	48	4	374	456	29	12	56					553						North Castle, N. Y. area
	Mass. militia	Jonathan Smith	23	40	4	362	429	34	33	38					534						North Castle, N. Y. area
Wadsworth	1st Conn. state	Gold Selleck Silliman	15	25	2	169	211	35	124	41					411						North Castle, N. Y. area
	2nd Conn. state	(late) Fisher Gay	21	32	5	202	260	30	73	71	1				435						North Castle, N. Y. area
	3rd Conn. state	Comfort Sage	15	30	2	205	252	61	126	50	1				490						North Castle, N. Y. area
	4th Conn. state	Lt. Col. Jonathan Lattimer	12	30	2	174	218	36	144	106					504						North Castle, N. Y. area
	5th Conn. state	William Douglas	20	36	4	207	267	25	122	71	3				488						North Castle, N. Y. area
	Conn. militia	Brig. Gen. David Wooster	71	104	9	303	487								487						North Castle, N. Y. area
	Conn. light horse	Maj. Elisha Sheldon	12	27	3	60	102	5		5	1				113						North Castle, N. Y. area
	TOTAL OF FORCES UNDER LEE		593	900	95	5952	7540	1295	1599	2140	48				12622						
	REMNANT OF NORTHERN DEPARTMENT (Serving as Garrison at Fort Ticonderoga and Mt. Independence) UNDER COLONEL ANTHONY WAYNE																				
	Cont'l. regt. (Conn.)	Charles Burrall	19	24	1	67	111	48	16	66	21				262						Ticonderoga, N. Y.
	2nd Pa. bn.	Joseph Wood	16	24	3	179	222	104	56	73	1				456						Ticonderoga, N. Y.
	4th Pa. bn.	Anthony Wayne	21	30	4	251	306	194	25	34	4				563						Ticonderoga, N. Y.
	6th Pa. bn.	William Irvine	15	19	4	104	142	246	70	32	13				503						Ticonderoga, N. Y.
	6th cont'l. (Mass.)	Asa Whitcomb	21	24	4	145	194	82	42	85	4				407						Ticonderoga, N. Y.
	3rd N. J.	Elias Dayton	27	45	3	363	438	94	53	6	1				592						Ticonderoga, N. Y,
	TOTAL OF FORCES UNDER WAYNE		119	166	19	1109	1413	768	262	296	44				2783						
	GRAND TOTAL		1388	2036	224	13159	16807	2825	3306	3636	198				26772						

NOVEMBER 1776
(continued)

SOURCES OF THIS REPORT

1. GENERAL RETURN OF THE ARMY [UNDER WASHINGTON], DECEMBER 1, 1776, RECORD GROUP 93, NATIONAL ARCHIVES.
   1a. General Return of the Army, printed in Peter Force, American Archives, ser. 5, 3: 1035-36.

2. A RETURN OF FOUR BRIGADES UNDER THE COMMAND OF MAJOR-GENERAL HEATH, NOVEMBER 24, 1776, PRINTED IN PETER FORCE, AMERICAN ARCHIVES, SER. 5, 3: 833-34.

3. A RETURN OF THE MEN IN GARRISON AT THE FORTS MONTGOMERY AND CONSTITUTION, NOVEMBER 23, 1776 [A RETURN TO THE REGIMENT LEVEL FOR JAMES CLINTON'S BRIGADE--BRIGADE TOTAL ONLY GIVEN IN THE RETURN LISTED ABOVE IN NUMBER 2], PRINTED IN PETER FORCE, AMERICAN ARCHIVES, SER. 5, 3: 823-24.

4. RETURN OF THE BRIGADE COMMANDED BY BRIGADIER-GENERAL GEORGE CLINTON, NOVEMBER 21, 1776 [LIKE NUMBER 3, THIS GIVES REGIMENTAL DETAIL FOR THE BRIGADE TOTAL FIGURES THAT WERE USED IN RETURN NUMBER 2], PRINTED IN PETER FORCE, AMERICAN ARCHIVES, SER. 5, 3: 791-92.

5. RETURN OF THE FORCES UNDER THE COMMAND OF GENERAL LEE, NOVEMBER 24, 1776, PRINTED IN PETER FORCE, AMERICAN ARCHIVES, SER. 5, 3: 831-32.

6. RETURN OF THE FORCES OF THE UNITED STATES OF AMERICA WHICH COMPOSE THE GARRISONS OF TICONDEROGA AND MOUNT INDEPENDENCE, NOVEMBER 29, 1776, GATES PAPERS, NEW-YORK HISTORICAL SOCIETY.
   6a. Return of...the Garrisons of Ticonderoga and Mount Independence, printed in Peter Force, American Archives, ser. 5, 3: 1589.

A. We have been unable to identify with certainty the first name of this officer, who also appears on the August 1776 return.

B. In addition to the men reported here, the return for George Clinton's brigade notes that there was also a detachment of Canadians under Pierre Regnier de Roussi at Kings Ferry on the Hudson. The detachment consisted of thirteen commissioned officers, nine noncommissioned officers, and seventy-two privates. Eight of these men were sick, and one was in New Jersey with the general's permission.

C. Although the return is headed both December 1 and Trenton, Washington did not reach that place in his retreat across New Jersey until December 3.

DECEMBER 1776

BRIGADE	UNIT	COMMANDING OFFICER	PRESENT FIT FOR DUTY & ON DUTY: COMMISSIONED OFFICERS	NONCOMMISSIONED OFFICERS	STAFF OFFICERS	RANK & FILE	TOTAL	RANK & FILE SICK, ON FURLOUGH, ETC.: SICK PRESENT	SICK ABSENT	ON COMMAND & EXTRA SERVICE	ON FURLOUGH	GRAND TOTAL	ALTERATIONS: DEATHS	DESERTED	TAKEN PRISONER	DISCHARGED	JOINED, ENLISTED, RECRUITED	LOCATION
	FORCES UNDER COMMANDER-IN-CHIEF GENERAL GEORGE WASHINGTON (Dated December 22--Before the Battle of Trenton)																	
Lord Stirling	1st Va.	Isaac Read	27	35	4	119	185	32	230	67		514						Banks of the Delaware, Pa.
	Del.	John Haslet	7	6	3	92	108	32				140						Banks of the Delaware, Pa.
	3rd Va.	George Weedon	18	26	3	134	181	19	360	62	11	633						Banks of the Delaware, Pa.
	6th Md.	Otho Holland Williams	18	20	1	160	199	19	188	98		504						Banks of the Delaware, Pa.
Mercer	20th cont'l. (Conn.)	John Durkee	28	35	2	248	313	8	148	58	3	530						Banks of the Delaware, Pa.
	1st Md.	Lt. Col. John Hawkins Stone	5	19		139	163	8			2	173						Banks of the Delaware, Pa.
	27th cont'l. (Mass.)	Israel Hutchinson	15	15	2	83	115	3	169	120		407						Banks of the Delaware, Pa.
	Conn. state	Philip Burr Bradley	16	30	2	94	142		153	73	5	373						Banks of the Delaware, Pa.
	Md. & Va. rifle regt.	Lt. Col. Moses Rawlings	3	9		93	105		19			124						Banks of the Delaware, Pa.
Stephen / De Fermoy	4th Va.	Thomas Elliott	29	31	2	167	229	14		19		262						Banks of the Delaware, Pa.
	5th Va.	Charles Scott	11	19	3	96	129	17		8		154						Banks of the Delaware, Pa.
	6th Va.	Mordecai Buckner	20	25	5	141	191	41		17		249						Banks of the Delaware, Pa.
	1st cont'l. (Pa.)	Edward Hand	23	42	5	194	264	36	211	76	3	590						Banks of the Delaware, Pa.
	German bn.	Nicholas Haussegger	35	40	5	294	374	36	18	10	11	449						Banks of the Delaware, Pa.
Ewing	Pa. bn. flying camp	Lt. Col. Frederick Watts	23	27	4	135	189	30	50	34		303						Banks of the Delaware, Pa.
	Pa. bn. flying camp	Jacob Klotz	17	21	1	130	169	16	15	2		202						Banks of the Delaware, Pa.
	Pa. bn. flying camp	William Montgomery	15	13		126	154	26	78	44	1	303						Banks of the Delaware, Pa.
	Pa. bn. flying camp	Richard McAllister	12	11	3	86	112	24	44	6	3	189						Banks of the Delaware, Pa.
	Pa. bn. flying camp	James Moore	15	14	2	70	101	8	50	10	7	176						Banks of the Delaware, Pa.
Hitchcock	4th cont'l. (Mass.)	Thomas Nixon	13	28	4	156	201					201						Banks of the Delaware, Pa.
	9th cont'l. (R. I.)	James Mitchell Varnum	15	17	1	131	164					164						Banks of the Delaware, Pa.
	11th cont'l. (R. I.)	Daniel Hitchcock	17	15	1	114	147					147						Banks of the Delaware, Pa.
	12th cont'l. (Mass.)	Moses Little	14	26	2	108	150					150						Banks of the Delaware, Pa.
	2nd R. I. militia	Christopher Lippitt	20	22	2	171	215					215						Banks of the Delaware, Pa.
Glover	3rd cont'l. (Mass.)	William Shepard	18	26	4	169	217	94	2	221	1	535						Banks of the Delaware, Pa.
	19th cont'l. (Conn.)	Charles Webb	18	23[B]	4	171	216	11	95	217	19	558						Banks of the Delaware, Pa.
	14th cont'l. (Mass.)	John Glover	27	23	3	124	177	10	2	207		396						Banks of the Delaware, Pa.
	23rd cont'l. (Mass.)	John Bailey	15	14	2	115	146	6	129	218		499						Banks of the Delaware, Pa.
	26th cont'l. (Mass.)	Loammi Baldwin	20	22	4	175	221	86	59	123		489						Banks of the Delaware, Pa.
Sargent	16th cont'l. (Mass.)	Paul Dudley Sargent	14	13	3	122	152	6	235	72		465						Banks of the Delaware, Pa.
	Ward's Conn.	Andrew Ward	11	18	2	126	157	7	205	60	20	449						Banks of the Delaware, Pa.
	6th Conn. state	John Chester	17	20	2	221	260					260						Banks of the Delaware, Pa.
	13th cont'l. (Mass.)	Joseph Read	15	1	1	105	122	3	103	230	1	459						Banks of the Delaware, Pa.
	1st N. Y.[A]	(late) Alexander McDougall	11	9		36	56		9			65						Banks of the Delaware, Pa.
	3rd N. Y.[A]	(late) Rudolphus Ritzema	13	3	2	62	80	8	8			96						Banks of the Delaware, Pa.
	TOTAL OF WASHINGTON'S INFANTRY		595	718	84	4707	6104	600	2580	2052	87	11423						

SOURCE OF THIS REPORT

1. RETURN OF THE FORCES IN THE SERVICE OF THE UNITED STATES...UNDER THE COMMAND OF HIS EXCELLENCY GEORGE WASHINGTON... DECEMBER 22, 1776, RECORD GROUP 93, NATIONAL ARCHIVES.

1a. Return of the Forces...under...Washington, printed in Peter Force, American Archives, ser. 5, 3: 1401-2.

A. Remnants of the old 1st and 3rd New York regiments whose terms of enlistment were expiring. Revamped regiments were organizing "for the war" in New York state.

B. The noncommissioned officer section of this return gives the number of sergeants in Colonel Webb's regiment as seventy-six; however, judging from the brigade total (and common sense), the correct number is sixteen.

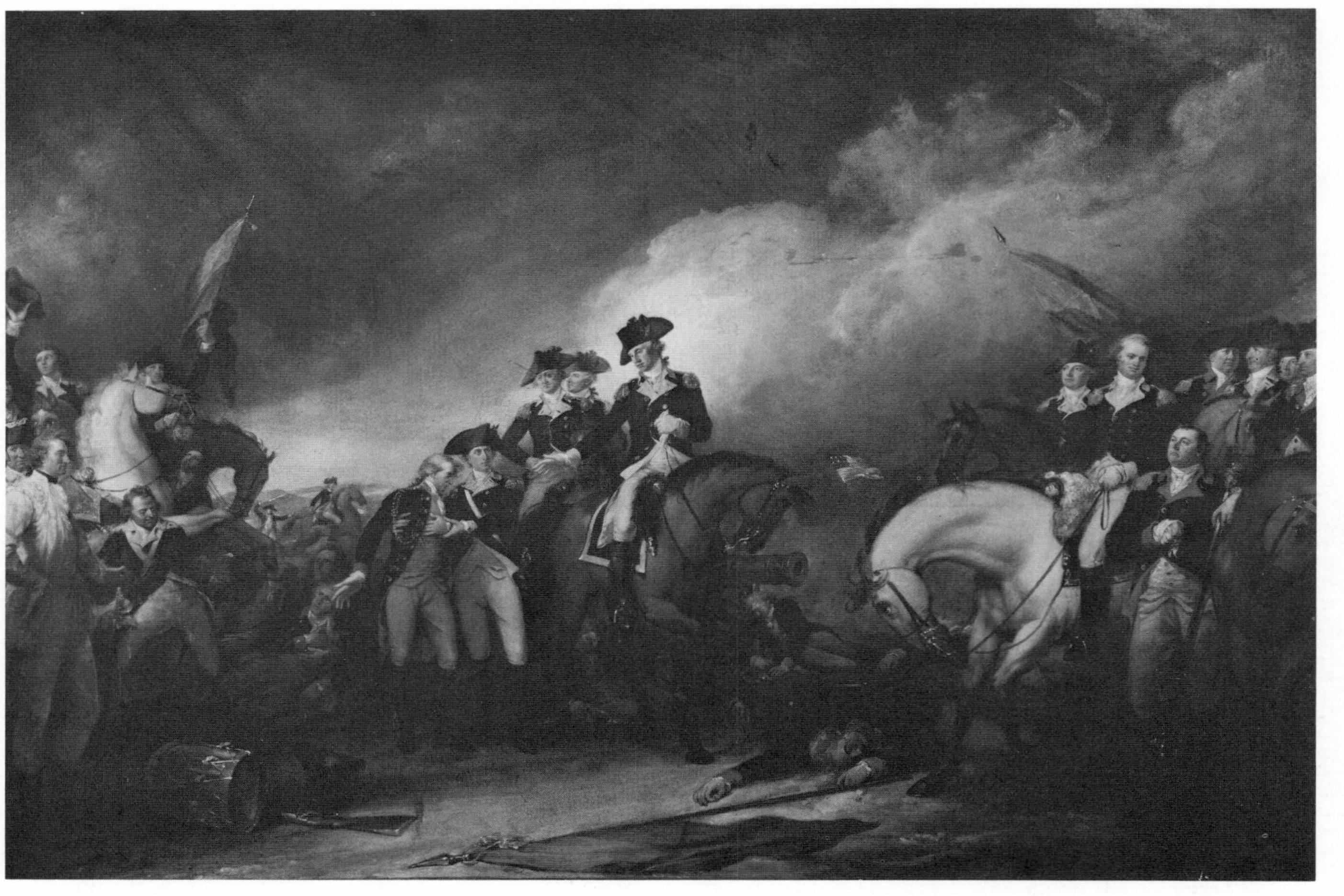

John Trumbull's small oil intended for engraving of *The Capture of the Hessians at Trenton*, December 26, 1776. Trumbull, who during the early part of the war served in the army in several capacities (including deputy adjutant general), took great pains to be accurate in his famous series of historical paintings. No matter how one judges the results, the several hundred sketches he did from life for those paintings remain an important archive of Revolutionary images. A few are reproduced in this volume. The scene shown here was painted (using some of the sketches) in London between 1786 and 1797. (Courtesy of the Yale University Art Gallery, New Haven, Conn.)

APRIL 1777

BRIGADE	UNIT	COMMANDING OFFICER	PRESENT FIT FOR DUTY & ON DUTY: COMMISSIONED OFFICERS	NONCOMMISSIONED OFFICERS	STAFF OFFICERS	RANK & FILE	TOTAL	RANK & FILE SICK, ON FURLOUGH, ETC.: SICK PRESENT	SICK ABSENT	ON COMMAND & EXTRA SERVICE	ON FURLOUGH				GRAND TOTAL	ALTERATIONS: DEATHS	DESERTED	TAKEN PRISONER	DISCHARGED	JOINED, ENLISTED, RECRUITED	LOCATION
	FORCES UNDER MAJOR GENERAL BENJAMIN LINCOLN AT OR NEAR BOUNDBROOK, NEW JERSEY[A]																				
	2nd Va.	Alexander Spotswood	18[B]	31	4	124	177		40						217						Boundbrook, N. J. area
	7th Va.	Alexander McClanachan	17	33	4	161	215		57	7					279						Boundbrook, N. J. area
	8th Va.	Abraham Bowman	10	14	1	94	119	15							134						Boundbrook, N. J. area
	11th Va.	Daniel Morgan	16	27	2	198	243	18	12						273						Boundbrook, N. J. area
	12th Va.	James Wood	2	4		36	42	5							47						Boundbrook, N. J. area
	10th Va.	Maj. George Nicholas	10	11		129	150	18							168						Boundbrook, N. J. area
	2nd Pa.	Capt. John Patterson	3	2		44	49								49						Boundbrook, N. J. area
	3rd Pa.	Maj. Josiah Harmar	7	14		108	129	5							134						Boundbrook, N. J. area
	4th Pa.	Capt. Robert Connelly	5	15		86	106	7	7	1					121						Boundbrook, N. J. area
	5th Pa.	Francis Johnston	12	30	2	189	233	35	27						295						Boundbrook, N. J. area
	8th Pa.	Daniel Brodhead	26	45	2	249	322	36	84	18	1				461						Boundbrook, N. J. area
	10th Pa.	Maj. Caleb North	4	15	1	82	102	16	2	2					122						Boundbrook, N. J. area
	Conn. det.	Lt. Col. Zebulon Butler	8	18	3	96	125	9		1					135						Boundbrook, N. J. area
	Independents		6	11		54	71	29	13	7	3				123						Boundbrook, N. J. area
	7th Md.	John Gunby	4	8		68	80	6	33						119						Boundbrook, N. J. area
	TOTAL OF FORCES UNDER LINCOLN		148	278	19	1718	2163	199	275	36	4				2677						

SOURCE OF THIS REPORT

1. A RETURN OF THE TROOPS...UNDER COMMAND OF MAJ. GEN. LINCOLN, MAY 3, 1777, BENJAMIN LINCOLN PAPERS, MASSACHUSETTS HISTORICAL SOCIETY.

A. This report represents those parts of various regiments which were in service in Lincoln's command at Boundbrook, New Jersey. Many of the new regiments under the reorganization of the Continental army still were being recruited and vaccinated against small pox. Detachments were being forwarded to the army as they were ready for service. In addition, some regiments were divided between different locations while the new formation remained incomplete.

B. In the commissioned officer section of this return, the number of cadets in the 3rd Virginia regiment is badly blurred but appears to be eight. Thus, there is no way to be certain about the number of commissioned officers in this regiment, since there are no totals given in the return.

BRIGADE	UNIT	COMMANDING OFFICER	PRESENT FIT FOR DUTY & ON DUTY: COMMISSIONED OFFICERS	NONCOMMISSIONED OFFICERS	STAFF OFFICERS	RANK & FILE	TOTAL	RANK & FILE SICK, ON FURLOUGH, ETC.: SICK PRESENT	SICK ABSENT	ON COMMAND & EXTRA SERVICE	ON FURLOUGH	ARTIFICERS			GRAND TOTAL	ALTERATIONS: DEATHS	DESERTED	TAKEN PRISONER	DISCHARGED	JOINED, ENLISTED, RECRUITED	LOCATION
	MAY 1777																				
	FORCES UNDER COMMANDER-IN-CHIEF GENERAL GEORGE WASHINGTON																				
	1st Va.	Isaac Read	12	25	2	98	137	15	17						169						New Jersey
	2nd Va.	Alexander Spotswood	15	25	3	130	173	48				4			225						New Jersey
	3rd Va.	Thomas Marshall	16	24	4	123	167	13	14						194						New Jersey
	4th Va.	Thomas Elliott	20	37	5	113	175	57	134	10					376						New Jersey
	5th Va.	Josiah Parker	20	19	2	92	133	12	20		3				168						New Jersey
	6th Va.	Lt. Col. James Hendricks	17	33	4	144	198	40	39						277						New Jersey
	7th Va.	Alexander McClanachan	43	58	4	221	326	60	114	4	73				577						New Jersey
	8th Va.	Abraham Bowman	15	22	3	130	170	27							197						New Jersey
	9th Va.	George Matthews	29	46	2	231	308	22	129		9				468						New Jersey
	10th Va.	Edward Stevens	19	22	1	253	295	42							337						New Jersey
	11th Va.	Daniel Morgan	26	38		257	321	23	93	4					441						New Jersey
	12th Va.	James Wood	4	11		94	109	19		4					132						New Jersey
	1st Md.	John Hawkins Stone	12	23	1	173	209	25		1					235						New Jersey
	2nd Md.	Thomas Price	10	17	2	97	126	12		9					147						New Jersey
	3rd Md.	Mordecai Gist	10	12		100	122	13		1					136						New Jersey
	4th Md.	Josias Carvil Hall	14	25	3	196	238	15	8	1					262						New Jersey
	6th Md.	Otho Holland Williams	7	15	2	93	117	12	13						142						New Jersey
	7th Md.	John Gunby	3	10	1	68	82	16	11						109						New Jersey
	Del.	David Hall	2	10	1	70	83	5	2	2					92						New Jersey
	1st Pa.	James Chambers	17	32	4	222	275	30	38	42		3			388						New Jersey
	2nd Pa.	James Irvine	2	2		14	18	2	1	4					25						New Jersey
	3rd Pa.	Joseph Wood	18	32		271	321	37	10			1			369						New Jersey
	4th Pa.	Lambert Cadwalader																			New Jersey
	5th Pa.	Francis Johnston	10	26	4	159	199	48	24	10					281						New Jersey
	9th Pa.	Anthony James Morris	11	11	1	182	205	5	6						216						New Jersey
	10th Pa.	Lt. Col. Adam Hubley	4	16	1	70	91	17	2						110						New Jersey
	11th Pa.	Richard Humpton	9	18	3	115	145	13		9	1				168						New Jersey
	12th Pa.	William Cooke	17	25	5	149	196	41	31	1	9				278						New Jersey
	1st N. J.	Matthias Ogden	13	32	2	116	163	26		35	7				231						New Jersey
	2nd N. J.	Israel Shreve	17	27	4	94	142	10	66	73	4				295						New Jersey
	3rd N. J.	Elias Dayton	25	21	2	125	173	66	21	48	40				348						New Jersey
	4th N. J.	Ephraim Martin	26	46	6	188	266	35	72	5	7				385						New Jersey
	Additional (5th N. J.) A	Oliver Spencer	14	18	2	92	126	45	23	16	10				220						New Jersey
	Conn. det.	Lt. Col. Zebulon Butler	10	17	3	85	115	11		6	1	13			146						New Jersey
	R. I. det.	Lt. Col. Jeremiah Olney	8	8	3	98	117	10	10	3					140						New Jersey
	2nd Canadian	Moses Hazen	21	42	4	344	411	49							460						New Jersey
	Additional	Thomas Hartley	9	19		141	169	10	4						183						New Jersey
	Additional	John Patton	8	14		84	106	16	6	18					146						New Jersey
	German bn.	Baron de Arendt	22	22	5	236	285	29	56	37	7				414						New Jersey
	Independent cos.		4	6			10	51	6	7	2				76						New Jersey
	8th Pa.	Daniel Brodhead	26	43	2	270	341	30	50	19					440						New Jersey
	TOTAL OF WASHINGTON'S INFANTRY		585	949	91	5738	7363	1057	1020	369	173	21			10003 B						

SOURCE OF THIS REPORT

1. A GENERAL RETURN OF THE CONTINENTAL FORCES. . . UNDER THE COMMAND OF HIS EXCELLENCY GENERAL WASHINGTON, MAY 21, 1777, RECORD GROUP 93, NATIONAL ARCHIVES.

A. Authorized by Congress December 27, 1776, Colonel Oliver Spencer's Additional regiment was often known as the 5th New Jersey because all or nearly all of its men were raised in New Jersey. This manuscript uses "5th N. J." to identify the regiment.

B. The manuscript notes that "No accurate returns are yet received of the light Corps & Artillery, being very much dispersed. There are about 500 Jersey Militia under the Command of General Heard."

BRIGADE

JULY 1777

UNIT	COMMANDING OFFICER	PRESENT FIT FOR DUTY & ON DUTY: COMMISSIONED OFFICERS	NONCOMMISSIONED OFFICERS	STAFF OFFICERS	RANK & FILE	TOTAL	RANK & FILE SICK, ON FURLOUGH, ETC.: SICK PRESENT	SICK ABSENT	ON COMMAND & EXTRA SERVICE	ON FURLOUGH			GRAND TOTAL	ALTERATIONS: DEATHS	DESERTED	TAKEN PRISONER	DISCHARGED	JOINED, ENLISTED, RECRUITED	LOCATION
CONTINENTAL TROOPS OF THE NORTHERN DEPARTMENT UNDER MAJOR GENERAL PHILIP SCHUYLER (To Brigade Level Only)																			
Nixon's brig.	Brig. Gen. John Nixon	89	145	15	853	1102	123	240	86	3			1554						Moses Creek, N. Y.
De Fermoy's brig.	Brig. Gen. Matthias De Fermoy	57	96	12	524	689	79	56	64	3			891						Moses Creek, N. Y.
Poor's brig.	Brig. Gen. Enoch Poor	51	94	11	542	698	114	54	90	1			957						Moses Creek, N. Y.
Paterson's brig.	Brig. Gen. John Paterson	79	95	14	528	716	84	73	82	2			957						Moses Creek, N. Y.
Learned's brig.	Brig. Gen. Ebenezer Learned	51	70	8	550	679	48	58	45	4			834						Moses Creek, N. Y.
TOTAL OF THE CONTINENTAL TROOPS UNDER SCHUYLER		327	500	60	2997	3884	448	481	367	13			5193[A]						

SOURCE OF THIS REPORT

1. A GENERAL RETURN OF THE CONTINENTAL TROOPS AT THIS POST COMMANDED BY THE HON. MAJOR GENERAL SCHUYLER, JULY 26, 1777, EMMET COLLECTION, MANUSCRIPTS AND ARCHIVES DIVISION, THE NEW YORK PUBLIC LIBRARY; ASTOR, LENOX, AND TILDEN FOUNDATIONS.

A. The manuscript notes, "The Artillery being Detached from the Army I have not been able to obtain a Return of it. The present Ignorance of the Brigade Majors, and the [illegible] of the Adjutants render it impossible for me to form Accurate or Correct Returns."

BRIGADE

AUGUST 1777

UNIT	COMMANDING OFFICER	PRESENT FIT FOR DUTY & ON DUTY: COMMISSIONED OFFICERS	NONCOMMISSIONED OFFICERS	STAFF OFFICERS	RANK & FILE	TOTAL	RANK & FILE SICK, ON FURLOUGH, ETC.: SICK PRESENT	SICK ABSENT	ON COMMAND & EXTRA SERVICE	ON FURLOUGH				GRAND TOTAL	ALTERATIONS: DEATHS	DESERTED	TAKEN PRISONER	DISCHARGED	JOINED, ENLISTED, RECRUITED	LOCATION
CONTINENTAL TROOPS OF THE NORTHERN DEPARTMENT UNDER MAJOR GENERAL HORATIO GATES (To Brigade Level Only)																				
Nixon's brig.	Brig. Gen. John Nixon	105	169	19	977	1270	115	191	167	4				1747						Van Schaicks Island, N. Y.
Poor's brig.	Brig. Gen. Enoch Poor	120	176	17	979	1292	181	175	153	7				1808						Van Schaicks Island, N. Y.
Glover's brig.	Brig. Gen. John Glover	87	139	14	915	1155	151	146	233	2				1687						Van Schaicks Island, N. Y.
Paterson's brig.	Brig. Gen. John Paterson	90	144	15	834	1083	114	156	173	4				1530						Van Schaicks Island, N. Y.
Learned's brig.	Brig. Gen. Ebenezer Learned	90	154	16	983	1243	94	135	54	2				1528						Van Schaicks Island, N. Y.
TOTAL OF THE CONTINENTAL TROOPS UNDER GATES		492	782	81	4688	6043	655	803	780	19				8300[A]						

SOURCE OF THIS REPORT

1. A GENERAL RETURN OF THE CONTINENTAL TROOPS UNDER THE COMMAND OF THE HON. MAJOR GENERAL GATES, SEPTEMBER 7, 1777, GATES PAPERS, NEW-YORK HISTORICAL SOCIETY.

A. The manuscript notes, "Rifle men & Militia not Included."

BRIGADE

OCTOBER 1777

UNIT	COMMANDING OFFICER	PRESENT FIT FOR DUTY & ON DUTY: COMMISSIONED OFFICERS	NONCOMMISSIONED OFFICERS	STAFF OFFICERS	RANK & FILE	TOTAL	RANK & FILE SICK, ON FURLOUGH, ETC.: SICK PRESENT	SICK ABSENT	ON COMMAND & EXTRA SERVICE	ON FURLOUGH	CONFINED	WITHOUT SHOES	GRAND TOTAL	ALTERATIONS: DEATHS	DESERTED	TAKEN PRISONER	DISCHARGED	JOINED, ENLISTED, RECRUITED	LOCATION
FORCES UNDER COMMANDER-IN-CHIEF GENERAL GEORGE WASHINGTON (To Brigade Level Only)																			
1st Md. brig.		89	131	20	577	817	91	344	188				1440						Pennsylvania
2nd Md. brig.		57	102	16	480	655	56	320	205	19		33	1288						Pennsylvania
Muhlenberg's brig.	Brig. Gen. Peter Muhlenberg	88	119	18	674	899	90	422	159	11			1581						Pennsylvania
Weedon's brig. A	Brig. Gen. George Weedon	65	133	15	834	1047	126	384	195	4			1756						Pennsylvania
Woodford's brig.	Brig. Gen. William Woodford	84	127	20	806	1037	86	406	234	26			1789						Pennsylvania
Scott's brig.	Brig. Gen. Charles Scott	86	135	20	728	969	75	329	161	8	6		1548						Pennsylvania
1st Pa. brig.		81	128	14	546	769	76	240	175	13			1273						Pennsylvania
2nd Pa. brig.	Richard Humpton	49	113	14	397	573	73	227	254				1127						Pennsylvania
Maxwell's brig.	Brig. Gen. William Maxwell	77	124	17	552	770	66	245	56	2	3		1142						Pennsylvania
Conway's brig.	Brig. Gen. Thomas Conway	107	129	21	640	897	54	302	134	10			1397						Pennsylvania
Huntington's brig.	Brig. Gen. Jedediah Huntington	71	127	13	876	1087	37	221	248	19			1612						Pennsylvania
N. C. brig.		93	174	31	514	812	59	168	110	3			1152						Pennsylvania
TOTAL OF WASHINGTON'S INFANTRY		947	1542	219	7624	10332	889	3608	2119	115	9	33	17105						
NORTHERN DEPARTMENT UNDER MAJOR GENERAL HORATIO GATES (Dated October 16; To Brigade Level Only)																			
Nixon's brig.	Brig. Gen. John Nixon	114	156	18	1257	1545	55	87	73	9			1769						Saratoga, N. Y.
Poor's brig.	Brig. Gen. Enoch Poor	112	160	19	1132	1423	48	64	61	11			1607						Saratoga, N. Y.
Learned's brig.	Brig. Gen. Ebenezer Learned	111	175	17	1498	1801	57	51	44	8			1961						Saratoga, N. Y.
Glover's brig.	Brig. Gen. John Glover	118	178	19	1776	2091	69	94	86	23			2363						Saratoga, N. Y.
Paterson's brig.	Brig. Gen. John Paterson	111	157	15	1255	1538	61	77	53	12			1741						Saratoga, N. Y.
Warner's brig.	Seth Warner B	111	136	14	1572	1833	95	83	68	32			2111						Saratoga, N. Y.
N. H. militia brig.	Brig. Gen. John Stark	113	149	15	220	497	25	32	1019	7			1580						Saratoga, N. Y.
Vt. militia brig.	Brig. Gen. Jacob Bayley	110	130	10	897	1147	30	23	48	13			1261						Saratoga, N. Y.
N. H. militia brig.	Brig. Gen. William Whipple	108	153	15	112	388	18	21	897	27			1351						Saratoga, N. Y.
Mass. militia brig.	Brig. Gen. James Brickett	115	120	8	776	1019	21	37	31	4			1112						Saratoga, N. Y.
Mass. militia brig.	Brig. Gen. John Fellows	110	164	16	132	422	40	31	884	10			1387						Saratoga, N. Y.
Conn. militia brig.	Brig. Gen. Oliver Wolcott	97	143	9	843	1092	27	34	38	7			1198						Saratoga, N. Y.
N. Y. militia brig.	Brig. Gen. Abraham Ten Broeck	112	149	12	987	1260	54	65	553	14			1946						Saratoga, N. Y.
TOTAL OF INFANTRY		1442	1970	187	12457	16056	600	699	3855	177			21387						
ARTILLERY																			
Artillery with Northern Dept.		18	34	8	438	498	17	25	8	2			550						Saratoga, N. Y.
CAVALRY																			
Cavalry with Northern Dept.		25	24	6	321	376	5	7	12	1			401						Saratoga, N. Y.
TOTAL OF NORTHERN DEPARTMENT		1485	2028	201	13216	16930	622	731	3875	180			22338 C						
GRAND TOTAL		2432	3570	420	20840	27262	1511	4339	5994	295	9	33	39443						

SOURCES OF THIS REPORT

1. A WEEKLY RETURN OF THE CONTINENTAL ARMY...UNDER THE COMMAND OF HIS EXCELLENCY GENERAL WASHINGTON, NOVEMBER 3, 1777, RECORD GROUP 93, NATIONAL ARCHIVES.

2. RETURN OF THE ARMY OF THE UNITED STATES, COMMANDED BY MAJOR GENERAL GATES, OCTOBER 16, 1777, GATES PAPERS, NEW-YORK HISTORICAL SOCIETY.
   2a. Return of the Army...Commanded by...Gates, printed in John Burgoyne, *A State of the Expedition from Canada, As Laid Before the House of Commons* (London: J. Almon, 1780), app. 16.

A. The manuscript notes, "Genl. Woodford's brigade includes the Farquhar [Fauquier?] Militia, amounting to 99 privates fit for duty."
B. The manuscript makes this appear to be a Brigadier General Warner, but the brigade would seem to be Colonel Seth Warner's, composed probably of his Additional regiment plus militia he had raised. Seth Warner became a brigadier general of militia officially in 1778. The only Warner who was officially a brigadier general at this time was Jonathan Warner of the Massachusetts militia, and he does not appear to have been present.
C. The manuscript notes, "Exclusive of the Numbers in the above Return, there are, the Upper Staff of the Army, the Batteaumen, the Artificers, and followers of the Camp. Colonel Morgan's Corps of Rifle Men, and the Light Infantry, are included in the Brigades."

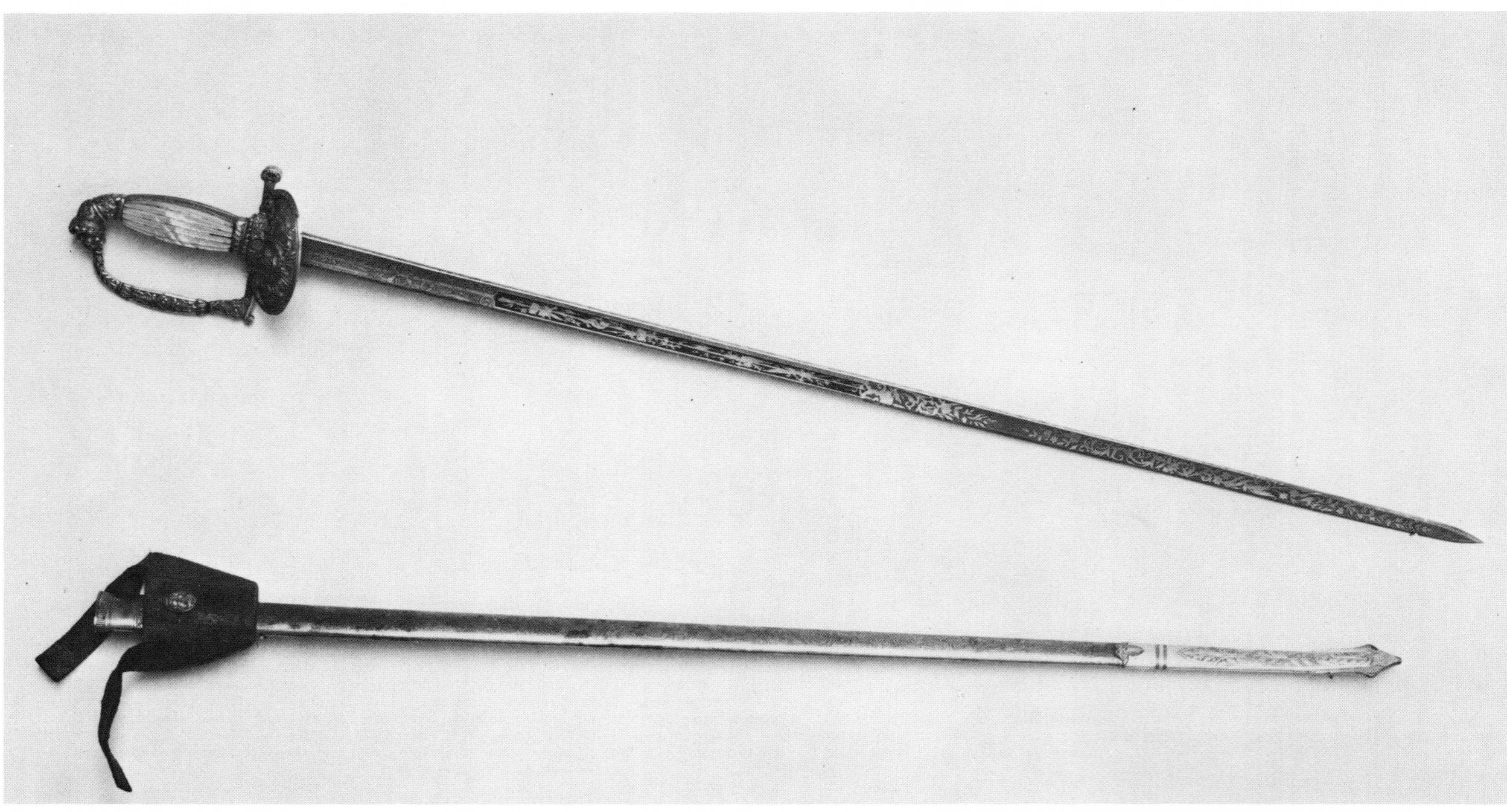

The sword worn by Major General Horatio Gates at Saratoga in 1777. (Courtesy of the New-York Historical Society, New York City)

BRIGADE

NOVEMBER 1777

UNIT	COMMANDING OFFICER	PRESENT FIT FOR DUTY & ON DUTY					RANK & FILE SICK, ON FURLOUGH, ETC.							GRAND TOTAL	ALTERATIONS					LOCATION
		COMMISSIONED OFFICERS	NONCOMMISSIONED OFFICERS	STAFF OFFICERS	RANK & FILE[A]	TOTAL	SICK PRESENT	SICK ABSENT	ON COMMAND & EXTRA SERVICE	ON FURLOUGH					DEATHS	DESERTED	TAKEN PRISONER	DISCHARGED	JOINED, ENLISTED, RECRUITED	
FORCES UNDER COMMANDER-IN-CHIEF GENERAL GEORGE WASHINGTON (For the Most Part, to Brigade Level Only)																				
1st Md. brig.		87	153	18	610	868	106	291	204	4				1473						White Marsh, Pa.
2nd Md. brig.		56	93	14	573	736	58	247	192	19				1252						White Marsh, Pa.
Muhlenberg's brig.	Brig. Gen. Peter Muhlenberg	119	149	22	639	929	104	367	167	48				1615						White Marsh, Pa.
Weedon's brig.	Brig. Gen. George Weedon	83	170	20	936	1209	163	486	145	9				2012						White Marsh, Pa.
Woodford's brig.	Brig. Gen. William Woodford	68	113	16	726	923	84	329	229	29				1594						White Marsh, Pa.
Scott's brig.	Brig. Gen. Charles Scott	89	155	18	772	1034	111	325	361	11				1842						White Marsh, Pa.
1st Pa. brig.		68	131	15	540	754	65	232	214	28				1293						White Marsh, Pa.
2nd Pa. brig..		50	118	11	433	612	58	214	257					1141						White Marsh, Pa.
Maxwell's brig.	Brig. Gen. William Maxwell	80	115	17	608	820	63	218	38	9				1148						White Marsh, Pa.
Conway's brig.	Brig. Gen. Thomas Conway	76	110	20	406	612	130	242	146	18				1148						White Marsh, Pa.
N. C. brig.		134	197	34	655	1020	58	200	120					1398						White Marsh, Pa.
Poor's brig.	Brig. Gen. Enoch Poor	78	144	17	632	871	296	288	124	70				1649						White Marsh, Pa.
Glover's brig.	Brig. Gen. John Glover	92	141	12	993	1238	33	292	70	112				1745						White Marsh, Pa.
Paterson's brig.	Brig. Gen. John Paterson	94	131	14	839	1078	88	175	81	153				1575						White Marsh, Pa.
Learned's brig.	Brig. Gen. Ebenezer Learned	64	99	9	501	673	24	155	87	61				1000						White Marsh, Pa.
Varnum's brig.	Brig. Gen. James M. Varnum	94	138	16	810	1058	112	310	188	7				1675						White Marsh, Pa.
Huntington's brig.	Brig. Gen. Jedediah Huntington[C]	60	119	15	811	1005	85	202	279	20				1591						White Marsh, Pa.
Additional	David Forman	4	7		31	42	2	1	4					49						White Marsh, Pa.
Additional[B]	William Malcolm	23	38	5	126	192	12	31	19	1				255						White Marsh, Pa.
Det. Lee's additional	William Lee	6	15	1	59	81	13	8	7					109						White Marsh, Pa.
Det. Jackson's additional	Henry Jackson	18	29	1	157	205	11	26		3				245						White Marsh, Pa.
Det. Henley's additional	David Henley	4	4		34	42	4	1						47						White Marsh, Pa.
Det. Webb's additional	Samuel Blatchley Webb	25	44	5	246	320	10	24	30	12				396						White Marsh, Pa.
Independent corps	(late) Tuffin Charles Armand	7	6	3	24	40	1	13	7					61						White Marsh, Pa.
TOTAL OF CONTINENTAL INFANTRY		1479	2419	303	12161	16362	1691	4677	2969	614				26313						
MILITIA																				
Pa. militia brig.	Brig. Gen. James Irving	195	231	19	1728	2173	90	75	175	35				2548						White Marsh, Pa.
Md. militia	Mordecai Gist[D]	77	80	10	713	880	40	2	32	2				956[E]						White Marsh, Pa.
TOTAL OF MILITIA		272	311	29	2441	3053	130	77	207	37				3504						
TOTAL OF WASHINGTON'S INFANTRY		1751	2730	332	14602	19415	1821	4754	3176	651				29817						

SOURCE OF THIS REPORT

1. A GENERAL RETURN OF THE ARMY UNDER THE COMMAND OF HIS EXCELLENCY GENERAL WASHINGTON. . . DECEMBER 3, 1777, RECORD GROUP 93, NATIONAL ARCHIVES.

A. The manuscript notes that "several hundred" men marked "fit for duty" and "some" marked "sick present" were "really unfit from the want of shoes [and] cloathing [sic.]."

B. A note indicates, "Malcom's [sic.] regt. was not included in the last Return of Conway's brigade, so the numbers are taken from Conway's last return, with the addition only of Colo. Malcom [sic.] himself."

C. The manuscript notes, "The return of Genl. Huntington's brigade was made Novr. 16.--In his return this minute brought in his fit for duty amount to 830 & the whole of the Rank & File to 1389."

D. A note indicates, "The return of the Maryland militia was made Novr. 14, but I believe no material change has since happened."

E. The manuscript notes that no return was available for James Potter's Pennsylvania militia brigade but that Colonel John Bull reported it had about eight hundred men present fit for duty.

DECEMBER 1777

BRIGADE	UNIT	COMMANDING OFFICER	PRESENT FIT FOR DUTY & ON DUTY: COMMISSIONED OFFICERS	NONCOMMISSIONED OFFICERS	STAFF OFFICERS	RANK & FILE	TOTAL	RANK & FILE SICK, ON FURLOUGH, ETC.: SICK PRESENT	SICK ABSENT	ON COMMAND & EXTRA SERVICE	ON FURLOUGH	WANTING SHOES, ETC.[D]	GRAND TOTAL	ALTERATIONS: DEATHS	DESERTED	TAKEN PRISONER	DISCHARGED	JOINED, ENLISTED, RECRUITED	LOCATION
		FORCES UNDER COMMANDER-IN-CHIEF GENERAL GEORGE WASHINGTON																	
1st Md.	1st Md.[A]	John Hawkins Stone	19	25	3	104	151	39	35	24		33	282						Wilmington, Del.
	Delaware	David Hall	18	37	4	90	149	14	54	38	2	22	279						Wilmington, Del.
	3rd Md.	Mordecai Gist	18	35	4	130	187	2	87	35		51	362						Wilmington, Del.
	5th Md.	William Richardson	14	28	3	105	150	35	75	49	2		311						Wilmington, Del.
	7th Md.	John Gunby	18	28	4	53	103	16	40	67		22	248						Wilmington, Del.
2nd Md.	2nd Canadian	Moses Hazen	20	40	6	150	216	20	79	98	16	50	479						Wilmington, Del.
	4th Md.	Josias Carvil Hall	11	23	3	92	129	16	64	36	1	59	305						Wilmington, Del.
	6th Md.	Otho Holland Williams	16	11	4	49	80	18	45	25		49	217						Wilmington, Del.
	2nd Md.	Thomas Price	9	19	1	57	86	4	59	33	2	67	251						Wilmington, Del.
Muhlenberg	1st Va.	James Hendricks	8	38	4	44	94	46	39	34	24		237				2	E	Valley Forge, Pa.
	5th & 9th Va.	Josiah Parker & George Mathews	15	20	4	59	98	17	139	42	61		357	3			1		Valley Forge, Pa.
	13th Va.	William Russell	8	13	4	44	69	1	80	25			175	1			2	6	Valley Forge, Pa.
	German bn.	Baron de Arendt	18	30	5	176	229	11	39	54	7		340		1				Valley Forge, Pa.
	1st Va. state	George Gibson	17	28	5	138	188	26	201	25	4		444	5	1				Valley Forge, Pa.
Weedon	2nd Va.	Christian Febiger	14	23	5	80	122	139	106	26	13		406		13		1		Valley Forge, Pa.
	6th Va.	John Gibson	6	20	2	54	82	67	65	6	17		237	4			5		Valley Forge, Pa.
	10th Va.	Edward Stevens	18	20	3	134	175	93	137	34	3		442	1	3				Valley Forge, Pa.
	14th Va.	Charles Lewis	13	25	5	75	118	64	85	19	2		288	3	1				Valley Forge, Pa.
	13th Pa.	Walter Stewart	25	40	5	282	352	104	91	44	10		601		4				Valley Forge, Pa.
Woodford	3rd Va.	Lt. Col. William Heth	11	8	5	47	71	16	59	40	53	70	309	1	1		1		Valley Forge, Pa.
	7th Va.	Alexander McClanachan	8	5	3	30	46	10	104	48	139	80	427	1			2		Valley Forge, Pa.
	11th Va.	Daniel Morgan	10	19	2	50	81	13	53	78	12	89	326		1		1		Valley Forge, Pa.
	15th Va.	David Mason	13	11	4	40	68	6	137	7	5	84	307						Valley Forge, Pa.
Scott	4th Va.	Isaac Read	9	17	5	43	74	12	63	34	29	71	283	1	1				Valley Forge, Pa.
	8th Va.	Abraham Bowman	4	16	1	32	53	8	4	21			86				2		Valley Forge, Pa.
	12th Va.	James Wood	15	27	3	119	164	127	130	67	7		495		6		3	1	Valley Forge, Pa.
	Additional	William Grayson	18	25	3	108	154	14	83	27	2		280	1	1				Valley Forge, Pa.
	Additional	John Patton	10	17	6	57	90	13	36	14	3		156	2	1				Valley Forge, Pa.
1st Pa.	1st Pa.	James Chambers	16	18	2	86	122	15	58	114	9	67	385	1	6		1		Valley Forge, Pa.
	2nd Pa.	Henry Bicker	12	23	3	67	105	7	12	10	2	12	148	1	1				Valley Forge, Pa.
	7th Pa.	William Irvine	15	20	4	66	105	12	54	20	5	43	239	2	14			2	Valley Forge, Pa.
	10th Pa.	Lt. Col. Adam Hubley	11	20	2	56	89	7	63	26	4	60	249	1	5				Valley Forge, Pa.
	Additional	Thomas Hartley	7	12	4	80	103	13	58	30	18	29	251		4				Valley Forge, Pa.
2nd Pa.	4th Pa.	Lambert Cadwalader	15	33	4	97	149	11	25	16			201	3	4				Valley Forge, Pa.
	5th Pa.	Francis Johnston	14	23	5	152	194	21	67	43			325		4			25	Valley Forge, Pa.
	8th Pa.	Daniel Brodhead	10	42	3	145	200	26	64	120			410	17	5				Valley Forge, Pa.
	11th Pa.	Richard Humpton	12	16	2	57	87	8	55	39			189	2	4				Valley Forge, Pa.
Maxwell	1st N. J.	Matthias Ogden	11	21	2	117	151	31	57	13	9		261		1				Valley Forge, Pa.
	2nd N. J.	Israel Shreve	18	29	2	155	204	11	42	18			275	1	1				Valley Forge, Pa.
	3rd N. J.	Elias Dayton	16	27	3	158	204	16	31	5	1		257						Valley Forge, Pa.
	4th N. J.	Ephraim Martin	14	24	3	145	186	17	76	13			292	1	6				Valley Forge, Pa.
(late) Conway	3rd Pa.	Thomas Craig	15	22	4	75	116	33	42	20	1		212						Valley Forge, Pa.
	6th Pa.	Robert Magaw	23	17	1	97	138	6	46	16			206	1					Valley Forge, Pa.
	9th Pa.	Richard Butler	18	19	2	107	146	12	50	16	5		229					3	Valley Forge, Pa.
	12th Pa.	William Cooke	12	15	2	104	133	15	47	37	5		237		2				Valley Forge, Pa.
	Additional	William Malcolm	11	34	4	109	158	28	31	12	2		231		7				Valley Forge, Pa.
	Additional	Oliver Spencer	11	24	2	90	127	28	50	22	6		233	4	4				Valley Forge, Pa.

DECEMBER 1777 (continued)

BRIGADE	UNIT	COMMANDING OFFICER	PRESENT FIT FOR DUTY & ON DUTY: COMMISSIONED OFFICERS	NONCOMMISSIONED OFFICERS	STAFF OFFICERS	RANK & FILE	TOTAL	RANK & FILE SICK, ON FURLOUGH, ETC.: SICK PRESENT	SICK ABSENT	ON COMMAND & EXTRA SERVICE	ON FURLOUGH	WANTING SHOES, ETC.[D]	GRAND TOTAL	ALTERATIONS: DEATHS	DESERTED	TAKEN PRISONER	DISCHARGED	JOINED, ENLISTED, RECRUITED	LOCATION
	FORCES UNDER COMMANDER-IN-CHIEF GENERAL GEORGE WASHINGTON (continued)																		
Poor	1st N. H.	Joseph Cilley	18	27	3	193	241	67	90	12	16		426	1				5	Valley Forge, Pa.
Poor	2nd N. H.	Nathan Hale	12	29	3	128	172	34	50	51	16		323	1	1				Valley Forge, Pa.
Poor	3rd N. H.	Alexander Scammell	17	33	3	184	237	31	47	20	34		369	2	1				Valley Forge, Pa.
Poor	2nd N. Y.	Philip Van Cortlandt	18	31	4	91	144	57	41	8	5		255		2				Valley Forge, Pa.
Poor	4th N. Y.	Henry Beekman Livingston	20	32	3	116	171	34	50	26	6		287		1				Valley Forge, Pa.
Glover	4th Mass.	William Shepard	23	33	4	227	287	12	72	40	26		437		5		1	3	Valley Forge, Pa.
Glover	13th Mass.	Edward Wigglesworth	18	41	2	222	283	16	75	34	44		452	4	2		2		Valley Forge, Pa.
Glover	1st Mass.	Joseph Vose	23	29	1	228	281	21	91	20	23		436		4				Valley Forge, Pa.
Glover	15th Mass.	Timothy Bigelow	21	29	2	170	222	16	77	46	49		410		1				Valley Forge, Pa.
Learned	2nd Mass.	John Bailey	23	34	5	235	297	13	58	60	31		459	3			1	9	Valley Forge, Pa.
Learned	9th Mass.	James Wesson	18	38	4	208	268	20	46	55	36		425	2	3		1		Valley Forge, Pa.
Learned	8th Mass.	Michael Jackson	22	35	3	176	236	20	58	43	11		368						Valley Forge, Pa.
Paterson	10th Mass.	Thomas Marshall	16	29	4	153	202	26	48	45	30		351	1	5			6	Valley Forge, Pa.
Paterson	12th Mass.	Samuel Brewer	18	32	4	185	239	24	38	23	45		369		1				Valley Forge, Pa.
Paterson	14th Mass.	Gamaliel Bradford	12	37	3	192	244	24	50	28	61		407	1					Valley Forge, Pa.
Paterson	11th Mass.	Benjamin Tupper	17	30	3	200	250	49	59	20	26		404	4	1				Valley Forge, Pa.
Varnum	4th Conn.	John Durkee	21	32	4	215	272	24	138	77	4		515	3	3			10	Valley Forge, Pa.
Varnum	1st R. I.	Christopher Greene	27	37	5	185	254	22	48	35			359	1					Valley Forge, Pa.
Varnum	8th Conn.	John Chandler	20	33	5	206	264	64	104	70	4		506	3					Valley Forge, Pa.
Varnum	2nd R. I.	Israel Angell	23	32	5	173	233	13	49	40			335		1				Valley Forge, Pa.
Huntington	1st Conn.	Lt. Col. Samuel Prentiss	24	44	5	320	393	35	62	64	8		562					3	Valley Forge, Pa.
Huntington	2nd Conn.	Charles Webb	19	39	3	201	262	24	30	38	8		362	1					Valley Forge, Pa.
Huntington	5th Conn.	Philip Burr Bradley	18	35	4	220	277	23	82	86	11		479						Valley Forge, Pa.
Huntington	7th Conn.	Heman Swift	17	41	4	296	358	17	78	79	4		536	2			1		Valley Forge, Pa.
	N. C. regts. 1-9[B]	Brig. Gen. Lachlan McIntosh	123	177	33	572	905	71	288	137	11		1412	4	4		1	1	Valley Forge, Pa.
	Det. Lee's additional[B]	William Lee	6	15		59	80	13	8	7			108						Lancaster, Pa.
	Det. Jackson's additional[B]	Henry Jackson	18	29	1	157	205	11	26		3		245						Lancaster, Pa.
	Det. Henley's additional[B]	David Henley	4	4		34	42	4	1				47						Lancaster, Pa.
	Independent corps	(late) Tuffin Charles Armand	7	8	3	25	43	1	13	9			66						
	TOTAL OF INFANTRY		1267	2132	283	9976	13658	2054	4994	2813	993	958	25470	90	137		28	74	
	CAVALRY																		
	1st cont'l.	Theodorick Bland	16	36	6	57	115	10	9	[C]	2		136						Valley Forge, Pa. area[G]
	4th cont'l.	Stephen Moylan	18	19	1	49	87	21	2		2		112						Valley Forge, Pa. area
	3rd cont'l.	George Baylor	11	19	5	92	127						127						Valley Forge, Pa. area
	2nd cont'l.	Elisha Sheldon	10	18	5	102	135	2	3				140						Valley Forge, Pa. area
	TOTAL OF CAVALRY		55	92	17	300	464	33	14		4		515						
	TOTAL OF WASHINGTON'S ARMY		1322	2224	300	10276	14122	2087	5008	2813	997	958	25985	90[F]	137		28	74	

DECEMBER 1777
(continued)

SOURCES OF THIS REPORT

1. A GENERAL RETURN OF THE CONTINENTAL ARMY...UNDER THE IMMEDIATE COMMAND OF HIS EXCELLENCY GEORGE WASHINGTON...DECEMBER 31, 1777, RECORD GROUP 93, NATIONAL ARCHIVES. [ALTHOUGH THE HEADING DOES NOT INDICATE THE FACT, THIS IS A MONTHLY RETURN; THE ALTERATIONS ARE MARKED "ALTERATIONS SINCE LAST RETURNS OF DEC. 1, 1777."]

1a. A General Return of the Continental Army under the command of his Excellency George Washington...December 31, 1777, Timothy Pickering Papers, Massachusetts Historical Society. [This version of the monthly return is almost entirely to the brigade level only but includes the detachments at Lancaster and (late) Armand's corps, which are not included on the National Archives return.]

2. A GENERAL RETURN OF THE CAVALRY IN MEN & HORSES, JANUARY 1, 1778, RECORD GROUP 93, NATIONAL ARCHIVES.

A. Both manuscript returns note that a return of December 1 was used for the two Maryland brigades. Thus, these figures are nearly the same as those of the November report; no recent return was available because these brigades had been detached to Wilmington.

B. Figures for these three units are nearly identical to the figures on the November report because, as the Pickering manuscript notes, these are from a return of December 1, after which most of these men soon went to Lancaster to be inoculated, and thus no recent return was available. Therefore, it must be kept in mind that, at the end of December, Washington really could not count on most of these men. Such was not the case, however, with the (late) Armand's Corps, which also was not included on the National Archives copy of the return; the Pickering Papers manuscript notes, "The return of Armand's Corps is as late as Jany. 5, 1778."

C. Under "Observations," the manuscript cavalry return indicates that fifty men from Bland's 1st Continental regiment were with Captain Lee, thirty men from Moylan's 4th Continental regiment were with Captain Craig, one troop of Baylor's 3rd Continental regiment was at Reading dismounted, and two troops of Sheldon's 2nd Continental were "on command in the north." These men would appear to be in addition to those included in the columns of the return and to be roughly those normally included in the "on command" column.

D. Only some units used this category in their returns. A note on both manuscripts indicates that many more men who were without shoes or clothes were included in either the "present fit for duty" or "sick present" columns, as all such men were on the November return. Washington reported to Congress on the 26th that a field return of the 23rd indicated that there were "not less than 2898 Men unfit for duty by reason of their being barefoot and otherwise naked." Fitzpatrick, Writings of Washington, 10:209.

E. The National Archives manuscript was damaged in this area, so it was necessary for the "joined, enlisted, recruited" column to use the figures from the Pickering Papers copy, which supplies figures only to the brigade level.

F. It will be noted that these alterations totals are only partial, as no monthly alterations figures were available for December for the Maryland brigades, the detachments at Lancaster, and the cavalry.

G. The cavalry had just been ordered (on December 31) to leave for a separate winter encampment.

Portrait of Brigadier General Lachlan McIntosh painted by Charles Willson Peale ca. 1783–1793. McIntosh was in command of the North Carolina regiments at Valley Forge. The following spring he was appointed to command the Western Department at Fort Pitt, but complaints by his subordinates led to a short tenure at that post. Apparently Peale painted this portrait for his "collection of great men" in his museum, but then did not exhibit it when he learned of McIntosh's dubious character (violent personal disputes and a duel were in McIntosh's background). (Courtesy of the Yale University Art Gallery, New Haven, Conn.)

BRIGADE

JANUARY 1778

UNIT	COMMANDING OFFICER	PRESENT FIT FOR DUTY & ON DUTY: COMMISSIONED OFFICERS	NONCOMMISSIONED OFFICERS	STAFF OFFICERS	RANK & FILE	TOTAL	RANK & FILE SICK, ON FURLOUGH, ETC.: SICK PRESENT	SICK ABSENT	ON COMMAND & EXTRA SERVICE	ON FURLOUGH	WANTING SHOES AND CLOTHES			GRAND TOTAL	ALTERATIONS: DEATHS	DESERTED	TAKEN PRISONER	DISCHARGED	JOINED, ENLISTED, RECRUITED	LOCATION
FORCES UNDER COMMANDER-IN-CHIEF GENERAL GEORGE WASHINGTON (For the Most Part, to Brigade Level Only)																				
Woodford's brig.	Brig. Gen. William Woodford	32	44	8	147	231	90	277	199	208	282			1287						Valley Forge, Pa.
Scott's brig.	Brig. Gen. Charles Scott	40	98	14	254	406	104	253	154	50	253			1220						Valley Forge, Pa.
1st Pa. brig.		47	60	11	163	281	55	143	150	32	280			941						Valley Forge, Pa.
2nd Pa. brig.		30	59	13	292	394	56	196	230	37	113			1026						Valley Forge, Pa.
Poor's brig.	Brig. Gen. Enoch Poor	60	139	17	252	468	116	261	164	73	484			1566						Valley Forge, Pa.
Glover's brig.	Brig. Gen. John Glover	77	121	10	374	582	91	236	201	124	379			1613						Valley Forge, Pa.
Learned's brig.	Brig. Gen. Ebenezer Learned	43	108	10	308	469	60	135	147	81	289			1181						Valley Forge, Pa.
Paterson's brig.	Brig. Gen. John Paterson	57	124	16	305	502	106	171	145	166	372			1462						Valley Forge, Pa.
Weedon's brig.	Brig. Gen. George Weedon	50	94	21	221	386	138	383	138	83	450			1578						Valley Forge, Pa.
Muhlenberg's brig.	Brig. Gen. Peter Muhlenberg	80	108	21	282	491	108	447	210	110	226			1592						Valley Forge, Pa.
Maxwell's brig.	Brig. Gen. William Maxwell	50	116	14	388	568	23	203	97	9	244			1144						Valley Forge, Pa.
Conway's brig.	(late) Brig. Gen. Thomas Conway	62	97	20	217	396	135	205	165	52	299			1252						Valley Forge, Pa.
Huntington's brig.	Brig. Gen. Jedediah Huntington	54	116	13	822	1005	131	181	301	42				1660						Valley Forge, Pa.
Varnum's brig.	Brig. Gen. James M. Varnum	48	101	13	652	814	124	213	198	18	69			1436						Valley Forge, Pa.
McIntosh's N. C. brig. A	Brig. Gen. Lachlan McIntosh	46	138	12	314	510	97	226	91	15	249			1188						Valley Forge, Pa.
Independent corps	(late) Tuffin Charles Armand	5	8	1	21	35	3	19	4					61						
TOTAL OF INFANTRY		781	1531	214	5012	7538	1437	3549	2594	1100	3989			20207						
ARTILLERY																				
3rd cont'l.	John Crane	18	98	2	88	206														Valley Forge, Pa.
2nd cont'l.	John Lamb	17	72		95	184	18	49	28	9				661						Valley Forge, Pa.
4th cont'l.	Thomas Proctor	14	84	4	65	167														Valley Forge, Pa.
TOTAL OF ARTILLERY		49	254	6	248	557	18	49	28	9				661 B						
TOTAL OF WASHINGTON'S ARMY		830	1785	220	5260	8095	1455	3598	2622	1109	3989			20868						

OFFICERS SICK, ON FURLOUGH, ETC.	WASHINGTON'S ARTILLERY (ONLY): COMMISSIONED	NONCOMMISSIONED	STAFF	TOTAL
Sick Present	2	13		15
Sick Absent	10	40	2	52
On Furlough	32	20	1	53
On Command	18	28	1	47
TOTAL	62	101	4	167

SOURCE OF THIS REPORT

1. RETURN OF THE CONTINENTAL ARMY UNDER THE COMMAND OF HIS EXCELLENCY GEORGE WASHINGTON, ESQ., JANUARY 31, 1778, RECORD GROUP 93, NATIONAL ARCHIVES.

A. The nine North Carolina regiments that were on the December report as the North Carolina brigade consolidated into reorganized 1st, 2nd, and 3rd North Carolina regiments.

B. The manuscript notes that no returns were available for the Maryland brigades at Wilmington, for Hartley's regiment at York, for Lee's, Henley's, or Jackson's detachments at Lancaster, or for the cavalry at Trenton.

BRIGADE

FEBRUARY 1778

UNIT	COMMANDING OFFICER	PRESENT FIT FOR DUTY & ON DUTY: COMMISSIONED OFFICERS	NONCOMMISSIONED OFFICERS	STAFF OFFICERS	RANK & FILE	TOTAL	RANK & FILE SICK, ON FURLOUGH, ETC.: SICK PRESENT	SICK ABSENT	ON COMMAND & EXTRA SERVICE	ON FURLOUGH	WANTING CLOTHES, ETC.	GRAND TOTAL	ALTERATIONS: DEATHS	DESERTED	TAKEN PRISONER	DISCHARGED	JOINED, ENLISTED, RECRUITED	LOCATION
FORCES UNDER COMMANDER-IN-CHIEF GENERAL GEORGE WASHINGTON (For the Most Part, to Brigade Level Only)																		
Woodford's brig.	Brig. Gen. William Woodford	31	23	8	57	119	94	200	134	195	246	988	20	9		273	26	Valley Forge, Pa.
Scott's brig.	Brig. Gen. Charles Scott	32	51	12	77	172	64	211	153	58	331	989	10	26		153	24	Valley Forge, Pa.
1st Pa. brig.		32	53	12	147	244	52	143	331	31	121	922	2	14		1	6	Valley Forge, Pa.
2nd Pa. brig.		25	63	13	148	249	70	190	375	58	71	1013	3	9		3	29	Valley Forge, Pa.
Poor's brig.	Brig. Gen. Enoch Poor	66	131	14	328	539	116	248	198	76	360	1537	15	6		4		Valley Forge, Pa.
Glover's brig.	Brig. Gen. John Glover	66	133	11	244	454	438	187	196	128	190	1593	13	11		1	6	Valley Forge, Pa.
Learned's brig.	Brig. Gen. Ebenezer Learned	28	50	7	106	191	594	126	91	87		1089	7			9	2	Valley Forge, Pa.
Paterson's brig.	Brig. Gen. John Paterson	36	61	14	85	196	576	159	117	174	142	1364	10	5		8	11	Valley Forge, Pa.
Weedon's brig.	Brig. Gen. George Weedon	43	66	17	192	318	136	354	150	95	283	1336	31	20		211	34	Valley Forge, Pa.
Muhlenberg's brig.	Brig. Gen. Peter Muhlenberg	48	78	19	138	283	92	330	190	123	228	1246	18	9		255	18	Valley Forge, Pa.
Maxwell's brig.	Brig. Gen. William Maxwell	33	93	10	351	487	56	202	146	24	180	1095	15	5			6	Valley Forge, Pa.
Conway's brig.	(late) Brig. Gen. Thomas Conway	54	83	16	227	380	139	192	189	58	242	1200	15	13				Valley Forge, Pa.
Huntington's brig.	Brig. Gen. Jedediah Huntington	43	102	9	532	686	180	154	542	41		1603	12	11		3	1	Valley Forge, Pa.
Varnum's brig.	Brig. Gen. James M. Varnum	48	92	9	528	677	140	176	229	32	127	1381	29	14		1	7	Valley Forge, Pa.
McIntosh's brig.	Brig. Gen. Lachlan McIntosh	52	192	13	490	747	178	210	100	16	30	1281	24			3	76	Valley Forge, Pa.
1st Md. brig.		82	103	17	314	516	91	282	214	19	228	1350	33	54		2	11	Wilmington, Del.
2nd Md. brig.		34	36	7	96	173	43	170	134	3	217	740	3	34		1		Wilmington, Del.
Additional	Thomas Hartley	17	31	3	81	132	24	48	20	15	29	268						York, Pa.
Det.	Lt. Col. William Stephens Smith	24	40	2	150	216	81	27	29	7		360		2				
Independent corps	(late) Tuffin Charles Armand	4	9	1	20	34		20			7	61	1					
TOTAL OF INFANTRY		798	1490	214	4311	6813	3164	3629	3538	1240	3032	21416	261	242		928	257	
ARTILLERY																		
3rd cont'l.	John Crane	19	104	2	95	220												Valley Forge, Pa.
2nd cont'l.	John Lamb	17	52		76	145	21	51	20	16		630	29	5		6	4	Valley Forge, Pa.
4th cont'l.	Thomas Proctor	21	70	3	63	157												Valley Forge, Pa.
Det.		12	79		130	221	16					237	2					Wilmington, Del.
TOTAL OF ARTILLERY		69	305	5	364	743	37	51	20	16		867	31	5		6	4	
TOTAL OF WASHINGTON'S ARMY		867	1795	219	4675	7556	3201	3680	3558	1256	3032	22283	292	247		934	261	

(The artillery figures 21, 51, 20, 16, 630, 29, 5, 6, 4 are bracketed jointly for the 3rd, 2nd and 4th cont'l.)

OFFICERS SICK, ON FURLOUGH, ETC.	WASHINGTON'S ARTILLERY (ONLY): COMMISSIONED	NONCOMMISSIONED	STAFF	TOTAL
Sick Present	3	17		20
Sick Absent	3	35	2	40
On Furlough	29	28	1	58
On Command	17	33	1	51
TOTAL	52	113	4	169

SOURCE OF THIS REPORT

1. MONTHLY RETURN OF THE TROOPS UNDER THE MORE IMMEDIATE COMMAND OF HIS EXCELLENCY GEORGE WASHINGTON... FEBRUARY 29, 1778, RECORD GROUP 93, NATIONAL ARCHIVES.

MARCH 1778

BRIGADE	UNIT	COMMANDING OFFICER	PRESENT FIT FOR DUTY & ON DUTY: COMMISSIONED OFFICERS	NONCOMMISSIONED OFFICERS	STAFF OFFICERS	RANK & FILE	TOTAL	RANK & FILE SICK, ON FURLOUGH, ETC.: SICK PRESENT	SICK ABSENT	ON COMMAND & EXTRA SERVICE	ON FURLOUGH	WITHOUT CLOTHES	GRAND TOTAL	ALTERATIONS: DEATHS	DESERTED	TAKEN PRISONER	DISCHARGED	JOINED, ENLISTED, RECRUITED	LOCATION
FORCES UNDER COMMANDER-IN-CHIEF GENERAL GEORGE WASHINGTON																			
Woodford	3rd Va. A	Lt. Col. William Heth	21	5	2	18	151	8	25	35	48	12	851					2 G	Valley Forge, Pa.
Woodford	7th Va.	Alexander McClanachan			1	2		8	1	12	103						82		Valley Forge, Pa.
Woodford	11th Va.	Daniel Morgan		13	3	48		25	30	59	14	52		3	1				Valley Forge, Pa.
Woodford	15th Va.	David Mason		8	3	27		75	68	59	6	60		13	5		1		Valley Forge, Pa.
Scott	4th Va.	Vacant	36	8	2	8	222	20	15	28	33	16	941				44	5	Valley Forge, Pa.
Scott	8th Va.	Abraham Bowman		1	1	3		2		1		2					5	12	Valley Forge, Pa.
Scott	12th Va.	James Wood		8	3	48		23	78	88	8	160		7	3		1	4	Valley Forge, Pa.
Scott	Additional	William Grayson		15	3	18		47	49	28	3	52		11	1		2	1	Valley Forge, Pa.
Scott	Additional	(late) John Patton		23	2	43		6	26	28	4	2		3	3			8	Valley Forge, Pa.
1st Pa.	1st Pa.	James Chambers	12	17	3	59	91	16	33	117	13	89	359	1	9			7	Valley Forge, Pa.
1st Pa.	2nd Pa.	Henry Bicker	9	17	2	37	65	9	7	36		17	134	1	2			5	Valley Forge, Pa.
1st Pa.	7th Pa.	William Irvine	6	8	1	58	73	17	24	38	8	18	178		9			1	Valley Forge, Pa.
1st Pa.	10th Pa.	George Nagel	9	9	4	39	61	15	47	54	8	36	221		3				Valley Forge, Pa.
2nd Pa.	4th Pa.	Lt. Col. William Butler	2	13	3	54	72	10	23	46	10	4	165	2	10		1	4	Valley Forge, Pa.
2nd Pa.	5th Pa.	Francis Johnston	6	12	6	72	96	20	46	74	10	39	285	3	7		4	8	Valley Forge, Pa.
2nd Pa.	8th Pa.	Daniel Brodhead	7	8	2	43	60	44	55	150	21	40	370	2	4		1	9	Valley Forge, Pa.
2nd Pa.	11th Pa.	Richard Humpton	5	8	1	28	42	10	33	50	9	4	148	3	6			2	Valley Forge, Pa.
Poor	1st N. H.	Joseph Cilley	9	24	2	60	95	150	77	42	15	12	391	3	1				Valley Forge, Pa.
Poor	2nd N. H.	Nathan Hale	8	24	1	41	74	84	43	68	18	19	306	2	1			2	Valley Forge, Pa.
Poor	3rd N. H.	Alexander Scammell	10	30	4	34	78	115	40	44	32	4	313	6				1	Valley Forge, Pa.
Poor	2nd N. Y.	Philip Van Cortlandt	13	30	3	46	92	22	34	7	56	30	241	5			1	8	Valley Forge, Pa.
Poor	4th N. Y.	Henry Beekman Livingston	19	26	4	33	82	31	40	45	3	69	270	4	1		1	1	Valley Forge, Pa.
Glover	4th Mass.	William Shepard	15	35	3	68	121	120	28	68	26	19	382	12				1	Valley Forge, Pa.
Glover	13th Mass.	Edward Wigglesworth	15	33	2	102	152	72	50	66	34	32	406	8	1		1	1	Valley Forge, Pa.
Glover	1st Mass.	Joseph Vose	16	32	2	90	140	68	57	59	23	70	417	8	3		1	10	Valley Forge, Pa.
Glover	15th Mass.	Timothy Bigelow	16	34	3	58	111	66	26	103	28	22	356	7	3		1	4	Valley Forge, Pa.
Learned	2nd Mass.	John Bailey	14	21	4	93	132	65	47	60	34	73	411	4	4		2		Valley Forge, Pa.
Learned	9th Mass.	James Wesson	9	21	3	23	56	41	31	49	36	138	351	9				11	Valley Forge, Pa.
Learned	8th Mass.	Michael Jackson	15	30	4	54	103	88	45	46	16	46	344	10			1		Valley Forge, Pa.
Paterson	10th Mass.	Thomas Marshall	8	26	4	61	99	48	33	87	35	6	308	6			3	1	Valley Forge, Pa.
Paterson	12th Mass.	Samuel Brewer	14	34	3	102	153	44	25	76	30	28	356	3	2		1	6	Valley Forge, Pa.
Paterson	14th Mass.	Gamaliel Bradford	10	24	3	62	99	60	38	72	59	19	347	14	3			1	Valley Forge, Pa.
Paterson	11th Mass.	Benjamin Tupper	12	21	4	43	80	64	31	71	36	85	367	7	2		1	1	Valley Forge, Pa.
Weedon	2nd Va.	Christian Febiger	6	18	4	62	90	29	31	54	21	21	246	12	2		29	1	Valley Forge, Pa.
Weedon	6th Va.	Vacant	1	4	1	10	16	2	11	3	17	4	53	1			21		Valley Forge, Pa.
Weedon	10th Va.	Vacant	13	22	3	48	86	49	107	51	14	82	389	17	5			3	Valley Forge, Pa.
Weedon	14th Va.	Charles Lewis	11	14	5	19	49	72	71	57	14	31	294	13	7		5	6	Valley Forge, Pa.
Weedon	13th Pa.	Walter Stewart	5	8		14	27	20	38	40	33	69	227	1	6		2	4	Valley Forge, Pa.
Muhlenberg	1st Va.	(late) James Hendricks	9	20	4	32	65	12	21	50	25	9	182	3			4	1	Valley Forge, Pa.
Muhlenberg	5th & 9th Va.	Josiah Parker & George Mathews	4	7	3	6	20	3	19	16	66	15	139	2			18	4	Valley Forge, Pa.
Muhlenberg	13th Va.	William Russell	6	7	2	12	27	20	46	28	6	42	169	6				1	Valley Forge, Pa.
Muhlenberg	1st Va. state	George Gibson	11	30	4	56	101	31	119	58	5	43	357	39	4		2		Valley Forge, Pa.
Muhlenberg	German bn.	Lt. Col. Ludowick Weltner	10	17	5	41	73	24	24	106	29	52	308	5	1		2		Valley Forge, Pa.
Maxwell	1st N. J. B	Matthias Ogden	9	16	4	38	67	30	62	80	6	29	274	8	4		1	11	Valley Forge, Pa.
Maxwell	2nd N. J.	Israel Shreve																	New Jersey
Maxwell	3rd N. J.	Elias Dayton	9	18	4	68	99	41	32	75	16		263	2	5			11	Valley Forge, Pa.
Maxwell	4th N. J.	Ephraim Martin	6	18	4	52	80	36	53	86	9	9	273	1			2	2	Valley Forge, Pa.

MARCH 1778 (continued)

BRIGADE	UNIT	COMMANDING OFFICER	PRESENT FIT FOR DUTY & ON DUTY: COMMISSIONED OFFICERS	NONCOMMISSIONED OFFICERS	STAFF OFFICERS	RANK & FILE	TOTAL	RANK & FILE SICK, ON FURLOUGH, ETC.: SICK PRESENT	SICK ABSENT	ON COMMAND & EXTRA SERVICE	ON FURLOUGH	WITHOUT CLOTHES	GRAND TOTAL	ALTERATIONS: DEATHS	DESERTED	TAKEN PRISONER	DISCHARGED	JOINED, ENLISTED, RECRUITED	LOCATION
	FORCES UNDER COMMANDER-IN-CHIEF GENERAL GEORGE WASHINGTON (continued)																		
(late) Conway	3rd Pa.	Thomas Craig	10	15	4	38	67	12	26	59	9	18	191	1	9			3	Valley Forge, Pa.
(late) Conway	6th Pa.	Robert Magaw	7	20	2	32	61	8	34	37	4	20	164	4	7		2	4	Valley Forge, Pa.
(late) Conway	9th Pa.	Richard Butler	8	18	4	37	67	13	32	40	7	48	207		20			6	Valley Forge, Pa.
(late) Conway	12th Pa.	(late) William Cooke	4	12	3	39	58	30	26	69	18		201	9	3		1	7	Valley Forge, Pa.
(late) Conway	Additional	William Malcolm	11	2	2	7	22	54	14	21	12	47	170	2	8		1		Valley Forge, Pa.
(late) Conway	Additional	Oliver Spencer	10	8	4	10	32	24	25	33	30	47	191	7	8		4		Valley Forge, Pa.
Huntington	1st & 5th Conn.	Lt. Col. S. Prentiss & P. Bradley	24	52	5	182	263	247	73	260	28		871	10				3	Valley Forge, Pa.
Huntington	2nd & 7th Conn.	(late) Charles Webb & Heman Swift	23	45	3	106	177	212	53	229	13	21	705	9	5		4	7	Valley Forge, Pa.
Varnum	4th & 8th Conn.	John Durkee & (late) John Chandler	22	48	2	146	218	284	81	175	41		799	19	2		7	16	Valley Forge, Pa.
Varnum	1st & 2nd R. I.	Christopher Greene & I. Angell	20	43	5	111	179	102	61	198	10	36	586	8	6		2	6	Valley Forge, Pa.
McIntosh	1st N. C.	Thomas Clark	25	65	5	113	208	90	50	58	2		408	39	4			1	Valley Forge, Pa.
McIntosh	2nd N. C.	John Patten	27	59	5	118	209	80	23	72	2		386	21			2	3	Valley Forge, Pa.
McIntosh	3rd N. C.	Jethro Sumner	25	56	5	121	207	66	51	52	11		387	14			1	5	Valley Forge, Pa.
1st Md.	1st Md.	John Hawkins Stone	13	21	3	71	108	11	32	37	2	28	218		1				Wilmington, Del.
1st Md.	Del. C	David Hall	10	8	3	72	93	6	30	57	13	41	240		2			1	Wilmington, Del.
1st Md.	3rd Md.	Mordecai Gist	15	24	2	104	145	17	70	81	4	16	333	3	9				Wilmington, Del.
1st Md.	5th Md.	William Richardson	12	18	4 D	90	124	26	63	24	28	4	269	4	1		2	7	Wilmington, Del.
1st Md.	7th Md.	John Gunby	13	24	5	79	121	9	35	41	5	31	242	1					Wilmington, Del.
2nd Md.	2nd Md.	Thomas Price	8	19		58	85	5	49	40	2	49	230		1		2		Wilmington, Del.
2nd Md.	4th Md.	Josias Carvil Hall	15	13	5 E	76	109	29	61	79	3	49	330	5	1			1	Wilmington, Del.
2nd Md.	6th Md.	Otho Holland Williams	11	15	5	33	64	9	46	42	2	36	199	1	2			10	Wilmington, Del.
	Det. Lee's additional	Lt. Col. William Stephens Smith	28	45	2	196	271		102	39	5		417					48	
	Independent corps	(late) Tuffin Charles Armand	3	9		22	34	2	14	6	2		58						
Lacey	York Co. Pa. militia	William Ross	20	18	3	69	110	15		39	1		165					26	Pennsylvania
Lacey	Northampton Co. Pa. militia	Jacob Stroud	33	52	3	246	334	11		8	10		363						Pennsylvania
	TOTAL OF INFANTRY		813	1526	218	4209	6766	3224	2890	4366	1304	2172	20722	424	207		268	314	
	ARTILLERY																		
	3rd cont'l.	John Crane	16	88	2	88	194							3	10		5	19	Valley Forge, Pa.
	2nd cont'l.	John Lamb	20	51		67	138	57	31	35	12		610	3	8			5	Valley Forge, Pa.
	4th cont'l.	Thomas Proctor	12	69	4	58	143							1	10		9	5	Valley Forge, Pa.
	Det.		7	32		36	75	4	2	3			84						Wilmington, Del.
	TOTAL OF ARTILLERY		55	240	6	249	550	61	33	38	12		694 F	7	28		14	29	
	TOTAL OF WASHINGTON'S ARMY		868	1766	224	4458	7316	3285	2923	4404	1316	2172	21416	431	235		282	343	

MARCH 1778
(continued)

OFFICERS SICK, ON FURLOUGH ETC.	WASHINGTON'S ARTILLERY (ONLY)			
	COMMISSIONED	NONCOMMISSIONED	STAFF	TOTAL
Sick Present	5	31		36
Sick Absent	3	24	1	28
On Furlough	34	30	1	65
On Command	14	32	1	47
TOTAL	56	117	3	176

SOURCE OF THIS REPORT

1. MONTHLY RETURN OF THE CONTINENTAL FORCES UNDER THE MORE IMMEDIATE COMMAND OF HIS EXCELLENCY GEORGE WASHINGTON...FOR MARCH 1778, ELEPHANT FOLIO OF WASHINGTON RETURNS, WILLIAM L. CLEMENTS LIBRARY. [THE HEADING AND A FEW OF THE FIGURES ON THIS RETURN HAVE BEEN DAMAGED, APPARENTLY BY MICE OR RATS; COMPARISON WITH THE NATIONAL ARCHIVES VERSION WHICH FOLLOWS ESTABLISHES THE IDENTITY OF THIS RETURN. THE ARTILLERY SECTION OF THIS RETURN IS SPECIFICALLY DATED MARCH 28, 1778, BUT CONTAINS THE MONTHLY ALTERATIONS.]

1a. Monthly Return of the Continental Forces under...Washington, March 30, 1778, Record Group 93, National Archives. [Like the rest of the National Archives copies of monthly returns through to the end of the war, this provides only brigade totals; see introduction. Comparison with the weekly returns and the Clements Library copy demonstrates that the column headings for the alterations in the artillery section of this return have been copied incorrectly.]

A. The names of the regiments and officers for Woodford's brigade and some of the figures for commissioned officers have been destroyed on this return. While comparison with the National Archives version of this return (which provides figures to the brigade level only, not for individual regiments) definitely establishes that the first four units are Woodford's brigade, identification of the individual regiments is based on the fact that they are arranged in this order on all the returns of the following months. Brigade totals for commissioned officers are supplied from the National Archives copy of this month's return for the damaged areas.
B. No figures are on the manuscript for this regiment, which was detached in New Jersey.
C. A careless ditto by the adjutant on the March and April returns in the Clements Library folio makes Hall's Delaware regiment appear to be from Maryland.
D. Four staff officers for John Gunby's 7th Maryland regiment plus one chaplain for the entire brigade.
E. Four staff officers for Otho Holland Williams's 6th Maryland regiment plus one chaplain for the entire brigade.
F. The National Archives return notes, "No monthly returns from the Cavalry, or Colo. Hartley's Regiment have come to hand this month."
G. Figure deduced from brigade total; regimental figure destroyed.

A nineteenth-century engraving of Major General John Sullivan. Sullivan, who was with the main army at Valley Forge at this time, had a number of significant commands during the war. His expedition against the Iroquois in 1779 was among the largest independent operations of the Revolution. This engraving, from the print collections of the Clements Library, is perhaps the most pleasing of a number of similar portraits, all of which are apparently based on a miniature by John Trumbull owned by Sullivan's descendants.

APRIL 1778

BRIGADE	UNIT	COMMANDING OFFICER	PRESENT FIT FOR DUTY & ON DUTY: COMMISSIONED OFFICERS	NONCOMMISSIONED OFFICERS	STAFF OFFICERS	RANK & FILE	TOTAL	RANK & FILE SICK, ON FURLOUGH, ETC.: SICK PRESENT	SICK ABSENT	ON COMMAND & EXTRA SERVICE	ON FURLOUGH	GRAND TOTAL	ALTERATIONS: DEATHS	DESERTED	TAKEN PRISONER	DISCHARGED	JOINED, ENLISTED, RECRUITED	LOCATION
FORCES UNDER COMMANDER-IN-CHIEF GENERAL GEORGE WASHINGTON																		
Woodford	3rd Va.	Lt. Col. William Heth	42 C	27	4	85	470	35	15	23	8	1159	23	6		2	D 218	Valley Forge, Pa.
	7th Va.	Alexander McClanachan		10	1	50		125	11	24	68							Valley Forge, Pa.
	11th Va.	Daniel Morgan		28	3	123		39	22	37	12							Valley Forge, Pa.
	15th Va.	David Mason		31	3	63		171	45	48	6							Valley Forge, Pa.
Scott	4th Va.	Vacant	7	13	3	60	83	48	10	21	10	172	21	17		39	230	Valley Forge, Pa.
	8th Va.	Abraham Bowman	11	27	4	68	110	20	7	28	14	179						Valley Forge, Pa.
	12th Va.	James Wood	17	29	5	238	289	40	33	61	8	431						Valley Forge, Pa.
	Additional	William Grayson	9	25	2	62	98	53	32	35	4	222						Valley Forge, Pa.
	Additional	(late) John Patton	8	23	2	55	88	16	17	17	2	140						Valley Forge, Pa.
1st Pa.	1st Pa.	James Chambers	11	21	3	172	207	27	23	95	9	361	13	35		2	62	Valley Forge, Pa.
	2nd Pa.	Henry Bicker	10	24	3	75	112	12	3	23	1	151						Valley Forge, Pa.
	7th Pa.	William Irvine	15	21	1	100	137	15	18	27	4	201						Valley Forge, Pa.
	10th Pa.	George Nagel	11	36	2	104	153	11	31	31	7	233						Valley Forge, Pa.
2nd Pa.	4th Pa.	Lt. Col. William Butler	9	29	3	98	139	17	15	34	6	211	4	14		2	54	Valley Forge, Pa.
	5th Pa.	Francis Johnston	7	23	4	150	184	27	34	54		299						Valley Forge, Pa.
	8th Pa.	Daniel Brodhead	3	18		117	138	61	25	136	10	370						Valley Forge, Pa.
	11th Pa.	Richard Humpton	7	14	2	51	74	10	27	35	6	152						Valley Forge, Pa.
Poor	1st N. H.	Joseph Cilley	18	24	2	176	220	91	63	28	10	412	23	5		6	53	Valley Forge, Pa.
	2nd N. H.	Nathan Hale	10	25	2	150	187	31	34	52	15	319						Valley Forge, Pa.
	3rd N. H.	Alexander Scammell	10	24	3	88	125	93	26	18	32	294						Valley Forge, Pa.
	2nd N. Y.	Philip Van Cortlandt	14	30	2	122	168	28	25	16	3	240						Valley Forge, Pa.
	4th N. Y.	Henry Beekman Livingston	14	19	4	103	140	81	25	13		259						Valley Forge, Pa.
Glover	4th Mass.	William Shepard	19	36	3	174	232	53	13	54	21	373	37	12		9	11	Valley Forge, Pa.
	13th Mass.	Edward Wigglesworth	16	32	3	184	235	51	34	47	28	395						Valley Forge, Pa.
	1st Mass.	Joseph Vose	21	30	2	201	254	42	25	48	27	396						Valley Forge, Pa.
	15th Mass.	Timothy Bigelow	17	32	4	164	217	60	28	38	14	357						Valley Forge, Pa.
/ Learned	2nd Mass.	John Bailey	14	27	4	195	240	63	38	28	37	406	20	3		2	6	Valley Forge, Pa.
	9th Mass.	James Wesson	16	31	5	202	254	29	21	22	37	363						Valley Forge, Pa.
	8th Mass.	Michael Jackson	14	32	4	124	174	59	43	42	19	337						Valley Forge, Pa.
Paterson	10th Mass.	Thomas Marshall	10	29	3	117	159	43	26	45	32	305	19	2		3	10	Valley Forge, Pa.
	12th Mass.	Samuel Brewer	15	43	4	163	225	46	21	42	27	361						Valley Forge, Pa.
	14th Mass.	Gamaliel Bradford	10	23	4	111	148	46	36	41	57	328						Valley Forge, Pa.
	11th Mass.	Benjamin Tupper	19	22	5	176	222	67	14	29	32	364						Valley Forge, Pa.
Weedon	2nd Va.	Christian Febiger	12	29	3	97	141	65	9	38	8	261	30	25		15	232	Valley Forge, Pa.
	6th Va.	Vacant	3	9	2	13	27	23	3	8	15	76						Valley Forge, Pa.
	10th Va.	John Green	20	29	3	51	103	213	32	33	16	397						Valley Forge, Pa.
	14th Va.	(late) Charles Lewis	17	33	4	76	130	151	41	30	16	368						Valley Forge, Pa.
	13th Pa.	Walter Stewart	19	24	4	145	192	22	25	61	22	322						Valley Forge, Pa.
Muhlenberg	1st Va.	Richard Parker	12	20	4	61	97	91	15	49	14	266	35	19		17	259	Valley Forge, Pa.
	5th & 9th Va.	Josiah Parker & George Mathews	8	19	4	46	77	93	13	30	20	233						Valley Forge, Pa.
	13th Va.	William Russell	8	10	3	65	86	21	26	18	5	156						Valley Forge, Pa.
	1st Va. state	George Gibson	17	34	3	156	210	60	35	27	4	336						Valley Forge, Pa.
	German bn.	Lt. Col. Ludowick Weltner	18	14	3	168	203	27	20	46	14	310						Valley Forge, Pa.
Maxwel	1st N. J. A	Matthias Ogden	14	28	4	113	159	49	30	38		276	9	48		8	65	Valley Forge, Pa.
	2nd N. J.	Israel Shreve																New Jersey
	3rd N. J.	Elias Dayton	15	30	4	115	164	41	26	43	5	279						Valley Forge, Pa.
	4th N. J.	Ephraim Martin	10	27	4	126	167	39	37	40	2	285						Valley Forge, Pa.

APRIL 1778 (continued)

BRIGADE	UNIT	COMMANDING OFFICER	PRESENT FIT FOR DUTY & ON DUTY: COMMISSIONED OFFICERS	NONCOMMISSIONED OFFICERS	STAFF OFFICERS	RANK & FILE	TOTAL	RANK & FILE SICK, ON FURLOUGH, ETC.: SICK PRESENT	SICK ABSENT	ON COMMAND & EXTRA SERVICE	ON FURLOUGH	GRAND TOTAL	ALTERATIONS: DEATHS	DESERTED	TAKEN PRISONER	DISCHARGED	JOINED, ENLISTED, RECRUITED	LOCATION
	FORCES UNDER COMMANDER-IN-CHIEF GENERAL GEORGE WASHINGTON (continued)																	
(late) Conway	3rd Pa.	Thomas Craig	8	13	4	100	125	19	23	14	6	187	14	19		3	48	Valley Forge, Pa.
(late) Conway	6th Pa.	Robert Magaw	10	26	2	96	134	13	29	10	5	191						Valley Forge, Pa.
(late) Conway	9th Pa.	Richard Butler	13	28	2	117	160	14	25	24	7	230						Valley Forge, Pa.
(late) Conway	Additional	William Malcolm	12	14	4	55	85	42	18	26	8	179						Valley Forge, Pa.
(late) Conway	12th Pa.	(late) William Cooke	4	19	3	85	111	8	29	42	20	210						Valley Forge, Pa.
(late) Conway	Additional	Oliver Spencer	6	16	3	48	73	27	27	31	22	180						Valley Forge, Pa.
Huntington	1st & 5th Conn.	Lt. Col. S. Prentiss & P. Bradley	27	64	5	402	498	134	69	133	23	857	48	8		4	29	Valley Forge, Pa.
Huntington	2nd & 7th Conn.	(late) Charles Webb & Heman Swift	21	68	6	357	452	108	49	92	12	713						Valley Forge, Pa.
Varnum	4th & 8th Conn.	John Durkee & (late) John Chandler	25	73	3	352	453	126	55	88	39	761	41	21		8	33	Valley Forge, Pa.
Varnum	1st & 2nd R. I.	Christopher Greene & I. Angell	18	41	2	216	277	130	31	75	6	519						Valley Forge, Pa.
McIntosh	1st N. C.	Thomas Clark	11	35	4	127	177	96	12	35	2	322	46	2		4	34	Valley Forge, Pa.
McIntosh	2nd N. C.	John Patten	15	36	5	115	171	126	25	32	1	355						Valley Forge, Pa.
McIntosh	3rd N. C.	Jethro Sumner	11	38	4	143	196	53	40	42	11	342						Valley Forge, Pa.
1st Md.	1st Md.	John Hawkins Stone	11	25	5	125	166		36	34	6	242	20	23		4	78	Wilmington, Del.
1st Md.	Del. B	David Hall	12	19	3	125	159	14	29	54	7	263						Wilmington, Del.
1st Md.	3rd Md.	Mordecai Gist	16	25		129	170	20	55	70	9	324						Wilmington, Del.
1st Md.	5th Md.	William Richardson	14	19	3	119	155	34	43	28	15	275						Wilmington, Del.
1st Md.	7th Md.	John Gunby	18	25	5	126	174	12	21	35	5	247						Wilmington, Del.
2nd Md.	2nd Md.	Thomas Price	11	28	2	199	240	6	33	18	2	299		4		1	65	Wilmington, Del.
2nd Md.	4th Md.	Josias Carvil Hall	12	17	5	246	280	20	34	26	8	368						Wilmington, Del.
2nd Md.	6th Md.	Otho Holland Williams	12	12	3	124	151	7	30	8	3	199						Wilmington, Del.
	Det. Lee's additional	Lt. Col. William Stephens Smith	27	42	2	200	271	28	85	14	1	399	4	16		2	19	The Gulph, Pa.
	1st N. Y.	Goose Van Schaick	26	49	4	347	426	10	21	27		484		16				
	Independent corps	(late) Tuffin Charles Armand	5	7		23	35	5	14	4	2	60						
	TOTAL OF INFANTRY		922	1903	223	9329	12377	3557	1985	2715	927	21561	407	295		131	1506	
	FORCES AT FISHKILL																	
	3rd Conn.	Samuel Wyllys	16	39	4	229	288	29	42	81	25	465	1	1		1	5	Fishkill, N. Y.
	Additional	Samuel Blatchley Webb	5	20		89	114	16	37	65	18	250					11	Fishkill, N. Y.
	Additional	Henry Sherburne	12	23	5	147	187	31	19	12	17	266					5	Fishkill, N. Y.
	5th Mass.	Rufus Putnam	22	39	3	277	341	37	6	25	5	414					4	Fishkill, N. Y.
	6th Conn.	Return Jonathan Meigs	15	42	2	297	356	41	28	50	50	525		1			19	Fishkill, N. Y.
	5th N. Y.	Lewis DuBois	9	24	3	78	114	15	25	99	3	256		6			3	Fishkill, N. Y.
	2nd Canadian	Moses Hazen	18	58	2	251	329	15	93	45	12	494						Fishkill, N. Y.
	6th Mass.	Thomas Nixon	21	43	3	122	189	19	11	123	44	386	1			1	5	Fishkill, N. Y.
	1st Canadian	James Livingston	22	35	5	120	182	7	33	7	2	231		2			5	Fishkill, N. Y.
	TOTAL AT FISHKILL		140	323	27	1610	2100	210	294	507	176	3287	2	10		2	57	
	ARTILLERY																	
	7 cos. 3rd cont'l.	John Crane	18	88	2	99	207	31	32	47	8	954	3	6		3	1	Valley Forge, Pa.
	5 cos. 2nd cont'l.	John Lamb	15	52		56	123							2		1	4	Valley Forge, Pa.
	4th cont'l.	Thomas Proctor	21	68	5	62	156						2	4			5	Valley Forge, Pa.
	5 ind. cos.		15	64		109	188										147	
	Artillery at Wilmington		11	57		94	162											Wilmington, Del.
	TOTAL OF ARTILLERY		80	329	7	420	836	31	32	47	8	954 F	5	12		4	157	
	TOTAL OF WASHINGTON'S ARMY		1142	2555	257	11359	15313	3798	2311	3269	1111	25802	414	317		137	1720	

BRIGADE

APRIL 1778 (continued)

UNIT	COMMANDING OFFICER	PRESENT FIT FOR DUTY & ON DUTY: COMMISSIONED OFFICERS	NONCOMMISSIONED OFFICERS	STAFF OFFICERS	RANK & FILE	TOTAL	RANK & FILE SICK, ON FURLOUGH, ETC.: SICK PRESENT	SICK ABSENT	ON COMMAND & EXTRA SERVICE	ON FURLOUGH	GRAND TOTAL	ALTERATIONS: DEATHS	DESERTED	TAKEN PRISONER	DISCHARGED	JOINED, ENLISTED, RECRUITED	LOCATION
SOUTH CAROLINA CONTINENTAL REGIMENTS																	
1st S. C.	Charles Cotesworth Pinckney	21	45	3	242	311	19	11	68	22	431		2		3		South Carolina
2nd S. C.	Isaac Motts	27	44	5	255	331	29		42	15	417						South Carolina
3rd S. C.	William Thompson	34	42	5	210	291	10		165	17	483	1	31		5		South Carolina
5th S. C.	Isaac Huger	19	27	5	110	161	10	2	17	3	193		4		4		South Carolina
6th S. C.	Thomas Sumter	17	29	5	125	176	6		7	14	203	2	2		1		South Carolina
TOTAL OF SOUTH CAROLINA INFANTRY		118	187	23	942	1270	74	13	299	71	1727	3	39		13		
ARTILLERY																	
4th S. C.	Owen Roberts	8	27	3	43	81	1 E		42		124	1	2		2		South Carolina
TOTAL OF SOUTH CAROLINA CONTINENTALS		126	214	26	985	1351	75	13	341	71	1851	4	41		15		
GRAND TOTAL		1268	2769	283	12344	16664	3873	2324	3610	1182	27653	418	358		152	1720	

OFFICERS SICK, ON FURLOUGH, ETC.	WASHINGTON'S ARTILLERY (ONLY): COMMISSIONED	NONCOMMISSIONED	STAFF	TOTAL	SOUTH CAROLINA ARTILLERY (ONLY): COMMISSIONED	NONCOMMISSIONED	STAFF	TOTAL	GRAND TOTAL
Sick Present	2	20		22	E 1	2		3	46
Sick Absent	1	19	1	21					
On Command	13	35		48	5	17		22	70
On Furlough	21	7	1	29	3		1	4	33
Recruiting					2			2	2
TOTAL	37	81	2	120	11	19	1	31	151

SOURCES OF THIS REPORT

1. MONTHLY RETURN OF THE CONTINENTAL ARMY UNDER THE COMMAND OF HIS EXCELLENCY GEORGE WASHINGTON... FOR APRIL 1778, ELEPHANT FOLIO OF WASHINGTON RETURNS, WILLIAM L. CLEMENTS LIBRARY. [THE HEADING AND A FEW OF THE FIGURES ON THIS RETURN ARE DAMAGED; COMPARISON WITH THE NATIONAL ARCHIVES VERSION WHICH FOLLOWS ESTABLISHES THE IDENTITY OF THIS RETURN. THE ARTILLERY SECTION OF THIS MONTHLY RETURN APPEARS TWO PAGES EARLIER IN THE FOLIO AND IS DATED MAY 2.]

1a. A General Return of the Continental Army under... Washington, May 2, 1778 [marked "Monthly Genl. Return" on the reverse], Record Group 93, National Archives. [To the brigade level only.]

2. RETURN OF THE FORCES AT FISHKILL, REMOVED FROM THE MAY MONTHLY RETURN [SOURCE 1 ON THIS VOLUME'S MAY 1778 MONTHLY REPORT] BECAUSE THE NATIONAL ARCHIVES VERSION OF THAT RETURN NOTES THAT THE RETURN OF THE FORCES AT FISHKILL WAS MADE APRIL 27. THEREFORE, THIS RETURN, WHICH WAS LATE IN ARRIVING, HAS BEEN MOVED TO ITS PROPER MONTH. SEE INTRODUCTION.

3. RETURN OF THE SOUTH CAROLINA CONTINENTAL REGIMENTS, REMOVED FROM THE MAY MONTHLY RETURN. [SEE SOURCE 2 ABOVE.] THE NATIONAL ARCHIVES VERSION OF THAT RETURN NOTES THAT THE RETURNS FROM SOUTH CAROLINA ARE DATED MAY 1. [THE ARTILLERY SECTION FOR THE SOUTHERN DEPARTMENT APPEARS SEVERAL PAGES EARLIER IN THE FOLIO THAN THE MAY MONTHLY INFANTRY RETURN AND IS UNDATED, BUT COMPARISON WITH THE NATIONAL ARCHIVES MANUSCRIPT ESTABLISHES ITS IDENTITY.]

A. The manuscript does not include any figures for this regiment, which was detached in New Jersey.
B. A careless ditto by the adjutant on the March and April returns in the Clements Library folio makes Hall's Delaware regiment appear to be from Maryland.
C. Because of the mutilation of this corner of the manuscript, no figures are available for the individual regiments.
D. With the exception of the grand total, all the alterations on the manuscript monthly return in the Clements folio for April are clearly in error. Thus, only the brigade figures for alterations (from the National Archives version of the return) can be provided. The figures on the Clements return do not add up to the totals given and do not agree with the brigade figures on the National Archives return. It seems that all the alterations except the grand total on the Clements return were copied from the wrong return by mistake.
E. The return gives only "sick," not "sick present" and "sick absent" for the South Carolina Continental artillery regiment (4th South Carolina).
F. The National Archives manuscript notes that no returns were received for the cavalry, for the Virginia state troops which had recently arrived, for Israel Shreve's 2nd New Jersey regiment, and for Thomas Hartley's Additional regiment.

John Trumbull's miniature of Charles Cotesworth Pinckney, painted in Charleston in 1791. Pinckney, whose 1st South Carolina Continental Regiment is included on the preceding page, was captured at the surrender of Charleston in May 1780. (Courtesy of the Yale University Art Gallery, New Haven, Conn.)

MAY 1778

BRIGADE	UNIT	COMMANDING OFFICER	PRESENT FIT FOR DUTY & ON DUTY: COMMISSIONED OFFICERS	NONCOMMISSIONED OFFICERS	STAFF OFFICERS	RANK & FILE	TOTAL	RANK & FILE SICK, ON FURLOUGH, ETC.: SICK PRESENT	SICK ABSENT	ON COMMAND & EXTRA SERVICE	ON FURLOUGH	GRAND TOTAL	ALTERATIONS: DEATHS	DESERTED	TAKEN PRISONER	DISCHARGED	JOINED, ENLISTED, RECRUITED	LOCATION
FORCES UNDER COMMANDER-IN-CHIEF GENERAL GEORGE WASHINGTON																		
Woodford	3rd Va.	William Heth	E	16	6	94	654	23	19	30		1213	4			3	7	Valley Forge, Pa.
	7th Va.	Lt. Col. Holt Richardson	50	31	3	184		81	24	42	12		4	2		2	62	Valley Forge, Pa.
	11th Va.	Daniel Morgan		25	3	122		45	10	34	8		6	7		5	6	Valley Forge, Pa.
	15th Va.	David Mason		28	3	89		118	56	52	5		14			2	4	Valley Forge, Pa.
Scott	4th Va.	Vacant	11	15	4	42	72	52	9	40	8	181	15	14		2	8	Valley Forge, Pa.
	8th Va.	Abraham Bowman	17	32	4	45	98	29	2	52	7	188	8	2		5	54	Valley Forge, Pa.
	12th Va.	James Wood	16	25	5	229	275	49	28	84	6	442	2	2		3		Valley Forge, Pa.
	Additional	William Grayson	11	23	2	70	106	46	13	35	2	202	10			5		Valley Forge, Pa.
	Additional	(late) John Patton	12	25	2	44	83	17	15	27	1	143	2					Valley Forge, Pa.
1st Pa.	1st Pa.	James Chambers	13	26	4	145	188	37	14	104	5	348	10	11		13	15	Valley Forge, Pa.
	2nd Pa.	Henry Bicker	15	24	3	72	114	15	1	24	2	156		5		1	6	Valley Forge, Pa.
	7th Pa.	William Irvine	11	19	1	101	132	22	4	37	2	197	1	6			21	Valley Forge, Pa.
	10th Pa.	George Nagel	14	31	4	86	135	25	19	51	6	236	6	5		2	20	Valley Forge, Pa.
2nd Pa.	4th Pa.	Lt. Col. William Butler	9	24	3	109	145	18	9	29	4	205	2	23		4	12	Valley Forge, Pa.
	5th Pa.	Francis Johnston	7	18	6	142	173	36	29	54	5	297	3	19			26	Valley Forge, Pa.
	8th Pa.	Daniel Brodhead	6	24	2	251	283	31	24	20	17	375	2	1		1	15	Valley Forge, Pa. G
	11th Pa.	Richard Humpton	7	14	4	46	71	16	13	38	7	145	2	4			9	Valley Forge, Pa.
Poor	1st N. H.	Joseph Cilley	16	22	4	176	218	94	55	29	8	404	8	4		1	10	Valley Forge, Pa.
	2nd N. H.	Nathan Hale	12	26	3	143	184	52	26	50	13	325	4	3			11	Valley Forge, Pa.
	3rd N. H.	Alexander Scammell	9	23	3	75	110	112	17	21	31	291	11	2		1	19	Valley Forge, Pa.
	2nd N. Y.	Philip Van Cortlandt	7	29	3	204	243	61	19	23	1	347	6	2		2	128	Valley Forge, Pa.
	4th N. Y.	Henry Beekman Livingston	7	18	4	160	189	111	15	14	2	331	7	9			104	Valley Forge, Pa.
Glover	4th Mass.	William Shepard	22	33	4	180	239	54	12	52	16	373	3			6	13	Valley Forge, Pa.
	13th Mass.	Edward Wigglesworth	21	35	3	184	243	40	26	61	15	385	9	1		8	2	Valley Forge, Pa.
	15th Mass.	Timothy Bigelow	16	26	4	170	216	34	34	42	11	337	9			6	3	Valley Forge, Pa.
	1st Mass.	Joseph Vose	22	32	2	185	241	55	19	54	22	391	5	1		3	2	Valley Forge, Pa.
(late) Learned	2nd Mass.	John Bailey	16	25	5	174	220	73	34	42	29	398	8	3			6	Valley Forge, Pa.
	8th Mass.	Michael Jackson	16	30	5	128	179	52	59	37	15	342	5			1	10	Valley Forge, Pa.
	9th Mass.	James Wesson	18	38	4	174	234	32	19	45	26	356	8	3		1	7	Valley Forge, Pa.
Paterson	12th Mass.	Samuel Brewer	23	42	5	137	207	50	24	47	14	342	7	8		14	4	Valley Forge, Pa.
	10th Mass.	Thomas Marshall	12	31	3	136	182	43	13	38	17	293	9	13		2	10	Valley Forge, Pa.
	14th Mass.	Gamaliel Bradford	14	29	2	125	170	46	27	36	34	313	13	2		13	12	Valley Forge, Pa.
	11th Mass.	Benjamin Tupper	20	24	5	187	236	60	10	30	16	352	7	1		8	4	Valley Forge, Pa.
Weedon	2nd Va.	Christian Febiger	11	28	4	107	150	71	4	29	8	262	5	2		2	12	Valley Forge, Pa.
	6th Va.	Lt. Col. Charles Simms	9	10	5	39	63	6	4	3	14	90	5				10	Valley Forge, Pa.
	10th Va.	John Green	19	33	3	197	252	88	17	26	16	399	12	2		5	18	Valley Forge, Pa.
	14th Va.	William Davies	25	36	5	152	218	132	24	31	9	414	3	3		4	41	Valley Forge, Pa.
	13th Pa.	Walter Stewart	22	28	3	184	237	20	17	36	15	325	7	17		1	22	Valley Forge, Pa.
Muhlenberg	1st Va.	Richard Parker	15	18	5	80	118	78	7	42	14	259	11			2	4	Valley Forge, Pa.
	5th & 9th Va.	Josiah Parker	19	28	4	113	164	46	11	30	10	261	5				14	Valley Forge, Pa.
	1st Va. state	George Gibson	16	31	4	168	219	59	19	36	2	335	2	2		2	18	Valley Forge, Pa.
	German bn.	Lt. Col. Ludowick Weltner	18	18	3	160	199	16	36	57	7	315	1			3	3	Valley Forge, Pa.
	13th Va. A	William Russell	9	11	4	51	75	23	20	35	5	158	1			2	2	Valley Forge, Pa. H
Maxwell	3rd N. J.	Elias Dayton	10	30	3	101	144	43	25	48	2	262	5	6			1	New Jersey
	4th N. J.	Ephraim Martin	7	25	2	98	132	55	17	53	1	258	3	17		1	2	New Jersey
	2nd N. J.	Israel Shreve	7	25		120	152	22	39	42	8	263						New Jersey
	1st N. J.	Matthias Ogden	14	28	4	151	197	49	30			276						New Jersey

MAY 1778 (continued)

BRIGADE	UNIT	COMMANDING OFFICER	PRESENT FIT FOR DUTY & ON DUTY: COMMISSIONED OFFICERS	NONCOMMISSIONED OFFICERS	STAFF OFFICERS	RANK & FILE	TOTAL	RANK & FILE SICK, ON FURLOUGH, ETC.: SICK PRESENT	SICK ABSENT	ON COMMAND & EXTRA SERVICE	ON FURLOUGH	GRAND TOTAL	ALTERATIONS: DEATHS	DESERTED	TAKEN PRISONER	DISCHARGED	JOINED, ENLISTED, RECRUITED	LOCATION
	FORCES UNDER COMMANDER-IN-CHIEF GENERAL GEORGE WASHINGTON (continued)																	
(late) Conway	3rd Pa.	Thomas Craig	8	18	4	109	139	16	21	13	6	195	2			1	10	Valley Forge, Pa.
(late) Conway	6th Pa.	Lt. Col. Josiah Harmar	10	27	3	83	123	15	23	27	3	191		6			5	Valley Forge, Pa.
(late) Conway	9th Pa.	Richard Butler	16	27	4	106	153	23	22	33	3	234	1	6		1	8	Valley Forge, Pa.
(late) Conway	12th Pa.	(late) William Cooke	3	27	4	76	110	18	23	61	10	222	1	1			8	Valley Forge, Pa.
(late) Conway	Malcolm's additional	Lt. Col. Aaron Burr	14	11	4	62	91	39	18	25	2	175	1	1				Valley Forge, Pa.
(late) Conway	Additional B	Oliver Spencer	5	17	3	64	89	26	21	27	7	170	1	6			3	Valley Forge, Pa.
Huntington	1st & 5th Conn. B	Philip B. Bradley	33	78	10	432	553	156	39	97	17	862	14	5		4	10	Valley Forge, Pa.
Huntington	2nd & 7th Conn.	Heman Swift	35	82	8	397	522	96	39	65	10	732	8	7		7	14	Valley Forge, Pa.
Varnum	4th & 8th Conn.	John Durkee & (late) John Chandler	32	82	6	440	560	102	33	53	26	774	19	5		9	30	Valley Forge, Pa.
Varnum	1st & 2nd R. I.	Israel Angell	18	42	2	252	314	120	20	30	5	489	16	4		11		Valley Forge, Pa.
McIntosh	1st N. C.	Thomas Clark	17	42	5	111	175	141	10	63		389	14	3			67	Valley Forge, Pa.
McIntosh	2nd N. C.	John Patten	15	35	6	140	196	116	17	21	1	351	19			1	16	Valley Forge, Pa.
McIntosh	3rd N. C.	Jethro Sumner	17	43	4	134	198	92	23	34	8	355	15			1	20	Valley Forge, Pa.
McIntosh	10th N. C.	Abraham Sheppard	15	37	4	178	234	21	45	2		302					2	Valley Forge, Pa.
1st Md.	1st Md. C	John Hawkins Stone	11	22	6	146	185	22	22	16	9	254					19	Valley Forge, Pa.
1st Md.	Del.	David Hall	13	27	3	160	203	16	32	67	3	321	1	1			37	Valley Forge, Pa.
1st Md.	3rd Md.	Mordecai Gist	13	21	4	163	201	23	44	81	11	360						Valley Forge, Pa.
1st Md.	5th Md.	William Richardson	13	18	5	100	136	33	43	47	14	273					1	Valley Forge, Pa.
1st Md.	7th Md.	John Gunby	12	21	5	93	131	17	22	60	5	235		2				Valley Forge, Pa.
2nd Md.	2nd Md.	Thomas Price	7	32	3	178	220	14	44	28	9	315					16	Chadds Ford, Pa.
2nd Md.	4th Md.	Josias Carvil Hall	12	22	5	212	251	33	32	61	8	385		1			2	Chadds Ford, Pa.
2nd Md.	6th Md.	Otho Holland Williams	7	20	2	94	123	7	28	40	3	201		1			1	Chadds Ford, Pa.
	Mass. det.	Henry Jackson	30	47	3	233	313	32	24	16	1	386	1	4			1	
	1st N. Y.	Goose Van Schaick	24	42	4	325	395	38	17	26	2	478	2	8		19	13	Valley Forge, Pa.
	2nd Va. state D	Gregory Smith	32	45	3	133	213	183	4	2		402	3	9				Valley Forge, Pa.
	Pa. independent co.	Capt. Anthony Selin	4	9		25	38	1	2	3	2	46						
	TOTAL OF INFANTRY		1067	2106	277	10576	14026	3737	1636	2840	643	22882	388	272		190	1040	
	ARTILLERY																	
	7 cos. 3rd cont'l.	John Crane	29	118	2	140	289						1	2		2	88	Valley Forge, Pa.
	5 cos. 2nd cont'l.	John Lamb	19	52		64	135							1		2	6	Valley Forge, Pa.
	4th cont'l.	John Proctor	21	66	4	68	159	29	34	34	1	1133	1	1		2	2	Valley Forge, Pa.
	1st cont'l.	Charles Harrison	35	102	4	148	289											Valley Forge, Pa.
	3 cos.		14	67		82	163										43	
	TOTAL OF ARTILLERY		118	405	10	502	1035	29	34	34	1	1133 F	2	4		6	139	
	TOTAL OF WASHINGTON'S ARMY		1185	2511	287	11078	15061	3766	1670	2874	644	24015	390	276		196	1179	

MAY 1778
(continued)

OFFICERS SICK, ON FURLOUGH, ETC.	WASHINGTON'S ARTILLERY (ONLY) COMMISSIONED	NONCOMMISSIONED	STAFF	TOTAL
Sick Present	3	28		31
Sick Absent	1	15		16
On Command	13	25	2	40
On Furlough	10	7	2	19
TOTAL	27	75	4	106

SOURCE OF THIS REPORT

1. MONTHLY RETURN OF THE CONTINENTAL ARMY UNDER THE COMMAND OF HIS EXCELLENCY GEORGE WASHINGTON...FOR MAY 1778, ELEPHANT FOLIO OF WASHINGTON RETURNS, WILLIAM L. CLEMENTS LIBRARY. [THE HEADING AND A FEW OF THE FIGURES ON THIS RETURN ARE DAMAGED; COMPARISON WITH THE NATIONAL ARCHIVES VERSION WHICH FOLLOWS ESTABLISHES THE IDENTITY OF THIS RETURN. SOME PORTIONS OF THIS RETURN HAVE BEEN REMOVED TO OUR APRIL REPORT. (SEE THAT REPORT.) THE ARTILLERY SECTION OF THE CLEMENTS MONTHLY RETURN FOR MAY APPEARS A FEW PAGES EARLIER IN THE FOLIO AND IS DATED MAY 30, 1778; IT IS NOT MARKED MONTHLY BUT CONTAINS THE MONTHLY ALTERATIONS.]

1a. A General Return of the Continental Army under...Washington, May 30, 1778 [marked "Monthly Genl. Return" on the reverse], Record Group 93, National Archives. [To the brigade level only.]

A. The National Archives return notes that the returns of the New Jersey brigade are partially from May 2 and partially from May 14.

B. The manuscript gives only 1st and 2nd as the designation of these temporarily combined units, but the names Bradley (of the 5th Connecticut) and Swift (of the 7th Connecticut) and a comparison of the figures make it certain that these are the correct components of these consolidated units.

C. The National Archives return notes that the returns for the Maryland brigades were dated the middle of May and that the first brigade since that time had been reinforced with 231 rank and file. The supplied location is as of the end of the month.

D. This is the same unit as "late Armand's Corps" on preceding reports and is marked so on the National Archives version of this return. Armand, who thought he deserved higher rank, had, as Washington put it, resigned "in a pet" (Writings of Washington, 10: 447) but by August had recruited (partly by enlisting deserters) a new corps, which appears on the August report in addition to Selin's company.

E. Because of the mutilation of this corner of the manuscript, no figures for the individual regiments are available.

F. The National Archives manuscript notes that no returns were received for the cavalry and for Thomas Hartley's Additional regiment.

G. Daniel Brodhead's 8th Pennsylvania regiment was under marching orders to go to the Western Department at Fort Pitt; Goose Van Schaick's 1st New York regiment was to take its place in this brigade.

H. The 13th Virginia regiment had just left or was about to leave for the Western Department at Fort Pitt; the 2nd Virginia state regiment was to take its place in this brigade.

Brigadier General Horatio Gates, Adjutant General of the forces of the United Colonies, June 17, 1775–June 5, 1776. The first of a series of portraits (on following pages) of men who filled this important office, this profile is by Pierre Eugène du Simitière, a Swiss artist and naturalist who arrived in the British colonies in 1765. Du Simitière, like Peale, was a collector at heart and advertised an "American Museum" in his residence at Philadelphia in 1782. Gates sat for this likeness in March 1777. Engraved by Burnet Reading, this profile (and others which follow) is from the first edition of Du Simitière's *Thirteen Portraits of American Legislators, Patriots, and Soldiers, Who Distinguished Themselves in Rendering Their Country Independent* (London: W. Richardson, 1783; from the copy in the Clements Library).

JUNE 1778

BRIGADE	UNIT	COMMANDING OFFICER	PRESENT FIT FOR DUTY & ON DUTY: COMMISSIONED OFFICERS	NONCOMMISSIONED OFFICERS	STAFF OFFICERS	RANK & FILE	TOTAL	RANK & FILE SICK, ON FURLOUGH, ETC.: SICK PRESENT	SICK ABSENT	ON COMMAND & EXTRA SERVICE	ON FURLOUGH	GRAND TOTAL	ALTERATIONS: DEATHS	DESERTED	TAKEN PRISONER	DISCHARGED	JOINED, ENLISTED, RECRUITED	LOCATION
	FORCES UNDER COMMANDER-IN-CHIEF GENERAL GEORGE WASHINGTON (Manuscript Completed After the Battle of Monmouth--Some Sections of Alterations Not Completed) A -																	
Woodford	3rd Va.	William Heth	11[D]	23	6	81	121	5	46	44		216	3			2	16	New Jersey
	7th Va.	Lt. Col. Holt Richardson	14	29	4	179	226	7	70	68	5	376	5	5		2	6	New Jersey
	11th Va.	Daniel Morgan	8	24	3	117	152	3	56	35	8	254	5	5		1	12	New Jersey
	15th Va.	David Mason	18	16	4	108	146	3	152	36		337	11	4		1	2	New Jersey
Scott	4th, 8th, 12th Va.	James Wood	18	69	10	303	400	25	204	114	9	752						New Jersey
	Additional	William Grayson	7	25	4	78	114	30	24	33	2	203	16	6		5	16	New Jersey
	Patton's additional	Lt. Col. John Parke	8	30	1	74	113	10	9	7	1	140						New Jersey
1st Pa.	1st Pa.	James Chambers	13	30	4	174	221	11	30	74	8	344						New Jersey
	2nd Pa.	Henry Bicker	11	25	1	81	118	8	5	15	2	148						New Jersey
	7th Pa.	William Irvine	12	23	1	139	175	8	16	11	1	211						New Jersey
	10th Pa.	George Nagel	11	34	3	120	168	13	23	15	9	228						New Jersey
2nd Pa.	1st N.Y.	Goose Van Schaick	23	44	4	316	387	5	57	26		475						New Jersey
	4th Pa.	Lt. Col. William Butler	10	28	3	116	157	6	38	16	5	222						New Jersey
	5th Pa.	Francis Johnston	11	29	4	150	194	21	57	32	2	306						New Jersey
	11th Pa.	Richard Humpton	9	14	2	65	90	5	15	24	6	140						New Jersey
Poor	1st N.H.	Joseph Cilley	18	23	3	198	242	7	182	31	5	467	7			1	71	New Jersey
	2nd N.H.	Nathan Hale	12	25	1	157	195	10	109	34	6	354	7				41	New Jersey
	3rd N.H.	Alexander Scammell	10	18	3	78	109	9	148	29	21	316	3				37	New Jersey
	2nd N.Y.	Philip Van Cortlandt	14	33	1	203	251	11	129	29	1	421	5	1		3	81	New Jersey
	4th N.Y.	Henry Beekman Livingston	11	17	2	152	182	11	155	33	2	383	5	1		8	74	New Jersey
Glover	4th Mass.	William Shepard	23	33	2	191	249	10	71	53	11	394	3			2	29	New Jersey
	13th Mass.	Edward Wigglesworth	21	39	3	187	250	6	59	49	10	374	13	5			6	New Jersey
	15th Mass.	Timothy Bigelow	16	28	3	150	197	11	62	44	8	322	3			6	2	New Jersey
	1st Mass.	Joseph Vose	25	29	3	175	232	17	80	41	16	386	2	3			1	New Jersey
(late) Learned	2nd Mass.	John Bailey	16	22	4	184	226	22	77	50	17	392	6	1		1	9	New Jersey
	8th Mass.	Michael Jackson	16	30	2	135	183	4	95	40	13	335	7	1		1	6	New Jersey
	9th Mass.	James Wesson	14	36	2	184	236	11	57	28	17	349	4	2			8	New Jersey
Paterson	12th Mass.	Samuel Brewer	22	36	3	122	183	10	86	42	9	330	7	3		2	11	New Jersey
	10th Mass.	Thomas Marshall	16	28	4	136	184	17	46	34	9	290	6	4		2	15	New Jersey
	14th Mass.	Gamaliel Bradford	14	31	4	136	185	6	89	24	23	327	11				22	New Jersey
	11th Mass.	Benjamin Tupper	20	31	5	155	211	15	91	33	12	362		1		2	11	New Jersey
(late) Weedon	2nd Va.	Christian Febiger	16	29	3	106	154	11	57	35	4	261	4	3		1	3	New Jersey
	6th Va.	John Gibson	8	9	5	25	47	6	14	10	11	88	2				3	New Jersey
	10th Va.	John Green	18	33	1	166	218	20	103	43	16	400	5	3		5	14	New Jersey
	14th Va.	William Davies	20	28	4	173	225	25	117	35	6	408	7				18	New Jersey
Muhlenberg	1st, 5th, 9th Va.	Richard Parker	16	56	8	201	281	16	130	62	18	507						New Jersey
	1st Va. state	George Gibson	20	30	3	150	203	18	71	41	2	335						New Jersey
	2nd Va. state	Gregory Smith	18	39	3	169	229	27	118	27		401						New Jersey
	German bn.	Lt. Col. Ludowick Weltner	16	25	3	269	313	4	40	35	5	397						New Jersey
Maxwell	1st N.J.	Matthias Ogden	18	29	4	345	396	49	55	29	9	538	2	6			74	New Jersey
	2nd N.J.	Israel Shreve	16	35	4	318	373	12	27	24	7	443	2	3		1	73	New Jersey
	3rd N.J.	Elias Dayton	16	33	5	240	294	18	51	14	1	378	5	1			59	New Jersey
	4th N.J.	Ephraim Martin	12	26	3	193	234	23	53	21	1	332	4	8			22	New Jersey
3rd Pa.	3rd Pa.	Thomas Craig	11	16	4	76	107	12	55	17	3	194						New Jersey
	6th Pa.	Lt. Col. Josiah Harmar	6	30	3	107	146		48	12	1	207						New Jersey
	9th Pa.	Richard Butler	6	23	4	84	117	7	56	30	2	212						New Jersey
	12th Pa.	(late) William Cooke	3	17	3	85	108	12	26	56	8	210						New Jersey
	Additional	William Malcolm	11	11	2	48	72	19	53	31		175						New Jersey
	Additional	Oliver Spencer	5	15	4	45	69	3	41	25	16	154						New Jersey

JUNE 1778 (continued)

BRIGADE: Varnum N.C. 1st Md. 2nd Md. Huntington

UNIT	COMMANDING OFFICER	PRESENT FIT FOR DUTY & ON DUTY: COMMISSIONED OFFICERS	NONCOMMISSIONED OFFICERS	STAFF OFFICERS	RANK & FILE	TOTAL	RANK & FILE SICK, ON FURLOUGH, ETC.: SICK PRESENT	SICK ABSENT	ON COMMAND & EXTRA SERVICE	ON FURLOUGH	GRAND TOTAL	ALTERATIONS: DEATHS	DESERTED	TAKEN PRISONER	DISCHARGED	JOINED, ENLISTED, RECRUITED	LOCATION
FORCES UNDER COMMANDER-IN-CHIEF GENERAL GEORGE WASHINGTON (continued)																	
2nd & 5th Conn.	(late) C. Webb & P. B. Bradley	28	71	8[E]	378	485	35	77	67	16	680	3	8		4	5	New Jersey
7th & 1st Conn.	H. Swift & (late) Lt. Col. Prentiss	32	77	9	433	551	61	138	107	12	869	10	3		9	13	New Jersey
4th Conn.	John Durkee	14	34	1	185	234	20	42	28	9	333						New Jersey
1st & 2nd R.I.	Israel Angell	22	48	2	257	329	21	101	34	2	487						New Jersey
8th Conn.	(late) John Chandler	16	36	3	178	233	32	35	36	10	346						New Jersey
1st N.C.	Thomas Clark	19	26	5	260	310	2	223	119	4	658	22	13		2	114	New Jersey
2nd N.C.	John Patten	17	34	4	254	309	23	215	109	3	659						New Jersey
1st Md.	John Hawkins Stone	9	22	3	169	203	5	47	38	12	305	3	1			31	New Jersey
Del.	David Hall	19	36	4	152	211	8	67	72	2	360	2	9		2	7	New Jersey
3rd Md.	Mordecai Gist	17	25	4	236	282	10	108	72	5	477	24	7		1	10	New Jersey
5th Md.	William Richardson	11	19	4[F]	149	183	14	151	31	4	383	2	3		2	73	New Jersey
7th Md.	John Gunby	12	34	4	228	278	4	74	38	4	398	7	5			157	New Jersey
2nd Md.	Lt. Col. Thomas Woolford	14	33	3	295	345	2	71	26	7	451						New Jersey
4th Md.	Josias Carvil Hall	17	22	5	225	269	7	53	119	7	455						New Jersey
6th Md.	Otho Holland Williams	10	28	3	265	306	8	56	23	2	395						New Jersey
Det.	Henry Jackson	22	28	3	197	250		82	17	3	352						New Jersey
Pa. independent co.	Capt. Anthony Selin	4	9		25	38		5	5	1	49		3			4	
TOTAL OF INFANTRY		971	1968	230	11330	14499	871	4998	2632	451	23451	233	118		66	1156	
ARTILLERY																	
9 cos. 3rd cont'l.	John Crane	34	133	4	149	320						5	2		1	1	New Jersey
5 cos. 2nd cont'l.	John Lamb	15	48		63	126	31	68	15	3	954	4	1		1		New Jersey
1st cont'l	Charles Harrison	40	111	6	174	331									2	26	New Jersey
3 cos.		8	29		23	60							1		1		New Jersey
TOTAL OF ARTILLERY		97	321	10	409	837	31	68	15	3	954	9	4		5	27	
TOTAL OF WASHINGTON'S ARMY		1068	2289	240	11739	15336	902	5066	2647	454	24405	242	122		71	1183	
EASTERN DEPARTMENT UNDER MAJOR GENERAL WILLIAM HEATH																	
Convention guards[B]	Jonathan Reed	28	35	3	230	296	27	13	127	12	475						Cambridge, Mass.
Convention guards[B]	Jacob Gerrish	19	29	3	243	294	18	22	81	16	431						Cambridge, Mass.
Convention guards[B]	Abijah Stearns	14	24	1	172	211	2	6	70	18	307						Roxbury & Dorchester Heights
Det. Stearns' guards	Maj. Reed[C]	6	10		92	108	1	4	1		114						Rutland, Mass.
Guard co.	Capt. John Morgan	4	7		117	128	1	4	4	4	141						Springfield & Brookfield[H]
Guard co.	Capt. Robinson[C]	2	14		76	92		1	[G]	1	94						Watertown, Mass., etc.[I]
TOTAL OF INFANTRY		73	119	7	930	1129	49	50	283	51	1562						
INVALIDS																	
Boston det.			12		43	55			4	5	64						Boston, Mass.
TOTAL OF EASTERN DEPARTMENT		73	131	7	973	1184	49	50	287	56	1626						
GRAND TOTAL		1141	2420	247	12712	16520	951	5116	2934	510	26031						

JUNE 1778
(continued)

OFFICERS SICK, ON FURLOUGH, ETC.	WASHINGTON'S ARTILLERY (ONLY)			
	COMMISSIONED	NONCOMMISSIONED	STAFF	TOTAL
Sick Present	1	10		11
Sick Absent	5	45		50
On Command	11	20		31
On Furlough	12	4	1	17
TOTAL	29	79	1	109

SOURCES OF THIS REPORT

1. MONTHLY RETURN OF THE CONTINENTAL ARMY UNDER THE COMMAND OF HIS EXCELLENCY GEORGE WASHINGTON... FOR JUNE 1778, ELEPHANT FOLIO OF WASHINGTON RETURNS, WILLIAM L. CLEMENTS LIBRARY. [THE HEADING AND ONE OF THE FIGURES ON THIS RETURN ARE DAMAGED; THE FORM OF THE RETURN, THE FIGURES IN IT, AND COMPARISON WITH THE NATIONAL ARCHIVES VERSION THAT FOLLOWS ESTABLISH THE IDENTITY OF THIS RETURN. THE ARTILLERY SECTION OF THIS MONTHLY RETURN APPEARS AT THE FOOT OF THE NEXT PAGE OF THE FOLIO; IT IS DATED JULY 5, AND NOT EXPLICITLY MARKED AS THE JUNE MONTHLY.]

1a. A General Return of the Continental Army under the Immediate Command of His Excellency George Washington ...July 4, 1778, Record Group 93, National Archives. [To the brigade level only. This copy is not marked "Monthly," nor is it headed "Weekly General Return" as are the weeklies in this period; it contains the same figures as the return in the Clements folio, which is clearly the monthly by its format.]

2. A GENERAL RETURN OF THE TROOPS DOING DUTY IN THE STATE OF MASSACHUSETTS BAY IN CONTINENTAL SERVICE, JUNE 25, 1778, WILLIAM HEATH PAPERS, MASSACHUSETTS HISTORICAL SOCIETY.

A. Although it is not indicated in any way, it would appear that no monthly alterations had come to hand for the 1st Pennsylvania, 2nd Pennsylvania, Muhlenberg's, 3rd Pennsylvania, Varnum's, and 2nd Maryland brigades, and for Jackson's detachment. There are no figures for these units in any of the alterations columns. The National Archives version of the return leaves blank the entire alterations section. Although the manuscripts were completed after Monmouth, there is no way of knowing whether the individual returns used in compiling the general return were made out before or after that engagement.
B. Massachusetts militia in the Continental service as Convention Guards.
C. We have been unable to further identify these officers.
D. Figure deduced from the brigade total; this one regimental figure destroyed on the Clements manuscript.
E. Eight staff officers in the combined 1st and 7th Connecticut regiments plus one chaplain for the entire brigade.
F. Three staff officers in John Gunby's 7th Maryland regiment plus one chaplain for the entire brigade.
G. The manuscript notes, "The officers & men on Command are doing Duty in Boston under Lieut. Col. Symmes except fifty-six of Col. Stearns who are doing duty under Lt. Col. Hitchburn at Dorchester Heights."
H. Guarding magazines at these places.
I. Guarding provision stores at Watertown, Sudbury, Worcester, Medford, Concord, Marlborough and Medfield.

Colonel Joseph Reed, Adjutant General of the Continental Army, June 5, 1776–January 13, 1777. Reed, who later served as president of the Supreme Executive Council of Pennsylvania between December 1778 and 1781, sat for this profile by Du Simitière in June 1779.

JULY 1778

BRIGADE	UNIT	COMMANDING OFFICER	PRESENT FIT FOR DUTY & ON DUTY: COMMISSIONED OFFICERS	NONCOMMISSIONED OFFICERS	STAFF OFFICERS	RANK & FILE	TOTAL	RANK & FILE SICK, ON FURLOUGH, ETC.: SICK PRESENT	SICK ABSENT	ON COMMAND & EXTRA SERVICE	ON FURLOUGH	CONFINED	GRAND TOTAL	ALTERATIONS: DEATHS	DESERTED	TAKEN PRISONER	DISCHARGED	JOINED, ENLISTED, RECRUITED	LOCATION
	FORCES UNDER COMMANDER-IN-CHIEF GENERAL GEORGE WASHINGTON																		
N.C.	1st N.C.	Thomas Clark	16	36	4 B	329	385	29	178	85			677	7	8			34	White Plains, N.Y. area
N.C.	2nd N.C.	John Patten	19	38	5	292	354	39	183	85	3		664	9	1		1	9	White Plains, N.Y. area
Woodford	2nd Va.	Christian Febiger	13	30	5	106	154	11	42	43	3		253	1					White Plains, N.Y. area
Woodford	3rd & 7th Va.	William Heth	18	45	8	254	325	31	111	94	2		563	2	3			3	White Plains, N.Y. area
Woodford	11th & 15th Va.	Lt. Col. John Cropper	13	46	6	265	330	18	161	71	3		583					5	White Plains, N.Y. area
Muhlenberg	1st, 5th, 9th Va.	Richard Parker	16	63	10	196	285	32	105	78	17		517	2	8		1	13	White Plains, N.Y. area
Muhlenberg	1st Va. state	George Gibson	15	31	3	165	214	25	54	37	2		332	1	2			6	White Plains, N.Y. area
Muhlenberg	2nd Va. state	Gregory Smith	20	30	2	190	242	39	115	25			421	3				32	White Plains, N.Y. area
Muhlenberg	14th Va.	William Davies	12	31	3	204	250	16	105	32	3		406					1	White Plains, N.Y. area
Scott	4th, 8th, 12th Va.	James Wood	13	66	11	330	420	49	156	126	8		759	4				20	White Plains, N.Y. area
Scott	6th & 10th Va.	John Green	20	41	7	197	265	20	99	85	17		486					4	White Plains, N.Y. area
Scott	Del.	David Hall	20	31	5	145	201	13	76	78	1		369	2	1		1	15	White Plains, N.Y. area
Scott	Additional	William Grayson	5	23	5	87	120	12	27	40	2		201	2				5	White Plains, N.Y. area
Smallwood	1st Md.	John Hawkins Stone	8	31	3	228	270	17	32	58	7		384					67	White Plains, N.Y. area
Smallwood	3rd Md.	Mordecai Gist	19	27	6	246	298	17	97	95	4		511	2	13		2	16	White Plains, N.Y. area
Smallwood	5th Md.	William Richardson	7	20	3	182	212	21	147	63	4		447	6	18		2	91	White Plains, N.Y. area
Smallwood	7th Md.	John Gunby	17	26	4	247	294	21	53	44	2		414		2		2	27	White Plains, N.Y. area
2nd Md.	2nd Md.	Lt. Col. Thomas Woolford	6	40	2	372	420	26	74	29	6		555	4	1		13	159	White Plains, N.Y. area
2nd Md.	German bn.	Lt. Col. Ludowick Weltner	17	30	4	249	300	4	48	44	3		399		2				White Plains, N.Y. area
2nd Md.	4th Md.	Josias Carvil Hall	13	36	5	333	387	23	51	67	2		530		9			82	White Plains, N.Y. area
2nd Md.	6th Md.	Otho Holland Williams	11	26	4	239	280	17	63	45	3		408	1	9		2	83	White Plains, N.Y. area
Wayne	1st Pa.	James Chambers	12	32	5	123	172	8	28	127	4		339	3	3		10	10	White Plains, N.Y. area
Wayne	2nd Pa.	Walter Stewart	12	43	5	239	299	16	42	106	5		468	2	5		14	38	White Plains, N.Y. area
Wayne	7th Pa.	William Irvine	13	29	4	119	165	18	15	42			240	2	2			48	White Plains, N.Y. area
Wayne	10th Pa.	Richard Humpton	13	44	4	181	242	12	26	64	10		354		21			11	White Plains, N.Y. area
2nd Pa.	3rd Pa.	Thomas Craig	9	40	6	173	228	18	77	73	11		407		3			11	White Plains, N.Y. area
2nd Pa.	5th Pa.	Francis Johnston	9	26	5	142	182	28	52	55			317	1	4			21	White Plains, N.Y. area
2nd Pa.	6th Pa.	Lt. Col. Josiah Harmar	5	33	3	89	130	9	38	35	1		213					1	White Plains, N.Y. area
2nd Pa.	9th Pa.	Richard Butler	6	20	5	84	115	11	46	45	2		219	1			1	10	White Plains, N.Y. area
Clinton	1st N.Y.	Goose Van Schaick	23	44	5	292	364	14	62	28			468	1	3			2	Hackensack, N.J.
Clinton	2nd N.Y.	Philip Van Cortlandt	15	28		199	242	13	92	46	21		414	6	5			7	White Plains, N.Y. area
Clinton	5th N.Y.	Lewis DuBois	9	45	2	241	297	4	21	11	1		334		2			14	White Plains, N.Y. area
Clinton	4th N.Y.	Henry Beekman Livingston	11	22	1	177	211	7	129	34	34		415	5	3			3	White Plains, N.Y. area
Clinton	N.Y. militia	Morris Graham	12	33	2	230	277	5	4	10	15		311		7				White Plains, N.Y. area
Parsons	3rd Conn.	Samuel Wyllys	22	45	5	449	521	22	19	45	2		609					3	White Plains, N.Y. area
Parsons	4th Conn.	John Durkee	17	42	3	208	270	19	26	41	11		367					12	White Plains, N.Y. area
Parsons	6th Conn.	Return Jonathan Meigs	27	55	4	503	589	42	22	20	4		677				1	6	White Plains, N.Y. area
Parsons	8th Conn.	(late) John Chandler	14	28	3	193	238	18	38	38	9		341	2				6	White Plains, N.Y. area
Huntington	1st Conn.	Lt. Col. David Fithian Sill A	16	38	4	227	285	30	64	64	10		453	2	2		2	6	White Plains, N.Y. area
Huntington	2nd Conn.	Lt. Col. Isaac Sherman	13	34	3	167	217	20	12	33	14		296				1	9	White Plains, N.Y. area
Huntington	5th Conn.	Philip Burr Bradley	14	36	3	193	246	24	51	58	10		389	5	5		1	12	White Plains, N.Y. area
Huntington	7th Conn.	Heman Swift	15	43	2	232	292	18	46	53	9		418	1	1		1	5	White Plains, N.Y. area
Nixon	3rd Mass.	John Greaton	27	48	6	258	339	17	22	11	1		390	1	1			4	White Plains, N.Y. area
Nixon	5th Mass.	Rufus Putnam	26	49	3	381	459	16	14	18			507	1				7	White Plains, N.Y. area
Nixon	6th Mass.	Thomas Nixon	30	50	5	353	438	9	7	4	6		464		1		1	74	White Plains, N.Y. area
Nixon	Mass. militia	Ezra Wood	27	49	4	314	394	16	1	19			430					15	White Plains, N.Y. area

JULY 1778
(continued)

BRIGADE	UNIT	COMMANDING OFFICER	DUTY & ON DUTY					ON FURLOUGH, ETC.							GRAND TOTAL						LOCATION
			COMMISSIONED OFFICERS	NONCOMMISSIONED OFFICERS	STAFF OFFICERS	RANK & FILE	TOTAL	SICK PRESENT	SICK ABSENT	ON COMMAND & EXTRA SERVICE	ON FURLOUGH	CONFINED				DEATHS	DESERTED	TAKEN PRISONER	DISCHARGED	JOINED, ENLISTED, RECRUITED	
	FORCES UNDER COMMANDER-IN-CHIEF GENERAL GEORGE WASHINGTON (continued)																				
Paterson	12th Mass.	Samuel Brewer	23	39	5	154	221	12	68	43	8				352	2	2		2	24	White Plains, N.Y. area
Paterson	10th Mass.	Thomas Marshall	15	26	3	136	180	14	39	46	9				288	3	3			8	White Plains, N.Y. area
Paterson	14th Mass.	Gamaliel Bradford	12	32	4	145	193	9	65	36	21				324	6				4	White Plains, N.Y. area
Paterson	11th Mass.	Benjamin Tupper	22	28	3	183	236	12	56	45	4				353	5				1	White Plains, N.Y. area
(late) Learned	2nd Mass.	John Bailey	15	28	3	204	250	16	61	51	14				392	6			1	4	White Plains, N.Y. area
(late) Learned	8th Mass.	Michael Jackson	17	35	4	153	209	12	56	45	11				333	15	3		2	12	White Plains, N.Y. area
(late) Learned	9th Mass.	James Wesson	18	39	4	202	263	12	30	38	12				355	6	2		1	7	White Plains, N.Y. area
Poor	1st N.H.	Joseph Cilley	17	29	2	247	295	16	115	47	4				477	7				14	White Plains, N.Y. area
Poor	2nd N.H.	Nathan Hale	13	28	3	149	193	10	86	80	5				374	8	1			26	White Plains, N.Y. area
Poor	3rd N.H.	Alexander Scammell	10	28	4	123	165	14	95	37	17				328	12	3			18	White Plains, N.Y. area
Poor	2nd Canadian	Moses Hazen	21	57	3	358	439	14	60	12	4				529	2	56			36	White Plains, N.Y. area
Glover	4th Mass.	William Shepard	23	33	2	191	249	10	71	53	11				394	3			2	29	Rhode Island
Glover	13th Mass.	Edward Wigglesworth	21	39	3	187	250	6	59	49	10				374	13	5			6	Rhode Island
Glover	15th Mass.	Timothy Bigelow	16	28	3	150	197	11	62	44	8				322	3			6	2	Rhode Island
Glover	1st Mass.	Joseph Vose	25	29	3	175	232	17	80	41	16				386	2	3			1	Rhode Island
	Additional	William Malcolm	12	15	1	74	102	14	46	9	6				177						West Point, N.Y.
	Patton's additional	Lt. Col. John Parke	8	29	1	75	113	6	8	7	1				135						West Point, N.Y.
	Conn. militia	Roger Enos	37	56	3	401	497	10	9	39					555				2	1	West Point, N.Y.
	Mass. militia	Thomas Poor	22	37	4	280	343	14	2	24					383					40	West Point, N.Y.
	Conn. militia	Samuel McLellan	11	14	3	104	132	6	3	14					155					1	West Point, N.Y.
	Conn. militia	Increase Moseley	14	21	2	147	184	2	2	126					314						West Point, N.Y.
	Pa. independent co.	Capt. Anthony Selin	4	9		26	39		5	3	1				48		1			1	
	TOTAL OF INFANTRY		1071	2382	260	14487	18200	1131	4009	3293	434				27067	172	224		72	1242	
	CAVALRY																				
	Conn. militia light horse	Capt. John Skinner	7	14	3	24	48	12		84					144						White Plains, N.Y. area
	2nd cont'l.	Elisha Sheldon	11	32	3	65	111	8	7	85	2	1			214		1		1	1	White Plains, N.Y. area
	TOTAL OF CAVALRY		18	46	6	89	159	20	7	169	2	1			358		1		1	1	
	ARTILLERY																				
	7 cos. 3rd cont'l.	John Crane	27	113	4	140	284														White Plains, N.Y. area
	8 cos. 2nd cont'l.	John Lamb	27	99		119	245														White Plains, N.Y. area
	11 cos. 1st cont'l.	Charles Harrison	35	128	7	200	370	24	63	22	3				1213						White Plains, N.Y. area
	3 cos.	Lt. Col. Ebenezer Stevens	18	63	5	70	156														White Plains, N.Y. area
	2 independent cos.		6	23		17	46														White Plains, N.Y. area
	TOTAL OF ARTILLERY		113	426	16	546	1101	24	63	22	3				1213						
	TOTAL OF WASHINGTON'S ARMY		1202	2854	282	15122	19460	1175	4079	3484	439	1			28638 C	D 172	225		73	1243	

JULY 1778
(continued)

OFFICERS SICK, ON FURLOUGH, ETC.	WASHINGTON'S ARTILLERY & 2ND CONT'L. CAVALRY (ONLY)			
	COMMISSIONED	NONCOMMISSIONED	STAFF	TOTAL
Sick Present	2	8		10
Sick Absent	11	49		60
On Command	21	24	4	49
On Furlough	5	3	2	10
TOTAL	39	84	6	129

SOURCE OF THIS REPORT

1. A GENERAL RETURN OF THE CONTINENTAL ARMY UNDER THE MORE IMMEDIATE COMMAND OF HIS EXCELLENCY GEORGE WASHINGTON...AUGUST 1, 1778, ELEPHANT FOLIO OF WASHINGTON RETURNS, WILLIAM L. CLEMENTS LIBRARY. [THE ARTILLERY SECTION OF THIS MONTHLY APPEARS SEVERAL PAGES EARLIER IN THE CLEMENTS LIBRARY FOLIO; THE COLUMN HEADINGS ON THIS ARTILLERY SECTION ARE DAMAGED ON THE MANUSCRIPT AND HAD TO BE PARTIALLY SUPPLIED ON THE BASIS OF THE NORMAL ORDER IN WHICH THEY APPEAR ON THE OTHER MONTHLY ARTILLERY RETURNS. NO ALTERATIONS ARE GIVEN FOR THE ARTILLERY. THE CAVALRY, WHICH APPEARS ON THE MANUSCRIPT WHICH FOLLOWS, IS NOT INCLUDED IN THE CLEMENTS FOLIO. THE FORMAT OF THE CLEMENTS FOLIO RETURN AND COMPARISON WITH THE RETURN WHICH FOLLOWS ESTABLISH THAT THIS IS THE MONTHLY RETURN, ALTHOUGH IT IS NOT HEADED EXPLICITLY AS SUCH.]

1a. Monthly Return of the Cont'l. Army...August 1, 1778, Record Group 93, National Archives. [To the brigade level only. The artillery, which is included in the Clements folio, is not on this manuscript.]

A. The manuscript returns in the Clements Library folio for July through November 1778 enter this officer as "Major Sills." Henry P. Johnston, editor, The Record of Connecticut Men in the Military and Naval Service During the War of the Revolution, 1775-1783 (Hartford: Case, Lockwood & Brainard, 1889), p. 145, records that Sills had been promoted to lieutenant colonel by a commission dated March 13, 1778; Heitman uses the same date.

B. Four commissioned officers in John Patten's 2nd North Carolina regiment plus one chaplain for the entire brigade.

C. The National Archives version of this return notes that no monthly returns had been received for July for the cavalry under Colonel Moylan's immediate command (in New Jersey), for Varnum's brigade in Rhode Island, for Maxwell's brigade in New Jersey, and for Spencer's regiment at Kings Ferry. Colonel Henry Jackson's detachment also had been ordered to Rhode Island and is not included.

Colonel George Weedon, Acting Adjutant General of the Continental Army, January 13–March 1, 1777. This pencil sketch by John Trumbull was drawn in Fredericksburg, Virginia, in 1791 and was used by Trumbull as the basis for his likeness of Weedon in *The Capture of the Hessians at Trenton*, reproduced on p. 44 above. Weedon, who was promoted to brigadier general early in 1777, appears on horseback at the far right in that painting. (Courtesy of the Yale University Art Gallery, New Haven, Conn.)

AUGUST 1778

BRIGADE	UNIT	COMMANDING OFFICER	PRESENT FIT FOR DUTY & ON DUTY: COMMISSIONED OFFICERS	NONCOMMISSIONED OFFICERS	STAFF OFFICERS	RANK & FILE	TOTAL	RANK & FILE SICK, ON FURLOUGH, ETC.: SICK PRESENT	SICK ABSENT	ON COMMAND & EXTRA SERVICE	ON FURLOUGH	CONFINED	NOT JOINED	GRAND TOTAL	ALTERATIONS: DEATHS	DESERTED	TAKEN PRISONER	DISCHARGED	JOINED, ENLISTED, RECRUITED	LOCATION
FORCES UNDER COMMANDER-IN-CHIEF GENERAL GEORGE WASHINGTON																				
N.C.	1st N. C.	Thomas Clark	16	37	4	287	344	55	131	137				667	11	1		5	9	White Plains, N. Y. area
	2nd N. C.	John Patten	11	37	3	287	338	49	130	128	3			648	3	4		1	3	White Plains, N. Y. area
Woodford	2nd & 6th Va.	Christian Febiger	14	40	7	143	204	46	33	54	2			339	2	2			5	White Plains, N. Y. area
	3rd & 7th Va.	William Heth	19	44	7	260	330	60	86	74	2			552	5	1		5	2	White Plains, N. Y. area
	11th & 15th Va.	Daniel Morgan	12	50	6	270	338	30	120	80	3			571		1		1	3	White Plains, N. Y. area
Muhlenberg	1st, 5th, 9th Va.	Richard Parker	12	66	8	193	279	30	84	107	17			517	4	1			9	White Plains, N. Y. area
	1st Va. state	George Gibson	15	30	4	137	186	27	46	69	1			329	3				1	White Plains, N. Y. area
	2nd Va. state	Gregory Smith	15	31	1	147	194	53	90	75				412	4			1	1	White Plains, N. Y. area
	14th Va.	William Davies	11	24	3	200	238	31	69	66	2			406	3			3	15	White Plains, N. Y. area
Scott	4th, 8th, 12th Va.	James Wood	19	65	8	363	455	77	106	109	6			753	13	1		1	7	White Plains, N. Y. area
	Del.	David Hall	12	30	4	145	191	46	57	62	2			358		4			5	White Plains, N. Y. area
	10th Va.	William Russell E	15	31	4	160	210	37	49	83	7			386					1	White Plains, N. Y. area
	Additional	William Grayson	4	23	5	96	128	29	14	27	1			199				2	3	White Plains, N. Y. area
Smallwood	1st Md.	John Hawkins Stone	10	29	4	182	225	33	33	81	3			375	1	9		2	4	White Plains, N. Y. area
	3rd Md.	Mordecai Gist	17	29	6	205	257	45	81	117	6			506	1	6		11	24	White Plains, N. Y. area
	5th Md.	William Richardson	6	31	5 F	126	168	30	98	92	5			393	10	36		18	7	White Plains, N. Y. area
	7th Md.	John Gunby	16	34	6 F	188	244	26	48	92	2			412	8	9		9	18	White Plains, N. Y. area
2nd Md.	2nd Md.	Thomas Price	7	29	2	344	382	42	61	54	5			544	10			3	19	White Plains, N. Y. area
	German bn.	Lt. Col. Ludowick Weltner	15	31	3	261	310	14	26	42	3			395	9	8		5	12	White Plains, N. Y. area
	4th Md.	Josias Carvil Hall	11	27	5	337	380	41	46	53				520	3	3		1	15	White Plains, N. Y. area
	6th Md.	Otho Holland Williams	13	30	3	269	315	26	60	37	2			440	2				36	White Plains, N. Y. area
Wayne	1st Pa.	James Chambers	15	32	6	156	209	21	17	79	9			335	1	5		8	7	White Plains, N. Y. area
	2nd Pa.	Walter Stewart	14	45	5	274	338	30	31	86	4			489	2	3		2	24	White Plains, N. Y. area
	7th Pa.	William Irvine	13	29	5	135	182	17	9	33				241					3	White Plains, N. Y. area
	10th Pa.	Richard Humpton	11	38	4	202	255	13	21	72	10			371				1	27	White Plains, N. Y. area
2nd Pa.	3rd Pa.	Thomas Craig	9	34	5	158	206	31	74	77	10			398	2	4		8	12	White Plains, N. Y. area
	5th Pa.	Francis Johnston	8	29	5	171	213	22	35	58				328	1	2			15	White Plains, N. Y. area
	6th Pa.	Lt. Col. Josiah Harmar	7	26	5	110	148	18	23	30				219		7		8	25	White Plains, N. Y. area
	9th Pa.	Richard Butler	5	16	3	103	127	17	32	40	3			219		3		2	16	White Plains, N. Y. area
Clinton	1st N. Y. A	Goose Van Schaick	13	32	2	229	276	30	55	74	3			438	1	4		1	4	White Plains, N. Y. area
	4th N. Y. A	Henry Beekman Livingston	7	23	3	186	219	16	74	61	4			374	8	5			3	White Plains, N. Y. area
	2nd N. Y. A	Philip Van Cortlandt	14	33	1 G	215	263	18	57	59	8			405	9	7		5	6	White Plains, N. Y. area
	5th N. Y. A	Lewis DuBois	6	38	3 G	185	232	22	13	74	1			342		2		1	23	White Plains, N. Y. area
Parsons	3rd Conn.	Samuel Wyllys	14	44	4	356	418	57	13	102	2			592		2		6	1	White Plains, N. Y. area
	4th Conn.	John Durkee	15	29	4	159	207	35	26	61	16			345	5	1		3	1	White Plains, N. Y. area
	6th Conn.	Return Jonathan Meigs	23	38	3	380	444	77	18	117	5			661	1	5		5	16	White Plains, N. Y. area
	8th Conn.	(late) John Chandler	9	33	3	164	209	30	38	56	5			338	1	3			5	White Plains, N. Y. area
Huntington	1st Conn.	Lt. Col. David Fithian Sill	10	36	4	206	256	44	50	77	13			440	5	2		2	2	White Plains, N. Y. area
	2nd Conn.	Lt. Col. Isaac Sherman	11	39	2	156	208	27	7	41	16			299	1	2		2	12	White Plains, N. Y. area
	5th Conn.	Philip Burr Bradley	14	36	3	171	224	40	38	71	13			386	7	2		2	11	White Plains, N. Y. area
	7th Conn.	Heman Swift	12	38	3	211	264	22	34	70	11			401	9	1		4	5	White Plains, N. Y. area
Nixon	3rd Mass.	John Greaton	23	47	6	296	372	40	14	50	1			477		4			98	White Plains, N. Y. area
	5th Mass.	Rufus Putnam	21	41	2	392	456	30	8	56				550		1		3	61	White Plains, N. Y. area
	6th Mass.	Thomas Nixon	24	48	5	339	416	26	13	51	3			509				1	54	White Plains, N. Y. area
	Mass. militia	Ezra Wood	29	41	5	260	335	63	3	22				423	1	1		16	17	White Plains, N. Y. area
Paterson	12th Mass.	Samuel Brewer	23	41	5	264	333	41	42	54	3			473	4	13		2	139	White Plains, N. Y. area
	10th Mass.	Thomas Marshall	18	28	3	258	307	37	23	52	4			423	9	11		14	166	White Plains, N. Y. area
	14th Mass.	Gamaliel Bradford	13	34	4	264	315	34	29	45	18			441	10	1		6	135	White Plains, N. Y. area
	11th Mass.	Benjamin Tupper	[illegible]	[illegible]	[illegible]	[illegible]	[illegible]	[illegible]	[illegible]	[illegible]	[illegible]			[illegible]	[illegible]	[illegible]		[illegible]	[illegible]	[illegible]

AUGUST 1778 (continued)

BRIGADE	UNIT	COMMANDING OFFICER	PRESENT FIT FOR DUTY & ON DUTY: COMMISSIONED OFFICERS	NONCOMMISSIONED OFFICERS	STAFF OFFICERS	RANK & FILE	TOTAL	RANK & FILE SICK, ON FURLOUGH, ETC.: SICK PRESENT	SICK ABSENT	ON COMMAND & EXTRA SERVICE	ON FURLOUGH	CONFINED	NOT JOINED	GRAND TOTAL	ALTERATIONS: DEATHS	DESERTED	TAKEN PRISONER	DISCHARGED	JOINED, ENLISTED, RECRUITED	LOCATION
	FORCES UNDER COMMANDER-IN-CHIEF GENERAL GEORGE WASHINGTON (continued)																			
(late) Learned	2nd Mass.	John Bailey	16	28	4	272	320	34	45	52	4			455	6	1		11	79	White Plains, N.Y. area
(late) Learned	8th Mass.	Michael Jackson	14	36	4	253	307	41	30	61	2			441	3	11		7	130	White Plains, N.Y. area
(late) Learned	9th Mass.	James Wesson	19	40	4	294	357	22	25	45	3			452		6		6	107	White Plains, N.Y. area
Poor	2nd Canadian	Moses Hazen	22	59	3	321	405	18	48	62	3			536		5		12	23	White Plains, N.Y. area
Poor	1st N.H.	Joseph Cilley	17	28	2	239	286	36	82	61	5			470	5	4			2	White Plains, N.Y. area
Poor	2nd N.H.	Nathan Hale	13	33	2	172	220	29	62	57	5			373	4	2			3	White Plains, N.Y. area
Poor	3rd N.H.	Alexander Scammell	8	23	1	152	184	28	53	38	12			315	4	1			1	White Plains, N.Y. area
Maxwell	1st N.J. B	Matthias Ogden	10	29	5	279	323	45	44	103	15			530	3	7			8	New Jersey
Maxwell	2nd N.J.	Israel Shreve	13	30	3	247	293	39	24	93	9			458		4		3	10	New Jersey
Maxwell	3rd N.J.	Elias Dayton	12	31	4	184	231	35	29	73	5			373		1			4	New Jersey
Maxwell	4th N.J. C	Ephraim Martin	11	27	4	148	190	36	23	79	3			331	2	6			2	New Jersey
Malcolm	Additional	William Malcolm	10	11	2	56	79	15	36	28	13			171	2				1	West Point, N.Y.
Malcolm	Patton's additional	Lt. Col. John Parke	6	28	1	65	100	8	8	16				132					1	West Point, N.Y.
Malcolm	Conn. militia	Roger Enos	36	55	3	364	458	46	15	29				548				11	4	West Point, N.Y.
Malcolm	Mass. militia	Thomas Poor	27	46	4	297	374	23	7	20				424					10	West Point, N.Y.
Malcolm	Conn. militia	Increase Moseley	12	20	3	129	164	18	2	4				188		2		5	8	West Point, N.Y.
Malcolm	Conn. militia	Samuel McLellan	9	18	2	90	119	12	7	13				151		2			1	West Point, N.Y.
	N.Y. militia D	Morris Graham	8	25	3	129	165	9	11	25	10			220						
	Armand's corps D	Tuffin Charles Armand	9	22	4	121	156							156		14				
	Pa. independent co. D	Capt. Anthony Selin	3	9		28	40	1	3	3				47					1	
	TOTAL OF INFANTRY		945	2328	262	14719	18254	2214	2850	4215	325			27858	201	244		230	1585	
	CAVALRY																			
	1st cont'l.	Theodorick Bland	6	10	4	58	78	8	4	77	5	1	4	177						White Plains, N.Y. area
	2nd cont'l.	Elisha Sheldon	13	18	2	117	150	7	8	48	1	2	1	217		4	2	1	1 J	White Plains, N.Y. area
	4th cont'l.	Stephen Moylan	8	13	4	70	95	14	4	74	3			190				2	3	White Plains, N.Y. area
	TOTAL OF CAVALRY		27	41	10	245	323	29	16	199	9	3	5	584		4	2	3	4	
	ARTILLERY																			
	7 cos. 3rd cont'l.	John Crane	25	113	3	129	270								1	2			1	White Plains, N.Y. area
	2nd cont'l.	John Lamb	42	134	3	171	350								2			1		White Plains, N.Y. area
	11 cos. 1st cont'l.	Charles Harrison	28	110	5	183	326	27	61	80	3			1267		1		1		White Plains, N.Y. area
	3 cos.	Lt. Col. Ebenezer Stevens	12	47	2	42	103									12				White Plains, N.Y. area
	3 independent cos.		5	24		18	47													White Plains, N.Y. area
	TOTAL OF ARTILLERY		112	428	13	543	1096	27	61	80	3			1267	3	15		2	1	
	TOTAL OF WASHINGTON'S ARMY		1084	2797	285	15507	19673	2270	2927	4494 H	337	3	5	29709 I	204	263	2	235	1590	

AUGUST 1778
(continued)

OFFICERS SICK, ON FURLOUGH, ETC.	WASHINGTON'S CAVALRY AND ARTILLERY (ONLY)			
	COMMISSIONED	NONCOMMISSIONED	STAFF	TOTAL
Sick Present	6	18	2	26
Sick Absent	17	47	2	66
On Command	45	91	4	140
On Furlough	9	5	4	18
TOTAL	77	161	12	250

SOURCE OF THIS REPORT

1. MONTHLY RETURN OF THE CONTINENTAL ARMY UNDER THE MORE IMMEDIATE COMMAND OF HIS EXCELLENCY GEORGE WASHINGTON...AUGUST 29, 1778, ELEPHANT FOLIO OF WASHINGTON RETURNS, WILLIAM L. CLEMENTS LIBRARY.

1a. Monthly Return of the Continental Army under...Washington...August 29 & 30, 1778, Record Group 93, National Archives. [The same figures, but to the brigade level only.]

A. The names of the commanders and the numbers of the regiments for these New York regiments do not match on the manuscript. Careful comparison of the figures makes it clear that the commanders are with the figures for their regiments, and the regiment numbers are wrong. We have corrected them.
B. The National Archives version of this return notes that the return of Maxwell's New Jersey brigade was dated August 5.
C. The National Archives version of this return notes that the return of the garrison at West Point under Malcolm was dated August 19.
D. See footnote D on the May 1778 report.
E. William Russell, colonel of the 13th Virginia regiment, had been temporarily put in command of the 10th Virginia regiment by Washington.
F. Five staff officers in Colonel John Gunby's 7th Maryland regiment plus one chaplain for the entire brigade.
G. Two staff officers in Lewis DuBois' 5th New York regiment plus one paymaster for the entire brigade.
H. The National Archives version of this return notes that 1,258 of the men included in the "on command" column were serving as light infantry under Brigadier General Scott. Morris Graham's New York militia also was serving with Scott in advanced positions nearer the enemy lines, and Armand's corps was doing similar duty. A further 150 of the men marked "on command" were with Lieutenant Colonel Carlton in the Terrytown area, another 150 with Major Fell at Hackensack, and 100 were with Major Gray at Norwalk.
I. The National Archives version of this return notes that no returns were received of the troops at Rhode Island, of Spencer's regiment at Kings Ferry, of the 3rd Continental cavalry at Hackensack, and of Lee's Partizan Corps of Horse, which had just arrived in camp.
J. Including two men classified as "returned from imprisonment."

Brigadier General Arthur St. Clair, who, with his aide-de-camp Isaac Budd Dunn, served as acting adjutant general of the Continental Army, March 1–April 9, 1777. While they were serving in this post (Dunn was the one actually named acting adjutant general in Washington's general orders), St. Clair was promoted to major general. Charles Willson Peale painted this portrait for his museum about 1782. (Courtesy of the Independence National Historical Park Collection, Philadelphia)

SEPTEMBER 1778

BRIGADE	UNIT	COMMANDING OFFICER	PRESENT FIT FOR DUTY & ON DUTY: COMMISSIONED OFFICERS	NONCOMMISSIONED OFFICERS	STAFF OFFICERS	RANK & FILE	TOTAL	RANK & FILE SICK, ON FURLOUGH, ETC.: SICK PRESENT	SICK ABSENT	ON COMMAND & EXTRA SERVICE	ON FURLOUGH	GRAND TOTAL	ALTERATIONS: DEATHS	DESERTED	TAKEN PRISONER	DISCHARGED	JOINED, ENLISTED, RECRUITED	LOCATION
FORCES UNDER COMMANDER-IN-CHIEF GENERAL GEORGE WASHINGTON																		
N.C.	1st N.C.	Thomas Clark	16	44	2	330	392	50	101	117		660						Danbury, Conn.
N.C.	2nd N.C.	John Patten	11	42	4	340	397	39	88	112	4	640						Danbury, Conn.
Woodford	2nd & 6th Va. A	Christian Febiger	14	36	6	144	200	39	33	53		325						New Jersey
Woodford	3rd & 7th Va.	William Heth	11	38	9	254	312	38	98	83	2	533						New Jersey
Woodford	11th & 15th Va.	Daniel Morgan	11	58	5	276	350	26	101	85	1	563						New Jersey
Muhlenberg	1st, 5th, 9th Va.	Richard Parker	9	57	8	162	236	52	97	91	15	491	11	1		2		vicinity of West Point
Muhlenberg	1st Va. state	George Gibson	9	25	4	117	155	25	40	89	1	310	6			1	2	vicinity of West Point
Muhlenberg	2nd Va. state	Gregory Smith	17	20	2	106	145	30	138	86		399	7	2		1	5	vicinity of West Point
Muhlenberg	14th Va.	William Davies	9	30	3	118	160	34	71	131	2	398	6	2				vicinity of West Point
Scott	4th, 8th, 12th Va.	James Wood	19	55	10	340	424	50	134	148	6	762						vicinity of West Point
Scott	10th Va.	William Russell	17	29	4	153	203	32	54	86	7	382						vicinity of West Point
Scott	Additional	William Grayson	4	20	4	83	111	13	39	23	2	188						vicinity of West Point
Smallwood	1st Md.	John Hawkins Stone	9	25	5	164	203	22	51	83	2	361	3	2		9	4	Fishkill, N. Y.
Smallwood	3rd Md.	Mordecai Gist	16	28	6	235	285	27	91	94	2	499	8	7		9	21	Fishkill, N. Y.
Smallwood	5th Md.	William Richardson	5	28	5 C	156	194	9	100	74	5	382	5	4		18	20	Fishkill, N. Y.
Smallwood	7th Md.	John Gunby	14	32	6	187	239	10	72	69	1	391	4	1		12	3	Fishkill, N. Y.
2nd Md.	2nd Md.	Thomas Price	7	38	2	292	339	10	135	51	5	540	3	7			2	near Fishkill, N. Y.
2nd Md.	German bn.	Lt. Col. Ludowick Weltner	12	39	4	254	309	7	34	45	2	397	2	2			1	near Fishkill, N. Y.
2nd Md.	4th Md.	Josias Carvil Hall	13	28	5	307	353	28	56	76		513	1	1		7	1	near Fishkill, N. Y.
2nd Md.	6th Md.	Otho Holland Williams	11	26	3	239	279	28	73	48	1	429	2	1			3	near Fishkill, N. Y.
Wayne	1st Pa.	James Chambers	7	27	4	151	189	13	16	77	7	302		2		7	23	Fredericksburg, N. Y.
Wayne	2nd Pa.	Walter Stewart	11	43	4	306	364	12	35	65		476	1	6		2	4	Fredericksburg, N. Y.
Wayne	7th Pa.	William Irvine	10	24	4	132	170	17	16	31		234	2	1			7	Fredericksburg, N. Y.
Wayne	10th Pa.	Richard Humpton	9	34	3	205	251	15	27	69	6	368					7	Fredericksburg, N. Y.
2nd Pa.	3rd Pa.	Thomas Craig	7	40	4	163	214	25	84	78	7	408	1			2	10	Fredericksburg, N. Y.
2nd Pa.	5th Pa.	Francis Johnston	7	32	4	163	206	29	40	48		323	2	3		1	2	Fredericksburg, N. Y.
2nd Pa.	6th Pa.	Lt. Col. Josiah Harmar	7	30	4	159	200	6	32	31	3	272	2				57	Fredericksburg, N. Y.
2nd Pa.	9th Pa.	Richard Butler	4	20	3	95	122	16	41	33	2	214		7			1	Fredericksburg, N. Y.
Clinton	1st N.Y.	Goose Van Schaick	13	36	3	239	291	16	71	65	1	444						near Continental Village, N. Y.
Clinton	2nd N.Y.	Philip Van Cortlandt	10	27	2	210	249	5	65	61	10	390						near Continental Village, N. Y.
Clinton	4th N.Y.	Henry B. Livingston	10	21	1 D	187	219	10	71	58	4	362						near Continental Village, N. Y.
Clinton	5th N.Y.	Lewis DuBois	7	38	3	183	231	7	39	69		346						near Continental Village, N. Y.
Parsons	3rd Conn.	Samuel Wyllys	16	42	4	311	373	40	69	103	3	588	1	4		4	1	Fredericksburg, N. Y.
Parsons	4th Conn.	John Durkee	13	35	4	145	197	21	50	63	15	346				3	2	Fredericksburg, N. Y.
Parsons	6th Conn.	Return Jonathan Meigs	15	43	4	365	427	43	70	103	11	654	2	1		1	3	Fredericksburg, N. Y.
Parsons	8th Conn.	(late) John Chandler	11	25	5	144	185	23	47	67	16	338	3	1			9	Fredericksburg, N. Y.
Huntington	1st Conn.	Lt. Col. David Fithian Sill	5	34	4	199	242	23	69	81	14	429	3					Fredericksburg, N. Y.
Huntington	2nd Conn.	Lt. Col. Isaac Sherman	7	41	2	142	192	20	23	49	12	296				2	4	Fredericksburg, N. Y.
Huntington	5th Conn.	Philip Burr Bradley	15	35	4 E	188	242	32	39	58	13	384	3	3			3	Fredericksburg, N. Y.
Huntington	7th Conn.	Heman Swift	15	38	5	197	255	20	47	76	7	405		2		1	3	Fredericksburg, N. Y.
Nixon	3rd Mass.	John Greaton	22	38	6	260	326	37	48	44	2	457				12	2	Danbury, Conn.
Nixon	5th Mass.	Rufus Putnam	23	42	4	361	430	37	22	57	1	547		2		1	4	Danbury, Conn.
Nixon	6th Mass.	Thomas Nixon	24	47	5	300	376	30	25	70	2	503	1	1		4	3	Danbury, Conn.
Nixon	Mass. militia	Ezra Wood	24	38	4	230	296	31	51	37		415	1	2		4	8	Danbury, Conn.
Paterson	12th Mass.	(late) Samuel Brewer	18	39	3	264	324	42	40	43	5	454	4	2		5	1	Danbury, Conn.
Paterson	10th Mass.	Thomas Marshall	15	29	5	233	282	42	32	60	3	419	1	3		2	1	Danbury, Conn.
Paterson	14th Mass.	Gamaliel Bradford	13	28	5	263	309	25	43	41	10	428	5			5	7	Danbury, Conn.
Paterson	11th Mass.	Benjamin Tupper	17	35	3	295	350	14	39	41	3	447		1			1	Danbury, Conn.

SEPTEMBER 1778 (continued)

BRIGADE	UNIT	COMMANDING OFFICER	PRESENT FIT FOR DUTY & ON DUTY: COMMISSIONED OFFICERS	NONCOMMISSIONED OFFICERS	STAFF OFFICERS	RANK & FILE	TOTAL	RANK & FILE SICK, ON FURLOUGH, ETC.: SICK PRESENT	SICK ABSENT	ON COMMAND & EXTRA SERVICE	ON FURLOUGH	GRAND TOTAL	ALTERATIONS: DEATHS	DESERTED	TAKEN PRISONER	DISCHARGED	JOINED, ENLISTED, RECRUITED	LOCATION
	FORCES UNDER COMMANDER-IN-CHIEF GENERAL GEORGE WASHINGTON (continued)																	
(late) Learned	2nd Mass.	John Bailey	17	32	4	254	307	22	63	58		450	5	1		4	1	Danbury, Conn.
	8th Mass.	Michael Jackson	12	34	4	253	303	37	39	51	1	431	3	3		1	1	Danbury, Conn.
	9th Mass.	James Wesson	20	42	4	273	339	32	30	50		451	3	1		2	2	Danbury, Conn.
Poor	2nd Canadian	Moses Hazen	18	49	2	272	341	12	68	76	10	507	1	17			3	Danbury, Conn.
	1st N.H.	Joseph Cilley	17	27	2	240	286	50	76	45	5	462	8	6		2	2	Danbury, Conn.
	2nd N.H.	Nathan Hale	14	32	2	186	234	23	50	41	5	353	14				2	Danbury, Conn.
	3rd N.H.	Alexander Scammell	10	26	1	150	187	30	55	39	10	321	1	1			4	Danbury, Conn.
Maxwell	1st N.J.	Matthias Ogden	17	23	4	253	297	84	43	100	7	531	3	1		1	6	New Jersey
	2nd N.J.	Israel Shreve	14	31	4	247	296	67	15	82	3	463	1	2			5	New Jersey
	3rd N.J.	Elias Dayton	5	31	4	181	221	41	23	72	4	361	1	3				New Jersey
	4th N.J.	Ephraim Martin	9	23	5	161	198	37	9	82	2	328	1	5			8	New Jersey
	Additional	William Malcolm	10	18	1	90	119	10	28	28	1	186						West Point, N.Y.
	Patton's additional	Lt. Col. John Parke	10	25	1	52	88	17	7	20		132						West Point, N.Y.
	3rd N.C.	James Hogun	19	45	4	379	447	50	57	9	1	564						West Point, N.Y.
	Mass. militia	Thomas Poor	26	44	4	214	288	47	9	84	1	429						West Point, N.Y.
Varnum	2nd R.I.	Israel Angell	68	131	12	787	998	62	56	65	4	1185						Rhode Island
	Additional	Henry Sherburne																Rhode Island
	Additional	Samuel Blatchley Webb																Rhode Island
	1st Canadian	James Livingston																Rhode Island
Glover	4th Mass.	William Shepard	74	146	12	785	1017	75	156	136	70	1454						Rhode Island
	13th Mass.	Edward Wigglesworth																Rhode Island
	1st Mass.	Joseph Vose																Rhode Island
	15th Mass.	Timothy Bigelow																Rhode Island
Cornell	1st R.I. state	John Topham	67	149	13	982	1211	106	132	235	10	1694						Rhode Island
	2nd R.I. state	Archibald Crary																Rhode Island
	Mass. militia	John Jacobs																Rhode Island
	Conn. militia brig.	Brig. Gen. John Tyler	35	51	7	333	426	21	10	36	6	499						Rhode Island
Col. Greene	1st R.I.	Christopher Greene	59	123	10	711	903	93	105	56	20	1177						Rhode Island
	Mass. militia	Nathaniel Wade																Rhode Island
	N.H. state	Lt. Col. Stephen Peabody																Rhode Island
	Det. additional	Henry Jackson	24	67	6	212	309	32	49	49	56	495						Rhode Island
	McIntosh's Mass. militia	William McIntosh	10	9	4	97	120	8	8	12	4	152						Rhode Island
	Gerrish's Mass. militia	Jacob Gerrish	28	66	3	431	528	28	51	176	17	800						Boston, Mass.
	Allen's Mass. militia	John Allen	8	7	4	144	163					163						Boston, Mass.
	Ft. Schuyler garrison	Peter Gansevoort	24	43	2	331	400	43	11	9		463						Fort Schuyler, N.Y.
	Additional	Oliver Spencer B	9	19	3	107	138	8	8	2	5	161	2					Kings Ferry, N.Y.
	N.Y. militia	Morris Graham																
	TOTAL OF INFANTRY		1213	2952	325	18472	22962	2255	4015	4935	457	34624	133	111		125	259	
	ARTILLERY																	
	7 cos. 3rd cont'l.	John Crane	11	41	4	52	108	19	47	358	1	1025	3	4				Fredericksburg, N.Y.
	2nd cont'l.	John Lamb	30	116	2	139	287						1			1		Fredericksburg, N.Y.
	11 cos. 1st cont'l.	Charles Harrison	12	40	4	47	103						1			1		Fredericksburg, N.Y.
	3 cont'l. cos.	Lt. Col. Ebenezer Stevens	8	42	1	33	84						1	5		1	1	Fredericksburg, N.Y.
	3 independent cos.		3	6		9	18										3	Fredericksburg, N.Y.
	TOTAL OF ARTILLERY		64	245	11	280	600	19	47	358	1	1025	6	9		3	4	
	TOTAL OF WASHINGTON'S ARMY		1277	3187	336	18752	23552	2274	4062	5293	458	35639	139	F 120		128	263	

SEPTEMBER 1778
(continued)

OFFICERS SICK, ON FURLOUGH, ETC.	WASHINGTON'S ARTILLERY (ONLY)			
	COMMISSIONED	NONCOMMISSIONED	STAFF	TOTAL
Sick Present	4	20	1	25
Sick Absent	8	19	3	30
On Command	82	268	2	352
On Furlough	6	5	1	12
TOTAL	100	312	7	419

SOURCE OF THIS REPORT

1. MONTHLY RETURN OF THE CONTINENTAL ARMY UNDER THE COMMAND OF HIS EXCELLENCY GEORGE WASHINGTON...OCTOBER 1, 1778, ELEPHANT FOLIO OF WASHINGTON RETURNS, WILLIAM L. CLEMENTS LIBRARY.

1a. Monthly Return of the Continental Army under...Washington...October 1, 1778 [marked "Monthly Genl. Return September" on reverse], Record Group 93, National Archives. [Same figures as the above, but to brigade level only.]

A. In the White Plains rearrangement, the depleted fifteen Virginia regiments were consolidated into eleven. The reorganization, however, had not been completed for this return, and all the Virginia regiment numbers on this report are those under the old organization. William Russell of the 13th had been temporarily put in command of the 10th by Washington.
B. No figures for this unit are given on the manuscripts.
C. Five staff officers in John Gunby's 7th Maryland regiment plus one chaplain for the entire brigade.
D. Two staff officers in Lewis DuBois' 5th New York regiment plus one chaplain for the entire brigade.
E. Four staff officers in Heman Swift's 7th Connecticut regiment plus one chaplain for the entire brigade.
F. Although it is not indicated in any way, monthly alterations must not have been available for several of the brigades, as there are no figures for them in any of the alterations columns. These alterations totals are therefore only partial.

Colonel Timothy Pickering, Adjutant General of the Continental Army, June 18, 1777–January 5, 1778. This portrait was painted by Charles Willson Peale for his museum, probably in 1792 when Pickering was postmaster general. Pickering and Peale had almost no ideas in common except an idealistic concern with preventing exploitation of the American Indian. Apparently Pickering's appointment as an Indian commissioner prompted Peale to do this, the earliest well-known likeness of Pickering, during a visit of Indian chiefs to Philadelphia. (Courtesy of the Independence National Historical Park Collection, Philadelphia)

OCTOBER 1778

BRIGADE	UNIT	COMMANDING OFFICER	PRESENT FIT FOR DUTY & ON DUTY: COMMISSIONED OFFICERS	NONCOMMISSIONED OFFICERS	STAFF OFFICERS	RANK & FILE	TOTAL	RANK & FILE SICK, ON FURLOUGH, ETC.: SICK PRESENT	SICK ABSENT	ON COMMAND & EXTRA SERVICE	ON FURLOUGH	NOT JOINED			GRAND TOTAL	ALTERATIONS: DEATHS	DESERTED	TAKEN PRISONER	DISCHARGED	JOINED, ENLISTED, RECRUITED	LOCATION
FORCES UNDER COMMANDER-IN-CHIEF GENERAL GEORGE WASHINGTON																					
1st N.C.	1st N.C.	Thomas Clark	17	40	3	317	377	31	79	130	2				619	16			30	7	Fredericksburg, N.Y.
	2nd N.C.	John Patten	13	37	5	333	388	30	59	85	4				566	8	2		67	4	Fredericksburg, N.Y.
Muhlenberg	1st (old 1 & 9) & old 5th Va. A	Richard Parker	13	62	8	196	279	41	65	92	14				491	9			1	4	vicinity of West Point
	1st Va. state	George Gibson	10	27	3	141	181	25	25	78	1				310	3				2	vicinity of West Point
	2nd Va. state	Gregory Smith	9	21	1 D	106	137	75	78	78	1				369	20	1		1	1	vicinity of West Point
	10th Va. (old 14th)	William Davies	10	28	5	149	192	48	61	88	2				391	6	1			4	vicinity of West Point
Scott	4th Va. (old 4th & 8th)	John Neville	3	35	4	154	196	21	43	40	1				301	2	1		1	5	vicinity of West Point
	Del.	David Hall	12	26	5	135	178	39	73	47	4				341	10			6	3	vicinity of West Point
	6th Va. (old 10th)	William Russell	12	26	4	195	237	33	22	68	7				367	4			3	2	vicinity of West Point
	8th Va. (old 12th)	James Wood	6	17	4 E	220	247	30	36	60	3				376	3	8		37	4	vicinity of West Point
Smallwood	Additional	William Grayson	6	18	5	98	127	15	21	23	2				188	2				1	vicinity of Fishkill, N.Y.
	1st Md.	John Hawkins Stone	8	27	2	173	210	12	32	105	1				360	9	2		1	14	vicinity of Fishkill, N.Y.
	3rd Md.	Mordecai Gist	15	33	6	278	332	28	59	134	2				555	8	3		7	79	vicinity of Fishkill, N.Y.
	5th Md.	William Richardson	6	23	4 F	142	175	18	90	94	3				380	6			4	16	vicinity of Fishkill, N.Y.
	7th Md.	John Gunby	13	38	6	200	257	18	61	90	1				427	6	3		2	51	vicinity of Fishkill, N.Y.
2nd Md.	2nd Md.	Thomas Price	6	33	1	222	262	29	99	136	2				528	3	2			4	vicinity of Fishkill, N.Y.
	Md. (German bn.)	Lt. Col. Ludowick Weltner	11	31	5	185	232	12	25	113	3				385						vicinity of Fishkill, N.Y.
	4th Md.	Josias Carvil Hall	10	27	5	267	309	18	47	134					508	4	1			5	vicinity of Fishkill, N.Y.
	6th Md.	Otho Holland Williams	5	27	3	223	258	8	74	73	2				415	9	2		1	4	vicinity of Fishkill, N.Y.
Wayne	1st Pa.	James Chambers	6	24	6	155	191	15	13	85	6				310		1		1	12	Fredericksburg, N.Y.
	2nd Pa.	Walter Stewart	9	41	4	273	327	48	25	69	2				471	4	3			9	Fredericksburg, N.Y.
	7th Pa.	William Irvine	10	26	4	141	181	11	9	33					234	1	1		1	1	Fredericksburg, N.Y.
	10th Pa.	Richard Humpton	10	32	3	188	233	7	26	90	4				360	2	2			4	Fredericksburg, N.Y.
2nd Pa.	3rd Pa.	Thomas Craig	9	43	5	195	252	34	54	71	7				418	5			2	14	Fredericksburg, N.Y.
	5th Pa.	Francis Johnston	8	26	5	180	219	20	30	47	1				317	6	1		1	9	Fredericksburg, N.Y.
	9th Pa.	Richard Butler	4	26	3	119	152	24	26	30	1				233	1	8			26	Fredericksburg, N.Y.
	6th Pa.	Lt. Col. Josiah Harmar	5	35	3	154	197	15	20	30	3				265		5		1	4	Fredericksburg, N.Y.
Clinton	1st N.Y.	Goose Van Schaick	18	32	3	249	302	13	92	26	5				438	5	1		1		New York state
	4th N.Y.	Henry Beekman Livingston	10	25	2	189	226	7	65	59	3				360		4		2	5	New York state
	5th N.Y.	Lewis DuBois	9	30	2	152	193	13	47	77	2				332		10			3	New York state
Parsons	3rd Conn.	Samuel Wyllys	9	39	4	267	319	33	42	141	45				580	9	6		6	11	New Milford, Conn.
	4th Conn.	John Durkee	9	34	2	139	184	16	29	73	28				330						New Milford, Conn.
	6th Conn.	Return Jonathan Meigs	10	31	3	299	343	19	36	177	53				628						New Milford, Conn.
	8th Conn.	(late) John Chandler	10	25	4	148	187	16	45	62	29				339						New Milford, Conn.
Huntington	1st Conn.	Lt. Col. David Fithian Sill	10	32	4	186	232	18	66	100	12				428	3	1		2	3	New Milford, Conn.
	2nd Conn.	Lt. Col. Isaac Sherman	4	34	4	132	174	10	36	58	11				289	3				3	New Milford, Conn.
	5th Conn.	Philip Burr Bradley	10	34	4 G	177	225	14	41	80	11				371	2	3		3	2	New Milford, Conn.
	7th Conn.	Heman Swift	16	32	5	189	242	8	41	97	10				398				2	1	New Milford, Conn.
Nixon	3rd Mass.	John Greaton	19	39	6	281	345	24	30	51	1				451	3	4		17	55	New Milford, Conn.
	5th Mass.	Rufus Putnam	21	40	3	345	409	26	25	75	3				538						New Milford, Conn.
	6th Mass.	Thomas Nixon	20	42	4	278	344	25	28	127	3				527						New Milford, Conn.
	Mass. militia	Ezra Wood	8	26	4	132	170	24	49	137	5				385						New Milford, Conn.
Paterson	12th Mass.	(late) Samuel Brewer	20	39	4	249	312	21	33	73	12				451	3	4			1	Hartford, Conn.
	10th Mass.	Thomas Marshall	16	31	4	237	288	14	32	76	3				413	5	3				Hartford, Conn.
	14th Mass.	Gamaliel Bradford	17	32	5	273	327	10	27	53	10				427	5	3			1	Hartford, Conn.
	11th Mass.	Benjamin Tupper	15	37	5	288	345	19	24	53	4				445	3				1	Hartford, Conn.
(late) Learned	2nd Mass.	John Bailey	17	28	5	244	294	35	39	75	3				446	1				1	Hartford, Conn.
	8th Mass.	Michael Jackson	10	37	4	242	293	28	34	69	1				425	1	2		4		Hartford, Conn.
	9th Mass.	James Wesson	17	39	2	272	330	21	23	66	3				443	4	1			5	Hartford, Conn.

OCTOBER 1778
(continued)

BRIGADE	UNIT	COMMANDING OFFICER	PRESENT FIT FOR DUTY & ON DUTY: COMMISSIONED OFFICERS	NONCOMMISSIONED OFFICERS	STAFF OFFICERS	RANK & FILE	TOTAL	RANK & FILE SICK, ON FURLOUGH, ETC.: SICK PRESENT	SICK ABSENT	ON COMMAND & EXTRA SERVICE	ON FURLOUGH	NOT JOINED	GRAND TOTAL	ALTERATIONS: DEATHS	DESERTED	TAKEN PRISONER	DISCHARGED	JOINED, ENLISTED, RECRUITED	LOCATION
	FORCES UNDER COMMANDER-IN-CHIEF GENERAL GEORGE WASHINGTON (continued)																		
Poor	2nd Canadian	Moses Hazen	19	49	2	276	346	15	54	81	10		506	4	2				Hartford, Conn.
Poor	1st N.H.	Joseph Cilley	15	29	2	241	287	38	54	71	7		457	2			2		Hartford, Conn.
Poor	2nd N.H.	Nathan Hale	11	33	2	183	229	27	26	58	5		345	5				2	Hartford, Conn.
Poor	3rd N.H.	Alexander Scammell	9	29	2	149	189	24	35	58	8		314	8					Hartford, Conn.
	Additional	William Malcolm	10	20	1	82	113	8	22	34	6		183						West Point, N.Y.
	Patton's additional	Lt. Col. John Parke	6	23	2	44	75	25	8	19			127	1					West Point, N.Y.
	3rd N.C.	James Hogun	18	42	3	312	375	79	77	19			550	2			2		West Point, N.Y.
	Mass. militia	Thomas Poor	15	41	3	151	210	60	11	130			411		1			1	West Point, N.Y.
	Additional	Oliver Spencer	11	19	4	110	144	2	13	5	3		167						
	Armand's corps	Tuffin Charles Armand	15	28	4	134	181	4	3	1			189						
	1st Canadian	James Livingston	13	22	4	106	145	7	15	19	2		188		1		1		Rhode Island
	Additional	Henry Sherburne	20	30	2	195	247	13	2	32	1		295	2				2	Rhode Island
	Additional	Samuel Blatchley Webb	14	32	3	173	222	30	8	40	6		306		1			5	Rhode Island
	2nd R.I.	Israel Angell	12	37	3	239	291	28	14	48	9		390	1	7			5	Rhode Island
	4th Mass.	William Shepard	22	33	3	193	251	12	41	63	19		386	2	6		2	2	Rhode Island
	13th Mass.	Edward Wigglesworth	17	32	2	151	202	19	25	85	22		353	3	2			3	Rhode Island
	1st Mass.	Joseph Vose	22	33	3	163	221	23	39	58	26		367	3	7		1	9	Rhode Island
	2nd R.I. state	Archibald Crary	16	39	5	219	279	2	33	113	8		435	3	7		6	20	Rhode Island
	Mass. militia[B]	John Jacobs	24	74	4	485	587	28	48	34	21		718	4	6		5	24	Rhode Island
	1st R.I. state	John Topham	19	34	4	293	350	11	12	130	14		517	3	6			13	Rhode Island
	1st R.I.	Christopher Greene	10	27	2	114	153	4	9	26	5		197	1	3				Rhode Island
	Mass. militia	Nathaniel Wade	24	44	3	371	442	32	46	113	19		652	2	9		10		Rhode Island
	N.H. state	Lt. Col. Stephen Peabody	11	27	3	177	218	11	18	18	9		274						Rhode Island
	Lee's additional	Lt. Col. William Stephens Smith	8	28	2	101	139	8	11	14	4		176		4			2	Rhode Island
	Additional	David Henley	10	16		52	78	9	4	29	5		125						Rhode Island
	Additional	Henry Jackson	6	29	2	112	149	11	13	21	8		202	2				1	Rhode Island
	15th Mass.	Timothy Bigelow	12	23	3	149	187	5	31	57	30		310	2	8			9	Rhode Island
Maxwell	1st N.J.	Matthias Ogden	14	34	5	299	352	28	86	47	12		525	2	17			4	New Jersey
Maxwell	2nd N.J.	Israel Shreve	14	33	5	267	319	45	28	56	5		453		14		1	2	New Jersey
Maxwell	3rd N.J.	Elias Dayton	15	36	4	203	258	37	28	42	8		373		3		2	2	New Jersey
Maxwell	4th N.J.	Ephraim Martin	12	29	3	194	238	24	16	46	3		327	1	6		1	1	New Jersey
Woodford	2nd Va. (old 2nd & 6th)[A]	Christian Febiger	12	30	3	160	205	20	34	47	2		308	3	1		2		New Jersey
Woodford	5th (old 7th) & old 3rd Va.	William Heth	12	39	9	285	345	33	82	67	2		529	3	2		2	1	New Jersey
Woodford	7th & 11th Va. (old 11 & 15)	Daniel Morgan	13	50	5	289	357	27	89	78	1		552	4	1				New Jersey
	TOTAL OF INFANTRY		1022	2691	302	16779	20794	1868	3171	5687	616		32136	257	203		241	489	
	CAVALRY																		
	1st cont'l.	Theodoric Bland	14	39	5	56	114	12	3	66	1		196						
	2nd cont'l.	Elisha Sheldon	19	43	5	62	129	16	5	60	4	2	216	1	1	6	2	1	
	Partizan corps[C]	Maj. Henry Lee	9	24	4	85	122			10			132			2			
	Marechaussie	Capt. Bartholomew Von Heer	3	7		28	38			7			45						
	TOTAL OF CAVALRY		45	113	14	231	403	28	8	143	5	2	589	1	1	8	2	1	

OCTOBER 1778 (continued)

BRIGADE / UNIT	COMMANDING OFFICER	PRESENT FIT FOR DUTY & ON DUTY: COMMISSIONED OFFICERS	NONCOMMISSIONED OFFICERS	STAFF OFFICERS	RANK & FILE	TOTAL	RANK & FILE SICK, ON FURLOUGH, ETC.: SICK PRESENT	SICK ABSENT	ON COMMAND & EXTRA SERVICE	ON FURLOUGH	NOT JOINED			GRAND TOTAL	ALTERATIONS: DEATHS	DESERTED	TAKEN PRISONER	DISCHARGED	JOINED, ENLISTED, RECRUITED	LOCATION
FORCES UNDER COMMANDER-IN-CHIEF GENERAL GEORGE WASHINGTON (continued)																				
ARTILLERY																				
7 cos. 3rd cont'l.	John Crane	10	40	4	58	112									4	1		1	1	Fredericksburg, N.Y.
2nd cont'l.	John Lamb	22	86	1	120	229									2	1		4	2	Fredericksburg, N.Y.
11 cos. 1st cont'l.	Charles Harrison	13	45	3	52	113	15	35	369	2				1035		1		4	2	Fredericksburg, N.Y.
3 cont'l. cos.	Lt. Col. Ebenezer Stevens	9	40	2	38	89													5	Fredericksburg, N.Y.
3 independent cos.		8	34		29	71													2	Fredericksburg, N.Y.
Det. 1st & 3rd cont'l.	(John Crane & Charles Harrison)	17	47		67	131 H								131		4				Providence, R.I.
R.I. state	Robert Elliot	20	65	2	262	349 H								349		2				Rhode Island
TOTAL OF ARTILLERY		99	357	12	626	1094	15	35	369	2				1515	6	9		9	12	
TOTAL OF WASHINGTON'S ARMY		1166	3161	328	17636	22291	1911	3214	6199 I	623	2			34240 J	264	213	8	252	502	

OFFICERS SICK, ON FURLOUGH, ETC.	WASHINGTON'S ARTILLERY IN NEW YORK (ONLY): COMMISSIONED	NONCOMMISSIONED	STAFF	TOTAL
Sick Present	2	15		17
Sick Absent	5	17	1	23
On Command	80	268	2	350
On Furlough	7	3	3	13
TOTAL	94	303	6	403

SOURCE OF THIS REPORT

1. MONTHLY RETURN OF THE CONTINENTAL ARMY UNDER THE COMMAND OF HIS EXCELLENCY GEORGE WASHINGTON . . . NOVEMBER 1, 1778, ELEPHANT FOLIO OF WASHINGTON RETURNS, WILLIAM L. CLEMENTS LIBRARY.

1a. Monthly Return of the Continental Army under. . . Washington. . . November 1, 1778 [marked "Monthly Genl. Ret. Oct. 1778" on reverse], Record Group 93, National Archives. [Same figures as the above, but to brigade level only.]

A. The depleted fifteen Virginia regiments had been consolidated into eleven at the White Plains rearrangement. The rearrangement was being completed at the time of the October return. We have indicated the old numbers in parentheses through the end of the year. William Russell, colonel of the old 13th Virginia, was temporarily put in command of the 6th Virginia (old 10th) by Washington. In Februrary, 1779, he assumed command of the 5th Virginia.

B. A careless ditto makes this appear to be a Rhode Island State regiment on the manuscript. There were only two Rhode Island State infantry regiments, and both are accounted for already. Subsequent returns do not repeat the error, and "Jacobs" on this manuscript, plus the designations on the following returns, make it clear that this is John Jacobs' Massachusetts militia regiment.

C. This was a provost company or horse police. The term comes from the French.

D. Four staff officers in William Davies' 10th Virginia (old 14th) regiment plus one chaplain for the entire brigade.

E. Four staff officers in William Grayson's Additional regiment plus one chaplain for the entire brigade.

F. Five staff officers in John Gunby's 7th Maryland regiment plus one chaplain for the entire brigade.

G. Four staff officers in Heman Swift's 7th Connecticut regiment plus one chaplain for the entire brigade.

H. These figures for the artillery stationed in Rhode Island may include all the men, not just "present fit for duty," although the manuscript does not explicitly say so. They may therefore inflate a little the totals of "present fit for duty."

I. The National Archives manuscript notes that 1,100 of those listed as "on command" were serving in Brigadier General Charles Scott's advanced detachment.

J. The National Archives manuscript notes that no returns were available for October for the 9th Virginia (old 13th) and 8th Pennsylvania regiments at Fort Pitt, Hartley's Additional and the 4th Pennsylvania regiments on the frontiers of Pennsylvania and New York, Gansevoort's 3rd New York regiment at Fort Schuyler, Warner's Additional regiment in the Green Mountains, Alden's 7th Massachusetts regiment at Cherry Valley, Van Cortlandt's 2nd New York regiment on the march to Schoharie, and Pulaski's Legion and Moylan's and Baylor's regiments of cavalry in New Jersey.

Colonel Otho Holland Williams, Acting Adjutant General of the Continental Army, December 25, 1779–April 11, 1780. Williams served while Adjutant General Alexander Scammell (of whom there is no contemporary likeness) was temporarily absent on leave. Later, Williams was deputy adjutant general for the Southern Department. This portrait is presumably a replica painted by Charles Willson Peale about 1782–1796. Peale was friendly with the Williams family and seems to have given them the original portriat that he painted for his museum in 1782. Williams, who was active in the Continental Army lodge of the Masons, wears a Masonic emblem with his military uniform. (Courtesy of the Independence National Historical Park Collection, Philadelphia)

NOVEMBER 1778

BRIGADE	UNIT	COMMANDING OFFICER	PRESENT FIT FOR DUTY & ON DUTY: COMMISSIONED OFFICERS	NONCOMMISSIONED OFFICERS	STAFF OFFICERS	RANK & FILE	TOTAL	RANK & FILE SICK, ON FURLOUGH, ETC.: SICK PRESENT	SICK ABSENT	ON COMMAND & EXTRA SERVICE	ON FURLOUGH	GRAND TOTAL	ALTERATIONS: DEATHS	DESERTED	TAKEN PRISONER	DISCHARGED	JOINED, ENLISTED, RECRUITED	LOCATION
	FORCES UNDER COMMANDER-IN-CHIEF GENERAL GEORGE WASHINGTON																	
N.C.	1st N.C.	Thomas Clark	17	38	4	296	355	30	68	110		563	1			4	1	New Jersey & Fort Clinton
N.C.	2nd N.C.	John Patten	11	42	5	246	304	21	41	120	4	490				2		New Jersey & Fort Clinton
Woodford	2nd Va. (old 2nd & 6th)	Christian Febiger	12	30	3	163	208	12	31	56	1	308				1	1	New Jersey & Fort Clinton
Woodford	3rd Va. (old 3rd & 5th)	William Heth	9	30	6	172	217	17	55	60		349						New Jersey & Fort Clinton
Woodford	5th Va. (old 7th)	Maj. John Webb	6	21	5	170	202	34	53	41	2	332	2				1	New Jersey & Fort Clinton
Woodford	7th & 11th Va. (old 11th & 15th)	Daniel Morgan	13	50	5	309	377	11	66	73	6	533				3		New Jersey & Fort Clinton
Muhlenberg	1st Va. (old 1st & 9th)	Richard Parker	6	32	5	130	173	27	31	62	16	309	6			1	3	New Jersey & Fort Clinton
Muhlenberg	1st Va. state	George Gibson	9	34	4	167	214	20	24	61	2	321					4	New Jersey & Fort Clinton
Muhlenberg	2nd Va. state	Gregory Smith	10	26	1	101	138	31	120	77	1	367	7	1				New Jersey & Fort Clinton
Muhlenberg	10th Va. (old 14th)	William Davies	6	25	4	172	207	26	81	62	3	379	9				5	New Jersey & Fort Clinton
Scott	4th Va. (old 4th & 8th)	John Neville	4	38	5	154	201	9	48	48	1	307	1				2	New Jersey & Fort Clinton
Scott	Del.	David Hall	11	31	4	149	195	24	61	50	1	331	14	1			3	New Jersey & Fort Clinton
Scott	6th Va. (old 10th)	William Russell	13	26	4	177	220	29	19	87	8	363	1	2		2	1	New Jersey & Fort Clinton
Scott	8th Va. (old 12th)	James Wood	5	22	3	197	227	24	45	76	6	378	3				4	New Jersey & Fort Clinton
Scott	Additional	William Grayson	2	25		86	113	14	15	32	8	182	2	1		5	4	New Jersey & Fort Clinton
Smallwood	1st Md.	John Hawkins Stone	6	21	2	138	167	16	31	139	1	354	3	2			5	New Jersey & Fort Clinton
Smallwood	3rd Md.	Mordecai Gist	7	31	5	183	226	19	71	219	2	537	5	3		5	7	New Jersey & Fort Clinton
Smallwood	5th Md.	William Richardson	6	25	3	107	141	7	88	133	3	372	6	3				New Jersey & Fort Clinton
Smallwood	7th Md.	John Gunby	8	39	5	135	187	13	49	173	1	423	3			3	9	New Jersey & Fort Clinton
2nd Md.	2nd Md.	Thomas Price	7	32	2	202	243	30	84	162	3	522	2	1		4		New Jersey & Fort Clinton
2nd Md.	Md. (German bn.)	Lt. Col. Ludowick Weltner	4	23	5	182	214	6	20	133	4	377		1			8	New Jersey & Fort Clinton
2nd Md.	4th Md.	Josias Carvil Hall	5	20	5	117	147	16	36	290	1	490	1	2		2		New Jersey & Fort Clinton
2nd Md.	6th Md.	Otho Holland Williams	4	24	5	187	220	12	50	119	7	408	2	3			5	New Jersey & Fort Clinton
Wayne	1st Pa.	James Chambers	3	18	5	121	147	15	10	127	6	305						New Jersey & Fort Clinton
Wayne	2nd Pa.	Walter Stewart	8	38	3	178	227	25	60	162	2	476	2	3		3	19	New Jersey & Fort Clinton
Wayne	7th Pa.	William Irvine	4	18	5	87	114	11	7	90		222	1				2	New Jersey & Fort Clinton
Wayne	10th Pa.	Richard Humpton	3	25	5	99	132	6	24	179	4	345	1	3			2	New Jersey & Fort Clinton
2nd Pa.	3rd Pa.	Thomas Craig	5	37	4	167	213	19	42	116	7	397		1				New Jersey & Fort Clinton
2nd Pa.	5th Pa.	Francis Johnston	5	24	5	123	157	13	37	105	2	314		1				New Jersey & Fort Clinton
2nd Pa.	6th Pa.	Robert Magaw	6	37	1	108	152	4	29	81	3	269						New Jersey & Fort Clinton
2nd Pa.	9th Pa.	Richard Butler	6	22	4	91	123	14	22	71	1	231		3				New Jersey & Fort Clinton
Maxwell	1st N.J.	Matthias Ogden	14	29	5	265	313	46	70	85	11	525	4	8			17	New Jersey & Fort Clinton
Maxwell	2nd N.J.	Israel Shreve	14	33	5	272	324	27	21	79	5	456		1		1	5	New Jersey & Fort Clinton
Maxwell	3rd N.J.	Elias Dayton	13	36	5	187	241	32	32	66	4	375		5			8	New Jersey & Fort Clinton
Maxwell	4th N.J.	Ephraim Martin	13	32	5	171	221	34	11	66	2	334					1	New Jersey & Fort Clinton
	Additional	William Malcolm	7	18	1	53	79	23	14	50	9	175		2			2	West Point, N.Y.
	Additional	(late) John Patton	6	23	2	60	91	9	8	19		127	1					West Point, N.Y.
	3rd N.C.	James Hogun	12	41	4	275	332	88	63	40	5	528	11			4	2	West Point, N.Y.
	Mass. militia	Thomas Poor	14	42	3	185	244	49	7	100		400		1		9		West Point, N.Y.
Clinton	4th N.Y.	Henry Beekman Livingston	9	28	2	201	240	17	48	55	4	364					3	New York state
Clinton	5th N.Y.	Lewis DuBois	11	38	2	172	223	17	36	64	2	342		3			3	New York state
Northern dept.	7th Mass.	(late) Ichabod Alden	18	43	2	209	272	17	10	53	1	353						Cherry Valley, N.Y.
Northern dept.	4th Pa.	Lambert Cadwalader	16	38	4	124	182	11	43	12		248						Schoharie, N.Y.
Northern dept.	Additional (Green Mt. boys)	Seth Warner	15	26	5	91	137	6	9	11	3	166						Fort Stark, Vt.
Northern dept.	2nd N.Y.	Philip Van Cortlandt	16	33	1	256	306	17	46	11	12	392	4	13		3	15	New York state
Northern dept.	1st N.Y.	Goose Van Schaick	16	33	4	244	297	16	90	27	5	435	1			1		New York state
Northern dept.	3rd N.Y.	Peter Gansevoort	24	43	2	331	400	43	11	9		463						New York state

NOVEMBER 1778 (continued)

BRIGADE	UNIT	COMMANDING OFFICER	PRESENT FIT FOR DUTY & ON DUTY: COMMISSIONED OFFICERS	NONCOMMISSIONED OFFICERS	STAFF OFFICERS	RANK & FILE	TOTAL	RANK & FILE SICK, ON FURLOUGH, ETC.: SICK PRESENT	SICK ABSENT	ON COMMAND & EXTRA SERVICE	ON FURLOUGH	GRAND TOTAL	ALTERATIONS: DEATHS	DESERTED	TAKEN PRISONER	DISCHARGED	JOINED, ENLISTED, RECRUITED	LOCATION
FORCES UNDER COMMANDER-IN-CHIEF GENERAL GEORGE WASHINGTON (continued)																		
Nixon	3rd Mass.	John Greaton	15	39	5	261	320	23	19	39	1	402				40		The Highlands, N.Y.
Nixon	5th Mass.	Rufus Putnam	23	41	2	363	429	35	13	59	2	538		1			2	The Highlands, N.Y.
Nixon	6th Mass.	Thomas Nixon	22	40	4	277	343	40	15	120	6	524	1	5			2	The Highlands, N.Y.
Nixon	Mass. militia	Ezra Wood	8	27	4	146	185	25	25	146	6	387					1	The Highlands, N.Y.
Paterson	12th Mass.	(late) Samuel Brewer	8	29	4	240	281	22	35	54	33	425	1	2		1		The Highlands, N.Y.
Paterson	10th Mass.	Thomas Marshall	9	30	4	195	238	13	34	82	27	394	2	3		1		The Highlands, N.Y.
Paterson	14th Mass.	Gamaliel Bradford	9	19	3	230	261	8	28	53	31	381	1	1			1	The Highlands, N.Y.
Paterson	11th Mass.	Benjamin Tupper	11	26	2	239	278	22	44	48	28	420		2				The Highlands, N.Y.
(late) Learned	2nd Mass.	John Bailey	41	102	11	763	917	79	92	200	21	1309	1	1		13	16	The Highlands, N.Y.
(late) Learned	8th Mass.	Michael Jackson																The Highlands, N.Y.
(late) Learned	9th Mass.	James Wesson																The Highlands, N.Y.
Parsons	3rd Conn.	Samuel Wyllys	9	38	5	255	307	28	35	155	53	578	1					Danbury, Conn.
Parsons	4th Conn.	John Durkee	7	33	1	138	179	19	21	71	27	317		3				Danbury, Conn.
Parsons	6th Conn.	Return Jonathan Meigs	12	35	2	289	338	30	29	179	52	628		1			1	Danbury, Conn.
Parsons	8th Conn.	(late) John Chandler	12	25	3	150	190	14	45	66	26	341					2	Danbury, Conn.
Huntington	1st Conn.	Lt. Col. David Fithian Sill	11	30	3	184	228	19	58	101	20	426		1				Danbury, Conn.
Huntington	2nd Conn.	Lt. Col. Isaac Sherman	3	34	2	128	167	12	29	63	11	282						Danbury, Conn.
Huntington	5th Conn.	Philip Burr Bradley	9	32	2 B	178	221	16	36	86	5	364						Danbury, Conn.
Huntington	7th Conn.	Heman Swift	13	32	4	184	233	11	31	111	8	394					1	Danbury, Conn.
Poor	2nd Canadian	Moses Hazen	46	142	8	844	1040	108	157	277	33	1615	3	2		1	5	Danbury, Conn.
Poor	1st N.H.	Joseph Cilley																Danbury, Conn.
Poor	2nd N.H.	Nathan Hale																Danbury, Conn.
Poor	3rd N.H.	Alexander Scammel																Danbury, Conn.
	1st Canadian	James Livingston	14	27	4	104	149	10	11	24	2	196						Rhode Island
	Additional	Henry Sherburne	16	26	4	194	240	6	1	38	1	286		4				Rhode Island
	Additional	Samuel Blatchley Webb	13	31	3	134	181	20	9	85	7	302		4			2	Rhode Island
	2nd R.I.	Israel Angell	10	26	3	210	249	6	13	105	1	374	1	2			1	Rhode Island
	4th Mass.	William Shepard	21	39	4	192	256	18	25	59	5	363	1			31	3	Rhode Island
	13th Mass.	Edward Wigglesworth	18	34	3	149	204	19	14	88	27	352	2	2		3	3	Rhode Island
	15th Mass.	Timothy Bigelow	12	28	2	158	200	15	25	56	17	313	1	1			1	Rhode Island
	1st Mass.	Joseph Vose	20	34	2	180	236	25	34	51	19	365	1	2			4	Rhode Island
	2nd R.I. state	Archibald Crary	19	42	4	248	313	6	22	96		437		3		2	2	Rhode Island
	Mass. militia	John Jacobs	34	73	4	533	644	20	35	38		737		1		4	15	Rhode Island
	1st R.I. state	John Topham	21	38	2	279	340	9	10	152		511	1	9			5	Rhode Island
	1st R.I.	Christopher Greene	11	30	1	132	174	6	6	14		200	1				2	Rhode Island
	Mass. militia	Nathaniel Wade	32	65	3	426	526	22	33	91	5	677		6		3	5	Rhode Island
	N.H. state	Lt. Col. Stephen Peabody	14	26	4	189	233	9	8	14	12	276				2	1	Rhode Island
	Lee's additional	Lt. Col. William Stephens Smith	5	30	1	110	146	6	7	16	3	178		2			3	Rhode Island
	Additional	David Henley	7	12		64	83	5	4	27	3	122						Rhode Island
	Additional	Henry Jackson	7	23	8 C	113	151	10	13	23	8	205		1				Rhode Island
	TOTAL OF INFANTRY		981	2778	295	16489	20543	1743	2953	6948	669	32856	111	123		154	220	

BRIGADE

NOVEMBER 1778 (continued)

UNIT	COMMANDING OFFICER	PRESENT FIT FOR DUTY & ON DUTY: COMMISSIONED OFFICERS	NONCOMMISSIONED OFFICERS	STAFF OFFICERS	RANK & FILE	TOTAL	RANK & FILE SICK, ON FURLOUGH, ETC.: SICK PRESENT	SICK ABSENT	ON COMMAND & EXTRA SERVICE	ON FURLOUGH				GRAND TOTAL	ALTERATIONS: DEATHS	DESERTED	TAKEN PRISONER	DISCHARGED	JOINED, ENLISTED, RECRUITED	LOCATION
FORCES UNDER COMMANDER-IN-CHIEF GENERAL GEORGE WASHINGTON (continued)																				
ARTILLERY																				
7 cos. 3rd cont'l.	John Crane	4	16	3	25	48												1		New Jersey
2nd cont'l.	John Lamb	20	88	3	121	232	6	26	410	11				928	2	3		2	3	New Jersey
11 cos. 1st cont'l.	Charles Harrison	10	46	4	45	105									2			2		New Jersey
3 cont'l cos. A	Lt. Col. Ebenezer Stevens	8	43	2	37	90												2		New Jersey
3 independent cos.																				
Det. 1st & 3rd cont'l.	(John Crane & Charles Harrison)	12	40		72	124 D								124	1				8	Providence, R.I.
R.I. state	Robert Elliot	16	53	2	263	334 D								334	2	1			6	Rhode Island
TOTAL OF ARTILLERY		70	286	14	563	933	6	26	410	11				1386	7	4		7	17	
TOTAL OF WASHINGTON'S ARMY		1051	3064	309	17052	21476	1749	2979	7358	680				34242 E	118	127		161	237	

OFFICERS SICK, ON FURLOUGH, ETC.	WASHINGTON'S ARTILLERY (EXCLUDING UNITS IN RHODE ISLAND): COMMISSIONED	NONCOMMISSIONED	STAFF	TOTAL
Sick Present		7		7
Sick Absent	3	11		14
On Command	87	303	2	392
On Furlough	13	16	2	31
TOTAL	103	337	4	444

SOURCE OF THIS REPORT

1. MONTHLY RETURN OF THE CONTINENTAL ARMY UNDER THE COMMAND OF HIS EXCELLENCY GEORGE WASHINGTON...FOR NOVEMBER 1778, ELEPHANT FOLIO OF WASHINGTON RETURNS, WILLIAM L. CLEMENTS LIBRARY. [THE ARTILLERY APPEARS ON THE PRECEDING PAGE OF THE FOLIO. WITH THIS RETURN, THE MONTHLIES BEGIN TO BE HEADED, FOR THE MOST PART, SIMPLY FOR A GIVEN MONTH, RATHER THAN WITH A SPECIFIC DATE; FOR THIS MONTH, A NOTE ON THE NATIONAL ARCHIVES VERSION LISTED BELOW EXPLAINS THAT THE MONTHLY WAS NOT COMPLETED UNTIL LATER THAN USUAL BECAUSE THE ARMY HAD BEEN MOVING INTO WINTER QUARTERS.]

1a. Monthly Return of the Continental Army under...Washington... for November 1778, Record Group 93, National Archives. [Same figures as the above, but to brigade level only.]

A. All columns on the manuscript are blank for this unit.
B. Three staff officers in Heman Swift's 7th Connecticut regiment plus one chaplain for the entire brigade.
C. Three staff officers in Henry Jackson's Additional regiment plus five chaplains for all the regiments stationed in Rhode Island.
D. These figures for the artillery stationed in Rhode Island may include all the men, not just "present fit for duty," although the manuscript does not explicitly say so. They may therefore inflate a little the totals of "present fit for duty."
E. The National Archives version of the return notes that no returns for the cavalry were available and that the return of "Foreman's Regiment consisting of 1 Capt., 1 Adjut., 5 Ser-

Brigadier General Edward Hand, Adjutant General of the Continental Army, January 8, 1781–November 3, 1783. This portrait by an unknown artist seems to have been painted after the war, even though Hand is depicted in his Continental uniform. Hand, born in Ireland in 1744 and a physician by profession, should not have appeared this aged during the Revolutionary years. He died in 1802. No other portrait is known. (Courtesy of The Historical Society of Pennsylvania, Philadelphia)

DECEMBER 1778

BRIGADE	UNIT	COMMANDING OFFICER	PRESENT FIT FOR DUTY & ON DUTY: COMMISSIONED OFFICERS	NONCOMMISSIONED OFFICERS	STAFF OFFICERS	RANK & FILE	TOTAL	RANK & FILE SICK, ON FURLOUGH, ETC.: SICK PRESENT	SICK ABSENT	ON COMMAND & EXTRA SERVICE	ON FURLOUGH	GRAND TOTAL	ALTERATIONS: DEATHS	DESERTED	TAKEN PRISONER	DISCHARGED	JOINED, ENLISTED, RECRUITED	LOCATION
FORCES UNDER COMMANDER-IN-CHIEF GENERAL GEORGE WASHINGTON																		
N.C.	1st N.C.	Thomas Clark	17	38	4	296	355	30	68	110		563						New Jersey
	2nd N.C.	John Patten	11	42	5	246	304	21	41	120	4	490						New Jersey
Woodford	2nd Va. (old 2nd & 6th)	Christian Febiger	13	24	1	101	139	16	47	27	73	302						New Jersey
	3rd Va. (old 3rd & 5th)	William Heth	11	32	6	116	165	35	54	56	42	352						New Jersey
	5th Va. (old 7th)	Maj. John Webb	14	18	4	107	143	17	83	37	48	328	4					New Jersey
	7th Va. (old 11th)	Daniel Morgan	5	14	4	67	90	4	24	27	87	232						New Jersey
	11th Va. (old 15th)	Abraham Buford	5	21	3	62	91	6	30	40	119	286						New Jersey
Muhlenberg	1st Va. (old 1st & 9th)	Richard Parker	11	36	5	153	205	8	50	22	32	317	3				3	New Jersey
	1st Va. state	George Gibson	15	35	3	201	254	14	21	26	2	317	1	3			2	New Jersey
	2nd Va. state	Gregory Smith	7	26	1	118	152	39	127	33	1	352	6	3			1	New Jersey
	10th Va. (old 14th)	William Davies	8	23	3	61	95	105	95	9	73	377		2				New Jersey
Scott	4th Va. (old 4th & 8th)	John Neville	12	29	4	116	161	11	52	19	61	304	3				2	New Jersey
	Del.	David Hall	11	26	3	153	193	21	72	34	2	322	2	5			4	New Jersey
	6th Va. (old 10th)	William Russell	6	21	2	138	167	19	39	14	110	349		1			1	New Jersey
	8th Va. (old 12th)	James Wood	10	20	4	150	184	20	49	30	88	371	2	8		2	2	New Jersey
	Additional	William Grayson	3	24	4	102	133	12	20	9	7	181	4	2			1	New Jersey
Smallwood	1st Md.	John Hawkins Stone	7	22	2	155	186	11	25	128	1	351		4		1	4	New Jersey
	3rd Md.	Mordecai Gist	10	37	5	289	341	19	71	104	3	538	2	9			3	New Jersey
	5th Md.	William Richardson	6	24	3	114	147	12	86	121	4	370	5	1			5	New Jersey
	7th Md.	John Gunby	13	28	4	168	213	8	47	147	1	416	1				1	New Jersey
2nd Md.	2nd Md.	Thomas Price	9	41	3	305	358	39	78	50	4	529	6			3		New Jersey
	4th Md.	Josias Carvil Hall	6	33	4	263	306	9	36	150	1	502		5			1	New Jersey
	6th Md.	Otho Holland Williams	6	28	4	239	277	23	50	34	22	406						New Jersey
Wayne	1st Pa.	James Chambers	8	30	6	186	230	13	20	67	6	336		4		1	18	New Jersey
	2nd Pa.	Walter Stewart	11	43	2	321	377	20	53	26	2	478	2	4			1	New Jersey
	7th Pa.	William Irvine	11	26	5	166	208	18	7	12		245	1	4			14	New Jersey
	10th Pa.	Richard Humpton	11	40	5	242	298	11	23	48	3	383		1			18	New Jersey
2nd Pa.	3rd Pa.	Thomas Craig	7	46	4	240	297	22	38	43	9	409		2			2	New Jersey
	5th Pa.	Francis Johnston	7	29	3	197	236	22	30	33	2	323		1			7	New Jersey
	6th Pa.	Robert Magaw	11	36	2	152	201	18	25	31	2	277	1				1	New Jersey
	9th Pa.	Richard Butler	6	27	4	154	191	9	21	19	2	242		2			7	New Jersey
Maxwell	1st N.J.	Matthias Ogden	14	26	5	295	340	51	48	63	16	518	4	4		1	7	New Jersey
	2nd N.J.	Israel Shreve	11	30	3	309	353	26	9	15	45	448	2	3			5	New Jersey
	3rd N.J.	Elias Dayton	14	36	4	345	399	23	27	14	11	474		2			1	New Jersey
	4th N.J.	Ephraim Martin	12	30	5	232	279	26	6	12	9	332		2			3	New Jersey
	Additional	David Forman [B]	1	6	1	28	36	11	6	17		70						New Jersey
	Additional	Oliver Spencer [B]																New Jersey
Northern dept.	1st N.Y.	Goose Van Schaick	17	36	3	245	301	27	77	27	3	435	3	2			2	Fort Schuyler, N.Y.
	3rd N.Y.	Peter Gansevoort	22	40	5	343	410	24	7	8	6	455				2	5	Albany, N.Y.
	4th N.Y.	Henry Beekman Livingston	11	29	2	233	275	11	46	30	4	366	2	5		1	7	Canajoharie, N.Y.
	5th N.Y.	Lewis DuBois	10	38	1	175	224	14	34	59	5	336	1	7			3	Schoharie, N.Y.
	4th Pa. [A]	Lt. Col. William Butler	14	33	5	131	183	8	41	9		241				2		Schoharie, N.Y.
	Rifle corps [A]	Maj. Thomas Posey																Schoharie, N.Y.
	Additional	Seth Warner	13	25	4	91	133	6	9	11	3	162						Fort Stark, Vt.
	Whitcomb's rangers	Maj. Benjamin Whitcomb	7	13		45	65	1	7		1	74						Rutland, Vt.
	7th Mass.	(late) Ichabod Alden	22	43	4	195	264	21	6	55	3	349	2	1		4		Cherry Valley, N.Y.
	Additional	William Malcolm	10	17	3	77	107	13	12	38	6	176		1			1	Haverstraw, N.Y.
	Patton's additional	(late) Lt. Col. John Parke	7	21		55	83	16	7	18	3	127					1	Haverstraw, N.Y.

DECEMBER 1778 (continued)

BRIGADE	UNIT	COMMANDING OFFICER	PRESENT FIT FOR DUTY & ON DUTY: COMMISSIONED OFFICERS	NONCOMMISSIONED OFFICERS	STAFF OFFICERS	RANK & FILE	TOTAL	RANK & FILE SICK, ON FURLOUGH, ETC.: SICK PRESENT	SICK ABSENT	ON COMMAND & EXTRA SERVICE	ON FURLOUGH	GRAND TOTAL	ALTERATIONS: DEATHS	DESERTED	TAKEN PRISONER	DISCHARGED	JOINED, ENLISTED, RECRUITED	LOCATION
	FORCES UNDER COMMANDER-IN-CHIEF GENERAL GEORGE WASHINGTON (continued)																	
Nixon	3rd Mass.	John Greaton	11	40	3	274	328	19	23	13	6	389						The Highlands, N.Y.
	5th Mass.	Rufus Putnam	17	42	4	394	457	37	15	20	8	537	4	20		4	9	The Highlands, N.Y.
	6th Mass.	Thomas Nixon	11	41	3	304	359	23	23	60	8	473						The Highlands, N.Y.
	Mass. militia	Ezra Wood	10	32	2	139	183	13	18	153	6	373						The Highlands, N.Y.
Paterson	12th Mass.	(late) Samuel Brewer	11	31	4	248	294	14	39	43	33	423		6			3	The Highlands, N.Y.
	10th Mass.	Thomas Marshall	11	26	4	202	243	20	37	58	30	388	2			3		The Highlands, N.Y.
	14th Mass.	Gamaliel Bradford	11	21	2	237	271	11	28	42	31	383		1				The Highlands, N.Y.
	11th Mass.	Benjamin Tupper	10	27	2	258	297	15	53	27	28	420	1				1	The Highlands, N.Y.
(late) Learned	2nd Mass.	John Bailey	11	28	1	236	276	11	52	53	34	426	2	6		7	20	The Highlands, N.Y.
	8th Mass.	Michael Jackson	10	28	2	214	254	16	34	74	22	400	3	10		10	12	The Highlands, N.Y.
	9th Mass.	James Wesson	10	30	2	220	262	15	32	74	32	415	1	12		4	29	The Highlands, N.Y.
	Mass. militia	Thomas Poor	14	37		220	271	8	37	65	2	383	2	7			2	The Highlands, N.Y.
Putnam's div.	3rd Conn.	Samuel Wyllys	12	33	3	307	355	45	70	90	10	570	2	1			2	Reading, Conn.
	4th Conn.	John Durkee	12	36	3	162	213	12	43	41	2	311	1	5		1	1	Reading, Conn.
	6th Conn.	Return Jonathan Meigs	14	35	3	353	405	42	58	98	17	620	1	6		1	1	Reading, Conn.
	8th Conn.	Giles Russell	9	30	2	150	191	37	43	42	23	336	2	3			5	Reading, Conn.
	1st Conn.	Josiah Starr	14	32	3	224	273	16	57	58	17	421	1	2				Reading, Conn.
	2nd Conn.	Zebulon Butler	11	35	5	171	222	6	30	28	8	294				1	3	Reading, Conn.
	5th Conn.	Philip Burr Bradley	14	30	3	212	259	19	32	55	2	367	2	1		1	3	Reading, Conn.
	7th Conn.	Heman Swift	16	37	4	236	293	12	32	58	3	398	1	2				Reading, Conn.
	2nd Canadian	Moses Hazen	13	46	2	321	382	25	48	20	20	495	1	8			3	Reading, Conn.
	1st N.H.	Joseph Cilley	9	19	2	270	300	26	58	19	21	424	5	3			1	Reading, Conn.
	2nd N.H.	Lt. Col. George Reid	8	20	2	187	217	27	32	22	20	318	1	8			1	Reading, Conn.
	3rd N.H.	Alexander Scammell	9	19	4	164	196	23	43	14	20	296	1	5			2	Reading, Conn.
	1st Canadian	James Livingston	14	23	4	91	132	24	11	19	5	191					1	Rhode Island
	Additional	Henry Sherburne	13	28	4	172	217	18	1	32	18	286					1	Rhode Island
	Additional	Samuel Blatchley Webb	11	22	1	141	175	33	12	45	24	289						Rhode Island
	2nd R.I.	Israel Angell	11	32	3	225	271	14	10	57	27	379		2				Rhode Island
	4th Mass.	William Shepard	18	42	3	190	253	17	18	60	8	356	2	3		1	6	Rhode Island
	13th Mass.	Edward Wigglesworth	16	34	4	163	217	18	13	79	25	352					1	Rhode Island
	15th Mass.	Timothy Bigelow	14	24	2	162	202	11	31	62	5	311		2			1	Rhode Island
	1st Mass.	Joseph Vose	17	33	2	183	235	22	33	53	17	360		2				Rhode Island
	1st R.I.	Christopher Greene	16	38	2	143	199	8	5	2	1	215	1				2	Rhode Island
	Mass. militia	Nathaniel Wade	30	67	4	447	548	24	31	61	5	669				9		Rhode Island
	N.H. state	Lt. Col. Stephen Peabody	15	30	5	196	246	7	12	12	5	282						Rhode Island
	2nd R.I. state	Archibald Crary	13	42	4	238	297	8	15	99	7	426		3		3	1	Rhode Island
	Mass. militia	John Jacobs	31	75	3	562	671	7	24	21	4	727		2		9	3	Rhode Island
	1st R.I. state	John Topham	11	35	3	272	321	5	8	144	23	501		4			8	Rhode Island
	Lee's additional	Lt. Col. William Stephens Smith	6	26	1	113	146	6	6	9	9	176						Rhode Island
	Additional	David Henley	6	10		62	78	5	3	27	3	116		4				Rhode Island
	Additional	Henry Jackson	5	20	2	103	130	10	12	36	5	193		2			1	Rhode Island
	TOTAL OF INFANTRY		998	2678	269	17343	21288	1639	3006	4047	1520	31500	93	E 218		71	256	

BRIGADE

DECEMBER 1778
(continued)

UNIT	COMMANDING OFFICER	PRESENT FIT FOR DUTY & ON DUTY: COMMISSIONED OFFICERS	NONCOMMISSIONED OFFICERS	STAFF OFFICERS	RANK & FILE	TOTAL	RANK & FILE SICK, ON FURLOUGH, ETC.: SICK PRESENT	SICK ABSENT	ON COMMAND & EXTRA SERVICE	ON FURLOUGH	GRAND TOTAL	ALTERATIONS: DEATHS	DESERTED	TAKEN PRISONER	DISCHARGED	JOINED, ENLISTED, RECRUITED	LOCATION
FORCES UNDER COMMANDER-IN-CHIEF GENERAL GEORGE WASHINGTON (continued)																	
ARTILLERY																	
4 cos. 3rd cont'l.	John Crane	8	54	2	59	123						F					New Jersey
7 cos. 2nd cont'l.	John Lamb	19	81	1	104	205	21	37	54	21	808						New Jersey
11 cos. 1st cont'l. B	Charles Harrison	26	133	4	184	347											New Jersey
3 independent cos.																	
Det. 1st & 3rd cont'l.	(John Crane & Charles Harrison)	11	38		72	121 C					121						Providence, R.I.
R.I. state	Robert Elliot	13	38	2	263	316 C					316						Rhode Island
TOTAL OF ARTILLERY		77	344	9	682	1112	21	37	54	21	1245						
ARTIFICERS																	
Artificer corps		34	119	3	510	666 C					666						
TOTAL OF WASHINGTON'S ARMY		1109	3141	281	18535	23066	1660	3043	4101	1541	33411 D						

OFFICERS SICK, ON FURLOUGH, ETC.	WASHINGTON'S INFANTRY & ARTILLERY (EXCLUDING ARTILLERY IN RHODE ISLAND): COMMISSIONED	NONCOMMISSIONED	STAFF	TOTAL
Sick Present	49	103	1	153
Sick Absent	74	207	9	290
On Furlough	427	312	66	805
Recruiting	40	17		57
On Command	260	337	13	610
On the Staff	52			52
Prisoners of War	60		2	62
In Arrest	5		1	6
TOTAL	967	976	92	2035

SOURCE OF THIS REPORT

1. MONTHLY RETURN OF THE CONTINENTAL ARMY UNDER THE COMMAND OF HIS EXCELLENCY GEORGE WASHINGTON...FOR DECEMBER 1778, ELEPHANT FOLIO OF WASHINGTON RETURNS, WILLIAM L. CLEMENTS LIBRARY. [THE ARTILLERY SECTION APPEARS ON THE PRECEDING PAGE OF THE FOLIO; THE ARTIFICERS ARE INCLUDED ONLY ON THE NATIONAL ARCHIVES MANUSCRIPT LISTED BELOW.]

1a. Monthly Return of the Continental Troops under...Washington... for the Month of December 1778, Record Group 93, National Archives. [Although the heading on this manuscript of the return differs slightly, this contains the same figures as the above, but only to the brigade level.]

A. No figures are entered on the manuscript for this unit because this corps was composed of detachments from various other regiments, and the men are therefore already included with their regiments as "on command." The National Archives manuscript notes that ninety-eight of those entered as rank and file on command and officers "in proportion" were serving in this unit at Schoharie. Washington at this time wanted to disband this corps.

B. All columns on the manuscript are blank for this unit.

C. The figures for the artillery stationed in Rhode Island and for the artificers may include all the men, not just "present fit for duty," although the manuscript does not explicitly say so. They may therefore inflate a little the totals of "present fit for duty."

D. The National Archives version of the return notes that no returns were received for December for the cavalry, for Pulaski's Legion, for the artillery attached to the divisions commanded by Generals Putnam and McDougall and attached to Clinton's Brigade and at Fort Schuyler, for the troops at Fort Pitt, for Van Cortlandt's 2nd New York, Spencer's Additional, Hartley's Additional and Proctor's artillery regiments, and for Armand's Corps.

E. The manuscript includes no figures in any of the alterations columns for a few units, probably because they were not available. These totals may therefore be a little less than the actual totals. The reader is cautioned that, in subsequent reports, there are also areas containing no alterations figures and that, therefore, the totals of alterations are sometimes partial. This matter can be noted by careful observation of the reports and generally has not been footnoted.

F. The alterations section for the artillery is blank on both manuscripts.

The Commander in Chief as depicted by Pierre Eugène du Simitière on February 1, 1779. About this time he also posed for the more famous portrait that is reproduced as the next illustration. That portrait, Charles Willson Peale's *George Washington at Princeton*, had been commissioned by the Supreme Executive Council of the state of Pennsylvania, and Washington sat for both artists during a visit to Philadelphia.

JANUARY 1779

BRIGADE	UNIT	COMMANDING OFFICER	PRESENT FIT FOR DUTY & ON DUTY: COMMISSIONED OFFICERS	NONCOMMISSIONED OFFICERS	STAFF OFFICERS	RANK & FILE	TOTAL	RANK & FILE SICK, ON FURLOUGH, ETC.: SICK PRESENT	SICK ABSENT	ON COMMAND & EXTRA SERVICE	ON FURLOUGH	CONFINED	GRAND TOTAL	ALTERATIONS: DEATHS	DESERTED	TAKEN PRISONER	DISCHARGED	JOINED, ENLISTED, RECRUITED	LOCATION
FORCES UNDER COMMANDER-IN-CHIEF GENERAL GEORGE WASHINGTON																			
N.C.	1st N.C.	Thomas Clark	17	37	4	298	356	36	49	107	1		549	2					New Jersey
	2nd N.C.	John Patten	13	38	5	250	306	34	28	110	5		483						New Jersey
Woodford	2nd Va.	Christian Febiger	10	13	2	102	127	11	29	43	82		292					4	New Jersey
	3rd Va.	William Heth	10	19	4	110	143	28	34	46	70		321	5	5		7		New Jersey
	5th Va.	Maj. John Webb	6	9	3	105	123	28	45	32	78		306	1				2	New Jersey
	7th Va.	Daniel Morgan	2	10	4	43	59	5	13	39	112		228	1			3	10	New Jersey
	11th Va.	Abraham Buford	4	15	3	74	96	13	25	21	125		280		1			3	New Jersey
Muhlenberg	1st Va.	Richard Parker	9	33	5	100	147	30	35	52	39		303	2			6	1	New Jersey
	1st Va. state	George Gibson	14	35	4	159	212	34	10	54	1		311	1	1				New Jersey
	2nd Va. state	Gregory Smith	6	26	1	118	151	62	74	39			326	17					New Jersey
	10th Va.	William Davies	7	18	5	88	118	66	58	25	88		355	14					New Jersey
Scott	4th Va.	John Neville	6	25	4	109	144	18	32	32	66		292	4	2			4	New Jersey
	Del.	David Hall	6	26	3	142	177	22	42	38	30		309	6			3	1	New Jersey
	6th Va.	William Russell	9	25	2	112	148	19	17	34	133		351	1	2		1	1	New Jersey
	8th Va.	James Wood	9	12	4	131	156	20	26	35	120		357	4	1		1	4	New Jersey
	Additional	William Grayson	1	18	4	82	105	11	12	20	21		169	3			1		New Jersey
Smallwood	1st Md.	John Hawkins Stone	4	17	4	141	166	21	24	108	28		347	2				5	New Jersey
	3rd Md.	(late) Mordecai Gist	4	30	4	306	344	41	38	77	31		531	5	3		18	26	New Jersey
	5th Md.	William Richardson	6	25	3 C	135	169	24	57	84	33		367	3	3		1	13	New Jersey
	7th Md.	John Gunby	8	35	2	246	291	24	33	43	15		406	2	10		5	6	New Jersey
2nd Md.	2nd Md.	Thomas Price	5	38	3	300	346	43	46	53	9		497	4	17		8	5	New Jersey
	4th Md.	Josias Carvil Hall	7	30	3	246	286	22	28	155	5		496	2	3		1	3	New Jersey
	6th Md.	Otho Holland Williams	5	26	2	231	264	18	48	43	23		396	3	3		1	2	New Jersey
Wayne	1st Pa.	James Chambers	8	28	4	154	194	14	6	69	22		305	2	1			34	New Jersey
	2nd Pa.	Walter Stewart	9	34	2	253	298	43	36	59	36		472	1	1			7	New Jersey
	7th Pa.	William Irvine	10	23	4	145	182	8	7	33	18		248					8	New Jersey
	10th Pa.	Richard Humpton	7	31	4	196	238	14	21	61	36		370		1			2	New Jersey
2nd Pa.	3rd Pa.	Thomas Craig	7	33	2	210	252	20	32	61	35		400	1	1			9	New Jersey
	5th Pa.	Francis Johnston	5	26	2	194	227	17	20	38	24		326	1				10	New Jersey
	6th Pa.	Robert Magaw	4	31	2	132	169	14	22	43	16		264	3	2			8	New Jersey
	9th Pa.	Richard Butler	6	24	4	133	167	19	14	31	21		252	2			1	19	New Jersey
Maxwell	1st N.J.	Matthias Ogden	13	28	5	302	348	54	56	31	19		508	1	9		1		New Jersey
	2nd N.J.	Israel Shreve	12	30	3	306	351	23	9	14	49		446	1	6		1	5	New Jersey
	3rd N.J.	Elias Dayton	12	37	5	264	318	20	15	4	18		375		4			5	New Jersey
	4th N.J.	Ephraim Martin	15	33	4	227	279	22	6	9	13		329		8		2	2	New Jersey
	Additional	William Malcolm	11	18	3	68	100	17	9	44	6		176						Haverstraw, N.Y.
	Patton's additional	(late) Lt. Col. John Parke	6	17		40	63	28	6	18	7		122						Haverstraw, N.Y.
Hand	2nd N.Y.	Philip Van Cortlandt	14	32	3	252	301	14	38	13	36		402		1		5	4	Rochester, N.Y.
	Pa. independent co.	Capt. John Paul Schott	3	6		28	37	3	3	5			48						Neversink, N.Y.
	Independent corps	Tuffin Charles Armand	7	24	4	81	116		1	7			124		6				Upper Smithfield, Pa.
	Additional	Oliver Spencer	8	14	3	96	121	3	7	8	10		149					7	Minisink (N.Y. or N.J.)
	Infantry, Pulaski's legion	Brig. Gen. Casimer Pulaski	6	8		120	134	10		5			149						Minisink (N.Y. or N.J.)
Clinton–Northern dept.	1st N.Y.	Goose Van Schaick	12	38	1	240	291	27	72	31	9		430	3				6	Fort Schuyler, N.Y.
	4th N.Y.	Lt. Col. Pierre Regnier de Roussi	14	30	2	221	267	34	43	18	3		365	1	4			2	Fort Plank, N.Y.
	7th Mass.	(late) Ichabod Alden	11	35	3	197	246	17	9	50	5		327				5	1	Cherry Valley, N.Y.
	5th N.Y.	Lewis DuBois	5	41	1	146	193	31	29	75	4		332	1	1		1	2	Schoharie, N.Y.
	4th Pa.A	Lt. Col. William Butler	21	48	6	227	302	20	44	21	3		390		4				Schoharie, N.Y.
	Additional	Seth Warner	11	23	2	75	111	3	5	36	2		157		1				Fort Stark, Vt.
	3rd N.Y.	Peter Gansevoort	16	29	6 D	250	301	25	7	18	15		266						

BRIGADE	UNIT	COMMANDING OFFICER	PRESENT FIT FOR DUTY & ON DUTY: COMMISSIONED OFFICERS	NONCOMMISSIONED OFFICERS	STAFF OFFICERS	RANK & FILE	TOTAL	RANK & FILE SICK, ON FURLOUGH, ETC.: SICK PRESENT	SICK ABSENT	ON COMMAND & EXTRA SERVICE	ON FURLOUGH	CONFINED			GRAND TOTAL	ALTERATIONS: DEATHS	DESERTED	TAKEN PRISONER	DISCHARGED	JOINED, ENLISTED, RECRUITED	LOCATION
JANUARY 1779 (continued)																					
FORCES UNDER COMMANDER-IN-CHIEF GENERAL GEORGE WASHINGTON (continued)																					
Nixon	3rd Mass.	John Greaton	9	39	5	244	297	25	11	24	23				380		8			1	The Highlands, N.Y.
	5th Mass.	Rufus Putnam	17	36	3	375	431	21	4	48	20				524		4		10	1	The Highlands, N.Y.
	6th Mass.	Thomas Nixon	10	25	2	269	306	54	16	82	15				473		6		2	27	The Highlands, N.Y.
	Mass. militia	Ezra Wood	16	36	4	222	278	20	17	18	8				341		22		15	9	The Highlands, N.Y.
	Mass. militia	Thomas Poor	15	39	3	220	277	56	17	28	5				383	2	1				The Highlands, N.Y.
Paterson	12th Mass.	(late) Samuel Brewer	13	33	4	187	237	20	27	88	26				398	1	12		17	3	The Highlands, N.Y.
	10th Mass.	Thomas Marshall	8	30	3	183	224	28	24	80	27				383	2	2		2	2	The Highlands, N.Y.
	14th Mass.	Gamaliel Bradford	9	24	3	193	229	20	18	81	28				376	1	7		1	2	The Highlands, N.Y.
	11th Mass.	Benjamin Tupper	12	24	2	197	235	27	40	86	27				415	3	1				The Highlands, N.Y.
(late) Learned	2nd Mass.	John Bailey	7	25	2	142	176	15	33	149	35				408	2	3		2		The Highlands, N.Y.
	8th Mass.	Michael Jackson	11	28	2	177	218	20	23	113	20				394		5		2		The Highlands, N.Y.
	9th Mass.	James Wesson	10	26	3	156	195	15	24	147	34				415	2	5		2	4	The Highlands, N.Y.
Putnam's div.	3rd Conn.	Samuel Wyllys	8	18	3	146	175	36	56	132	60				459	1	4		86	1	Reading, Conn.
	4th Conn.	John Durkee	9	26	3	77	115	16	40	67	32				270	1	1		27	1	Reading, Conn.
	6th Conn.	Return Jonathan Meigs	9	27	2	228	266	23	50	139	66				544	1	1		60		Reading, Conn.
	8th Conn.	Giles Russell	12	27	3	123	165	29	40	63	23				320		4		10		Reading, Conn.
	1st Conn.	Josiah Starr	6	26	4	189	225	17	69	79	13				403	2	1		4	1	Reading, Conn.
	2nd Conn.	Zebulon Butler	6	16	4	114	140	8	46	47	24				265	1			4	1	Reading, Conn.
	5th Conn.	Philip Burr Bradley	8	30	3	156	197	23	27	89	21				357		1				Reading, Conn.
	7th Conn.	Heman Swift	8	22	3	187	220	4	35	88	24				371		1		3	1	Reading, Conn.
	2nd Canadian	Moses Hazen	13	42	2	291	348	23	37	64	13				485	1	10			7	Reading, Conn.
	1st N.H.	Joseph Cilley	6	16	4	243	269	24	52	52	24				421		4			3	Reading, Conn.
	2nd N.H.	Lt. Col. George Reid	6	16	3	166	191	25	29	36	20				301	3	10			1	Reading, Conn.
	3rd N.H.	Alexander Scammell	5	20	2	144	171	15	40	42	20				288	2					Reading, Conn.
	German bn.	Lt. Col. Ludowick Weltner	14	30	5	221	270	12	15	38	53				388	1	2		1	3	Easton, Pa.
Sullivan's div.	1st Canadian	James Livingston	10	20	2	77	109	10	17	29	14				179	2	3		1	4	Rhode Island
	Additional	Samuel Blatchley Webb	12	23	2	166	203	15	10	25	35				288				3	2	Rhode Island
	Additional	Henry Sherburne	15	23	2	172	212	8	1	37	15				273		3		5		Rhode Island
	2nd R.I.	Israel Angell	13	32	3	221	269	13	11	49	37				379		2				Rhode Island
	4th Mass.	William Shepard	12	32	2	155	201	16	14	98	19				348		1		3	13	Rhode Island
	13th Mass.	Edward Wigglesworth	12	24	5	137	178	14	11	97	40				340				1	2	Rhode Island
	15th Mass.	Timothy Bigelow	11	23	3	129	166	11	29	85	19				310	1	1			4	Rhode Island
	1st Mass.	Joseph Vose	14	27	3	162	206	16	31	74	19				346	2	2				Rhode Island
	2nd R.I. state	Archibald Crary	18	37	3	195	253	2	11	149	8				423		4			2	Rhode Island
	1st R.I. state	John Topham	13	31	7	197	248	5	6	222	14				495		3		4	1	Rhode Island
	1st R.I.	Christopher Greene	16	34	1	138	189	11	1	2	6				209	1					Rhode Island
	Lee's additional	Lt. Col. William Stephens Smith	5	19	1	67	92	3	5	56	17				173		3			1	Rhode Island
	Additional	David Henley	3	8		31	42	7	3	49	11				112					2	Rhode Island
	Additional	Henry Jackson	3	19	1	69	92	6	8	61	19				186	1	2			1	Rhode Island
	TOTAL OF INFANTRY		825	2314	265	14951	18355	1843	2268	5005	2456				29927	132	241		337	326	

JANUARY 1779 (continued)

BRIGADE	UNIT	COMMANDING OFFICER	PRESENT FIT FOR DUTY & ON DUTY: COMMISSIONED OFFICERS	NONCOMMISSIONED OFFICERS	STAFF OFFICERS	RANK & FILE	TOTAL	RANK & FILE SICK, ON FURLOUGH, ETC.: SICK PRESENT	SICK ABSENT	ON COMMAND & EXTRA SERVICE	ON FURLOUGH	CONFINED	GRAND TOTAL	ALTERATIONS: DEATHS	DESERTED	TAKEN PRISONER	DISCHARGED	JOINED, ENLISTED, RECRUITED	LOCATION
	FORCES UNDER COMMANDER-IN-CHIEF GENERAL GEORGE WASHINGTON (continued)																		
	CAVALRY																		
	2nd cont'l.	Elisha Sheldon	14	45	5	62	126	6	5	25	58		220				4	2	Durham, Conn.
	3rd cont'l.	George Baylor	5	9	3	89	106	4	13	26	14		163						Frederick, Md.
	4th cont'l.	Stephen Moylan	9	32	5	91	137	11	6	25	7	10	196						Lancaster, Pa.
	Marechaussie	Capt. Bartholomew Von Heer	3	9		33	45	8					53						Somerset Court House, N.J.
	TOTAL OF CAVALRY		31	95	13	275	414	29	24	76	79	10	632				4	2	
	ARTILLERY IN RHODE ISLAND																		
	2 cos. 3rd cont'l.	John Crane	8	35	1	43	87	1	3	3	3		97						Rhode Island
	1 co. 1st cont'l.	Charles Harrison	2	10		18	30						30						Rhode Island
	R.I. state	Robert Elliot	9	39	2	125	175		10	117	10		312						Rhode Island
	TOTAL OF ARTILLERY IN RHODE ISLAND		19	84	3	186	292	1	13	120	13		439						
	ARTIFICERS																		
	Artificers at Middle Brook		9	16		138 E	163	2	5	3	6		179				2	3	Middlebrook, N.J.
	TOTAL OF WASHINGTON'S ARMY		884	2509	281	15550	19224	1875	2310	5204	2554	10	31177	132	241		343	331	
	SOUTHERN DEPARTMENT UNDER MAJOR GENERAL BENJAMIN LINCOLN (Partial Report)																		
Huger	1st S.C.	Charles Cotesworth Pinckney	20	33	5	129	187	13	16		6	2	224		3				Purysburg, S.C.
Huger	3rd S.C. (rangers)	William Thompson	11	28	3	187	229	22	24	19	21		315	1	25	100			Purysburg, S.C.
Huger	5th S.C. (rifles)	Isaac Huger	4	19		99	122		19	36			177		4	59	1		Purysburg, S.C.
Huger	6th S.C. (rifles)	Lt. Col. William Henderson	11	29	4	129	173	11	18	2	8		212		3				Purysburg, S.C.
	TOTAL OF HUGER'S BRIGADE		46	109	12	544	711	46	77 G	57	35	2	928	1	35	159	1		
Williamson	Ga. cont'l. troops	Samuel Elbert					100						100						opposite Augusta, in S.C.
Williamson	S.C. independents						50						50						opposite Augusta, in S.C.
Williamson	Light troops B	Lt. Col. Archibald Lytle					250						250						opposite Augusta, in S.C.
Williamson	S.C. militia						370						370						opposite Augusta, in S.C.
Williamson	Ga. militia						100						100						opposite Augusta, in S.C.
Rutherford	N.C. new levies	Jethro Sumner					370						370						Purysburg, S.C.
Rutherford	N.C. militia	James Sanders					70						70						Purysburg, S.C.
Rutherford	N.C. militia	Francis Locke					120						120						Purysburg, S.C.
	TOTAL OF LINCOLN'S INFANTRY						2141						2358						
	GRAND TOTAL						21365 F						33535 H	133 I	276	159	344	331	

OFFICERS SICK, ON FURLOUGH, ETC.	WASHINGTON'S ARMY (EXCEPT CAVALRY)				SOUTHERN DEPARTMENT (HUGER'S BRIGADE ONLY)				GRAND TOTAL
	COMMISSIONED	NONCOMMISSIONED	STAFF	TOTAL	COMMISSIONED	NONCOMMISSIONED	STAFF	TOTAL	
Sick Present	60	137	2	199		3 G		3	202
Sick Absent	61	160	5	226		5		5	231
On Furlough	499	527	105	1131					1131
Recruiting	27	9		36	16			16	52
On Command	285	394	21	700	5	1		6	706
On the Staff	96			96					96
Prisoners of War	55	3	2	60	7			7	67
In Arrest	2		1	3					3
On Parole	1	1		2	2			2	4
Absent J					8		1	9	9
TOTAL	1086	1231	136	2453	38	9	1	48	2501

SOURCES OF THIS REPORT

1. MONTHLY RETURN OF THE CONTINENTAL ARMY UNDER THE COMMAND OF HIS EXCELLENCY GEORGE WASHINGTON... FOR JANUARY 1779, ELEPHANT FOLIO OF WASHINGTON RETURNS, WILLIAM L. CLEMENTS LIBRARY. [ARTILLERY AND CAVALRY APPEAR ON THE PRECEDING PAGE OF THE FOLIO.]
   1a. Monthly Return of the Continental Army under... Washington... for January 1779, Record Group 93, National Archives. [Contains the same figures as the above except that it does not include the artificers and is to the brigade level only.]

2. MONTHLY RETURN OF THE FIRST BRIGADE OF THE CONTINENTAL OF SOUTH CAROLINA COMMANDED BY COLONEL HUGER, FEBRUARY 1, 1779, BENJAMIN LINCOLN PAPERS, MASSACHUSETTS HISTORICAL SOCIETY.

3. A RETURN OF THE SOLDIERS FIT FOR DUTY AND CARTRIDGES NOW IN CAMP IN GENL. RUTHERFORD'S BRIGADE, JANUARY 31, 1779, BENJAMIN LINCOLN PAPERS, MASSACHUSETTS HISTORICAL SOCIETY.

4. REPORT OF THE TROOPS UNDER THE COMMAND OF BRIGADIER GENERAL WILLIAMSON, FEBRUARY 1, 1779, BENJAMIN LINCOLN PAPERS, MASSACHUSETTS HISTORICAL SOCIETY.

A. The National Archives version of the manuscript notes that these figures for Lieutenant Colonel William Butler's 4th Pennsylvania regiment include the small "rifle corps" composed of men detached from other regiments that is discussed in footnote A on the December 1778 report. The note refers to these men as "heretofore returned on Command," but from a later return (see footnote K on our March 1779 report), it would appear that these men also still were being included in the "on command" column of their nominal regiments and are therefore included twice.

B. The manuscript notes that these light troops include "Col. McIntosh's" (probably John McIntosh of Georgia).

C. One staff officer in John Gunby's 7th Maryland regiment plus one chaplain for the entire brigade.

D. Five staff officers in Peter Gansevoort's 3rd New York regiment plus one chaplain for the entire Northern Department.

E. Including fourteen smiths and carpenters that are termed "draughted" on the manuscript.

F. Since the returns for Williamson's and Rutherford's brigades give only a total figure, we have brought only the total figures down to the Grand Total line.

G. Of the seventy-seven rank and file in Huger's brigade included in "sick absent," fifty-four are actually marked "sick in hospital" on the manuscript. The five "sick absent" officers in the brigade are also marked "sick in hospital" on the manuscript. See footnote C on our August 1775 report.

H. The National Archives version of the Washington return notes that no monthly returns were available for the artillery stationed at Pluckemin, New Jersey, or at Philadelphia, for Bland's 1st Continental cavalry, for Lee's Partizan Corps at Burlington, for the Southern Department (partially supplied here on our report), for the troops at Fort Pitt, and for Hartley's Additional and the 3rd North Carolina regiments. It is noted also that Whitcomb's Rangers had deserted their post at Rutland, Vermont and had gone home and that several companies of Gansevoort's 3rd New York regiment at an advanced post are omitted in the return.

I. It will be noted that no alterations are available for a portion of our partial return of the Southern Department and these totals are accordingly smaller than they otherwise would be.

J. Officers simply marked "absent," with no further explanation on the manuscript.

FEBRUARY 1779

Brigade	Unit	Commanding Officer	Present Fit for Duty & on Duty: Commissioned Officers	Noncommissioned Officers	Staff Officers	Rank & File	Total	Rank & File Sick, on Furlough, etc.: Sick Present	Sick Absent	On Command & Extra Service	On Furlough	Confined	Recruiting	Grand Total	Alterations: Deaths	Deserted	Taken Prisoner	Discharged	Joined, Enlisted, Recruited	Location
FORCES UNDER COMMANDER-IN-CHIEF GENERAL GEORGE WASHINGTON																				
N.C.	1st N.C.	Thomas Clark	18	38	4	302	362	28	35	125	1			551		2			3	New Jersey
N.C.	2nd N.C.	John Patten	12	39	5	223	279	44	16	127	7			473	10	3			3	New Jersey
Woodford	2nd Va.	Christian Febiger	10	14	3	72	99	17	14	38	84			252	1			36		New Jersey
Woodford	3rd Va.	William Heth	8	18	4	53	83	20	16	33	68			220	3			96	2	New Jersey
Woodford	5th Va.	William Russell	6	9	4	42	61	8	9	17	76			171	1			136	2	New Jersey
Woodford	7th Va.	Daniel Morgan	4	9	3	40	56	3	10	38	114			221				5		New Jersey
Woodford	11th Va.	Abraham Buford	3	16	3	64	86	5	14	19	123			247				23		New Jersey
Muhlenberg	1st Va.	Richard Parker	8	29	3	58	98	14	21	46	39			218	5			73		New Jersey
Muhlenberg	1st Va. state	George Gibson	15	43	4	162	224	28	6	50	3			311	2	1		2		New Jersey
Muhlenberg	2nd Va. state	Gregory Smith	6	33	1	145	185	57	27	52				321	8			1	2	New Jersey
Muhlenberg	10th Va.	William Davies	7	17	5	76	105	28	35	38	91			297	1			63	7	New Jersey
Scott	4th Va.	John Neville	8	13	4	68	93	8	15	25	77			218	8	3		54	1	New Jersey
Scott	Del.	David Hall	5	21	5	162	193	17	10	35	35			290	4			14	3	New Jersey
Scott	6th Va.	John Green	3	19	2	91	115	9	8	35	135			302	1	2		34	1	New Jersey
Scott	8th Va.	James Wood	6	14	4	129	153	18	17	17	126			331				23		New Jersey
Scott	Additional	William Grayson		19	4	93	116	6	6	14	24			166	4	1		2	3	New Jersey
Smallwood	1st Md.	John Hawkins Stone	4	20	4	148	176	14	19	98	30			337	2	1		19	11	New Jersey
Smallwood	3rd Md.	(late) Mordecai Gist	6	30	5	311	352	26	37	73	34			522		3		16	10	New Jersey
Smallwood	5th Md.	William Richardson	3	27	4	149	183	24	41	73	39			360	4	2		3	4	New Jersey
Smallwood	7th Md.	John Gunby	9	33	3	244	289	23	30	44	14			400	3	2		4	5	New Jersey
2nd Md.	2nd Md.	Thomas Price	7	35	3	286	331	40	37	47	14			469	10	2		12		New Jersey
2nd Md.	4th Md.	Josias Carvil Hall	7	26	3	279	315	27	33	51	22			448	2	6		36	1	New Jersey
2nd Md.	6th Md.	Otho Holland Williams	7	27	2	223	259	15	44	41	28			387	2	3		10	3	New Jersey
Wayne	1st Pa.	James Chambers	4	29	1	169	203	14	6	59	22			304	1	4		3	15	New Jersey
Wayne	2nd Pa.	Walter Stewart	9	35	4	282	330	29	22	53	35			469	1	5		2	3	New Jersey
Wayne	7th Pa.	William Irvine	6	23	4	138	171	9	4	31	27			242	2	1		1	2	New Jersey
Wayne	10th Pa.	Richard Humpton	7	30	3	202	242	5	21	61	37			366		4			4	New Jersey
2nd Pa.	3rd Pa.	Thomas Craig	8	32	4	212	256	18	29	69	26			398		1			4	New Jersey
2nd Pa.	5th Pa.	Francis Johnston	3	25	4	182	214	22	22	37	28			323	1	2			2	New Jersey
2nd Pa.	6th Pa.	Robert Magaw	5	24	2	134	165	5	20	43	23			256		1				New Jersey
2nd Pa.	9th Pa.	Richard Butler	4	26	5	137	172	18	15	26	20			251		4			5	New Jersey
Maxwell	1st N.J.	Matthias Ogden	20	48	5	413	486	43	39	8	22			598		5		18	6	New Jersey
Maxwell	2nd N.J.	Israel Shreve	18	38	5	420	481	25	5	8	40			559						New Jersey
Maxwell	3rd N.J.	Elias Dayton	18	42	6	343	409	16	13	7	22			467				3	8	New Jersey
	3rd N.C.	Lt. Col. William Lee Davidson	16	15	4	35	70	62	263	64				459	24					
Hand	2nd N.Y.	Philip Van Cortlandt	14	32	3	252	301	14	38	13	36			402						Minisink area
Hand	Independent co.	Capt. John Paul Schott	3	8		28	39	2	3	4	2			50						Minisink area
Hand	Independent corps	Tuffin Charles Armand	10	23	5	84	122		1		6			129						Minisink area
Hand	Additional	Oliver Spencer	7	16	2	95	120	5	3	4	16			148	1	4		1	2	Minisink area
McIntosh-Western dept.	8th Pa.	Daniel Brodhead	11	46	2	193	252	9	15	138	29			443		2			1	Fort Pitt, Pa.
McIntosh-Western dept.	9th Va.	John Gibson	13	36	2	191	242	9		38				289		1				Fort Pitt, Pa.
McIntosh-Western dept.	Independent co.	Capt. Samuel Moorhead	2	4		23	29							29						Fort Pitt, Pa.
McIntosh-Western dept.	Independent co.	Capt. Henry Heth	3	7		39	49	4	3	9				65		3				Fort Pitt, Pa.
McIntosh-Western dept.	Independent co.	(late) Capt. James O'Hara		5		27	32							32						Fort Pitt, Pa.
McIntosh-Western dept.	Independent co.	Capt. Thomas Ferroll	4	5		31	40	6	1	18				65						Fort Pitt, Pa.
McIntosh-Western dept.	Independent co.	Capt. John Rust	2	5		10	17	13						30						Fort Pitt, Pa.
	Additional	William Malcolm	8	18	2	76	104	11	12	41	5			173		1				Haverstraw, N.Y.
	Patton's additional	(late) Lt. Col. John Parke	7	14		53	74	11	4	21	9			119		1			2	Haverstraw, N.Y.

FEBRUARY 1779
(continued)

BRIGADE	UNIT	COMMANDING OFFICER	DUTY & ON DUTY					ON FURLOUGH, ETC.						GRAND TOTAL						LOCATION
			COMMISSIONED OFFICERS	NONCOMMISSIONED OFFICERS	STAFF OFFICERS	RANK & FILE	TOTAL	SICK PRESENT	SICK ABSENT	ON COMMAND & EXTRA SERVICE	ON FURLOUGH	CONFINED	RECRUITING		DEATHS	DESERTED	TAKEN PRISONER	DISCHARGED	JOINED, ENLISTED, RECRUITED	
	FORCES UNDER COMMANDER-IN-CHIEF GENERAL GEORGE WASHINGTON (continued)																			
Nixon	3rd Mass.	John Greaton	7	24	3	190	224	10	19	79	19			351		11		1	2	The Highlands, N. Y.
	5th Mass.	Rufus Putnam	11	25	3	267	306	5	7	158	19			495	4	9			1	The Highlands, N. Y.
	6th Mass.	Thomas Nixon	9	26	3	232	270	3	24	148	20			465	1	4		4	1	The Highlands, N. Y.
Paterson	12th Mass.	(late) Samuel Brewer	11	26	3	159	199	18	20	119	21			377		1		12	3	The Highlands, N. Y.
	10th Mass.	Thomas Marshall	8	25	2	181	216	18	14	85	23			356		6		9	2	The Highlands, N. Y.
	14th Mass.	Gamaliel Bradford	10	21	5	181	217	12	13	90	20			352	1	3		22	2	The Highlands, N. Y.
	11th Mass.	Benjamin Tupper	9	28	3	204	244	24	24	97	21			410	2	1		12	8	The Highlands, N. Y.
(late) Learned	2nd Mass.	John Bailey	8	26	2	132	168	17	37	124	28			374		4		37	1	The Highlands, N. Y.
	8th Mass.	Michael Jackson	15	24	4	164	207	.6	38	92	18			361		12		21		The Highlands, N. Y.
	9th Mass.	James Wesson	8	22	4	86	120	6	29	220	26			401	1	1		8	1	The Highlands, N. Y.
Putnam's div.	3rd Conn.	Samuel Wyllys	7	26	5	139	177	26	45	196	20			464	2	5		1	7	Reading, Conn.
	4th Conn.	John Durkee	5	29	3	80	117	5	23	104	16			265	1	2				Reading, Conn.
	6th Conn.	Return Jonathan Meigs	5	28	2	216	251	25	43	200	20			539		4		1	8	Reading, Conn.
	8th Conn.	Giles Russell	11	26	3	101	141	29	37	98	9			314		6		1	4	Reading, Conn.
	1st Conn.	Josiah Starr	7	28	3	135	173	14	64	140	5			396		10		1	2	Reading, Conn.
	2nd Conn.	Zebulon Butler	8	24	2	97	131	7	38	90	8			274		1			2	Reading, Conn.
	5th Conn.	Philip Burr Bradley	10	23	3	130	166	12	29	137	9			353		1			2	Reading, Conn.
	7th Conn.	Heman Swift	9	26	1	150	186	12	26	147	2			373		1			2	Reading, Conn.
	2nd Canadian	Moses Hazen	12	32	3	192	239	16	30	166	16			467		8			3	Reading, Conn.
	1st N.H.	Joseph Cilley	8	17	4	175	204	15	46	141	19			425	1			2	5	Reading, Conn.
	2nd N.H.	Lt. Col. George Reid	4	13	4	117	138	19	21	109	17			304					6	Reading, Conn.
	3rd N.H.	Alexander Scammell	3	15	2	109	129	6	31	102	19			287					7	Reading, Conn.
Sullivan's div.	1st Canadian	James Livingston	12	23	2	77	114	13	16	22	15			180		3			3	Rhode Island
	Additional	Henry Sherburne	15	26	4	176	221	10	1	27	14			273		7			2	Rhode Island
	Additional	Samuel Blatchley Webb	11	31	2	175	219	15	13	4	38			289	1	5			1	Rhode Island
	2nd R.I.	Israel Angell	18	30	4	254	306	9	9	14	37			375	2	4		3	1	Rhode Island
	4th Mass.	William Shepard	11	33	2	163	209	21	13	94	16			353		4		2	11	Rhode Island
	13th Mass.	Edward Wigglesworth	12	27	4	122	165	12	14	109	40			340	1					Rhode Island
	15th Mass.	Timothy Bigelow	11	20	1	106	138	7	24	107	26			302	1	1				Rhode Island
	1st Mass.	Joseph Vose	17	40	2	156	215	16	25	88	14			358		3		1	1	Rhode Island
	2nd R.I. state	Archibald Crary	19	40	5	240	304	5	9	104	7			429		3			3	Rhode Island
	1st R.I. state	John Topham	17	41	4	247	309	15	3	169	3			499		5		2	15	Rhode Island
	1st R.I.	Christopher Greene	17	35	1	134	187	8	7	3	1			206	2	5			2	Rhode Island
	Lee's additional	Lt. Col. William Stephens Smith	4	16	2	41	63	5	5	76	16			165		4		1		Rhode Island
	Additional	David Henley	4	8		29	41	11	3	50	7			112				2	2	Rhode Island
	Additional	Henry Jackson	6	19	2	44	71	10	8	74	24			187	1	2				Rhode Island
	TOTAL OF INFANTRY		723	2058	247	12590	15618	1291	1847	5671	2222			26649	122	206		833	225	
	CAVALRY																			
	2nd cont'l.	Elisha Sheldon	6	38	2	94	140	1	3	26	31			201				1	1	Durham, Conn.
	3rd cont'l.	George Baylor	5	11	1	111	128	18	3	20	16	1		186						Frederick, Md.
	4th cont'l.	Stephen Moylan	8	28	4	106	146	8	3	13	6	9		185		3				Lancaster, Pa.
	Marechaussie	Capt. Bartholomew Von Heer	4	6		36	46		1		2	3		52						New Jersey
	TOTAL OF CAVALRY		23	83	7	347	460	27	10	59	55	13		624		3		1	1	

FEBRUARY 1779 (continued)

BRIGADE UNIT	COMMANDING OFFICER	PRESENT FIT FOR DUTY & ON DUTY: COMMISSIONED OFFICERS	NONCOMMISSIONED OFFICERS	STAFF OFFICERS	RANK & FILE	TOTAL	RANK & FILE SICK, ON FURLOUGH, ETC.: SICK PRESENT	SICK ABSENT	ON COMMAND & EXTRA SERVICE	ON FURLOUGH	CONFINED	RECRUITING	GRAND TOTAL	ALTERATIONS: DEATHS	DESERTED	TAKEN PRISONER	DISCHARGED	JOINED, ENLISTED, RECRUITED	LOCATION
FORCES UNDER COMMANDER-IN-CHIEF GENERAL GEORGE WASHINGTON (continued)																			
ARTILLERY A																			
4 cos. 3rd cont'l.	John Crane	9	54	3	67	133											2		Pluckemin, N.J.
7 cos. 2nd cont'l.	John Lamb	18	75	3	91	187									1		1	7	Pluckemin, N.J.
11 cos. 1st cont'l. B	Charles Harrison	25	114	3	172	314	31	26	77	23			1227	3			1	1	Pluckemin, N.J.
3 independent cos. B																			
Det. 1st & 3rd cont'l.	(John Crane & Charles Harrison)	12	43	1	69	125									2			3	Providence, R.I.
R.I. state	Robert Elliot	10	38	2	261	311											1		Rhode Island
TOTAL OF ARTILLERY		74	324	12	660	1070	31	26	77	23			1227	3	3		5	11	
TOTAL OF WASHINGTON'S ARMY		820	2465	266	13597	17148	1349	1883	5807	2300			28500	125	212		839	237	
SOUTHERN DEPARTMENT UNDER MAJOR GENERAL BENJAMIN LINCOLN (Partial Report)																			
S.C. brig.	Brig. Gen. Isaac Huger	42	104	7	635	788	38	71	54	6			957	4	28		3	80	Purysburg, S.C.
N.C. brig. (new levies)	Brig. Gen. Jethro Sumner	40	82	10	625	757	33	11	13				814		2			64	Purysburg, S.C.
TOTAL OF INFANTRY		82	186	17	1260	1545	71	82	67	6			1771	4	30		3	144	
CAVALRY																			
Det. N.C. dragoons	Lt. Edmund Gamble	1	4	1	6	12	2		2				16						Purysburg, S.C.
Det. S.C. dragoons	Maj. Hezekiah Maham	12	20	6	100	138							138						
TOTAL OF CAVALRY		13	24	7	106	150	2		2				154						
ARTILLERY																			
4th S.C.	Owen Roberts	11	28	1	53	93		5 D	20 E			1	119		10 G				Purysburg, S.C.
TOTAL OF LINCOLN'S ARMY		106	238	25	1419	1788	73	87	89	6		1	2044	4	40		3	144	
GRAND TOTAL		926	2703	291	15016	18936	1422	1970	5896	2306	13	1	30544 F	129	252		842	381	

OFFICERS SICK, ON FURLOUGH, ETC.	WASHINGTON'S ARMY				LINCOLN'S INFANTRY & ARTILLERY H				GRAND TOTAL
	COMMISSIONED	NONCOMMISSIONED	STAFF	TOTAL	COMMISSIONED	NONCOMMISSIONED	STAFF	TOTAL	
Sick Present	30	114		144					144
Sick Absent	43	127	4	174		5 D		5	179
On Furlough	516	545	65	1126					1126
Recruiting	10	3		13	4			4	17
On Command or Detachment	329	434	20	783	3	13		16	799
On the Staff	83	1	3	87	7		11	18	105
Prisoners of War	48	2	4	54					54
In Arrest	4			4					4
TOTAL	1063	1226	96	2385	14	18	11	43	2428

SOURCES OF THIS REPORT

1. MONTHLY RETURN OF THE CONTINENTAL ARMY UNDER THE COMMAND OF HIS EXCELLENCY GEORGE WASHINGTON. . . FOR FEBRUARY 1779, ELEPHANT FOLIO OF WASHINGTON RETURNS, WILLIAM L. CLEMENTS LIBRARY. [THE ARTILLERY AND CAVALRY SECTIONS APPEAR ON THE FOLLOWING PAGES OF THE FOLIO; SEE ALSO FOOTNOTE A ON THIS REPORT.]

   1a. Monthly Return of the Continental Troops under. . . Washington. . . February 28, 1779, Record Group 93, National Archives. [Although the heading on this manuscript of the return differs slightly, this contains the same figures as the above, but only to the brigade level.]

2. RETURN OF THE TROOPS [HUGER'S AND SUMNER'S BRIGADES ONLY] UNDER THE COMMAND OF MAJ. GEN. LINCOLN, MARCH 4, 1779, BENJAMIN LINCOLN PAPERS, MASSACHUSETTS HISTORICAL SOCIETY. [THIS CONTAINS THE MONTHLY ALTERATIONS EVEN THOUGH THE HEADING DOES NOT NOTE EXPLICITLY THAT IT IS THE MONTHLY RETURN.]

3. A MONTHLY RETURN OF A DETACHMENT OF CAPT. [UNCLEAR] TROOP OF LIGHT DRAGOONS COMMANDED BY EDMD. GAMBLE, MARCH 4, 1779, BENJAMIN LINCOLN PAPERS, MASSACHUSETTS HISTORICAL SOCIETY.

4. A GENERAL RETURN OF A DETACH. OF HORSE UNDER THE COMMAND OF MJR. MAHAM, MARCH 4, 1779, BENJAMIN LINCOLN PAPERS, MASSACHUSETTS HISTORICAL SOCIETY.

5. MONTHLY RETURN OF THE SOUTH CAROLINA CONTINENTAL REGIMENT OF ARTILLERY. . . MARCH 1, 1779, BENJAMIN LINCOLN PAPERS, MASSACHUSETTS HISTORICAL SOCIETY.

A. The artillery section of this monthly return in both the Clements folio and the National Archives manuscript, though marked "monthly," also is marked "For January & February 1779." The strength figures obviously represent the end of February, when it was made out like the rest of the monthly, but the alterations probably represent the total of alterations for both months. It will be noted that no alterations for artillery appear on the January monthly.

B. All columns are blank for this unit on the Clements Library manuscript; the National Archives copy omits the unit.

C. Five staff officers in Elias Dayton's 3rd New Jersey regiment plus one chaplain for the entire brigade.

D. The five rank and file and the five noncommissioned officers in the 4th South Carolina artillery regiment that appear in "sick absent" on our report actually are marked "sick in hospital" on the manuscript. See footnote C on our August 1775 report.

E. Gunners (who were noncommissioned officers) are lumped together with matrosses (the equivalent for the artillery of rank and file) in two columns on the manuscript. Thus we are unable to extract a few noncommissioned officers included in the figure of twenty men on command and extra service who really should appear in the section of officers sick, on furlough, etc. below.

F. The National Archives manuscript notes that no monthly returns were available for Lee's Partizan Corps and Bland's 1st Continental cavalry regiment, for the troops at Boston and the Northern and Southern Departments (the last partially supplied on our report), for Weltner's German and Hartley's Additional regiments, and for fifteen companies of artillery in the Northern and Middle Departments. It also is noted that Thomas Poor's and Ezra Wood's regiments of Massachusetts militia had been discharged because their terms of service had expired.

G. This figure also includes an undetermined number of gunners, although they normally might not have been included in the alterations section of returns. See Introduction on the question of who was included in the alterations that were reported on the returns.

H. The return for the infantry of the Southern Department used here does not report on the full range of officers sick, on furlough, etc., but only on the eighteen who were on the staff.

MARCH 1779

BRIGADE	UNIT	COMMANDING OFFICER	PRESENT FIT FOR DUTY & ON DUTY: COMMISSIONED OFFICERS	NONCOMMISSIONED OFFICERS	STAFF OFFICERS	RANK & FILE	TOTAL	RANK & FILE SICK, ON FURLOUGH, ETC.: SICK PRESENT	SICK ABSENT	ON COMMAND & EXTRA SERVICE	ON FURLOUGH	CONFINED	RECRUITING	GRAND TOTAL	ALTERATIONS: DEATHS	DESERTED	TAKEN PRISONER	DISCHARGED	JOINED, ENLISTED, RECRUITED	LOCATION
		FORCES UNDER COMMANDER-IN-CHIEF GENERAL GEORGE WASHINGTON																		
N.C.	1st N.C.	Thomas Clark	14	36	4	246	300	30	26	176	1			533	8	1		3	1	New Jersey
	2nd N.C.	John Patten								398				398	15	2		2	1	The Highlands, N.Y.
Woodford	2nd Va.	Christian Febiger	9	12	3	102	126	9	10	16	85			246						New Jersey
	3rd Va.	William Heth	7	20	2	89	118	8	11	13	67			217	2	1		2	4	New Jersey
	5th Va.	William Russell	6	14	4	58	82	6	7	8	77			180					3	New Jersey
	7th Va.	Daniel Morgan	2	9	2	67	80		8	19	113			220					2	New Jersey
	11th Va.	Abraham Buford	4	15	3	69	91	4	9	19	123			246						New Jersey
Muhlenberg	1st Va.	Richard Parker	6	32	3	76	117	11	17	34	39			218		1				New Jersey
	1st Va. state	George Gibson	12	39	4	160	215	28	4	57	3			307					3	New Jersey
	2nd Va. state	Gregory Smith	12	31	4	177	224	41	20	32				317	3			8		New Jersey
	10th Va.	William Davies	7	20	5	114	146	20	20	27	88			301	2				4	New Jersey
Scott	4th Va.	John Neville	6	22	3	83	114	8	10	12	79			223	1	1		1	4	New Jersey
	Del.	David Hall	4	29	2	168	203	16	7	31	36			293				2		New Jersey
	6th Va.	John Green	6	23	4	101	134	12	8	23	134			311		1			1	New Jersey
	8th Va.	James Wood	10	19	5	132	166	16	9	29	120			340	1	1			1	New Jersey
	Additional	William Grayson	2	18	4	80	104	13	4	17	26			164		2		2	1	New Jersey
Smallwood	1st Md.	John Hawkins Stone	7	28	4	199	238	13	16	33	35			335	1	7		9	8	New Jersey
	3rd Md.	(late) Mordecai Gist	6	26	3	328	363	36	21	48	37			505	2	3		10	4	New Jersey
	5th Md.	William Richardson	2	28	4	163	197	22	36	25	45			325		10		27	2	New Jersey
	7th Md.	John Gunby	11	34	4	244	293	20	26	29	17			385		1		20	2	New Jersey
2nd Md.	2nd Md.	Thomas Price	6	33	3	300	342	44	22	31	13			452	7	3		7	4	New Jersey
	4th Md.	Josias Carvil Hall	6	27	5	276	314	38	21	54	21			448		2		3	5	New Jersey
	6th Md.	Otho Holland Williams	6	28	3	218	255	18	34	31	29			367	2	4		13		New Jersey
Wayne	1st Pa.	James Chambers	5	29	3	180	217	15	6	50	15			303		6			3	New Jersey
	2nd Pa.	Walter Stewart	10	38	4	288	340	26	17	48	31			462	1	12			2	New Jersey
	7th Pa.	William Irvine	9	27	3	148	187	13	2	13	31			246	1	2			1	New Jersey
	10th Pa.	Richard Humpton	7	29	3	203	242	14	20	55	29			360		1		2		New Jersey
3rd Pa.	3rd Pa.	Thomas Craig	10	36	3	221	270	33	20	53	19			395	3	5		1	6	New Jersey
	5th Pa.	Francis Johnston	1	22	4	190	217	19	20	34	30			320		2			4	New Jersey
	6th Pa.	Robert Magaw	8	31	3	150	192	8	14	29	22			265	3	1		2	4	New Jersey
	9th Pa.	Richard Butler	2	23	4	141	170	18	15	30	10			243		3		1	3	New Jersey
Maxwell	1st N.J.	Matthias Ogden	18	38	4	204	264	44	19	14	8			349		11		227	6	New Jersey
	2nd N.J.	Israel Shreve	14	40	5 F	269	328	11	5	11	42			397		3		158	2	New Jersey
	3rd N.J.	Elias Dayton	18	42	6 F	230	296	13	20	8	31			368		7		102	10	New Jersey
	Additional	William Malcolm	6	18	4	79	107	10	8	40	7			172	1	1			2	Haverstraw, N.Y.
	Patton's additional	(late) Lt. Col. John Parke	8	17		41	66	9	3	39	5			122		1			4	Haverstraw, N.Y.
Nixon	3rd Mass.	John Greaton	9	27	3	146	185	9	18	79	13			304		23		33	4	The Highlands, N.Y.
	5th Mass.	Rufus Putnam	14	31	3	232	280	5	1	126	5			417	1	3		85	2	The Highlands, N.Y.
	6th Mass.	Thomas Nixon	2	24	4	82	112	17	12	204	13			358		7		93	2	The Highlands, N.Y.
Paterson	12th Mass.	(late) Samuel Brewer	12	29	3	105	149	14	17	91	14			285	3	1		94	2	The Highlands, N.Y.
	10th Mass.	Thomas Marshall	9	25	3	144	181	15	12	65	15			288		2		72	5	The Highlands, N.Y.
	14th Mass.	Gamaliel Bradford	11	26	5	111	153	11	8	87	10			269	1	5		85	4	The Highlands, N.Y.
(late) Learned	11th Mass.	Benjamin Tupper	13	31	4	164	212	17	17	85	14			345				72		The Highlands, N.Y.
	2nd Mass.	John Bailey	14	29	3	140	186	13	23	117	13			352	2	4		25		The Highlands, N.Y.
	8th Mass.	Michael Jackson	14	25	5	92	136	9	18	128	11			302	1	4		57	1	The Highlands, N.Y.
	9th Mass.	James Wesson	12	27	5	91	135	15	15	154	15			334	1	8		67		The Highlands, N.Y.

MARCH 1779 (continued)

BRIGADE	UNIT	COMMANDING OFFICER	PRESENT FIT FOR DUTY & ON DUTY: COMMISSIONED OFFICERS	NONCOMMISSIONED OFFICERS	STAFF OFFICERS	RANK & FILE	TOTAL	RANK & FILE SICK, ON FURLOUGH, ETC.: SICK PRESENT	SICK ABSENT	ON COMMAND & EXTRA SERVICE	ON FURLOUGH	CONFINED	RECRUITING	GRAND TOTAL	ALTERATIONS: DEATHS	DESERTED	TAKEN PRISONER	DISCHARGED	JOINED, ENLISTED, RECRUITED	LOCATION
FORCES UNDER COMMANDER-IN-CHIEF GENERAL GEORGE WASHINGTON (continued)																				
Putnam's div.	3rd Conn.	Samuel Wyllys	5	18	4	99	126	28	36	239	19			448	1	7		1	5	Reading, Conn.
	4th Conn.	John Durkee	7	15	3	45	70	10	20	126	22			248		3		2		Reading, Conn.
	6th Conn.	Return Jonathan Meigs	5	21	1	137	164	15	30	288	26			523		6		3	1	Reading, Conn.
	8th Conn.	Giles Russell	7	28	4	70	109	21	22	133	24			309		5		3	4	Reading, Conn.
	1st Conn.	Josiah Starr	7	22	2	100	131	8	48	180	21			388		2		2	3	Reading, Conn.
	2nd Conn.	Zebulon Butler	6	21	1	63	91	6	23	122	24			266	1				1	Reading, Conn.
	5th Conn.	Philip Burr Bradley	4	18	3	85	110	9	25	172	25			341	1	2			4	Reading, Conn.
	7th Conn.	Heman Swift	8	16	4	92	120	7	26	185	25			363						Reading, Conn.
	2nd Canadian	Moses Hazen	15	40	3	245	303	15	28	116	14			476		6			6	Reading, Conn.
	1st N.H.	Joseph Cilley	9	22	4	144	179	13	43	186	12			433	1				3	Reading, Conn.
	2nd N.H.	Lt. Col. George Reid	6	22	4	99	131	25	15	137	8			316	1	2		2	10	Reading, Conn.
	3rd N.H.	Alexander Scammell	4	17	4	86	111	9	17	133	16			286	7			1	2	Reading, Conn.
Hand	2nd N.Y.	Philip Van Cortlandt	13	34	3	162	212	15	16	11	12			266		5		117	14	Minisink area
	Pa. independent co.	Capt. John Paul Schott	4	8		32	44	1	2	4	4			55						Minisink area
	Independent corps	Tuffin Charles Armand	5	16	3	64	88	3		5	1			97						Minisink area
	Additional	Oliver Spencer	6	14	4	92	116	9	4	3	18			150					2	Minisink area
	German bn.	Lt. Col. Ludowick Weltner	13	32	5	236	286	2	19	27	49			383						Minisink area
Clinton	1st N.Y.	Goose Van Schaick	11	42	2	237	292	19	40	77	10			438	4				26	Fort Schuyler, N.Y.
	3rd N.Y.	Peter Gansevoort	10	21	4	159	194	23	1	20	15			253	1	3			1	Albany, N.Y.
	5th N.Y.	Lewis DuBois	7	36	1	161	205	21	17	84	4			331				1	4	Schoharie, N.Y.
	4th N.Y.	Lt. Col. Pierre Regnier de Roussi	13	28	2	152	195	9	9	18	4			235		1		7	1	Fort Plank, N.Y.
	7th Mass.	(late) Ichabod Alden	14	37	2	206	259	13	10	36	5			323				5		Cherry Valley, N.Y.
	Additional	Seth Warner	9	20	2	55	86	2	6	58	3			155					3	Fort Edward, N.Y.
	4th Pa.	Lt. Col. William Butler	9	37	5	145	196	9	12	31	1			249	1	2		3	21	Schoharie, N.Y.
	Rifle corps		5	13	3	83	104	7	1	9	1			122					3	Schoharie, N.Y.
Sullivan's div.	1st Canadian	James Livingston	6	23	2	67	98	3	11	46	9			167		1		1	2	Rhode Island
	Additional	Henry Sherburne	15	35	4	176	230	6	1	18	20			275		4		1		Rhode Island
	Additional	Samuel Blatchley Webb	13	30	4	158	205	8	19	20	31			283	2	4		2		Rhode Island
	2nd R.I.	Israel Angell	18	27	6	212	263	8	7	68	24			370		2		3		Rhode Island
	4th Mass.	William Shepard	12	32	1	131	176	28	9	119	18			350	1	2		3	4	Rhode Island
	13th Mass.	(late) Edward Wigglesworth	11	22	4	127	164	20	12	102	38			336					2	Rhode Island
	15th Mass.	Timothy Bigelow	10	18	2	67	97	9	19	147	26			298				1	1	Rhode Island
	1st Mass.	Joseph Vose	16	26	1	139	182	21	23	105	12			343		1			3	Rhode Island
	1st R.I. A	Christopher Greene	16	32	1	140	189	7	5	3				204					1	Rhode Island
	Lee's additional	Lt. Col. William Stephens Smith	3	20		45	68	2	6	57	27			160	1	1				Rhode Island
	Additional	David Henley	3	7		26	36	2	3	55	12			108		1			1	Rhode Island
	Additional B	Henry Jackson	4	18	2	47	71	7	7	65	27			177		1				Rhode Island
	Additional	(late) Thomas Hartley	9	31		168	208	8	2	30	26			274						Sunbury, Pa.
	TOTAL OF INFANTRY		715	2126	262	11653	14756	1199	1250	5957	2224			25386	84	213		1443	245	

MARCH 1779 (continued)

BRIGADE	UNIT	COMMANDING OFFICER	PRESENT FIT FOR DUTY & ON DUTY: COMMISSIONED OFFICERS	NONCOMMISSIONED OFFICERS	STAFF OFFICERS	RANK & FILE	TOTAL	RANK & FILE SICK, ON FURLOUGH, ETC.: SICK PRESENT	SICK ABSENT	ON COMMAND & EXTRA SERVICE	ON FURLOUGH	CONFINED	RECRUITING	GRAND TOTAL	ALTERATIONS: DEATHS	DESERTED	TAKEN PRISONER	DISCHARGED	JOINED, ENLISTED, RECRUITED	LOCATION
	FORCES UNDER COMMANDER-IN-CHIEF GENERAL GEORGE WASHINGTON (continued)																			
	CAVALRY																			
	1st cont'l.	Theodorick Bland	16	27	5	78	126	6	5	11 J	5			153				1	11	Virginia
	3rd cont'l.	George Baylor	6	15	3	93	117	16	2	37	17			189						Frederick, Md.
	4th cont'l.	Stephen Moylan	7	45	3	105	160	11	4	6		10		191						Lancaster, Pa.
	Partizan corps	Maj. Henry Lee	8	30	2	115	155							155						
	Marechaussie	Capt. Bartholomew Von Heer	2	5		28	35	3		11	2			51						Somerset, N.J.
	TOTAL OF CAVALRY		39	122	13	419	593	36	11	65	24	10		739				1	11	
	ARTILLERY																			
	4 cos. 3rd cont'l.	John Crane	7	54	3	64	128									1				Pluckemin, N.J.
	7 cos. 2nd cont'l.	John Lamb	17	73	3	96	189									1				Pluckemin, N.J.
	11 cos. 1st cont'l. C	Charles Harrison	25	115	4	169	313	30	22	82	22			907	4				1	Pluckemin, N.J.
	3 independent cos.																	1		
	Det. 3rd cont'l.	John Crane	6	31	1	52	90									1			2	Rhode Island
	Det. 1st cont'l.	Charles Harrison	3	10		18	31													Rhode Island
	TOTAL OF ARTILLERY		58	283	11	399	751	30	22	82	22			907	4	3		1	3	
	TOTAL OF WASHINGTON'S ARMY		812	2531	286	12471	16100	1265	1283	6104	2270	10		27032	88	216		1445	259	
	SOUTHERN DEPARTMENT UNDER MAJOR GENERAL BENJAMIN LINCOLN																			
Huger	1st S.C.	Charles Cotesworth Pinckney	14	36	5	130	185	12	12	43	3			255	1	4				Black Swamp, S.C.
Huger	Det. 2nd S.C.	Isaac Motte	11	12	1	89	113	16		22				151		17				Black Swamp, S.C.
Huger	3rd S.C. (rangers)	William Thompson	13	33	3	291	340	25	17	51	1			434		13		1	113	Black Swamp, S.C.
Huger	5th S.C. (rifles)	Isaac Huger	9	27		92	128	20	26	14				188		25			27	Black Swamp, S.C.
Huger	6th S.C. (rifles)	Lt. Col. William Henderson	10 D	21	2	118	151	14	5 H	38				208		5		1	33	Black Swamp, S.C.
Sumner	Pt. 4th N.C.	Lt. Col. James Thackston	11 E	38	4 G	201	254	23	30 H	55	1			363	1	2		1	8	Black Swamp, S.C.
Sumner	5th N.C.	James Armstrong	14	41	4	269	328	31	20	56	1			436		6		1		Black Swamp, S.C.
Sumner	1 co. 4th N.C.	Capt. William Goodman	4	4		55	63		9					72						Black Swamp, S.C.
Sumner	1 co. 3rd N.C.	Christopher Goodin	3	4		50	57		10					67						Black Swamp, S.C.
	Ga. cont'l. troops	John White	10	19	5	50	84	13						97						
	TOTAL OF INFANTRY		99	235	24	1345	1703	154	129	279	6			2271	2	72		4	181	
	CAVALRY																			
	Light horse		4	4		24	32	1	6	1				40						Black Swamp, S.C.
	ARTILLERY																			
	4th S.C.	Owen Roberts	9	23		40	72	6	7 I	22	2		1	110						Black Swamp, S.C.
	TOTAL OF LINCOLN'S ARMY		112	262	24	1409	1807	161	142	302	8		1	2421	2	72		4	181	
	GRAND TOTAL		924	2793	310	13880	17907	1426	1425	6406	2278	10	1	29453 K	90	288		1449	440	

OFFICERS SICK, ON FURLOUGH, ETC.	WASHINGTON'S ARMY				LINCOLN'S ARMY (CAVALRY & GEORGIA CONTINENTALS EXCLUDED)				GRAND TOTAL
	COMMISSIONED	NONCOMMISSIONED	STAFF	TOTAL	COMMISSIONED	NONCOMMISSIONED	STAFF	TOTAL	
Sick Present	43	108	1	152	7 L	10		17 M	169
Sick Absent	37	95	2	134	1	2		3	137
On Furlough	374	389	51	814	1			1	815
Recruiting	22			22	4			4	26
On Command	423	531	34	988	3	19		22	1010
Prisoners of War	79	1	2	82					82
In Arrest	3	2		5					5
On the Staff	114		1	115	8		11	19	134
Absent L					44	18	8	70	70
TOTAL	1095	1126	91	2312	68	49	19	136	2448

SOURCES OF THIS REPORT

1. MONTHLY RETURN OF THE CONTINENTAL ARMY UNDER THE COMMAND OF HIS EXCELLENCY GEORGE WASHINGTON. . . FOR MARCH 1779, ELEPHANT FOLIO OF WASHINGTON RETURNS, WILLIAM L. CLEMENTS LIBRARY. [THE ARTILLERY AND CAVALRY SECTIONS APPEAR ON THE FOLLOWING PAGES OF THE FOLIO.]

1a. Monthly Return of the Continental Army under. . . Washington. . . March 1779, Record Group 93, National Archives. [The same return, but only to the brigade level.]

2. RETURN OF THE TROOPS UNDER THE COMMAND OF MAJOR GENL. LINCOLN, APRIL 1, 1779, BENJAMIN LINCOLN PAPERS, MASSACHUSETTS HISTORICAL SOCIETY AND THE INDIVIDUAL RETURNS FOR HUGER'S AND SUMNER'S BRIGADES AND THE ARTILLERY THAT WERE USED IN COMPILING THE GENERAL RETURN. [INDIVIDUAL RETURNS ARE ALSO IN THE LINCOLN PAPERS. THEY SUPPLY MORE DETAILED DATA THAN THEIR TOTALS THAT WERE USED IN THE GENERAL RETURN. THEIR HEADINGS CONFIRM THAT THE GENERAL RETURN IS THE MONTHLY ONE, THOUGH NOT SO HEADED.]

A. The Clements folio manuscript for March and April erroneously indicates this regiment as "R.I. state," and the May return shows evidence of a "state" having been erased after "R.I." Greene's name and the figures given make it clear that the "state" designation was an error and that the figures are for the 1st Rhode Island Continental regiment.

B. While Congress had resolved on January 13, 1779 to incorporate other units with this regiment and make it the 11th Pennsylvania, the changes actually had not yet taken place by the time of this return.

C. With the exception of the one matross discharged, the columns are blank for this unit on the Clements folio; the National Archives manuscript does not include the unit or the one man discharged. These three companies surely are not included in the combined figures that are given for the rank and file sick, on furlough, etc. in the artillery. How the adjutant came to know of the one man discharged in these companies for which he had no return is unknown.

D. Including one officer of the 6th regiment acting in the 4th.

E. Including nine officers of the 6th regiment acting in the 5th.

F. Five staff officers in Elias Dayton's 3rd New Jersey regiment plus one chaplain for the entire brigade.

G. Including one staff officer from the 6th regiment acting in the 5th.

H. These men are given as "sick in hospital" on the manuscript; see footnote C on our August 1775 report.

I. Three men sick in a fixed hospital, four sick in a general hospital.

J. Including the sole private in a column simply headed "waggoners"; from the position of the column it would appear that the meaning is that the private was doing detached service as a waggoner and therefore normally would have been included in this column.

K. The National Archives manuscript notes that no returns were received for the troops in the Western Department, for the troops in the Southern Department (supplied, at least as far as Continentals, here), for the forces in Boston and Philadelphia, for the Additional regiment formerly commanded by David Forman, for Sheldon's 2nd Continental cavalry, and for seven companies of artillery detached to the Northern Department. It is also noted that Topham's and Crary's Rhode Island state infantry regiments and Elliot's Rhode Island state artillery regiment had been discharged because their terms of service had expired. In addition, the manuscript notes that the 122 men of the rifle corps (see footnote A on the December 1778 report) are included twice in the return because they were also included as "on command" in the returns of the regiments to which they nominally belonged.

L. For some of the officers of the Southern Department who were not present fit for duty, the manuscripts detail only whether they were "absent" or "sick present." For Huger's brigade, the division is "sick" and "absent," but because the "absent" column presumably includes "sick absent," the "sick" column on that brigade has been assumed to enumerate the sick present only.

M. Sick in fixed hospital.

APRIL 1779

BRIGADE	UNIT	COMMANDING OFFICER	PRESENT FIT FOR DUTY & ON DUTY: COMMISSIONED OFFICERS	NONCOMMISSIONED OFFICERS	STAFF OFFICERS	RANK & FILE	TOTAL	RANK & FILE SICK, ON FURLOUGH, ETC.: SICK PRESENT	SICK ABSENT	ON COMMAND & EXTRA SERVICE	ON FURLOUGH	GRAND TOTAL	ALTERATIONS: DEATHS	DESERTED	TAKEN PRISONER	DISCHARGED	JOINED, ENLISTED, RECRUITED	LOCATION
FORCES UNDER COMMANDER-IN-CHIEF GENERAL GEORGE WASHINGTON																		
N.C.	1st N.C.	Thomas Clark	12	38	4	273	327	27	13	140		507	15	3		4	4	New Jersey
	2nd N.C.	John Patten	5	24	3	142	174	19	10	216	7	426		2			1	New Jersey
Woodford	2nd Va.	Christian Febiger	8	22	3	140	173	7	6	14	58	258					2	New Jersey
	3rd Va.	William Heth	8	26	4	115	153	15	6	18	34	226						New Jersey
	5th Va.	William Russell	3	16	4	64	87	7	4	9	70	177				1		New Jersey
	7th Va.	Daniel Morgan	7	27	3	129	166	3	5	14	56	244				3	3	New Jersey
	11th Va.	Abraham Buford	8	15	2	106	131	5	5	19	92	252					3	New Jersey
Muhlenberg	1st Va.	Richard Parker	8	33	3	82	126	9	11	35	22	203				1		New Jersey
	1st Va. state	George Gibson	16	40	4	158	218	28	2	62	3	313						New Jersey
	2nd Va. state	(late) Gregory Smith	6	34	4	184	228	28	20	38		314					3	New Jersey
	10th Va.	William Davies	10	23	5	120	158	21	14	31	71	295						New Jersey
Scott	4th Va.	John Neville	4	26	4	103	137	10	8	13	55	223				3		New Jersey
	Del.	David Hall	6	27	4	160	197	16	6	34	38	291	1	1		1	1	New Jersey
	6th Va.	John Green	9	26	5	144	184	10	4	22	98	318				1	1	New Jersey
	8th Va.	James Wood	9	27	5	143	184	27	6	28	98	343	1	1		2		New Jersey
	Additional	William Grayson	3	21	4	88	116	18	2	13	20	169					1	New Jersey
Smallwood	1st Md.	John Hawkins Stone	9	25	3	189	226	17	13	29	30	315	1	4		21	8	New Jersey
	3rd Md.	(late) Mordecai Gist	3	24	3	316	346	27	16	51	39	479	1	4		20	4	New Jersey
	5th Md.	William Richardson	2	27	5	181	215	12	40	29	25	321		3		4	4	New Jersey
	7th Md.	John Gunby	10	30	5	212	257	13	23	31	17	341	1	14		33	8	New Jersey
2nd Md.	2nd Md.	Thomas Price	7	33	3	250	293	27	23	35	10	388	1	8		58	3	New Jersey
	4th Md.	Josias Carvil Hall	6	25	3	293	327	24	18	56	10	435		6		5	2	New Jersey
	6th Md.	Otho Holland Williams	7	25	5	195	232	14	26	42	17	331	1	3		35	4	New Jersey
Wayne	1st Pa.	James Chambers	4	32	4	187	227	8	8	50	11	304		4			5	New Jersey
	2nd Pa.	Walter Stewart	13	36	5	303	357	17	20	37	24	455		9			6	New Jersey
	7th Pa.	William Irvine	8	29	4	167	208	12	2	14	9	245		4			3	New Jersey
	10th Pa.	Richard Humpton	7	38	5	221	271	11	13	58	12	365	4	2			4	New Jersey
2nd Pa.	3rd Pa.	Thomas Craig	9	40	3	232	284	30	19	53	7	393		10		1	8	New Jersey
	5th Pa.	Francis Johnston	5	27	3	206	241	24	13	34	22	334					7	New Jersey
	6th Pa.	Robert Magaw	10	33	4 C	156	203	14	11	26	11	265		4		2	3	New Jersey
	9th Pa.	Richard Butler	5	29	6	148	188	16	10	23	8	245	7	4		1	4	New Jersey
Maxwell	1st N.J.	Matthias Ogden	21	41	4	208	274	42	11	11	11	349		5		6	8	New Jersey
	2nd N.J.	Israel Shreve	18	39	4 D	256	317	18	4	12	27	378		17		2	1	New Jersey
	3rd N.J.	Elias Dayton	18	41	6	226	291	21	15	10	18	355		8		4	2	New Jersey
Nixon	3rd Mass.	John Greaton	12	32	2	176	222	14	11	41	9	297	2	6		11	6	The Highlands, N.Y.
	5th Mass.	Rufus Putnam	10	35	3	256	304	8	3	83	8	406	2	4		16	12	The Highlands, N.Y.
	6th Mass.	Thomas Nixon	13	37	4	224	278	18	7	38	7	348	1	6		32	5	The Highlands, N.Y.
Paterson	12th Mass.	(late) Samuel Brewer	14	38	5	143	200	7	13	48	8	276		7		16	3	The Highlands, N.Y.
	10th Mass.	Thomas Marshall	9	32	4	149	194	11	11	31	9	256	1	6		42	12	The Highlands, N.Y.
	14th Mass.	Gamaliel Bradford	11	31	5	151	198	10	9	31	11	259		5		12	5	The Highlands, N.Y.
	11th Mass.	Benjamin Tupper	12	34	4	197	247	18	11	48	11	335	2	1		10	4	The Highlands, N.Y.
(late) Learned	2nd Mass.	John Bailey	10	30	3	156	199	8	19	106	10	342		1		8	3	The Highlands, N.Y.
	8th Mass.	Michael Jackson	13	27	2	117	159	19	7	73	11	269	1	3		27	2	The Highlands, N.Y.
	9th Mass.	James Wesson	9	34	5	133	181	13	12	104	11	321		2		18	3	The Highlands, N.Y.
Poor	1st N.H.	Joseph Cilley	12	21	4	205	242	10	38	66	71	427	3	4		3	2	The Highlands, N.Y.
	2nd N.H.	Lt. Col. George Reid	8	22	2	154	186	8	23	46	46	309				9	3	The Highlands, N.Y.
	3rd N.H.	Alexander Scammell	5	25	2	131	163	9	19	40	56	287		5		3	4	The Highlands, N.Y.

APRIL 1779 (continued)

BRIGADE	UNIT	COMMANDING OFFICER	PRESENT FIT FOR DUTY & ON DUTY: COMMISSIONED OFFICERS	NONCOMMISSIONED OFFICERS	STAFF OFFICERS	RANK & FILE	TOTAL	RANK & FILE SICK, ON FURLOUGH, ETC.: SICK PRESENT	SICK ABSENT	ON COMMAND & EXTRA SERVICE	ON FURLOUGH	GRAND TOTAL	ALTERATIONS: DEATHS	DESERTED	TAKEN PRISONER	DISCHARGED	JOINED, ENLISTED, RECRUITED	LOCATION
	FORCES UNDER COMMANDER-IN-CHIEF GENERAL GEORGE WASHINGTON (continued)																	
Putnam's div.	3rd Conn.	Samuel Wyllys	4	24	5	100	133	17	25	258	21	454		6			7	Reading, Conn.
	4th Conn.	John Durkee	5	18	5	78	106	3	12	112	19	252		1			3	Reading, Conn.
	6th Conn.	Return Jonathan Meigs	3	26	1	145	175	3	20	290	36	524	2	4		2	6	Reading, Conn.
	8th Conn.	Giles Russell	7	24	4	90	125	21	25	107	24	302		5			3	Reading, Conn.
	1st Conn.	Josiah Starr	6	17	1	85	109	12	42	179	39	381						Reading, Conn.
	2nd Conn.	Zebulon Butler	2	21	1	68	92	8	28	105	30	263					2	Reading, Conn.
	5th Conn.	Philip Burr Bradley	3	14	2 E	78	97	5	26	177	34	339					4	Reading, Conn.
	7th Conn.	Heman Swift	4	15	3	71	93	2	26	207	28	356					1	Reading, Conn.
Clinton	1st N.Y.	Goose Van Schaick	17	44	4	281	346	19	24	56	7	452	3			1	6	Fort Schuyler, N.Y.
	4th N.Y.	Lt. Col. Pierre Regnier de Roussi	16	24	2	108	150	13	3	69	3	238						Fort Plank, N.Y.
	3rd N.Y.	Peter Gansevoort	14	34	4	254	306	19	7	98	9	439		24				Albany, N.Y.
	5th N.Y.	Lewis DuBois	4	31	2	117	154	11	13	137	6	321						Schoharie, N.Y.
	7th Mass.	(late) Ichabod Alden	14	36	2	183	235	17	5	41	3	301		1		21	1	Cherry Valley, N.Y.
	Additional	Seth Warner	9	20	3	56	88	5	3	59		155		1		1		Fort Edward, N.Y.
	4th Pa.	Lt. Col. William Butler	6	36	4	99	145	10	11	72	1	239		1			1	Schoharie, N.Y.
	2nd N.Y.	Philip Van Cortlandt	15	34	4	180	233	13	8	10	2	266	2	6		4	11	Rochester, N.Y.
McIntosh-Western dept.	8th Pa.	Daniel Brodhead	3	22	2	152	179	18	6	203	14	420	4					Fort Pitt, Pa.
	9th Va.	John Gibson	19	35		200	254	13	2	46	14	329	19					Fort Pitt, Pa.
	Va. independent co.	Capt. Henry Heth	2	6		43	51	3		7		61						Fort Pitt, Pa.
	Independent co.	Capt. James O'Hara	1	6		20	27			12		39					3	Fort Pitt, Pa.
	Independent co.	Capt. Samuel Moorhead	2	4		19	25					25				4		Fort Pitt, Pa.
Gates' div.	4th Mass.	William Shepard	14	33	4	186	237	26	4	81	4	352	1	3		3	5	Rhode Island
	13th Mass.	(late) Edward Wigglesworth	20	38	4	184	246	10	7	63	23	349	2	1		4		Rhode Island
	15th Mass.	Timothy Bigelow	12	23	2	116	153	13	17	106	8	297		2		3		Rhode Island
	1st Mass.	Joseph Vose	11	33	4	170	218	18	21	79	10	346		1		1		Rhode Island
	1st Canadian	James Livingston	12	22	4	70	108	2	9	52	4	175		1		1	2	Rhode Island
	Additional	Samuel Blatchley Webb	17	41	4	197	259	13	14	5	3	294		3		1		Rhode Island
	R.I. militia	——— Hathway B	14	30	2	212	258	5	2	4	5	274						Rhode Island
	Additional	Henry Sherburne	13	26	4	206	249	4	1	5	4	263		3		1	4	Rhode Island
	2nd R.I.	Israel Angell	13	34	4	238	289	13	6	53	1	362		8			1	Rhode Island
	1st R.I.	Christopher Greene	16	34	2	145	197	5	6	2		210	1			1	2	Rhode Island
	Additional	Henry Jackson	10	50		166	226	16	11	164	34	451		7			9	Rhode Island
	TOTAL OF INFANTRY		730	2252	264	12606	15852	1087	974	4921	1684	24518	79	244		463	238	
	CAVALRY																	
	2nd cont'l.	Elisha Sheldon	9	44	4	129	186	1	3	12	11	213				2		
	3rd cont'l.	George Baylor	8	18	2	107	135	16	2	30	19	202						
	Partizan corps	Maj. Henry Lee	7	24	3	94	128	10		5		143						
	Marechaussie	Capt. Bartholomew Von Heer	2	5		26	33	4		12	1	50						
	TOTAL OF CAVALRY		26	91	9	356	482	31	5	59	31	608				2		
	ARTILLERY																	
	4 cos. 3rd cont'l.	John Crane	5	40	4	49	98							2			1	Pluckemin, N.J.
	7 cos. 2nd cont'l.	John Lamb	16	57	2	84	159							1				Pluckemin, N.J.
	11 cos. 1st cont'l.	Charles Harrison	21	79	4	121	225	25	14	186	14	829	2	8		2		Pluckemin, N.J.
	Det. 3rd cont'l.	John Crane	10	34	1	37	82							4				Rhode Island
	Det. 1st cont'l.	Charles Harrison	3	8	1	14	26											Rhode Island
	TOTAL OF ARTILLERY		55	218	12	305	590	25	14	186	14	829	2	15		2	1	

BRIGADE	UNIT	COMMANDING OFFICER	PRESENT FIT FOR DUTY & ON DUTY: COMMISSIONED OFFICERS	NONCOMMISSIONED OFFICERS	STAFF OFFICERS	RANK & FILE	TOTAL	RANK & FILE SICK, ON FURLOUGH, ETC.: SICK PRESENT	SICK ABSENT	ON COMMAND & EXTRA SERVICE	ON FURLOUGH			GRAND TOTAL	ALTERATIONS: DEATHS	DESERTED	TAKEN PRISONER	DISCHARGED	JOINED, ENLISTED, RECRUITED	LOCATION
	APRIL 1779 (continued)																			
	FORCES UNDER COMMANDER-IN-CHIEF GENERAL GEORGE WASHINGTON (continued)																			
	INVALIDS[A]																			
	Philadelphia unit	Lewis Nicola	6	38		224	268							268						Philadelphia, Pa.
	Boston det.	Capt. Moses McFarland	1	8		108	117							117						Boston, Mass.
	TOTAL OF INVALIDS		7	46		332	385							385						
	TOTAL OF WASHINGTON'S ARMY		818	2607	285	13599	17309	1143	993	5166	1729			26340	81	257		467	239	
	SOUTHERN DEPARTMENT UNDER MAJOR GENERAL BENJAMIN LINCOLN (Partial Report)																			
Pinckney	1st S.C.	Charles Cotesworth Pinckney	20	39	5	156	220	7	25	15	1			268	1	22				Georgia
Pinckney	3rd S.C. (rangers)	William Thompson	15	30	1	348	394	24	38	19	3			478	2	30		4	85	Georgia
Pinckney	6th S.C. (rifles)	Lt. Col. William Henderson	15	29	3	112	159	11	8	25	4			207		15			39	Georgia
	Forces under Brig. Gen. Andrew Williamson		195	196	22	2076	2489				11			2500[F]						
	TOTAL OF PART OF THE SOUTHERN ARMY		245	294	31	2692	3262	42	71	59	19			3453	3	67		4	124	
	GRAND TOTAL		1063	2901	306	16291	20571	1185	1064	5225	1748			29793[G]	84	326		471	363	

OFFICERS SICK, ON FURLOUGH, ETC.	WASHINGTON'S ARMY (EXCEPT INVALID CORPS): COMMISSIONED	NONCOMMISSIONED	STAFF	TOTAL	SOUTHERN DEPARTMENT (PINCKNEY'S BRIGADE ONLY): COMMISSIONED	NONCOMMISSIONED	STAFF	TOTAL	GRAND TOTAL
Sick Present	46	90	2	138	2	5		7	145
Sick Absent	38	87	2	127	2	6		8	135
On Furlough	337	319	52	708	1	2	4	7	715
On Command	414	610	26	1050	2	5		7	1057
Recruiting	13	22		35			1	1	36
Prisoners of War	71	1	4	76	5			5	81
On the Staff	200		1	201	2		20	22	223
In Arrest	3			3					3
Prisoners on Parole					2			2	2
TOTAL	1122	1129	87	2338	16	18	25	59	2397

SOURCES OF THIS REPORT

1. MONTHLY RETURN OF THE CONTINENTAL ARMY UNDER THE COMMAND OF HIS EXCELLENCY GEORGE WASHINGTON. . . FOR APRIL 1779, ELEPHANT FOLIO OF WASHINGTON RETURNS, WILLIAM L. CLEMENTS LIBRARY. [THE CAVALRY AND ARTILLERY SECTIONS APPEAR ON THE FOLLOWING PAGE OF THE FOLIO; THE INVALID CORPS SECTION APPEARS ONLY ON THE NATIONAL ARCHIVES COPY BELOW.]

   1a. Monthly Return of the Continental Troops under. . . Washington. . . for April 1779, Record Group 93, National Archives. [Same figures, but to the brigade level only.]

2. RETURN OF THE FIRST S. CAROLINA BRIGADE OF FOOT, COMMANDED BY CHARLES COTESWORTH PINCKNEY, ESQ., MAY 1, 1779 [INSCRIBED "MONTHLY RETURN" ON THE REVERSE], BENJAMIN LINCOLN PAPERS, MASSACHUSETTS HISTORICAL SOCIETY.

3. A GENERAL RETURN OF THE ARMY UNDER THE COMMAND OF BRIGADIER GENERAL WILLIAMSON INCLUDING THOSE ON DUTY IN GEORGIA AND FRONTIERS OF GEORGIA, APRIL 29, 1779, BENJAMIN LINCOLN PAPERS, MASSACHUSETTS HISTORICAL SOCIETY.

A. With this monthly return the manuscript for the first time includes a separate section for the Invalid Corps, established by Congress on June 20, 1777. Such a report on the Invalid Corps was not always available for inclusion in later returns. When it was, until January 1782 the adjutant used a more abbreviated form for the Invalid Corps than for other sections of the monthly returns. (A few exceptions exist when the Invalids were included in returns of the Eastern Department.) These abbreviated sections for the Invalids do not have separate columns for different conditions (sick absent, on furlough, etc.), but simply give numbers of men under various ranks. We have entered these men under present fit for duty, but it is likely that these figures include other men in addition to those present and able to do the guard duty, etc., for which the Corps was established. With the January 1782 monthly return a full form began to be used for the Invalid Corps, but before that date when an Invalid section appears, it may inflate a little the totals of present fit for duty.

B. We have been unable to identify this officer further. The National Archives version of the manuscript notes that this unit was discharged after having been included in the return.

C. Five staff officers in Richard Butler's 9th Pennsylvania regiment plus one chaplain for the entire brigade.

D. Five staff officers in Elias Dayton's 3rd New Jersey regiment plus one chaplain for the entire brigade.

E. Two staff officers in Heman Swift's 7th Connecticut regiment plus one chaplain for the entire division.

F. Williamson's return also shows fifty-three men serving as waggoners not included here. Judging from the return, these men appear to be civilians, rather than enlisted men. However, because the return is in a form that is quite different from the usual return and is difficult to decipher, it is possible that we have erred and that the waggoners are enlisted men acting as waggoners and should have been included here.

G. The National Archives manuscript notes that no returns were available for the troops at Boston, for Malcolm's and Spencer's Additional regiments "now joined," for the old Additional regiments formerly commanded by Hartley and Patton which had been joined to form the 11th Pennsylvania, for the German battalion, for Pulaski's Legion, for Proctor's 4th Continental artillery, for twelve companies of artillery with Putnam's and McDougall's divisions and with the Northern Department, and for the 1st and 4th Continental cavalry regiments.

MAY 1779

BRIGADE	UNIT	COMMANDING OFFICER	PRESENT FIT FOR DUTY & ON DUTY: COMMISSIONED OFFICERS	NONCOMMISSIONED OFFICERS	STAFF OFFICERS	RANK & FILE	TOTAL	RANK & FILE SICK, ON FURLOUGH, ETC.: SICK PRESENT	SICK ABSENT	ON COMMAND & EXTRA SERVICE	ON FURLOUGH	GRAND TOTAL	ALTERATIONS: DEATHS	DESERTED	TAKEN PRISONER	DISCHARGED	JOINED, ENLISTED, RECRUITED	LOCATION
FORCES UNDER COMMANDER-IN-CHIEF GENERAL GEORGE WASHINGTON																		
N.C.	1st N.C.	Thomas Clark	10	29	3	206	248	24	10	169	2	453	4	8		27	1	New Jersey
N.C.	2nd N.C.	John Patten								398		398						New Jersey
Woodford	2nd Va.	Christian Febiger	5	30	4	171	210	11	2	16	24	263	1	1		1	2	New Jersey
Woodford	3rd & 4th Va.	John Neville	15	53	5	266	339	23	9	29	50	450		1		1		New Jersey
Woodford	5th & 11th Va.	William Russell	9	31	4	218	262	14	14	21	111	422						New Jersey
Woodford	7th Va.	Daniel Morgan	8	22	3	161	194	10	10	14	13	241		1		2	1	New Jersey
Woodford	8th Va.	James Wood	8	20	5	196	229	11	4	29	34	307					2	New Jersey
Muhlenberg	1st & 10th Va.	William Davies	8	47	8	261	324	12	20	52	70	478	1	4		1	11	New Jersey
Muhlenberg	Additional	Nathaniel Gist	10	32	3	145	190	16	9	19	12	246	1					New Jersey
Muhlenberg	2nd Va. state	William Brent	12	37	4	220	273	12	11	30		326	3				3	New Jersey
Muhlenberg	1st Va. state	George Gibson	19	38	4	213	274	11	4	23	2	314	1	1			1	New Jersey
Muhlenberg	6th Va.	John Green	9	29	6	185	229	14	3	21	55	322	1	1			1	New Jersey
Smallwood	1st Md.	John Hawkins Stone	4	27	2	217	250	12	11	31	8	312				2	6	New Jersey
Smallwood	3rd Md.	Maj. Forrest A	6	26	3	337	372	30	10	40	14	466	3	1			15	New Jersey
Smallwood	5th Md.	William Richardson	10	27	4	204	245	20	28	23	6	322	9	2			12	New Jersey
Smallwood	7th Md.	John Gunby	11	29	4	212	256	20	23	28	9	336	2	2		1	2	New Jersey
2nd Md.	Del.	David Hall	11	31	4	196	242	15	6	27	17	307		2		3	15	New Jersey
2nd Md.	2nd Md.	Thomas Price	6	34	1	262	303	21	24	33	6	387		3			6	New Jersey
2nd Md.	4th Md.	Josias Carvil Hall	6	22	3	319	350	22	12	41	2	427	2	1		1	1	New Jersey
2nd Md.	6th Md.	Otho Holland Williams	6	27	5	205	243	18	20	30	13	324	3	2		2	5	New Jersey
Irvine	1st Pa.	James Chambers	7	32	6	194	239	14	4	50	6	313		3		3	14	New Jersey
Irvine	2nd Pa.	Walter Stewart	13	41	5	334	393	22	15	30	8	468	1	1		1	11	New Jersey
Irvine	7th Pa.	Lt. Col. Samuel Hay	8	30	4	171	213	20	22	10	1	266	1	4		1	7	New Jersey
Irvine	10th Pa.	Richard Humpton	8	42	5	242	297	11	11	52	9	380	2	2			20	New Jersey
2nd Pa.	3rd Pa.	Thomas Craig	8	36	4	246	294	21	24	48	3	390	1	2		1	6	New Jersey
2nd Pa.	5th Pa.	Francis Johnston	10	29	4	227	270	24	16	28	4	342		7		1	9	New Jersey
2nd Pa.	6th Pa.	Robert Magaw	9	34	4 C	178	225	7	11	20	4	267		1			2	New Jersey
2nd Pa.	9th Pa.	Richard Butler	6	29	6	159	200	9	8	20	3	240	1	10			7	New Jersey
Parsons	3rd Conn.	Samuel Wyllys	19	37	5	281	342	11	43	72		468						The Highlands, N.Y.
Parsons	4th Conn.	John Durkee	13	38		153	204	1	18	42		265						The Highlands, N.Y.
Parsons	6th Conn.	Return Jonathan Meigs	15	42	3	333	393	8	44	94	1	540						The Highlands, N.Y.
Parsons	8th Conn.	Giles Russell	13	33	3	156	205	6	32	71		314						The Highlands, N.Y.
Huntington	1st Conn.	Josiah Starr	16	29	3	261	309	15	45	21		390		12		1	1	The Highlands, N.Y.
Huntington	2nd Conn.	Zebulon Butler	15	42	3	200	260	5	27	4	1	297		5		1	4	The Highlands, N.Y.
Huntington	5th Conn.	Philip Burr Bradley	18	36	3 D	231	288	7	23	42	4	364	1	15			3	The Highlands, N.Y.
Huntington	7th Conn.	Heman Swift	18	38	6	273	335	4	27	25	3	394	1	4			3	The Highlands, N.Y.
Nixon	3rd Mass.	John Greaton	16	35	3	195	249	11	20	12	16	308	1	6			11	The Highlands, N.Y.
Nixon	5th Mass.	Rufus Putnam	10	36	3	249	298	8	2	84	12	404	1	1		4	5	The Highlands, N.Y.
Nixon	6th Mass.	Thomas Nixon	15	39	3	244	301	13	8	12	11	345		5		5	1	The Highlands, N.Y.
Paterson	12th Mass.	(late) Samuel Brewer	16	39	5	165	225	10	10	23	8	276						The Highlands, N.Y.
Paterson	10th Mass.	Thomas Marshall	13	35	4	150	202	12	10	25	12	261	2	8		1	7	The Highlands, N.Y.
Paterson	14th Mass.	Gamaliel Bradford	9	26	4	98	137	12	8	84	9	250	1	2		7	6	The Highlands, N.Y.
Paterson	11th Mass.	Benjamin Tupper	13	32	4	174	223	6	5	83	11	328		6			7	The Highlands, N.Y.
(late) Learned	2nd Mass.	John Bailey	11	28	3	133	175	6	14	137	9	341	1	3		3	1	The Highlands, N.Y.
(late) Learned	8th Mass.	Michael Jackson	11	28	2	110	151	12	10	83	12	268						The Highlands, N.Y.
(late) Learned	9th Mass.	James Wesson	12	34	5	168	219	11	8	72	8	318		1		1	4	The Highlands, N.Y.

MAY 1779 (continued)

BRIGADE	UNIT	COMMANDING OFFICER	PRESENT FIT FOR DUTY & ON DUTY: COMMISSIONED OFFICERS	NONCOMMISSIONED OFFICERS	STAFF OFFICERS	RANK & FILE	TOTAL	RANK & FILE SICK, ON FURLOUGH, ETC.: SICK PRESENT	SICK ABSENT	ON COMMAND & EXTRA SERVICE	ON FURLOUGH	GRAND TOTAL	ALTERATIONS: DEATHS	DESERTED	TAKEN PRISONER	DISCHARGED	JOINED, ENLISTED, RECRUITED	LOCATION
	FORCES UNDER COMMANDER-IN-CHIEF GENERAL GEORGE WASHINGTON (continued)																	
Maj. Gen. Gates' div.	4th Mass.	William Shepard	16	37	3	199	255	26	2	56	6	345		7				Rhode Island
	13th Mass.	(late) Edward Wigglesworth	14	37	5	187	243	23	2	66	7	341		6		3	1	Rhode Island
	15th Mass.	Timothy Bigelow	14	32	4	168	218	18	15	51	3	305		1		5	7	Rhode Island
	1st Mass.	Joseph Vose	17	34	3	193	247	16	22	48	6	339	1				1	Rhode Island
	1st Canadian	James Livingston	10	18	4	72	104	4	3	47		158	1	2		6	2	Rhode Island
	Additional	Henry Sherburne	15	31	5	208	259	6	1	5	1	272		5		3	3	Rhode Island
	Additional	Samuel Blatchley Webb	15	41	4	215	275	10	11	2		298		3			4	Rhode Island
	2nd R.I.	Israel Angell	13	38	5	219	275	17	7	60		359		1			7	Rhode Island
	1st R.I.	Christopher Greene	13	28	4	140	185	5	2	2		194		7			4	Rhode Island
	Additional	Henry Jackson	8	58	3	181	250	9	14	170	13	456		1		1		Rhode Island
	2nd R.I. state	(late) Archibald Crary	8	23		57	88			8		96		12			9	Rhode Island
	1st R.I. state	John Topham	12	21	1	41	75			39		114		1		1		Rhode Island
	R.I. militia		2	5		83	90					90					6	Rhode Island
Maj. Gen. Heath	Invalids	Capt. Moses McFarland	2	12		60	74	14	6	26	11	131					4	Boston, Mass.
	Militia		9	27		166	202	11	11	143		367				4		Boston, Mass.
Clinton	1st N.Y.	Goose Van Schaick	19	45	1	274	339	27	21	56	8	451		1				Fort Schuyler, N.Y.
	3rd N.Y.	Peter Gansevoort	22	40	6	305	373	25	6	32	1	437	1	22		2	13	Albany, N.Y.
	4th N.Y.	Lt. Col. Frederick Weisenfels	12	31	2	151	196	10	1	29	1	237				2	1	Fort Plank, N.Y.
	5th N.Y.	Lewis DuBois	6	39	3	152	200	41	11	75	4	331		1		1	2	Johnstown, N.Y.
	7th Mass.	(late) Ichabod Alden	13	33	2	156	204	9	3	84		300		1		1	5	Cherry Valley, N.Y.
	Additional	Seth Warner	11	25	3	77	116	4	5	33	1	159		2		1		Fort George, N.Y.
	4th Pa.	Lt. Col. William Butler	10	39	4	164	217	7	10	12	1	247					3	Schoharie, N.Y.
	Rifle corps		4	14	3	86	107	9	1	2	1	120		2			12	Schoharie, N.Y.
Hand	German bn.	Lt. Col. Ludowick Weltner	14	36	5	250	305	22	16	20	18	381						Wyoming Valley, Pa.
	11th Pa.	(late) Thomas Hartley	14	48	2	276	340	16	3	18	18	395						Wyoming Valley, Pa.
	Independent corps	Tuffin Charles Armand	2	15	2	54	73	5		11		89						Wyoming Valley, Pa.
	Pa. independent corps	Capt. John Paul Schott	3 B	3		31	37	2	5	3	2	49						Wyoming Valley, Pa.
	Wyoming Valley co.	Capt. Simon Spalding	3	9	1	60	73	10	4	3	9	99						Wyoming Valley, Pa.
	TOTAL OF INFANTRY		796	2310	250	13744	17100	948	877	3419	714	23058	48	203		101	297	
	ARTILLERY																	
	4 cos. 3rd cont'l.	John Crane	10	54	3	59	126							2		4		Pluckemin, N.J.
	7 cos. 2nd cont'l.	John Lamb	24	78	3	109	214							2		1	2	Pluckemin, N.J.
	11 cos. 1st cont'l.	Charles Harrison	28	120	4	183	335							1		4	10	Pluckemin, N.J.
	3 independent cos.		1	9		16	26	27	13	137	4	1042		1		1		
	Det. 3rd cont'l.	John Crane	8	31	1	35	75							1			1	Rhode Island
	Det. 1st cont'l.	Charles Harrison	2	9		13	24											Rhode Island
	R.I. state	Robert Elliot	13	19		29	61										3	Rhode Island
	TOTAL OF ARTILLERY		86	320	11	444	861	27	13	137	4	1042		7		10	16	
	TOTAL OF WASHINGTON'S ARMY		882	2630	261	14188	17961	975	890	3556	718	24100	48	210		111	313	

MAY 1779
(continued)

BRIGADE	UNIT	COMMANDING OFFICER	PRESENT FIT FOR DUTY & ON DUTY: COMMISSIONED OFFICERS	NONCOMMISSIONED OFFICERS	STAFF OFFICERS	RANK & FILE	TOTAL	RANK & FILE SICK, ON FURLOUGH, ETC.: SICK PRESENT	SICK ABSENT	ON COMMAND & EXTRA SERVICE	ON FURLOUGH	GRAND TOTAL	ALTERATIONS: DEATHS	DESERTED	TAKEN PRISONER	DISCHARGED	JOINED, ENLISTED, RECRUITED	LOCATION
	SOUTHERN DEPARTMENT UNDER MAJOR GENERAL BENJAMIN LINCOLN (Partial Report)																	
Thompson	1st S.C.	Charles Cotesworth Pinckney	22	42	5	161	230	4	27	2		263	5	4		1	2	Stono, S.C.
Thompson	3rd S.C. (rangers)	William Thompson	18	32	2	337	389	13	74	22	3	501	3	23		1	48	Stono, S.C.
Thompson	6th S.C. (rifles)	Lt. Col. William Henderson	12	23	4	118	157	7	21	22	1	208	1	7			1	Stono, S.C.
Armstrong	4th N.C.	Lt. Col. James Thackston	11	28	5	239	283	14	100	73 E	5	475	4	2		2	9	Stono, S.C.
Armstrong	5th N.C.	James Armstrong	12	38	4	241	295	9	99	105 E	1	509		4			7	Stono, S.C.
Butler	N.C. militia	Jonas Johnston	25	15	3	322	365	34	26	54		479						Stono, S.C.
Butler	N.C. militia	Charles McDowell	19	17	2	222	260	22	21	157		460						Stono, S.C.
	S.C. militia brig.	Brig. Gen. Andrew Williamson	44	50	12	433	539	31				570						Stono, S.C.
	Va. militia brig.	David Mason	30	35	2	333	400	13	15			428						Stono, S.C.
	TOTAL OF LINCOLN'S INFANTRY		193	280	39	2406	2918	147	383	435	10	3893	13	40		4	67	
	GRAND TOTAL		1075	2910	300	16594	20879	1122	1273	3991	728	27993	61	250		115	380	

OFFICERS SICK, ON FURLOUGH, ETC.	WASHINGTON'S ARMY: COMMISSIONED	NONCOMMISSIONED	STAFF	TOTAL	LINCOLN'S ARMY (EXCEPT SOUTH CAROLINA AND VIRGINIA MILITIA): COMMISSIONED	NONCOMMISSIONED	STAFF	TOTAL	GRAND TOTAL
Sick Present	43	79	4	126	6	8		14	140
Sick Absent	39	72	3	114	5	9	1	15	129
On Command	353	412	35	800	15	15		30	830
On Furlough	159	129	29	317	2		2	4	321
Recruiting	23	33		56					56
On the Staff	154	1		155	13		2	15	170
Prisoners of War	46			46	5	4		9	55
In Arrest	10			10	1			1	11
Prisoners on Parole					2			2	2
TOTAL	827	726	71	1624	49	36	5	90	1714

SOURCES OF THIS REPORT

1. MONTHLY RETURN OF THE CONTINENTAL ARMY UNDER THE COMMAND OF HIS EXCELLENCY GEORGE WASHINGTON... FOR MAY 1779, ELEPHANT FOLIO OF WASHINGTON RETURNS, WILLIAM L. CLEMENTS LIBRARY. [ARTILLERY SECTION APPEARS ON THE PRECEDING PAGE OF THE FOLIO.]

1a. A General Return of the Troops in the State of Rhode Island Commanded by the Honourable Major General Gates, May 22, 1779, Gates Papers, New York Historical Society. [Marked monthly elsewhere on the return; this is the return that was used by the adjutant in the compilation of the general monthly return above.]

2. RETURN OF THE INFANTRY WITH MAJOR GENERAL LINCOLN, JUNE 1, 1779, BENJAMIN LINCOLN PAPERS, MASSACHUSETTS HISTORICAL SOCIETY, AND THE INDIVIDUAL RETURNS FOR THOMPSON'S, ARMSTRONG'S, AND BUTLER'S BRIGADES THAT WERE USED IN COMPILING THE GENERAL RETURN. [INDIVIDUAL RETURNS ARE ALSO IN THE LINCOLN PAPERS AND ARE ALSO DATED JUNE 1, WITH THE EXCEPTION OF THE ONE FOR BUTLER'S BRIGADE, WHICH IS DATED JUNE 7. THESE INDIVIDUAL RETURNS SUPPLY MORE DETAILED DATA THAN THEIR TOTALS, WHICH WERE USED IN THE GENERAL RETURN. THEIR HEADINGS CONFIRM THAT THE GENERAL RETURN IS THE MONTHLY ONE, THOUGH NOT SO HEADED.]

A. The manuscript for this month lists "Major Forrest" as commander of the 3rd Maryland regiment and on the June return lists "Lt. Col. Forrest." This was perhaps Uriah Forrest, who had long since been promoted to lieutenant colonel, although none of the sources in print connect him with this regiment at this time.
B. Two commissioned officers in Spalding's Wyoming Valley company plus one colonel not attached to any particular unit in Hand's brigade.
C. Five staff officers in Richard Butler's 9th Pennsylvania regiment plus one chaplain for the entire brigade.
D. Five staff officers in Heman Swift's 7th Connecticut regiment plus one chaplain for the entire brigade.
E. The manuscript notes that 120 of these 178 North Carolina Continentals on command and doing extra service were serving with the light infan[illegible]

George Washington at Princeton, by Charles Willson Peale. (Courtesy of the Pennsylvania Academy of the Fine Arts, Philadelphia)

JUNE 1779

BRIGADE	UNIT	COMMANDING OFFICER	PRESENT FIT FOR DUTY & ON DUTY: COMMISSIONED OFFICERS	NONCOMMISSIONED OFFICERS	STAFF OFFICERS	RANK & FILE	TOTAL	RANK & FILE SICK, ON FURLOUGH, ETC.: SICK PRESENT	SICK ABSENT	ON COMMAND & EXTRA SERVICE	ON FURLOUGH	PRISONERS OF WAR	EXCUSED FROM DUTY	GRAND TOTAL	ALTERATIONS: DEATHS	DESERTED	TAKEN PRISONER	DISCHARGED	JOINED, ENLISTED, RECRUITED	LOCATION
FORCES UNDER COMMANDER-IN-CHIEF GENERAL GEORGE WASHINGTON																				
Woodford	2nd Va.	Christian Febiger	2	23	4	137	166	10	9	42	23			250	1					The Clove, N.Y.
	3rd & 4th Va.	John Neville	17	58	4	271	350	17	23	20	43			453	1	2		2	6	The Clove, N.Y.
	5th & 11th Va.	William Russell	7	33	3	178	221	10	24	66	100			421				1	3	The Clove, N.Y.
	7th Va.	Daniel Morgan	6	24	3	145	178	7	12	29	13			239		2			1	The Clove, N.Y.
	8th Va.	James Wood	10	23	5	166	204	19	8	49	31			311					5	The Clove, N.Y.
Muhlenberg	1st & 10th Va.	William Davies	8	45	7	224	284	11	24	88	68			475		3		1	7	The Clove, N.Y.
	Additional	Nathaniel Gist	9	31	4	121	165	8	18	45	7			243		1			1	The Clove, N.Y.
	2nd Va. state	William Brent	13	35	4	173	225	11	19	71				326					2	The Clove, N.Y.
	1st Va. state	George Gibson	25	39	3	177	244	16	9	50	1			320		1			1	The Clove, N.Y.
	6th Va.	John Green	8	25	5	140	178	12	14	57	55			316				1		The Clove, N.Y.
Smallwood	1st Md.	John Hawkins Stone	4	23	2	140	169	3	15	113	5			305						The Clove, N.Y.
	3rd Md.	Lt. Col. Forrest [B]	8	24	4	256	292	7	28	88	9			424						The Clove, N.Y.
	5th Md.	William Richardson	6	26	5 [C]	159	196	6	25	77	5			309						The Clove, N.Y.
	7th Md.	John Gunby	12	35	5 [C]	170	222	3	25	71	5			326						The Clove, N.Y.
2nd Md.	2nd Md.	Thomas Price	6	30	1	120	157	16	30	69	6			278	1	8		1	6	The Clove, N.Y.
	4th Md.	Josias Carvil Hall	7	20	3	276	306	14	23	85	1			429		3		1	16	The Clove, N.Y.
	6th Md.	Otho Holland Williams	7	30	4	218	259	9	23	19	3			313		8		5	1	The Clove, N.Y.
Irvine	1st Pa.	James Chambers	10	31	5	176	222	10	10	59	4			305		1			1	The Clove, N.Y.
	2nd Pa.	Walter Stewart	15	34	5	313	367	15	19	52	5			458	1	5			4	The Clove, N.Y.
	7th Pa.	Lt. Col. Samuel Hay	8	29	4 [D]	166	207	13	5	21				246		1			2	The Clove, N.Y.
	10th Pa.	Richard Humpton	11	43	5 [D]	250	309	11	7	33	1			361	4	10		4		The Clove, N.Y.
2nd Pa.	3rd Pa.	Thomas Craig	11	37	5	207	260	25	20	78	1			384					4	The Clove, N.Y.
	5th Pa.	Francis Johnston	8	19	5	145	177	30	17	89	1			314		12			12	The Clove, N.Y.
	6th Pa.	Robert Magaw	12	30	4	143	189	13	11	44	2			259		2				The Clove, N.Y.
	9th Pa.	Richard Butler	5	21	4	107	137	19	15	46	2			219	1	15			7	The Clove, N.Y.
N.C.	1st N.C.	Thomas Clark	15	36	3	233	287	8	24	121	1			441	4	7		19	9	West Point, N.Y.
	2nd N.C.	John Patten	9	38	5	187	239	21	8	96	7			371						West Point, N.Y.
Paterson	12th Mass.	(late) Samuel Brewer	20	42	4	171	237	6	9	22	5			279	3	1			2	West Point, N.Y.
	10th Mass.	Thomas Marshall	13	35	4	154	206	7	10	23	9			255		5				West Point, N.Y.
	14th Mass.	Gamaliel Bradford	12	35	5 [E]	167	219	3	13	16	7			258		6				West Point, N.Y.
	11th Mass.	Benjamin Tupper	20	36	5 [E]	227	288	21	4	16	11			340					1	West Point, N.Y.
(late) Learned	2nd Mass.	John Bailey	14	36	3	203	256	13	13	64	5			351						West Point, N.Y.
	8th Mass.	Michael Jackson	19	32	2	173	226	11	10	24	12			283					2	West Point, N.Y.
	9th Mass.	James Wesson	14	36	5	177	232	15	9	59	7			322					1	West Point, N.Y.
Parsons	3rd Conn.	Samuel Wyllys	17	33	5	266	321	16	38	84				459		5		1	10	Highlands & east of the Hudson
	4th Conn.	John Durkee	14	40	4	147	205	2	13	51				271		5			6	Highlands & east of the Hudson
	6th Conn.	Return Jonathan Meigs	20	43	4	332	399	13	38	95	1			546	1	5			3	Highlands & east of the Hudson
	8th Conn.	Giles Russell	12	40	4	174	230	11	26	49				316		5		1	2	Highlands & east of the Hudson
Huntington	1st Conn.	Josiah Starr	17	39	3	231	290	19	38	38	1			386				2		Highlands & east of the Hudson
	2nd Conn.	Zebulon Butler	12	36	3	179	230	18	19	12	2			281					1	Highlands & east of the Hudson
	5th Conn.	Philip Burr Bradley	15	36	4	218	273	13	24	36				346		5				Highlands & east of the Hudson
	7th Conn.	Heman Swift	14	41	5	265	325	11	24	29	1			390					1	Highlands & east of the Hudson
Nixon	3rd Mass.	John Greaton	18	36	3	198	255	10	23	7	9			304	1	6			4	Highlands & east of the Hudson
	5th Mass.	Rufus Putnam	17	40	3	299	359	13	4	28	9			413		6		1	7	Highlands & east of the Hudson
	6th Mass.	Thomas Nixon	16	38	3	243	300	5	20	12	7			344		1		1	2	Highlands & east of the Hudson

JUNE 1779 (continued)

BRIGADE	UNIT	COMMANDING OFFICER	DUTY & ON DUTY: COMMISSIONED OFFICERS	NONCOMMISSIONED OFFICERS	STAFF OFFICERS	RANK & FILE	TOTAL	ON FURLOUGH, ETC.: SICK PRESENT	SICK ABSENT	ON COMMAND & EXTRA SERVICE	ON FURLOUGH	PRISONERS OF WAR	EXCUSED FROM DUTY	GRAND TOTAL	DEATHS	DESERTED	TAKEN PRISONER	DISCHARGED	JOINED, ENLISTED, RECRUITED	LOCATION
	FORCES UNDER COMMANDER-IN-CHIEF GENERAL GEORGE WASHINGTON (continued)																			
Maj. Gen. Gates' div.	4th Mass.	William Shepard	16	36	3	196	251	19	5	59	4			338		6			2	Rhode Island
	13th Mass.	(late) Edward Wigglesworth	14	39	4	179	236	18	4	71	5			334		6		3	3	Rhode Island
	15th Mass.	Timothy Bigelow	12	34	4	174	224	8	14	55	1			302		3			1	Rhode Island
	1st Mass.	Joseph Vose	12	33	3	175	223	20	17	46	4			310	2	21				Rhode Island
	1st Canadian	James Livingston	13	26	4	89	132	3	3	24				162		9		1	3	Rhode Island
	Additional	Henry Sherburne	17	32	5	210	264	4	1	5				274						Rhode Island
	Additional	Samuel Blatchley Webb	15	41	3	209	268	17	9	2				296				1	1	Rhode Island
	2nd R.I.	Israel Angell	16	41	5	252	314	11	3	37				365		1			1	Rhode Island
	1st R.I.	Christopher Greene	12	26	4	137	179	8	1	2				190		2				Rhode Island
	Additional	Henry Jackson	16	54	2	218	290	8	19	98	7			422		39			1	Rhode Island
	2nd R.I. state	(late) Archibald Crary	7	24	1	58	90			16				106		1			12	Rhode Island
	1st R.I. state	John Topham	11	22	1	42	76			44				120				1	10	Rhode Island
	Mass. militia	Lt. Col. Samuel Pierce	17	31	4	276	328	5		87				420					14	Rhode Island
Clinton	3rd N.Y.	Peter Gansevoort	21	37	6	309	373	7	11	38	1			430	1	5			3	Canajohary, N.Y.
	4th N.Y.	Lt. Col. Frederick Weisenfels	19	39	5	249	312	8	1	18	2			341		3		2	101	Canajohary, N.Y.
	5th N.Y.	Lewis DuBois	11	41	2	279	333	3	30	8	1			375	2	2			44	Canajohary, N.Y.
	Rifle corps	Maj. James Parr	4	12	4	58	78	6	1	34	1			120						Canajohary, N.Y.
	4th Pa. A	Lt. Col. William Butler	11	35	4	148	198	5	8	32				243	1			1		Canajohary, N.Y.
	7th Mass.	(late) Ichabod Alden	13	33	1	156	203	9	3	84				299		1		1	1	Canajohary, N.Y.
	1st N.Y.	Goose Van Schaick	20	48	1	319	388	10	14	30	2			444						Fort Schuyler, N.Y.
	TOTAL OF INFANTRY		820	2200	246	12555	15821	720	944	3133	513			21131	24	230		51	327	
	ARTILLERY																			
	3 cos. 3rd cont'l.	John Crane	7	29	3	39	78									1		1	2	Chester, N.Y.
	7 cos. 2nd cont'l.	John Lamb	24	81	4	121	230												3	Chester, N.Y.
	11 cos. 1st cont'l.	Charles Harrison	32	118	4	199	353									2			2	Chester, N.Y.
	3 independent cos.		5	19		17 F	41	23	20	77	2			1244						Chester, N.Y.
	Det. 1st & 3rd cont'l.	John Crane & Charles Harrison	8	39	1	48 F	96									3			1	Rhode Island
	R.I. state	Robert Elliot	11	27		42	80									10			6	Rhode Island
	Det. 2nd cont'l.	John Lamb	24	109		111	244									4		1	2	The Highlands, N.Y.
	TOTAL OF ARTILLERY		111	422	12	577	1122	23	20	77	2			1244		20		2	16	
	TOTAL OF WASHINGTON'S ARMY		931	2622	258	13132	16943	743	964	3210	515			22375	24	250		53	343	
	EASTERN DEPARTMENT (Formerly under Major General William Heath, Who Left June 11)																			
	Det. Mass. militia	Maj. Nathaniel Heath	7	24	1	123	155	3		64	3			225					36	in and around Boston
	Invalids	Capt. Moses McFarland	3	15		32	50	40	3	44	8			145				1	2	Boston, Mass.
	Mass. militia co.	Capt. John Carpenter	2	5		35	42	2	1					45						Springfield, Mass.
	Mass. militia co.	Capt. Elias Pratt	2	6		38	46				2			48				2		Rutland, Mass.
	TOTAL OF EASTERN DEPARTMENT		14	50	1	228	293	45	4	108	13			463				3	38	

JUNE 1779 (continued)

BRIGADE	UNIT	COMMANDING OFFICER	PRESENT FIT FOR DUTY & ON DUTY: COMMISSIONED OFFICERS	NONCOMMISSIONED OFFICERS	STAFF OFFICERS	RANK & FILE	TOTAL	RANK & FILE SICK, ON FURLOUGH, ETC.: SICK PRESENT	SICK ABSENT	ON COMMAND & EXTRA SERVICE	ON FURLOUGH	PRISONERS OF WAR	EXCUSED FROM DUTY	GRAND TOTAL	ALTERATIONS: DEATHS	DESERTED	TAKEN PRISONER	DISCHARGED	JOINED, ENLISTED, RECRUITED	LOCATION
	SOUTHERN DEPARTMENT UNDER MAJOR GENERAL BENJAMIN LINCOLN																			
Pinckney	1st S.C.	Charles Cotesworth Pinckney	14	38	5	134	191	10	27	7		3		238						Stono, S.C.
Pinckney	3rd S.C. (rangers)	William Thompson	15	31	2	305	353	9	76	57	3	89		587						Port Royal Ferry, S.C.
Pinckney	6th S.C. (rifles)	Lt. Col. William Henderson	8	20	2	103	133	17	30	14	5			199						Stono, S.C.
Armstrong	4th N.C.	Lt. Col. James Thackston	6	26	5	184	221	14	97	21	3			356						Stono, S.C.
Armstrong	5th N.C.	James Armstrong	6	36	4	217	263	34	60	56	1			414						Stono, S.C.
Williamson	Independent cos.		2	6		47	55						5	60						Stono, S.C.
Williamson	S.C. militia	Robert Goodwin	4	3	1	23	31							31						Stono, S.C.
Williamson	S.C. militia	James Lyles	8	4	2	11	25							25						Stono, S.C.
Williamson	S.C. militia	LeRoy Hammond	6	6	1	37	50							50						Stono, S.C.
Williamson	S.C. militia	Samuel Watson	2	1	1	9	13							13						Stono, S.C.
Williamson	S.C. militia	John Thomas	2	1	2	10	15							15						Stono, S.C.
Williamson	S.C. militia	James Williams	5	3		31	39	73 G						112						Stono, S.C.
	N.C. militia brig.	Brig. Gen. John Butler	28	45	3	271	347	44 H						391 L						Stono, S.C.
	Va. militia brig.	David Mason	22	27	3	199	251	51	45	18 J				365 M						Stono, S.C.
Moore	1st Ga. bn.	Robert Rae												38						Stono, S.C.
Moore	2nd Ga. bn.	Samuel Elbert												66						Stono, S.C.
Moore	3rd Ga. bn.	John Stirk												44						Stono, S.C.
Moore	4th Ga. bn.	John White												37 M						Stono, S.C.
	TOTAL OF INFANTRY		128	247	31	1581	1987	252 H	335	173	12	92	5	3041						
	ARTILLERY																			
	4th S.C.	Maj. John Grimké	8	32	1	53	94		11 I	19 K	1			125						Stono, S.C.
	TOTAL OF LINCOLN'S ARMY		136	279	32	1634	2081	252	346	192	13	92	5	3166						
	GRAND TOTAL		1081	2951	291	14994	19317	1040	1314	3510	541	92	5	26004 M						

OFFICERS SICK, ON FURLOUGH, ETC.	WASHINGTON'S ARMY				EASTERN DEPARTMENT (EXCLUDING CARPENTER'S & PRATT'S COMPANIES)				LINCOLN'S ARMY (EXCLUDING ARMSTRONG'S AND MOORE'S BRIGADES)				GRAND TOTAL
	COMMISSIONED	NONCOMMISSIONED	STAFF	TOTAL	COMMISSIONED	NONCOMMISSIONED	STAFF	TOTAL	COMMISSIONED	NONCOMMISSIONED	STAFF	TOTAL	
Sick Present	18	56	3	77		2		2	19	13	3	35 H	114
Sick Absent	43	82	5	130					13	16	1	30	160
On Command	270	338	13	621	4	18		22	6	15		21	664
On Furlough	85	88	19	192	2	1		3	4	2	3	9	204
On the Staff	146			146							3	3	149
Recruiting	15	29		44									44
Prisoners of War	59	11	4	74					7	9		16	90
In Arrest	3			3									3
Wounded									3	1	1	5	5
TOTAL	639	604	44	1287	6	21		27	52	56	11	119	1433

SOURCES OF THIS REPORT

1. MONTHLY RETURN OF THE CONTINENTAL ARMY UNDER THE COMMAND OF HIS EXCELLENCY GEORGE WASHINGTON. . . FOR THE MONTH OF JUNE 1779, ELEPHANT FOLIO OF WASHINGTON RETURNS, WILLIAM L. CLEMENTS LIBRARY.

1a. Monthly Return of the Continental Army under. . . Washington. . . June 1779, Record Group 93, National Archives. [The same figures but only to the brigade level.]

1b. A General Return of the Troops in the State of Rhode Island Commanded by the Honourable Major General Gates, June 19, 1779, Gates Papers, New-York Historical Society. [Although not so headed, this is the monthly return used by the adjutant in compiling the general monthly return above.]

2. A MONTHLY GENERAL RETURN OF THE TROOPS DOING DUTY IN THE EASTERN DEPARTMENT, JUNE 30, 1779, GATES PAPERS, NEW-YORK HISTORICAL SOCIETY.

3. SOUTHERN DEPARTMENT REPORT COMPILED FROM MONTHLY RETURNS FOR PINCKNEY'S BRIGADE AND THE 4th SOUTH CAROLINA (ARTILLERY) AND FROM RETURNS DATED JUNE 21 (ARMSTRONG'S BRIGADE), AND JULY 3, 4 and 5, 1779 (THE OTHER BRIGADES), ALL IN THE BENJAMIN LINCOLN PAPERS, MASSACHUSETTS HISTORICAL SOCIETY.

A. The manuscript returns for both June and July have 6th Massachusetts for this regiment; although there is some confusion in other records as well, Nixon's 6th Massachusetts regiment is elsewhere on both returns, and the regiment is usually cited as the 7th.

B. See footnote A on the previous report.

C. Four staff officers in John Gunby's 7th Maryland regiment plus one chaplain for the entire brigade.

D. Four staff officers in Richard Humpton's 10th Pennsylvania regiment plus one chaplain for the entire brigade.

E. Four staff officers in Benjamin Tupper's 11th Massachusetts regiment plus one chaplain for the entire brigade.

F. For the months of June and October 1779, there is a discrepancy between the original return of the artillery in the Northern Department (found in the Gates Papers) and the figures for the Northern Department artillery as transcribed in the general returns of Washington's command. In compiling the general return, the adjutant mistook a total of rank and file (fit for duty, sick present, sick absent, on command, and on furlough) for the column of rank and file fit for duty. We have corrected the fit for duty figures on our report, so that they agree with the original return. However, because the general return of Washington's command gives only totals of matrosses sick present, sick absent, etc., it is not possible to be certain whether the sick present, sick absent, etc., from the Northern Department were included in these combined figures. It seems reasonable to conclude that they were, since the other mistake was simply the copying of a wrong column, but it is possible that fifty-six matrosses who were sick present, sick absent, etc., in the Northern Department have been excluded here.

G. These men are in a column headed "sick in camp hospital or gone home" on the manuscript. Thus, an undetermined number of these men were actually not "sick present."

H. The return of Butler's North Carolina militia brigade does not distinguish between "sick present" and "sick absent" but simply enters the men as "sick." Since the return does not report on other types of absences, the designation actually may have meant "sick present," but these forty-four men should be kept in mind in considering the total of "sick present" for the rank and file of the Southern Department. Similarly, there are seven commissioned, seven noncommissioned, and one staff officer included in "sick present" of the officers section that are marked only "sick" on the manuscript.

I. Including two men sick at Silver Bluff, six in a fixed hospital, and three in a Charleston hospital.

J. This column is headed simply "1st Battalion" on the manuscript; apparently these men were on some sort of detached duty.

K. Including two men in Charleston, three acting as orderlies in hospitals, and fourteen on detachment.

L. Butler's return also notes seventeen waggoners, but, judging from their position on the manuscript, they apparently were civilians rather than enlisted men and have been excluded here.

M. The return for the Georgia brigade is in a form that is very unlike the standard form used for returns; moreover, much of the form is illegible. Consequently, only totals, including all the men in the brigade, are given here, and therefore this report has a difference in its horizontal and vertical totals. The National Archives manuscript notes that no monthly returns were available for the Southern Department (supplied here), for the Western Department with the exception of Clinton's brigade, for the 2nd Canadian and Warner's Additional regiments in the Northern Department, and for the cavalry. It is also noted that the "monthly alterations of the first Maryland Brigade are omitted as being inaccurate."

JULY 1779

BRIGADE	UNIT	COMMANDING OFFICER	Present Fit for Duty & on Duty: COMMISSIONED OFFICERS	NONCOMMISSIONED OFFICERS	STAFF OFFICERS	RANK & FILE	TOTAL	Rank & File Sick, on Furlough, etc.: SICK PRESENT	SICK ABSENT	ON COMMAND & EXTRA SERVICE	ON FURLOUGH	PRISONERS OF WAR	ON THE STAFF	NONEFFECTIVE	GRAND TOTAL	Alterations: DEATHS	DESERTED	TAKEN PRISONER	DISCHARGED	JOINED, ENLISTED, RECRUITED	LOCATION
FORCES UNDER COMMANDER-IN-CHIEF GENERAL GEORGE WASHINGTON																					
Woodford	2nd Va.	Christian Febiger	5	19	5	123	152	10	5	84					251						The Highlands, N.Y.
Woodford	3rd & 4th Va.	John Neville	16	56	5	276	353	10	25	21	39				448						The Highlands, N.Y.
Woodford	5th & 11th Va.	William Russell	9	31	3	146	189	8	33	185	1				416	6	5		14	14	The Highlands, N.Y.
Woodford	7th Va.	Daniel Morgan	6	17	3	110	136	4	12	55	13				220						The Highlands, N.Y.
Woodford	8th Va.	James Wood	9	21	4	137	171	12	15	104					302						The Highlands, N.Y.
Muhlenberg	1st & 10th Va.	William Davies	13	37	6	224	280	12	26	156					474	1	2		2		The Highlands, N.Y.
Muhlenberg	Additional	Nathaniel Gist	10	29	4	133	176	6	18	36	5				241		1		2	2	The Highlands, N.Y.
Muhlenberg	2nd Va. state	William Brent	13	30	4	189	236	8	11	64					319			1	2	1	The Highlands, N.Y.
Muhlenberg	1st Va. state	George Gibson	23	34	4	176	237	10	9	56	1				313	1			1		The Highlands, N.Y.
Muhlenberg	6th Va.	John Green	10	37	6	146	199	9	9	60	45				322		3		7	1	The Highlands, N.Y.
Smallwood	1st Md.	John Hawkins Stone	7	39	2	224	272	16	16	25	6				335	2	8		1	22	The Highlands, N.Y.
Smallwood	3rd Md.	Lt. Col. Nathaniel Ramsay	9	25	5	321	360	14	28	65	8				475		3		1	22	The Highlands, N.Y.
Smallwood	5th Md.	William Richardson	7	24	3	194	228	5	26	36	3				298	5	11			1	The Highlands, N.Y.
Smallwood	7th Md.	John Gunby	9	33	4	228	274		17	30	5				326	5			1	7	The Highlands, N.Y.
Gist	2nd Md.	Thomas Price	5	29	1	214	249	7	20	106	4				386	1	2		1	15	The Highlands, N.Y.
Gist	4th Md.	Josias Carvil Hall	6	26	3	227	262	10	29	117					418	1	6		4	1	The Highlands, N.Y.
Gist	6th Md.	Otho Holland Williams	7	32	1	193	233	4	26	47	2				312		9		4	16	The Highlands, N.Y.
Irvine	1st Pa.	James Chambers	12	29	4	170	215	7	11	39	4				276	1	26			3	The Highlands, N.Y.
Irvine	2nd Pa.	Walter Stewart	15	30	4	295	344	28	11	61	4				448	3	5		1	3	The Highlands, N.Y.
Irvine	7th Pa.	Lt. Col. Morgan Connor	8	31	4 D	171	214	14	8	3					239	1	9			2	The Highlands, N.Y.
Irvine	10th Pa.	Richard Humpton	11	43	6	244	304	17	11	35					367		2			8	The Highlands, N.Y.
2nd Pa.	3rd Pa.	Thomas Craig	13	37	5	240	295	18	19	41	2				375	6	7	1	4	4	The Highlands, N.Y.
2nd Pa.	5th Pa.	Francis Johnston	12	34	5	201	252	38	16	23	1				330	1	2		1	7	The Highlands, N.Y.
2nd Pa.	6th Pa.	Robert Magaw	9	27	5	162	203	16	11	15					245		8	1	7	3	The Highlands, N.Y.
2nd Pa.	9th Pa.	Richard Butler	10	25	5	138	178	23	11	16	1				229	1	7			6	The Highlands, N.Y.
N.C.	1st N.C.	Thomas Clark	18	44	3	288	353	24	6	47	2				432		4		14	8	West Point, N.Y.
N.C.	2nd N.C.	John Patten	12	44	5	253	314	22	5	19	3				363		8		9	1	West Point, N.Y.
Paterson	12th Mass.	(late) Samuel Brewer	11	41	3	241	296	9	8	18	2				333	2	7		2	78	West Point, N.Y.
Paterson	10th Mass.	Thomas Marshall	14	39	4	243	300	13	7	17					337	1	5			86	West Point, N.Y.
Paterson	14th Mass.	Gamaliel Bradford	13	37	4 E	251	305	9	10	14	1				339	1	4			85	West Point, N.Y.
Paterson	11th Mass.	Benjamin Tupper	16	37	4	246	303	17	10	12					342		7			14	West Point, N.Y.
4th Mass.	2nd Mass.	John Bailey	13	35	5	193	246	12	16	67					341	3	7			1	West Point, N.Y.
4th Mass.	8th Mass.	Michael Jackson	16	37	4	230	287	25	10	17	3				342	1	7			64	West Point, N.Y.
4th Mass.	9th Mass.	James Wesson	13	36	5	205	259	17	9	50	3				338		4			21	West Point, N.Y.
Parsons	3rd Conn.	Samuel Wyllys	11	36	5	246	298	13	35	101					447	4	3			1	Highlands & east of the Hudson
Parsons	4th Conn.	John Durkee	10	32	5	130	177	7	16	61					261		1			2	Highlands & east of the Hudson
Parsons	6th Conn.	Return Jonathan Meigs	13	36	5	288	342	18	44	123					527	2	4		1	3	Highlands & east of the Hudson
Parsons	8th Conn.	Giles Russell	9	33	3	134	179	15	33	77					304		2			1	Highlands & east of the Hudson
Huntington	1st Conn.	Josiah Starr	11	40	2	201	254	17	36	63	1				371	4	2		4	1	Highlands & east of the Hudson
Huntington	2nd Conn.	Zebulon Butler	9	29	3	137	178	7	30	55	1				271		1		1	3	Highlands & east of the Hudson
Huntington	5th Conn.	Philip Burr Bradley	14	32	4 F	169	219	13	30	76	2				340	1	8			6	Highlands & east of the Hudson
Huntington	7th Conn.	Heman Swift	11	36	5	220	272	6	28	69					375		7			2	Highlands & east of the Hudson
Nixon	3rd Mass.	John Greaton	11	38	5	220	274	8	20	11					313		15			30	Highlands & east of the Hudson
Nixon	5th Mass.	Rufus Putnam	15	39	3	287	344	15	13	24	2				398	1	10	5		5	Highlands & east of the Hudson
Nixon	6th Mass.	Thomas Nixon	16	37	4	245	302	4	18	14	2				340		5		1	2	Highlands & east of the Hudson
Glover	4th Mass.	William Shepard	17	40	5	246	308	5	13	7	5				338		8		1	5	Highlands & east of the Hudson
Glover	13th Mass.	Lt. Col. Ebenezer Sprout B	19	37	4	204	264	11	15	34	7				331		5		1	2	Highlands & east of the Hudson
Glover	15th Mass.	Timothy Bigelow	15	36	4	201	256	10	11	13	4				294		11				Highlands & east of the Hudson
Glover	1st Mass.	Joseph Vose	17	34	3	196	250	15	29	6	6				306		10		2	2	Highlands & east of the Hudson

JULY 1779 (continued)

BRIGADE	UNIT	COMMANDING OFFICER	PRESENT FIT FOR DUTY & ON DUTY: COMMISSIONED OFFICERS	NONCOMMISSIONED OFFICERS	STAFF OFFICERS	RANK & FILE	TOTAL	RANK & FILE SICK, ON FURLOUGH, ETC.: SICK PRESENT	SICK ABSENT	ON COMMAND & EXTRA SERVICE	ON FURLOUGH	PRISONERS OF WAR	ON THE STAFF	NONEFFECTIVE	GRAND TOTAL	ALTERATIONS: DEATHS	DESERTED	TAKEN PRISONER	DISCHARGED	JOINED, ENLISTED, RECRUITED	LOCATION
	FORCES UNDER COMMANDER-IN-CHIEF GENERAL GEORGE WASHINGTON (continued)																				
Maj. Gen. Gates' div.	1st Canadian	James Livingston	11	28	4	92	135	7	3	19					164		3			6	Rhode Island
	Additional	Henry Sherburne	16	37	5	207	265	2	1	5					273						Rhode Island
	Additional	Samuel Blatchley Webb	12	40	5	210	267	11	7	8					293				1		Rhode Island
	2nd R.I.	Israel Angell	15	38	5	210	268	5	7	78					358	2	3			6	Rhode Island
	1st R.I.	Christopher Greene	11	26	4	138	179	2	1	6					188		1			3	Rhode Island
	Additional	Henry Jackson	16	63	3	266	348	15	14	34					411		22		1	8	Rhode Island
	1st R.I. state	John Topham	13	42	1	87	143	3		74					220		1		2	6	Rhode Island
	Mass. state	Nathan Tyler	13	24	2	268	307	8		42					357						Rhode Island
	R.I. militia	Lt. Col. Nathaniel Church	6	6		121	133								133						Rhode Island
Clinton	4th Pa.	Lt. Col. William Butler C	11	38	5	178	232		1	2					235						Otsego Lake, N.Y.
	Rifle corps	Lt. Col. William Butler	5	13	3	88	109		6	1					116						Otsego Lake, N.Y.
	3rd N.Y.	Peter Gansevoort	25	43	4	328	400		14	21					435		1			1	Otsego Lake, N.Y.
	4th N.Y.	Lt. Col. Frederick Weisenfels	19	39	4	245	307		11	7	2				327	1	6				Otsego Lake, N.Y.
	5th N.Y. A	Lewis DuBois	12	40	4	274	330		33	11					374						Otsego Lake, N.Y.
	7th Mass.	Maj. Daniel Whiting	18	44	4	229	295		19	5					319		1	9			Otsego Lake, N.Y.
Maxwell	1st N.J.	Matthias Ogden	19	49	5	241	314	18	17	2					351		2			2	Wyoming Valley, Pa.
	2nd N.J.	Israel Shreve	19	40	5	264	328	13	19	10	1				371		1				Wyoming Valley, Pa.
	3rd N.J.	Elias Dayton	16	43	4	253	316	8	16	13					353					1	Wyoming Valley, Pa.
	Additional	Oliver Spencer	11	42	4	210	267	20	15	15	2				319		2		1		Wyoming Valley, Pa.
Poor	1st N.H.	Joseph Cilley	20	33	5	282	340	16	38	9	44				447						Wyoming Valley, Pa.
	2nd N.H.	Lt. Col. George Reid	18	33	3	214	268	11	21	14	18				332						Wyoming Valley, Pa.
	3rd N.H.	Alexander Scammell	17	32	4	169	222	13	17	11	25				288	1	3				Wyoming Valley, Pa.
	2nd N.Y.	Philip Van Cortlandt	15	31	3	170	219	14	10	5					248						Wyoming Valley, Pa.
Hand	German bn.	Lt. Col. Ludowick Weltner	17	42	2	280	341	5	9	15	2				372		6		1		Wyoming Valley, Pa.
	11th Pa.	Lt. Col. Adam Hubley	16	45	2	267	330	14	19		3				366						Wyoming Valley, Pa.
	Pa. independent co.	Capt. John Paul Schott	4	7		38	49				2				51				3		Wyoming Valley, Pa.
	Independent corps		4	6	1	69	80	6	1	1	1				89		3				Wyoming Valley, Pa.
	2nd Canadian	Moses Hazen	17	31	3	173	224	15	19	217	4				479					3	Coos (Vt. & N.H.)
	TOTAL OF INFANTRY		974	2615	292	15727	19608	824	1193	3100	292				25017	59	316	17	98	597	
	ARTILLERY																				
	3 cos. 3rd cont'l.	John Crane	7	29	3	43	82														Chester, N.Y.
	7 cos. 2nd cont'l.	John Lamb	32	82	4	135	253									1			2	5	Chester, N.Y.
	11 cos. 1st cont'l.	Charles Harrison	35	139	4	216	394													2	Chester, N.Y.
	3 independent cos.		4	18		20	42												2	1	Chester, N.Y.
	5 cos. 3rd cont'l.	John Crane	16	74		79	169	5	17	110					1377		1			1	West Point, N.Y.
	2 cos. 2nd cont'l.	John Lamb	10	30		42	82													2	West Point, N.Y.
	Det. 3rd cont'l.	John Crane	11	52	1	47	111									1	3			1	Rhode Island
	Det. 1st cont'l.	Charles Harrison	2	7		19	28													3	Rhode Island
	R.I. state	Robert Elliot	10	29		45	84														Rhode Island
	TOTAL OF ARTILLERY		127	460	12	646	1245	5	17	110					1377	2	4		4 N	15	
	TOTAL OF WASHINGTON'S ARMY		1101	3075	304	16373	20853	829	1210	3210	292				26394	61	320	17	102	612	

JULY 1779 (continued)

BRIGADE	UNIT	COMMANDING OFFICER	PRESENT FIT FOR DUTY & ON DUTY: COMMISSIONED OFFICERS	NONCOMMISSIONED OFFICERS	STAFF OFFICERS	RANK & FILE	TOTAL	RANK & FILE SICK, ON FURLOUGH, ETC.: SICK PRESENT	SICK ABSENT	ON COMMAND & EXTRA SERVICE	ON FURLOUGH	PRISONERS OF WAR	ON THE STAFF	NONEFFECTIVE	GRAND TOTAL	ALTERATIONS: DEATHS	DESERTED	TAKEN PRISONER	DISCHARGED	JOINED, ENLISTED, RECRUITED	LOCATION
	SOUTHERN DEPARTMENT UNDER MAJOR GENERAL BENJAMIN LINCOLN																				
Scott	1st S.C.	Charles Cotesworth Pinckney	10	31	2	125	168	8	38		13	3			230	3[K]	6			2	Sheldon Plantation, S.C.
Scott	3rd S.C. (rangers)	William Thompson	14	32	3	301	350	16	87	21	19	5			498	69[L]	37[M]		3[O]	14	Sheldon Plantation, S.C.
Scott	6th S.C. (rifles)	Lt. Col. William Henderson	6	21	4	100	131	11[G]	24		16				182	9	4				Sheldon Plantation, S.C.
	5th S.C. (rifles)	Lt. Col. Alexander McIntosh	20	24		77	121	35			17				173	2	12	8			"the New Barracks"
Lt. Col. Thackston	4th N.C.	Lt. Col. James Thackston	16	29	6	211	262	77	74	13	37				463						
Lt. Col. Thackston	5th N.C.	James Armstrong	11	38	3	238	290	68	64	8	34				464						
Ga.	1st Ga.	Robert Rae	3	4	2	8	17	2	2	1	3	6[H]	1		32						Augusta, Ga.
Ga.	2nd Ga.	Samuel Elbert	1	4		17	22	2	3	11	5		4		47						Augusta, Ga.
Ga.	3rd Ga.	John Stirk		4	1	10	15	3	1	1	1	2[H]	5		28						Augusta, Ga.
Ga.	4th Ga.	John White	1	5	1	3	10	1	3	4	2		1		21						Augusta, Ga.
	TOTAL OF INFANTRY		82	192	22	1090	1386	223[G]	296	59	147	16	11		2138	83	59	8		16	
	CAVALRY AND LEGIONARY CORPS																				
	Pulaski's legion	Casimir Pulaski	15	30	5	142	192							126[I]	318						South Carolina
	Ga. cavalry		6	3		13	22			1	3				26						Augusta, Ga.
	TOTAL OF CAVALRY		21	33	5	155	214			1	3			126	344						
	ARTILLERY																				
	4th S.C.	Barnard Beekman	5	19		45	69								69						Sheldon Plantation, S.C.
	TOTAL OF LINCOLN'S ARMY		108	244	27	1290	1669	223[G]	296	60	150	16	11	126	2551						
	GRAND TOTAL		1209	3319	331	17663	22522	1052[G]	506	3270	442	16	11	126	28945[J]						

OFFICERS SICK, ON FURLOUGH, ETC.	WASHINGTON'S ARMY: COMMISSIONED	NONCOMMISSIONED	STAFF	TOTAL	LINCOLN'S ARMY (EXCEPT ARTILLERY): COMMISSIONED	NONCOMMISSIONED	STAFF	TOTAL	GRAND TOTAL
Sick Present	41	64	5	110	1	10[G]		11	121
Sick Absent	67	111	8	186	10	21	1	32	218
On Command	248	320	18	586	2	10		12	598
On Furlough	73	46	18	137	24	23	4	51	188
Recruiting	16	42		58					58
On the Staff	225			225	10	7	3	20	245
Prisoners of War	68	3	2	73	32		1	33	106
In Arrest	3		1	4					4
Prisoners on Parole					11			11	11
Noneffective[P]						9		1	1
Wounded					3	1	1	5	5
TOTAL	741	586	53	1379	93	73	10	176	1555

SOURCES OF THIS REPORT

1. MONTHLY RETURN OF THE CONTINENTAL ARMY UNDER THE COMMAND OF HIS EXCELLENCY GEORGE WASHINGTON. . . FOR THE MONTH OF JULY 1779, ELEPHANT FOLIO OF WASHINGTON RETURNS, WILLIAM L. CLEMENTS LIBRARY.

   1a. Monthly Return of the Continental Army under. . . Washington. . . July 1779, Record Group 93, National Archives. [The same figures, but only to the brigade level.]

   1b. A General Return of the Troops in the State of Rhode Island Commanded by the Honourable Major General Gates, July 24, 1779, Gates Papers, New-York Historical Society. [Although not so headed, this is the monthly return used by the adjutant in compiling the general monthly return above.]

2. REPORT FOR THE SOUTHERN DEPARTMENT COMPILED FROM MONTHLY RETURNS FOR SCOTT'S BRIGADE, THE 5th SOUTH CAROLINA REGIMENT, AND THE 4th SOUTH CAROLINA (ARTILLERY) REGIMENT AND RETURNS DATED JULY 27, AUGUST 4, AND AUGUST 5, 1779, FOR PULASKI'S LEGION, THACKSTON'S BRIGADE AND THE GEORGIA BRIGADE, RESPECTIVELY, BENJAMIN LINCOLN PAPERS, MASSACHUSETTS HISTORICAL SOCIETY.

A. See footnote A on the previous return; one of the records abstracted in Massachusetts Soldiers and Sailors of the Revolutionary War agrees exactly with this by making Whiting Major Commandant of the 7th Massachusetts; other records have him promoted to Lieutenant Colonel of the 6th Massachusetts at an earlier date.
B. Gates, in a letter dated June 16, 1779, recommended Sprout for the command of the 13th Massachusetts, and Sprout temporarily served in that regiment. However, he eventually became Lieutenant Colonel Commandant of the 12th Massachusetts.
C. The rifle corps was incorporated in the command of Butler of the 4th Pennsylvania; see footnote A on our December 1778 report and footnote K on our March 1779 report. Presumably, by this time these men were no longer being included as "on command" from the regiments from which they had been drawn.
D. Five staff officers in Richard Humpton's 10th Pennsylvania regiment plus one chaplain for the entire brigade.
E. Three staff officers in Benjamin Tupper's 11th Massachusetts regiment plus one chaplain for the entire brigade.
F. Four staff officers in Heman Swift's 7th Connecticut regiment plus one chaplain for the entire brigade.
G. The manuscript for the 5th South Carolina regiment does not distinguish between "sick present" and "sick absent." Since we have put the thirty-five rank and file "sick" into the "sick present" column, these men should be kept in mind in considering the totals of "sick present." Seven noncommissioned officers "sick" are also entered in "sick present."
H. Prisoners on parole.
I. A total of all noneffective enlisted men in Pulaski's Legion; the manuscript does not divide them into categories.
J. The National Archives manuscript notes that no monthly returns were available for the Southern Department (the Continental units of which are supplied here), for the 8th Pennsyl- and 9th Virginia (old 13th) regiments at Fort Pitt, for Van Schaick's 1st New York regiment at Fort Schuyler, for Warner's Additional regiment at Fort George, for the Delaware Continental regiment at Middle Brook, for Armand's Corps on the east side of the Hudson, for the cavalry, for one company of artillery at Fort Schuyler, for three companies of artillery with General Clinton's brigade, and for two companies of artillery with the Connecticut brigades.
K. Including one missing.
L. Including sixty-four who died while prisoners of war.
M. Including thirty who enlisted with the British while prisoners of war.
N. Including fifty men in Washington's infantry discharged for inability.
O. The manuscript notes that two of these men were "ruptured" and that one's time had expired.
P. Eight officers from Pulaski's Legion, marked simply "noneffective" and not further distinguished, and one fife major in Thackston's brigade who was noneffective (it is not possible to decipher in what way because of a crease in the manuscript).

AUGUST 1779

BRIGADE	UNIT	COMMANDING OFFICER	PRESENT FIT FOR DUTY & ON DUTY: COMMISSIONED OFFICERS	NONCOMMISSIONED OFFICERS	STAFF OFFICERS	RANK & FILE	TOTAL	RANK & FILE SICK, ON FURLOUGH, ETC.: SICK PRESENT	SICK ABSENT	ON COMMAND & EXTRA SERVICE	ON FURLOUGH	NOT JOINED	PRISONERS OF WAR	GRAND TOTAL	ALTERATIONS: DEATHS	DESERTED	TAKEN PRISONER	DISCHARGED	JOINED, ENLISTED, RECRUITED	LOCATION
	FORCES UNDER COMMANDER-IN-CHIEF GENERAL GEORGE WASHINGTON																			
Woodford	2nd Va.	Christian Febiger	8	24	6	184	222	14	3	54				293	1	1	1	1	1	The Highlands, N.Y.
Woodford	3rd & 4th Va.	John Neville	17	53	5	267	342	16	9	81				448	1	1		1	6	The Highlands, N.Y.
Woodford	5th & 11th Va.	William Russell	13	33	4	204	254	12	10	145	1			422				2	1	The Highlands, N.Y.
Woodford	7th Va.	Daniel Morgan	8	18	3	133	162	5	5	18	14			204				20	1	The Highlands, N.Y.
Woodford	8th Va.	James Wood	12	24	4	181	221	9	6	66	1			303	2	1			1	The Highlands, N.Y.
Muhlenberg	1st & 10th Va.	William Davies	14	36	6	178	234	13	20	152	1			420				43	2	The Highlands, N.Y.
Muhlenberg	Additional	Nathaniel Gist	9	25	4	124	162	12	11	40	3			228		6	3		3	The Highlands, N.Y.
Muhlenberg	2nd Va. state	William Brent	11	34	4	184	233	16	9	63				321	1	1			1	The Highlands, N.Y.
Muhlenberg	1st Va. state	George Gibson	14	39	4	170	227	17	6	57	2			309					1	The Highlands, N.Y.
Muhlenberg	6th Va.	John Green	10	30	6	178	224	8	6	30	45			313	1	2		1	2	The Highlands, N.Y.
Smallwood	1st Md.	(late) John Hawkins Stone	8	40	3	222	273	18	14	35	4			344	4	1		5	19	The Highlands, N.Y.
Smallwood	3rd Md.	Lt. Col. Nathaniel Ramsay	11	29	5	339	384	12	21	58	3			478		5		1	6	The Highlands, N.Y.
Smallwood	5th Md.	William Richardson	4	32	4	215	255	20	15	28	2			320				1	21	The Highlands, N.Y.
Smallwood	7th Md.	John Gunby	9	38	4	222	273	15	14	30	5			337	1				17	The Highlands, N.Y.
Gist	2nd Md.	Thomas Price	8	36	4	264	312	14	18	51	3			398	1	3			9	The Highlands, N.Y.
Gist	4th Md.	Josias Carvil Hall	7	34	3 A	303	347	16	21	48				432	1	1			4	The Highlands, N.Y.
Gist	6th Md.	Otho Holland Williams	9	31	2	209	251	12	18	35	1			317	1	2			6	The Highlands, N.Y.
Irvine	1st Pa.	James Chambers	9	27	3	162	201	12	8	41	4			266		4		3	6	The Highlands, N.Y.
Irvine	2nd Pa.	Walter Stewart	14	39	5	339	397	16	14	23	3			453	1	5			4	The Highlands, N.Y.
Irvine	7th Pa.	Lt. Col. Morgan Connor	11	29	4	161	205	21	5	7				238		4			2	The Highlands, N.Y.
Irvine	10th Pa.	Richard Humpton	11	42	3	245	301	12	9	43				365					2	The Highlands, N.Y.
2nd Pa.	3rd Pa.	Thomas Craig	12	38	4	223	277	18	16	55	3			369	1	6			4	The Highlands, N.Y.
2nd Pa.	5th Pa.	Francis Johnston	12	27	4	200	243	33	18	25	1			320	1	2			2	The Highlands, N.Y.
2nd Pa.	6th Pa.	Robert Magaw	10	29	5	157	201	18	8	14				241		3		5	3	The Highlands, N.Y.
2nd Pa.	9th Pa.	Richard Butler	12	28	5	158	203	15	6	8				232		5		1	4	The Highlands, N.Y.
N.C.	1st N.C.	Thomas Clark	16	42	2	291	351	31	8	42	3			435		2		7	10	West Point, N.Y.
N.C.	2nd N.C.	John Patten	12	49	5	296	362	28	4	19				413				3	55	West Point, N.Y.
Paterson	12th Mass.	(late) Samuel Brewer	12	41	2	282	337	14	7	19	1			378		5		4	54	West Point, N.Y.
Paterson	10th Mass.	Thomas Marshall	12	36	5	268	321	19	3	32	1			376		3		3	50	West Point, N.Y.
Paterson	14th Mass.	Gamaliel Bradford	13	38	4 B	280	335	18	11	19	1			384		3		1	50	West Point, N.Y.
Paterson	11th Mass.	Benjamin Tupper	16	38	3	294	351	18	9	15				393					53	West Point, N.Y.
4th Mass.	2nd Mass.	John Bailey	16	39	6	267	328	21	12	31	1			393	1	1			47	West Point, N.Y.
4th Mass.	8th Mass.	Michael Jackson	13	41	5	272	331	38	5	17	2			393		3			52	West Point, N.Y.
4th Mass.	9th Mass.	James Wesson	14	39	3	271	327	26	9	21	3			386					48	West Point, N.Y.
Parsons	3rd Conn.	Samuel Wyllys	14	38	5	285	342	22	27	53	3			447		4		1		Highlands & east of the Hudson
Parsons	4th Conn.	John Durkee	10	34	3	155	202	16	11	36	2			267		4			10	Highlands & east of the Hudson
Parsons	6th Conn.	Return Jonathan Meigs	16	46	4	351	417	19	39	63	3			541	1	2			6	Highlands & east of the Hudson
Parsons	8th Conn.	Giles Russell	12	39	4	190	245	10	30	23	3			311	2	2		1	2	Highlands & east of the Hudson
Huntington	1st Conn.	Josiah Starr	11	42	2	233	288	21	28	27	4			368		1		4		Highlands & east of the Hudson
Huntington	2nd Conn.	Zebulon Butler	14	34	2	189	239	9	30	17	1			296		1			17	Highlands & east of the Hudson
Huntington	5th Conn.	Philip Burr Bradley	13	32	4 C	211	260	18	28	34	2			342	2	1		2	7	Highlands & east of the Hudson
Huntington	7th Conn.	Heman Swift	13	37	6	253	309	6	30	30	3			378					2	Highlands & east of the Hudson
Nixon	3rd Mass.	John Greaton	13	41	4	278	336	25	16	10				387		2		2	75	Highlands & east of the Hudson
Nixon	5th Mass.	Rufus Putnam	16	34	3	283	336	18	11	21	1			387		5				Highlands & east of the Hudson
Nixon	6th Mass.	Thomas Nixon	16	40	4	281	341	20	14	16				391	1	2		2	58	Highlands & east of the Hudson
Glover	4th Mass.	William Shepard	9	29	4	128	170	6	12	156	4			348		5			36	Highlands & east of the Hudson
Glover	13th Mass.	Lt. Col. Ebenezer Sprout	16	30	4	205	255	12	12	77	4			360		2			40	Highlands & east of the Hudson
Glover	15th Mass.	Timothy Bigelow	7	22	1	150	180	4	12	132	3			331	1	2		1	67	Highlands & east of the Hudson
Glover	1st Mass.	Joseph Vose	15	[illegible]	4	237	[illegible]	13	21	[illegible]	6			358		1		1	[illegible]	Highlands & east of the Hudson

AUGUST 1779 (continued)

BRIGADE	UNIT	COMMANDING OFFICER	PRESENT FIT FOR DUTY & ON DUTY: COMMISSIONED OFFICERS	NONCOMMISSIONED OFFICERS	STAFF OFFICERS	RANK & FILE	TOTAL	RANK & FILE SICK, ON FURLOUGH, ETC.: SICK PRESENT	SICK ABSENT	ON COMMAND & EXTRA SERVICE	ON FURLOUGH	NOT JOINED	PRISONERS OF WAR	GRAND TOTAL	ALTERATIONS: DEATHS	DESERTED	TAKEN PRISONER	DISCHARGED	JOINED, ENLISTED, RECRUITED	LOCATION
	FORCES UNDER COMMANDER-IN-CHIEF GENERAL GEORGE WASHINGTON (continued)																			
	Independent corps	Tuffin Charles Armand	12	21	4	127	164	3	1	2				170				1	1	Highlands & east of the Hudson
Maj. Gen. Gates' div.	1st Canadian	James Livingston	11	25	4	85	125	1	4	24				154		7				Rhode Island
	Additional	Henry Sherburne	16	38	5	207	266		1	5				272		1				Rhode Island
	Additional	Samuel Blatchley Webb	12	43	5	190	250	17	7	21				295					1	Rhode Island
	2nd R.I.	Israel Angell	17	40	5	220	282	8	4	66				360		1				Rhode Island
	1st R.I.	Christopher Greene	11	27	5	137	180	3	1	9	1			193					3	Rhode Island
	1st R.I. state	John Topham	12	47	4	115	178	2		49				229				2	5	Rhode Island
	Mass. state	Nathan Tyler	18	33	5	410	466	24	1	67				558		2				Rhode Island
	N.H. state	Hercules Mooney	14	24	1	187	226	1		3				230						Rhode Island
	R.I. militia	Lt. Col. Nathaniel Church	5	8		138	151							151 F	1		3	11	34	Rhode Island
	Mass. militia		14	33	2	288	337	8		2				348						Rhode Island
	Mass. militia	Maj. Nathaniel Heath	8	17	2	85	112	1		55	5			173						Boston, Mass.
	Mass. militia	Capt. John Carpenter	2	5		34	41	3	3					47						Springfield, Mass.
	1st N.Y.	Lt. Col. Cornelius Van Dyke	19	43	2	274	338	16	14	25	2			395	5		28		5	Fort Schuyler, N.Y.
	TOTAL OF INFANTRY		753	2113	237	13669	16772	893	715	2474	155			21009	31	115	35	130	973	
	CAVALRY																			
	2nd cont'l.	Elisha Sheldon						1	14	132	3	2		154	1				2	
	4th cont'l.	Stephen Moylan	1	2	2	11	16		2	128				146						
	Partizan corps	Maj. Henry Lee	12	38	2	142	194	4						198						
	Marechaussie	Capt. Bartholomew Von Heer	4	7		31	42	2	1	9				54						
	Independent corps	Capt. Henry Bedkin	2	3		18	23	1						24						
	TOTAL OF CAVALRY		19	50	4	202	275	8	17	269	3	2		576	1				2	
	ARTILLERY																			
	11 cos. 1st cont'l.	Charles Harrison	34	137	4	217	392											1	2	Chester, N.Y.
	5 cos. 2nd cont'l.	John Lamb	19	68	5	89	181									1			1	Chester, N.Y.
	2 cos. 3rd cont'l.	John Crane	5	26	1	29	61													Chester, N.Y.
	2 independent cos.		3	15		13	31												1	Chester, N.Y.
	4 cos. 2nd cont'l.	John Lamb	13	45		73	131	9	22	106	3			1380	1					West Point, N.Y.
	6 cos. 3rd cont'l.	John Crane	20	81	1	93	195									1			12	West Point, N.Y.
	2 independent cos.			5		7	12											1		West Point, N.Y.
	Det. 1st cont'l.	Charles Harrison	3	7		20	30												1	Rhode Island
	Det. 3rd cont'l.	John Crane	12	56	1	51	120									1		1		Rhode Island
	R.I. state	Robert Elliot	5	31		51	87									2		1		Rhode Island
	TOTAL OF ARTILLERY		114	471	12	643	1240	9	22	106	3			1380	1	5		4	17	
	INVALIDS																			
	Philadelphia unit	Lewis Nicola	5	31		243	279							279						Philadelphia, Pa.
	Boston det.	Capt. Moses McFarland	9	20		133	162							162						Boston, Mass.
	TOTAL OF INVALIDS		14	51		376	441							441						
	TOTAL OF WASHINGTON'S ARMY		900	2685	253	14890	18728	910	754	2849	161	2		23406	33	120	35	134	992	

AUGUST 1779
(continued)

BRIGADE	UNIT	COMMANDING OFFICER	PRESENT FIT FOR DUTY & ON DUTY: COMMISSIONED OFFICERS	NONCOMMISSIONED OFFICERS	STAFF OFFICERS	RANK & FILE	TOTAL	RANK & FILE SICK, ON FURLOUGH, ETC.: SICK PRESENT	SICK ABSENT	ON COMMAND & EXTRA SERVICE	ON FURLOUGH	NOT JOINED	PRISONERS OF WAR	GRAND TOTAL	ALTERATIONS: DEATHS	DESERTED	TAKEN PRISONER	DISCHARGED	JOINED, ENLISTED, RECRUITED	LOCATION
	SOUTH CAROLINA UNITS IN THE SOUTHERN DEPARTMENT UNDER MAJOR GENERAL BENJAMIN LINCOLN																			
Lt. Col. Wm. Scott	1st S.C.	Charles Cotesworth Pinckney	9	23	2	82	116	17	34	19	20		3	209	2	10		1		Sheldon Plantation, S.C.
	3rd S.C. (rangers)	William Thompson	7	32	1	284	324	46	62	19	28		4	483	4	11		2	11	Sheldon Plantation, S.C.
	6th S.C. (rifles)	Lt. Col. William Henderson	5	19	2	96 D	122	7	23		18			170	4	3			3	Sheldon Plantation, S.C.
	TOTAL OF SOUTH CAROLINA UNITS		21	74	5	462	562	70	119	38	66		7	862	10	24		3	14	
	ARTILLERY																			
	1st, 2nd, 3rd cos., 4th S.C.	Barnard Beekman		16		26	42	7 E		26	1			76						Sheldon Plantation, S.C.
	TOTAL OF LINCOLN'S ARMY		21	90	5	488	604	77	119	64	67		7	938	10	24		3	14	
	GRAND TOTAL		921	2775	258	15378	19332	987	873	2913	228	2	7	24344 G	43	144	35	137 H	1006	

OFFICERS SICK, ON FURLOUGH, ETC.	WASHINGTON'S ARMY (EXCEPT INVALIDS): COMMISSIONED	NONCOMMISSIONED	STAFF	TOTAL	SOUTH CAROLINA UNITS: COMMISSIONED	NONCOMMISSIONED	STAFF	TOTAL	GRAND TOTAL
Sick Present	43	80	2	125	5 E	5 E		10	135
Sick Absent	60	95	12	167	8	12	1	21	188
On Command	251	387	22	660	2	20		22	682
On Furlough	68	28	17	113	22	20	7	49	162
Recruiting	12	34		46					46
On the Staff	205			205			3	3	208
Prisoners of War	48		4	52	6			6	58
In Arrest	3		1	4					4
Wounded					3	1		4	4
TOTAL	690	624	58	1372	46	58	11	115	1487

SOURCES OF THIS REPORT

1. MONTHLY RETURN OF THE CONTINENTAL ARMY UNDER THE COMMAND OF HIS EXCELLENCY GEORGE WASHINGTON... FOR THE MONTH OF AUGUST 1779, ELEPHANT FOLIO OF WASHINGTON RETURNS, WILLIAM L. CLEMENTS LIBRARY. [ARTILLERY AND CAVALRY SECTIONS OF THIS RETURN APPEAR ON THE PRECEDING PAGES OF THE FOLIO.]
   1a. Monthly Return of the Continental Army under... Washington... August 1779, Record Group 93, National Archives. [Contains the same figures, but only to the brigade level.]
   1b. A General Return of the Troops in the State of Rhode Island Commanded by the Honourable Major General Gates, August 21, 1779, Gates Papers, New-York Historical Society. [Although not so headed, this is the monthly return used by the adjutant in compiling the general monthly return above.]

2. MONTHLY RETURN OF THE SOUTH CAROLINA CONTINENTAL BRIGADE, COMMANDED BY LIEUTENANT COLONEL WILLIAM SCOTT, SEPTEMBER 1, 1779, BENJAMIN LINCOLN PAPERS, MASSACHUSETTS HISTORICAL SOCIETY.

3. MONTHLY RETURN OF THE FIRST, SECOND, AND THIRD COMPANIES OF THE S. CAROLINA CONTINENTAL REGIMENT OF ARTILLERY, SEPTEMBER 1, 1779, BENJAMIN LINCOLN PAPERS, MASSACHUSETTS HISTORICAL SOCIETY.

A. One staff officer in Otho Holland Williams' 6th Maryland regiment plus one chaplain for the entire brigade.
B. Two staff officers in Benjamin Tupper's 11th Massachusetts regiment plus one chaplain for the entire brigade.
C. Five staff officers in Heman Swift's 7th Connecticut regiment plus one chaplain for the entire brigade.
D. Of these 462 rank and file present fit for duty the manuscript notes that 16 men were wanting arms and 24 were serving as waggoners.
E. The return of the South Carolina artillery gives only "sick," not "sick present" and "sick absent." Seven rank and file, two commissioned officers, and two noncommissioned officers marked only "sick" have been included in "sick present."
F. Including the one rank and file on furlough in Gates' Division whose regiment is not indicated.
G. The National Archives manuscript notes that no monthly returns were received for the Southern Department (partially supplied on our report), for the troops at Fort Pitt, for the Western Army (i. e., Sullivan's expedition), for the Delaware Continental regiment stationed in New Jersey, for Warner's Additional regiment at Fort George, for Hazen's 2nd Canadian regiment, for Jackson's Additional regiment in Massachusetts, and for Baylor's 3rd Continental cavalry.
H. Including thirty men discharged for inability in Washington's infantry. The manuscript for the South Carolina Continental brigade notes that of the three men marked discharged, one's time had expired, one was a prisoner of war, and one had bodily infirmities

Portrait of Major General Benjamin Lincoln by Charles Willson Peale. Lincoln, part of whose command in the Southern Department is reported on the previous page, sat for this likeness about 1781 or 1782 when he was secretary of war. Although Lincoln was of sufficient stature in society that his portrait would have been painted anyway, it is fortunate for historians of the Revolution that both Peale and Du Simitière collected portraits from life for their collections with the same élan that they expended on bones, antiquities, and curiosities. (Courtesy of the Independence National Historical Park Collection, Philadelphia)

SEPTEMBER 1779

BRIGADE	UNIT	COMMANDING OFFICER	PRESENT FIT FOR DUTY & ON DUTY: COMMISSIONED OFFICERS	NONCOMMISSIONED OFFICERS	STAFF OFFICERS	RANK & FILE	TOTAL	RANK & FILE SICK, ON FURLOUGH, ETC.: SICK PRESENT	SICK ABSENT	ON COMMAND & EXTRA SERVICE	ON FURLOUGH	CONFINED	NOT JOINED	GRAND TOTAL	ALTERATIONS: DEATHS	DESERTED	TAKEN PRISONER	DISCHARGED	JOINED, ENLISTED, RECRUITED	LOCATION
	FORCES UNDER COMMANDER-IN-CHIEF GENERAL GEORGE WASHINGTON																			
Woodford	2nd Va.	Christian Febiger	8	21	5	108	142	14	3	60				219		2		30	3	The Highlands, N.Y.
	3rd & 4th Va.	John Neville	17	50	5	291	363	7	11	62				443				4	2	The Highlands, N.Y.
	5th & 11th Va.	William Russell	12	35	4	200	251	13	12	143	1			420	1	1		1		The Highlands, N.Y.
	7th Va.	Daniel Morgan	7	16	3	123	149	6	5	23	10			193		1		7	2	The Highlands, N.Y.
	8th Va.	James Wood	11	27	5	163	206	8	12	72	1			299		6			2	The Highlands, N.Y.
Muhlenberg	1st & 10th Va.	William Davies	10	30	7	216	263	19	12	111	1			406	1	1	2	3		The Highlands, N.Y.
	Additional	Nathaniel Gist	14	27	4	132	177	11	12	32	3			235	1	1			2	The Highlands, N.Y.
	2nd Va. state	William Brent	13	34	4	216	267	14	4	38				323					1	The Highlands, N.Y.
	1st Va. state	George Gibson	23	40	4	181	248	17	4	47	1			317	1					The Highlands, N.Y.
	6th Va.	John Green	9	27	6	159	201	16	5	50	37			309		1				The Highlands, N.Y.
Smallwood	1st Md.	Lt. Col. Uriah Forrest	10	43	3	250	306	15	11	15	4			351		1			5	The Highlands, N.Y.
	3rd Md.	Lt. Col. Nathaniel Ramsay	11	34	4	363	412	15	17	38				482	1	4			9	The Highlands, N.Y.
	5th Md.	William Richardson	6	32	2	205	245	18	15	38	5			321		1			3	The Highlands, N.Y.
	7th Md.	John Gunby	9	38	3	245	295	12	11	15	5			338	1	3	1		6	The Highlands, N.Y.
Gist	2nd Md.	Thomas Price	9	40	4	276	329	23	17	39	2			410	1			1	9	The Highlands, N.Y.
	4th Md.	Josias Carvil Hall	7	38	4 C	329	378	16	15	34				443	2	2			13	The Highlands, N.Y.
	6th Md.	Otho Holland Williams	11	34	3	217	265	12	17	28	1			323						The Highlands, N.Y.
Irvine	1st Pa.	James Chambers	8	34	4	168	214	8	6	40	5			273		1			5	The Highlands, N.Y.
	2nd Pa.	Walter Stewart	17	43	5	328	393	21	17	17	1			449	1	7			2	The Highlands, N.Y.
	7th Pa.	Lt. Col. Morgan Connor	11	27	4	172	214	12	4	9				239		2			5	The Highlands, N.Y.
	10th Pa.	Richard Humpton	10	38	2	234	284	17	9	45	1			356	1	2			2	The Highlands, N.Y.
2nd Pa.	3rd Pa.	Thomas Craig	15	38	4	236	293	27	18	36	3			377				1	6	The Highlands, N.Y.
	5th Pa.	Francis Johnston	12	29	3	205	249	33	11	30	1			324		2		1	8	The Highlands, N.Y.
	6th Pa.	Robert Magaw	11	28	5	150	194	25	3	11				233		7	1	1	1	The Highlands, N.Y.
	9th Pa.	Richard Butler	10	28	5	148	191	20	10	10				231	1			1	3	The Highlands, N.Y.
N.C.	1st N.C.	Thomas Clark	14	45	3	284	346	36	5	42	1			430	1	2		2	5	West Point, N.Y.
	2nd N.C.	John Patten	14	47	5	293	359	35	1	16				411		1		3	1	West Point, N.Y.
Paterson	10th Mass.	Thomas Marshall	10	38	5	279	332	18	4	25	2			381	1	5			11	West Point, N.Y.
	11th Mass.	Benjamin Tupper	15	37	3	293	348	24	8	16				396	2				7	West Point, N.Y.
	12th Mass.	(late) Samuel Brewer	13	42	2	218	275	20	9	19				323	3	2			9	West Point, N.Y.
	14th Mass.	Gamaliel Bradford	14	36	5 D	284	339	17	13	18	2			389	1	2		1	10	West Point, N.Y.
4th Mass.	2nd Mass.	John Bailey	14	36	6	255	311	19	23	37				390					7	West Point, N.Y.
	8th Mass.	Michael Jackson	14	36	4	256	310	40	8	33	3			394		2			8	West Point, N.Y.
	9th Mass.	James Wesson	10	41	4	254	309	24	13	36	1			383	2	5			7	West Point, N.Y.
Parsons	3rd Conn.	Samuel Wyllys	15	34	4	281	334	26	30	53				443		3			3	Highlands & east of the Hudson
	4th Conn.	John Durkee	10	30	3	236	279	25	11	46	1			362		2			102	Highlands & east of the Hudson
	6th Conn.	Return Jonathan Meigs	14	40	4	360	418	19	40	52	2			531		1		1	1	Highlands & east of the Hudson
	8th Conn.	Giles Russell	10	39	3	242	294	12	32	28	2			368					61	Highlands & east of the Hudson
Huntington	1st Conn.	Josiah Starr	14	40	2	230	286	22	29	27	5			369	2	1			3	Highlands & east of the Hudson
	2nd Conn.	Zebulon Butler	13	35	3	248	299	14	34	19	1			367		1			73	Highlands & east of the Hudson
	5th Conn.	Philip Burr Bradley	16	42	4	227	289	16	33	36	1			375		4			25	Highlands & east of the Hudson
	7th Conn.	Heman Swift	14	40	6 E	245	305	14	29	33	1			382		2			2	Highlands & east of the Hudson
Nixon	3rd Mass.	John Greaton	15	41	5	277	338	17	22	11	1			389	1	4		4	8	Highlands & east of the Hudson
	5th Mass.	Rufus Putnam	16	36	2 F	263	317	26	18	21	1			383	1	3			2	Highlands & east of the Hudson
	6th Mass.	Thomas Nixon	17	40	5	280	342	20	19	18				399				1	7	Highlands & east of the Hudson
Glover	1st Mass.	Joseph Vose	11	37	5	251	304	15	16	41	3			379	3	2			25	Highlands & east of the Hudson
	4th Mass.	William Shepard	13	38	4	222	277	8	17	77	5			384	1		1		26	Highlands & east of the Hudson
	13th Mass.	Lt. Col. Ebenezer Sprout	16	37	4	255	312	21	14	36	3			386		2			23	Highlands & east of the Hudson
	15th Mass.	Timothy Bigelow	[illegible]	34	3	[illegible]	[illegible]	[illegible]	[illegible]	[illegible]	[illegible]			[illegible]				[illegible]	[illegible]	[illegible]

SEPTEMBER 1779 (continued)

BRIGADE	UNIT	COMMANDING OFFICER	PRESENT FIT FOR DUTY & ON DUTY: COMMISSIONED OFFICERS	NONCOMMISSIONED OFFICERS	STAFF OFFICERS	RANK & FILE	TOTAL	RANK & FILE SICK, ON FURLOUGH, ETC.: SICK PRESENT	SICK ABSENT	ON COMMAND & EXTRA SERVICE	ON FURLOUGH	CONFINED	NOT JOINED	GRAND TOTAL	ALTERATIONS: DEATHS	DESERTED	TAKEN PRISONER	DISCHARGED	JOINED, ENLISTED, RECRUITED	LOCATION
	FORCES UNDER COMMANDER-IN-CHIEF GENERAL GEORGE WASHINGTON (continued)																			
	Independent corps	Tuffin Charles Armand	12	21	4	130	167	3	1	2				173					4	Highlands & east of the Hudson
Maj. Gen. Gates' div.	1st Canadian	James Livingston	8	24	3	79	114	6	4	21				145		4				Rhode Island
	Additional	Henry Sherburne	12	36	4	192	244	2	1	13				260		6			1	Rhode Island
	Additional	Samuel Blatchley Webb	10	42	5	194	251	15	11	12				289		4			1	Rhode Island
	2nd R.I.	Israel Angell	15	41	5	216	277	10	5	60				352		7				Rhode Island
	1st R.I.	Christopher Greene	10	25	5	134	174	11	1	1				187		3		1		Rhode Island
	R.I. state	William Barton	4	10	1	60	75	1	2	1	1			80						Rhode Island
	1st R.I. state	John Topham	11	44	3	115	173	4		52				229		1			1	Rhode Island
	Mass. state	John Jacobs	2	7		32	41			15				56						Rhode Island
	Mass. state	Nathan Tyler	19	37	5	374	435	38	1	96	2			572		6				Rhode Island
	N.H. state	Hercules Mooney	13	26	3	146	188	6		41				235		1		1	5	Rhode Island
	R.I. militia		6	9		143	158							158						Rhode Island
	Mass. militia	Maj. Nathaniel Heath	11	21	2	131	165	2	1	15	4			187						Boston, Mass.
	Mass. militia co.	Capt. John Carpenter	4	8		33	45	38	5	41	12			141		2			4	Springfield, Mass.
	2nd Canadian	Moses Hazen	24	43	3	301	371	2	13	100	4			490						
	Additional	Seth Warner	14	15	2	66	97	3	9	28	1			138						Fort George, N.Y.
	1st N.Y.	Goose Van Schaick	17	40	2	277	336	20	15	14	4			389		1				Fort Schuyler, N.Y.
	N.H. & N.Y. militia		12	15		253	280							280						N.Y. frontiers
	Del.	David Hall	11	26	5	208	250	16	13	46	13			338	2	12			50	
	TOTAL OF INFANTRY		821	2242	248	14660	17971	1073	788	2411	159			22402	32	136	5	65	606	
	CAVALRY																			
	2nd cont'l.	Elisha Sheldon							9	135	3	2	2	151		1				
	3rd cont'l.	George Baylor	8	7	2	53	70	21	23	59				173		7				
	4th cont'l.	Stephen Moylan	1	2	3	3	9	10	3	129				151					4	
	Partizan corps	Maj. Henry Lee	8	28	3	120	159	2		26				187						
	TOTAL OF CAVALRY		17	37	8	176	238	33	35	349	3	2	2	662		8			4	
	ARTILLERY																			
	11 cos. 1st cont'l.	Charles Harrison	32	135	4	218	389												1	Chester, N.Y.
	5 cos. 2nd cont'l.	John Lamb	19	67	5	90	181													Chester, N.Y.
	2 cos. 3rd cont'l.	John Crane	5	27	1	29	62								1					Chester, N.Y.
	2 independent cos.		3	15		13	31													Chester, N.Y.
	4 cos. 2nd cont'l.	John Lamb	13	42		73	128	13	21	100	6			1378						West Point, N.Y.
	6 cos. 3rd cont'l.	John Crane	21	78	1	85	185									2		1		West Point, N.Y.
	2 independent cos.			4		7	11									1				West Point, N.Y.
	Det. 1st cont'l.	Charles Harrison	3	8		20	31													Rhode Island
	Det. 3rd cont'l.	John Crane	12	62	1	59	134									4			2	Rhode Island
	R.I. state	Robert Elliot	6	32		48	86												3	Rhode Island
	TOTAL OF ARTILLERY		114	470	12	642	1238	13	21	100	6			1378	1	7		1	6	
	INVALIDS																			
	Philadelphia unit	Lewis Nicola	5	32		279	316							316						Philadelphia, Pa.
	Boston det.	Capt. Moses McFarland	5	18		126	149							149						Boston, Mass.
	TOTAL OF INVALIDS		10	50		405	465							465						
	TOTAL OF WASHINGTON'S ARMY		962	2799	268	15883	19912	1119	844	2860	168	2	2	24907	33	151	5	66	616	

SEPTEMBER 1779 (continued)

BRIGADE	UNIT	COMMANDING OFFICER	PRESENT FIT FOR DUTY & ON DUTY: COMMISSIONED OFFICERS	NONCOMMISSIONED OFFICERS	STAFF OFFICERS	RANK & FILE	TOTAL	RANK & FILE SICK, ON FURLOUGH, ETC.: SICK PRESENT	SICK ABSENT	ON COMMAND & EXTRA SERVICE	ON FURLOUGH	CONFINED	NOT JOINED	GRAND TOTAL	ALTERATIONS: DEATHS	DESERTED	TAKEN PRISONER	DISCHARGED	JOINED, ENLISTED, RECRUITED	LOCATION
	SOUTHERN DEPARTMENT UNDER MAJOR GENERAL BENJAMIN LINCOLN																			
McIntosh	1st S.C.	Charles Cotesworth Pinckney	17	21	3	66	107	18	50	12	3			190						near Savannah, Ga.
McIntosh	3rd S.C. (rangers)	William Thompson	12	25	1	154	192	18	19	10				239						near Savannah, Ga.
McIntosh	6th S.C. (rifles)	Lt. Col. William Henderson	9	15	1	57	82	21	36	10	23			172						near Savannah, Ga.
McIntosh	Ga. militia	William Few	9	5	1	44	59	5		6				70						near Savannah, Ga.
McIntosh	Ga. militia	John Dooley	14	16	2	84	116	19		13	3			151						near Savannah, Ga.
McIntosh	Ga. militia	John Twiggs	15	11	2	77	105	11	6	23				145						near Savannah, Ga.
McIntosh	Ga. militia	Robert Middleton	14	4	2	27	47	11		7				65						near Savannah, Ga.
Huger	Cont'l. troops	Brig. Gen. Isaac Huger	28	54	4	360	446	46	65	17	2			576						near Savannah, Ga.
Huger	S.C. militia	William Skirving	30	18	5	160	213	33	6	4	2			258						near Savannah, Ga.
Huger	S.C. militia	William Harden	9	7	2	89	107	2	7	10	4			130						near Savannah, Ga.
Huger	S.C. militia	Lt. Col. Benjamin Garden	14	7	3	97	121	8 G	6	26	3			164						near Savannah, Ga.
	Charleston militia	Maurice Simons	31	34	4	242	311	13		2	6			332						near Savannah, Ga.
	Light troops A	Lt. Col. John Laurens	16	29	2	128	175	3						178						near Savannah, Ga.
	TOTAL OF INFANTRY		218	246	32	1585	2081	208	195	140	46			2670						
	CAVALRY B																			
	1st cont'l.	Lt. Col. Benjamin Temple																		near Savannah, Ga.
	Pulaski's legion	Casimir Pulaski																		near Savannah, Ga.
	S.C. dragoons	Daniel Horry																		near Savannah, Ga.
	S.C. militia	Capt. William Clay Snipes																		near Savannah, Ga.
	Militia	Capt. Charles Elliott	2			10	12							12						near Savannah, Ga.
	ARTILLERY																			
	4th S.C.	Barnard Beekman	12	16	2	71	101		31	35	4			171						near Savannah, Ga.
	TOTAL OF LINCOLN'S ARMY		232	262	34	1666	2194	208 G	226	175	50			2853						
	VIRGINIA STATE AND MILITIA FORCES IN THE CONTINENTAL SERVICE AS GUARDS FOR THE CONVENTION TROOPS																			
	Va. convention guards	Francis Taylor	11	30	1	147	189		24	51 I	34	1	12	311	1	3		2		Albemarle Barracks, Va.
	6 cos. Va. militia		13	15		120	148		6 H	14	1			169				5		Albemarle Barracks, Va.
	TOTAL OF CONVENTION GUARDS		24	45	1	267	337		30	65	35	1	12	480	1	3		7		
	GRAND TOTAL		1218	3106	303	17816	22443	1327	1100	3100	253	3	14	28240 J	34	154	5	73 K	616	

OFFICERS SICK, ON FURLOUGH, ETC.	WASHINGTON'S ARMY (EXCEPT INVALIDS)				4th SOUTH CAROLINA (ARTILLERY)				CONVENTION GUARDS				GRAND TOTAL
	COMMISSIONED	NONCOMMISSIONED	STAFF	TOTAL	COMMISSIONED	NONCOMMISSIONED	STAFF	TOTAL	COMMISSIONED	NONCOMMISSIONED	STAFF	TOTAL	
Sick Present	38	89	2	129	1			1	1	3		4	336
Sick Absent	85	101	14	200	1	1		2					
On Command	236	373	23	632					1	1		2	634
On Furlough	66	28	14	108					1	2		3	111
Recruiting	17	25		42									42
On the Staff	212			212									212
Prisoners of War	61	1		62									62
In Arrest	5		2	7									7
TOTAL	720	617	55	1392	2	1		3	3	6		9	1404

SOURCES OF THIS REPORT

1. MONTHLY RETURN OF THE CONTINENTAL ARMY UNDER THE COMMAND OF HIS EXCELLENCY GEORGE WASHINGTON. . . FOR THE MONTH OF SEPTEMBER 1779, ELEPHANT FOLIO OF WASHINGTON RETURNS, WILLIAM L. CLEMENTS LIBRARY. [THE CAVALRY AND ARTILLERY SECTIONS OF THIS RETURN APPEAR SEVERAL PAGES EARLIER IN THE FOLIO.]

 1a. Monthly Return of the Continental Army under. . . Washington. . . September 1779, Record Group 93, National Archives. [Contains the same figures, but only to the brigade level.]

 1b. A General Return of the Troops in the State of Rhode Island Commanded by the Honourable Major General Gates, September 18, 1779, Gates Papers, New-York Historical Society. [Although not so marked, this is the monthly return used by the adjutant in compiling the general monthly return above.]

2. REPORT OF THE SOUTHERN DEPARTMENT COMPILED FROM A GENERAL RETURN OF LINCOLN'S COMMAND DATED SEPTEMBER 21, 1779 AND INDIVIDUAL MONTHLY RETURNS FOR THE MILITIA IN HUGER'S BRIGADE, THE CHARLESTON MILITIA, AND THE ARTILLERY PLUS WEEKLY RETURNS DATED SEPTEMBER 26 AND OCTOBER 1, 1779 FOR ELLIOT'S MILITIA LIGHT HORSE AND McINTOSH'S BRIGADE, RESPECTIVELY, ALL IN THE BENJAMIN LINCOLN PAPERS, MASSACHUSETTS HISTORICAL SOCIETY.

3. A RETURN OF COLONEL TAYLOR'S REGIMENT OF GUARDS AND MILITIA, COLONEL JAMES WOOD MANUSCRIPTS, VIRGINIA STATE LIBRARY.

A. Companies detached from the Continental regiments.
B. The cavalry section is blank on the general return. We have been able to supply figures from individual returns for only Elliot's militia light horse.
C. Two staff officers in Otho Holland Williams' 6th Maryland regiment plus one chaplain for the entire brigade.
D. Four staff officers in Gamaliel Bradford's 14th Massachusetts regiment plus one chaplain for the entire brigade.
E. Five staff officers in Heman Swift's 7th Connecticut regiment plus one chaplain for the entire brigade.
F. Four staff officers in Thomas Nixon's 6th Massachusetts regiment plus one chaplain for the entire brigade.
G. The return of the Charleston militia does not distinguish between "sick present" and "sick absent." We have placed the thirteen men "sick" in "sick present," and this should be remembered in considering the total of "sick present."
H. All of the returns for the Albemarle Convention Guards have only a "in hospital" category, rather than "sick present" and "sick absent." We have included all these men in "sick absent."
I. Including seven men who were serving as camp color men. On August 1, 1775, Washington ordered the appointment of one camp color man for every company of every regiment of the army. Their duties were "to sweep the Streets of their respective encampments, to fill up the old necessary Houses and dig new ones, to bury all Offal, Filth, and Nastiness." Normally the returns do not specifically enumerate the camp color men, but a column for them was included on the returns of the Convention Guards. We have placed them in the "On Command & Extra Service" column and noted the matter in a footnote. Perhaps the men could be considered "Present Fit for Duty."
J. The National Archives manuscript notes that no monthly returns were received for the Southern Department (supplied here), for the troops at Fort Pitt, for Sullivan's army, for Whitcomb's Rangers, for Jackson's Additional regiment, for the Marechaussie, for Captain Henry Bedkin's Independent corps of cavalry, and for four companies of artillery.
K. Including sixteen men in Washington's infantry discharged for inability.

OCTOBER 1779

BRIGADE	UNIT	COMMANDING OFFICER	PRESENT FIT FOR DUTY & ON DUTY: COMMISSIONED OFFICERS	NONCOMMISSIONED OFFICERS	STAFF OFFICERS	RANK & FILE	TOTAL	RANK & FILE SICK, ON FURLOUGH, ETC.: SICK PRESENT	SICK ABSENT	ON COMMAND & EXTRA SERVICE	ON FURLOUGH	CONFINED	ABSENT WITHOUT LEAVE	GRAND TOTAL	ALTERATIONS: DEATHS	DESERTED	TAKEN PRISONER	DISCHARGED	JOINED, ENLISTED, RECRUITED	LOCATION
		FORCES UNDER COMMANDER-IN-CHIEF GENERAL GEORGE WASHINGTON																		
Woodford	2nd Va.	Christian Febiger	8	21	4	127	160	2	6	50				218				3	4	The Highlands, N.Y.
	3rd & 4th Va.	John Neville	16	46	6	276	344	4	19	71				438	1	1			1	The Highlands, N.Y.
	5th & 11th Va.	William Russell	10	38	3	223	274	3	11	132				420		1			3	The Highlands, N.Y.
	7th Va.	Daniel Morgan	7	19	4	123	153	4	2	22	11			192	1			2	1	The Highlands, N.Y.
	8th Va.	James Wood	12	24	5	168	209	10	10	65	3			297		1		1	4	The Highlands, N.Y.
Muhlenberg	1st & 10th Va.	William Davies	14	32	7	228	281	2	10	118	2			413			1		1	The Highlands, N.Y.
	Additional	Nathaniel Gist	10	39	4	146	199	1	6	33	4			243						The Highlands, N.Y.
	2nd Va. state	William Brent	16	32	4	213	265		5	54				324						The Highlands, N.Y.
	1st Va. state	George Gibson	22	36	3	200	261	5	5	41				312					1	The Highlands, N.Y.
	6th Va.	John Green	10	28	6	162	206	3	10	67	24			310				1	1	The Highlands, N.Y.
Smallwood	1st Md.	Lt. Col. Uriah Forrest	10	42	2	207	261	19	7	66	4			357					8	The Highlands, N.Y.
	3rd Md.	Lt. Col. Nathaniel Ramsay	10	31	4	334	379	18	14	58				469		7			3	The Highlands, N.Y.
	5th Md.	(late) William Richardson	8	34	5	170	217	27	21	59	3			327	2			1		The Highlands, N.Y.
	7th Md.	John Gunby	11	35	4	230	280	19	11	23	3			336	1	1			1	The Highlands, N.Y.
Gist	2nd Md.	Thomas Price	10	33	3	261	307	24	17	53	4			405		2		1	3	The Highlands, N.Y.
	4th Md.	Josias Carvil Hall	9	35	3	320	367	20	12	42				441	1	1			3	The Highlands, N.Y.
	6th Md.	Otho Holland Williams	11	37	2	228	278	16	16	26	2			338		3			18	The Highlands, N.Y.
Irvine	1st Pa.	James Chambers	11	32	5	165	213	15	7	39	1			275		3		2	9	The Highlands, N.Y.
	2nd Pa.	Walter Stewart	19	41	4	319	383	25	18	22				448		3			3	The Highlands, N.Y.
	7th Pa.	Lt. Col. Morgan Connor	9	30	4	171	214	11	3	11				239		2			2	The Highlands, N.Y.
	10th Pa.	Richard Humpton	14	37	2	233	286	10	12	53	1			362	1				4	The Highlands, N.Y.
2nd Pa.	3rd Pa.	Thomas Craig	11	38	4	225	278	28	9	48	1			364	5	3		1	1	The Highlands, N.Y.
	5th Pa.	Francis Johnston	13	26	5	210	254	28	10	31	1			324					1	The Highlands, N.Y.
	6th Pa.	Robert Magaw	11	29	5	153	198	16	2	18				234		1		1	1	The Highlands, N.Y.
	9th Pa.	Richard Butler	10	28	5	136	179	22	12	13	1			227		3			1	The Highlands, N.Y.
N.C.	1st N. C.	Thomas Clark	13	46	3	264	326	31	3	60	2			422	2			3	2	West Point, N.Y.
	2nd N.C.	John Patten	12	44	5	272	333	22	2	48	1			406		1			1	West Point, N.Y.
Paterson	10th Mass.	Thomas Marshall	11	41	4	227	283	25	4	77	1			390		1			7	West Point, N.Y.
	11th Mass.	Benjamin Tupper	10	33	4	267	314	26	8	45				393				2	8	West Point, N.Y.
	12th Mass.	(late) Samuel Brewer	13	37	3	247	300	23	5	59	1			388	1	2			10	West Point, N.Y.
	14th Mass.	Gamaliel Bradford	11	36	5	281	333	18	11	29	1			392	1	1			8	West Point, N.Y.
4th Mass.	2nd Mass.	John Bailey	14	37	6	239	296	13	14	72				395	1	2			12	West Point, N.Y.
	8th Mass.	Michael Jackson	14	34	4	239	291	29	9	65	1			395	1	1			6	West Point, N.Y.
	9th Mass.	James Wesson	12	37	4	233	286	25	13	61	1			386					8	West Point, N.Y.
Parsons	3rd Conn.	Samuel Wyllys	13	37	4	255	309	23	21	85	1			439		5			3	Highlands & east of the Hudson
	4th Conn.	John Durkee	11	36	5	213	265	35	17	64	1			382	2	2			16	Highlands & east of the Hudson
	6th Conn.	Return Jonathan Meigs	17	42	5	343	407	18	35	72	1			533		3		1		Highlands & east of the Hudson
	8th Conn.	Giles Russell	11	39	4	213	267	12	38	59				376	1	3		1	13	Highlands & east of the Hudson
Huntington	1st Conn.	Josiah Starr	15	41	3	239	298	20	34	19	4			375		2		1	6	Highlands & east of the Hudson
	2nd Conn.	Zebulon Butler	13	39	3	348	403	13	30	25	4			475		4			9	Highlands & east of the Hudson
	5th Conn.	Philip Burr Bradley	18	36	4[B]	236	294	13	31	41	2			381		4			15	Highlands & east of the Hudson
	7th Conn.	Heman Swift	17	38	6	258	319	8	30	27				384	1	2			4	Highlands & east of the Hudson
Nixon	3rd Mass.	John Greaton	14	40	3	284	341	20	15	12	1			389		3			7	Highlands & east of the Hudson
	5th Mass.	Rufus Putnam	18	38	1[C]	273	330	21	15	17	1			384	1				7	Highlands & east of the Hudson
	6th Mass.	Thomas Nixon	16	39	5	296	356	14	12	18	1			401		2			5	Highlands & east of the Hudson
Glover	1st Mass.	Joseph Vose	12	29	2	229	272	16	11	68	3			370	1				7	Highlands & east of the Hudson
	4th Mass.	William Shepard	14	33	4	224	275	7	15	84	3			384		2		1	7	Highlands & east of the Hudson
	13th Mass.	Lt. Col. Ebenezer Sprout	14	39	4[D]	242	299	5	16	67	2			389		2			6	Highlands & east of the Hudson
	15th Mass.	Timothy Bigelow	11	36	4	217	268	13	15	79				375		1			5	Highlands & east of the Hudson

OCTOBER 1779 (continued)

BRIGADE	UNIT	COMMANDING OFFICER	PRESENT FIT FOR DUTY & ON DUTY: COMMISSIONED OFFICERS	NONCOMMISSIONED OFFICERS	STAFF OFFICERS	RANK & FILE	TOTAL	RANK & FILE SICK, ON FURLOUGH, ETC.: SICK PRESENT	SICK ABSENT	ON COMMAND & EXTRA SERVICE	ON FURLOUGH	CONFINED	ABSENT WITHOUT LEAVE	GRAND TOTAL	ALTERATIONS: DEATHS	DESERTED	TAKEN PRISONER	DISCHARGED	JOINED, ENLISTED, RECRUITED	LOCATION
FORCES UNDER COMMANDER-IN-CHIEF GENERAL GEORGE WASHINGTON (continued)																				
	2nd Canadian	Moses Hazen	24	42	3	316	385	16	23	43	9			476		1				Highlands & east of the Hudson
	Independent corps	Tuffin Charles Armand	12	22	4	120	158		1	1				160		3			1	Highlands & east of the Hudson
Maj. Gen. Gates' div.	1st Canadian	James Livingston	8	29	4	100	141	1	4	3				149		1			2	Rhode Island
Maj. Gen. Gates' div.	Additional	Henry Sherburne	14	37	5	194	250	4	2	5				261		4			1	Rhode Island
Maj. Gen. Gates' div.	Additional	Samuel Blatchley Webb	10	43	5	215	273		14	2				289		1				Rhode Island
Maj. Gen. Gates' div.	2nd R.I.	Israel Angell	17	40	5	217	279	12	4	57				352		3			2	Rhode Island
Maj. Gen. Gates' div.	1st R.I.	Christopher Greene	9	24	5	139	177	9	4	1				191		2			8	Rhode Island
Maj. Gen. Gates' div.	Additional	Henry Jackson	18	58	4	275	355	9	20	25	1			410		29			32	Rhode Island
Maj. Gen. Gates' div.	R.I. state	William Barton	4	9	1	57	71	1	3	1	1			77	1	10			9	Rhode Island
Maj. Gen. Gates' div.	1st R.I. state	John Topham	13	42	4	126	185	1		45				231					1	Rhode Island
Maj. Gen. Gates' div.	Mass. state	Nathan Tyler	24	40	5	386	455	7	38	117	1			618		10			52	Rhode Island
Maj. Gen. Gates' div.	N.H. state	Hercules Mooney	15	27	4	164	210	8		23				241					4	Rhode Island
Maj. Gen. Gates' div.	Mass. state	John Jacobs	13	24	2	139	178		1	166				345		3			9	Rhode Island
Maj. Gen. Gates' div.	R.I. militia		4	7		90	101							101						Rhode Island
Sullivan's div. — Hand	4th Pa.	Lt. Col. William Butler	8	29	3	118	158	8	12	29	1			208					1	
Sullivan's div. — Hand	11th Pa.	Lt. Col. Adam Hubley	14	44	4	236	298	4	33	28	4			367						
Sullivan's div. — Maxwell	1st N.J.	Matthias Ogden	15	45	2	219	281	16	31	8	2			338					1	
Sullivan's div. — Maxwell	2nd N.J.	Israel Shreve	16	44	3	245	308	22	30	8	6			374					2	
Sullivan's div. — Maxwell	3rd N.J.	Elias Dayton	9	35	1	233	278	8	23	21				330	1	1				
Sullivan's div. — Maxwell	Additional	Oliver Spencer	13	30	3	173	219	17	37	20	3			296						
Sullivan's div. — Clinton	2nd N.Y.	Philip Van Cortlandt	13	32	3	159	207	10	18	10	2			247						
Sullivan's div. — Clinton	3rd N.Y.	Peter Gansevoort	16	29	3	228	276	21	45	60				402		1				
Sullivan's div. — Clinton	4th N.Y.	Lt. Col. Frederick Weisenfels	18	28	3	182	231	20	27	36	1			315						
Sullivan's div. — Clinton	5th N.Y.	Lewis DuBois	9	38	3	183	233	14	64	45				356						
Sullivan's div. — Poor	1st N.H.	Joseph Cilley	17	34	3	302	356	16	44	8	22			446	1					
Sullivan's div. — Poor	2nd N.H.	Lt. Col. George Reid	14	30	3	190	237	41	27	19	7			331					5	
Sullivan's div. — Poor	3rd N.H.	Alexander Scammell	15	28	5 E	180	228	12	21	8	15			284	1				3	
Sullivan's div. — Poor	7th Mass.	(late) Ichabod Alden	16	40	4	160	220	20	36	34				310						
	1st N.Y.	Goose Van Schaick	12	41	1	268	322	15	19	19	8			383	1					Fort Schuyler, N.Y.
	Additional	Seth Warner	9	15	2	70	96	2	6	16	2			122		3		5		Lake George, N.Y.
	Mass. militia	Maj. Nathaniel Heath	6	16	1	125	148	2		7				157						In & about Boston, Mass.
	Mass. militia co.	Capt. John Carpenter	2	4		20	26							26						Springfield, Mass.
	TOTAL OF INFANTRY		1023	2736	296	17196	21251	1098	1246	3333	182			27110	29	147	1	27	380	

OCTOBER 1779 (continued)

BRIGADE	UNIT	COMMANDING OFFICER	PRESENT FIT FOR DUTY & ON DUTY: COMMISSIONED OFFICERS	NONCOMMISSIONED OFFICERS	STAFF OFFICERS	RANK & FILE	TOTAL	RANK & FILE SICK, ON FURLOUGH, ETC.: SICK PRESENT	SICK ABSENT	ON COMMAND & EXTRA SERVICE	ON FURLOUGH	CONFINED	ABSENT WITHOUT LEAVE	GRAND TOTAL	ALTERATIONS: DEATHS	DESERTED	TAKEN PRISONER	DISCHARGED	JOINED, ENLISTED, RECRUITED	LOCATION
	FORCES UNDER COMMANDER-IN-CHIEF GENERAL GEORGE WASHINGTON (continued)																			
	CAVALRY																			
	2nd cont'l.	Elisha Sheldon	4	7	2	45	58	7	9	157	2	4		237		1			11	
	3rd cont'l.	George Baylor	10	13	5	51	79	2	35	67			6	189		1			2	
	4th cont'l.	Stephen Moylan	3	1	4	1	9	12	3	126				150	1					
	Partizan corps	Maj. Henry Lee	12	36	3	148	199	2	3	4				208			1			
	Marechaussie	Capt. Bartholomew Von Heer	4	7		22	33		1	16				50		1				
	TOTAL OF CAVALRY		33	64	14	267	378	23	51	370	2	4	6	834	1	3	1		13	
	ARTILLERY																			
	11 cos. 1st cont'l.	Charles Harrison	35	127	5	215	382								2	1			1	Chester, N.Y.
	4 cos. 2nd cont'l.	John Lamb	12	52	5	73	142									1		1	3	Chester, N.Y.
	2 cos. 3rd cont'l.	John Crane	5	27	1	27	60													Chester, N.Y.
	2 independent cos.		11	41		95	147											2	1	Chester, N.Y.
Lamb's det.	5 cos. 2nd cont'l.	John Lamb	16	51		87	154									1				
Lamb's det.	6 cos. 3rd cont'l.	John Crane	19	78	1	91	189	23	30	62	4			1626	1	1			2	
Lamb's det.	Independent co.			5		7	12													
	Det. 3rd cont'l.	John Crane	14	59	1	59 F	133									4			1	Rhode Island
	Det. 1st cont'l.	Charles Harrison	2	6		15 F	23													Rhode Island
	Det. R.I. state	Robert Elliot	12	36		70 F	118												3	Rhode Island
	4th cont'l. A	Thomas Proctor	14	64	2	67	147													
	TOTAL OF ARTILLERY		140	546	15	806	1507	23	30	62	4			1626	3	8		3	11	
	INVALIDS																			
	Philadelphia unit	Lewis Nicola	8	30		234	272							272						Philadelphia, Pa.
	Boston det.	Capt. Moses McFarland	4	7		144	155							155						Boston, Mass.
	TOTAL OF INVALIDS		12	37		378	427							427						
	TOTAL OF WASHINGTON'S ARMY		1208	3383	325	18647	23563	1144	1327	3765	188	4	6	29997 G	33	158	2	30 H	404	

OFFICERS SICK, ON FURLOUGH, ETC.	WASHINGTON'S ARMY (EXCEPT INVALIDS)			
	COMMISSIONED	NONCOMMISSIONED	STAFF	TOTAL
Sick Present	32	103	4	139
Sick Absent	90	130	20	240
On Command	277	428	23	728
On Furlough	74	41	25	140
Recruiting	7	16		23
On the Staff	201			201
Prisoners of War	79	8	2	89
In Arrest	10			10
TOTAL	770	726	74	1570

SOURCE OF THIS REPORT

1. MONTHLY RETURN OF THE CONTINENTAL ARMY UNDER THE COMMAND OF HIS EXCELLENCY GEORGE WASHINGTON... FOR THE MONTH OF OCTOBER 1779, ELEPHANT FOLIO OF WASHINGTON RETURNS, WILLIAM L. CLEMENTS LIBRARY. [THE CAVALRY SECTION OF THE RETURN APPEARS ON THE FOLLOWING PAGE OF THE FOLIO.]

1a. Monthly Return of the Continental Army under... Washington... October 1779, Record Group 93, National Archives. [Contains the same figures, but only to the brigade level.]

1b. A General Return of the Troops in the State of Rhode Island Commanded by the Honourable Major General Gates, October 23, 1779, Gates Papers, New-York Historical Society. [Alterations marked "since last Monthly Return"; this is the return from which the adjutant compiled the general monthly return above.]

A. This regiment was also known as the Pennsylvania state regiment or Proctor's artillery regiment; the manuscript for this month has "Proctor's State regiment."
B. Five staff officers in Heman Swift's 7th Connecticut regiment plus one chaplain for the entire brigade.
C. Four staff officers in Thomas Nixon's 6th Massachusetts regiment plus one chaplain for the entire brigade.
D. Three staff officers in Timothy Bigelow's 15th Massachusetts regiment plus one chaplain for the entire brigade.
E. Three staff officers in (late) Ichabod Alden's 7th Massachusetts regiment plus one chaplain for the entire brigade.
F. There is a discrepancy between the original return of the artillery in the Northern Department (found in the Gates Papers) and the figures for the Northern Department artillery as transcribed in the general returns of Washington's command. We have corrected the error. However, it is possible that twenty-seven matrosses who were sick present, sick absent, etc., in the Northern Department have been excluded here, although we do not believe that to be the case. For a fuller description of the problem, see footnote F on our June 1779 report.
G. The National Archives manuscript notes that no returns had arrived for the Southern Department, for the troops at Fort Pitt, and for the Delaware regiment.
H. Including six men in Washington's infantry discharged for inability.

NOVEMBER 1779

FORCES UNDER COMMANDER-IN-CHIEF GENERAL GEORGE WASHINGTON

BRIGADE	UNIT	COMMANDING OFFICER	Present Fit for Duty & on Duty: COMMISSIONED OFFICERS	NONCOMMISSIONED OFFICERS	STAFF OFFICERS	RANK & FILE	TOTAL	Rank & File Sick, on Furlough, etc.: SICK PRESENT	SICK ABSENT	ON COMMAND & EXTRA SERVICE	ON FURLOUGH	CONFINED			GRAND TOTAL	Alterations: DEATHS	DESERTED	TAKEN PRISONER	DISCHARGED	JOINED, ENLISTED, RECRUITED	LOCATION
Woodford	2nd Va.	Christian Febiger	9	21	5	130	165	9	2	41					217				4	1	New Jersey[E]
	3rd & 4th Va.	John Neville	18	43	6	263	330	13	10	83					436	1					New Jersey
	5th & 11th Va.	William Russell	12	38	5	233	288	12	6	120	1				427	1			1	8	New Jersey
	7th Va.	Daniel Morgan	8	20	4	115	147	7	2	20	13				189				21	17	New Jersey
	8th Va.	James Wood	14	23	4	170	211	13	9	61	3				297		8			6	New Jersey
Muhlenberg	1st & 10th Va.	William Davies	14	33	7	217	271	13	10	115	4				413				1	1	New Jersey
	Additional	Nathaniel Gist	7	26	4	144	181	9	8	22	4				224		2				New Jersey
	2nd Va. state	William Brent	14	33	4	208	259	13	4	45					321				2		New Jersey
	1st Va. state	George Gibson	22	35	3	202	262	14	3	31					310	1					New Jersey
	6th Va.	John Green	9	27	6	166	208	14	5	55	26				308				1		New Jersey
Smallwood	1st Md.	Lt. Col. Uriah Forrest	11	41	3	240	295	14	13	32	4				358		1				New Jersey
	3rd Md.	Lt. Col. Nathaniel Ramsay	12	33	4	367	416	8	12	35					471		2			2	New Jersey
	5th Md.	(late) William Richardson	7	31	5	206	249	17	18	31	4				319	2	1			2	New Jersey
	7th Md.	John Gunby	11	36	4	251	302	6	15	10	4				337		2			3	New Jersey
Gist	2nd Md.	Thomas Price	10	40	3	294	347	15	19	26	4				411	1	2			1	New Jersey
	4th Md.	Josias Carvil Hall	10	37	4	331	382	16	15	31					444		1				New Jersey
	6th Md.	Otho Holland Williams	13	36	3	236	288	10	19	16	4				337	2	1				New Jersey
Irvine	1st Pa.	James Chambers	13	35	5	180	233	7	8	16	5				269	4	4		1		New Jersey
	2nd Pa.	Walter Stewart	19	41	4	329	393	20	20	16	1				450				1	3	New Jersey
	7th Pa.	Lt. Col. Morgan Connor	6	29	4	176	215	7	2	5					229		6			3	New Jersey
	10th Pa.	Richard Humpton	13	38	3	235	289	8	15	47	1				360		3				New Jersey
2nd Pa.	3rd Pa.	Thomas Craig	12	37	3	243	295	23	12	18	6				354	3	2			3	New Jersey
	5th Pa.	Francis Johnston	13	35	5	235	288	19	14	11	1				333	1	1			3	New Jersey
	6th Pa.	Robert Magaw	10	26	5	167	208	4	3	12					227		2			2	New Jersey
	9th Pa.	Richard Butler	11	28	5	147	191	19	9	6	1				226	1	1				New Jersey
Hand	4th Pa.	Lt. Col. William Butler	10	31	5	147	193	7	12	9					221						New Jersey
	11th Pa.	Lt. Col. Adam Hubley	13	38	4	233	288	29	14	21	6				358	1			1		New Jersey
Maxwell	1st N.J.	Matthias Ogden	17	38	4	206	265	17	24	19	14				339		1			5	New Jersey
	2nd N.J.	Israel Shreve	15	45	4	260	324	9	21	11	11				376		1		1	3	New Jersey
	3rd N.J.	Elias Dayton	12	37	3	232	284	6	18	15	11				334	1	2			1	New Jersey
	Additional	Oliver Spencer	14	27	3	197	241	12	20	16	3				292		3		3	4	New Jersey
Clinton	2nd N.Y.	Philip Van Cortlandt	10	29	4	158	201	10	11	12	9				243		1			2	New Jersey
	3rd N.Y.	Peter Gansevoort	15	32	4	286	337	26	11	30	1				405		4		2	3	New Jersey
	4th N.Y.	Lt. Col. Frederick Weisenfels	16	36	4[A]	199	255	21	18	23	3				320				1	2	New Jersey
	5th N.Y.	Lewis DuBois	7	30	4	212	253	24	26	35	6				344				4	1	New Jersey
Parsons	3rd Conn.	Samuel Wyllys	10	38	4	282	334	27	14	55	7				437		2		2	2	New Jersey
	4th Conn.	John Durkee	10	32	5	221	268	19	19	62	5				373				3	1	New Jersey
	6th Conn.	Return Jonathan Meigs	15	42	4	370	431	9	31	53	3				527	1	2		4	4	New Jersey
	8th Conn.	(late) Giles Russell	11	36	3	213	263	12	31	60	6				372				5	5	New Jersey
Huntington	1st Conn.	Josiah Starr	13	41	3	246	303	12	32	24	5				376		2			5	New Jersey
	2nd Conn.	Zebulon Butler	10	38	3	242	293	13	31	26	7				370				1	1	New Jersey
	5th Conn.	Philip Burr Bradley	11	37	2[B]	220	270	15	35	44	6				370		3		1	2	New Jersey
	7th Conn.	Heman Swift	12	39	3	263	317	6	35	21	1				380					2	New Jersey

NOVEMBER 1779 (continued)

BRIGADE	UNIT	COMMANDING OFFICER	PRESENT FIT FOR DUTY & ON DUTY: COMMISSIONED OFFICERS	NONCOMMISSIONED OFFICERS	STAFF OFFICERS	RANK & FILE	TOTAL	RANK & FILE SICK, ON FURLOUGH, ETC.: SICK PRESENT	SICK ABSENT	ON COMMAND & EXTRA SERVICE	ON FURLOUGH	CONFINED	GRAND TOTAL	ALTERATIONS: DEATHS	DESERTED	TAKEN PRISONER	DISCHARGED	JOINED, ENLISTED, RECRUITED	LOCATION
	FORCES UNDER COMMANDER-IN-CHIEF GENERAL GEORGE WASHINGTON (continued)																		
Stark	1st Canadian	James Livingston	6	26	3	89	124	9	5	5	1		144					1	New Jersey
Stark	Additional	Henry Sherburne	12	36	5	174	227	4	7	4	9		251						New Jersey
Stark	Additional	Samuel Blatchley Webb	10	40	4	203	257	6	17	4			284						New Jersey
Stark	2nd R.I.	Israel Angell	13	37	4	240	294	6	22	12	4		338		1			1	New Jersey
Stark	Additional	Henry Jackson	15	58	3	261	337	13	16	34			400					1	New Jersey
	2nd Canadian	Moses Hazen	25	39	1	315	380	16	29	39	4		468	1			2	2	New Jersey
	Del.	David Hall	12	26	4	224	266	24	3	39	4		336	1	3				New Jersey
Nixon	3rd Mass.	John Greaton	12	34	4	268	318	24	17	11	1		371	3	1		8	3	The Highlands, N. Y.
Nixon	5th Mass.	Rufus Putnam	17	41	1	263	322	18	11	28	1		380		2			8	The Highlands, N. Y.
Nixon	6th Mass.	Thomas Nixon	12	40	3	288	343	15	6	33	3		400		2			8	The Highlands, N. Y.
Glover	1st Mass.	Joseph Vose	11	29	4	231	275	19	11	66	3		374		3		1	11	The Highlands, N. Y.
Glover	4th Mass.	William Shephard	11	39	3	239	292	13	16	64	2		387		1		1	16	The Highlands, N. Y.
Glover	13th Mass.	Lt. Col. Calvin Smith	12	33	4	234	283	14	10	62	1		370		5			1	The Highlands, N. Y.
Glover	15th Mass.	Timothy Bigelow	8	38	4	226	276	17	12	74			379					6	The Highlands, N. Y.
Paterson	7th Mass.	Lt. Col. John Brooks	16	42	4	212	274	23	8	5	3		313		1			2	The Highlands, N. Y.
Paterson	10th Mass.	Thomas Marshall	13	39	3	239	294	22	6	65			387		2			4	The Highlands, N. Y.
Paterson	11th Mass.	Benjamin Tupper	14	37	4	276	331	19	4	40			394	2			4	2	The Highlands, N. Y.
Paterson	14th Mass.	Gamaliel Bradford	12	36	4	294	346	13	10	21	1		391	1				1	The Highlands, N. Y.
4th Mass.	2nd Mass.	John Bailey	15	39	5	260	319	18	9	54	1		401				2	7	The Highlands, N. Y.
4th Mass.	8th Mass.	Michael Jackson	10	34	4	249	297	30	8	47			382		1			1	The Highlands, N. Y.
4th Mass.	9th Mass.	James Wesson	13	42	4	255	314	12	11	52	1		390	1	1			1	The Highlands, N. Y.
	8th Pa.	Daniel Brodhead	18	30	5	138	191	10			11		212						Fort Pitt, Pa.
	9th Va.	John Gibson	21	35	5	253	314	20		2	5		341						Fort Pitt, Pa.
	Rifle corps (Md.)	(late) Moses Rawlings	3	7	3	43	56	3					59						Fort Pitt, Pa.
	Va. independent co.	Capt. Henry Heth	1	6		48	55	1			1		57						Fort Pitt, Pa.
	Independent co.	Capt. Samuel Moorhead	1	2		16	19						19						Fort Pitt, Pa.
	TOTAL OF INFANTRY		832	2333	262	15210	18637	953	894	2202	246		22932	29	83		78	174	
	CAVALRY																		
	2nd cont'l.	Elisha Sheldon	10	32	5	153	200	10	15	40	4	2	271						
	Partizan corps	Maj. Henry Lee	11	36	3	141	191	7	1	8			207			1			
	TOTAL OF CAVALRY		21	68	8	294	391	17	16	48	4	2	478			1			
	ARTILLERY																		
	10 cos. 1st cont'l.	Charles Harrison	30	110	5	179	324												
	7 cos. 2nd cont'l.	John Lamb	19	63	5	114	201								7		1	14	
	2 cos. 3rd cont'l.	John Crane	5	27	1	26	59	20	22	44	1		923		1				
	8 cos. 4th cont'l.	Thomas Proctor	13	70	3	67	153												
	4 independent cos.		8	40		51	99							1	4		1		
	TOTAL OF ARTILLERY		75	310	14	437	836	20	22	44	1		923 C	1	12		2 D	14	
	TOTAL OF WASHINGTON'S ARMY		928	2711	284	15941	19864	990	932	2294	251	2	24333	30	95	1	80	188	

NOVEMBER 1779
(continued)

OFFICERS SICK, ON FURLOUGH, ETC.	WASHINGTON'S ARMY			
	COMMISSIONED	NONCOMMISSIONED	STAFF	TOTAL
Sick Present	47	93	6	146
Sick Absent	70	117	8	195
On Command	215	288	18	521
On Furlough	116	53	30	199
Recruiting	6	16		22
On the Staff	217			217
Prisoners of War	70	4	2	76
In Arrest	3			3
TOTAL	744	571	64	1379

SOURCE OF THIS REPORT

1. MONTHLY RETURN OF THE CONTINENTAL ARMY UNDER THE COMMAND OF HIS EXCELLENCY GEORGE WASHINGTON... FOR THE MONTH OF NOVEMBER 1779, ELEPHANT FOLIO OF WASHINGTON RETURNS, WILLIAM L. CLEMENTS LIBRARY. [ARTILLERY APPEARS ON THE FOLLOWING PAGE OF THE FOLIO.]
   1a. Monthly Return of the Continental Army under... Washington... November 1779, Record Group 93, National Archives. [Contains the same figures, but to the brigade level only.]

A. Three staff officers in Lewis DuBois' 5th New York regiment plus one chaplain for the entire brigade.
B. Two staff officers in Heman Swift's 7th Connecticut regiment plus one chaplain for the entire brigade.
C. The National Archives manuscript notes that no returns were received for the Southern Department, for the garrison at Fort Schuyler, for Warner's Additional regiment at Lake George, for Whitcomb's Rangers at Rutland, for Poor's brigade at Danbury, for Moylan's 4th Continental and Baylor's 3rd Continental cavalry, for the Marechaussie, and for Captain Henry Bedkin's Independent Corps of cavalry.
D. Including twenty-six men in Washington's infantry discharged for inability.
E. The locations given here are as on the manuscript, which may well have been made out in the first few days of December. On the last day of November Washington himself had

Colonel Samuel Blatchley Webb as depicted by Charles Willson Peale. Webb, who is nominally listed as commander of an Additional regiment on the preceding report, actually was a prisoner of the British at that time. The miniature (on ivory) reproduced here was painted in February 1779 when Webb had a six-week pass to go to Philadelphia to present a petition from prisoners to Continental Congress. The star on his epaulette and the insignia of the Order of Cincinnati, which can be faintly seen on his lapel, were added in 1790 when Webb gave the miniature to Catherine Hogeboom, whom he was then courting. She became his second wife. Webb merited the star by virtue of his brevet brigadier general rank at the end of the war. (Courtesy of the New-York Historical Society, New York City)

DECEMBER 1779

BRIGADE	UNIT	COMMANDING OFFICER	PRESENT FIT FOR DUTY & ON DUTY: COMMISSIONED OFFICERS	NONCOMMISSIONED OFFICERS	STAFF OFFICERS	RANK & FILE	TOTAL	RANK & FILE SICK, ON FURLOUGH, ETC.: SICK PRESENT	SICK ABSENT	ON COMMAND & EXTRA SERVICE	ON FURLOUGH	GRAND TOTAL	ALTERATIONS: DEATHS	DESERTED	TAKEN PRISONER	DISCHARGED	JOINED, ENLISTED, RECRUITED	LOCATION
FORCES UNDER COMMANDER-IN-CHIEF GENERAL GEORGE WASHINGTON																		
Smallwood	1st Md.	Lt. Col. Uriah Forrest	10	41	3	236	290	11	10	36	4	351	1	2		2		New Jersey
	3rd Md.	Lt. Col. Nathaniel Ramsay	6	34	4	318	362	20	19	55	2	458		8		2	2	New Jersey
	5th Md.	Lt. Col. John Eager Howard	6	30	3	169	208	27	20	38	12	305	1	3		10	3	New Jersey
	7th Md.	John Gunby	10	28	3	197	238	19	10	40	4	311		2		13		New Jersey
Gist	2nd Md.	Thomas Price	7	37	4	267	315	16	14	39	12	396	3	2		5		New Jersey
	4th Md.	Josias Carvil Hall	8	30	4	269	311	21	10	59	5	406		5		23	7	New Jersey
	6th Md.	Otho Holland Williams	8	34	3	207	252	12	16	31	13	324					1	New Jersey
	Del.	David Hall	7	25	3	205	240	30	3	49	5	327	1	5			6	New Jersey
Irvine	1st Pa.	James Chambers	9	34	5	158	206	13	4	35	2	260	1	6			2	New Jersey
	2nd Pa.	Walter Stewart	12	36	4	276	328	29	18	62		437		1				New Jersey
	7th Pa.	Lt. Col. Morgan Connor	8	31	4	149	192	16	2	26		236					4	New Jersey
	10th Pa.	Richard Humpton	11	33	3	209	256	11	14	75	1	357					4	New Jersey
2nd Pa.	3rd Pa.	Thomas Craig	9	29	3	212	253	33	8	41	5	340						New Jersey
	5th Pa.	Francis Johnston	6	30	5	191	232	39	11	38	3	323	2	6			7	New Jersey
	6th Pa.	Robert Magaw	9	26	5	124	164	24	2	33	2	225						New Jersey
	9th Pa.	Richard Butler	10	29	5	117	161	32	8	22	1	224						New Jersey
Hand	4th Pa.	Lt. Col. William Butler	7	29	4	115	155	11	8	40		214		2				New Jersey
	2nd Canadian	Moses Hazen	10	32	1	210	253	41	23	123	5	445						New Jersey
	1st Canadian	James Livingston	3	28	3	81	115	8	6	4	9	142					2	New Jersey
	11th Pa.	Lt. Col. Adam Hubley	10	34	3	169	216	26	14	83	7	346	4	2				New Jersey
Maxwell	1st N.J.	Matthias Ogden	14	30	3	189	236	14	25	39	11	325		2				New Jersey
	2nd N.J.	Israel Shreve	9	38	3	230	280	9	21	40	7	357		4				New Jersey
	3rd N.J.	Elias Dayton	17	32	4 A	213	266	8	17	39	6	336						New Jersey
	Additional	Oliver Spencer	14	27	5	193	239	8	14	25	10	296					2	New Jersey
Clinton	2nd N.Y.	Philip Van Cortlandt	7	21	4	127	159	12	10	32	4	217	1	3		12	3	New Jersey
	3rd N.Y.	Peter Gansevoort	11	27	4	224	266	37	7	69	2	381		1		17	2	New Jersey
	4th N.Y.	Lt. Col. Frederick Weisenfels	13	29	3	178	223	19	11	41	3	297	3	1		9	3	New Jersey
	5th N.Y.	Lewis DuBois	3	26	3	193	225	19	21	52	14	331	3			3	2	New Jersey
Parsons	3rd Conn.	Samuel Wyllys	11	35	5	258	309	26	14	73	8	430		4				New Jersey
	4th Conn.	John Durkee	6	27	5	220	258	18	23	55	13	367		5			10	New Jersey
	6th Conn.	Return Jonathan Meigs	12	42	3	354	411	17	25	58	4	515		7			1	New Jersey
	8th Conn.	Lt. Col. Isaac Sherman	9	41	3	206	259	29	30	48	10	376					2	New Jersey
Huntington	1st Conn.	Josiah Starr	10	31	3	214	258	11	33	53	7	362		1				New Jersey
	2nd Conn.	Zebulon Butler	8	38	2	213	261	19	29	40	13	362					2	New Jersey
	5th Conn.	Philip Burr Bradley	11	35	4	200	250	18	31	54	10	363		8			2	New Jersey
	7th Conn.	Heman Swift	8	36	4	219	267	15	32	43	14	371						New Jersey
Stark	2nd R.I.	Israel Angell	17	42	5	254	318	12	8	11		349					4	New Jersey
	Additional	Henry Sherburne	6	37	4	172	219	4	13	7	1	244	1					New Jersey
	Additional	Samuel Blatchley Webb	8	41	5	191	245	9	21	8	2	285					2	New Jersey
	Additional	Henry Jackson	14	56	4	242	316	16	22	38		392					4	New Jersey

DECEMBER 1779
(continued)

BRIGADE	UNIT	COMMANDING OFFICER	PRESENT FIT FOR DUTY & ON DUTY: COMMISSIONED OFFICERS	NONCOMMISSIONED OFFICERS	STAFF OFFICERS	RANK & FILE	TOTAL	RANK & FILE SICK, ON FURLOUGH, ETC.: SICK PRESENT	SICK ABSENT	ON COMMAND & EXTRA SERVICE	ON FURLOUGH	GRAND TOTAL	ALTERATIONS: DEATHS	DESERTED	TAKEN PRISONER	DISCHARGED	JOINED, ENLISTED, RECRUITED	LOCATION
	FORCES UNDER COMMANDER-IN-CHIEF GENERAL GEORGE WASHINGTON (continued)																	
	Armand's corps	Tuffin Charles Armand	12	22	4	128	166	3	1	1	1	172		1			1	New Jersey
	3rd Mass.	John Greaton	6	32	4	246	288	22	12	11	20	353						The Highlands, N.Y.
	5th Mass.	Rufus Putnam	10	34	2	232	278	20	5	32	27	362	1	1	1	9	18	The Highlands, N.Y.
	6th Mass.	Thomas Nixon	8	37	1	253	299	9	6	29	37	380						The Highlands, N.Y.
	12th Mass.	Lt. Col. Ebenezer Sprout	11	36	4	235	286	14	5	45	17	367						The Highlands, N.Y.
	1st Mass.	Joseph Vose	11	33	4	228	276	9	13	49	28	375		1		4	3	The Highlands, N.Y.
	4th Mass.	William Shepard	10	34	3	224	271	6	15	62	23	377		4			3	The Highlands, N.Y.
	13th Mass.	Lt. Col. Calvin Smith	12	25	2	218	257	12	8	43	37	357		2			6	The Highlands, N.Y.
	15th Mass.	Timothy Bigelow	11	32	3	200	246	18	14	73	24	375					2	The Highlands, N.Y.
	8th Pa.	Daniel Brodhead	18	30	5	138	191	10			11	212		2		233		Fort Pitt, Pa.
	9th Va.	John Gibson	21	34	5	253	313	20		2	5	340						Fort Pitt, Pa.
	Rifle corps (Md.)	(late) Moses Rawlings	4	7	3	43	57	3				60						Fort Pitt, Pa.
	Va. independent co.	Capt. Henry Heth	1	6		48	55	1			1	57	1					Fort Pitt, Pa.
	Independent co.	Capt. Samuel Moorhead	1	2		16	19					19						Fort Pitt, Pa.
	TOTAL OF INFANTRY		510	1685	188	10631	13014	906	706	2101	462	17189	23	91	1	342	110	
	CAVALRY																	
	Independent corps	Capt. Henry Bedkin	1	3		8	12			5		17						New Jersey
	ARTILLERY																	
	10 cos. 1st cont'l.	Charles Harrison	15	82	4	145	246						1			43		New Jersey
	8 cos. 2nd cont'l.	John Lamb	16	69	5	122	212									1	5	New Jersey
	6 cos. 3rd cont'l.	John Crane	15	79	2	82	178	25	54	60	54	1319		1				New Jersey
	4th cont'l.	Thomas Proctor	10	61	2	65	138											New Jersey
	4 independent cos.		5	34		50	89						1			1	3	New Jersey
	West Point garrison		19	98	2	144	263											West Point, N.Y.
	TOTAL OF ARTILLERY		80	423	15	608	1126	25	54	60	54	1319	2	1		45	8	
	INVALIDS																	
	Boston det.	Capt. Moses McFarland	5	33		137	175					175					7	Boston, Mass.
	TOTAL OF WASHINGTON'S ARMY		596	2144	203	11384	14327	931	760	2166	516	18700 B	25	92	1	387 C	125	

DECEMBER 1779
(continued)

OFFICERS SICK, ON FURLOUGH, ETC.	WASHINGTON'S ARMY (EXCEPT INVALIDS AND CAVALRY)			
	COMMISSIONED	NONCOMMISSIONED	STAFF	TOTAL
Sick Present	40	94	2	136
Sick Absent	52	99	4	155
On Command	143	237	11	391
On Furlough	199	164	42	405
Recruiting	9	5		14
On the Staff	169			169
Prisoners of War	52	2	1	55
In Arrest	2		1	3
TOTAL	666	601	61	1328

SOURCE OF THIS REPORT

1. MONTHLY RETURN OF THE CONTINENTAL ARMY UNDER THE COMMAND OF HIS EXCELLENCY GEORGE WASHINGTON... FOR DECEMBER 1779, ELEPHANT FOLIO OF WASHINGTON RETURNS, WILLIAM L. CLEMENTS LIBRARY. [ARTILLERY SECTION APPEARS TWO PAGES EARLIER IN THE FOLIO.]

1a. Monthly Return of the Continental Army under... Washington... December 1779, Record Group 93, National Archives. [Contains the same figures, but to the brigade level only.]

A. Four staff officers in Oliver Spencer's Additional regiment plus one chaplain for the entire brigade.

B. The National Archives manuscript notes that no returns were received for the Southern Department, for the North Carolina brigade, for Woodford's and Muhlenberg's brigades, for Paterson's and the 4th Massachusetts brigades at West Point, for Poor's brigade at Danbury, for the troops at Rhode Island and at Boston, for Warner's Additional regiment at Fort George, for Van Schaick's 1st New York regiment at Fort Schuyler, and for the cavalry (except for Bedkin's Independent Corps).

C. Including six men in Washington's infantry who were discharged for inability.

Brigadier General William Irvine, whose brigade of Pennsylvania troops appears on the preceding report, was commander of the Western Department at Fort Pitt after 1781. A Scotch Ulsterman by birth, Irvine held a number of important political and military posts after the war. This portrait by James Reid Lambdin is one of several early nineteenth-century copies after an original by Robert Edge Pine (owned by Irvine's descendants) for which Irvine sat while he was a delegate to the Confederation Congress of 1786–1788. (Courtesy of the New-York Historical Society, New York City)

JANUARY 1780

BRIGADE	UNIT	COMMANDING OFFICER	PRESENT FIT FOR DUTY & ON DUTY: COMMISSIONED OFFICERS	NONCOMMISSIONED OFFICERS	STAFF OFFICERS	RANK & FILE	TOTAL	RANK & FILE SICK, ON FURLOUGH, ETC.: SICK PRESENT	SICK ABSENT	ON COMMAND & EXTRA SERVICE	ON FURLOUGH	CONFINED			GRAND TOTAL	ALTERATIONS: DEATHS	DESERTED	TAKEN PRISONER	DISCHARGED	JOINED, ENLISTED, RECRUITED	LOCATION
FORCES UNDER COMMANDER-IN-CHIEF GENERAL GEORGE WASHINGTON																					
Woodford	1st, 10th, 5th, 11th, 7th Va.	William Russell	22	56	6	420	504	1	12	334	13				864		4		44		
Woodford	2nd, 3rd, 4th Va.	John Neville	20	65	9	359	453	28	9	139	7				636		1		8	1	
Woodford	6th, 8th Va. and Gist's	Nathaniel Gist	19	50	14	349	432	13	14	260	18				737		2		3		
Smallwood	1st Md.	Lt. Col. Uriah Forrest	5	23	2	97	127	12	11	81	22				253		4		67	3	New Jersey
Smallwood	3rd Md.	Lt. Col. Nathaniel Ramsay	4	17	4	194	219	17	14	118	35				403		17		18	2	New Jersey
Smallwood	5th Md.	Lt. Col. John Eager Howard	3	16	2	102	123	19	16	64	31				253		14		19	1	New Jersey
Smallwood	7th Md.	John Gunby	1	19	4	116	140	16	5	74	42				277	1	7		6	1	New Jersey
Gist	2nd Md.	Thomas Price	5	24	2	132	163	15	15	70	14				277	2	3		85	3	New Jersey
Gist	4th Md.	Josias Carvil Hall	3	22	5	136	166	20	10	119	32				347		21		23	4	New Jersey
Gist	6th Md.	Otho Holland Williams	4	29	3	133	169	22	14	71	26				302		6		10	2	New Jersey
Gist	Del.	David Hall	4	21	3	149	177	24	9	117	5				332	2	2			18	New Jersey
Irvine	1st Pa.	James Chambers	4	25	3	93	125	13	7	70	29				244		1			1	New Jersey
Irvine	2nd Pa.	Walter Stewart	4	32	4	190	230	30	12	109	33				414		9		1		New Jersey
Irvine	7th Pa.	Lt. Col. Morgan Connor	5	26	3	100	134	10	2	52	24				222		4		1		New Jersey
Irvine	10th Pa.	Richard Humpton	5	29	4	128	166	18	12	105	35				336	1	9				New Jersey
2nd Pa.	3rd Pa.	Thomas Craig	4	32	4	133	173	33	8	94	24				332	1	7			4	New Jersey
2nd Pa.	5th Pa.	Francis Johnston	5	22	5	143	175	30	9	77	20				311	1	3			1	New Jersey
2nd Pa.	6th Pa.	Robert Magaw	4	17	3	84	108	15	2	67	18				210		1			2	New Jersey
2nd Pa.	9th Pa.	Richard Butler	3	20	4	68	95	26	6	58	15				200	1	2		1	1	New Jersey
Hand	4th Pa.	Lt. Col. William Butler	3	21	4	72	100	14	8	70	6				198		4				New Jersey
Hand	2nd Canadian	Moses Hazen	2	25	3	138	168	15	7	108	24				322	2	4				New Jersey
Hand	1st Canadian	James Livingston	7	25	2	143	177	46	23	181	6				433	1	5			4	New Jersey
Hand	11th Pa.	Lt. Col. Adam Hubley	2	24	2	58	86	8	5	22	5				126		10				New Jersey
Maxwell	1st N.J.	Matthias Ogden	8	16		103	127	17	18	90	37				289		5		13	5	New Jersey
Maxwell	2nd N.J.	Israel Shreve	3	22	4	95	124	15	22	153	21				335	2	3		4	8	New Jersey
Maxwell	3rd N.J.	Elias Dayton	3	24	3	84	114	11	14	131	33				303	1	3		2	3	New Jersey
Maxwell	Additional	Oliver Spencer	3	8	4	103	118	24	12	79	27				260		5		4	4	New Jersey
Clinton	2nd N.Y.	Philip Van Cortlandt	4	16	3	86	109	16	6	33	33				197	1	3		9	2	New Jersey
Clinton	3rd N.Y.	Peter Gansevoort	6	25	3	184	218	22	8	87	32				367		3		5	3	New Jersey
Clinton	4th N.Y.	Lt. Col. Frederick Weisenfels	9	21	3	97	130	18	14	50	24				236		2		50	6	New Jersey
Clinton	5th N.Y.	(late) Lewis DuBois	5	15	2	72	94	15	18	47	61				235		5	1	82	2	New Jersey
Parsons	3rd Conn.	Samuel Wyllys	4	31	1	146	182	35	17	158	5				397	1	3		17	3	New Jersey
Parsons	4th Conn.	John Durkee	2	23	5	67	97	21	17	96	7				238		1		120	1	New Jersey
Parsons	6th Conn.	Return Jonathan Meigs	2	35	1 B	207	245	45	25	166	4				485				12		New Jersey
Parsons	8th Conn.	Lt. Col. Isaac Sherman	4	33	5	94	136	16	26	102	10				290		4		71		New Jersey
Huntington	1st Conn.	Josiah Starr	1	22	2	120	145	19	26	107	5				302				42	1	New Jersey
Huntington	2nd Conn.	Zebulon Butler	3	23	3	98	127	17	21	32	11				208	1	3		130		New Jersey
Huntington	5th Conn.	Philip Burr Bradley	4	23	1 C	85	113	26	23	112	7				281		3		59		New Jersey
Huntington	7th Conn.	Heman Swift	2	27	3	116	148	24	25	116	12				325		3	2	25	1	New Jersey
Stark	2nd R.I.	Israel Angell	7	26	1	170	204	28	5	36	32				305	1	3		10		New Jersey
Stark	Additional	Henry Sherburne	2	33	3	103	141	7	13	74					235						New Jersey
Stark	Additional	Samuel Blatchley Webb	1	33	4	131	169	23	20	50	5				267				3	1	New Jersey
Stark	Additional	Henry Jackson	3	38	3	131	175	35	12	97	33				352		6				New Jersey

JANUARY 1780 (continued)

BRIGADE	UNIT	COMMANDING OFFICER	PRESENT FIT FOR DUTY & ON DUTY: COMMISSIONED OFFICERS	NONCOMMISSIONED OFFICERS	STAFF OFFICERS	RANK & FILE	TOTAL	RANK & FILE SICK, ON FURLOUGH, ETC.: SICK PRESENT	SICK ABSENT	ON COMMAND & EXTRA SERVICE	ON FURLOUGH	CONFINED			GRAND TOTAL	ALTERATIONS: DEATHS	DESERTED	TAKEN PRISONER	DISCHARGED	JOINED, ENLISTED, RECRUITED	LOCATION
	FORCES UNDER COMMANDER-IN-CHIEF GENERAL GEORGE WASHINGTON (continued)																				
Nixon	3rd Mass.	John Greaton	9	21	2	192	224	32	7	15	25				303				3		The Highlands, N. Y.
Nixon	5th Mass.	Rufus Putnam	5	28	2	192	227	16	6	26	37				312				1		The Highlands, N. Y.
Nixon	6th Mass.	Thomas Nixon	8	27	1	209	245	10	5	46	46				342				7	3	The Highlands, N. Y.
Nixon	12th Mass.	Lt. Col. Ebenezer Sprout	10	30	2	150	192	20	3	38	21				284		2		3		The Highlands, N. Y.
Glover	1st Mass.	Joseph Vose	12	20	4	116	152	21	12	79	46				310	1	2		50	2	The Highlands, N. Y.
Glover	4th Mass.	William Shepard	11	25	3	159	198	19	17	66	51				351		6		15	10	The Highlands, N. Y.
Glover	13th Mass.	Lt. Col. Calvin Smith	7	19	3	144	173	19	10	53	59				314	1	4		28	5	The Highlands, N. Y.
Glover	15th Mass.	Timothy Bigelow	8	24	3	173	208	28	17	67	40				360		57		1	60	The Highlands, N. Y.
Paterson	7th Mass.	Lt. Col. John Brooks	7	31	3	113	154	23	7	32	36				252	1	1		22		The Highlands, N. Y.
Paterson	10th Mass.	Thomas Marshall A	8	15	2	146	171	13	10	45	45				284		1		58	8	The Highlands, N. Y.
Paterson	11th Mass.	Benjamin Tupper A	7	18	3	142	170	11	4	28	47				260				80	10	The Highlands, N. Y.
Paterson	14th Mass.	Gamaliel Bradford A	7	25	2	198	232	15	10	32	27				316		5		37	3	The Highlands, N. Y.
4th Mass.	2nd Mass.	John Bailey	10	30	3	187	230	27	7	62	42				368	1			9	3	The Highlands, N. Y.
4th Mass.	8th Mass.	Michael Jackson	5	28	3	189	225	26	8	50	37				346	1			7		The Highlands, N. Y.
4th Mass.	9th Mass.	James Wesson	8	28	2	189	227	15	9	40	45				336		1		28	6	The Highlands, N. Y.
	1st N. Y.	Goose Van Schaick	13	41	2	223	279	19	16	23	35				372				13	8	Fort Schuyler, N. Y.
	Additional	Seth Warner	9	10	1	38	58		6	33	16				113		1		9	16	Fort George, N. Y.
	TOTAL OF INFANTRY		358	1554	190	8589	10691	1193	727	5011	1538				19160	24	275	3	1315	222	
	CAVALRY																				
	2nd cont'l.	Elisha Sheldon	10	26	2	131	169	5	7	6	18	2			207					20	Connecticut
	4th cont'l.	Stephen Moylan	6	34	2	109	151		6	13	14				184				1		Connecticut
	Partizan corps	Maj. Henry Lee	8	25	3	99	135	5		11	48				199						New Jersey
	Marechaussie	Capt. Bartholomew Von Heer	3	9		27	39			13					52					2	
	Independent corps	Capt. Henry Bedkin	1	1		2	4		1	6					11			4			New Jersey
	TOTAL OF CAVALRY		28	95	7	368	498	10	14	49	80	2			653			4	1	22	
	ARTILLERY																				
	10 cos. 1st cont'l.	Charles Harrison	8	47	4	92	151										1		53		New Jersey
	8 cos. 2nd cont'l.	John Lamb	18	61	5	97	181									1	9		6	3	New Jersey
	7 cos. 3rd cont'l.	John Crane	8	75	2	88	173	41	53	93	94				1177	2	8		4		New Jersey
	8 cos. 4th cont'l.	Thomas Proctor	9	45	2	47	103														New Jersey
	3 independent cos.		5	26		38	69										1		15		New Jersey
	West Point garrison		16	91	2	110	219												27	13	West Point, N. Y.
	TOTAL OF ARTILLERY		64	345	15	472	896	41	53	93	94				1177	3	19		105	16	
	INVALIDS																				
	Philadelphia unit	Lewis Nicola	7	47		217	271								271						Philadelphia, Pa.
	TOTAL OF WASHINGTON'S ARMY		457	2041	212	9646	12356	1244	794	5153	1712	2			21261 D	27	294	7	1421 E	260	

JANUARY 1780
(continued)

OFFICERS SICK, ON FURLOUGH, ETC.	WASHINGTON'S ARMY (EXCEPT INVALIDS) COMMISSIONED	NONCOMMISSIONED	STAFF	TOTAL
Sick Present	67	111	4	182
Sick Absent	52	102	5	159
On Command	341	428	27	796
On Furlough	443	395	83	921
On Extra Service		20		20
Recruiting	19	42	1	62
On the Staff	213	1	7	221
Prisoners of War	75	5	1	81
In Arrest	6		1	7
TOTAL	1216	1104	129	2449

SOURCE OF THIS REPORT

1. MONTHLY RETURN OF THE CONTINENTAL ARMY UNDER THE COMMAND OF HIS EXCELLENCY GEORGE WASHINGTON... FOR JANUARY 1780, ELEPHANT FOLIO OF WASHINGTON RETURNS, WILLIAM L. CLEMENTS LIBRARY.

1a. Monthly Return of the Continental Army under... Washington... January 1780, Record Group 93, National Archives. [Contains the same figures, but to the brigade level only.]

A. The Clements Library manuscript has Tupper's and Bradford's names with the wrong regiments; comparison of figures makes it clear that the regiment numbers were entered correctly and the commanders' names reversed erroneously. We have corrected them.
B. Four staff officers in Lieutenant Colonel Isaac Sherman's 8th Connecticut regiment plus one chaplain for the entire brigade.
C. Two staff officers in Heman Swift's 7th Connecticut regiment plus one chaplain for the entire brigade.
D. The National Archives manuscript notes that no returns were received for the Southern Department, for the troops at Fort Pitt, for the German regiment at Wyoming, for Poor's brigade at Danbury, for the troops in Rhode Island and at Boston, and for Armand's Corps.
E. Including twenty men in Washington's infantry discharged for inability.

Henry Knox, at this time a brigadier general, was promoted to major general in 1781. Knox was chief of artillery throughout the war, and it was he who conceived the idea for the Society of Cincinnati. One of the society's original eagle badges, which were made in France, is prominent in this portrait painted by Charles Willson Peale for his museum in late 1783. (Courtesy of the Independence National Historical Park Collection, Philadelphia)

FEBRUARY 1780

BRIGADE	UNIT	COMMANDING OFFICER	PRESENT FIT FOR DUTY & ON DUTY: COMMISSIONED OFFICERS	NONCOMMISSIONED OFFICERS	STAFF OFFICERS	RANK & FILE	TOTAL	RANK & FILE SICK, ON FURLOUGH, ETC.: SICK PRESENT	SICK ABSENT	ON COMMAND & EXTRA SERVICE	ON FURLOUGH	CONFINED	NOT JOINED	GRAND TOTAL	ALTERATIONS: DEATHS	DESERTED	TAKEN PRISONER	DISCHARGED	JOINED, ENLISTED, RECRUITED	LOCATION
FORCES UNDER COMMANDER-IN-CHIEF GENERAL GEORGE WASHINGTON																				
Smallwood	1st Md.	Lt. Col. Uriah Forrest	3	25	2	138	168	7	12	23	24			234		2	13	6	2	New Jersey
Smallwood	3rd Md.	Lt. Col. Nathaniel Ramsay A	5	20	4	251	280	16	12	25	33			366	1	20	2	15	1	New Jersey
Smallwood	5th Md.	(Lt. Col. John Eager Howard) A	5	21	3	135	164	17	15	18	30			244		3	2	12	2	New Jersey
Smallwood	7th Md.	John Gunby	6	22	4	156	188	15	6	20	41			270		10		5	2	New Jersey
Gist	2nd Md.	Thomas Price	4	20	3	188	215	14	12	39	32			312		18			2	New Jersey
Gist	4th Md.	Josias Carvil Hall	4	24	5	214	247	16	9	23	35			330		13	2	10	5	New Jersey
Gist	6th Md.	Otho Holland Williams	8	32	3	175	218	21	10	8	27			284	3	8	4	8	2	New Jersey
Gist	Del.	David Hall	3	25	4	151	183	12	11	24	34			264		3	3	5	1	New Jersey
Irvine	1st Pa.	James Chambers	5	28	3	143	179	19	5	19	26			248		1			4	New Jersey
Irvine	2nd Pa.	Walter Stewart	9	34	5	252	300	27	13	34	39			413		3	8		2	New Jersey
Irvine	7th Pa.	Lt. Col. Morgan Connor	6	28	3	127	164	12	2	15	28			221			3	1		New Jersey
Irvine	10th Pa.	Richard Humpton	8	31	4	191	234	11	10	45	30			330		4	6			New Jersey
2nd Pa.	3rd Pa.	Thomas Craig	8	36	4	183	231	26	8	27	37			329		7	1		5	New Jersey
2nd Pa.	5th Pa.	Francis Johnston	9	27	5	173	214	35	10	30	20			309	1	7	5		4	New Jersey
2nd Pa.	6th Pa.	Robert Magaw	5	18	3	127	153	12	2	19	20			206		3	3			New Jersey
2nd Pa.	9th Pa.	Richard Butler	3	20	3	92	118	22	8	24	18			190		9		1		New Jersey
Hand	4th Pa.	Lt. Col. William Butler	6	37	4	119	166	14	6	10	6			202		8				New Jersey
Hand	11th Pa.	Lt. Col. Adam Hubley	7	36	3	213	259	14	7	23	20			323	1	17		2	3	New Jersey
Hand	2nd Canadian	Moses Hazen	13	43	1	274	331	38	14	48	5			436		14		2	1	New Jersey
Hand	1st Canadian	James Livingston	5	21	3	58	87	13	5	19	2			126		1				New Jersey
Maxwell	1st N.J.	Matthias Ogden	9	28	3	108	148	33	8	69	20			278		14	2	4	12	New Jersey
Maxwell	2nd N.J.	Israel Shreve	5	20	5	119	149	19	22	126	14			330		2	5	2	6	New Jersey
Maxwell	3rd N.J.	Elias Dayton	6	24	5	139	174	11	4	71	30			290	2	8	1	14	11	New Jersey
Maxwell	Additional	Oliver Spencer	7	30	5	139	181	21	12	34	16			264	1	1	1	14	10	New Jersey
Clinton	2nd N.Y.	Philip Van Cortlandt	8	23	2	100	133	11	5	12	37			198		4		5		New Jersey
Clinton	3rd N.Y.	Peter Gansevoort	8	24	3	229	264	27	7	32	23			353		12		5	2	New Jersey
Clinton	4th N.Y.	Lt. Col. Frederick Weisenfels	9	22	2	117	150	13	13	23	32			231	1	2		1		New Jersey
Clinton	5th N.Y.	Lt. Col. Jacobus S. Bruyn	4	18	3	88	113	20	13	20	61			227	1	7		3	1	New Jersey
Parsons	3rd Conn.	Samuel Wyllys	6	37	1	257	301	18	19	40	4			342				15	1	New Jersey
Parsons	4th Conn.	John Durkee	4	30	4	129	167	8	16	41	5			277				1		New Jersey
Parsons	6th Conn.	Return Jonathan Meigs	9	37	2 D	335	383	12	37	39	3			474				4		New Jersey
Parsons	8th Conn.	Lt. Col. Isaac Sherman	10	39	4 D	162	215	12	26	34	12			299						New Jersey
Huntington	1st Conn.	Josiah Starr	8	25	1	187	221	3	20	23	3			270		12		28	1	New Jersey
Huntington	2nd Conn.	Zebulon Butler	8	17	1	118	144	7	15	21	5			192				15	1	New Jersey
Huntington	5th Conn.	Philip Burr Bradley	8	22	2	131	163	7	27	41	6			244		4	2	35		New Jersey
Huntington	7th Conn.	Heman Swift	6	28	2	185	221	8	33	38	6			306				23		New Jersey
Stark	2nd R.I.	Israel Angell	9	22	3	198	232	15	3	14	35			299				7	3	New Jersey
Stark	Additional	Henry Sherburne	6	33	4	152	195	12	11	19				237		1	1	1		New Jersey
Stark	Additional	Samuel Blatchley Webb	4	37	3	156	200	28	20	16	4			268				6	2	New Jersey
Stark	Additional	Henry Jackson	9	37	3	188	237	15	11	44	41			348			1	10		New Jersey
Nixon	3rd Mass.	John Greaton	7	18	2	172	189	21	7	17	22			256	4	4	9	23		The Highlands, N.Y.
Nixon	5th Mass.	Rufus Putnam	4	23	3	172	202	10	6	20	39			277	1	2	4	24	1	The Highlands, N.Y.
Nixon	6th Mass.	Thomas Nixon	10	23	1	170	204	8	5	40	51			308	1	1	15	27	18	The Highlands, N.Y.
Nixon	12th Mass.	Lt. Col. Ebenezer Sprout	10	26	2	149	187	12	3	36	20			258		1		16	7	The Highlands, N.Y.

FEBRUARY 1780
(continued)

BRIGADE	UNIT	COMMANDING OFFICER	DUTY & ON DUTY: COMMISSIONED OFFICERS	NONCOMMISSIONED OFFICERS	STAFF OFFICERS	RANK & FILE	TOTAL	ON FURLOUGH, ETC.: SICK PRESENT	SICK ABSENT	ON COMMAND & EXTRA SERVICE	ON FURLOUGH	CONFINED	NOT JOINED	GRAND TOTAL	DEATHS	DESERTED	TAKEN PRISONER	DISCHARGED	JOINED, ENLISTED, RECRUITED	LOCATION
	FORCES UNDER COMMANDER-IN-CHIEF GENERAL GEORGE WASHINGTON (continued)																			
Glover	1st Mass.	Joseph Vose	5	13	4	101	123	24	11	73	51			282		1		13	2	The Highlands, N. Y.
Glover	4th Mass.	William Shepard	10	18	1	125	154	17	16	75	57			319	1	4	9	9	5	The Highlands, N. Y.
Glover	13th Mass.	Lt. Col. Calvin Smith	6	15	2	92	125	12	10	67	65			279		1		39	1	The Highlands, N. Y.
Glover	15th Mass.	Timothy Bigelow	4	20	1	153	178	26	20	61	54			339	2	2	10	1	1	The Highlands, N. Y.
Paterson	7th Mass.	Lt. Col. John Brooks	4	27	3	112	146	15	6	30	30			227		3	1	15	3	The Highlands, N. Y.
Paterson	10th Mass.	Thomas Marshall B	9	12	2	125	148	18	6	48	49			269			1	12	1	The Highlands, N. Y.
Paterson	11th Mass.	Benjamin Tupper B	6	11	3	96	116	7	2	25	51			201	1		1	48	1	The Highlands, N. Y.
Paterson	14th Mass.	Gamaliel Bradford	8	18	2	170	198	11	8	39	26			282	1	1		28	2	The Highlands, N. Y.
4th Mass.	2nd Mass.	John Bailey	8	25	2	151	186	15	8	63	47			319	5	1	10	27	2	The Highlands, N. Y.
4th Mass.	8th Mass.	Michael Jackson	7	14	3	125	149	22	5	55	39			270	3	8	12	37	1	The Highlands, N. Y.
4th Mass.	9th Mass.	James Wesson	10	19	2	137	168	16	9	43	48			284			9	31		The Highlands, N. Y.
Poor	1st N.H.	Joseph Cilley	8	18	4	221	251	22	23	24	38			358						Danbury, Conn.
Poor	2nd N.H.	Lt. Col. George Reid	9	23	4	183	219	35	14	34	32			334		21		107	10	Danbury, Conn.
Poor	3rd N.H.	Alexander Scammell	9	20	4	181	214	31	9	25	36			315						Danbury, Conn.
	1st N.Y.	Goose Van Schaick	12	38	1	235	286	11	16	22	32			367				6	7	Fort Schuyler, N. Y.
	Additional	Seth Warner	6	7		35	48	1	9	30	9			97		5		4		Fort George, N. Y.
	TOTAL OF INFANTRY		417	1489	173	9502	11581	995	692	2077	1660			17005	30	273	146	727	148	
	CAVALRY																			
	2nd cont'l.	Elisha Sheldon	11	29	3	118	161		14	21	26	3	8	233		1		2	16	Connecticut
	Independent corps	Capt. Henry Bedkin	1	3		3	7		1	6				14						New Jersey
	TOTAL OF CAVALRY		12	32	3	121	168		15	27	26	3	8	247		1		2	16	
	ARTILLERY																			
	10 cos. 1st cont'l.	Charles Harrison	9	41	4	81	135											34		New Jersey
	8 cos. 2nd cont'l.	John Lamb	19	71	5	105	200									1		8		New Jersey
	7 cos. 3rd cont'l.	John Crane	12	69	3	90	174	34	48	75	97			1154		2		2	4	New Jersey
	8 cos. 4th cont'l.	Thomas Proctor	12	56	3	54	125									3				New Jersey
	2 independent cos.		3	23		30	56													New Jersey
	West Point garrison		15	86	2	107	210									1		8	4	West Point, N. Y.
	TOTAL OF ARTILLERY		70	346	17	467	900	34	48	75	97			1154		7		52	8	
	INVALIDS																			
	Philadelphia unit	Lewis Nicola	7	47		224	278							278						Philadelphia, Pa.
	Boston det.	Capt. Moses McFarland	5	21		96	122							122						Boston, Mass.
	TOTAL OF INVALIDS		12	68		320	400							400						
	TOTAL OF WASHINGTON'S ARMY		511	1935	193	10410	13049	1029	755	2179	1783	3	8	18806	30	281	146	781	172	

FEBRUARY 1780
(continued)

BRIGADE	UNIT	COMMANDING OFFICER	PRESENT FIT FOR DUTY & ON DUTY: COMMISSIONED OFFICERS	NONCOMMISSIONED OFFICERS	STAFF OFFICERS	RANK & FILE	TOTAL	RANK & FILE SICK, ON FURLOUGH, ETC.: SICK PRESENT	SICK ABSENT	ON COMMAND & EXTRA SERVICE	ON FURLOUGH	CONFINED	NOT JOINED	GRAND TOTAL	ALTERATIONS: DEATHS	DESERTED	TAKEN PRISONER	DISCHARGED	JOINED, ENLISTED, RECRUITED	LOCATION
	WESTERN DEPARTMENT UNDER COLONEL DANIEL BRODHEAD																			
	8th Pa.	Daniel Brodhead	9	28	4	126	167	3	2	14	9			195		2		10	31	Fort Pitt, Pa.
	9th Va.	John Gibson	12	36	4	216	268	8	3	6	20			305		7		16	1	Fort Pitt, Pa.
	Additional (Md. corps)	(late) Moses Rawlings	1	8	1	36	46		2	9	1			58						Fort Pitt, Pa.
	Va. independent corps	Capt. Henry Heth	2	6		39	47	3		4	1			55	2	1				Fort Pitt, Pa.
	TOTAL OF WESTERN DEPARTMENT		24	78	9	417	528	14	7	33	31			613	2	10		26	32	
	PART OF MAJOR GENERAL BENJAMIN LINCOLN'S SOUTHERN DEPARTMENT																			
	3rd S.C.	William Thompson	10	30	3	126	169	32	29	107	20			357	1	3		6		Charleston, S.C.
Simons	Charleston militia bn.	Lt. Col. Smith C	20	26	1	176 E	223	24	8	36				291						Charleston, S.C.
Simons	Charleston militia bn.	Lt. Col. Huger C	18	26	1	169	214	47	13	36				310						Charleston, S.C.
	TOTAL OF PART OF INFANTRY		48	82	5	471	606	103	50	179	20			958	1	3		6		
	SOUTH CAROLINA ARTILLERY BRIGADE																			
Beekman	4th S.C.	Barnard Beekman	14	16	4	96	130	11	1	22	1			165	1	7			1	Charleston, S.C.
Beekman	Charleston bn.		11	18	2	133	164	8						172						Charleston, S.C.
Beekman	Cannoniers		4	5	1	83	93		7					100						Charleston, S.C.
Beekman	Berkley Co. militia		5	5		56	66							66						Charleston, S.C.
	TOTAL OF SOUTH CAROLINA ARTILLERY BRIGADE		34	44	7	368	453	19	8	22	1			503	1	7			1	
	TOTAL OF PART OF SOUTHERN ARMY		82	126	12	839	1059	122	58	201	21			1461	2	10		6	1	

OFFICERS SICK, ON FURLOUGH, ETC.	WASHINGTON'S ARMY (EXCEPT INVALIDS)				3rd SOUTH CAROLINA & SOUTH CAROLINA ARTILLERY BRIGADE				GRAND TOTAL
	COMMISSIONED	NONCOMMISSIONED	STAFF	TOTAL	COMMISSIONED	NONCOMMISSIONED	STAFF	TOTAL	
Sick Present	59	76	8	143	1			1	144
Sick Absent	53	103	6	162	1	4		5	167
On Command	152	207	14	373	6	9		15	388
On Extra Service		19		19					19
On Furlough	402	429	83	914	1			1	915
Recruiting	24	42	1	67					67
On the Staff	201	4		205	1		5	6	211
Prisoners of War	64	3	1	68					68
In Arrest	10			10					10
Prisoners on Parole					1			1	1
Absent G					5	3		8	8
TOTAL	965	883	113	1961	16	16	5	37	1998

SOURCES OF THIS REPORT

1. MONTHLY RETURN OF THE CONTINENTAL ARMY UNDER THE COMMAND OF HIS EXCELLENCY GEORGE WASHINGTON... FOR FEBRUARY 1780, ELEPHANT FOLIO OF WASHINGTON RETURNS, WILLIAM L. CLEMENTS LIBRARY.

2. RETURN OF THE WESTERN DEPARTMENT, REMOVED FROM THE APRIL 1780 MONTHLY RETURN [SOURCE 1 ON THIS VOLUME'S APRIL MONTHLY REPORT] BECAUSE THE NATIONAL ARCHIVES VERSION OF THAT RETURN NOTES THAT THE RETURN OF THE WESTERN DEPARTMENT WAS DATED FEBRUARY 29. THEREFORE, THIS RETURN, WHICH WAS LATE IN ARRIVING, HAS BEEN MOVED TO ITS PROPER MONTH. SEE INTRODUCTION.

3. MONTHLY RETURNS OF THE CHARLESTON BRIGADE OF MILITIA, OF THE 3rd SOUTH CAROLINA CONTINENTAL REGIMENT, AND OF BARNARD BEEKMAN'S BRIGADE OF SOUTH CAROLINA ARTILLERY DATED FEBRUARY 26, FEBRUARY 29, AND MARCH 1, 1780, RESPECTIVELY, BENJAMIN LINCOLN PAPERS, MASSACHUSETTS HISTORICAL SOCIETY.

A. Lieutenant Colonel Howard was under arrest, awaiting a court-martial.
B. The names of these officers are reversed erroneously on the manuscript and have been corrected here. See footnote A on our January 1780 report.
C. We have been unable to establish the first names of these officers.
D. Three staff officers in Lieutenant Colonel Isaac Sherman's 8th Connecticut regiment plus one chaplain for the entire brigade.
E. Including twenty-nine "Alarm Men" in Huger's battalion.
F. Including eighteen men in Washington's infantry discharged for inability.
G. The return of the South Carolina artillery brigade divides its officers who were not present fit for duty into only "sick present" and "absent." We are therefore unable to say why these eight men were absent.

MARCH 1780

BRIGADE	UNIT	COMMANDING OFFICER	PRESENT FIT FOR DUTY & ON DUTY: COMMISSIONED OFFICERS	NONCOMMISSIONED OFFICERS	STAFF OFFICERS	RANK & FILE	TOTAL	RANK & FILE SICK, ON FURLOUGH, ETC.: SICK PRESENT	SICK ABSENT	ON COMMAND & EXTRA SERVICE	ON FURLOUGH	CONFINED	NOT JOINED	GRAND TOTAL	ALTERATIONS: DEATHS	DESERTED	TAKEN PRISONER	DISCHARGED	JOINED, ENLISTED, RECRUITED	LOCATION
FORCES UNDER COMMANDER-IN-CHIEF GENERAL GEORGE WASHINGTON																				
Smallwood	1st Md.	Lt. Col. Peter Adams	6	21	2	129	158	10	4	20	24			216		2		15	1	New Jersey
	3rd Md.	Lt. Col. Nathaniel Ramsay	3	22	4	243	272	15	10	32	32			361	1	1		3	5	New Jersey
	5th Md.	Lt. Col. Thomas Woolford	5	23	3	135	166	12	11	18	28			235		4		9	6	New Jersey
	7th Md.	John Gunby	7	20	4	150	181	16	5	22	39			263		2		5	2	New Jersey
Gist	2nd Md.	Thomas Price	1	23	3	158	185	2	8	23	34			252	3	1	1	4	1	New Jersey
	4th Md.	Josias Carvil Hall	2	22	5	196	225	16	9	27	37			314		7		7	4	New Jersey
	6th Md.	Otho Holland Williams	7	29	3	184	223	12	5	12	23			275	1	2		7	7	New Jersey
	Del.	David Hall	7	25	4	184	220	20	10	30	30			310		12			3	New Jersey
Irvine	1st Pa.	James Chambers	8	34	4	150	196	7	6	31	17			257		4			3	New Jersey
	2nd Pa.	Walter Stewart	7	27	4	243	281	18	13	46	46			404					1	New Jersey
	7th Pa.	Lt. Col. Morgan Connor	6	32	3	121	162	9	3	18	26			218		3				New Jersey
	10th Pa.	Richard Humpton	7	26	5	193	231	9	10	49	27			326		3			5	New Jersey
2nd Pa.	3rd Pa.	Thomas Craig	5	30	4	174	213	26	5	38	36			318		3			1	New Jersey
	5th Pa.	Francis Johnston	8	21	4	180	213	25	10	31	20			299		3		3	5	New Jersey
	6th Pa.	Robert Magaw	8	18	3	124	153	15	2	21	16			207		4			2	New Jersey
	9th Pa.	Richard Butler	3	24	4	92	123	21	8	29	12			193		2		1	1	New Jersey
Hand	4th Pa.	Lt. Col. William Butler	7	35	4	117	163	9	6	18	4			200	1	3			2	New Jersey
	11th Pa.	Lt. Col. Adam Hubley	7	37	3	189	236	15	9	37	18			315		11				New Jersey
	2nd Canadian	Moses Hazen	13	34	2	256	305	31	20	55	4			415	1	13		3	5	New Jersey
	1st Canadian	James Livingston	5	25	3	70	103	9	6	10				128	1	1				New Jersey
Maxwell	1st N.J.	Matthias Ogden	8	22	3	133	166	15	6	53	26			266		4		4	5	New Jersey
	2nd N.J.	Israel Shreve	7	27	3	138	175	18	20	105	15			333		5		1	3	New Jersey
	3rd N.J.	Elias Dayton	7	32	4	145	188	18	9	67	9			291		1		4	9	New Jersey
	Additional	Oliver Spencer	9	20	4	136	169	18	11	35	11			244		1		12		New Jersey
Clinton	2nd N.Y.	Philip Van Corlandt	6	24	3	111	144	6	7	15	22			194		5			3	New Jersey
	3rd N.Y.	Peter Gansevoort	7	26	3	229	265	17	8	44	12			346		3		8	3	New Jersey
	4th N.Y.	Lt. Col. Frederick Weisenfels	12	20	2	124	158	9	8	23	31			229	2	2		2	5	New Jersey
	5th N.Y.	Lt. Col. Jacobus S. Bruyn	3	20	3	99	125	22	10	24	44			225		4			2	New Jersey,
Parsons	3rd Conn.	Samuel Wyllys	8	29	1	232	270	23	16	40	14			363		1		14	2	New Jersey
	4th Conn.	John Durkee	7	31	4	109	151	8	13	37	10			219		1		18	1	New Jersey
	6th Conn.	Return Jonathan Meigs	12	28	3	315	358	20	28	40	16			462	1	1		7	3	New Jersey
	8th Conn.	Lt. Col. Isaac Sherman	12	36	5	173	226	11	15	32	7			291		2		7	1	New Jersey
Huntington	1st Conn.	Josiah Starr	8	21		163	192	7	17	22	9			247		2		16		New Jersey
	2nd Conn.	Zebulon Butler	8	15	1	98	122	3	14	18	9			166		1		22		New Jersey
	5th Conn.	Philip Burr Bradley	10	16	2	117	145	7	21	38	11			222	1			19	2	New Jersey
	7th Conn.	Heman Swift	8	27	3	168	206	5	22	36	8			277		1		30	1	New Jersey
Stark	2nd R.I.	Israel Angell	10	24	3	164	201	14	3	34	40			292		2		9	4	New Jersey
	Additional	Henry Sherburne	6	21	4	106	137	15	11	20				183				44	2	New Jersey
	Additional	Samuel Blatchley Webb	4	35	4	134	177	22	18	21	3			241				26		New Jersey
	Additional	Henry Jackson	10	41	3	201	255	14	10	35	40			354				2	3	New Jersey
Nixon	3rd Mass.	John Greaton	10	17	3	112	142	6	6	73	20			247			2	15	1	The Highlands, N.Y.
	5th Mass.	Rufus Putnam	4	17	3	98	122	17	4	58	36			237	1			32	1	The Highlands, N.Y.
	6th Mass.	Thomas Nixon	11	21	3	113	148	7	4	56	46			261		2		42	1	The Highlands, N.Y.
	12th Mass.	Lt. Col. Ebenezer Sprout	9	24	3	176	212	8	2	11	19			252				16	13	The Highlands, N.Y.

MARCH 1780
(continued)

BRIGADE	UNIT	COMMANDING OFFICER	COMMISSIONED OFFICERS	NONCOMMISSIONED OFFICERS	STAFF OFFICERS	RANK & FILE	TOTAL	SICK PRESENT	SICK ABSENT	ON COMMAND & EXTRA SERVICE	ON FURLOUGH	CONFINED	NOT JOINED	GRAND TOTAL	DEATHS	DESERTED	TAKEN PRISONER	DISCHARGED	JOINED, ENLISTED, RECRUITED	LOCATION
	FORCES UNDER COMMANDER-IN-CHIEF GENERAL GEORGE WASHINGTON (continued)																			
Glover	1st Mass.	Joseph Vose	11	13	3	82	109	10	8	89	49			265				27	6	The Highlands, N. Y.
Glover	4th Mass.	William Shepard	6	18		110	134	12	13	78	50			287	2	2		32	9	The Highlands, N. Y.
Glover	13th Mass.	Lt. Col. Calvin Smith	6	15	3	77	101	11	6	65	58			241				38	11	The Highlands, N. Y.
Glover	15th Mass.	Timothy Bigelow	2	15	3	96	116	22	20	74	67			299			1	38	5	The Highlands, N. Y.
Paterson	7th Mass.	Lt. Col. John Brooks	10	18	2	68	98	17	5	58	28			206				19	3	The Highlands, N. Y.
Paterson	10th Mass.	Thomas Marshall	8	8	3	89	108	14	3	64	48			237	1	1		26	1	The Highlands, N. Y.
Paterson	11th Mass.	Benjamin Tupper	5	5	4	59	73	6		28	50			157				38	1	The Highlands, N. Y.
Paterson	14th Mass.	Gamaliel Bradford	10	12	1	133	156	5	8	62	14			245		1		27		The Highlands, N. Y.
4th Mass.	2nd Mass.	John Bailey	12	20	4	114	150	10	6	84	40			290				30	1	The Highlands, N. Y.
4th Mass.	8th Mass.	Michael Jackson	9	15	4	117	145	10	4	51	38			248	1			26	3	The Highlands, N. Y.
4th Mass.	9th Mass.	James Wesson	9	17	3	125	154	15	7	46	46			268		1		13	1	The Highlands, N. Y.
Poor	1st N.H.	Joseph Cilley	7	18	4	216	245	16	20	29	41			351						Danbury, Conn.
Poor	2nd N.H.	Lt. Col. George Reid	8	22	4 B	183	217	26	11	41	29			324	5	5		4	7	Danbury, Conn.
Poor	3rd N.H.	Alexander Scammell	7	18	4	170	199	22	8	33	41			303						Danbury, Conn.
	Mass. militia	Maj. Nathaniel Heath	6	10	1	28	45			45				90				2		Boston, Mass.
	Mass. militia co.	Capt. John Carpenter	1	1		15	17							17				43	15	Springfield, Mass.
	Mass. militia co.	Capt. Ephraim Hartwell	2	6		37	45	1	2		1			49					1	Rutland, Mass.
	TOTAL OF INFANTRY		437	1353	184	8601	10575	804	564	2351	1531			15825	22	129	4	770	183	
	CAVALRY																			
	2nd cont'l.	Elisha Sheldon	11	33	2	143	189	7	7	10	22	3	4	242				4	13	Connecticut
	4th cont'l.	Stephen Moylan	6	27	2	104	139	1	4	11	17			172				8	5	Connecticut
	Independent corps	Capt. Henry Bedkin	1	3		10	14							14						New Jersey
	TOTAL OF CAVALRY		18	63	4	257	342	8	11	21	39	3	4	428				12	18	
	ARTILLERY																			
	10 cos. 1st cont'l.	Charles Harrison	11	35	4	73	123								1	1		18		New Jersey
	9 cos. 2nd cont'l.	John Lamb	21	78	5	110	214									6		14 D	2	New Jersey
	7 cos. 3rd cont'l.	John Crane	9	57	2	77	145	31	23	94	81			1078		5		27	1	New Jersey
	8 cos. 4th cont'l.	Thomas Proctor	8	51	3	44	106									2			3	New Jersey
	2 independent cos.		3	23		36	62											E		New Jersey
	West Point garrison		16	76	2	105	199									2		34	4	West Point, N. Y.
	TOTAL OF ARTILLERY		68	320	16	445	849	31	23	94	81			1078	1	16		93	10	
	INVALIDS																			
	Philadelphia unit	Lewis Nicola	4	43	3	234	284							284						Philadelphia, Pa.
	Boston det.	Capt. Moses McFarland	4	15		90	109							109						Boston, Mass.
	TOTAL OF INVALIDS		8	58	3	324	393							393 C				F		
	TOTAL OF WASHINGTON'S ARMY		531	1794	207	9627	12159	843	598	2466	1651	3	4	17724	23	145	4	875	211	

MARCH 1780
(continued)

OFFICERS SICK, ON FURLOUGH, ETC.	WASHINGTON'S ARMY (EXCEPT INVALIDS)			
	COMMISSIONED	NONCOMMISSIONED	STAFF	TOTAL
Sick Present	61	75	4	140
Sick Absent	49	95	7	151
On Command	167	205	18	390
On Extra Service	1	25		26
On Furlough	360	417	75	852
Recruiting	17	33	1	51
On the Staff	214			214
Prisoners of War	71	5	1	77
In Arrest	4		1	5
TOTAL	944	855	107	1906

SOURCE OF THIS REPORT

1. MONTHLY RETURN OF THE CONTINENTAL ARMY UNDER THE COMMAND OF HIS EXCELLENCY GEORGE WASHINGTON. . . FOR MARCH 1780, ELEPHANT FOLIO OF WASHINGTON RETURNS, WILLIAM L. CLEMENTS LIBRARY.

1a. Monthly Return of the Continental Army under. . . Washington. . . March 1780, Record Group 93, National Archives. [Contains the same figures, but only to the brigade level.]

A. Four staff officers in Lieutenant Colonel Isaac Sherman's 8th Connecticut regiment plus one chaplain for the entire brigade.

B. Three staff officers in Alexander Scammell's 3rd New Hampshire regiment plus one chaplain for the entire brigade.

C. The National Archives manuscript notes that no returns were available for the Southern Department, for the troops at Fort Pitt, for the German regiment at Wyoming, for Van Schaick's 1st New York regiment at Fort Schuyler, for Warner's Additional regiment at Fort George, for Lee's Partizan Corps, for Von Heer's Marechaussie, or for the troops in Rhode Island.

D. Including two men listed on the manuscript as "resigned."

E. Including one man listed on the manuscript as "resigned."

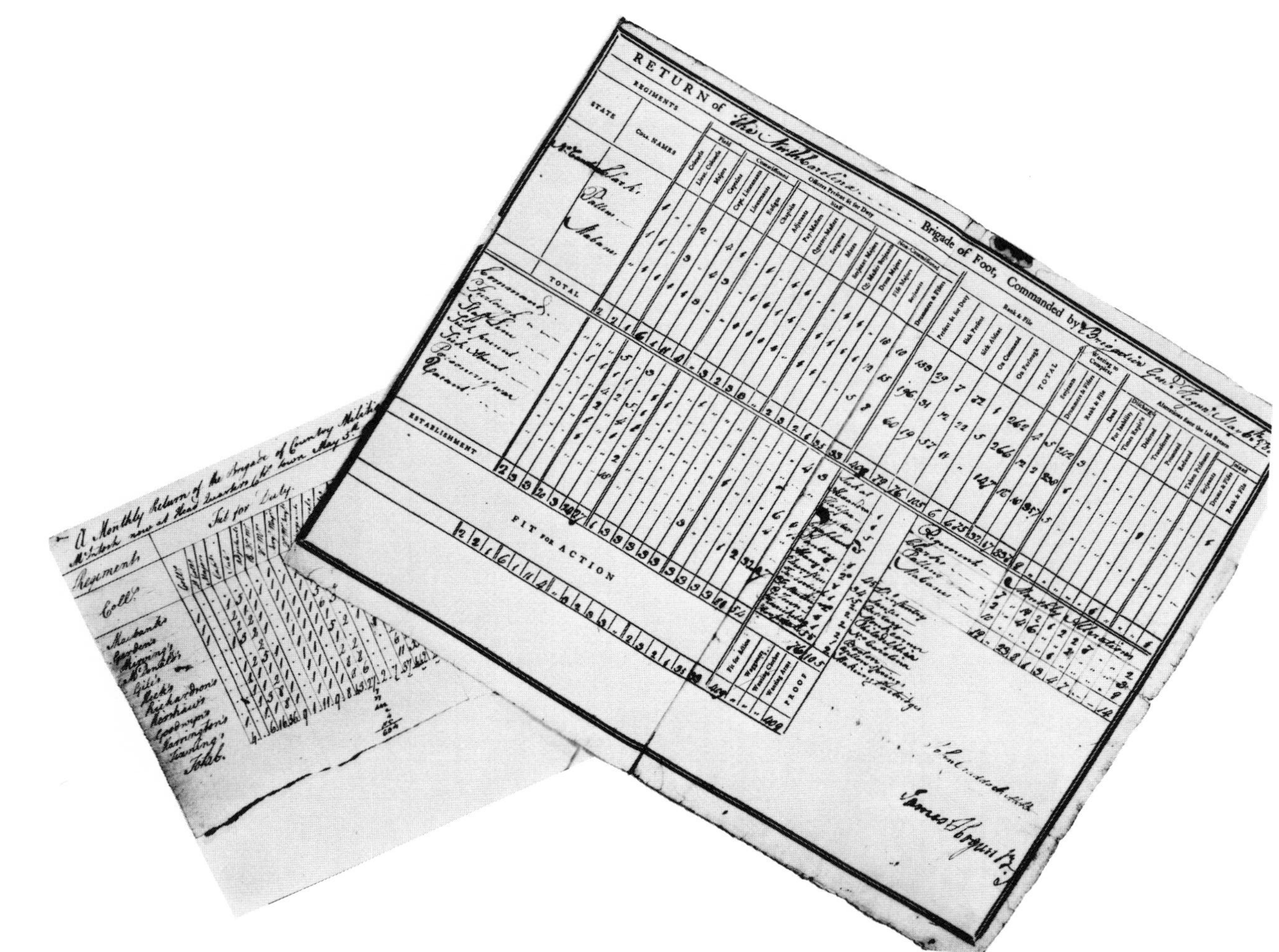

Two of the six captured returns used to compile the report on the Southern Department in the next monthly report. The captured returns were found in the Sir Henry Clinton Papers, Clements Library.

APRIL 1780

BRIGADE	UNIT	COMMANDING OFFICER	PRESENT FIT FOR DUTY & ON DUTY: COMMISSIONED OFFICERS	NONCOMMISSIONED OFFICERS	STAFF OFFICERS	RANK & FILE	TOTAL	RANK & FILE SICK, ON FURLOUGH, ETC.: SICK PRESENT	SICK ABSENT	ON COMMAND & EXTRA SERVICE	ON FURLOUGH	CONFINED	ABSENT	ABSENT WITHOUT LEAVE	GRAND TOTAL	ALTERATIONS: DEATHS	DESERTED	TAKEN PRISONER	DISCHARGED	JOINED, ENLISTED, RECRUITED	LOCATION
		FORCES UNDER COMMANDER-IN-CHIEF GENERAL GEORGE WASHINGTON																			
Irvine	1st Pa.	James Chambers	10	33	5	138	186	12	7	43	8				256		7			4	New Jersey
	2nd Pa.	Walter Stewart	11	30	4	250	295	18	9	56	14				392		13	5	1	1	New Jersey
	7th Pa.	Lt. Col. Morgan Connor	7	28	5	117	157	13	5	24	4				203		17	1		4	New Jersey
	10th Pa.	Richard Humpton	7	32	5	174	218	14	8	66	16				322	2	10	2		2	New Jersey
2nd Pa.	3rd Pa.	Thomas Craig	9	31	4	165	209	33	4	51	13				310	2	2	8	2	6	New Jersey
	5th Pa.	Francis Johnston	7	28	3	181	219	19	12	32	9				291	2	9	3	1	3	New Jersey
	6th Pa.	Robert Magaw	13	24	5 H	119	161	18	3	33	3				218	2	4	2	1	9	New Jersey
	9th Pa.	Richard Butler	6	21	6	86	119	20	7	30	5				181		10	4		3	New Jersey
Hand	4th Pa.	Lt. Col. William Butler	11	35	4	118	168	6	4	14					192	2	6	6		2	New Jersey
	11th Pa.	Lt. Col. Adam Hubley	7	36	3	195	241	10	6	38	5				300	2	16	6	1	14	New Jersey
	2nd Canadian	Moses Hazen	11	38	3	240	292	36	23	62	1				414		5	4		6	New Jersey
	1st Canadian	James Livingston	5	23	4	59	91	14	4	15					124		1	2	1	1	New Jersey
Maxwell	1st N.J.	Matthias Ogden	3	18	5	117	143	14	6	69	18				250		12	6	1	14	New Jersey
	2nd N.J.	Israel Shreve C	4	22	4	148	178	14	19	90	3				304	2	20	5		5	New Jersey
	3rd N.J.	Elias Dayton																			New Jersey
	Additional	Oliver Spencer	4	9	3	66	82	15	10	81	7				195		6	3	27	6	New Jersey
Clinton	2nd N.Y.	Philip Van Cortlandt	10	24	5	88	127	14	4	30	5				180	1	12	1	6	1	New Jersey
	5th N.Y.	Lt. Col. Jacobus S. Bruyn	5	27	4	114	150	30	8	25	12				225		3		7	4	New Jersey
	4th N.Y.	Lt. Col. Frederick Weisenfels	12	26	4	109	151	21	7	40	7				226	1	6			1	New Jersey
	3rd N.Y.	Peter Gansevoort	9	33	3	226	271	24	9	40	2				346		8		6	7	New Jersey
Parsons	3rd Conn.	Samuel Wyllys	8	24	4	195	231	22	10	41	12				316	1	3		40	2	New Jersey
	4th Conn.	John Durkee	5	23		77	105	8	10	37	8				168				34	1	New Jersey
	6th Conn.	Return Jonathan Meigs	8	34	3 I	273	318	26	20	53	12				429				30	3	New Jersey
	8th Conn.	Lt. Col. Isaac Sherman	5	22	4	125	156	7	14	40	5				222		3		40		New Jersey
Huntington	1st Conn.	Josiah Starr	5	19	2	98	124	10	12	44	5				195		1		46	4	New Jersey
	2nd Conn.	Zebulon Butler	3	14	2	70	89	5	9	21	8				132				29	1	New Jersey
	5th Conn.	Philip Burr Bradley	8	19	3	101	131	5	13	38	5				192		1		26	2	New Jersey
	7th Conn.	Heman Swift	4	20	3	116	143	4	13	40	2				202				52		New Jersey
Stark	2nd R.I.	Israel Angell	10	36	2	184	232	24	1	37	5				299		6	1	11	18	New Jersey
	Additional	Henry Sherburne	1	15	2	86	104	5	7	13					129		1		40		New Jersey
	Additional	Samuel Blatchley Webb	4	25	5	116	150	12	17	21					200		3		29	1	New Jersey
	Additional	Henry Jackson	5	48	3	216	272	18	11	41	20				362			2		10	New Jersey
Nixon	3rd Mass.	John Greaton	8	15	4	53	80	3	6	62	9				160						The Highlands, N.Y.
	5th Mass.	Rufus Putnam	7	18	3	93	121	9	2	38	25				195		11		278	13	The Highlands, N.Y.
	6th Mass.	Thomas Nixon	5	24	3	82	114	3	2	51	15				185						The Highlands, N.Y.
	12th Mass.	Lt. Col. Ebenezer Sprout	14	18	4	99	135	8	4	7	6				160						The Highlands, N.Y.
Glover	1st Mass.	Joseph Vose	13	16	4	104	137	11	4	62	32				246				26	3	The Highlands, N.Y.
	4th Mass.	William Shepard	10	23	2	123	158	11	12	65	20				266	1			33	3	The Highlands, N.Y.
	13th Mass.	Lt. Col. Calvin Smith	10	21	4	84	119	4	6	55	31				215		1	1	40	6	The Highlands, N.Y.
	15th Mass.	Timothy Bigelow	5	16	2	50	73	7	15	70	41				206	1			99	8	The Highlands, N.Y.
Paterson	7th Mass.	Lt. Col. John Brooks	12	19	1	64	96	6	3	66	11				182		5		21	2	The Highlands, N.Y.
	10th Mass.	Thomas Marshall	7	18	3	75	103	11		31	23				168			1	74	2	The Highlands, N.Y.
	11th Mass.	Benjamin Tupper	4	11	2	62	79	2		18	20				119		1		46	12	The Highlands, N.Y.
	14th Mass.	Gamaliel Bradford	10	9	2	56	77	4	3	61	7				152	1			88		The Highlands, N.Y.
4th Mas	2nd Mass.	John Bailey	15	29	3	111	158	5	5	88	14				270				27	4	The Highlands, N.Y.
	8th Mass.	Michael Jackson	11	11	3	55	80	5	3	46	28				162	1	1		82	2	The Highlands, N.Y.
	[illegible]	[illegible]	[illegible]	[illegible]	[illegible]	[illegible]	[illegible]	[illegible]	[illegible]	[illegible]	[illegible]				[illegible]		[illegible]		[illegible]	[illegible]	[illegible]

APRIL 1780 (continued)

BRIGADE	UNIT	COMMANDING OFFICER	PRESENT FIT FOR DUTY & ON DUTY: COMMISSIONED OFFICERS	NONCOMMISSIONED OFFICERS	STAFF OFFICERS	RANK & FILE	TOTAL	RANK & FILE SICK, ON FURLOUGH, ETC.: SICK PRESENT	SICK ABSENT	ON COMMAND & EXTRA SERVICE	ON FURLOUGH	CONFINED	ABSENT	ABSENT WITHOUT LEAVE	GRAND TOTAL	ALTERATIONS: DEATHS	DESERTED	TAKEN PRISONER	DISCHARGED	JOINED, ENLISTED, RECRUITED	LOCATION
	FORCES UNDER COMMANDER-IN-CHIEF GENERAL GEORGE WASHINGTON (continued)																				
Poor	1st N.H.	Joseph Cilley	9	15	4	153	181	10	15	52	21				279						The Highlands, N.Y.
Poor	2nd N.H.	Lt. Col. George Reid	5	18	3 J	135	161	12	9	67	21				270	2	13		197	32	The Highlands, N.Y.
Poor	3rd N.H.	Alexander Scammell	7	14	4	104	129	16	7	51	30				233						The Highlands, N.Y.
	1st N.Y.	Goose Van Schaick	9	38	1	209	257	11	15	43	27				353		1		11	3	Fort Schuyler, N.Y.
	Additional	Seth Warner	13	13		51	77	2	8	18	3				108		3		3	5	Fort George, N.Y.
	TOTAL OF INFANTRY		397	1180	167	6217	7961	643	417	2277	627				11925	23	224	63	1498	231	
	ARTILLERY																				
	8 cos. 2nd cont'l.	John Lamb	32	64	6	98	200										2		3 W	4	New Jersey
	7 cos. 3rd cont'l.	John Crane	12	45	3	56	116	17	14	91	25				824	1			31 W	2	New Jersey
	8 cos. 4th cont'l.	Thomas Proctor	9	55	3	52	119										1		1 W	3	New Jersey
	West Point garrison		19	83	1	139	242										38		23	6	West Point, N.Y.
	TOTAL OF ARTILLERY		72	247	13	345	677	17	14	91	25				824	1	41		58 X	15	
	TOTAL OF WASHINGTON'S ARMY		469	1427	180	6562	8638	660	431	2368	652				12749	24	265	63	1556	246	
	SOUTHERN DEPARTMENT UNDER MAJOR GENERAL BENJAMIN LINCOLN (Incomplete) T																				
Hogun	1st N.C.	Thomas Clark	8	30	3	153	194	29	7	72	1				303	7	2	7	19	2	Charleston, S.C.
Hogun	2nd N.C.	John Patten	12	31	4	196	243	31	12	22	5				313	2	6		4	3	Charleston, S.C.
Hogun	3rd N.C. A	Lt. Col. Robert Mebane	7	15	4	60	86	19	57	11					173	10				9	Charleston, S.C.
Woodford	1st Va. A	William Russell	20	47	4	236	307	21	32	115	22				497						Charleston, S.C.
Woodford	3rd Va. A	Nathaniel Gist	12	39	5 K	190	246	7	29	55	28				365						Charleston, S.C.
Woodford	2nd Va. B	John Neville	22	49	6	232	309	32	42	91	7				481						Charleston, S.C.
Scott	1st Va. det. B	Lt. Col. Samuel Hopkins	9	12	4	132	157	36	39	24					256						Charleston, S.C.
Scott	2nd Va. det.	William Heth	11	21	3	179	214	22	63	24					323						Charleston, S.C.
Scott	2nd S.C.	Lt. Col. Francis Marion	6	16	4	53	79	22	44	106	1				252						Charleston, S.C.
Scott	3rd S.C.	William Thompson	9	29	4	109	151 N	28	58	60	8				305						Charleston, S.C.
Scott	N.C. militia	Archibald Lytle D	11	19	3	142	175	18	5	1					199						Charleston, S.C.
Simons	1st bn. Charleston militia	Lt. Col. Smith D	22	1	25	174	222	37 O		54 Q			12		325						Charleston, S.C.
Simons	2nd bn. Charleston militia	Lt. Col. Huger	20 E	1	G 28	161	210	82 O		41 R			8	16	357						Charleston, S.C.
Simons	Bretigny's corps	Marquis de Bretigny	8	3	10	64	85	5 O					2		92						Charleston, S.C.
McIntosh	S.C. militia	Joseph Maybank		1	1	12	14	8				1			23						Charleston, S.C.
McIntosh	S.C. militia	Benjamin Garden	7	9	3	46	65	32							97						Charleston, S.C.
McIntosh	S.C. militia	William Skirving	4	4	2	18	28	5							33						Charleston, S.C.
McIntosh	Militia (N.C. or S.C.)	______ McDonald D	5	14	2	66	87	11							98						Charleston, S.C.
McIntosh	S.C. militia	Hugh Giles	6	12	2	52	72	5							77						Charleston, S.C.
McIntosh	S.C. militia	George Hicks	2	3	1	10	16	4							20				5		Charleston, S.C.
McIntosh	S.C. militia	Richard Richardson	8	11	2	36	57	11		2				1	71						Charleston, S.C.
McIntosh	S.C. militia	Joseph Kershaw	3	3	2	18	26	12							38						Charleston, S.C.
McIntosh	S.C. militia	Robert Goodwin	4	5	2	26	37	2							39						Charleston, S.C.
McIntosh	N.C. militia	Henry William Harrington	12	18	2	103	135	15							150						Charleston, S.C.
McIntosh	N.C. militia	Hugh Tinning	11	16	2	55 M	84	10							94						Charleston, S.C.
	TOTAL OF SOUTHERN INFANTRY		239	409	128	2523	3299	504	388	678	72	1	22	17	4981						
	ARTILLERY																				
Beekman	4th S.C.	Barnard Beekman	18	14	5	68	105	10	1	27	1				144	4	10			1	Charleston, S.C.
Beekman	Cont'l. independent co.		3	7		22	32			1					33						Charleston, S.C.
Beekman	Charleston bn.		12	16	3	106	137	16	2	40	1				196	1	2 V		6		Charleston, S.C.
Beekman	Cannoniers C																				Charleston, S.C.
Beekman	1st S.C. cont'l. bn. C																				Charleston, S.C.
	TOTAL OF ARTILLERY		33	37	8	196	274	26	3	68	2				373	5	12		6	1	
	TOTAL OF SOUTHERN ARMY		272	446	136	2719	3573	530	391	746	74	1	22	17	5354						

BRIGADE

APRIL 1780
(continued)

UNIT	COMMANDING OFFICER	PRESENT FIT FOR DUTY & ON DUTY: COMMISSIONED OFFICERS	NONCOMMISSIONED OFFICERS	STAFF OFFICERS	RANK & FILE	TOTAL	RANK & FILE SICK, ON FURLOUGH, ETC.: SICK PRESENT	SICK ABSENT	ON COMMAND & EXTRA SERVICE	ON FURLOUGH	CONFINED	ABSENT	ABSENT WITHOUT LEAVE	GRAND TOTAL	ALTERATIONS: DEATHS	DESERTED	TAKEN PRISONER	DISCHARGED	JOINED, ENLISTED, RECRUITED	LOCATION
VIRGINIA STATE FORCES IN THE CONTINENTAL SERVICE AS GUARDS FOR THE CONVENTION TROOPS																				
Va. convention guards	Francis Taylor	11	24		164	199		5	25	10	1			240						Albemarle Barracks, Va.
Va. western bn.	Lt. Col. Joseph Crockett	12 [F]	14	3 [L]	75	105		14 [P]	15 [S]	6	1			141	1	8				Albemarle Barracks, Va.
TOTAL OF CONVENTION GUARDS		24	38	3	239	304		19	40	16	2			381	1	8				
GRAND TOTAL		765	1911	319	9520	12515	1190	841	3154	742	3	22	17	18484 [U]						

OFFICERS SICK, ON FURLOUGH, ETC.	WASHINGTON'S ARMY[Y]: COMMISSIONED	NONCOMMISSIONED	STAFF	TOTAL	SOUTHERN ARMY (NO FIGURES FOR CHARLESTON MILITIA & ONLY PARTIAL FOR McINTOSH'S BRIGADE & THE ARTILLERY): COMMISSIONED	NONCOMMISSIONED	STAFF	TOTAL	CONVENTION GUARDS: COMMISSIONED	NONCOMMISSIONED	STAFF	TOTAL	GRAND TOTAL
Sick Present	49	56	3	108	29	45		74					182
Sick Absent	46	50	6	102	12	46	1	59					161
On Command	178	190	12	380	29	39	5	73	1			1	454
On Furlough	150	136	41	327	18	15	7	40	4	2		6	373
On Extra Service	2	17		19									19
Recruiting	100	38	3	141									141
On the Staff	191			191	18		1	19					210
Prisoners of War	61	10		71	5			5					76
In Arrest	4		3	7									7
Furlough Expired/AWOL	2			2	1			1					3
Absent					2			2					2
TOTAL	783	497	68	1348	114	145	14	273	5	2		7	1628

SOURCES OF THIS REPORT

1. MONTHLY RETURN OF THE CONTINENTAL ARMY UNDER THE COMMAND OF HIS EXCELLENCY GEORGE WASHINGTON... FOR APRIL 1780, ELEPHANT FOLIO OF WASHINGTON RETURNS, WILLIAM L. CLEMENTS LIBRARY. [THE PORTION OF THIS RETURN GIVING THE STATE OF THE FORCES AT FORT PITT, WHICH ORIGINALLY WAS MADE OUT ON FEBRUARY 29, HAS BEEN MOVED TO ITS PROPER PLACE IN OUR FEBRUARY REPORT. SEE THAT REPORT. THE ARTILLERY SECTION OF THIS RETURN IS ON THE PRECEDING PAGE OF THE FOLIO.]

1a. Monthly Return of the Continental Army under... Washington... April 1780, Record Group 93, National Archives. [Contains the same figures, but only to the brigade level.]

2. REPORT FOR THE SOUTHERN DEPARTMENT AT CHARLESTON COMPILED FROM THE FOLLOWING CAPTURED RETURNS IN THE SIR HENRY CLINTON PAPERS, WILLIAM L. CLEMENTS LIBRARY: RETURN OF THE NORTH CAROLINA BRIGADE OF FOOT, COMMANDED BY BRIGADIER GENL. HOGUN, MAY 6, 1780; A WEEKLY RETURN OF THE 1st VIRGINIA BRIGADE COMMANDED BY WILLIAM WOODFORD ESQR. BRIGADIER GENERAL, MAY 1, 1780; RETURN OF THE BRIGADE OF FOOT COMMANDED BY CHARLES SCOTT ESQUIRE BRIGADIER GENERAL, MAY 9, 1780; GENERAL RETURN OF THE BRIGADE COMMANDED BY COL. MAURICE SIMONS, APRIL 25, 1780; A MONTHLY RETURN OF THE BRIGADE OF COUNTRY MILITIA UNDER THE COMMAND OF BRIGADIER GENL. McINTOSH, MAY 5, 1780; AND MONTHLY RETURN OF THE BRIGADE OF SOUTH CAROLINA ARTILLERY UNDER THE COMMAND OF BARNARD BEEKMAN ESQR., MAY 1, 1780. [ALTHOUGH IT IS NOT HEADED AS A MONTHLY RETURN, THE RETURN OF THE NORTH CAROLINA BRIGADE DOES CONTAIN THE MONTHLY ALTERATIONS. FOR MORE INFORMATION ABOUT THESE RETURNS, SEE FOOTNOTE T.]

3. A RETURN OF COLONEL TAYLOR'S REGIMENT OF GUARDS & COLO. CROCKETT'S REGT., MAY 1, 1780, COLONEL JAMES WOOD MANUSCRIPTS, VIRGINIA STATE LIBRARY. [ALTHOUGH THEY ARE NOT SO HEADED, THIS SERIES OF RETURNS FOR THE CONVENTION GUARDS APPARENTLY CONTAINS THE MONTHLY ALTERATIONS.]

A. These are not the 1st, 2nd, and 3rd Virginia regiments of the White Plains rearrangement, but a new consolidation of the 1st, 10th, 5th, 11th, and 7th regiments under Russell; the 2nd, 3rd, and 4th regiments under Neville; and the 6th, 8th, and Gist's under Gist. See our January 1780 report.

B. Officers were elected to recruit three Virginia detachments to go South in May 1779. The 1st and 2nd of these units, included in this report, recruited sufficient men by early 1780, but the third detachment under Colonel Abraham Buford encountered difficulties and did not leave Virginia in time to reach Charleston; they were cut to pieces at Hanging Rock, near Wax Haws, South Carolina, May 29, 1780. For the officers, see Lieutenant Colonel Gustavus Brown Wallace to Colonel John Cropper, May 12, 1779, Executive Department--Executive Papers, Box 1, Archives Division, Virginia State Library. E.M. Sanchez-Saavedra of the Publications Branch of the Archives Division was most helpful in straightening out these Virginia detachments at Charleston. C.A. Flagg and W.O. Waters, "Virginia Soldiers in the Revolution," Virginia Magazine of History and Biography, 19: 406-7, is in error as to the makeup of the Virginia units at Charleston.

C. No figures are given for this unit on the manuscript.

D. We have been unable to further identify this officer.

E. Including one colonel with Simons' brigade who was not connected with any particular unit in the brigade.

F. Including two majors who were not specifically assigned to either of the two guard units on the original return.

G. Two noncommissioned officers in Marquis de Bretigny's Corps plus one quartermaster for the entire brigade.

H. Five staff officers in Richard Butler's 9th Pennsylvania regiment plus one chaplain for the entire brigade.

I. Three staff officers in Lieutenant Colonel Isaac Sherman's 8th Connecticut regiment plus one chaplain for the entire brigade.

J. Three staff officers in Alexander Scammell's 3rd New Hampshire regiment plus one chaplain for the entire brigade.

K. Five staff officers in John Neville's 2nd Virginia regiment plus one chaplain for the entire brigade.

L. This figure represents the two surgeons and the brigade major at Albemarle who were not specifically part of either unit.

M. In addition to the figures for rank and file present fit for duty included here, this brigade also had an additional thirty-seven men who are marked as "servants" in a separate column. We have not included the men here because it seems most probable that they were slaves who accompanied their masters, not privates serving as orderlies. Therefore, these "servants" were probably not soldiers at all.

N. Of the 615 enlisted men given as present fit for duty in the five units of Scott's brigade, the manuscript further specifies that 8 were waggoners and 27 were wanting clothes.

O. The heading for this column for Simons' brigade reads "Sick and Alarm Men." Therefore, these figures include more than just those men sick present. The men who were sick absent are probably included in the "Absent" column.

P. This column on the original manuscript reads "in hospital," rather than "sick absent."

Q. Of this total, forty-three men are indicated as on "public service."

R. Of this total, thirty-three men are indicated as on "public service."

S. Including six men in Taylor's regiment and two in Crockett's classified as camp color men. See footnote I on our September 1779 report.

T. The captured returns from which these figures for the Southern Department are compiled offer the best and most detailed report of the strength of Lincoln's forces at about the end of April, shortly before they surrendered to Sir Henry Clinton. Although nearly complete, there are no returns for Colonel Charles Pinckney's 1st South Carolina regiment (with a total of 231 men according to the British return of the captured), the Light Dragoons (most of whom escaped; 41 men on the British return of the captured) and Virginia and Georgia officers without regiments under them (52 according to the British return). The South Carolina Continentals had been reduced and consolidated to only three infantry regiments, two of which are included here. Two other reports on the forces at Charleston exist: (1) the totals of rank and file fit for duty (only) at various dates in a letter from Jean Baptiste Ternant (Lincoln's adjutant general), Charleston, May 24, 1780, to Benjamin Lincoln, Emmet Collection No. 7726, New York Public Library; and (2) a British "Return of the Rebel Forces, Commanded by Major Genl. Lincoln at the Surrender of Charlestown; the 12th of May 1780; Now Prisoners of War" enclosed in Sir Henry Clinton, June 4, 1780, to George Sackville Germain, Sir Henry Clinton Papers, William L. Clements Library. The latter is printed in William Moultrie, Memoirs of the American Revolution (New York: Printed by David Longworth, 1802), 2: 114.

U. The National Archives manuscript notes that no returns were available for the troops at Rhode Island, for the German battalion, for the cavalry, for Dayton's regiment on the lines, for the invalids, for the Delaware and Maryland troops, and for the Southern Department (the last largely supplied on our report).

V. The manuscript notes that these two men who deserted were Negroes. They have been included on the assumption that they were actually serving in the artillery; otherwise they probably would not have been counted as deserted. Perhaps they were slaves who were freed to serve as substitutes for their masters. It is possible, however, that these men were not soldiers but were slaves serving as laborers, particularly since, throughout the war, South Carolina strongly resisted the suggestion that slaves could bear arms.

W. Including one man classified as resigned.

X. Including nineteen men in Washington's infantry discharged for inability.

Y. This section may include a very few men from the return of the Western Department made out at the end of February and included on our February report. Since the returns did not break down the figures for officers sick, on furlough, etc., it is not possible to determine how many of these men, if any, were from the Fort Pitt units, but the number would have had to be so small as to not alter significantly these totals.

MAY 1780

BRIGADE	UNIT	COMMANDING OFFICER	PRESENT FIT FOR DUTY & ON DUTY: COMMISSIONED OFFICERS	NONCOMMISSIONED OFFICERS	STAFF OFFICERS	RANK & FILE	TOTAL	RANK & FILE SICK, ON FURLOUGH, ETC.: SICK PRESENT	SICK ABSENT	ON COMMAND & EXTRA SERVICE	ON FURLOUGH	CONFINED	NOT JOINED	FURLOUGH EXPIRED	GRAND TOTAL	ALTERATIONS: DEATHS	DESERTED	TAKEN PRISONER	DISCHARGED	JOINED, ENLISTED, RECRUITED	LOCATION
FORCES UNDER COMMANDER-IN-CHIEF GENERAL GEORGE WASHINGTON																					
Irvine	1st Pa.	James Chambers	12	34	5	158	209	5	6	30	5				255		3		1	5	New Jersey
	2nd Pa.	Walter Stewart	12	32	4	249	297	14	10	55	2				378	2	14	1		2	New Jersey
	7th Pa.	Lt. Col. Morgan Connor	6	28	5	127	166	9	4	20					199		7			3	New Jersey
	10th Pa.	Richard Humpton	6	31	5	191	233	10	10	53	8				314		11			5	New Jersey
2nd Pa.	3rd Pa.	Thomas Craig	11	33	5	172	221	32	5	46	6				310		7		1	4	New Jersey
	5th Pa.	Francis Johnston	8	25	4	168	205	17	15	34	3				274		11				New Jersey
	6th Pa.	Robert Magaw	13	22	5	121	161	16	4	26					207	1	11			3	New Jersey
	9th Pa.	Richard Butler	5	21	6 [A]	88	120	21	9	25	4				179		3			2	New Jersey
Hand	4th Pa.	Lt. Col. William Butler	10	30	4	112	156	11	5	13					185						New Jersey
	11th Pa.	Lt. Col. Adam Hubley	9	34	3	180	226	18	5	37	5				291						New Jersey
	2nd Canadian	Moses Hazen	14	39	3	235	291	32	20	68	1				412	1	18	1	9	8	New Jersey
	1st Canadian	James Livingston	7	25	3	61	96	10	5	14					125						New Jersey
Maxwell	1st N.J.	Matthias Ogden	8	27	4	176	215	9	9	28	4				265		6			9	New Jersey
	2nd N.J.	Israel Shreve	9	24	5	195	233	20	19	55	3				330		3		3	24	New Jersey
	3rd N.J.	Elias Dayton	17	39	4	215	275	12	4	17	1				309		5			10	New Jersey
	Additional	Oliver Spencer	9	18	4	103	134	16	9	16	10				185		3	3	21	1	New Jersey
Clinton	2nd N.Y.	Philip Van Cortlandt	12	22	3	97	134	9	4	22	1				170		5		1	3	New Jersey
	5th N.Y.	Lt. Col. Jacobus S. Bruyn	5	27	4	109	145	21	8	31	4				209		7		6	2	New Jersey
	4th N.Y.	Lt. Col. Frederick Weisenfels	15	19	5	124	163	13	3	30	2				211	1	3		9	1	New Jersey
	3rd N.Y.	Peter Gansevoort	11	28	3	231	273	26	7	28	1				335	2			6	2	New Jersey
Parsons	3rd Conn.	Samuel Wyllys	6	22	4	149	181	13	12	41	8				255	1	3		50		New Jersey
	4th Conn.	John Durkee	6	19	2	69	96	8	10	31	6				151		1		16		New Jersey
	6th Conn.	Return Jonathan Meigs	8	32	2	261	303	25	22	34	8				392				35	1	New Jersey
	8th Conn.	Lt. Col. Isaac Sherman	7	15	5	103	130	10	9	9	6				164		1		53	2	New Jersey
Huntington	1st Conn.	Josiah Starr	6	15	3	93	117	5	10	16	5				153		3		36		New Jersey
	2nd Conn.	Zebulon Butler	3	16	3	58	80	5	6	16	6				113				18	1	New Jersey
	5th Conn.	Philip Burr Bradley	6	19	3	96	124	4	12	30	6				176	1	1	1	11		New Jersey
	7th Conn.	Heman Swift	5	14	1 [B]	90	110	3	13	42	3				171		1		23	1	New Jersey
Stark	2nd R.I.	Israel Angell	13	38	2	193	246	17	9	28					300		4		24	30	New Jersey
	Additional	Samuel Blatchley Webb	5	34	5	144	188	7	16	15					226				23	51	New Jersey
	Additional	Henry Jackson	6	52	4	203	265	25	11	48	12				361		1		23	28	New Jersey
Nixon	3rd Mass.	John Greaton	7	19	3	53	82	8	3	46	6				145			2	39	7	The Highlands, N.Y.
	5th Mass.	Rufus Putnam	6	17	3	80	106	10	2	27	17				162			2	34	1	The Highlands, N.Y.
	6th Mass.	Thomas Nixon	6	22	3	79	110	3		31	12				156		1		50	3	The Highlands, N.Y.
	12th Mass.	Lt. Col. Ebenezer Sprout	10	18	4	69	101	1	4	16	2				124		7		49		The Highlands, N.Y.
Glover	1st Mass.	Joseph Vose	13	19	2	72	106	11	1	56	22				196				26	1	The Highlands, N.Y.
	4th Mass.	William Shepard	9	30	4	89	132	3	7	63	5				210		7	2	28	1	The Highlands, N.Y.
	13th Mass.	Lt. Col. Calvin Smith	7	22	4	61	94	3	6	45	19				167		2		20	3	The Highlands, N.Y.
	15th Mass.	Timothy Bigelow	6	14	4 [C]	23	47	1	9	62	22				141		1		51	1	The Highlands, N.Y.

MAY 1780 (continued)

BRIGADE	UNIT	COMMANDING OFFICER	PRESENT FIT FOR DUTY & ON DUTY: COMMISSIONED OFFICERS	NONCOMMISSIONED OFFICERS	STAFF OFFICERS	RANK & FILE	TOTAL	RANK & FILE SICK, ON FURLOUGH, ETC.: SICK PRESENT	SICK ABSENT	ON COMMAND & EXTRA SERVICE	ON FURLOUGH	CONFINED	NOT JOINED	FURLOUGH EXPIRED	GRAND TOTAL	ALTERATIONS: DEATHS	DESERTED	TAKEN PRISONER	DISCHARGED	JOINED, ENLISTED, RECRUITED	LOCATION
	FORCES UNDER COMMANDER-IN-CHIEF GENERAL GEORGE WASHINGTON (continued)																				
Paterson	7th Mass.	Lt. Col. John Brooks	8	17	1	49	75	6	4	66	5				156		1		19	1	The Highlands, N.Y.
Paterson	10th Mass.	Thomas Marshall	5	22	3	56	86	6	1	33	15				141				29	3	The Highlands, N.Y.
Paterson	11th Mass.	Benjamin Tupper	3	16	4 D	33	56	6	1	22	1				86		9	1	31	4	The Highlands, N.Y.
Paterson	14th Mass.	Gamaliel Bradford	6	9	5	32	52		2	21	1				76		5	1	72	4	The Highlands, N.Y.
4th Mass.	2nd Mass.	John Bailey	10	25	3	77	115	1	4	78	8				206		3		54	3	The Highlands, N.Y.
4th Mass.	8th Mass.	Michael Jackson	11	15	3	34	63	4	1	33	13				114		4		49	5	The Highlands, N.Y.
4th Mass.	9th Mass.	James Wesson	8	15	2	64	89	9	3	53	14				168		6	1	47	1	The Highlands, N.Y.
Poor	1st N.H.	Joseph Cilley	10	19	4	142	175	8	12	58	11				264		11		18	12	The Highlands, N.Y.
Poor	2nd N.H.	Lt. Col. George Reid	8	22	3 E	140	173	9	7	58	14				261	1	3		20	11	The Highlands, N.Y.
Poor	3rd N.H.	Alexander Scammell	10	17	5	110	142	18	6	52	17				235	1			13	13	The Highlands, N.Y.
	8th Pa.	Daniel Brodhead	9	27	4	137	177	2	1	2	4				186		5		6	3	Fort Pitt, Pa.
	9th Va.	John Gibson	14	29	4	147	194	1		8	14				217		7		73	4	Fort Pitt, Pa.
	Additional (Md. corps)	(late) Moses Rawlings	1	8	1	35	45		2	9	1				57		1				Fort Pitt, Pa.
	Va. independent corps	Capt. Henry Heth	2	5		39	46	4		1	3				54						Fort Pitt, Pa.
	1st N.Y.	Goose Van Schaick	15	41	2	238	296	16	15	18	8				353	1	6		5	2	Fort Schuyler, N.Y.
	Additional	Seth Warner	13	16	2	60	91	2	8	16	2				119		2		3	19	Fort George, N.Y.
	TOTAL OF INFANTRY		467	1298	191	6490	8446	575	390	1832	356				11599	12	213	15	1105	300	
	CAVALRY																				
	2nd cont'l.	Elisha Sheldon	16	29	4	170	219	6	7	18	7	2	2		261		7			8	
	4th cont'l.	Stephen Moylan	4	24	3	84	115	4	1	15	16	1			152		1		2		
	TOTAL OF CAVALRY		20	53	7	254	334	10	8	33	23	3	2		413		8		2	8	
	ARTILLERY																				
	8 cos. 2nd cont'l.	John Lamb	23	56	5	96	180												8	4	New Jersey
	7 cos. 3rd cont'l.	John Crane	15	46	3	75	139	18	12	80	16			3	811				13 G	22	New Jersey
	8 cos. 4th cont'l.	Thomas Proctor	11	50	2	57	120										1		2	2	New Jersey
	West Point garrison		21	77	1	144	243										2		12	15	West Point, N.Y.
	TOTAL OF ARTILLERY		70	229	11	372	682	18	12	80	16			3	811 F		3		35 H	43	
	TOTAL OF WASHINGTON'S ARMY		557	1580	209	7116	9462	603	410	1945	395	3	2	3	12823	12	224	15	1142	351	

MAY 1780
(continued)

OFFICERS SICK, ON FURLOUGH, ETC.	WASHINGTON'S ARMY			
	COMMISSIONED	NONCOMMISSIONED	STAFF	TOTAL
Sick Present	34	62	3	99
Sick Absent	37	56	7	100
On Command	137	161	6	304
On Extra Service	27	63	2	92
On Furlough	80	104	34	218
Recruiting	129	35	5	169
On the Staff	194			194
Prisoners of War	66	9	1	76
Furlough Expired	28	9	6	43
In Arrest	3	1	1	5
TOTAL	735	500	65	1300

SOURCE OF THIS REPORT

1. MONTHLY RETURN OF THE CONTINENTAL ARMY UNDER THE COMMAND OF HIS EXCELLENCY GEORGE WASHINGTON... FOR MAY 1780, ELEPHANT FOLIO OF WASHINGTON RETURNS, WILLIAM L. CLEMENTS LIBRARY. [THE ARTILLERY SECTION OF THE RETURN APPEARS ON THE NEXT PAGE OF THE FOLIO.]

1a. Monthly Return of the Continental Army under... Washington... May 1780, Record Group 93, National Archives. [Contains the same figures, but only to the brigade level.]

A. Five staff officers in Richard Butler's 9th Pennsylvania regiment plus one chaplain for the entire brigade.
B. One chaplain for the entire brigade; there were no staff officers present fit for duty in Heman Swift's 7th Connecticut regiment.
C. Three staff officers in Timothy Bigelow's 15th Massachusetts regiment plus one chaplain for the entire brigade.
D. Four staff officers in Gamaliel Bradford's 14th Massachusetts regiment plus one chaplain for the entire brigade.
E. Four staff officers in Alexander Scammell's 3rd New Hampshire regiment plus one chaplain for the entire brigade.
F. The National Archives manuscript notes that no returns had been received for the Maryland and Delaware troops, for the German regiment, and for Lee's Partizan Corps.
G. Including one man listed on the manuscript as "resigned."
H. Including twelve men in Washington's infantry discharged for inability.

Louis le Bèque Duportail, who had been an engineer in the French army, was one of a very few foreign officers whose services were really useful to the rebel army. Duportail became chief engineer of the Continental Army and rose to the rank of major general. Although captured in the fall of Charleston (May 12, 1780), he was promptly exchanged, serving to the end of the war. Peale's museum portrait dates from 1781 or 1782. The two other most significant foreign officers are shown in the next two illustrations. (Courtesy of the Independence National Historical Park Collection, Philadelphia)

JUNE 1780

BRIGADE	UNIT	COMMANDING OFFICER	PRESENT FIT FOR DUTY & ON DUTY: COMMISSIONED OFFICERS	NONCOMMISSIONED OFFICERS	STAFF OFFICERS	RANK & FILE	TOTAL	RANK & FILE SICK, ON FURLOUGH, ETC.: SICK PRESENT	SICK ABSENT	ON COMMAND & EXTRA SERVICE	ON FURLOUGH	CONFINED	FURLOUGH EXPIRED	WANTING CLOTHES	GRAND TOTAL	ALTERATIONS: DEATHS	DESERTED	TAKEN PRISONER	DISCHARGED	JOINED, ENLISTED, RECRUITED	LOCATION
FORCES UNDER COMMANDER-IN-CHIEF GENERAL GEORGE WASHINGTON																					
Wayne	1st Pa.	James Chambers	15	30	4	160	209	7	6	18					240	2	11		2	2	New Jersey
	2nd Pa.	Walter Stewart	13	34	5	265	317	8	21	27					373	3	11			10	New Jersey
	7th Pa.	Lt. Col. Morgan Connor	6	30	5	131	172	2	11	13					198		2				New Jersey
	10th Pa.	Richard Humpton	8	35	5	213	261	7	9	17	1				295	2	22	2	1	5	New Jersey
Irvine	3rd Pa.	Thomas Craig	11	38	4	198	251	12	21	22	6				312		2		1	1	New Jersey
	5th Pa.	Francis Johnston	9	28	5	181	223	5	23	20	2				273	3	3		1	2	New Jersey
	6th Pa.	Robert Magaw	14	26	5	145	190	2	9	12					213		2			3	New Jersey
	9th Pa.	Richard Butler	9	26	5	111	151	4	19	13	2				189		4			6	New Jersey
Hand	4th Pa.	Lt. Col. William Butler	11	33	5	107	156	4	9	14					183		12 (for 4th Pa., 11th Pa., 2nd Canadian, 1st Canadian)			3 (for 4th Pa., 11th Pa., 2nd Canadian, 1st Canadian)	New Jersey
	11th Pa.	Lt. Col. Adam Hubley	12	40	4	196	252	4	15	21	3				295						New Jersey
	2nd Canadian	Moses Hazen	24	39	3	252	318	17	30	59	1				425						New Jersey
	1st Canadian	James Livington	4	23	3	67	97	2	8	11	1				119						New Jersey
Maxwell	1st N.J.	Matthias Ogden	13	39	3	179	234	10	17	15	1				277		8			10	New Jersey
	2nd N.J.	Israel Shreve	17	38	5	218	278	5	39	30	1				353	4	11	8	3	35	New Jersey
	3rd N.J.	Elias Dayton	12	40	3 B	189	244	4	20	20	2				290	4	4	5	2	3	New Jersey
	Additional	Oliver Spencer	10	15	6	92	123	4	22	11	9				169		2		16	2	New Jersey
Stark	2nd R.I.	Israel Angell	12	34	3	159	208	8	31	29					276	4	7	1	3	1	New Jersey
	Additional	Samuel Blatchley Webb	3	29	5	119	156	11	15	22					204	1			14		New Jersey
	Additional	Henry Jackson	6	32	4	156	198	24	17	61	6				306		1		35	2	New Jersey
Clinton	2nd N.Y.	Philip Van Cortlandt	7	22	3	114	146	5	4	11	1				167	1	1		1	3	The Highlands, N.Y.
	5th N.Y.	Lt. Col. Marinus Willett	6	22	3	132	163	9	6	23	2				203		3		3	6	The Highlands, N.Y.
	4th N.Y.	Lt. Col. Frederick Weisenfels	13	27	4	141	185	8	5	18	2				218		1		1	4	The Highlands, N.Y.
	3rd N.Y.	Peter Gansevoort	11	31	3	241	286	5	11	19					321		14		5	4	The Highlands, N.Y.
Parsons	3rd Conn.	Samuel Wyllys	8	24	4	144	180	14	10	48	2				254		3 (for 3rd, 4th, 6th, 8th Conn.)	2 (for 3rd, 4th, 6th, 8th Conn.)	15 (for 3rd, 4th, 6th, 8th Conn.)	2 (for 3rd, 4th, 6th, 8th Conn.)	The Highlands, N.Y.
	4th Conn.	John Durkee	7	26	2	53	88	9	7	38	3				145						The Highlands, N.Y.
	6th Conn.	Return Jonathan Meigs	9	34	1 C	261	305	6	23	49	5				388						The Highlands, N.Y.
	8th Conn.	Lt. Col. Isaac Sherman	8	18	6	99	131	7	11	16	1				166						The Highlands, N.Y.
Huntington	1st Conn.	Josiah Starr	5	15	3	83	106	4	13	20	1				144				10	2	The Highlands, N.Y.
	2nd Conn.	Zebulon Butler	5	16	4	51	76	9	7	14	3				109				9	2	The Highlands, N.Y
	5th Conn.	Philip Burr Bradley	5	20	5	90	120	4	13	21	2				160				18		The Highlands, N.Y.
	7th Conn.	Heman Swift	5	13	4 D	70	92	1	22	26	1				142				30		The Highlands, N.Y.
Nixon	3rd Mass.	John Greaton	9	19	3	58	89	4	7	35	6				141			1	8	3	The Highlands, N.Y.
	5th Mass.	Rufus Putnam	8	17	4	64	93	8	3	27	9				140				27	3	The Highlands, N.Y.
	6th Mass.	Thomas Nixon	6	21	5	64	96	3	4	35	8				146		2		11	2	The Highlands, N.Y.
	12th Mass.	Lt. Col. Ebenezer Sprout	10	19	3	71	103	1	3	5	1				113				10		The Highlands, N.Y.
Glover	1st Mass.	Joseph Vose	12	20	2	78	112	2	4	52	20				190		1		6	1	The Highlands, N.Y.
	4th Mass.	William Shepard	14	28	2	59	103	8	7	84	3				205		2		6	2	The Highlands, N.Y.
	13th Mass.	Lt. Col. Calvin Smith	7	25	3	62	97	1	5	33	15				151		2	1	15		The Highlands, N.Y.
	15th Mass.	Timothy Bigelow	4	15	3	29	51		10	50	15				126				12	2	The Highlands, N.Y.
Paterson	7th Mass.	Lt. Col. John Brooks	7	18	4	35	64	8	5	60	5				142		4		13	1	The Highlands, N.Y.
	10th Mass.	Thomas Marshall	6	22	5	44	77	7		38	10				132				12	1	The Highlands, N.Y.
	11th Mass.	Benjamin Tupper	6	15	5	33	59	3	1	20	1				84				4	2	The Highlands, N.Y.
	14th Mass.	Gamaliel Bradford	6	13	6 E	24	49	2	1	22	1				75				3		The Highlands, N.Y.
4th Mass.	2nd Mass.	John Bailey	10	24	4	46	84	5	2	62	6				159		1		45	2	The Highlands, N.Y.
	8th Mass.	Michael Jackson	14	14	3	36	67	4	2	35	3				111		5		3	3	The Highlands, N.Y.
	9th Mass.	James Wesson	8	16	3	51	78	11	3	57	7				156		3		11	2	The Highlands, N.Y.

JUNE 1780 (continued)

BRIGADE	UNIT	COMMANDING OFFICER	DUTY & ON DUTY: COMMISSIONED OFFICERS	NONCOMMISSIONED OFFICERS	STAFF OFFICERS	RANK & FILE	TOTAL	ON FURLOUGH, ETC.: SICK PRESENT	SICK ABSENT	ON COMMAND & EXTRA SERVICE	ON FURLOUGH	CONFINED	FURLOUGH EXPIRED	WANTING CLOTHES	GRAND TOTAL	DEATHS	DESERTED	TAKEN PRISONER	DISCHARGED	JOINED, ENLISTED, RECRUITED	LOCATION
	FORCES UNDER COMMANDER-IN-CHIEF GENERAL GEORGE WASHINGTON (continued)																				
Poor	1st N.H.	Joseph Cilley	10	21	3	147	181	9	8	54	5				257	2	3		5	7	The Highlands, N.Y.
Poor	2nd N.H.	Lt. Col. George Reid	11	29	5 F	148	193	12	6	44	6				261		4	2	4	4	The Highlands, N.Y.
Poor	3rd N.H.	Alexander Scammell	13	21	5	113	152	20	5	42	10				229		2		17	8	The Highlands, N.Y.
	Pa. independent co.	Capt. John Paul Schott	1			3	4								4						Wyoming Valley, Pa.
	Pa. independent co.	Capt. Anthony Selin	1	5		11	17	2		4					23						Wyoming Valley, Pa.
	Wyoming Valley co.	Capt. Simon Spalding	4 A	8		50	62	2	2	10					76						Wyoming Valley, Pa.
	Militia	Capt. John Franklin	2		2 G		4			31					35						Wyoming Valley, Pa.
	TOTAL OF INFANTRY		467	1247	194	5843	7751	333	552	1538	189				10363	26	153	22	382	151	
	CAVALRY																				
	4th cont'l.	Stephen Moylan	5	18	4	46	73	1	2	70	2	1			149		1	1		2	New Jersey
	Marechaussie	Capt. Bartholomew Von Heer	2	7		30	39			13					52			1			
	Independent corps	Capt. Henry Bedkin	1	3		9	13		1						14	1					
	TOTAL OF CAVALRY		8	28	4	85	125	1	3	83	2	1			215	1	1	2		2	
	ARTILLERY																				
	8 cos. 2nd cont'l.	John Lamb	20	66	4	84	174	8	16	122	5		9		785	3	2		4 J	10	New Jersey
	7 cos. 3rd cont'l.	John Crane	12	39	3	67	121									1	5		7	4	New Jersey
	7 cos. 4th cont'l.	Thomas Proctor	10	52	2	45	109													1	New Jersey
	West Point garrison		21	78	1	121	221										6		7	14	West Point, N.Y.
	TOTAL OF ARTILLERY		63	235	10	317	625	8	16	122	5		9		785	4	13		18	29	
	INVALIDS																				
	Philadelphia unit	Lewis Nicola	6	33		235	274								274						Philadelphia, Pa.
	Boston det.	Capt. Moses McFarland	5	14		76	95								95						Boston, Mass.
	TOTAL OF INVALIDS		11	47		311	369								369						
	TOTAL OF WASHINGTON'S ARMY		549	1557	208	6556	8870	342	571	1743	196	1	9		11732	31	167	24	400	182	
	WESTERN DEPARTMENT UNDER COLONEL DANIEL BRODHEAD																				
Brodhead	8th Pa.	Daniel Brodhead	13	24	5	127	169	6		6	2				183		7		1	3	Fort Pitt, Pa.
Brodhead	9th Va.	John Gibson	18	30	5	159	212	2		6	6				226		2			4	Fort Pitt, Pa.
Brodhead	Additional (Md. corps)	(late) Moses Rawlings	2	7	1	42	52	3	1	1					57				1		Fort Pitt, Pa.
Brodhead	Va. independent co.	Capt. Henry Heth	1	2		29	32	4							36				5		Fort Pitt, Pa.
	TOTAL OF WESTERN DEPARTMENT		34	63	11	357	465	15	1	13	8				502		9		7	7	
	VIRGINIA STATE FORCES IN THE CONTINENTAL SERVICE AS GUARDS FOR THE CONVENTION TROOPS																				
	Va. convention guards	Francis Taylor	14	22		162	198		8	20	12				238						Albemarle Barracks, Va.
	Va. western bn.	Lt. Col. Joseph Crockett	16	20	1	74	111		8 H	19 I	4			38	180					1	Albemarle Barracks, Va.
	TOTAL OF CONVENTION GUARDS		30	42	1	236	309		16	39	16			38	418					1	
	GRAND TOTAL		613	1662	220	7149	9644	357	588	1795	220	1	9	38	12652 K	31	176	24	407 L	190	

JUNE 1780
(continued)

OFFICERS SICK, ON FURLOUGH, ETC.	WASHINGTON'S ARMY (EXCEPT INVALIDS)				CONVENTION GUARDS				GRAND TOTAL
	COMMISSIONED	NONCOMMISSIONED	STAFF	TOTAL	COMMISSIONED	NONCOMMISSIONED	STAFF	TOTAL	
Sick Present	24	46		70					70
Sick Absent	47	62	9	118					118
On Command	110	148	7	265					265
On Extra Service	22	39	1	62					62
On Furlough	59	49	25	133	5			5	138
Recruiting	123	23	4	150					150
On the Staff	184			184					184
Prisoners of War	66	5	1	72					72
Furlough Expired	20	8	3	31					31
In Arrest	7		1	8					8
TOTAL	662	380	51	1093	5			5	1098

SOURCES OF THIS REPORT

1. MONTHLY RETURN OF THE CONTINENTAL ARMY UNDER THE COMMAND OF HIS EXCELLENCY GEORGE WASHINGTON... FOR JUNE 1780, ELEPHANT FOLIO OF WASHINGTON RETURNS, WILLIAM L. CLEMENTS LIBRARY.
   1a. Monthly Return of the Continental Army under... Washington... June 1780, Record Group 93, National Archives. [Contains the same figures, but only to the brigade level.]

2. RETURN OF THE WESTERN DEPARTMENT REMOVED FROM THE JULY 1780 RETURN [SOURCE ONE ON OUR JULY 1780 REPORT] BECAUSE IT IS CLEARLY A REPORT OF EARLIER DATE. THE RETURN OF THE WESTERN DEPARTMENT ON THE AUGUST 1780 RETURN [SOURCE ONE ON OUR REPORT FOR THAT MONTH] WAS THE MONTHLY RETURN MADE OUT AT FORT PITT JULY 30 AND IS IDENTICAL TO A MANUSCRIPT SO DATED IN THE PENNSYLVANIA STATE ARCHIVES. THEREFORE, IT HAS BEEN MOVED BACK TO JULY AND THE SECTION FOR FORT PITT ON THAT RETURN MOVED BACK TO THIS REPORT. SEE THE JULY AND AUGUST REPORTS.

3. A RETURN OF COLONEL TAYLOR'S REGIMENT OF GUARDS AND A RETURN OF LT. COLONEL CROCKETT'S WESTERN REGIMENT, BOTH DATED JULY 1, 1780, COLONEL JAMES WOOD MANUSCRIPTS, VIRGINIA STATE LIBRARY.

A. One commissioned officer for Captain John Franklin's militia plus one colonel for all the forces at Wyoming.
B. Five staff officers in Oliver Spencer's Additional regiment plus one chaplain for the entire brigade.
C. Five staff officers in Lieutenant Colonel Isaac Sherman's 8th Connecticut regiment plus one chaplain for the entire brigade.
D. Three staff officers in Heman Swift's 7th Connecticut regiment plus one chaplain for the entire brigade.
E. Five staff officers in Gamaliel Bradford's 14th Massachusetts regiment plus one chaplain for the entire brigade.
F. Four staff officers in Alexander Scammell's 3rd New Hampshire regiment plus one chaplain for the entire brigade.
G. This figure represents two staff officers for all the forces at Wyoming, not staff officers in Captain John Franklin's militia.
H. This column on the original manuscript for the convention guards reads "in hospital" rather than "sick absent."
I. Including six men in Francis Taylor's regiment and two men in Lieutenant Colonel Crockett's battalion classified as camp color men. See footnote I on our September 1779 report.
J. Including one man classified as "resigned."
K. The National Archives manuscript of this monthly return notes that no returns were received for Van Schaick's regiment at Fort Schuyler, for Warner's regiment at Fort George, for Greene's regiment in Rhode Island, for the German battalion on the frontiers, for Sheldon's Light Dragoons, for Lee's Partizan Corps, or for the troops at Fort Pitt and to the southward. Our report supplies the figures for the troops at Fort Pitt.

Charles Willson Peale's three-quarter-length portrait of the Marquis de Lafayette, commissioned by George Washington and completed in 1781. (Courtesy of Washington and Lee University, Lexington, Va.)

JULY 1780

BRIGADE	UNIT	COMMANDING OFFICER	PRESENT FIT FOR DUTY & ON DUTY: COMMISSIONED OFFICERS	NONCOMMISSIONED OFFICERS	STAFF OFFICERS	RANK & FILE	TOTAL	RANK & FILE SICK, ON FURLOUGH, ETC.: SICK PRESENT	SICK ABSENT	ON COMMAND & EXTRA SERVICE	ON FURLOUGH	CONFINED	FURLOUGH EXPIRED	GRAND TOTAL	ALTERATIONS: DEATHS	DESERTED	TAKEN PRISONER	DISCHARGED	JOINED, ENLISTED, RECRUITED	LOCATION
FORCES UNDER COMMANDER-IN-CHIEF GENERAL GEORGE WASHINGTON																				
Wayne	1st Pa.	James Chambers	8	22	3	147	180	18	21	30				249	10	2	1		41	New Jersey
Wayne	2nd Pa.	Walter Stewart	12	36	5	243	296	16	21	34				367		3			1	New Jersey
Wayne	7th Pa.	Lt. Col. Morgan Connor	4	30	3	187	224	18	7	19				268		3			78	New Jersey
Wayne	10th Pa.	Richard Humpton	8	33	4	183	228	16	15	29				288			4			New Jersey
Irvine	3rd Pa.	Thomas Craig	15	38	4	178	235	20	16	28	2			301	2	10	1	1	5	New Jersey
Irvine	5th Pa.	Francis Johnston	9	29	4	170	212	10	18	28				268	1	10		1	10	New Jersey
Irvine	6th Pa.	Robert Magaw	12	26	4 B	190	232	19	4	24				279		2		5	86	New Jersey
Irvine	9th Pa.	Richard Butler	10	22	6	159	197	19	16	31	2			265	1	6		3	97	New Jersey
Hand	4th Pa.	Lt. Col. William Butler	9	34	5	171	219	6	5	36				266					97	New Jersey
Hand	11th Pa.	Lt. Col. Adam Hubley	12	33	5	183	233	7	13	25	1			279		4				New Jersey
Hand	2nd Canadian	Moses Hazen	14	34	3	223	274	25	24	87	1			411						New Jersey
Hand	1st Canadian	James Livingston A																		New Jersey
N.J.	1st N.J.	Matthias Ogden	10	29	3	160	202	6	12	53	3			276		19		1	35	New Jersey
N.J.	2nd N.J.	Israel Shreve	12	35	5	205	257	6	30	62	1			356						New Jersey
N.J.	3rd N.J.	Elias Dayton	11	34	4	166	215	9	20	60	5			309	1	7		1	34	New Jersey
N.J.	Additional	Oliver Spencer	6	13	3	34	56	3	25	56	5			145	1	9		2	2	New Jersey
Stark	2nd R.I.	Israel Angell	14	41	5	155	215	14	19	38				286		1		2	4	New Jersey
Stark	Additional	Samuel Blatchley Webb	7	32	4	142	185	12	12	21				230		1		8	29	New Jersey
Stark	Additional	Henry Jackson	9	38	4	162	213	6	14	54	4			291	1	9		26	15	New Jersey
Clinton	2nd N.Y.	Philip Van Cortlandt	9	20	3	95	127	6	4	21	5			163		3		2		The Highlands, N.Y.
Clinton	5th N.Y.	Lt. Col. Marinus Willett	3	16	3	95	117	11	7	46	11			192		8			6	The Highlands, N.Y.
Clinton	4th N.Y.	Lt. Col. Frederick Weisenfels	12	23	3	114	152	8	5	37	7			209		2		1	3	The Highlands, N.Y.
Clinton	3rd N.Y.	Peter Gansevoort	15	30	3	176	224	34	12	48				318	1	6			2	The Highlands, N.Y.
Parsons	3rd Conn.	Samuel Wyllys	9	25	3	191	228	17	10	46	1			302	1	1			50	The Highlands, N.Y.
Parsons	4th Conn.	John Durkee	5	26	3	120	154	7	8	40	2			211		1		1	70	The Highlands, N.Y.
Parsons	6th Conn.	Return Jonathan Meigs	12	36	2	254	304	13	21	50	4			392	1			1	2	The Highlands, N.Y.
Parsons	8th Conn.	Lt. Col. Isaac Sherman	4	21	3	132	160	7	11	20	3			201		2			42	The Highlands, N.Y.
Huntington	1st Conn.	Josiah Starr	4	22	2	180	208	9	11	27	2			257						The Highlands, N.Y.
Huntington	2nd Conn.	Zebulon Butler	8	27	5	186	226	11	6	11	4			258		4 (1st–7th Conn.)		1 (1st–7th Conn.)	449 (1st–7th Conn.)	The Highlands, N.Y.
Huntington	5th Conn.	Philip Burr Bradley	6	25	5	130	166	10	9	20	2			207						The Highlands, N.Y.
Huntington	7th Conn.	Heman Swift	9	20	3	208	240	6	12	25	1			284						The Highlands, N.Y.
Nixon	3rd Mass.	John Greaton	11	22	2	169	204	6	4	48				262	1	8			130	The Highlands, N.Y.
Nixon	5th Mass.	Rufus Putnam	6	22	5	146	179	5	4	41				229		8		4	101	The Highlands, N.Y.
Nixon	6th Mass.	Thomas Nixon	9	22	5	185	221	3	3	40				267		9		4	130	The Highlands, N.Y.
Nixon	12th Mass.	Lt. Col. Ebenezer Sprout	11	22	5	187	225	4	2	4				235	1	4			124	The Highlands, N.Y.
Glover	1st Mass.	Joseph Vose	12	17	4	165	198	4	6	42				250		21		2	85	The Highlands, N.Y.
Glover	4th Mass.	William Shepard	14	29	3	176	222	5	9	48				284		1		1	83	The Highlands, N.Y.
Glover	13th Mass.	Lt. Col. Calvin Smith	7	26	4	198	235	4	3	30	1			273		15		1	138	The Highlands, N.Y.
Glover	15th Mass.	Timothy Bigelow	8	22	4	161	195	2	6	43	8			254	3	2		12	143	The Highlands, N.Y.
Paterson	7th Mass.	Lt. Col. John Brooks	8	20	3	162	193	4	3	55				255		7		2	123	The Highlands, N.Y.
Paterson	10th Mass.	Thomas Marshall	9	25	4	197	235	7		41	1			284		6	1	2	157	The Highlands, N.Y.
Paterson	14th Mass.	Gamaliel Bradford	9	17	4 C	219	249	1	1	12	1			264		2		1	192	The Highlands, N.Y.
Paterson	11th Mass.	Benjamin Tupper	5	16	5	201	227	6		23				256		5			176	The Highlands, N.Y.
1st Mass.	2nd Mass.	John Bailey	13	29	4	171	217	12	2	49				280		5		5	126	The Highlands, N.Y.
1st Mass.	8th Mass.	Michael Jackson	14	16	3	189	222	5	1	36	1			265		3		1	158	The Highlands, N.Y.
1st Mass.	9th Mass.	James Wesson	9	24	3	185	221	5	2	45	1			274	1	10		2	128	The Highlands, N.Y.
Poor	1st N.H.	Joseph Cilley	8	31	4	225	268	11	7	43	2			331		21		9	102	The Highlands, N.Y.
Poor	2nd N.H.	Lt. Col. George Reid	12	34	5 D	203	254	13	3	37	2			309		9		40	107	The Highlands, N.Y.
Poor	3rd N.H.	Alexander Scammell	13	38	4	193	227	7	9	34				277	1	10		65	222	The Highlands, N.Y.

BRIGADE	UNIT	JULY 1780 (continued) COMMANDING OFFICER	PRESENT FIT FOR DUTY & ON DUTY: COMMISSIONED OFFICERS	NONCOMMISSIONED OFFICERS	STAFF OFFICERS	RANK & FILE	TOTAL	RANK & FILE SICK, ON FURLOUGH, ETC.: SICK PRESENT	SICK ABSENT	ON COMMAND & EXTRA SERVICE	ON FURLOUGH	CONFINED	FURLOUGH EXPIRED	GRAND TOTAL	ALTERATIONS: DEATHS	DESERTED	TAKEN PRISONER	DISCHARGED	JOINED, ENLISTED, RECRUITED	LOCATION
	FORCES UNDER COMMANDER-IN-CHIEF GENERAL GEORGE WASHINGTON (continued)																			
	1st N.Y.	Goose Van Schaick	14	36	3	217	270	17	14	13	2			316				2	2	Fort Schuyler, N.Y.
	Additional	Seth Warner	12	16	2	66	96	1	2	15	2			116					3	Fort Edward, N.Y.
	TOTAL OF INFANTRY		482	1324	188	8553	10547	491	489	1795	87			13409	27	259	7	209	3594	
	CAVALRY																			
	2nd cont'l.	Elisha Sheldon	11	38	4	154	207	6	14	21	2			250		5				
	4th cont'l.	Stephen Moylan	9	18	3	98	128	4	1	13	1	5		152		4				
	Marechaussie	Capt. Bartholomew Von Heer	1	4		5	10	2	2	31				45						
	TOTAL OF CAVALRY		21	60	7	257	345	12	17	65	3	5		447		9				
	ARTILLERY																			
	5 cos. 2nd cont'l.	John Lamb	11	37	6	47	101									7		3	3	
	7 cos. 3rd cont'l.	John Crane	14	48	3	175	240	12	20	110	1		1	912		2			128	
	7 cos. 4th cont'l.	Thomas Proctor	10	50	2	47	109									4				
	West Point garrison		29	111	1	177	318									13		3	99	West Point, N.Y.
	Pa. independent co.	(late) Capt. Gibbs Jones[A]																		
	TOTAL OF ARTILLERY		64	246	12	446	768	12	20	110	1		1	912		26		6	230	
	TOTAL OF WASHINGTON'S ARMY		567	1630	207	9256	11660	515	526	1970	91	5	1	14768	27	294	7	215	3824	
	WESTERN DEPARTMENT UNDER COLONEL DANIEL BRODHEAD																			
Brodhead	8th Pa.	Daniel Brodhead	12	23	5	120	160	4		8	2			174		3				Fort Pitt, Pa.
Brodhead	9th Va.	John Gibson	16	27	5	148	196	4		6	2			208	1	9				Fort Pitt, Pa.
Brodhead	Additional (Md. corps)	(late) Moses Rawlings	1	7	1	43	52	1	1	2				56						Fort Pitt, Pa.
Brodhead	Va. independent co.	Capt. Henry Heth	2	4		25	31	5		1				37						Fort Pitt, Pa.
	TOTAL OF INFANTRY		31	61	11	336	439	14	1	17	4			475	1	12				
	ARTILLERY																			
	1 co. 4th cont'l.	Capt. Isaac Craig	3	13		10	26[E]							26						Fort Pitt, Pa.
	TOTAL OF WESTERN DEPARTMENT		34	74	11	346	465	14	1	17	4			501	1	12				
	VIRGINIA STATE FORCES IN THE CONTINENTAL SERVICE AS GUARDS FOR THE CONVENTION TROOPS																			
	Va. convention guards	Francis Taylor	14	20		166	200	5[F]	3	16	13			237						Albemarle Barracks, Va.
	Va. western bn.	Lt. Col. Joseph Crockett	15	18	1	104	138		8	17	5			168		10			1	Albemarle Barracks, Va.
	TOTAL OF CONVENTION GUARDS		29	38	1	270	338	5	11[G]	33[H]	18			405		10			1	
	GRAND TOTAL		630	1742	219	9872	12463	534	538	2020	113	5	1	15674	28	316	7	215	[I] 3825	

JULY 1780
(continued)

OFFICERS SICK, ON FURLOUGH, ETC.	WASHINGTON'S ARMY[J]				WESTERN DEPARTMENT				CONVENTION GUARDS				GRAND TOTAL
	COMMISSIONED	NONCOMMISSIONED	STAFF	TOTAL	COMMISSIONED	NONCOMMISSIONED	STAFF	TOTAL	COMMISSIONED	NONCOMMISSIONED	STAFF	TOTAL	
Sick Present	33	38	2	73									73
Sick Absent	45	64	12	121									121
On Command	127	160	14	301	2			2					303
On Extra Service	27	56		83									83
On Furlough	64	33	25	122	3			3	5			5	130
Recruiting	80	21	6	107									107
On the Staff	205			205	8			8					213
Prisoners of War	72	7	1	80	1			1					81
Furlough Expired	11	3		14									14
In Arrest	6			6									6
TOTAL	670	382	60	1112	14			14	5			5	1131

SOURCES OF THIS REPORT

1. MONTHLY RETURN OF THE CONTINENTAL ARMY UNDER THE COMMAND OF HIS EXCELLENCY GEORGE WASHINGTON. . . FOR JULY 1780, ELEPHANT FOLIO OF WASHINGTON RETURNS, WILLIAM L. CLEMENTS LIBRARY. [THE PORTION OF THIS RETURN GIVING THE STATE OF THE FORCES AT FORT PITT HAS BEEN MOVED BACK TO OUR JUNE 1780 REPORT BECAUSE THE RETURNS OF THE WESTERN DEPARTMENT WERE TAKING AT LEAST A MONTH TO ARRIVE AT HEADQUARTERS IN THIS PERIOD, AND THE ACTUAL JULY MONTHLY RETURN OF THE WESTERN DEPARTMENT WAS AVAILABLE TO REPLACE IT ON THIS MONTHLY REPORT. SEE SOURCE 2 BELOW.]

2. A MONTHLY RETURN OF THE TROOPS IN THE WESTERN DEPARTMENT COMMANDED BY COL. DANL. BRODHEAD, JULY 30, 1780, RECORD GROUP 27 C, DIVISION OF ARCHIVES AND MANUSCRIPTS, PENNSYLVANIA HISTORICAL AND MUSEUM COMMISSION. [THE FIGURES FOR THE INFANTRY FROM THIS JULY MONTHLY RETURN OF THE WESTERN DEPARTMENT APPEAR ON THE AUGUST GENERAL RETURN (SOURCE 1 ON OUR AUGUST 1780 REPORT). SINCE WE HAVE PLACED THEM HERE WHERE THEY BELONG, WE HAVE REMOVED THEM FROM THE AUGUST REPORT. THE RETURN OF THE ARTILLERY COMPANY INCLUDED HERE IS NOT INCLUDED ON THE MANUSCRIPT OF THE AUGUST RETURN, AND, SINCE THAT MANUSCRIPT ONLY REPORTS ON THE USUAL SEVEN COMPANIES OF THE 4th CONTINENTAL ARTILLERY, THE COMPANY COULD NOT HAVE BEEN INCORPORATED INTO THE REPORT ON THE REGIMENT TO WHICH IT NOMINALLY BELONGED.]

3. A RETURN OF COLONEL TAYLOR'S REGIMENT OF GUARDS AND A RETURN OF LIEUT. COLONEL CROCKETT'S BATTALION, BOTH DATED AUGUST 1, 1780. COLONEL JAMES WOOD MANUSCRIPTS, VIRGINIA STATE LIBRARY.

A. No figures for this unit are given on the manuscript.
B. Five staff officers in Richard Butler's 9th Pennsylvania regiment plus one chaplain for the entire brigade.
C. Four staff officers in Benjamin Tupper's 11th Massachusetts regiment plus one chaplain for the entire brigade.
D. Three staff officers in Alexander Scammell's 3rd New Hampshire regiment plus one chaplain for the entire brigade.
E. The manuscript does not indicate whether these twenty-six men are those present fit for duty or whether they are all the men in the artillery company. The figure therefore may include a few men who were sick, on furlough, etc.
F. Given on the original manuscript as "invalids."
G. Given on the original manuscript as "in hospital."
H. Including six men in Taylor's regiment and one man in Crockett's battalion classified as camp color men. See footnote I on our September 1779 report.
I. Including five men in Washington's infantry discharged for inability.
J. This section of the report on officers who were sick, on furlough, etc. may include a few officers for the portion of the return for the Western Department that has been moved back to the June 1780 report. Because the manuscripts do not break down to the regiment or brigade level the information on those officers who were not present fit for duty, it is not possible to know how many such officers may be included, but, if any were, they would have been so few as to not affect the totals enough to be statistically significant. It will be

Profile of Baron von Steuben by Du Simitière. A Prussian professional soldier who had served as a staff officer and aide-de-camp to Frederick the Great, Steuben brought much-needed military expertise to the rebel army. Appointed inspector general of the Continental Army early in 1778, he served as a critical instrument in turning the rebels into a disciplined and trained force.

AUGUST 1780

FORCES UNDER COMMANDER-IN-CHIEF GENERAL GEORGE WASHINGTON

BRIGADE	UNIT	COMMANDING OFFICER	PRESENT FIT FOR DUTY & ON DUTY: COMMISSIONED OFFICERS	NONCOMMISSIONED OFFICERS	STAFF OFFICERS	RANK & FILE	TOTAL	RANK & FILE SICK, ON FURLOUGH, ETC.: SICK PRESENT	SICK ABSENT	ON COMMAND & EXTRA SERVICE	ON FURLOUGH	PRISONERS OF WAR	WANTING ARMS	WANTING CLOTHES	GRAND TOTAL	ALTERATIONS: DEATHS	DESERTED	TAKEN PRISONER	DISCHARGED	JOINED, ENLISTED, RECRUITED	LOCATION
1st Pa.	1st Pa.	James Chambers	11	25	3	182	221	17	24	27					289		6			14	New Jersey
1st Pa.	2nd Pa.	Walter Stewart	13	35	5	231	284	10	30	36					360	1	6			2	New Jersey
1st Pa.	4th Pa.	Lt. Col. William Butler	12	34	5	197	248	12	12	11					283		1		1	10	New Jersey
1st Pa.	7th Pa.	Lt. Col. Josiah Harmar	9	29	4	198	240	16	9	15					280		8			17	New Jersey
1st Pa.	10th Pa.	Richard Humpton	9	32	4	189	234	9	20	24					287	1	3		2	7	New Jersey
2nd Pa.	3rd Pa.	Thomas Craig	11	33	3	182	229	15	22	36	3				305	1	2			20	New Jersey
2nd Pa.	5th Pa.	Francis Johnston	10	31	4	177	222	9	15	26					272		2			6	New Jersey
2nd Pa.	6th Pa.	Robert Magaw	12	27	5	196	240	4	6	24					274	1	5			23	New Jersey
2nd Pa.	9th Pa.	Richard Butler	12	22	5 B	177	216	17	15	27					275		10		1	20	New Jersey
2nd Pa.	11th Pa.	Lt. Col. Adam Hubley	9	36	6	178	229	8	26	17	1				281	4				5	New Jersey
N.J.	1st N.J.	Matthias Ogden	15	38	4	196	253	8	15	26	2				304		5			18	New Jersey
N.J.	2nd N.J.	Israel Shreve	12	38	5	240	295	21	30	28	1				375		3			25	New Jersey
N.J.	3rd N.J.	Elias Dayton	10	37	4	203	254	15	22	21	2				314	1	5		2	17	New Jersey
N.J.	Additional	Oliver Spencer	8	18	5	76	107	8	25	12	6				158		2		1	4	New Jersey
N.Y.	2nd N.Y.	Philip Van Cortlandt	10	28	4	127	169	7	11	19					206		1			42	New Jersey
N.Y.	5th N.Y.	Lt. Col. Marinus Willett	9	27	4	156	196	14	7	19					236		6		2	38	New Jersey
N.Y.	4th N.Y.	Lt. Col. Frederick Weisenfels	16	30	4 C	208	258	24	9	31	1				323		2			111	New Jersey
N.Y.	3rd N.Y.	Peter Gansevoort	15	37	5	220	277	21	15	24	1				338	1	8			22	New Jersey
1st Conn.	3rd Conn.	Samuel Wyllys	10	34	4	235	283	19	16	32					350		5		2	59	New Jersey
1st Conn.	4th Conn.	John Durkee	8	31	3	237	279	10	16	35					340		3		5	137	New Jersey
1st Conn.	6th Conn.	Return Jonathan Meigs	15	39	3	256	313	26	22	36	2				399		3	1	5	15	New Jersey
1st Conn.	8th Conn.	Lt. Col. Isaac Sherman	9	28	4	245	286	11	24	18					339		6		7	146	New Jersey
2nd Conn.	1st Conn.	Josiah Starr	11	29	3	255	298	17	10	23	1				349						New Jersey
2nd Conn.	2nd Conn.	Zebulon Butler	10	29	5	255	299	28	7	15	2				351		17		10	394	New Jersey
2nd Conn.	5th Conn.	Philip Burr Bradley	12	29	4 D	239	284	17	17	25					343						New Jersey
2nd Conn.	7th Conn.	Heman Swift	12	21	4	244	281	14	17	24	1				337						New Jersey
1st Mass.	3rd Mass.	John Greaton	14	27	3	217	261	8	13	26					308		10			53	New Jersey
1st Mass.	5th Mass.	Rufus Putnam	11	29	5	208	253	23	7	27					310		1		2	79	New Jersey
1st Mass.	6th Mass.	Thomas Nixon	11	31	4 E	240	286	16	9	21					332		1			64	New Jersey
1st Mass.	12th Mass.	Lt. Col. Ebenezer Sprout	10	34	5	218	267	10	14	21					312		3		2	87	New Jersey
2nd Mass.	1st Mass.	Joseph Vose	15	27	3	226	271	9	15	26					321		4		2	76	New Jersey
2nd Mass.	4th Mass.	William Shepard	15	37	3	223	278	18	15	24					335		3		1	51	New Jersey
2nd Mass.	13th Mass.	Lt. Col. Calvin Smith	14	36	4	235	289	8	17	22					336		1			55	New Jersey
2nd Mass.	15th Mass.	Timothy Bigelow	10	29	4	215	258	6	12	39	2				317		4		8	76	New Jersey
3rd Mass.	7th Mass.	Lt. Col. John Brooks	9	24	3	270	306	11	10	14					341		1		3	85	New Jersey
3rd Mass.	10th Mass.	Thomas Marshall	12	35	5	242	294	32	3	19					348	1	3			64	New Jersey
3rd Mass.	11th Mass.	Benjamin Tupper	9	26	4	261	300	17	8	15					340				1	86	New Jersey
3rd Mass.	14th Mass.	Gamaliel Bradford	14	27	5	248	294	15	8	31					348		1		1	82	New Jersey
4th Mass.	2nd Mass.	John Bailey	14	33	5	226	278	17	17	34	1				347					67	New Jersey
4th Mass.	8th Mass.	Michael Jackson	17	28	4	231	280	9	20	22					331		2		3	67	New Jersey
4th Mass.	9th Mass.	James Wesson	12	34	4	241	291	15	7	30	1				344		1			66	New Jersey
Stark	2nd R.I. A	Israel Angell	14	42	5	161	222	21	13	34					290		1		1	7	New Jersey
Stark	9th Conn.	Samuel Blatchley Webb	7	31	4	230	272	17	15	18	1				323		1		8	104	New Jersey
Stark	16th Mass.	Henry Jackson	13	36	3	214	266	7	30	45	1				349		4		18	80	New Jersey
Poor	1st N.H.	Joseph Cilley	12	34	4	246	296	16	14	26	1				353		1		3	23	New Jersey
Poor	2nd N.H.	Lt. Col. George Reid	15	34	4	254	307	19	5	22	2				355		2		5	48	New Jersey
Poor	3rd N.H.	Alexander Scammell	16	33	2 F	261	312	9	14	16					351				2	72	New Jersey
Poor	2nd Canadian	Moses Hazen	19	35	4	238	296	27	27	58	2				410		8			1	New Jersey

AUGUST 1780 (continued)

BRIGADE	UNIT	COMMANDING OFFICER	PRESENT FIT FOR DUTY & ON DUTY: COMMISSIONED OFFICERS	NONCOMMISSIONED OFFICERS	STAFF OFFICERS	RANK & FILE	TOTAL	RANK & FILE SICK, ON FURLOUGH, ETC.: SICK PRESENT	SICK ABSENT	ON COMMAND & EXTRA SERVICE	ON FURLOUGH	PRISONERS OF WAR	WANTING ARMS	WANTING CLOTHES	GRAND TOTAL	ALTERATIONS: DEATHS	DESERTED	TAKEN PRISONER	DISCHARGED	JOINED, ENLISTED, RECRUITED	LOCATION
	FORCES UNDER COMMANDER-IN-CHIEF GENERAL GEORGE WASHINGTON (continued)																				
	1st Canadian	James Livingston	4	22	2	72	100	3	8	9	2				122						King's Ferry, N. Y.
	1st R.I.	Christopher Greene	8	42	4	524	578	20	32	5	3				638	6	32		1	531	Rhode Island
Malcolm	N.Y. levies	William Malcolm	18	28	2	227	275	23	2	80					380					5	New York state
Malcolm	N.Y. levies	Lewis DuBois	15	23	2	177	217	6	19	75	3				320		4			3	New York state
Malcolm	N.Y. levies	Morris Graham	16	25	3	205	249	9	11	107	1				377		5			18	New York state
Col. Lamb	Mass. militia	Nathaniel Wade	9	21	3	172	205	14		195					414						West Point, N. Y.
Col. Lamb	Mass. militia	Seth Murray	9	20	5	196	230	26	3	201	1				461					15	West Point, N. Y.
Col. Lamb	Mass. militia	John Rand	10	27	5	255	297	21	11	229	3				561					2	West Point, N. Y.
Col. Lamb	Pt. Mass. state	Ebenezer Thayer	6	13	2	106	127	8	2	59					196						West Point, N. Y.
Col. Lamb	Mass. militia	Jonathan Brown	1	1		6	8			1					9						West Point, N. Y.
Col. Lamb	Pt. Mass. state	Ezekiel Howe								13					13						West Point, N. Y.
Col. Lamb	N.H. militia	Thomas Bartlett	21	39	4	262	326	46	4	24	2				402					5	West Point, N. Y.
	N.H. militia	Moses Nichols	18	31	2	286	337	22	10	34	3				406		1			4	
Wells	Conn. militia	Levi Wells	18	26	4	85	133	18	3	38					192		1		41		
Wells	Conn. militia	Bezaleel Beebe	21	38	4	125	188	13	17	26	4				248		2		98		
Wells	Conn. militia	Lt. Col. Samuel Canfield	17	34	4	278	333	15	4	1	59				412		2				
	Partizan rangers	Maj. Henry Lee	2	12		69	83	10	1	3					97		12			1	
	N.J. militia	Maj. John Mauritius Goetschius	6	8	2	107	123	9	9	11	6				158		2				
	Del. militia	Lt. Col. Henry Neill	19	33	3	187	242	13	1	1					257					14	
	Pt. Mass. state	Ebenezer Thayer	15	30	3	186	234	7		68	1				310					48	Rhode Island
	Mass. state	John Jacobs	24	46	3	254	327	10	5	37	1				380					93	Rhode Island
	Pt. Mass. state	Ezekiel Howe	26	52	4	444	526	17	1	65					609					17	Rhode Island
	Mass. state	Abiel Mitchel	19	35	4	164	222	8	1	66					297						Rhode Island
	TOTAL OF INFANTRY		875	2105	261	14791	18032	1025	879	2569	123				22628	17	222	1	238	3301	
	CAVALRY																				
	4th cont'l.	Stephen Moylan	12	21	2	75	110	5	1	19	2		15		152		4	1	1	2	New Jersey
	Partizan corps	Maj. Henry Lee	10	29	3	80	122	3		10					135						New Jersey
	Independent corps	Capt. Henry Bedkin	1	3		7	11			2					13						New Jersey
	TOTAL OF CAVALRY		23	53	5	162	243	8	1	31	2		15		300		4	1	1	2	
	ARTILLERY																				
	10 cos. 2nd cont'l.	John Lamb	25	94	5	170	294													26	New Jersey
	9 cos. 3rd cont'l.	John Crane	25	88	3	252	368	18	29	92	1	1			1137		8			54	New Jersey
	7 cos. 4th cont'l.	Thomas Proctor	11	55	2	61	129													20	New Jersey
	West Point det.		17	64	1	123	205									1	2			47	West Point, N. Y.
	TOTAL OF ARTILLERY		78	301	11	606	996	18	29	92	1	1			1137	1	10			147	
	INVALIDS																				
	Philadelphia unit	Lewis Nicola	5	49	3	224	281								281						Philadelphia, Pa.
	Boston det.	Capt. Thomas Arnold	6	16		60	82								82						Boston, Mass.
	TOTAL OF INVALIDS		11	65	3	284	363								363						
	TOTAL OF WASHINGTON'S ARMY		987	2524	280	15843	19634	1051	909	2692	126	1	15		24428	18	236	2	239	3450	
	VIRGINIA STATE FORCES IN THE CONTINENTAL SERVICE AS GUARDS FOR THE CONVENTION TROOPS																				
	Va. convention guards	Francis Taylor	14	20		152	186	G	6	16	17			7	232		1			1	Albemarle Barracks, Va.
	Va. western bn.	Lt. Col. Joseph Crockett	15	8	2	107	132	4	6	16 I	10				168						Albemarle Barracks, Va.
	TOTAL OF CONVENTION GUARDS		29	28	2	259	318	4	12 H	32	27			7	400		1			1	
	GRAND TOTAL		1016	2552	282	16102	19952	1055	921	2724	153	1	15	7	24828 J	18	237	2	239	K 3451	

AUGUST 1780
(continued)

OFFICERS SICK, ON FURLOUGH, ETC.	WASHINGTON'S ARMY (EXCEPT INVALIDS)L				CONVENTION GUARDS				GRAND TOTAL
	COMMISSIONED	NONCOMMISSIONED	STAFF	TOTAL	COMMISSIONED	NONCOMMISSIONED	STAFF	TOTAL	
Sick Present	34	62	3	99					99
Sick Absent	57	74	11	142					142
On Command	49	48	13	110					110
On Extra Service	31	62	4	97					97
On Furlough	27	18	9	54	7			7	61
Recruiting	17	2		19					19
On the Staff	188			188					188
Prisoners of War	64	7	1	72					72
Furlough Expired	9		4	13					13
In Arrest	8		2	10					10
TOTAL	484	273	47	804	7			7	811

SOURCES OF THIS REPORT

1. MONTHLY RETURN OF THE CONTINENTAL ARMY UNDER THE COMMAND OF HIS EXCELLENCY GEORGE WASHINGTON. . . FOR THE MONTH OF AUGUST 1780, ELEPHANT FOLIO OF WASHINGTON RETURNS, WILLIAM L. CLEMENTS LIBRARY. [THE CAVALRY SECTION OF THE RETURN AND A SECTION CONTAINING RETURNS THAT ARRIVED LATE APPEAR ON THE FOLLOWING PAGE OF THE FOLIO. THE SECTION OF THIS RETURN CONTAINING FIGURES FOR THE WESTERN DEPARTMENT AT FORT PITT ACTUALLY WAS THE JULY MONTHLY RETURN FOR THAT DEPARTMENT AND, THEREFORE, HAS NOT BEEN INCLUDED ON THIS AUGUST MONTHLY REPORT. SEE OUR JULY MONTHLY REPORT.]

1a. Monthly Return of the Continental Army under. . . Washington. . . August 1780, Record Group 93, National Archives. [Contains the same figures, but only to the brigade level.]

2. A RETURN OF COLONEL TAYLOR'S REGIMENT OF GUARDS AND A RETURN OF LT. COLONEL CROCKETT'S W. BATTALION, BOTH DATED SEPTEMBER 1, 1780, COLONEL JAMES WOOD MANUSCRIPTS, VIRGINIA STATE LIBRARY.

A. Webb's Additional regiment was designated as the 9th Connecticut regiment from August through December 1780.
B. Five staff officers in Lieutenant Colonel Adam Hubley's 11th Pennsylvania regiment plus one chaplain for the entire brigade.
C. Four staff officers in Peter Gansevoort's 3rd New York regiment plus one chaplain for the entire brigade.
D. Three staff officers in Heman Swift's 7th Connecticut regiment plus one chaplain for the entire brigade.
E. Four staff officers in Lieutenant Colonel Ebenezer Sprout's 12th Massachusetts regiment plus one chaplain for the entire brigade.
F. Three staff officers in Moses Hazen's 2nd Canadian regiment plus one chaplain for the entire brigade.
G. Given as "invalids" on the original manuscript.
H. Given as "in hospital" on the original manuscript.
I. Including five men in Taylor's regiment and two in Crockett's battalion who are specified as camp color men on the original manuscript. See footnote I on our September 1779 report.
J. The National Archives manuscript notes that the return of Sheldon's cavalry regiment, consisting of sixty-three mounted and forty-nine dismounted dragoons at Bedford, was not included "on account of its incorrectness."
K. Including thirteen men in Washington's infantry discharged for inability.
L. The officers who were sick, on furlough, etc., from the Western Department (removed from this report because those figures represented the July monthly return) have been subtracted from these figures. Although the figures for officers sick, on furlough, etc., on the general monthly returns are not broken down to the brigade or regiment level, the separate manuscript for the Western Department for July that we have used on our July report enables us to determine how many noneffective officers to remove here.

Museum portrait of Henry Lee by Charles Willson Peale. Lee, who probably sat for this portrait in April 1782, when he was resigning his commission in order to marry his cousin Matilda Lee, gained acclaim as "Light-Horse Harry Lee" for his brilliant service during the Revolution. Commander of a mixed infantry and cavalry force which appears in the previous monthly report, Lee was promoted to lieutenant colonel in November 1780. (Courtesy of the Independence National Historical Park Collection, Philadelphia)

SEPTEMBER 1780

BRIGADE	UNIT	COMMANDING OFFICER	PRESENT FIT FOR DUTY & ON DUTY: COMMISSIONED OFFICERS	NONCOMMISSIONED OFFICERS	STAFF OFFICERS	RANK & FILE	TOTAL	RANK & FILE SICK, ON FURLOUGH, ETC.: SICK PRESENT	SICK ABSENT	ON COMMAND & EXTRA SERVICE	ON FURLOUGH	CONFINED	PRISONERS OF WAR	WANTING CLOTHES	GRAND TOTAL	ALTERATIONS: DEATHS	DESERTED	TAKEN PRISONER	DISCHARGED	JOINED, ENLISTED, RECRUITED	LOCATION
FORCES UNDER COMMANDER-IN-CHIEF GENERAL GEORGE WASHINGTON																					
1st Pa.	1st Pa.	James Chambers	10	28	4	212	254	6	17	27					304		2	1		17	West Point, N.Y. area
1st Pa.	2nd Pa.	Walter Stewart	12	38	5	220	275	16	20	36					347		13				West Point, N.Y. area
1st Pa.	4th Pa.	Lt. Col. William Butler	12	34	4	209	259	7	8	20					294		2			17	West Point, N.Y. area
1st Pa.	7th Pa.	Lt. Col. Josiah Harmar	7	32	4	206	249	16	10	18					293	1	6			20	West Point, N.Y. area
1st Pa.	10th Pa.	Richard Humpton	8	33	5 A	183	229	10	13	38					290	2	4		1	12	West Point, N.Y. area
2nd Pa.	3rd Pa.	Thomas Craig	12	29	4	194	239	21	14	28	3				305		5			9	West Point, N.Y. area
2nd Pa.	5th Pa.	Francis Johnston	11	26	5	189	231	15	11	25	1				283		9			26	West Point, N.Y. area
2nd Pa.	6th Pa.	Robert Magaw	9	27	5	201	242	7	9	28					286		8		1	31	West Point, N.Y. area
2nd Pa.	9th Pa.	Richard Butler	12	24	4	197	237	12	13	28					290	1	7			24	West Point, N.Y. area
2nd Pa.	11th Pa.	Lt. Col. Adam Hubley	11	35	5	194	245	8	17	22					292	2	6		1	23	West Point, N.Y. area
N.J.	1st N.J.	Matthias Ogden	16	37	3	199	255	7	17	20	2				301	1	4		1	6	Tappan, N.Y. area
N.J.	2nd N.J.	Israel Shreve	13	36	5	272	326	7	27	39	2				401	1	3			31	Tappan, N.Y. area
N.J.	3rd N.J.	Elias Dayton	12	35	5 B	216	268	8	18	28	1				323		1		1	10	Tappan, N.Y. area
N.J.	German bn.	Lt. Col. Ludowick Weltner	12	20	6	132	170	10	1	12	2				195					4	Tappan, N.Y. area
N.Y.	2nd N.Y.	Philip Van Cortlandt	12	25	3	121	161	5	15	24					205		1			1	Tappan, N.Y. area
N.Y.	5th N.Y.	Lt. Col. Marinus Willett	8	25	5	149	187	7	11	25					230		5		3	2	Tappan, N.Y. area
N.Y.	4th N.Y.	Lt. Col. Frederick Weisenfels	17	32	4 C	218	271	7	14	34	2				328		2		1	5	Tappan, N.Y. area
N.Y.	3rd N.Y.	Peter Gansevoort	14	31	5	222	272	8	8	36	1				325		5		2	1	Tappan, N.Y. area
1st Conn.	3rd Conn.	Samuel Wyllys	14	40	5	249	308	17	12	33	1				371		1			19	Tappan, N.Y. area
1st Conn.	4th Conn.	John Durkee	10	33	4 D	236	283	18	9	49	1				360		3		2	21	Tappan, N.Y. area
1st Conn.	8th Conn.	Lt. Col. Isaac Sherman	13	27	2	253	295	26	9	25					355		1		4	21	Tappan, N.Y. area
2nd Conn.	1st Conn.	Josiah Starr	11	26	3	267	307	12	12	31					362		2		1	18	Tappan, N.Y. area
2nd Conn.	2nd Conn.	Zebulon Butler	11	33	3	267	314	8	13	27					362	1	2		1	15	Tappan, N.Y. area
2nd Conn.	5th Conn.	Philip Burr Bradley	14	30	5 E	252	301	22	12	30					365	1	1		1	22	Tappan, N.Y. area
2nd Conn.	7th Conn.	Heman Swift	13	27	3	259	302	11	10	35	2				360		1		5	23	Tappan, N.Y. area
1st Mass.	3rd Mass.	John Greaton	14	34	3	211	262	11	12	31					316	2	1		4	12	Tappan, N.Y. area
1st Mass.	5th Mass.	Rufus Putnam	10	31	5	206	252	9	21	29					311		1		2	6	Tappan, N.Y. area
1st Mass.	6th Mass.	Thomas Nixon	15	32	4 F	224	275	19	14	31					339	2	1			4	Tappan, N.Y. area
1st Mass.	12th Mass.	Lt. Col. Ebenezer Sprout	12	34	6	208	260	12	16	29					317	1	3		1	9	Tappan, N.Y. area
2nd Mass.	1st Mass.	Joseph Vose	16	24	3	226	269	12	11	36	1				329	1	6			17	Tappan, N.Y. area
2nd Mass.	4th Mass.	William Shepard	14	37	3	215	269	18	12	41					340		2		1	11	Tappan, N.Y. area
2nd Mass.	13th Mass.	Lt. Col. Calvin Smith	13	36	4	226	279	10	10	19					318				1	4	Tappan, N.Y. area
2nd Mass.	15th Mass.	Timothy Bigelow	11	28	4	219	262	20	6	38					326		1		4	18	Tappan, N.Y. area
3rd Mass.	7th Mass.	Lt. Col. John Brooks	11	27	4	242	284	11	18	26					339	1			1	1	Tappan, N.Y. area
3rd Mass.	10th Mass.	Thomas Marshall	11	37	3	252	303	23	5	26					357				3	13	Tappan, N.Y. area
3rd Mass.	11th Mass.	Benjamin Tupper	9	33	4 G	247	293	10	14	26					343	2			1	6	Tappan, N.Y. area
3rd Mass.	14th Mass.	Gamaliel Bradford	14	32	6	237	289	12	8	39					348	1	1		1	2	Tappan, N.Y. area
4th Mass.	2nd Mass.	John Bailey	18	34	4	217	273	22	10	42					347		4		2	2	Tappan, N.Y. area
4th Mass.	8th Mass.	Michael Jackson	14	31	4 H	219	268	18	8	34					328		1		1	2	Tappan, N.Y. area
4th Mass.	9th Mass.	James Wesson	13	36	5	225	279	12	6	43					340		8		4	7	Tappan, N.Y. area
Stark (late)	2nd R.I.	Israel Angell	15	40	5	165	225	19	10	31	1				286		1		3	2	Tappan, N.Y. area
Stark (late)	9th Conn.	Samuel Blatchley Webb	8	32	4	232	276	17	15	27	1				336	1	1		4	19	Tappan, N.Y. area
Stark (late)	16th Mass.	Henry Jackson	10	24	3	180	217	10	14	41					282		2		53	2	Tappan, N.Y. area
Poor	1st N.H.	Joseph Cilley	12	37	4	245	298	5	12	37	1				353		1			2	Tappan, N.Y. area
Poor	2nd N.H.	Lt. Col. George Reid	15	38	5	255	313	13	4	29	2				361		1		2	4	Tappan, N.Y. area
Poor	3rd N.H.	Alexander Scammell	16	34	3 I	265	318	14	6	20					358				3	9	Tappan, N.Y. area
Poor	2nd Canadian	Moses Hazen	16	37	4	241	298	15	34	54	2				403		5		2	3	Tappan, N.Y. area
	Del. militia	Lt. Col. Henry Neill	17	29	3	150	199	22	5	25					251		1		4		Tappan, N.Y. area
	N.J. militia	Maj. John Mauritius Goetschius	5	12	2	67	86	11	10	51	11				169						Tappan, N.Y. area

SEPTEMBER 1780 (continued)

BRIGADE	UNIT	COMMANDING OFFICER	PRESENT FIT FOR DUTY & ON DUTY: COMMISSIONED OFFICERS	NONCOMMISSIONED OFFICERS	STAFF OFFICERS	RANK & FILE	TOTAL	RANK & FILE SICK, ON FURLOUGH, ETC.: SICK PRESENT	SICK ABSENT	ON COMMAND & EXTRA SERVICE	ON FURLOUGH	CONFINED	PRISONERS OF WAR	WANTING CLOTHES	GRAND TOTAL	ALTERATIONS: DEATHS	DESERTED	TAKEN PRISONER	DISCHARGED	JOINED, ENLISTED, RECRUITED	LOCATION
	FORCES UNDER COMMANDER-IN-CHIEF GENERAL GEORGE WASHINGTON (continued)																				
	1st Canadian	James Livingston	5	24	2	69	100	4	9	9					122		1				West Point & dependencies
	Additional	Oliver Spencer	6	11	2	45	64	4	23	45	6				142		2		1	1	West Point & dependencies
	6th Conn.	Return Jonathan Meigs	15	39	2	257	313	16	26	47					402					1	West Point & dependencies
	Conn. militia	Levi Wells	17	20	2	191	230	14	11	31	8				294				3	120	West Point & dependencies
	Conn. militia	Bezaleel Beebe	22	41	3	169	235	14	23	25	7				304				1	17	West Point & dependencies
	Mass. militia	Nathaniel Wade	10	28	4	199	241	25		181					447						West Point & dependencies
	Mass. militia	Seth Murray	15	24	4	211	254	22	12	200	1				489		1				West Point & dependencies
	Mass. militia	John Rand	13	32	4	246	295	31	7	249	1				583					1	West Point & dependencies
	Pt. Mass. state	Ebenezer Thayer	6	22		110	138	5		69	1				213		1			1	West Point & dependencies
	N.H. militia	Thomas Bartlett	18	27	4	160	209	47	11	121	2				390						West Point & dependencies
	N.H. militia	Moses Nichols	18	30	2	226	276	21	17	96	2				412		2		1		West Point & dependencies
	1st R.I.	Christopher Greene	9	41	3	522	575	27	27	26	6				661	3	4			32	Rhode Island
Jacobs	Mass. state	John Jacobs	20	33	3	213	269	9	5	63					346					32	Rhode Island
Jacobs	Pt. Mass. state	Ebenezer Thayer	16	30	3	190	239	5	5	69					318					12	Rhode Island
Jacobs	Mass. state	Ezekiel Howe	19	38	4	355	416	29	4	87					536				2	85	Rhode Island
Jacobs	Mass. state	Abiel Mitchel	18	37	4	205	264	13	1	75					353					64	Rhode Island
Jacobs	Mass. state	Lt. Col. Enoch Hallett	12	24	2	226	264	13		31					308					2	Rhode Island
Malcolm	N.Y. levies	William Malcolm	17	28	3	247	295	11	5	74	6				391						Albany, N.Y.
Malcolm	N.Y. levies	Lewis DuBois	9	22	3	208	242	2	9	63	2				318		2		1	1	Albany, N.Y.
Malcolm	N.Y. levies	Morris Graham	17	27	3	209	256	9	1	110	6				382		1			3	Albany, N.Y.
	1st N.Y.	Goose Van Schaick	13	36	1	213	263	17	14	15					309						Fort Schuyler, N.Y.
	Additional	Seth Warner	11	18	3	67	99	1	2	14					116		2		1	4	Fort Edward, N.Y.
	TOTAL OF INFANTRY		909	2164	262	15029	18364	975	813	3223	85				23460	24	151	1	132	909	
	CAVALRY																				
	4th cont'l.	Stephen Moylan	11	21	2	75	109	24	1	19		1			154			1	2	5	Tappan, N.Y. area
	Marechaussie	Capt. Bartholomew Von Heer	3	11		32	46		5	3					54						Tappan, N.Y. area
	Independent corps	Capt. Henry Bedkin	1	2		8	11	2							13						Tappan, N.Y. area
	TOTAL OF CAVALRY		15	34	2	115	166	26	6	22		1			221			1	2	5	
	ARTILLERY																				
	10 cos. 2nd cont'l.	John Lamb	24	94	3	174	295	15	34	82			2		1136	2	5		2	8	
	9 cos. 3rd cont'l.	John Crane	24	90	3	238	355										14			3	
	7 cos. 4th cont'l.	Thomas Proctor	10	57	3	80	150										2			26	
	West Point det.		19	60	1	123	203									1			1		West Point, N.Y.
	TOTAL OF ARTILLERY		77	301	10	615	1003	15	34	82			2		1136	3	21		3	37	
	INVALIDS																				
	Boston det.	Capt. Thomas Arnold	6	13		65	84								84						Boston, Mass.
	TOTAL OF WASHINGTON'S ARMY		1007	2512	274	15824	19617	1016	853	3327	85	1	2		24901	27	172	2	137	951	
	VIRGINIA STATE FORCES IN THE CONTINENTAL SERVICE AS GUARDS FOR THE CONVENTION TROOPS																				
	Va. convention guards	Francis Taylor	14	17		119	150		3 J	25 K	31 L	1		20	230		1		1		Albemarle Barracks, Va.
	GRAND TOTAL		1021	2529	274	15943	19767	1016	856	3352	116	2	2	20	25131 M	27	173	2	138 N	951	

SEPTEMBER 1780
(continued)

OFFICERS SICK, ON FURLOUGH, ETC.	WASHINGTON'S ARMY (EXCEPT INVALIDS)				CONVENTION GUARDS				GRAND TOTAL
	COMMISSIONED	NONCOMMISSIONED	STAFF	TOTAL	COMMISSIONED	NONCOMMISSIONED	STAFF	TOTAL	
Sick Present	36	63	3	102	1			1	266
Sick Absent	73	72	18	163					
On Command	109	132	9	250					250
On Extra Service	34	66	3	103					103
On Furlough	42	23	11	76	2			2	78
Recruiting	8	3		11					11
On the Staff	219			219					219
Prisoners of War	68	17	1	86					86
Furlough Expired	12		2	14					14
In Arrest	4		1	5					5
TOTAL	605	376	48	1029	3			3	1032

SOURCES OF THIS REPORT

1. MONTHLY RETURN OF THE CONTINENTAL ARMY UNDER THE COMMAND OF HIS EXCELLENCY GEORGE WASHINGTON... FOR THE MONTH OF SEPTEMBER 1780, ELEPHANT FOLIO OF WASHINGTON RETURNS, WILLIAM L. CLEMENTS LIBRARY.
   1a. Monthly Return of the Continental Army under... Washington... September 1780, Record Group 93, National Archives. [Contains the same figures, but only to the brigade level.]

2. A RETURN OF COLONEL F. TAYLOR'S REGIMENT OF GUARDS, OCTOBER 1, 1780, COLONEL JAMES WOOD MANUSCRIPTS, VIRGINIA STATE LIBRARY.

A. Four staff officers in Richard Humpton's 10th Pennsylvania regiment plus one chaplain for the entire brigade.
B. Five staff officers in Lieutenant Colonel Ludowick Weltner's German battalion plus one chaplain for the entire brigade.
C. Four staff officers in Peter Gansevoort's 3rd New York regiment plus one chaplain for the entire brigade.
D. One staff officer in Lieutenant Colonel Isaac Sherman's 8th Connecticut regiment plus one chaplain for the entire brigade.
E. Two staff officers in Heman Swift's 7th Connecticut regiment plus one chaplain for the entire brigade.
F. Five staff officers in Lieutenant Colonel Ebenezer Sprout's 12th Massachusetts regiment plus one chaplain for the entire brigade.
G. Five staff officers in Gamaliel Bradford's 14th Massachusetts regiment plus one chaplain for the entire brigade.
H. Four staff officers in James Wesson's 9th Massachusetts regiment plus one chaplain for the entire brigade.
I. Three staff officers in Moses Hazen's 2nd Canadian regiment plus one chaplain for the entire brigade.
J. The manuscript reads "in hospital" for this figure.
K. Including five men classified as camp color men. See footnote I on our September 1779 report.
L. The manuscript notes that most of the thirty-one men on furlough were "Naked."
M. The National Archives manuscript notes that no returns were received for the troops "at the Southward," for the troops at Fort Pitt and the Wyoming Valley, for Sheldon's regiment of cavalry, and for Lee's Partizan Corps.
N. Including nineteen men in Washington's infantry discharged for inability.

Benedict Arnold sat for this profile by Du Simitière in July 1777. Arnold was then in Philadelphia trying to resign his commission as major general because Continental Congress had not given him that rank ahead of four other officers, as he felt they should have in recognition of his considerable military exploits. Arnold's desertion to the British at the time of this report is clearly the reason why his profile, which appeared as the last of Du Simitière's *Thirteen Portraits*. . . in the first edition, was omitted from later editions.

OCTOBER 1780

BRIGADE	UNIT	COMMANDING OFFICER	PRESENT FIT FOR DUTY & ON DUTY: COMMISSIONED OFFICERS	NONCOMMISSIONED OFFICERS	STAFF OFFICERS	RANK & FILE	TOTAL	RANK & FILE SICK, ON FURLOUGH, ETC.: SICK PRESENT	SICK ABSENT	ON COMMAND & EXTRA SERVICE	ON FURLOUGH	CONFINED	DISMOUNTED	PRISONERS OF WAR	GRAND TOTAL	ALTERATIONS: DEATHS	DESERTED	TAKEN PRISONER	DISCHARGED	JOINED, ENLISTED, RECRUITED	LOCATION
FORCES UNDER COMMANDER-IN-CHIEF GENERAL GEORGE WASHINGTON																					
1st Pa.	1st Pa.	James Chambers	10	27	4	204	245	7	16	30					298		3		1	6	New Jersey
	2nd Pa.	Walter Stewart	14	41	4	228	287	9	17	35					348	1	1		1	1	New Jersey
	4th Pa.	Lt. Col. William Butler	10	33	4	202	249	7	8	26					290		5		1	5	New Jersey
	7th Pa.	Lt. Col. Josiah Harmar	5	29	3 A	208	245	18	5	19					287					1	New Jersey
	10th Pa.	Richard Humpton	7	34	5	196	242	10	10	29	1				292					2	New Jersey
2nd Pa.	3rd Pa.	Thomas Craig	12	32	4	196	244	21	13	25	4				307	1	3			5	New Jersey
	5th Pa.	Francis Johnston	10	25	5	190	230	11	9	25					275	2	4			1	New Jersey
	6th Pa.	Robert Magaw	11	25	5	199	240	11	5	28	1				285		1				New Jersey
	9th Pa.	Richard Butler	12	24	4	194	234	10	14	30	1				289		4			8	New Jersey
	11th Pa.	Lt. Col. Adam Hubley	10	34	4	188	236	10	13	26					285	1	3		1	2	New Jersey
1st Conn.	3rd Conn.	Samuel Wyllys	14	33	5	243	295	12	12	39	1				359	1			4	1	New Jersey
	4th Conn.	John Durkee	10	34	2	229	275	20	11	44	1				351		2		4	2	New Jersey
	6th Conn.	Return Jonathan Meigs	13	40	2	264	319	16	31	28	2				396				1	1	New Jersey
	8th Conn.	Lt. Col. Isaac Sherman	13	26	4	246	289	22	4	30	1				346		1		7	3	New Jersey
2nd Conn.	1st Conn.	Josiah Starr	16	24	3	259	302	20	9	32	1				364		2			2	New Jersey
	2nd Conn.	Zebulon Butler	12	31	3	254	300	10	13	26	8				357	1	1		1	1	New Jersey
	5th Conn.	Philip Burr Bradley	14	24	5 B	245	288	22	11	37					358	2	2			2	New Jersey
	7th Conn.	Heman Swift	15	26	5	251	297	12	8	35					352		3		2	1	New Jersey
1st Mass.	3rd Mass.	John Greaton	14	33	3	219	269	6	8	31					314	1			1	3	New Jersey
	5th Mass.	Rufus Putnam	8	32	3	214	257	12	8	22					299		11			3	New Jersey
	6th Mass.	Thomas Nixon	13	30	4 C	237	284	11	10	28					333				1		New Jersey
	12th Mass.	Lt. Col. Ebenezer Sprout	12	35	5	211	263	16	11	27					317	1			1	1	New Jersey
2nd Mass.	1st Mass.	Joseph Vose	14	24	4	227	269	12	7	29					317	1	9				New Jersey
	4th Mass.	William Shepard	13	36	4	228	281	12	9	34	1				337	1	1		1	1	New Jersey
	13th Mass.	Lt. Col. Calvin Smith	12	34	4	239	289	8	6	31					334		1			1	New Jersey
	15th Mass.	Timothy Bigelow	14	27	5	223	269	12	9	35					325	1			2		New Jersey
3rd Mass.	7th Mass.	Lt. Col. John Brooks	11	27	4	245	287	9	21	26					343				2	10	New Jersey
	10th Mass.	Thomas Marshall	11	35	4	259	309	14	5	27					355						New Jersey
	11th Mass.	Benjamin Tupper	7	36	5	233	281	11	14	35	1				342		2		1	3	New Jersey
	14th Mass.	Gamaliel Bradford	11	33	5	238	287	11	7	39					344	1			1	1	New Jersey
4th Mass.	2nd Mass.	John Bailey	16	35	5	221	277	4	7	58					346		4			5	New Jersey
	8th Mass.	Michael Jackson	15	28	4	211	258	13	7	49					327		1			1	New Jersey
	9th Mass.	James Wesson	11	36	5	207	259	12	8	58					337		3			3	New Jersey
N.J.	1st N.J.	Matthias Ogden	12	32	3	141	188	12	13	80	1				294	1	4		1	3	West Point & dependencies
	2nd N.J.	Israel Shreve	14	33	5	198	250	9	25	107	7				398		4			4	West Point & dependencies
	3rd N.J.	Elias Dayton	11	29	5	186	231	3	14	59	5				312	1	3				West Point & dependencies
	German bn.	Lt. Col. Ludowick Weltner	8	22	5	96	131	8	1	54					194		2			6	West Point & dependencies
N.Y.	1st N.Y.	Goose Van Schaick	16	36	3	197	252	10	18	20	4				304	5	10		5	6	West Point & dependencies
	5th N.Y.	Lt. Col. Marinus Willett	7	25	4 D	148	184	8	7	22	1				222		4				West Point & dependencies
	2nd N.Y.	Philip Van Cortlandt	11	29	4	120	164	6	5	18					193		6		14	5	West Point & dependencies

OCTOBER 1780 (continued)

BRIGADE	UNIT	COMMANDING OFFICER	PRESENT FIT FOR DUTY & ON DUTY: COMMISSIONED OFFICERS	NONCOMMISSIONED OFFICERS	STAFF OFFICERS	RANK & FILE	TOTAL	RANK & FILE SICK, ON FURLOUGH, ETC.: SICK PRESENT	SICK ABSENT	ON COMMAND & EXTRA SERVICE	ON FURLOUGH	CONFINED	DISMOUNTED	PRISONERS OF WAR	GRAND TOTAL	ALTERATIONS: DEATHS	DESERTED	TAKEN PRISONER	DISCHARGED	JOINED, ENLISTED, RECRUITED	LOCATION
	FORCES UNDER COMMANDER-IN-CHIEF GENERAL GEORGE WASHINGTON (continued)																				
Stark	2nd R.I.	Israel Angell	12	36	5	125	178	18	7	76	1				280	1	2			6	West Point & dependencies
Stark	9th Conn.	Samuel Blatchley Webb	5	28	4	171	208	16	10	94					328				1	1	West Point & dependencies
Stark	16th Mass.	Henry Jackson	9	27	3	121	160	5	10	94					269				12	2	West Point & dependencies
N.H.	1st N.H.	Joseph Cilley	11	29	4	165	209	3	11	122					345						West Point & dependencies
N.H.	2nd N.H.	Lt. Col. George Reid	11	32	5	162	210	9	11	120	1				351						West Point & dependencies
N.H.	3rd N.H.	Alexander Scammell	14	30	3	196	243	11	3	92					349	2			2	3	West Point & dependencies
N.H.	2nd Canadian	Moses Hazen	20	32	3	184	239	16	34	99	2				390	1	13			3	West Point & dependencies
	1st Canadian	James Livingston	4	23	2	58	87	2	12	14	3				118	1					Verplancks Point, N. Y.
	Additional	Oliver Spencer	4	8	1	40	53	2	20	46	7				128		2				Stony Point, N. Y.
	8th Pa.	Daniel Brodhead	12	23	5	122	162	4		3	4				173		1				Fort Pitt, Pa.
	9th Va.	John Gibson	15	25	5	145	190	9		3	2				204		3			2	Fort Pitt, Pa.
	Additional (Md. corps)	(late) Moses Rawlings	1	7	1	43	52	1	1	2					56						Fort Pitt, Pa.
	Va. independent co.	Capt. Henry Heth	2	4		22	28	5	1	3					37						Fort Pitt, Pa.
	TOTAL OF INFANTRY		589	1533	205	10048	12375	568	549	2201	61				15754	27	121		68	117	
	CAVALRY																				
	4th cont'l.	Stephen Moylan	10	14	4	47	75	12	4	49		2	7		149		2			1	New Jersey
	Marechaussie	Capt. Bartholomew Von Heer	3	10		35	48		2	5					55						New Jersey
	Independent corps	Capt. Henry Bedkin	1	3		6	10			3					13						New Jersey
	TOTAL OF CAVALRY		14	27	4	88	133	12	6	57		2	7		217		2			1	
	ARTILLERY																				
	8 cos. 2nd cont'l.	John Lamb	17	75	2	149	243	11	26	84	1			2	1090		3		3	1	New Jersey
	8 cos. 3rd cont'l.	John Crane	23	76	5	208	312										3				New Jersey
	7 cos. 4th cont'l.	Thomas Proctor	11	62	3	86	162													1	New Jersey
	West Point det.		24	74		151	249										5				West Point, N. Y.
	TOTAL OF ARTILLERY		75	287	10	594	966	11	26	84	1			2	1090		11		3	2	
	INVALIDS																				
	Philadelphia unit	Lewis Nicola	9	45		224	278								278						Philadelphia, Pa.
	Boston det.	Capt. Thomas Arnold	5	13		67	85								85						Boston, Mass.
	TOTAL OF INVALIDS		14	58		291	363								363						
	TOTAL OF WASHINGTON'S ARMY		692	1905	219	11021	13837	591	581	2342	62	2	7	2	17424	27	134		71	120	
	VIRGINIA STATE FORCES IN THE CONTINENTAL SERVICE AS GUARDS FOR THE CONVENTION TROOPS																				
	Va. western bn.	Lt. Col. Joseph Crockett	14	20		95	129	7[E]	6[F]	13[G]	4	3			162					2	Albemarle Barracks, Va.
	GRAND TOTAL		706	1925	219	11116	13966	598	587	2355	66	5	7	2	17586[H]	27	134		71[I]	122	

OCTOBER 1780
(continued)

OFFICERS SICK, ON FURLOUGH, ETC.	WASHINGTON'S ARMY (EXCEPT INVALIDS)			
	COMMISSIONED	NONCOMMISSIONED	STAFF	TOTAL
Sick Present	24	73	5	102
Sick Absent	51	69	15	135
On Command	71	108	8	187
On Extra Service	32	63	3	98
On Furlough	50	23	9	82
Recruiting	3	1		4
On the Staff	210			210
Prisoners of War	66	11	1	78
Furlough Expired	6		1	7
In Arrest	5			5
Dismounted		1		1
Unfit for Duty		1		1
TOTAL	518	350	42	910

SOURCES OF THIS REPORT

1. MONTHLY RETURN OF THE CONTINENTAL ARMY UNDER THE COMMAND OF HIS EXCELLENCY GEORGE WASHINGTON. . . FOR THE MONTH OF OCTOBER 1780, ELEPHANT FOLIO OF WASHINGTON RETURNS, WILLIAM L. CLEMENTS LIBRARY.
   1a. Monthly Return of the Continental Army under. . . Washington. . . October 1780, Record Group 93, National Archives. [Contains the same figures, but only to the brigade level.]

2. A RETURN OF COLO. JOSEPH CROCKETT'S BATTALION, NOVEMBER 1, 1780, COLONEL JAMES WOOD MANUSCRIPTS, VIRGINIA STATE LIBRARY.

A. Four staff officers in Richard Humpton's 10th Pennsylvania regiment plus one chaplain for the entire brigade.
B. Four staff officers in Heman Swift's 7th Connecticut regiment plus one chaplain for the entire brigade.
C. Four staff officers in Lieutenant Colonel Ebenezer Sprout's 12th Massachusetts regiment plus one chaplain for the entire brigade.
D. Three staff officers in Philip Van Cortlandt's 2nd New York regiment plus one chaplain for the entire brigade.
E. These seven men are given simply as "unfit for duty" on the manuscript, but this may mean "sick present."
F. The manuscript marks these men as "in hospital."
G. Including three men serving as camp color men. See footnote I on our September 1779 report.
H. The National Archives manuscript notes that no returns were received for the Southern Department, for Sheldon's 2nd Continental cavalry, for Lee's Partizan Corps, and for Warner's Additional, Gansevoort's 3rd New York, and Lieutenant Colonel Weisenfels' 4th New York regiments. It is also noted that a return of Greene's 1st Rhode Island regiment dated October 21 arrived too late to be included in the return, but the regiment reported 608 rank and file. Also arriving too late to be included was a return of John Jacobs' brigade of Massachusetts state troops (see the September report), dated October 21 and consisting of 1,530 effective rank and file.
I. Including twenty-seven men in Washington's infantry discharged for inability.

America Presenting at the Altar of Liberty, Medallions of Her Illustrious Sons, an English printed cotton of about 1783. Pink and white in color, the fabric depicts the full figure of Washington (being crowned with a laurel wreath) as well as a variety of other important Revolutionary political and military figures. The medallion between the two standing female figures at the right, for example, has profiles of Horatio Gates and Joseph Reed. (Courtesy of the New-York Historical Society, New York City)

NOVEMBER 1780

BRIGADE	UNIT	COMMANDING OFFICER	PRESENT FIT FOR DUTY & ON DUTY: COMMISSIONED OFFICERS	NONCOMMISSIONED OFFICERS	STAFF OFFICERS	RANK & FILE	TOTAL	RANK & FILE SICK, ON FURLOUGH, ETC.: SICK PRESENT	SICK ABSENT	ON COMMAND & EXTRA SERVICE	ON FURLOUGH	CONFINED	PRISONERS OF WAR	GRAND TOTAL	ALTERATIONS: DEATHS	DESERTED	TAKEN PRISONER	DISCHARGED	JOINED, ENLISTED, RECRUITED	LOCATION
FORCES UNDER COMMANDER-IN-CHIEF GENERAL GEORGE WASHINGTON																				
1st Pa.	1st Pa.	James Chambers	10	25	4	174	213	5	25	52				295						near Morristown, N.J. D
	2nd Pa.	Walter Stewart	12	37	3	216	268	6	17	52	2			345		3			8	near Morristown, N.J.
	4th Pa.	Lt. Col. William Butler	9	28	4	183	224	2	14	40				280	1	2		2	1	near Morristown, N.J.
	7th Pa.	Lt. Col. Josiah Harmar	7	29	2	179	217	6	30	38				291		1			4	near Morristown, N.J.
	10th Pa.	Richard Humpton	7	32	4	177	220	9	13	47	3			292		1			4	near Morristown, N.J.
2nd Pa.	3rd Pa.	Thomas Craig	9	30	3	182	224	13	20	41	4			302					2	near Morristown, N.J.
	5th Pa.	Francis Johnston	7	22	4	181	214	6	11	39				270		1			5	near Morristown, N.J.
	6th Pa.	Robert Magaw	12	21	5	181	219	2	18	41				280	1	1		2	3	near Morristown, N.J.
	9th Pa.	Richard Butler	10	23	5	163	201	11	32	42	1			287					2	near Morristown, N.J.
	11th Pa.	Lt. Col. Adam Hubley	10	32	4	173	219	9	21	34				283						near Morristown, N.J.
N.J.	1st N.J.	Matthias Ogden	13	34	4	159	210	7	14	50	3			284		9		1	2	moving to winter quarters
	2nd N.J.	Israel Shreve	12	34	5	230	281	13	20	72	10			396		2			2	moving to winter quarters
	3rd N.J.	Elias Dayton	8	29	3	190	230	6	14	46	3			299		8		3	3	moving to winter quarters
	German bn.	Lt. Col. Ludowick Weltner	13	25	5	121	164	4	1	15				184		14		3		moving to winter quarters
N.Y.	1st N.Y.	Goose Van Schaick	11	32	3	158	204	9	19	37	14			283		9				vicinity of West Point, N.Y. E
	5th N.Y.	Marinus Willett	7	21	4	131	163	13	8	22	5			211	1	7		1	2	vicinity of West Point, N.Y.
	2nd N.Y.	Philip Van Cortlandt	7	28	2	113	150	8	5	22	1			186		1			1	vicinity of West Point, N.Y.
1st Conn.	3rd Conn.	Samuel Wyllys	10	30	3	167	210	5	19	94	3			331		1		7	2	moving to winter quarters
	4th Conn.	John Durkee	5	27	3	151	186	8	23	107	2			326				16	4	moving to winter quarters
	6th Conn.	Return Jonathan Meigs	13	38	2	244	297	8	43	40	3			391					2	moving to winter quarters
	8th Conn.	Lt. Col. Isaac Sherman	10	22	3	178	213	9	30	74	4			330				6		moving to winter quarters
2nd Conn.	1st Conn.	Josiah Starr	5	21	2	187	215	7	15	98	1			336						moving to winter quarters
	2nd Conn.	Zebulon Butler	6	31	3	181	221	1	17	92	9			340		4		40	4	moving to winter quarters
	5th Conn.	Philip Burr Bradley	6	21	4	184	215	9	16	85				325						moving to winter quarters
	7th Conn.	Heman Swift	6	24	4	205	239	3	12	76				330						moving to winter quarters
Stark	2nd R.I.	Israel Angell	11	35	5	126	177	26	4	63				270		1		8	1	vicinity of West Point, N.Y.
	9th Conn.	Samuel Blatchley Webb	3	27	5	179	214	26	10	72				322				4		vicinity of West Point, N.Y.
	16th Mass.	Henry Jackson	9	27	3	102	141	22	8	87				258				11	1	vicinity of West Point, N.Y.
1st Mass.	3rd Mass.	John Greaton	9	25	4	148	186	4	23	79				292	1	2		5		moving to winter quarters
	5th Mass.	Rufus Putnam	7	30	3	169	209	6	14	59				288		1		7	2	moving to winter quarters
	6th Mass.	Thomas Nixon	8	28	4	202	242	3	17	56				318		1		7		moving to winter quarters
	12th Mass.	Lt. Col. Ebenezer Sprout	8	30	4	161	203	4	26	67				300	1			5		moving to winter quarters
2nd Mass.	1st Mass.	Joseph Vose	11	23	4	191	229	1	15	64				309				5	2	moving to winter quarters
	4th Mass.	William Shepard	10	27	2	161	200	6	20	90	3			319		1		5	3	moving to winter quarters
	13th Mass.	Lt. Col. Calvin Smith	10	29	4	188	231	5	19	69	1			325				2	1	moving to winter quarters
	15th Mass.	Timothy Bigelow	9	24	5	185	223	7	25	52				307		2		10	1	moving to winter quarters
3rd Mass.	7th Mass.	Lt. Col. John Brooks	8	26	3	197	234	6	12	69				321	2			14		moving to winter quarters
	10th Mass.	Thomas Marshall	9	35	4	205	253	9	28	59				349		1		4	1	moving to winter quarters
	11th Mass.	Benjamin Tupper	5	33	5	184	227	2	14	81	1			325		1		12	1	moving to winter quarters
	14th Mass.	Gamaliel Bradford	11	31	5	207	254		17	67				338				4		moving to winter quarters

NOVEMBER 1780 (continued)

BRIGADE	UNIT	COMMANDING OFFICER	PRESENT FIT FOR DUTY & ON DUTY: COMMISSIONED OFFICERS	NONCOMMISSIONED OFFICERS	STAFF OFFICERS	RANK & FILE	TOTAL	RANK & FILE SICK, ON FURLOUGH, ETC.: SICK PRESENT	SICK ABSENT	ON COMMAND & EXTRA SERVICE	ON FURLOUGH	CONFINED	PRISONERS OF WAR	GRAND TOTAL	ALTERATIONS: DEATHS	DESERTED	TAKEN PRISONER	DISCHARGED	JOINED, ENLISTED, RECRUITED	LOCATION
	FORCES UNDER COMMANDER-IN-CHIEF GENERAL GEORGE WASHINGTON (continued)																			
4th Mass.	2nd Mass.	John Bailey	14	28	4	182	228	1	16	95				340		2		2	8	moving to winter quarters
4th Mass.	8th Mass.	Michael Jackson	12	24	4	176	216	4	20	92				332	1			3	17	moving to winter quarters
4th Mass.	9th Mass.	James Wesson	9	34	5	168	216	5	19	91				331				2		moving to winter quarters
N.H.	1st N.H.	Joseph Cilley	9	28	3	170	210	11	11	108				340	1			1		vicinity of West Point, N.Y.
N.H.	2nd N.H.	Lt. Col. George Reid	12	34	5	185	236	9	9	96	1			351				1		vicinity of West Point, N.Y.
N.H.	3rd N.H.	Alexander Scammell	12	30	3	185	230	17	3	96				346						vicinity of West Point, N.Y.
N.H.	2nd Canadian	Moses Hazen	21	33	3	166	223	25	30	109	3			390	1	1		1	1	vicinity of West Point, N.Y.
	Additional	Oliver Spencer	5	9	2	47	63	3	18	36	6			126		1		4	2	Stony Point, N.Y.
	1st Canadian	James Livingston	2	22	2	63	89	6	9	14				118				1		Verplancks Point, N.Y.
	1st R.I.	Christopher Greene	4	32	3	364	403	58	32	147				640	2	6		1	1	Rhode Island
	TOTAL OF INFANTRY		453	1400	182	8719	10754	445	876	3274	83			15432	12	84		200	93	
	CAVALRY																			
	2nd cont'l.	Elisha Sheldon	6	22	4	85	117	6	14	76		2		215		3	1	2	4	vicinity of West Point, N.Y. [F]
	Independent corps	Capt. Henry Bedkin	1	3		5	9			4				13						
	TOTAL OF CAVALRY		7	25	4	90	126	6	14	80		2		228		3	1	2	4	
	ARTILLERY																			
	8 cos. 2nd cont'l.	John Lamb	17	77	3	145	242	14	24	120	2		2	1038		4		2		moving to winter quarters
	8 cos. 3rd cont'l.	John Crane	23	69	4	202	298									7		5	2	moving to winter quarters
	7 cos. 4th cont'l.	Thomas Proctor	11	62	3	86	162													moving to winter quarters
	West Point det.		17	47		110	174									2	1	2	2	West Point, N.Y.
	TOTAL OF ARTILLERY		68	255	10	543	876	14	24	120	2		2	1038		13	1	9	4	
	INVALIDS																			
	Philadelphia unit	Lewis Nicola	10	50	2	236	298							298						Philadelphia, Pa.
	Boston det.	Capt. Thomas Arnold	5	17		67	89							89						Boston, Mass.
	TOTAL OF INVALIDS		15	67	2	303	387							387						
	TOTAL OF WASHINGTON'S ARMY		543	1747	198	9655	12143	465	914	3474	85	2	2	17085	12	100	2	211 [C]	101	
	SOUTHERN DEPARTMENT UNDER MAJOR GENERAL HORATIO GATES (To Brigade Level Only)																			
	Cont'l. brig.		29	96	9	609	743	38	198	199	9			1187						Providence, N.C. [G]
	Morgan's brig.	Brig. Gen. Daniel Morgan	23	45	4	358	430	31	4	6	5			476						Providence, N.C.
	N.C. militia brig.	Brig. Gen. William Lee Davidson	61	65	10	737	873	75	85	155	95			1283 [A]						Providence, N.C.
	TOTAL OF SOUTHERN ARMY		113	206	23	1704	2046	144	287	360	109			2946						
	GRAND TOTAL		656	1953	221	10759	14189	609	1201	3834	194	2	2	20031 [B]						

NOVEMBER 1780
(continued)

OFFICERS SICK, ON FURLOUGH, ETC.	WASHINGTON'S ARMY (EXCEPT INVALIDS) COMMISSIONED	NONCOMMISSIONED	STAFF	TOTAL
Sick Present	20	31	5	56
Sick Absent	45	99	14	158
On Command	146	239	13	398
On Extra Service	29	59	1	89
On Furlough	108	27	26	161
Recruiting	1	1		2
On the Staff	207			207
Prisoners of War	62	12	1	75
Furlough Expired	5		1	6
In Arrest	4			4
TOTAL	627	468	61	1156

SOURCES OF THIS REPORT

1. MONTHLY RETURN OF THE CONTINENTAL ARMY UNDER THE COMMAND OF HIS EXCELLENCY GEORGE WASHINGTON. . . FOR THE MONTH OF NOVEMBER 1780, ELEPHANT FOLIO OF WASHINGTON RETURNS, WILLIAM L. CLEMENTS LIBRARY.
   1a. Monthly Return of the Continental Army under. . . Washington. . . November 1780, Record Group 93, National Archives. [Contains the same figures, but only to the brigade level.]

2. A FIELD RETURN OF THE SOUTHERN ARMY UNDER COMMAND OF HIS EXCELLENCY MAJ. GENERAL GATES, NOVEMBER 25, 1780, GATES PAPERS, NEW-YORK HISTORICAL SOCIETY.
   2a. A Field Return of the Southern Army under Command of Major General Gates, November 25, 1780, Record Group 360, National Archives. [Another manuscript of the same return.]

A. The manuscripts used for the Southern Department (dated November 25) both note that Colonel Peasley's regiment of militia, consisting of four captains, five subalterns, eight sergeants, and two hundred privates, would be discharged two days later and that the terms of service of the militia in general would expire by December 5.
B. The National Archives manuscript notes that no returns were received for the troops at Fort Pitt, for the 3rd and 4th New York regiments on the frontiers, for the 4th cavalry regiment, for Lee's Partizan Corps, for Von Heer's Marechaussie, and for the Southern Department (the last supplied on our report).
C. Including 123 men in Washington's infantry discharged for inability.
D. Washington broke up his camp near the falls of the Passaic River on November 27, and some of the units from that camp and from West Point were still marching to their winter quarters at the end of the month. Many of the figures used in compiling this monthly return were probably collected before they broke camp, but the locations (largely supplied) are as of the end of the month.
E. During November, much of the New York line was shifted back and forth between the Albany area and West Point due to various alarms. At the end of the month, it finally had been decided to winter the whole line in the vicinity of Albany, but those at West Point probably had not yet received that order.
F. On November 27 Washington wrote Sheldon ordering his regiment to winter at Colchester, Connecticut. They probably had not left the West Point area by the end of the month. When forage was found to be inadequate in the Colchester area and the Connecticut authorities requested that they winter elsewhere, Washington reluctantly allowed them to winter in Massachusetts.
G. A few miles south of Charlotte and called "New Providence" on the manuscript

Major General Horatio Gates at this time was about to be relieved by Nathanael Greene as commander of the Southern Department. This replacement was ordered by Continental Congress in a resolution which also called for an inquiry into Gates's disastrous defeat at Camden, S.C. (August 16, 1780). Gates objected to this treatment and twice went to Philadelphia demanding exoneration. Charles Willson Peale apparently painted this portrait there in 1782, when Congress finally repealed its resolution calling for investigation of Gates's conduct, and Gates's restored good name entitled him to a place in the museum. (Courtesy of the Independence National Historical Park Collection, Philadelphia)

DECEMBER 1780

BRIGADE	UNIT	COMMANDING OFFICER	PRESENT FIT FOR DUTY & ON DUTY: COMMISSIONED OFFICERS	NONCOMMISSIONED OFFICERS	STAFF OFFICERS	RANK & FILE	TOTAL	RANK & FILE SICK, ON FURLOUGH, ETC.: SICK PRESENT	SICK ABSENT	ON COMMAND & EXTRA SERVICE	ON FURLOUGH	CONFINED	PRISONERS OF WAR	GRAND TOTAL	ALTERATIONS: DEATHS	DESERTED	TAKEN PRISONER	DISCHARGED	JOINED, ENLISTED, RECRUITED	LOCATION
	FORCES UNDER COMMANDER-IN-CHIEF GENERAL GEORGE WASHINGTON																			
N.J.	1st N.J.	Matthias Ogden	12	31	4	150	197	8	14	39	12			270		5		1	2	near Pompton, N.J.
	2nd N.J.	Israel Shreve	9	30	5	222	266	25	20	55	19			385		5		5	6	near Pompton, N.J.
	3rd N.J. A	Elias Dayton	9	25	3	180	217	12	14	36	9			288		5	3			near Pompton, N.J.
	German bn.	Lt. Col. Ludowick Weltner	13	22	5	95	135	5	1	36	1			178		3				
1st Conn.	3rd Conn.	Samuel Wyllys	7	19	4	63	93	14	10	75	19			211				107	1	West Point & vicinity
	4th Conn.	John Durkee	5	14	3	33	55	4	5	55	13			132		2		184	5	West Point & vicinity
	6th Conn.	Return Jonathan Meigs	5	31	3	134	173	12	28	100	14			327	1	6		40	1	West Point & vicinity
	8th Conn.	Lt. Col. Isaac Sherman	4	19	2	48	73	12	3	49	6			143	1	9		169	2	West Point & vicinity
2nd Conn.	1st Conn.	Josiah Starr	6	15	2	38	61	7	4	47	9			128		1		201		West Point & vicinity
	2nd Conn.	Zebulon Butler	5	21	2	30	58		5	21	13			97		1		228		West Point & vicinity
	5th Conn.	Philip Burr Bradley	5	12	3	46	66	6	3	55	10			140		3		171		West Point & vicinity
	7th Conn.	Heman Swift	3	16	4	33	56	5	5	38	9			113		1		207	1	West Point & vicinity
	9th Conn.	Samuel Blatchley Webb	3	22	2	60	87	14	9	51	11			172				142		West Point & vicinity
1st Mass.	3rd Mass.	John Greaton	8	26	2	85	121	10	6	51				188				104	4	West Point & vicinity
	5th Mass.	Rufus Putnam	5	29	4	71	109	14	8	53				184				109	8	West Point & vicinity
	6th Mass.	Thomas Nixon	9	26	4 E	105	144	5	7	59				215	1			113	12	West Point & vicinity
	12th Mass.	Lt. Col. Ebenezer Sprout	7	20	5	86	118	6	7	45				176		1		113		West Point & vicinity
2nd Mass.	1st Mass.	Joseph Vose	8	18	3	89	118	9	8	64	1			200		4		101	6	West Point & vicinity
	4th Mass.	William Shepard	7	32	3	89	131	4	6	72	3			216		2		107	4	West Point & vicinity
	13th Mass.	Lt. Col. Calvin Smith	6	28	2	96	132	7	9	52	2			202				121	4	West Point & vicinity
	15th Mass.	Timothy Bigelow	6	23	2	88	119	15	6	50	1			191				108	1	West Point & vicinity
3rd Mass.	7th Mass.	Lt. Col. John Brooks	8	28	4	105	145	6	6	30	3			190		1		133	1	West Point & vicinity
	10th Mass.	Thomas Marshall	5	25	4	101	135	14	2	34	1			186		3		146	1	West Point & vicinity
	11th Mass.	Benjamin Tupper	4	24	5	79	112	9	4	29	1			155	2	1		162	5	West Point & vicinity
	14th Mass.	Gamaliel Bradford	7	21	5	81	114	7	2	47	1			171		1		151		West Point & vicinity
4th Mass.	2nd Mass.	John Bailey	8	30	4	80	122	12	5	74	2			215		2		126	10	West Point & vicinity
	8th Mass.	Michael Jackson	13	25	3	68	109	7	2	57				175	1	3		156	3	West Point & vicinity
	9th Mass.	James Wesson	7	30	4	83	124	9	6	65				204		2		119	3	West Point & vicinity
	16th Mass.	Henry Jackson	9	21	3	62	95	2	6	62				165		7		80	1	West Point & vicinity
Stark	1st N.H.	Joseph Cilley	8	30	3	98	139	3	8	67	6			223	1	1	1	117	2	West Point & vicinity
	2nd N.H.	Lt. Col. George Reid	9	29	5	91	134	7	7	54	1			203		1		137		West Point & vicinity
	3rd N.H. B	Alexander Scammell	6	30	3	65	104	8	4	46	3			165				176	1	West Point & vicinity
	R.I. C	Israel Angell	9	40	4	153	206	29	7	30				272						West Point & vicinity
	2nd Canadian	Moses Hazen	18	37	3	233	291	13	23	91	5			423						Fishkill, N.Y.
	8th Pa.	Daniel Brodhead	10	23	5	110	148	2		1	4			155		5		2	1	Fort Pitt, Pa.
	9th Va.	John Gibson	16	18	5	124	163	3		3	7			176		1		12		Fort Pitt, Pa.
	Additional (Md. corps)	(late) Moses Rawlings	1	7	1	38	47	3			1			51				1		Fort Pitt, Pa.
	Va. independent co.	Capt. Henry Heth	2	4		25	31	2	1	3				37						Fort Pitt, Pa.
	Pa. independent co.	Capt. John Paul Schott	1			1	2			1				3						Wyoming Valley, Pa.
	Pa. independent co.	Capt. Anthony Selin	1 D	6	F	13	20			3	1			24						Wyoming Valley, Pa.
	Wyoming Valley co.	Capt. Simon Spalding	5	9	2	43	59	3	2	11	3			78						Wyoming Valley, Pa.
	TOTAL OF INFANTRY		289	916	130	3494	4829	333	263	1811	191			7427	7	76	4	3849	85	
	CAVALRY																			
	2nd cont'l.	Elisha Sheldon	9	25	3	127	164	1	11	11	32	2		221		2	1	1	4	Springfield, Mass. area
	ARTILLERY																			
	8 cos. 2nd cont'l.	John Lamb	15	76	3	88	182									1		63	2	New Windsor, N.Y.
	8 cos. 3rd cont'l.	John Crane	16	59	4	89	168	15	11	46	9		2	652				154	3	New Windsor, N.Y.
	West Point det.		18	68		133	219											3	3	West Point, N.Y.
	TOTAL OF ARTILLERY		49	203	7	310	569	15	11	46	9		2	652		1		220	8	

DECEMBER 1780 (continued)

BRIGADE / UNIT	COMMANDING OFFICER	PRESENT FIT FOR DUTY & ON DUTY: COMMISSIONED OFFICERS	NONCOMMISSIONED OFFICERS	STAFF OFFICERS	RANK & FILE	TOTAL	RANK & FILE SICK, ON FURLOUGH, ETC.: SICK PRESENT	SICK ABSENT	ON COMMAND & EXTRA SERVICE	ON FURLOUGH	CONFINED	PRISONERS OF WAR	GRAND TOTAL	ALTERATIONS: DEATHS	DESERTED	TAKEN PRISONER	DISCHARGED	JOINED, ENLISTED, RECRUITED	LOCATION
FORCES UNDER COMMANDER-IN-CHIEF GENERAL GEORGE WASHINGTON (continued)																			
SAPPERS AND MINERS																			
Sapper and miner cos.	Lt. Col. Jean Baptiste Gouvion	3	2	1	32	38	5	2	4	11			60		2			1	West Point & vicinity
INVALIDS																			
Philadelphia unit	Lewis Nicola	10	46	2	237	295							295						Philadelphia, Pa.
Boston det.	Capt. Thomas Arnold	5	16		66	87							87						Boston, Mass.
TOTAL OF INVALIDS		15	62	2	303	382							382						
TOTAL OF WASHINGTON'S ARMY		365	1208	143	4266	5982	354	287	1872	243	2	2	8742	7	81	5	4070[G]	98	

OFFICERS SICK, ON FURLOUGH, ETC.	WASHINGTON'S ARMY (EXCEPT INVALIDS): COMMISSIONED	NONCOMMISSIONED	STAFF	TOTAL
Sick Present	25	53	2	80
Sick Absent	33	41	6	80
On Command	72	91	8	171
On Extra Service	24	49	2	75
On Furlough	189	103	30	322
Recruiting	4	2		6
On the Staff	154			154
Prisoners of War	31	4	1	36
Furlough Expired	6	1	1	8
In Arrest	3		1	4
TOTAL	541	344	51	936

SOURCE OF THIS REPORT

1. MONTHLY RETURN OF THE CONTINENTAL ARMY UNDER THE COMMAND OF HIS EXCELLENCY GEORGE WASHINGTON...FOR THE MONTH OF DECEMBER 1780, ELEPHANT FOLIO OF WASHINGTON RETURNS, WILLIAM L. CLEMENTS LIBRARY.

A. At the end of December, the German battalion either had just disbanded or was about to disband. Those men from the battalion who were from Pennsylvania were ordered to join the Pennsylvania line, and those from Maryland, the Maryland line.
B. These figures represent Israel Angell's old 2nd Rhode Island regiment, which was in the process of consolidating with Christopher Greene's old 1st Rhode Island regiment to form one Rhode Island Continental regiment.
C. The 1st Canadian regiment had just been disbanded. Those of its men who were not reassigned to specific state regiments were added to Moses Hazen's 2nd Canadian regiment, which was also known as Congress's Own or Hazen's Own. Although Hazen was promoted to Brevet Brigadier General on June 29, 1781, he continued to be associated with the regiment until the end of the war. The men in the regiment were not all Canadian.
D. Four commissioned officers in Captain Simon Spalding's Wyoming Valley company plus one colonel for all the companies in the Wyoming Valley.
E. Four staff officers in Lieutenant Colonel Ebenezer Sprout's 12th Massachusetts regiment plus one chaplain for the entire brigade.
F. This figure represents one adjutant and one surgeon for all of the companies in the Wyoming Valley, not staff officers in Captain Simon Spalding's Wyoming Valley company.
G. Including 916 men in Washington's infantry discharged for inability.

JANUARY 1781

BRIGADE	UNIT	COMMANDING OFFICER	PRESENT FIT FOR DUTY & ON DUTY: COMMISSIONED OFFICERS	NONCOMMISSIONED OFFICERS	STAFF OFFICERS	RANK & FILE	TOTAL	RANK & FILE SICK, ON FURLOUGH, ETC.: SICK PRESENT	SICK ABSENT	ON COMMAND & EXTRA SERVICE	ON FURLOUGH	CONFINED	FURLOUGH EXPIRED	RECRUITING	GRAND TOTAL	ALTERATIONS: DEATHS	DESERTED	TAKEN PRISONER	DISCHARGED	JOINED, ENLISTED, RECRUITED	LOCATION
	FORCES UNDER COMMANDER-IN-CHIEF GENERAL GEORGE WASHINGTON																				
1st Conn.	1st Conn. A	John Durkee	2	22	3	41	68	10	20	181	41				320		1		3	10	West Point & vicinity
1st Conn.	3rd Conn.	Samuel Blatchley Webb	1	22	3	35	61	16	13	108	19				217		5		5	4	West Point & vicinity
1st Conn.	5th Conn.	Lt. Col. Isaac Sherman	3	21	3	33	60	16	7	145	17				245		2		1	5	West Point & vicinity
2nd Conn.	2nd Conn.	Heman Swift		15	2	25	42	9	16	151	16				234				2	10	West Point & vicinity
2nd Conn.	4th Conn.	Zebulon Butler		20	3	33	56	15	27	181	34				313	1	1		6	10	West Point & vicinity
1st Mass.	3rd Mass.	John Greaton	4	31	4	42	81	5	12	104	6				208		2		68	7	West Point & vicinity
1st Mass.	6th Mass.	Lt. Col. Calvin Smith	4	27	4	44	79	6	4	98	3				190		1		63	1	West Point & vicinity
1st Mass.	8th Mass.	Michael Jackson	9	30	4	42	85	3	7	82	5				182				51		West Point & vicinity
1st Mass.	10th Mass.	Benjamin Tupper	5	27	4	54	90	13	2	98	2				205				85	2	West Point & vicinity
2nd Mass.	2nd Mass.	Lt. Col. Ebenezer Sprout	8	32	4	31	75	11	5	109	3				203		1		75	2	West Point & vicinity
2nd Mass.	4th Mass.	William Shepard	3	25	4	49	81	10	3	84	3				181				20	1	West Point & vicinity
2nd Mass.	9th Mass.	Henry Jackson	5	29	2	29	65	4	6	110	9				194				47	3	West Point & vicinity
3rd Mass.	1st Mass.	Joseph Vose	10	20	3	33	66	12	6	132	2				218				48	3	West Point & vicinity
3rd Mass.	5th Mass.	Rufus Putnam	5	30	4	21	60	11	11	109	9				200		1		100	1	West Point & vicinity
3rd Mass.	7th Mass.	Lt. Col. John Brooks	8	34	4	29	75	7	2	108	6				198		1		93		West Point & vicinity
Stark	1st N.H.	Alexander Scammell	1	28	2	30	61	8	4	174	7				254				2		West Point & vicinity
Stark	2nd N.H.	Lt. Col. George Reid	1	29	1	22	53	8	10	159	7				237		7		11	2	West Point & vicinity
Stark	R.I. B	Israel Angell		30	4	45	79	21	5	143	3				251	1			1	2	West Point & vicinity
	Canadian B	Moses Hazen	18	37	3	203	261	23	28	100	3				415			2	8	29	Fishkill, N.Y.
	R.I. det.	Christopher Greene		8		26	34	11	1	28					74						Rhode Island
Clinton	1st N.Y.	Goose Van Schaick	22	63	5	371	461	41	14	41	42				599						Albany, N.Y. area
Clinton	2nd N.Y.	Philip Van Cortlandt	4	31	2	138	175	31	18	273	43				540						Albany, N.Y. area
	TOTAL OF INFANTRY		113	611	68	1376	2168	291	221	2718	280				5678	2	22	2	689	92	
	CAVALRY																				
	2nd cont'l.	Elisha Sheldon	7	25	3	126	161		5	10	45	2			223				2	158 E	Springfield, Mass. area
	ARTILLERY																				
	7 cos. 2nd cont'l.	John Lamb	7	51	3	48	109	40	7	83	28		1	1	527				2	5	New Windsor, N.Y.
	7 cos. 3rd cont'l.	John Crane	8	37	4	54	103										2		3		New Windsor, N.Y.
	1 co. 4th cont'l.	Thomas Proctor	1	1		5	7														New Windsor, N.Y.
	West Point det.		13	60		75	148									1	2		50	2	West Point, N.Y.
	TOTAL OF ARTILLERY		29	149	7	182	367	40	7	83	28		1	1	527	1	4		55	7	
	SAPPERS AND MINERS																				
	Sapper and miner cos.	Lt. Col. Jean Baptiste Gouvion	2	2	1	19	24	2		23	8				57		2				West Point & vicinity
	INVALIDS																				
	Philadelphia unit	Lewis Nicola	7	45	5	215	272								272						Philadelphia, Pa.
	Boston det.	Capt. Thomas Arnold	7	15		74	96								96						Boston, Mass.
	TOTAL OF INVALIDS		14	60	5	289	368								368 C						
	TOTAL OF WASHINGTON'S ARMY		165	847	84	1992	3088	333	233	2834	361	2	1	1	6853	3	28	2	746 D	257	

OFFICERS SICK, ON FURLOUGH, ETC.	WASHINGTON'S ARMY (EXCEPT INVALIDS)			
	COMMISSIONED	NONCOMMISSIONED	STAFF	TOTAL
Sick Present	22	56		78
Sick Absent	30	31	1	62
On Command	188	311	10	509
On Extra Service	29	34	2	65
On Furlough	206	137	27	370
Recruiting	22	25		47
On the Staff	90			90
Prisoners of War	17	3		20
Fourlough Expired	9	3		12
In Arrest	1			1
TOTAL	614	600	40	1254

SOURCE OF THIS REPORT

1. MONTHLY RETURN OF THE CONTINENTAL ARMY UNDER THE COMMAND OF HIS EXCELLENCY GEORGE WASHINGTON. . . FOR JANUARY 1781, ELEPHANT FOLIO OF WASHINGTON RETURNS, WILLIAM L. CLEMENTS LIBRARY.

1a. Monthly Return of the Continental Army under. . . Washington. . . January 1781, Record Group 93, National Archives. [Contains the same figures, but only to the brigade level.]

A. These units are not identical to those that appeared on the December report. A major reduction in the number of regiments and consolidation and reorganization had gone into effect.
B. Israel Angell's old 2nd Rhode Island regiment and Christopher Greene's old 1st Rhode Island regiment had been consolidated into one Rhode Island Continental regiment, but they had not yet actually physically joined.
C. The National Archives manuscript notes that no returns were received for the Southern and Western Departments, for the Pennsylvania and New Jersey lines, and for the cavalry, except for Sheldon's regiment.
D. Including twelve men in Washington's infantry discharged for inability.
E. This figure may mislead the reader. Although this large number of men had been recruited or had joined Elisha Sheldon's 2nd Continental cavalry from other troops, the manuscript also contains an unusual counterbalancing entry of 130 men "Transfered to other Troops."

FEBRUARY 1781

BRIGADE	UNIT	COMMANDING OFFICER	PRESENT FIT FOR DUTY & ON DUTY: COMMISSIONED OFFICERS	NONCOMMISSIONED OFFICERS	STAFF OFFICERS	RANK & FILE	TOTAL	RANK & FILE SICK, ON FURLOUGH, ETC.: SICK PRESENT	SICK ABSENT	ON COMMAND & EXTRA SERVICE	ON FURLOUGH	CONFINED	RECRUITING	GRAND TOTAL	ALTERATIONS: DEATHS	DESERTED	TAKEN PRISONER	DISCHARGED	JOINED, ENLISTED, RECRUITED	LOCATION
	FORCES UNDER COMMANDER-IN-CHIEF GENERAL GEORGE WASHINGTON																			
1st Conn.	1st Conn.	John Durkee	6	21	3	50	80	9	22	168	28			307		20		7	9	West Point & vicinity
	3rd Conn.	Samuel Blatchley Webb	7	21	3	32	63	14	15	98	18			208		5		15	3	West Point & vicinity
	5th Conn.	Lt. Col. Isaac Sherman	6	16	4	28	54	10	8	143	19			234		14		3	8	West Point & vicinity
2nd Conn.	2nd Conn.	Heman Swift	4	27	3	48	82	10	12	139	15			258		4		5	20	West Point & vicinity
	4th Conn.	Zebulon Butler	7	24	1	68	100	18	26	148	22			314		3	1		5	West Point & vicinity
1st Mass.	3rd Mass.	John Greaton	3	27	2	40	72	5	11	96	8			192				11	2	West Point & vicinity
	6th Mass.	Lt. Col. Calvin Smith	4	28	5	41	78	7	4	91	3			183				9		West Point & vicinity
	8th Mass.	Michael Jackson	15	27	4	35	81	4	4	74	9			172		1	1	9		West Point & vicinity
	10th Mass.	Benjamin Tupper	5	23	3	42	73	11	3	89	7			183	2	1	1	14	1	West Point & vicinity
2nd Mass.	2nd Mass.	Lt. Col. Ebenezer Sprout	8	34	4	30	76	6	2	94	10			188	1			15		West Point & vicinity
	4th Mass.	William Shepard	5	25	4	47	81	6	3	85	4			179		1		2		West Point & vicinity
	9th Mass.	Henry Jackson	4	24	2	36	66	6	5	99	9			185		1		2	1	West Point & vicinity
3rd Mass.	1st Mass.	Joseph Vose	8	20	3	71	102	7	5	71	6			191	1	3	2	22	3	West Point & vicinity
	5th Mass.	Rufus Putnam	9	30	4	42	85	7	10	72	10			184	1	4		16	1	West Point & vicinity
	7th Mass.	Lt. Col. John Brooks	9	37	3	46	95	7	2	78	7			189			1	11		West Point & vicinity
Stark	1st N.H.	Alexander Scammell	1	19	2	36	58	16	6	142	9			231		1	1	12		West Point & vicinity
	2nd N.H.	Lt. Col. George Reid	3	28	2	30	63	12	9	134	10			228			3	8		West Point & vicinity
	R.I.	Christopher Greene	5	23	1	130	159	2	55	161	14			391	2				58	West Point & vicinity
	Canadian	Moses Hazen	19	44	3	216	282	27	19	87	4			419		4			3	West Point & vicinity
	TOTAL OF INFANTRY		128	498	56	1068	1750	184	221	2069	212			4436	7	62	10	161	114	
	CAVALRY																			
	2nd cont'l.	Elisha Sheldon	5	24	4	141	174		5	12	30	2		223				1	3	Springfield, Mass. area
	ARTILLERY																			
	7 cos. 2nd cont'l.	John Lamb	5	40	3	54	102	48	6	75	44		8	529		3		2	31	New Windsor, N.Y.
	6 cos. 3rd cont'l.	John Crane	8	36	3	46	93											2		New Windsor, N.Y.
	1 co. 4th cont'l.	Thomas Proctor	1	1		3	5									1				New Windsor, N.Y.
	West Point det.		11	58		79	148									3		3	6	West Point, N.Y.
	TOTAL OF ARTILLERY		25	135	6	182	348	48	6	75	44		8	529		7		7	37	
	TOTAL OF WASHINGTON'S ARMY		158	657	66	1391	2272	232	232	2156	286	2	8	5188	7	69	10	169	B 154	
	WESTERN DEPARTMENT UNDER COLONEL DANIEL BRODHEAD																			
Brodhead	8th Pa.[A]	Daniel Brodhead	9	25	4	103	141	4		4	6			155						Fort Pitt, Pa.
	9th Va.[A]	John Gibson	11	21	5	125	162	10	2	5	10			189						Fort Pitt, Pa.
	Additional (Md. corps)	(late) Moses Rawlings		8		39	47	2			1			50						Fort Pitt, Pa.
	TOTAL OF WESTERN DEPARTMENT		20	54	9	267	350	16	2	9	17			394						
	SOUTHERN DEPARTMENT UNDER MAJOR GENERAL NATHANAEL GREENE (Effectives Only)																			
	Va. cont'l. brig.		21	51	4	472	548													High Rock Ford, N.C.
	Md. cont'l. brig.		32	80	5	496	613													High Rock Ford, N.C.
	Va. militia	Gen. Edward Stevens	53	60	5	609	727													High Rock Ford, N.C.
	N.C. militia	Francis Locke	29	28	1	281	339													High Rock Ford, N.C.
	TOTAL OF INFANTRY		135	219	15	1858	2227													
	ARTILLERY																			
	Artillery in Southern Department		6	7		55	68													High Rock Ford, N.C.
	TOTAL OF GREENE'S ARMY		141	226	15	1913	2295													
	GRAND TOTAL		319	937	90	3571	4917													

OFFICERS SICK, ON FURLOUGH, ETC.	WASHINGTON'S ARMY			
	COMMISSIONED	NONCOMMISSIONED	STAFF	TOTAL
Sick Present	14	57		71
Sick Absent	28	36	1	65
On Command	127	245	11	383
On Extra Service	32	34	1	67
On Furlough	210	146	28	384
Recruiting	20	37		57
On the Staff	84			84
Prisoners of War	9	2		11
Furlough Expired	14	1	1	16
TOTAL	538	558	42	1138

SOURCES OF THIS REPORT

1. MONTHLY RETURN OF THE CONTINENTAL ARMY UNDER THE COMMAND OF HIS EXCELLENCY GEORGE WASHINGTON. . . FOR THE MONTH OF FEBRUARY 1781, ELEPHANT FOLIO OF WASHINGTON RETURNS, WILLIAM L. CLEMENTS LIBRARY. [THE ARTILLERY SECTION OF THE RETURN APPEARS ON THE FOLLOWING PAGE OF THE FOLIO.]

1a. Monthly Return of the Continental Army under. . . Washington. . . February 1781, Record Group 93, National Archives. [Contains the same figures, but only to the brigade level.]

2. RETURN OF THE WESTERN DEPARTMENT UNDER COLONEL DANIEL BRODHEAD, REMOVED FROM THE APRIL MONTHLY RETURN [SOURCE 1 ON THIS VOLUME'S APRIL 1781 REPORT] BECAUSE THE NATIONAL ARCHIVES VERSION OF THAT RETURN NOTES THAT THE FIGURES FOR THE WESTERN DEPARTMENT DATED FROM FEBRUARY 26. THEREFORE THIS SECTION, WHICH WAS LATE IN ARRIVING, HAS BEEN MOVED TO ITS PROPER MONTH. SEE INTRODUCTION.

3. FIELD RETURN OF THE ARMY COMMANDED BY THE HONBLE. MAJOR GENERAL GREENE, MARCH 1, 1781, GREENE PAPERS, WILLIAM L. CLEMENTS LIBRARY.

A. These units and commanders are old designations that were still in effect at the remote Fort Pitt, although they officially had been changed. In the reduction and rearrangement of the Pennsylvania line, which was put into effect after the mutiny of that line, Daniel Brodhead became colonel of the 1st Pennsylvania regiment. During February 1781, Virginia's eleven Continental regiments were consolidated into eight, and the 9th Virginia ceased to exist officially as a separate organization.

B. Including seven men in Washington's infantry and one man in Washington's cavalry discharged for inability.

MARCH 1781

BRIGADE	UNIT	COMMANDING OFFICER	PRESENT FIT FOR DUTY & ON DUTY: COMMISSIONED OFFICERS	NONCOMMISSIONED OFFICERS	STAFF OFFICERS	RANK & FILE	TOTAL	RANK & FILE SICK, ON FURLOUGH, ETC.: SICK PRESENT	SICK ABSENT	ON COMMAND & EXTRA SERVICE	ON FURLOUGH	CONFINED	FURLOUGH EXPIRED	RECRUITING	GRAND TOTAL	ALTERATIONS: DEATHS	DESERTED	TAKEN PRISONER	DISCHARGED	JOINED, ENLISTED, RECRUITED	LOCATION
	FORCES UNDER COMMANDER-IN-CHIEF GENERAL GEORGE WASHINGTON																				
1st Conn.	1st Conn.	John Durkee	12	37	3	153	205	10	16	174	22				427						West Point & vicinity
	3rd Conn.	Samuel Blatchley Webb	8	36	2A	85	131	12	9	92	11				255		19		4	192	West Point & vicinity
	5th Conn.	Lt. Col. Isaac Sherman	8	21	4	69	102	9	9	123	19				262						West Point & vicinity
2nd Conn.	2nd Conn.	Heman Swift	7	35	2	81	125	9	10	138	5				287		5		2	27	West Point & vicinity
	4th Conn.	Zebulon Butler	8	38	1	103	150	9	22	154	7				342		4		1	25	West Point & vicinity
1st Mass.	3rd Mass.	John Greaton	6	35	2	42	85	5	7	91	10				198		1	1	3	1	West Point & vicinity
	6th Mass.	Lt. Col. Calvin Smith	5	23	4	58	90	5	2	84	3				184				2	8	West Point & vicinity
	8th Mass.	Michael Jackson	12	25	4	64	105	6	4	64	10				189		1		6	27	West Point & vicinity
	10th Mass.	Benjamin Tupper	7	28	4	49	88	13	2	74	6				183		2		11	6	West Point & vicinity
2nd Mass.	2nd Mass.	Lt. Col. Ebenezer Sprout	11	30	4	46	91	3	1	82	8				185		2	1	5	4	West Point & vicinity
	4th Mass.	William Shepard	6	27	2	43	78	5	1	90	3				177		2		2	2	West Point & vicinity
	9th Mass.	Henry Jackson	5	17	2	45	69	3	6	87	9				174		1		4		West Point & vicinity
3rd Mass.	1st Mass.	Joseph Vose	9	19	3	63	94	4	5	81	6				190				2	2	West Point & vicinity
	5th Mass.	Rufus Putnam	8	26	4	62	100	4	9	61	12				186				2	8	West Point & vicinity
	7th Mass.	Lt. Col. John Brooks	9	38	3	55	105	4	2	70	4				185	1	2		4	2	West Point & vicinity
	1st N.Y.	Goose Van Schaick	12	36	3	148	199	19	43	286	9				556	1	5				West Point & vicinity
Stark	1st N.H.	Alexander Scammell	5	27	2	70	104	10	5	117	9				245			1	3	6	West Point & vicinity
	2nd N.H.	Lt. Col. George Reid	3	29	2	31	65	11	8	130	11				225				3		West Point & vicinity
	R.I.	Chrisopher Greene	4	27	4	171	206	30	104	120	11				471	1	8			86	West Point & vicinity
	Canadian	Moses Hazen	13	37	3	139	192	36	14	164	16				422		3			4	West Point & vicinity
	TOTAL OF INFANTRY		158	591	58	1577	2384	207	279	2282	191				5343	3	55	3	54	400	
	CAVALRY																				
	2nd cont'l.	Elisha Sheldon	2	22	2	162	188	6	6	15	19	1			235					19	Springfield, Mass. area
	ARTILLERY																				
	7 cos. 2nd cont'l.	John Lamb	6	47	3	79	135										6		3	22	New Windsor, N.Y.
	6 cos. 3rd cont'l.	John Crane	8	40	3	51	102	38	8	76	30		1	6	542		2		1	1	New Windsor, N.Y.
	West Point det. (7 cos.)		12	53		81	146												6	6	West Point, N.Y.
	TOTAL OF ARTILLERY		26	140	6	211	383	38	8	76	30		1	6	542		8		10	29	
	TOTAL OF WASHINGTON'S ARMY		186	753	66	1950	2955	251	293	2373	240	1	1	6	6120	3	63	3	64B	448	

OFFICERS SICK, ON FURLOUGH, ETC.	WASHINGTON'S ARMY			
	COMMISSIONED	NONCOMMISSIONED	STAFF	TOTAL
Sick Present	12	39		51
Sick Absent	29	38	1	68
On Command	136	281	9	426
On Extra Service	36	31	2	69
On Furlough	195	119	34	348
Recruiting	23	34		57
On the Staff	84			84
Prisoners of War	6	2		8
Furlough Expired	10	3	1	14
TOTAL	531	547	47	1125

SOURCE OF THIS REPORT

1. MONTHLY RETURN OF THE CONTINENTAL ARMY UNDER THE COMMAND OF HIS EXCELLENCY GEORGE WASHINGTON. . . FOR THE MONTH OF MARCH 1781, ELEPHANT FOLIO OF WASHINGTON RETURNS, WILLIAM L. CLEMENTS LIBRARY. [THE ARTILLERY SECTION OF THE RETURN APPEARS ON THE FOLLOWING PAGE OF THE FOLIO.]

1a. Monthly Return of the Continental Army under. . . Washington. . . March 1781, Record Group 93, National Archives. [Contains the same figures, but only to the brigade level.]

A. Three staff officers in Lieutenant Colonel Isaac Sherman's 5th Connecticut regiment plus one chaplain for the entire brigade.
B. Including four men in Washington's infantry discharged for inability.

APRIL 1781

BRIGADE	UNIT	COMMANDING OFFICER	PRESENT FIT FOR DUTY & ON DUTY: COMMISSIONED OFFICERS	NONCOMMISSIONED OFFICERS	STAFF OFFICERS	RANK & FILE	TOTAL	RANK & FILE SICK, ON FURLOUGH, ETC.: SICK PRESENT	SICK ABSENT	ON COMMAND & EXTRA SERVICE	ON FURLOUGH	RECRUITING	FURLOUGH EXPIRED	GRAND TOTAL	ALTERATIONS: DEATHS	DESERTED	TAKEN PRISONER	DISCHARGED	JOINED, ENLISTED, RECRUITED	LOCATION
	FORCES UNDER COMMANDER-IN-CHIEF GENERAL GEORGE WASHINGTON																			
1st Conn.	1st Conn.	John Durkee	8	39	3	155	205	6	74	133	11			429		9		7	29	West Point & vicinity
	3rd Conn.	Samuel Blatchley Webb	10	34	3	113	160	9	35	78	2			284	1	1		5	52	West Point & vicinity
	5th Conn.	Lt. Col. Isaac Sherman	10	25	2	110	147	13	30	107	11			308				1	52	West Point & vicinity
2nd Conn.	2nd Conn.	Heman Swift	7	31	2	149	189	15	25	125				354		9		4	89	West Point & vicinity
	4th Conn.	Zebulon Butler	7	34	4	109	154	11	44	139	1			349		7	2		28	West Point & vicinity
1st Mass.	3rd Mass.	John Greaton	8	21	2	78	109	10	12	81	7			219		3		5	45	West Point & vicinity
	6th Mass.	Lt. Col. Calvin Smith	6	25	4	92	127	6	12	81	3			229				1	48	West Point & vicinity
	8th Mass.	Michael Jackson	15	22	4	94	135	3	19	50	4			211		13		11	50	West Point & vicinity
	10th Mass.	Benjamin Tupper	7	25	2	83	117	16	8	71	5			217	1	1		5	51	West Point & vicinity
2nd Mass.	2nd Mass.	Lt. Col. Ebenezer Sprout	7	29	2	79	117	4	9	80	7			217				5	47	West Point & vicinity
	4th Mass.	William Shepard	9	33	4	82	128	9	7	85	4			233		1			51	West Point & vicinity
	9th Mass.	Henry Jackson	6	23	3	77	109	3	17	78	8			215				15	50	West Point & vicinity
3rd Mass.	1st Mass.	Joseph Vose	7	16	2	96	121	6	1	87	4			219	1	4		4	49	West Point & vicinity
	5th Mass.	Rufus Putnam	4	27	3	96	130	2	17	70	8			227					48	West Point & vicinity
	7th Mass.	Lt. Col. John Brooks	10	26	2	85	123	1	4	79	3			210		4			44	West Point & vicinity
	1st N.Y.	Goose Van Schaick	14	37	3	187	241	30	35	256	7			569		10			16	West Point & vicinity
Stark	1st N.H.	Alexander Scammell	4	21	3	32	60	59	2	111	8			240	1	1		2	9	West Point & vicinity
	2nd N.H.	Lt. Col. George Reid	4	21	2	14	41	43	8	120	11			223		1			7	West Point & vicinity
	R.I.	Christopher Greene	8	25	4	87	124	35	99	223				481	5	14			32	West Point & vicinity
	Canadian	Moses Hazen	16	48	3	187	254	51	11	108	13			437	1	3			31	West Point & vicinity
	TOTAL OF INFANTRY		167	562	57	2005	2791	332	469	2162	117			5871	10	81	2	65	828	
	CAVALRY																			
	2nd cont'l.	Elisha Sheldon	6	23	3	193	225	4	7	11	18			265	1	1		3	31	Springfield, Mass. area
	ARTILLERY																			
	7 cos. 2nd cont'l.	John Lamb	7	54	3	86	150									5		1	7	New Windsor, N.Y.
	6 cos. 3rd cont'l.	John Crane	8	40	3	55	106	30	14	72	21	8	3	517		1		2	1	New Windsor, N.Y.
	West Point det.		9	41		63	113								1	3			8	West Point, N.Y.
	TOTAL OF ARTILLERY		24	135	6	204	369	30	14	72	21	8	3	517	1	9		3	16	
	SAPPERS AND MINERS																			
	3 cos.		2	2	1	31	36		4	8	4			52		4			5	West Point & vicinity
	INVALIDS																			
	Philadelphia unit	Lewis Nicola	10	40	5	206	261							261						Philadelphia, Pa.
	Boston det.	Capt. Moses McFarland	9	19		116	144							144						Boston, Mass.
	TOTAL OF INVALIDS		19	59	5	322	405							405						
	TOTAL OF WASHINGTON'S ARMY		218	781	72	2755	3826	366	494	2253	160	8	3	7110	12	95	2	71	880	
	FOURTH CONTINENTAL CAVALRY UNDER COLONEL STEPHEN MOYLAN																			
	4th cont'l.	Stephen Moylan	8	16	2	73	99	3		6	4	1		113		1		1	3	Lancaster, Pa.
	GRAND TOTAL		226	797	74	2828	3925	369	494	2259	164	9	3	7223	12	96	2	72[A]	883	

APRIL 1781
(continued)

OFFICERS SICK, ON FURLOUGH, ETC.	WASHINGTON'S ARMY (EXCEPT INVALIDS)[B]			
	COMMISSIONED	NONCOMMISSIONED	STAFF	TOTAL
Sick Present	9	45		54
Sick Absent	30	91	2	123
On Command	163	282	17	462
On Extra Service	36	30	4	70
On Furlough	90	48	16	154
Recruiting	20	35	1	56
On the Staff	98			98
Prisoners of War	6	3		9
Furlough Expired	70	10	8	88
In Arrest	1			1
TOTAL	523	544	48	1115

SOURCES OF THIS REPORT

1. MONTHLY RETURN OF THE CONTINENTAL ARMY UNDER THE COMMAND OF HIS EXCELLENCY GEORGE WASHINGTON...APRIL 1781, ELEPHANT FOLIO OF WASHINGTON RETURNS, WILLIAM L. CLEMENTS LIBRARY. [THE PORTION OF THIS RETURN GIVING THE STATE OF THE FORCES AT FORT PITT, WHICH ORIGINALLY WAS MADE OUT ON FEBRUARY 26, HAS BEEN MOVED TO ITS PROPER PLACE ON OUR FEBRUARY REPORT. SEE THAT REPORT.]

1a. Monthly Return of the Continental Army under...Washington...April 1781, Record Group 93, National Archives. [Contains the same figures, but only to the brigade level.]

2. RETURN OF THE FOURTH CONTINENTAL CAVALRY UNDER COLONEL STEPHEN MOYLAN, REMOVED FROM THE MAY MONTHLY RETURN [SOURCE 1 ON THIS VOLUME'S MAY 1781 REPORT] BECAUSE THE NATIONAL ARCHIVES VERSION OF THAT RETURN NOTES THAT THE FIGURES FOR THIS REGIMENT DATED FROM APRIL 16. THEREFORE, THIS SECTION, WHICH WAS LATE IN ARRIVING, HAS BEEN MOVED TO ITS PROPER MONTH. SEE INTRODUCTION.

A. Including thirteen men in Washington's infantry and one man in Moylan's cavalry discharged for inability.

B. This section of officers sick, on furlough, etc., may include a few men from the February 26 return of the Western Department, which we have moved back to its proper place on our February 1781 monthly report. It is likely, however, that this is not the case, because that return was incomplete. It included no figures for alterations or for vacancies and may well have not reported officers beyond those who were present fit for duty. Since the section for officers who were sick, etc. is not broken down, it is not possible to be certain, but in any case, only a few men would have been involved.

MAY 1781

UNIT	COMMANDING OFFICER	PRESENT FIT FOR DUTY & ON DUTY: COMMISSIONED OFFICERS	NONCOMMISSIONED OFFICERS	STAFF OFFICERS	RANK & FILE	TOTAL	RANK & FILE SICK, ON FURLOUGH, ETC.: SICK PRESENT	SICK ABSENT	ON COMMAND & EXTRA SERVICE	ON FURLOUGH	CONFINED	FURLOUGH EXPIRED	RECRUITING	GRAND TOTAL	ALTERATIONS: DEATHS	DESERTED	TAKEN PRISONER	DISCHARGED	JOINED, ENLISTED, RECRUITED	LOCATION
FORCES UNDER COMMANDER-IN-CHIEF GENERAL GEORGE WASHINGTON																				
1st Conn.	John Durkee	10	31	4	147	192	17	10	198	9				426		2		3	11	West Point & vicinity
3rd Conn.	Samuel Blatchley Webb	6	33	3 B	187	229	25	7	110	2				373		5		2	102	West Point & vicinity
5th Conn.	Lt. Col. Isaac Sherman	9	26	4	118	157	14	14	142	7				334		4		1	32	West Point & vicinity
2nd Conn.	Heman Swift	12	40	3 C	157	212	14	5	156					387	4	5			28	West Point & vicinity
4th Conn.	Zebulon Butler	8	40	4	122	174	9	18	166					367		3		1	16	West Point & vicinity
3rd Mass.	John Greaton	9	29	3	114	155	17	8	99	4				283	2	2		7	69	West Point & vicinity
6th Mass.	Lt. Col. Calvin Smith	5	31	5	111	152	8	4	115	2				281		3		6	55	West Point & vicinity
8th Mass.	Michael Jackson	15	27	2 D	145	189	8	7	92	3				299		2		3	92	West Point & vicinity
10th Mass.	Benjamin Tupper	6	28	3	131	168	13	6	98	4				289				2	75	West Point & vicinity
2nd Mass.	Lt. Col. Ebenezer Sprout	9	31	1	103	144	10		121	5				280		2			64	West Point & vicinity
4th Mass.	William Shepard	9	30	4	93	136	12	2	127	1				278				3	54	West Point & vicinity
9th Mass.	Henry Jackson	7	26	3	104	140	25	6	112	5				288	3	4		6	88	West Point & vicinity
1st Mass.	Joseph Vose	3	16	2	109	130	8	1	124	4				267	1	1		4	62	West Point & vicinity
5th Mass.	Rufus Putnam	7	28	4	100	139	12	11	112	4				278				3	58	West Point & vicinity
7th Mass.	Lt. Col. John Brooks	7	30	2	128	167	7	2	112	3				291	1	3			86	West Point & vicinity
1st N.Y.	Goose Van Schaick	9	34	2	166	211	29	26	292	8				566	1	8			16	West Point & vicinity
1st N.H.	Alexander Scammell	13	29	5	166	213	14	3	119	4				353		2	5	2	106	West Point & vicinity
2nd N.H.	Lt. Col. George Reid	10	35	4 E	151	200	10	4	126	4				344	1	1	1	4	114	West Point & vicinity
R.I.	Lt. Col. Jeremiah Olney	9	36	4	224	273	47	17	145					482	10	19	21		39	West Point & vicinity
Canadian A	Moses Hazen	18	45	2	183	248	47	10	104	10				419					6	West Point & vicinity
1st N.J.	Matthias Ogden	4	16	3	70	93	4	15	255	19				386						New Jersey
2nd N.J.	Elias Dayton	7	21	3	64	95	22	14	287	22				440						New Jersey
TOTAL OF INFANTRY		192	662	70	2893	3817	372	190	3212	120				7711	23	66	27	47	1173	
CAVALRY																				
2nd cont'l.	Elisha Sheldon	7	27	4	202	240	9	7	10	18	6			290		3		1	24	Springfield, Mass. area
ARTILLERY																				
6 cos. 2nd cont'l.	John Lamb	8	47	2	94	151	24	10	30	2		5	2	458		2			10	New Windsor, N. Y.
7 cos. 3rd cont'l.	John Crane	16	77	3	138	234										7			81	New Windsor, N. Y.
TOTAL OF ARTILLERY		24	124	5	232	385	24	10	30	2		5	2	458 F		9			91	
SAPPERS AND MINERS																				
3 cos.		4	2	1	38	45	1	1	7	1				55					1	West Point & vicinity
TOTAL OF WASHINGTON'S ARMY		227	815	80	3365	4487	406	208	3259	141	6	5	2	8514	23	78	27	48 G	1289	

BRIGADE: 1st Conn. | 2nd Conn. | 1st Mass. | 2nd Mass. | 3rd Mass. | Stark

OFFICERS SICK, ON FURLOUGH, ETC.	WASHINGTON'S ARMY[H]			
	COMMISSIONED	NONCOMMISSIONED	STAFF	TOTAL
Sick Present	9	43		52
Sick Absent	23	31	3	57
On Command	196	350	20	566
On Extra Service	27	20	5	52
On Furlough	78	36	16	130
Recruiting	27	52		79
On the Staff	94			94
Prisoners of War	10	4	1	15
Furlough Expired	46	6	1	53
Confined		1		1
TOTAL	510	543	46	1099

SOURCE OF THIS REPORT

1. MONTHLY RETURN OF THE CONTINENTAL ARMY UNDER THE COMMAND OF HIS EXCELLENCY GEORGE WASHINGTON...MAY 1781, ELEPHANT FOLIO OF WASHINGTON RETURNS, WILLIAM L. CLEMENTS LIBRARY. [THE SECTIONS FOR THE CAVALRY, ARTILLERY, AND SAPPERS AND MINERS APPEAR ON THE FOLLOWING PAGE OF THE FOLIO. THE PORTION OF THIS RETURN GIVING THE STATE OF STEPHEN MOYLAN'S 4th CONTINENTAL CAVALRY, WHICH WAS ORIGINALLY MADE OUT ON APRIL 16, HAS BEEN MOVED TO ITS PROPER PLACE IN OUR APRIL REPORT. SEE THAT REPORT.]

1a. Monthly Return of the Continental Army under... Washington... May 1781, Record Group 93, National Archives. [Contains the same figures, but only to the brigade level.]

A. The National Archives manuscript notes that the return of the New Jersey brigade had been dated May 10.
B. Three staff officers in Lieutenant Colonel Isaac Sherman's 5th Connecticut regiment plus one chaplain for the entire brigade.
C. Three staff officers in Zebulon Butler's 4th Connecticut regiment plus one chaplain for the entire brigade.
D. Two staff officers in Benjamin Tupper's 10th Massachusetts regiment plus one chaplain for the entire brigade.
E. Three staff officers in Lieutenant Colonel Jeremiah Olney's Rhode Island regiment plus one chaplain for the entire brigade.
F. The National Archives manuscript notes that no monthly return was received from the six companies of artillery serving as the artillery detachment at West Point.
G. Including fourteen men in Washington's infantry discharged for inability.
H. This section of officers sick, on furlough, etc., may include a very few men from Stephen Moylan's 4th Continental cavalry. The National Archives manuscript notes that the figures for Moylan's regiment, which has been moved back to its proper place on our April report, not only arrived late but also included no figures for the vacant and wanting to complete categories. Since the section for officers who were sick, etc., is never broken down to the regiment level, it is not possible to remove any officers sick, etc., if any were included. Since the regiment was small, any men from it that may still remain in these totals would be very few and would not distort these figures significantly.

JUNE 1781

BRIGADE	UNIT	COMMANDING OFFICER	PRESENT FIT FOR DUTY & ON DUTY: COMMISSIONED OFFICERS	NONCOMMISSIONED OFFICERS	STAFF OFFICERS	RANK & FILE	TOTAL	RANK & FILE SICK, ON FURLOUGH, ETC.: SICK PRESENT	SICK ABSENT	ON COMMAND & EXTRA SERVICE	ON FURLOUGH	CONFINED	FURLOUGH EXPIRED	RECRUITING	GRAND TOTAL	ALTERATIONS: DEATHS	DESERTED	TAKEN PRISONER	DISCHARGED	JOINED, ENLISTED, RECRUITED	LOCATION
	FORCES UNDER COMMANDER-IN-CHIEF GENERAL GEORGE WASHINGTON																				
N.J.	1st N.J.	Matthias Ogden	7	22	4	87	120	7	11	251	4	8			401		4			11	New Jersey
N.J.	2nd N.J.	Elias Dayton	11	27	3	115	156	10	15	246	19	5			451		5			12	New Jersey
N.Y.	1st N.Y.	Goose Van Schaick	16 A	38	4	437	495	16	18	46	8	2			585		24		2	26	Albany, N.Y. area
N.Y.	2nd N.Y.	Philip Van Cortlandt	17	64	3	379	463	22	17	68	11	2			583	1	16		1	11	Albany, N.Y. area
1st Conn.	1st Conn.	John Durkee	13	40	4	207	264	7	6	157	1				435	3	4		1	7	near Peekskill, N.Y.
1st Conn.	3rd Conn.	Samuel Blatchley Webb	9 B	38	4	204	255	7	10	112					384		1			9	near Peekskill, N.Y.
1st Conn.	5th Conn.	Lt. Col. Isaac Sherman	14	29	4 D	172	219	2	16	129					366		3		1	29	near Peekskill, N.Y.
2nd Conn.	2nd Conn.	Heman Swift	15	39	5	176	235	5	1	143		2			386	1	5		2	8	near Peekskill, N.Y.
2nd Conn.	4th Conn.	Zebulon Butler	11	37	4	158	210	8	15	142					375		1		1	15	near Peekskill, N.Y.
2nd Conn.	R.I.	Lt. Col. Jeremiah Olney	7	35	3	253	298	14	14	151					477	1	10	2		19	near Peekskill, N.Y.
1st Mass.	1st Mass.	Joseph Vose	5	23	2	142	172	4	2	141	3	1			323	1	4		1	63	near Peekskill, N.Y.
1st Mass.	4th Mass.	William Shepard	8	27	4	173	212	6	2	116					336		6			68	near Peekskill, N.Y.
1st Mass.	7th Mass.	Lt. Col. John Brooks	7	27	4 E	175	213	4	3	114	2				336		4			54	near Peekskill, N.Y.
2nd Mass.	2nd Mass.	Lt. Col. Ebenezer Sprout	10	29	2	165	206	7	3	121	2				339		4	1		63	near Peekskill, N.Y.
2nd Mass.	5th Mass.	Rufus Putnam	5 C	30	4	159	198	3	16	118	2	1			338		2		2	69	near Peekskill, N.Y.
2nd Mass.	8th Mass.	Michael Jackson	14	34	3	193	244	6	6	97	1				354	1	5			65	near Peekskill, N.Y.
3rd Mass.	3rd Mass.	John Greaton	9	29	3	150	191	3	11	122	2				329	1	2			55	near Peekskill, N.Y.
3rd Mass.	6th Mass.	Lt. Col. Calvin Smith	7	35	5	161	208	4	9	119					340		4			68	near Peekskill, N.Y.
3rd Mass.	9th Mass.	Henry Jackson	6	29	3	166	204	9	1	111	3				328		5		2	55	near Peekskill, N.Y.
Stark	1st N.H.	Alexander Scammell	10	28	5	234	277	8	5	61	1				352		10		2	21	near Peekskill, N.Y.
Stark	2nd N.H.	Lt. Col. George Reid	9	34	3 F	236	282	10	4	66	3				365	1				29	near Peekskill, N.Y.
Stark	10th Mass.	Benjamin Tupper	8	32	5	220	265	3	9	63	2				342		5			55	near Peekskill, N.Y.
	Canadian	Brevet Brig. Gen. Moses Hazen	9	37	3	179	228	4	43	126	2				403		3			4	Albany, N.Y. area
	Officers present on duty		63	108	4		175								175						
	TOTAL OF INFANTRY		290	871	88	4541	5790	169	237	2820	66	21			9103	10	127	3	15	816	
	CAVALRY																				
	2nd cont'l.	Elisha Sheldon	10	31	4	165	210	3	9	87 G			2		311	1	5		2	123 J	New York state K
	ARTILLERY																				
	2nd cont'l.	John Lamb	7	46	4	77	134	22	21	61	1	2	2	2	421		7			7	New York state K
	3rd cont'l.	John Crane	6	68	3	99	176										4			23	New York state K
	Present on duty		22	84	1	173	280								280						
	TOTAL OF ARTILLERY		35	198	8	349	590	22	21	61	1	2	2	2	701		11			30	
	SAPPERS AND MINERS																				
	3 cos.	Brig. Gen. Louis le Bèque Duportail	3	3		68	74	5	4	3	1				87		1			41	New York state K
	INVALIDS																				
	Philadelphia unit	Lewis Nicola	13	42		188	243								243						Philadelphia, Pa.
	TOTAL OF WASHINGTON'S ARMY		351	1145	100	5311	6907	199	271	2971 H	68	23	4	2	10445	11	144	3	17 I	1010	

OFFICERS SICK, ON FURLOUGH, ETC.	WASHINGTON'S ARMY (EXCEPT INVALIDS)			
	COMMISSIONED	NONCOMMISSIONED	STAFF	TOTAL
Sick Present	6	25	1	32
Sick Absent	31	30	3	64
On Command	188	328	16	532
On Extra Service	15	17	1	33
On Furlough	45	14	9	68
Furlough Expired	33	3	2	38
Absent without Leave		1		1
Recruiting	23	37		60
On the Staff	113			113
Prisoners of War	9	3	1	13
In Arrest	1	1		2
TOTAL	464	459	33	956

SOURCE OF THIS REPORT

1. MONTHLY RETURN OF THE CONTINENTAL ARMY UNDER THE COMMAND OF HIS EXCELLENCY GEORGE WASHINGTON... FOR THE MONTH OF JUNE 1781, ELEPHANT FOLIO OF WASHINGTON RETURNS, WILLIAM L. CLEMENTS LIBRARY.

1a. Monthly Return of the Continental Army under... Washington... June 1781, Record Group 93, National Archives. [Contains the same figures, but only to the brigade level.]

A. Although until this time brigadier generals were generally not included in this section of the returns, from this time on they sometimes do appear here. This figure represents sixteen commissioned officers in Philip Van Cortlandt's 2nd New York regiment plus one brigadier general for the entire brigade.
B. Thirteen commissioned officers in Lieutenant Colonel Isaac Sherman's 5th Connecticut regiment plus one brigadier general for the entire brigade.
C. Thirteen commissioned officers in Michael Jackson's 8th Massachusetts regiment plus one brigadier general for the entire brigade.
D. Three staff officers in Lieutenant Colonel Isaac Sherman's 5th Connecticut regiment plus one chaplain for the entire brigade.
E. Three staff officers in Lieutenant Colonel John Brooks' 7th Massachusetts regiment plus one chaplain for the entire brigade.
F. Four staff officers in Benjamin Tupper's 10th Massachusetts regiment plus one chaplain for the entire brigade.
G. Seventy-three of these men were waiting for horses at Hartford.
H. In his letter to Congress of August 2, 1781, Washington especially noted that the "on command" column on the June monthly return included the large detachment of light infantry with Lafayette in addition to the usual small detached guards for various purposes, boatmen, waggoners, extra artificers, etc.
I. Including three men in Washington's infantry and one man in Washington's cavalry discharged for inability.
J. This large figure for men who were by one method or another added to the regiment (the manuscript in this case says simply "Joined") was counterbalanced by ninety-four men who were "Transferred." For a discussion of these columns see the introduction.
K. In the general area of New Windsor, West Point, and Peekskill; joining or about to join the main army at Peekskill.

JULY 1781

BRIGADE	UNIT	COMMANDING OFFICER	PRESENT FIT FOR DUTY & ON DUTY: COMMISSIONED OFFICERS	NONCOMMISSIONED OFFICERS	STAFF OFFICERS	RANK & FILE	TOTAL	RANK & FILE SICK, ON FURLOUGH, ETC.: SICK PRESENT	SICK ABSENT	ON COMMAND & EXTRA SERVICE	ON FURLOUGH	CONFINED	FURLOUGH EXPIRED	GRAND TOTAL	ALTERATIONS: DEATHS	DESERTED	TAKEN PRISONER	DISCHARGED	JOINED, ENLISTED, RECRUITED	LOCATION
	FORCES UNDER COMMANDER-IN-CHIEF GENERAL GEORGE WASHINGTON																			
N.J.	1st N.J.	Matthias Ogden	11	22	3	149	185	6	15	198		4		408		17		1	34	west bank of the Hudson
N.J.	2nd N.J.	Elias Dayton	14	37	4	171	226	13	23	180	5			447	1	12		3	7	west bank of the Hudson
1st Conn.	1st Conn.	John Durkee	11	38	4	197	250	16	7	154				427		7	2		6	near Dobbs Ferry, N.Y.
1st Conn.	3rd Conn.	Samuel Blatchley Webb	6 [A]	38	4 [E]	208	256	9	6	135				406		2		1	32	near Dobbs Ferry, N.Y.
1st Conn.	5th Conn.	Lt. Col. Isaac Sherman	11	29	4	176	220	14	12	143				389	2	1	1		32	near Dobbs Ferry, N.Y.
2nd Conn.	2nd Conn.	Heman Swift	11	35	5	188	239	8	3	147				397		4		1	25	near Dobbs Ferry, N.Y.
2nd Conn.	4th Conn.	Zebulon Butler	9	40	4	180	233	10	13	147				403	1	1	3		33	near Dobbs Ferry, N.Y.
2nd Conn.	R.I.	Lt. Col. Jeremiah Olney	11	35	5	247	298	10	15	156		1		480	3	3	1		7	near Dobbs Ferry, N.Y.
1st Mass.	1st Mass.	Joseph Vose	8	26	4	162	200	4	2	144	1	1		352	1	2	2		29	near Dobbs Ferry, N.Y.
1st Mass.	4th Mass.	William Shepard	10 [B]	28	3 [F]	152	193	9	7	140		1		350		2			15	near Dobbs Ferry, N.Y.
1st Mass.	7th Mass.	Lt. Col. John Brooks	7	28	4	153	192	6	8	146		1		353		3		1	21	near Dobbs Ferry, N.Y.
2nd Mass.	2nd Mass.	Lt. Col. Ebenezer Sprout	12	31	3	169	215	6	6	134	1			362		4		1	23	near Dobbs Ferry, N.Y.
2nd Mass.	5th Mass.	Rufus Putnam	8 [C]	26	4	147	185	11	14	129		1		340	1	12		4	20	near Dobbs Ferry, N.Y.
2nd Mass.	8th Mass.	Michael Jackson	13	29	3	178	223	9	9	113	1			355	2	5			15	near Dobbs Ferry, N.Y.
3rd Mass.	3rd Mass.	John Greaton	7	27	4	155	193	11	11	134				349	1	6			31	near Dobbs Ferry, N.Y.
3rd Mass.	6th Mass.	Lt. Col. Calvin Smith	8	32	5	162	207	5	9	134				355	1	2		1	23	near Dobbs Ferry, N.Y.
3rd Mass.	9th Mass.	Henry Jackson	9	31	2	181	223	6	2	132				363		4			37	near Dobbs Ferry, N.Y.
N.H.	1st N.H.	Alexander Scammell	6	27	5	176	214	12	4	127				357	1				13	near Dobbs Ferry, N.Y.
N.H.	2nd N.H.	Lt. Col. George Reid	10	34	2 [G]	166	212	8	12	133	1			366		1		1	4	near Dobbs Ferry, N.Y.
N.H.	10th Mass.	Benjamin Tupper	10	28	5	160	203	16	13	122	1			355	1	2	2		21	near Dobbs Ferry, N.Y.
	1st N.Y.	Goose Van Schaick	25	48	4	361	438	31	33	53	3	9		567		2		1	5	West Point, N.Y.
	Canadian	Brevet Brig. Gen. Moses Hazen	14	38	3	208	263	30	26	85	4			408		1			1	West Point, N.Y.
Waterbury	1st bn., Conn. state brig.	Maj. Edward Shipman	8 [D]	23	5	184	220	9		6	4			239		9	2		10	near Dobbs Ferry, N.Y.
Waterbury	2nd bn., Conn. state brig.	Maj. Elijah Humphrys	7	14	2	163	186	4	4	2	6			202		1	1		4	near Dobbs Ferry, N.Y.
	Officers present on duty		59	89	2		150							150						
	TOTAL OF INFANTRY		305	833	93	4393	5624	263	254	2994	27	18		9180	15	103	14	15	448	
	CAVALRY																			
	2nd cont'l.	Elisha Sheldon	9	36	4	185	234	13	12	45				304		5			4	near Dobbs Ferry, N.Y.
	ARTILLERY																			
	2nd cont'l.	John Lamb	20	57	3	83	163	7	23	140	1	2	1	542	1	8			12	near Dobbs Ferry, N.Y.
	3rd cont'l.	John Crane	15	82	3	105	205								1	1		1	1	near Dobbs Ferry, N.Y.
	Present on duty		15	48	1	89	153							153						
	TOTAL OF ARTILLERY		50	187	7	277	521	7	23	140	1	2	1	695	2	9		1	13	
	SAPPERS AND MINERS																			
	3 cos.	Brig. Gen. Louis le Bèque Duportail	2	2		42	46	3	3	32 [H]	2			86 [I]				[J]	1	near Dobbs Ferry, N.Y.
	TOTAL OF WASHINGTON'S ARMY		366	1058	104	4897	6425	286	292	3211	30	20	1	10265	17	117	14	16	466	

OFFICERS SICK, ON FURLOUGH, ETC.	WASHINGTON'S ARMY			
	COMMISSIONED	NONCOMMISSIONED	STAFF	TOTAL
Sick Present	17	34		51
Sick Absent	30	44	3	77
On Command	190	338	12	540
On Extra Service	10	20	3	33
On Furlough	20	5	9	34
Furlough Expired	22	2	1	25
Recruiting	21	31		52
On the Staff	110			110
Prisoners of War	11	4	2	17
In Arrest	2	1		3
TOTAL	433	479	30	942

SOURCE OF THIS REPORT

1. MONTHLY RETURN OF THE CONTINENTAL ARMY UNDER THE IMMEDIATE COMMAND OF HIS EXCELLENCY GEORGE WASHINGTON. . . FOR THE MONTH OF JULY 1781, ELEPHANT FOLIO OF WASHINGTON RETURNS, WILLIAM L. CLEMENTS LIBRARY.

1a. Monthly Return of the Continental Army under. . . Washington. . . July 1781, Record Group 93, National Archives. [Contains the same figures, but only to the brigade level.]

A. Ten commissioned officers in Lieutenant Colonel Isaac Sherman's 5th Connecticut regiment plus a brigadier general for the entire brigade.
B. Six commissioned officers in Lieutenant Colonel John Brooks' 7th Massachusetts regiment plus a brigadier general for the entire brigade.
C. Twelve commissioned officers in Michael Jackson's 8th Massachusetts regiment plus a brigadier general for the entire brigade.
D. Six commissioned officers in Major Elijah Humphrys' 2nd battalion of the Connecticut state brigade plus a brigadier general for the entire brigade.
E. Three staff officers in Lieutenant Colonel Isaac Sherman's 5th Connecticut regiment plus one chaplain for the entire brigade.
F. Three staff officers in Lieutenant Colonel John Brooks' 7th Massachusetts regiment plus one chaplain for the entire brigade.
G. Four staff officers in Benjamin Tupper's 10th Massachusetts regiment plus one chaplain for the entire brigade.
H. See footnote H on our June 1781 report.
I. The National Archives manuscript notes that no return was received for the 2nd New York regiment and that one brigade major, one forage master, one armorer, and fifteen light dragoons present fit for duty in Waterbury's brigade, and a volunteer company of one captain, one lieutenant, one sergeant, two music, and twenty-one rank and file serving with Hazen's regiment are not included in the return.
J. Including two men in Washington's infantry discharged for inability.

SEPTEMBER 1781

BRIGADE	UNIT	COMMANDING OFFICER	PRESENT FIT FOR DUTY & ON DUTY: COMMISSIONED OFFICERS	NONCOMMISSIONED OFFICERS	STAFF OFFICERS	RANK & FILE	TOTAL	RANK & FILE SICK, ON FURLOUGH, ETC.: SICK PRESENT	SICK ABSENT	ON COMMAND & EXTRA SERVICE	ON FURLOUGH			GRAND TOTAL	ALTERATIONS: DEATHS	DESERTED	TAKEN PRISONER	DISCHARGED	JOINED, ENLISTED, RECRUITED	LOCATION
FORCES UNDER COMMANDER-IN-CHIEF GENERAL GEORGE WASHINGTON																				
Muhlenberg	Mass. det.[A]	Joseph Vose	19	41	2	247	309	32	33	18				392						besieging Yorktown, Va.[E]
Muhlenberg	N.J. det.[A]	Lt. Col. Francis Barber	19	36	2	300	357	41	18	24	1			441						besieging Yorktown, Va.
Muhlenberg	Det.[A]	Jean Joseph Gimat	15	42	2	241	300	25	51	35				411						besieging Yorktown, Va.
Hazen	Det.[A]	Alexander Scammell	20	26	4	328	378	2		4				384						besieging Yorktown, Va.
Hazen	Det.[A]	Lt. Col. Alexander Hamilton	13	26	3	205	247	13	3	2				265						besieging Yorktown, Va.
Hazen	Canadian	Brevet Brig. Gen. Moses Hazen	20	42	1	204	267	10		1				278						besieging Yorktown, Va.
Wayne	3rd Va.	Lt. Col. Thomas Gaskins	22	46	5	302	375	83	126	78	39			701						besieging Yorktown, Va.
Wayne	5th Pa.	Richard Butler	17	35	4	254	310	48	47	39	2			446						besieging Yorktown, Va.
Wayne	2nd Pa.	Walter Stewart	16	36	3	231	286	59	49	30				424						besieging Yorktown, Va.
Dayton	1st N.J.	Matthias Ogden	11	20	4	130	165	5						170						besieging Yorktown, Va.
Dayton	2nd N.J.	Elias Dayton	13	20	5	121	159	6						165						besieging Yorktown, Va.
Gist	R.I.	Lt. Col. Jeremiah Olney	21	43	4	291	359	33						392						besieging Yorktown, Va.
Gist	3rd Md.	Lt. Col. Peter Adams	23	60	4	344	431	46	69	22	11			579						besieging Yorktown, Va.
Gist	4th Md.	Lt. Col. Thomas Woolford[C]																		besieging Yorktown, Va.
Clinton	1st N.Y.	Goose Van Schaick	20	46	4	321	391							391						besieging Yorktown, Va.
Clinton	2nd N.Y.[B]	Philip Van Cortlandt	19	54	4	344	421	8						429						besieging Yorktown, Va.
	Va. state	Charles Dabney	7	11		182	200			19				219						besieging Yorktown, Va.
	TOTAL OF WASHINGTON'S ARMY		275	584	51	4045	4955	411	396	272	53			6087[D]						

SOURCE OF THIS REPORT

1. RETURN OF THE CONTINENTAL AND VIRGINIA STATE TROOPS UNDER THE IMMEDIATE COMMAND OF HIS EXCELLENCY GENERAL WASHINGTON, SEPTEMBER 26, 1781, RECORD GROUP 93, NATIONAL ARCHIVES.

A. Light infantry companies and other companies had been detached from the New York, New Jersey, Massachusetts, Rhode Island, and New Hampshire Continental lines to form special temporary light infantry battalions. These figures are for those temporary battalions. The battalion under Colonel Gimat consisted of two light infantry companies from Massachusetts regiments plus detached light infantry companies from Connecticut and Rhode Island. The battalion under Alexander Scammell consisted of two New Hampshire companies, three Massachusetts companies, and three Connecticut companies. That under Hamilton consisted of the light infantry companies of the 1st and 2nd New York regiments plus two companies of New York levies and two additional detached Connecticut companies. There were also two Delaware companies present which Washington ordered annexed to the 3rd Maryland regiment on September 27. They may or may not be included somewhere in these figures.

B. This is apparently not Dabney's 2nd Virginia state regiment, but rather the remnants of various Virginia state regiments which were collected for the Yorktown campaign by Colonel Charles Dabney in the summer of 1781. See *Virginia Magazine of History and Biography* 21 (1913): 340.

C. The line for this regiment is left blank on the manuscript without explanation (see footnote D below).

D. The manuscript notes that 34 men of the 2nd New York regiment, about 50 men from New Jersey, and nearly two companies of the detachments had not yet arrived and were omitted in the return. It also notes that 22 men from the New York line on extra service and 30 men with the French army are omitted as well, making about 216 men omitted in the totals. Although it is not indicated on the manuscript, two brigades of Virginia militia, the artillery, and the sappers and miners were also present and are not included in the return.

E. The manuscript was made out just before these men marched from Williamsburg to lay siege to Yorktown.

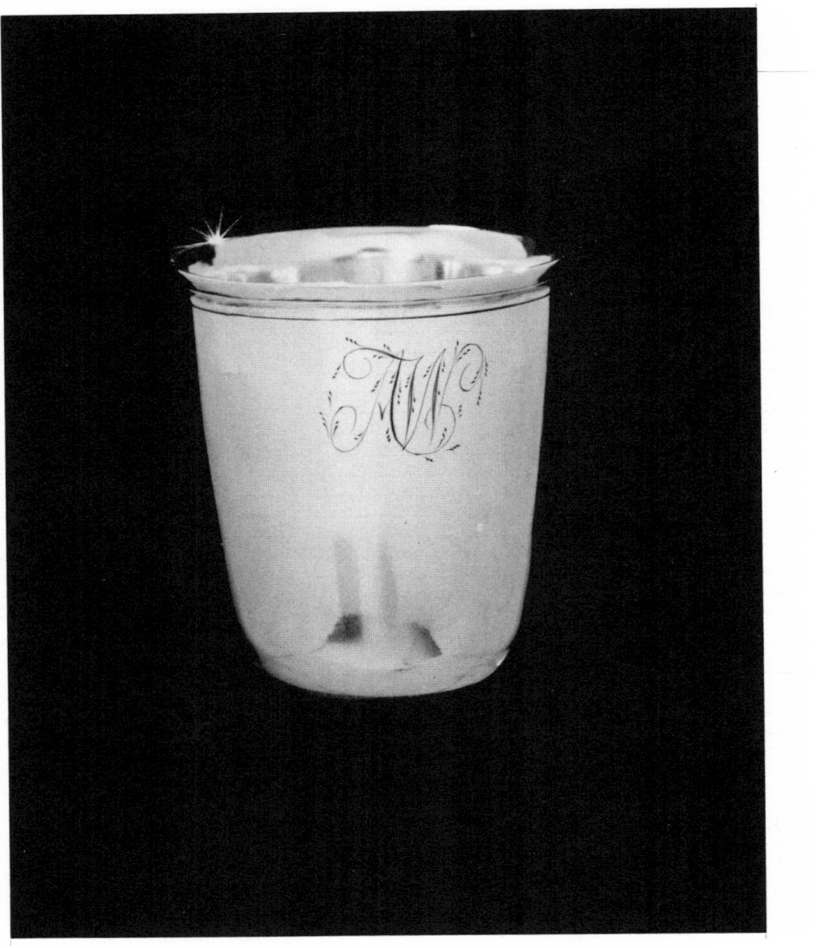

Anthony Wayne's sterling silver wine cup, bearing his initials, in the Clements Library. Originally part of a set of twenty-four, designed to be carried in a leather pouch on his campaigns, the cup measures only 4.8 centimeters in diameter at the top and 5 centimeters high.

OCTOBER 1781

Brigade	Unit	Commanding Officer	Present Fit for Duty & on Duty: Commissioned Officers	Noncommissioned Officers	Staff Officers	Rank & File	Total	Rank & File Sick, on Furlough, etc.: Sick Present	Sick Absent	On Command & Extra Service[B]	On Furlough	Confined	Grand Total[B]	Alterations: Deaths	Deserted	Taken Prisoner	Discharged	Joined, Enlisted, Recruited	Location
	FORCES UNDER COMMANDER-IN-CHIEF GENERAL GEORGE WASHINGTON (To Brigade Level Only)[C]																		
	Muhlenberg's brig.	Brig. Gen. Peter Muhlenberg	46	101	9	716	872	161	116	53	2	2	1206						
	Hazen's brig.	Brevet Brig. Gen. Moses Hazen	48	87	10	633	778	153	87	110	4	2	1134						Yorktown, Va. area
	N.J. & R.I. brig.	Elias Dayton	39	95	12	592	738	84	58	430	1	1	1312						Yorktown, Va. area
	N.Y. brig.	Brig. Gen. James Clinton	32	101	10	623	766	75	54	195	1	6	1097						Yorktown, Va. area
	Pa. & Va. brig.	Brig. Gen. Anthony Wayne	55	101	10	702	868	167	94	83	1	10	1223						Yorktown, Va. area
	Md. brig.	Brig. Gen. Mordecai Gist	24	87	8	568	687	136	119	50	7		999						Yorktown, Va. area
	Officers present on duty		9	13			22						22						Yorktown, Va. area
	TOTAL OF WASHINGTON'S INFANTRY		253	585	59	3834	4731	776	528	921[B]	16	21	6993[C]						
	EASTERN DEPARTMENT UNDER MAJOR GENERAL WILLIAM HEATH																		
Huntington	1st Conn.	John Durkee	7	22	5	196	230	26	13	149[B]	11	1	430		4		3	5	protecting the Highlands, N.Y.
Huntington	5th Conn.	Lt. Col. Isaac Sherman	10	29	3	238	280	26	21	127	5	1	460		3		4	8	protecting the Highlands, N.Y.
Huntington	3rd Conn.	Samuel Blatchley Webb	4	30	3	203	240	24	20	153	5		442				4	1	protecting the Highlands, N.Y.
Swift	2nd Conn.	Heman Swift	8	33	5	197	243	24	10	175	2	1	455		1		2	2	protecting the Highlands, N.Y.
Swift	4th Conn.	Zebulon Butler	6	28	4	171	209	35	16	175		2	437		2		7	1	protecting the Highlands, N.Y.
Glover	1st Mass.	Joseph Vose	8	27	5	199	239	17	9	133			398		3	1		2	protecting the Highlands, N.Y.
Glover	4th Mass.	William Shepard	9	33	4	179	225	18	14	137	1		395	1	2	4		6	protecting the Highlands, N.Y.
Glover	7th Mass.	Lt. Col. John Brooks	10	24	4	208	246	10	15	116			387	1	3	8		4	protecting the Highlands, N.Y.
Paterson	2nd Mass.	Lt. Col. Ebenezer Sprout	10	30	5	215	260	13	13	117		1	404	1	1			5	protecting the Highlands, N.Y.
Paterson	5th Mass.	Rufus Putnam	13	34	4	218	269	26	15	94		1	405		1			5	protecting the Highlands, N.Y.
Paterson	8th Mass.	Michael Jackson	11	32	3	234	280	27	14	82	2		405	3	1			6	protecting the Highlands, N.Y.
Greaton	3rd Mass.	John Greaton	7	29	4	185	225	28	14	117		1	385	1		1	1	7	protecting the Highlands, N.Y.
Greaton	6th Mass.	Lt. Col. Calvin Smith	6	34	2	200	242	19	5	126	2		394	1	6			15	protecting the Highlands, N.Y.
Greaton	9th Mass.	Henry Jackson	10	33	3	198	244	20	15	128			407				2	7	protecting the Highlands, N.Y.
	Officers present on duty		44	80			124						124						
	TOTAL OF CONTINENTAL INFANTRY		163	498	54	2841	3556	313	194	1829[B]	28	8	5928	8	27	14	23	74	
	MILITIA AND STATE TROOPS																		
	Conn. levies brig.	Brig. Gen. David Waterbury	51	100	6	876	1033	45	28	64	25		1195		13	22		31	protecting the Highlands, N.Y.
	Mass. militia	Lt. Col. Joseph Webb	24	50	3	313	390	16	10	151		1	568					6	protecting the Highlands, N.Y.
	Mass. militia	Lt. Col. Luke Drury																	protecting the Highlands, N.Y.
	Mass. militia	Lt. Col. Enoch Putnam	49	82	11	767	909	69	23	33	2	2	1038	2			236	5	protecting the Highlands, N.Y.
	Conn. militia	Lt. Col. Samuel Canfield																	protecting the Highlands, N.Y.
	N.J. levies	Sylvanus Seely[A]																	New Jersey
	TOTAL OF MILITIA AND STATE INFANTRY		124	232	20	1956	2332	130	61	248	27	3	2801	2	13	22	236	42	
	ARTILLERY																		
	3rd cont'l.	John Crane	39	132	5	280	456						456	3	1	1		6	protecting the Highlands, N.Y.
	CAVALRY																		
	2nd cont'l.	Elisha Sheldon	5	18	4	101	128	1	10	140		1	280					3	protecting the Highlands, N.Y.
	INVALIDS																		
	Invalid corps	Lewis Nicola	16	37	5	185	243	13	12	33	10		311[D]		1			26	West Point, N.Y.
	TOTAL OF HEATH'S ARMY		347	917	88	5363	6715	457	277	2250	65	12	9776[D]	13	42	37	259[E]	151	
	GRAND TOTAL		600	1502	147	9197	11446	1233	805	3171[B]	81	33	16769[B]						

(The Lt. Col. Luke Drury, Lt. Col. Enoch Putnam and Lt. Col. Samuel Canfield rows are bracketed together, sharing one set of figures.)

OFFICERS SICK, ON FURLOUGH, ETC.	WASHINGTON'S ARMY				EASTERN DEPARTMENT (CONTINENTAL INFANTRY AND CAVALRY ONLY)				GRAND TOTAL
	COMMISSIONED	NONCOMMISSIONED	STAFF	TOTAL	COMMISSIONED	NONCOMMISSIONED	STAFF	TOTAL	
Sick Present	32	72		104	14	31	2	47	151
Sick Absent	34	38	2	74	33	18	3	54	128
On Command	42	69	6	117	115	196	9	320	437
On Extra Service		12	1	13	11	13		24	37
On Furlough	6	1	1	8	21	14	5	40	48
Leave of Absence Expired	1			1	2	1		3	4
Absent without Leave	1			1	1			1	2
Recruiting	4	10		14	10	8		18	32
On the Staff	40			40	63	1	1	65	105
Prisoners of War	4			4	4	1		5	9
In Arrest			1	1					1
TOTAL	64	202	11	377	274	283	20	577	954

SOURCES OF THIS REPORT

1. STATE OF THE CONTINENTAL ARMY UNDER THE IMMEDIATE COMMAND OF HIS EXCELLENCY GENERAL WASHINGTON, OCTOBER 29, 1781, ELEPHANT FOLIO OF WASHINGTON RETURNS, WILLIAM L. CLEMENTS LIBRARY.

2. RETURN OF THE TROOPS OF THE UNITED STATES OF NORTH AMERICA UNDER THE COMMAND OF THE HONBLE. MAJR. GENERAL HEATH, OCTOBER 29, 1781, RECORD GROUP 93, NATIONAL ARCHIVES. [ALTHOUGH MONTHLY DOES NOT APPEAR IN THE HEADING OF THE RETURN, THE ALTERATIONS ARE MARKED "MONTHLY ALTERATIONS."]

A. The line for the New Jersey levies is blank on the manuscript, which indicates in a note that no return was received for these troops, which were protecting the New Jersey side of the Hudson.

B. The figures for on command and extra service on this monthly report (and, as a result, the figures in the grand total column as well) should be used with extreme caution or ignored because of the probability that the same men are included more than once. The return for the regiments under the command of Heath may include as "on command" those companies that were detached to form the special light infantry regiments that were at Yorktown. (See our September 1781 report.) These men would therefore appear twice here, once in the figures for Muhlenberg's and Hazen's brigades at Yorktown and also in the "on command & extra service" column for the regiments under Heath from which they had been detached. Of those on command from the forces at Yorktown, the manuscript notes that 443 were doing duty in the light infantry. If, as seems to be the case, by "light infantry" the manuscript means the light infantry detachments in Muhlenberg's and Hazen's brigades, then these men are also included twice.

C. It will be noted that figures are provided on this manuscript for only the Continental infantry brigades.

D. The manuscript notes that in addition to having received no return for the New Jersey levies under Sylvanus Seely, no return had arrived for the New Hampshire brigade (then serving on the frontier).

E. Including seventeen men in Heath's Continental regiments and seventy-nine in the militia and state troops discharged for inability.

BRIGADE

JANUARY 1782

UNIT	COMMANDING OFFICER	PRESENT FIT FOR DUTY & ON DUTY: COMMISSIONED OFFICERS	NONCOMMISSIONED OFFICERS	STAFF OFFICERS	RANK & FILE	TOTAL	RANK & FILE SICK, ON FURLOUGH, ETC.: SICK PRESENT	SICK ABSENT	ON COMMAND & EXTRA SERVICE	ON FURLOUGH	CONFINED			GRAND TOTAL	ALTERATIONS: DEATHS	DESERTED	TAKEN PRISONER	DISCHARGED	JOINED, ENLISTED, RECRUITED	LOCATION
FORCES UNDER COMMANDER-IN-CHIEF GENERAL GEORGE WASHINGTON (Mostly to the Brigade Level Only)																				
1st Conn. brig.	Brig. Gen. Jedediah Huntington	15	99	7	438	559	318	79	92	59				1107	11	15		51	11	West Point & dependencies
2nd Conn. brig.	Heman Swift	14	70	4 A	290	378	196	48	74	40	1			737	4	1		24	1	West Point & dependencies
1st Mass. brig.	Brig. Gen. John Glover	15	85	14	719	833	93	61	148	39	1			1175	9	3		4	28	West Point & dependencies
2nd Mass. brig.	Brig. Gen. John Paterson	16	72	10	717	815	84	62	130	50				1141	7	8		1	20	West Point & dependencies
3rd Mass. brig.	John Greaton	19	94	8	422	543	442	49	92	43				1169	4	13	1	1	21	West Point & dependencies
N.H. brig.		16	81	8	459	564	175	62	236	32				1069	16	7		177	20	Albany, N.Y. area
Conn. state brig.	Brig. Gen. David Waterbury	21	49	6	390	466	46	12	94	10	1			629		11		3	2	West Point & dependencies
N.Y. brig.	Brig. Gen. James Clinton	26	91	5	645	767	87	51	115	24	6			1050	4	5	1	1	9	Pompton, N.J.
N.J. brig.	Elias Dayton	38	77	9	418	542	78	59	117	60				856	12	24		5	38	near Morristown, N.J.
R.I.	Lt. Col. Jeremiah Olney	12	35	3	197	247	61	71	26		1			406	46			1	5	Philadelphia, Pa.
Canadian	Brevet Brig. Gen. Moses Hazen	10	26	3	187	226	27	28	118	23	4			426	2	4			23	Lancaster, Pa.
TOTAL OF INFANTRY		202	779	77	4882	5940	1607	582	1242	380	14			9765	115	91	2	268	178	
CAVALRY																				
2nd cont'l.	Elisha Sheldon	9	17	3	111	140	2	2	131	5	1			281	1				1	Connecticut
ARTILLERY																				
2nd cont'l.	John Lamb	25	74	4	132	235	25	7	14	9	1			291	1				15	Burlington, N.J.
INVALIDS																				
Invalid corps	Lewis Nicola	4	17		110	131	30	10	78	14				263		1			1	
SAPPERS AND MINERS																				
3 cos.		2	5		41 B	48	12	19 B	6		2			87	2					Burlington, N.J.
TOTAL OF WASHINGTON'S ARMY		242	892	84	5276	6494	1676 C	620	1471	408	18			10687	119	92	2	268 D	195	

OFFICERS SICK, ON FURLOUGH, ETC.	WASHINGTON'S ARMY			
	COMMISSIONED	NONCOMMISSIONED	STAFF	TOTAL
Sick Present	29	147		176
Sick Absent	34	57	6	97
On Command	61	85	9	155
On Extra Service	19	15		34
On Furlough	210	175	40	425
Furlough Expired	6	1	1	8
Absent without Leave	1	2		3
Recruiting	19	16		35
On the Staff	101	2		103
Prisoners of War	4	1		5
In Arrest or in Gaol	3	1		4
TOTAL	487	502	56	1045

SOURCE OF THIS REPORT

1. MONTHLY RETURN OF THE CONTINENTAL ARMY UNDER THE IMMEDIATE COMMAND OF HIS EXCELLENCY GEORGE WASHINGTON. . . FOR THE MONTH OF JANUARY 1782, RECORD GROUP 93, NATIONAL ARCHIVES.

A. This figure has been derived from a total, as the manuscript is illegible at this point.
B. The figures for the sappers and miners are badly creased, making those "present fit for duty" and "sick absent" almost illegible. The total of all enlisted men is eighty, and the missing figures have in part been deduced from this total.
C. The unusually large numbers of sick present on this report and on the February report can be accounted for by both an outbreak of smallpox and extensive innoculation for smallpox.
D. Including twelve men in Washington's infantry discharged for inability.

FEBRUARY 1782

BRIGADE	UNIT	COMMANDING OFFICER	PRESENT FIT FOR DUTY & ON DUTY: COMMISSIONED OFFICERS	NONCOMMISSIONED OFFICERS	STAFF OFFICERS	RANK & FILE	TOTAL	RANK & FILE SICK, ON FURLOUGH, ETC.: SICK PRESENT	SICK ABSENT	ON COMMAND & EXTRA SERVICE	ON FURLOUGH	CONFINED	FURLOUGH EXPIRED	PRISONERS OF WAR	GRAND TOTAL	ALTERATIONS: DEATHS	DESERTED	TAKEN PRISONER	DISCHARGED	JOINED, ENLISTED, RECRUITED	LOCATION
	FORCES UNDER COMMANDER-IN-CHIEF GENERAL GEORGE WASHINGTON																				
1st Conn.	1st Conn.	John Durkee	5	40	2	180	227	69	17	31	20	1			365	4	5		3	3	West Point & dependencies
1st Conn.	3rd Conn.	Samuel Blatchley Webb	6	39	3	143	191	122	25	21	18				377	7	1			6	West Point & dependencies
1st Conn.	5th Conn.	Lt. Col. Isaac Sherman	7	36	2	160	205	92	20	29	16				362	7	7			4	West Point & dependencies
2nd Conn.	2nd Conn.	Heman Swift	7	43	1	173	224	82	17	36	19				378	5	2			3	West Point & dependencies
2nd Conn.	4th Conn.	Zebulon Butler	10	43	3	164	220	66	27	35	20				368	1	3		3	2	West Point & dependencies
1st Mass.	1st Mass.	Joseph Vose	6	19	4	132	161	148	15	40	16				380	6	3		1	6	West Point & dependencies
1st Mass.	4th Mass.	William Shepard	4	22	4	123	153	148	18	39	18				376	8			1	6	West Point & dependencies
1st Mass.	7th Mass.	Lt. Col. John Brooks	7	28	5	234	274	53	17	34	13				391	7	2			7	West Point & dependencies
2nd Mass.	2nd Mass.	Lt. Col. Ebenezer Sprout	6	21	3	131	161	141	9	50	21				382	3	1		1	5	West Point & dependencies
2nd Mass.	5th Mass.	Rufus Putnam	5	28	5	195	233	77	20	41	12				383	9	3			15	West Point & dependencies
2nd Mass.	8th Mass.	Michael Jackson	8	22	3	148	181	109	20	44	22				376	10	1			5	West Point & dependencies
3rd Mass.	3rd Mass.	John Greaton	7	34	2	184	227	100	14	27	17				385	4	7		1	9	West Point & dependencies
3rd Mass.	6th Mass.	Lt. Col. Calvin Smith	9	23	3	195	230	98	10	32	14				384	4	5			10	West Point & dependencies
3rd Mass.	9th Mass.	Henry Jackson	8	29	3	220	260	76	10	28	17	1			392	12	1		1	13	West Point & dependencies
	10th Mass.	Benjamin Tupper	5	27	3	213	248	48	27	33	22				378	9	3			13	
N.H.	1st N.H.	Lt. Col. Henry Dearborn	8	26	3	219	256	10	13	26	32	2			339	4	2			3	Albany, N.Y. area
N.H.	2nd N.H.	Lt. Col. George Reid	9	26	1	157	193	3	19	31	30				276	13	3		1		Albany, N.Y. area
N.Y.	1st N.Y.	Goose Van Schaick	20	43	2	294	359	24	26	66	33	4			512	1	9			9	Pompton, N.J.
N.Y.	2nd N.Y.	Philip Van Cortlandt	16	46	5	331	398	32	12	62	30	2			536	2	8		2	6	Pompton, N.J.
N.J.	1st N.J.	Matthias Ogden	15	29	4	180	228	16	20	106	41				411					6	near Morristown, N.J.
N.J.	2nd N.J.	Elias Dayton	13	30	4	145	192	34	30	117	46				419	2	2		2	2	near Morristown, N.J.
	R.I.	Lt. Col. Jeremiah Olney	12	41	3	219	275	44	64	13		1			397	16			1	2	Philadelphia, Pa.
	Canadian	Brevet Brig. Gen. Moses Hazen	12	32	2	175	221	34	21	123	28	3			430	1	3			3	Lancaster, Pa.
	Officers present on duty		65	63	1		129								129						
	TOTAL OF INFANTRY		270	790	71	4315	5446	1626	471	1064	505	14			9126	135	71		17	138	
	CAVALRY																				
	2nd cont'l.	Elisha Sheldon	14	40	4	100	158	4	2	133	9	2			308		1		1		Connecticut
	ARTILLERY																				
	2nd cont'l.	John Lamb	13	55	4	53	125	81	12	151[A]	23	1	3	1	693		1		9	1	Burlington, N.J.
	3rd cont'l.	John Crane	24	94	3	175	296									1	3		1	9	West Point & dependencies
	Present on duty		5	11		14	30								30						
	TOTAL OF ARTILLERY		42	160	7	242	451	81	12	151	23	1	3	1	723	1	4		10	10	
	SAPPERS AND MINERS																				
	3 cos.		2	1		30	33	14	4	27	1	1			80	3					Burlington, N.J.
	INVALIDS																				
	Invalid corps	Lewis Nicola	6	23		111	140	27	14	77	15				273						
	TOTAL OF WASHINGTON'S ARMY		334	1014	82	4798	6228	1752	503	1452	553	18	3	1	10510	139	76		28[B]	148	

OFFICERS SICK, ON FURLOUGH, ETC.	WASHINGTON'S ARMY			
	COMMISSIONED	NONCOMMISSIONED	STAFF	TOTAL
Sick Present	18	116		134
Sick Absent	34	62	6	102
On Command	61	138	9	208
On Extra Service	18	25		43
On Furlough	225	206	38	469
Furlough Expired	8	18	3	29
Absent without Leave	2			2
Recruiting	21	20		41
On the Staff	108			108
Prisoners of War	4	1		5
Confined or in Arrest	1	1	1	3
TOTAL	500	587	57	1144

A. Including three men "recruiting."
B. Including nine men in Washington's infantry discharged for inability.

SOURCE OF THIS REPORT

1. MONTHLY RETURN OF THE CONTINENTAL ARMY UNDER THE IMMEDIATE COMMAND OF HIS EXCELLENCY GEORGE WASHINGTON. . . FOR THE MONTH OF FEBRUARY 1782, ELEPHANT FOLIO OF WASHINGTON RETURNS, WILLIAM L. CLEMENTS LIBRARY.

1a. Monthly Return of the Continental Army under. . . Washington. . . February 1782, Record Group 93, National Archives. [Contains the same figures, but only to the brigade level.]

MARCH 1782

BRIGADE	UNIT	COMMANDING OFFICER	PRESENT FIT FOR DUTY & ON DUTY: COMMISSIONED OFFICERS	NONCOMMISSIONED OFFICERS	STAFF OFFICERS	RANK & FILE	TOTAL	RANK & FILE SICK, ON FURLOUGH, ETC.: SICK PRESENT	SICK ABSENT	ON COMMAND & EXTRA SERVICE	ON FURLOUGH	CONFINED	FURLOUGH EXP. OR AWOL	PRISONERS OF WAR	GRAND TOTAL	ALTERATIONS: DEATHS	DESERTED	TAKEN PRISONER	DISCHARGED	JOINED, ENLISTED, RECRUITED	LOCATION
	FORCES UNDER COMMANDER-IN-CHIEF GENERAL GEORGE WASHINGTON																				
1st Conn.	1st Conn.	John Durkee	8	36	4	203	251	35	16	38	17				357	2	2		7	2	West Point & dependencies
1st Conn.	3rd Conn.	Samuel Blatchley Webb	5	33	3	200	241	56	22	29	18				366	5	3			3	West Point & dependencies
2nd Conn.	5th Conn.	Lt. Col. Isaac Sherman	12	32	4	198	246	44	16	35	20	1			362		10		1	8	West Point & dependencies
2nd Conn.	2nd Conn.	Heman Swift	11	42	4	225	282	30	10	39	16				377	2	5		1	1	West Point & dependencies
2nd Conn.	4th Conn.	Zebulon Butler	9	42	4	187	242	38	23	41	18	1			363		3		4	4	West Point & dependencies
1st Mass.	1st Mass.	Joseph Vose	8	28	4	247	287	28	12	47	15	1			390	4			2	4	West Point & dependencies
1st Mass.	4th Mass.	William Shepard	8	26	4	215	253	35	18	46	25				377	8	2			2	West Point & dependencies
1st Mass.	7th Mass.	Lt. Col. John Brooks	6	25	4	227	262	45	12	41	14				374	10	6			3	West Point & dependencies
2nd Mass.	2nd Mass.	Lt. Col. Ebenezer Sprout	5	23	3	221	252	42	8	54	19	2			377	6	3			5	West Point & dependencies
2nd Mass.	5th Mass.	Rufus Putnam	4	28	5	221	258	43	14	49	11				375	8			1	3	West Point & dependencies
2nd Mass.	8th Mass.	Michael Jackson	12[D]	28	2	175	217	71	25	43	22				378	9	2		1	6	West Point & dependencies
3rd Mass.	3rd Mass.	John Greaton	9	31	4	238	282	47	9	29	14				381	4	10			10	West Point & dependencies
3rd Mass.	6th Mass.	Lt. Col. Calvin Smith	9	28	3	222	262	60	8	38	15				383	5	5			4	West Point & dependencies
3rd Mass.	9th Mass.	Henry Jackson	9	33	3	233	278	53	6	37	16				390	6	2			3	West Point & dependencies
	10th Mass.	Benjamin Tupper	11	28	4	229	272	33	14	32	26				377	11	1			5	
	1st N.H.	Lt. Col. Henry Dearborn	9	29	3	198	239	37	7	27	32				342	1					Albany, N.Y. area
	2nd N.H.	Lt. Col. George Reid	2	12	2	31	47	6	21	211	31				316						Albany, N.Y. area
	1st N.Y.	Goose Van Schaick	20	42	3	287	352	33	18	72	28	5			508	4	7		2	8	Pompton, N.J.
	2nd N.Y.	Philip Van Cortlandt	18	41	4	342	405	23	7	56	42				533	2	3	1	2	11	Pompton, N.J.
	1st N.J.	Matthias Ogden	15	33	4	198	250	13	15	103	39				420				4	12	near Morristown, N.J.
	2nd N.J.	Elias Dayton	11	19	3	191	224	21	23	82	55				405		1		1	3	near Morristown, N.J.
	R.I.	Lt. Col. Jeremiah Olney	14	40	4	236	294	55	22	17		6			394	7				2	Philadelphia, Pa.
	Canadian	Brevet Brig. Gen. Moses Hazen[A]																			Lancaster, Pa.
	TOTAL OF INFANTRY		215	679	78	4724	5696	848	326	1166	493	16			8545	94	65	1	26	99	
	CAVALRY																				
	2nd cont'l.	Elisha Sheldon	9	31	3	104	147		120	15	14				296	1				4	Connecticut
	ARTILLERY																				
	9 cos. 2nd cont'l.	John Lamb	21	70	3	103	197	45	16	97	21	1	4	1	706		4			3	Burlington, N.J.
	3rd cont'l. & 1 co. 2nd cont'l.	John Crane	20	93	3	208	324									1	1			5	West Point & dependencies
	Present on duty					14	14								14						
	TOTAL OF ARTILLERY		41	163	6	325	535	45	16	97	21	1	4	1	720	1	5			8	
	SAPPERS AND MINERS																				
	3 cos.	Maj. Gen. Louis le Bèque Duportail	2	5		52	59	6	1	7	9				82	1					Burlington, N.J.
	TOTAL OF WASHINGTON'S ARMY		267	878	87	5205	6437	899	463	1285	537	17	4	1	9643	97	70	1	26	111	
	WESTERN DISTRICT UNDER BRIGADIER GENERAL WILLIAM IRVINE																				
	7th Va.	John Gibson	6	10	5	77	98	9	2	32	6	1			148		2		1		Fort Pitt, Pa.
	Pa. det.	Lt. Col. Samuel Bayard	5[E]	13	2	57	77	15		25	4				121		1			2	Fort Pitt, Pa.
	Officers present on duty		1	1			2								2						Fort Pitt, Pa.
	TOTAL OF INFANTRY		12	24	7	134	177	24	2	57	10	1			271		3		1	2	
	ARTILLERY AND ARTIFICERS																				
	Det. 4th cont'l. & artificers		2	10		18	30	1		4[F]	2				37					3	Fort Pitt, Pa.
	TOTAL OF WESTERN DISTRICT		14	34	7	152	207	25	2	61	12	1			308		3		1	5	

MARCH 1782 (continued)

BRIGADE	UNIT	COMMANDING OFFICER	PRESENT FIT FOR DUTY & ON DUTY: COMMISSIONED OFFICERS	NONCOMMISSIONED OFFICERS	STAFF OFFICERS	RANK & FILE	TOTAL	RANK & FILE SICK, ON FURLOUGH, ETC.: SICK PRESENT	SICK ABSENT	ON COMMAND & EXTRA SERVICE	ON FURLOUGH	CONFINED	FURLOUGH EXP. OR AWOL	PRISONERS OF WAR	GRAND TOTAL	ALTERATIONS: DEATHS	DESERTED	TAKEN PRISONER	DISCHARGED	JOINED, ENLISTED, RECRUITED	LOCATION
	SOUTHERN DEPARTMENT UNDER MAJOR GENERAL NATHANAEL GREENE																				
N.C.	1st N.C.	Lt. Col. Hardy Murfree	8	23	3	268	302	31	52	98	4	2			489	7	2		5	11	Ashley River, S.C.
N.C.	2nd N.C.	Lt. Col. Henry Dixon	8	24	3	225	260	17	41	124	7				449	2	2		2	8	Ashley River, S.C.
N.C.	3rd N.C.	Maj. Griffith John McRae	4	17	2	184	207			2					209		1				Ashley River, S.C.
Md.	1st Md. B	Lt. Col. Peter Adams	20	45	5	215	285	19	123	174	34				635	3	2			5	Ashley River, S.C.
Md.	2nd Md. B	Lt. Col. John Stewart	14	50	4	242	310	13	76	145	68				612	8	4			3	Ashley River, S.C.
Pa.	Del. C	David Hall	4	18	2	105	129	9	26	27	8				199	1	1		3		Ashley River, S.C.
Pa.	1st Pa. C	Thomas Craig	17	41	4	289	351	17	59	111	1				539	6	3			7	Ashley River, S.C.
Pa.	2nd Pa. C	Lt. Col. Josiah Harmar	17	48	3	281	349	23	60	106		1			539	2	6		2	3	Ashley River, S.C.
	Officers present on duty		6	25			31								31						
	TOTAL OF INFANTRY		98	291	26	1809	2224	129	437	787	122	3			3702	29	21		12	37	
	CAVALRY AND LEGIONARY CORPS																				
	Partizan corps cavalry	Lt. Col. Henry Lee	5	7	2	70	84	1	26	1	7				119						on detachment M
	Partizan corps infantry	Lt. Col Henry Lee	5	11		102	118	7	17	35	2				179						on detachment M
	3rd cont'l. cavalry	Maj. Richard Call	5	5	2	43	55	6	21	28					110						on detachment M
	Officers present on duty		1				1								1						
	TOTAL OF CAVALRY AND LEGIONARY CORPS		16	23	4	215	258	14	64	64	9				409						
	ARTILLERY																				
	Va. co., 1st cont'l.	Capt. Lt. Lewis Booker	4	16		41	61	1	1	12					75						Ashley River, S.C.
	Md. co., 1st cont'l.	Capt. William Brown	2	14		25	41	1	1	3					46						Ashley River, S.C.
	Md. co., 1st cont'l.	Capt. James Smith	1	9		11	21		2	13					36						Ashley River, S.C.
	Pa. co., 4th cont'l.	Capt. William Ferguson	5	22		44	71	1	1	6					79						Camden, S.C.
	Pa. co., 4th cont'l.	Capt. John Brice	3	9		23	35			6					41						Georgia
	TOTAL OF ARTILLERY		15	70		144	229	3	5	40					277 J						
	TOTAL OF GREENE'S ARMY		129	384	30	2168	2711	146	506	891	131	3			4388 J	29	21		12	37	
	GEORGIA EXPEDITION UNDER BRIGADIER GENERAL ANTHONY WAYNE																				
	1st cont'l. cavalry	Anthony Walton White	7	10	2	93	112	7	3	22 G					144	1	5			4	Georgia
	4th cont'l. cavalry	Stephen Moylan	3	6	1	31	41	2	1	6 H					50						Georgia
	Ga. legion horse	James Jackson	4	3	3	30	40	2	1	7					50						Georgia
	Ga. legion infantry	James Jackson	4	3		23	30	9		15	3				57						Georgia
	Va. bn.	Lt. Col. Thomas Posey	19	45	4	240	308	15	10	46 I					379		5			2	Georgia
	Ga. militia		9	8		44	61			5 I					66						Georgia
	TOTAL OF WAYNE'S EXPEDITION		46	75	10	461	592	35	15	101	3				746 K	1	10			6	
	GRAND TOTAL		456	1371	134	7986	9947	1105	986	2338	683	21	4	1	15085	127	104	1	39 L	159	

MARCH 1782
(continued)

OFFICERS SICK, ON FURLOUGH, ETC.	WASHINGTON'S ARMY (EXCEPT INFANTRY)N				WESTERN DISTRICT				SOUTHERN DEPARTMENT				GEORGIA EXPEDITION				GRAND TOTAL
	COMMISSIONED	NONCOMMISSIONED	STAFF	TOTAL	COMMISSIONED	NONCOMMISSIONED	STAFF	TOTAL	COMMISSIONED	NONCOMMISSIONED	STAFF	TOTAL	COMMISSIONED	NONCOMMISSIONED	STAFF	TOTAL	
Sick Present	1	13	1	15		5		5	5	13		18	1	1		2	40
Sick Absent	6	10		16					12	24		36	4			4	56
On Command	10	41	2	53	1	4		5	40	46	1	87	3	2	1	6	151
On Extra Service	1	5		6	2	8		10	1	38		39		2		2	57
On Furlough	25	29	2	56	1	1		2	26	25	3	54					112
Furlough Expired		4		4	1			1									5
Recruiting	6	6		12	2	2		4	9		1	10					26
On the Staff	15			15	4			4	20			20			2	2	41
Prisoners of War	1			1					9	1	1	11	1			1	13
In Arrest	4			4					1			1					5
Absent without Leave									1			1					1
Wounded													1	1		2	2
TOTAL	69	108	5	182	11	20		31	124	147	6	277	10	6	3	19	509

SOURCES OF THIS REPORT

1. MONTHLY RETURN OF THE CONTINENTAL ARMY UNDER THE IMMEDIATE COMMAND OF HIS EXCELLENCY GEORGE WASHINGTON. . . FOR THE MONTH OF MARCH 1782, ELEPHANT FOLIO OF WASHINGTON RETURNS, WILLIAM L. CLEMENTS LIBRARY.

2. RETURN OF THE TROOPS IN THE WESTERN DISTRICT IN SERVICE OF THE U.S., COMMANDED BY WILLIAM IRVINE. . . MARCH 28, 1782, WILLIAM IRVINE PAPERS, THE HISTORICAL SOCIETY OF PENNSYLVANIA. [CONTAINS A SECTION FOR THE MONTHLY ALTERATIONS, EVEN THOUGH IT IS NOT HEADED AS A MONTHLY RETURN.]

3. MONTHLY RETURN OF THE INFANTRY OF THE SOUTHERN ARMY COMMANDED BY THE HONOURABLE MAJOR GENERAL GREENE. . . APRIL 1, 1782, RECORD GROUP 93, NATIONAL ARCHIVES. [ALSO CONTAINS SECTIONS FOR THE ARTILLERY AND CAVALRY AND LEGIONARY CORPS.]

4. GENERAL RETURN OF THE ARMY SERVING IN GEORGIA, UNDER THE COMMAND OF THE HONORABLE BRIGADIER GENERAL ANTHONY WAYNE. . . MARCH 29, 1782, RECORD GROUP 93, NATIONAL ARCHIVES [MARKED "MONTHLY RETURN" ON THE REVERSE].

A. The line for the Canadian regiment is blank on the manuscript.
B. These units represent a recent consolidation of the Maryland forces serving with the Southern Department, a reorganization that apparently has not previously been discussed in print. See footnote C below.
C. These are the new 1st and 2nd Pennsylvania regiments under the rearrangement of the Pennsylvania line ordered by Greene in January 1782. The 2nd, 3rd, and 5th Pennsylvania regiments had been ordered to reinforce Greene's Southern Department in November 1781, and this consolidation was effected on their arrival in January. See Lieutenant Colonel Josiah Harmar, January 11, 1782, to Nathanael Greene, Greene Papers, William L. Clements Library. This consolidation is not noted in either Heitman or the Pennsylvania Archives.
D. Eleven commissioned officers in Michael Jackson's 8th Massachusetts regiment plus one brigadier general for the entire brigade.
E. Four commissioned officers for the Pennsylvania detachment under Lieutenant Colonel Samuel Bayard plus one brigadier general for the Western District.
F. Including one matross in a column headed "recruiting." Men doing such duty were usually included by the adjutants in the columns for on command and on extra service.
G. Including five waggoners. Presumably these were enlisted men doing this extra duty rather than civilians, since the waggoner column is included under rank and file.
H. Including one waggoner.
I. Including three waggoners.
J. The manuscript notes that Lieutenant Colonel Maham's corps of cavalry with about fifty men and Lieutenant Colonel Horry's corps of cavalry also with about fifty men were on the lines and detached and had not sent in their returns. The manuscript also notes that General Francis Marion had about two hundred dismounted militia under his command between the Cooper and Santee Rivers; these men were not included in the return. Additional militia had been ordered out, but there was "little prospect" of this resulting in any addition to the forces.
K. The manuscript notes that in addition to the men included in the return there were 2 sergeants and 18 rank and file of the Pennsylvania line that had arrived and 150 "Reclaimed Citizens, outlayers, and Crackers, that have lately surrendered and joined our Arms."
L. Including thirteen men in Washington's infantry, nine men in Greene's infantry, and one man in the Western District discharged for inability.
M. The cavalry and the light troops under Lieutenant Colonel John Laurens had been detached on March 30 to cooperate with the forces under Francis Marion in an attempt to capture a British foraging party. The manuscript notes this as the reason for the incomplete state of the cavalry return. It will be noted that no alterations are given for either the cavalry or the artillery of the Southern Department.
N. The section of the return for officers sick, on furlough, etc., for the infantry of Washington's army is blank on the manuscript.
O. For this one man the column is headed simply "prisoners." This probably means prisoner of war, but could possibly indicate that the man was in arrest or confined.

APRIL 1782

BRIGADE	UNIT	COMMANDING OFFICER	PRESENT FIT FOR DUTY & ON DUTY: COMMISSIONED OFFICERS	NONCOMMISSIONED OFFICERS	STAFF OFFICERS	RANK & FILE	TOTAL	RANK & FILE SICK, ON FURLOUGH, ETC.: SICK PRESENT	SICK ABSENT	ON COMMAND & EXTRA SERVICE	ON FURLOUGH	CONFINED	PRISONERS OF WAR	GRAND TOTAL	ALTERATIONS: DEATHS	DESERTED	TAKEN PRISONER	DISCHARGED	JOINED, ENLISTED, RECRUITED	LOCATION
	FORCES UNDER COMMANDER-IN-CHIEF GENERAL GEORGE WASHINGTON																			
1st Conn.	1st Conn.	John Durkee	13	45	4	238	300	30	7	26	1			364	1	18		4	16	West Point & dependencies
1st Conn.	3rd Conn.	Samuel Blatchley Webb	12	44	3 C	244	303	45	10	18				376	1	4		2		West Point & dependencies
2nd Conn.	5th Conn.	Lt. Col. Isaac Sherman	10	44	5	253	312	36	10	26				384		5		1	20	West Point & dependencies
2nd Conn.	2nd Conn.	Heman Swift	15	43	6	247	311	30	7	37				385		5		2	8	West Point & dependencies
2nd Conn.	4th Conn.	Zebulon Butler	13	51	4	218	286	34	16	38	1			375		3	1	1	4	West Point & dependencies
1st Mass.	1st Mass.	Joseph Vose	10	34	5	262	311	28	12	41		1		393	3	11	1	1	11	West Point & dependencies
1st Mass.	4th Mass.	William Shepard	12	38	4 D	247	301	30	10	44	2			387	6	7			7	West Point & dependencies
1st Mass.	7th Mass.	Lt. Col. John Brooks	13	34	6	251	304	45	9	38				396	2	12			17	West Point & dependencies
2nd Mass.	2nd Mass.	Lt. Col. Ebenezer Sprout	14	32	4	262	312	21	13	48				394	4	6			7	West Point & dependencies
2nd Mass.	5th Mass.	Rufus Putnam	13	36	5 E	241	295	30	14	47	3			389	4	4			7	West Point & dependencies
2nd Mass.	8th Mass.	Michael Jackson	15	38	5	217	275	38	37	41				391	1	11		1	14	West Point & dependencies
3rd Mass.	3rd Mass.	John Greaton	12	37	2	295	346	18	9	19				392	1	7		1	8	West Point & dependencies
3rd Mass.	6th Mass.	Lt. Col. Calvin Smith	15	43	4	274	336	28	8	32	1			405	2	7			8	West Point & dependencies
3rd Mass.	9th Mass.	Henry Jackson	15	40	4	267	326	31	9	28	4	1		399	3	4		1	4	West Point & dependencies
	10th Mass.	Benjamin Tupper	15	44	3	268	330	25	9	25				389		14			16	
N.H.	1st N.H.	Lt. Col. Henry Dearborn	10	30	4	237	281	14	2	38	19			354	1	1		1	13	Albany, N.Y. area
N.H.	2nd N.H.	Lt. Col. George Reid	2	15	2	37	56	2	17	212	31	1		319	1				1	Albany, N.Y. area
N.Y.	1st N.Y.	Goose Van Schaick	19	48	5	327	399	37	10	64		7		517		6		1	10	Pompton, N.J.
N.Y.	2nd N.Y.	Philip Van Cortlandt	20	54	4	368	446	34	11	51		4		546	1	5		2	6	Pompton, N.J.
N.J.	1st N.J.	Matthias Ogden	17	36	5 F	251	309	14	14	89		6		432		3			9	near Morristown, N.J.
N.J.	2nd N.J.	Elias Dayton	15	37	5	242	299	36	16	77		4		432				2	6	near Morristown, N.J.
	R.I.	Lt. Col. Jeremiah Olney	15	40	5	314	374	52	23	20		4		473	2				82	Philadelphia, Pa.
	Canadian	Brevet Brig.Gen. Moses Hazen	14	30	2	207	253	16	16	143	10	2		440		7			8	Lancaster, Pa.
	Officers present on duty		70	91	2		163							163						
	TOTAL OF INFANTRY		379	984	98	5767	7228	674	289	1202	72	30		9495	33	140	2	20	282	
	CAVALRY																			
	2nd cont'l.	Elisha Sheldon	13	41	4	216	274	13	6	13	1	1		308	1	5			3	Connecticut
	ARTILLERY																			
	1 co., Lamb's 2nd cont'l.	Capt. Andrew Moodie	4	8		16	28	13	13	79		1	1	479		1			4	West Point & dependencies
	3rd cont'l.	John Crane	26	103	4	211	344								1	12			1	West Point & dependencies
	TOTAL OF ARTILLERY		30	111	4	227	372	13	13	79		1	1	479	1	13			5	
	INVALIDS																			
	Invalid corps	Lewis Nicola	7	22	1	142	172	36	12	45				265 G					1	
	TOTAL OF WASHINGTON'S ARMY		429	1158	107	6352	8046	736	320	1339	73	32	1	10547	35	158	2	20	291	

BRIGADE	UNIT	COMMANDING OFFICER	PRESENT FIT FOR DUTY & ON DUTY: COMMISSIONED OFFICERS	NONCOMMISSIONED OFFICERS	STAFF OFFICERS	RANK & FILE	TOTAL	RANK & FILE SICK, ON FURLOUGH, ETC.: SICK PRESENT	SICK ABSENT	ON COMMAND & EXTRA SERVICE	ON FURLOUGH	CONFINED	PRISONERS OF WAR	GRAND TOTAL	ALTERATIONS: DEATHS	DESERTED	TAKEN PRISONER	DISCHARGED	JOINED, ENLISTED, RECRUITED	LOCATION
	SOUTHERN DEPARTMENT UNDER MAJOR GENERAL NATHANAEL GREENE																			
N.C. Md. Pa.	1st N.C.[A]	Lt. Col. Hardy Murfree	10	35	3	309	357	31	15	86	6	1		496	1	14		64	7	Ashley River, S.C.
	2nd N.C.[A]	Lt. Col. Henry Dixon	16	25	5	264	310	15	18	92	6			441	4	12		117	3	Ashley River, S.C.
	1st Md.[B]	Lt. Col. Peter Adams	18	47	10	258	333	30	93	119	42			617	5	11	3		11	Ashley River, S.C.
	2nd Md.[B]	Lt. Col. John Stewart	7	47	12	288	354	19	63	111	66			613	5	10	1	1	22	Ashley River, S.C.
	Del.	David Hall	4	20	2	112	138	10	20	21	10			199	2					Ashley River, S.C.
	1st Pa.[B]	Thomas Craig	17	45	5	309	376	30	17	70	2			495	2	8			2	Ashley River, S.C.
	2nd Pa.[B]	Lt. Col. Josiah Harmar	18	49	6	301	374	24	36	74				508	8	14		2	5	Ashley River, S.C.
	Officers present on duty			13			13							13						
	TOTAL OF INFANTRY		90	281	43	1841	2255	159	262	573	132	1		3382	27	69	4	184	50	
	CAVALRY AND LEGIONARY CORPS																			
	Partizan corps cavalry	Lt. Col. Henry Lee	4	7	2	79	92	4		2	9			107			11			Ashley River, S.C.
	Partizan corps infantry	Lt. Col. Henry Lee	9	11		133	153	3	8	18	3			185				5	7	Ashley River, S.C.
	3rd cavalry	Maj. Richard Call	4	7	2	38	51	9	12	35				107				3	1	Ashley River, S.C.
	Officers present on duty		1	2			3							3						
	TOTAL OF CAVALRY AND LEGIONARY CORPS		18	27	4	250	299	16	20	55	12			402			11	8	8	
	ARTILLERY																			
	Va. co., 1st cont'l.	Capt. Lt. Lewis Booker	5	15		37	57		1	16				74		1			2	Ashley River, S.C.
	Md. co., 1st cont'l.	Capt. William Brown	1	13		20	34		2	6				42						Ashley River, S.C.
	Md. co., 1st cont'l.	Capt. James Smith	1	8		16	25		1	9				35						Ashley River, S.C.
	Pa. co., 4th cont'l.	Capt. William Ferguson	5	22		44	71	1	1	6				79						Camden, S.C.
	Pa. co., 4th cont'l.	Capt. John Brice	3	10		25	38							38					1	Georgia
	TOTAL OF ARTILLERY		15	68		142	225	1	5	37				268[H]		1			3	
	TOTAL OF GREENE'S ARMY		124	374	47	2233	2778	176	287	665	144	1		4051[H]	27	70	15	192	61	
	GEORGIA EXPEDITION UNDER BRIGADIER GENERAL ANTHONY WAYNE																			
	1st cont'l. cavalry	Anthony Walton White	4	11	3	112	130	10	6					146	1[J]				4	Georgia
	4th cont'l. cavalry	Stephen Moylan	2	4	1	38	45	2						47						Georgia
	Ga. legion horse	James Jackson	4	3	2	36	45	2	1					48		1				Georgia
	Va. det.	Lt. Col. Thomas Posey	20	42	3	289	354	14	11					379					6	Georgia
	Ga. legion infantry	James Jackson	4	3		41	48	9						57						Georgia
	Ga. militia		4	3		21	28	4						32[I]		28[J]				Georgia
	TOTAL OF WAYNE'S EXPEDITION		38	66	9	537	650	41	18					709[I]	1[J]	29[J]			10[J]	
	GRAND TOTAL		591	1598	163	9122	11474	953	625	2004	217	33	1	15307	63[J]	257	17	212[K]	362	

APRIL 1782
(continued)

OFFICERS SICK, ON FURLOUGH, ETC.	WASHINGTON'S ARMY				SOUTHERN DEPARTMENT				GEORGIA EXPEDITION				GRAND TOTAL
	COMMISSIONED	NONCOMMISSIONED	STAFF	TOTAL	COMMISSIONED	NONCOMMISSIONED	STAFF	TOTAL	COMMISSIONED	NONCOMMISSIONED	STAFF	TOTAL	
Sick Present	28	71		99	8	24		32		2		2	133
Sick Absent	28	40	4	72	7	19	1	27	5			5	104
On Command	81	134	7	222	30	31	2	63		2	1	3	288
On Extra Service	12	14	1	27	2	37		39					66
On Furlough	32	19	7	58	31	23	5	59	5		1	6	123
Furlough Expired	19	13	4	36									36
Absent without Leave	1			1									1
Recruiting	15 L	7		22	2			2					24
On the Staff	109 L			109	24		2	26			2	2	137
Prisoners of War	3	1		4	1			1					5
In Arrest or Confined	5	4	1	10	1			1					11
TOTAL	333	303	24	660	106	134	10	250	10	4	4	18	928

SOURCES OF THIS REPORT

1. MONTHLY RETURN OF THE CONTINENTAL ARMY UNDER THE IMMEDIATE COMMAND OF HIS EXCELLENCY GEORGE WASHINGTON... FOR APRIL 1782, ELEPHANT FOLIO OF WASHINGTON RETURNS, WILLIAM L. CLEMENTS LIBRARY. [THE SECTION OF THIS RETURN FOR THE INVALIDS APPEARS ON THE FOLLOWING PAGE OF THE FOLIO.]

1a. Monthly Return of the Continental Army under...Washington... April 1782, Record Group 93, National Archives. [Contains the same figures, but only to the brigade level.]

2. MONTHLY RETURN OF THE INFANTRY OF THE SOUTHERN ARMY, COMMANDED BY THE HONORABLE MAJOR GENERAL GREENE... MAY 1, 1782, RECORD GROUP 93, NATIONAL ARCHIVES. [ALSO CONTAINS SECTIONS FOR THE ARTILLERY AND CAVALRY AND LEGIONARY CORPS.]

3. RETURN OF THE TROOPS IN GEORGIA, COMMANDED BY THE HONORABLE BRIGADIER GENERAL WAYNE...APRIL 29, 1782, RECORD GROUP 93, NATIONAL ARCHIVES. [ALTHOUGH IT IS NOT SO HEADED, THIS IS APPARENTLY THE MONTHLY RETURN.]

A. The manuscript notes that Major Griffith John McRae's battalion (included separately on the March return) had been "incorporated."
B. See footnotes B and C on our March 1782 report.
C. Four staff officers in Lieutenant Colonel Isaac Sherman's 5th Connecticut regiment plus one chaplain for the entire brigade.
D. Five staff officers in Lieutenant Colonel John Brooks' 7th Massachusetts regiment plus one chaplain for the entire brigade.
E. Four staff officers in Michael Jackson's 8th Massachusetts regiment plus one chaplain for the entire brigade.
F. Four staff officers in Elias Dayton's 2nd New Jersey regiment plus one chaplain for the entire brigade.
G. The National Archives manuscript notes that no returns were received for this month for the 2nd regiment of artillery and for the sappers and miners.
H. The manuscript notes that General Francis Marion had under his command Lieutenant Colonel Maham's corps of state cavalry with 72 men fit for action, militia cavalry with 12 men fit for action, and South Carolina militia (chiefly unarmed) with 364 men fit for action. Lieutenant Colonel Horry's corps of cavalry had been incorporated with Lieutenant Colonel Maham's. These troops under Marion "have joined and are doing duty with the main army," even though they are not included in the main body of the return.
I. The manuscript notes that there were an additional 150 volunteers, reclaimed citizens, etc., doing duty between the Ogeechee and Altamaha Rivers and elsewhere. It is also noted that General Wayne's guard of thirteen Pennsylvanians was omitted here because they were returned as "on command" in the return of the Pennsylvania troops in the Southern Department; similarly, Captain Brice's company of artillery was also excluded because they were in the general return of the Southern Department.
J. The manuscript return for the Georgia expedition indicates that the alterations are not "regularly accounted for"; apparently these alterations figures are therefore incomplete.
K. Including ten men in Washington's infantry and two men in Greene's infantry discharged for inability.
L. Both manuscripts of this return have a note after the "on the staff" heading which relates that two second lieutenants and one captain lieutenant who were really on the staff had been included in the main body of the return. It is not clear whether these men were also included in the "Officers sick, on furlough, etc." section; if they were, these men are then counted twice on this report.

Brigadier General Anthony Wayne's 1782 expedition against the British, Loyalist, and Indian forces in Georgia brought this Pennsylvania soldier considerable credit. Wayne's later victory over the Indians in the Northwest, resulting in the Treaty of Greenville in August 1795, further enhanced his military fame. The John Trumbull pencil sketch reproduced here was drawn either in Philadelphia in 1790 or at New York in 1791–1792. (Courtesy of the Fordham University Library, Bronx, N.Y.)

MAY 1782

BRIGADE	UNIT	COMMANDING OFFICER	PRESENT FIT FOR DUTY & ON DUTY: COMMISSIONED OFFICERS	NONCOMMISSIONED OFFICERS	STAFF OFFICERS	RANK & FILE	TOTAL	RANK & FILE SICK, ON FURLOUGH, ETC.: SICK PRESENT	SICK ABSENT	ON COMMAND & EXTRA SERVICE	ON FURLOUGH	CONFINED	PRISONERS OF WAR	GRAND TOTAL	ALTERATIONS: DEATHS	DESERTED	TAKEN PRISONER	DISCHARGED	JOINED, ENLISTED, RECRUITED	LOCATION
	FORCES UNDER COMMANDER-IN-CHIEF GENERAL GEORGE WASHINGTON																			
1st Conn.	1st Conn.	John Durkee	14	43	5	267	329	20	5	27				381	1	1	1	1	22	West Point, N.Y. area
	3rd Conn.	Samuel Blatchley Webb	15	45	4 [E]	280	344	37	14	17				412	2	2		1	36	West Point, N.Y. area
	5th Conn.	Lt. Col. Isaac Sherman	12	44	5	267	328	43	9	25				405		9		1	28	West Point, N.Y. area
2nd Conn.	2nd Conn.	Heman Swift	19	44	4	311	378	26	4	22				430	1			1	44	West Point, N.Y. area
	4th Conn.	Zebulon Butler	16	56	4	257	333	36	13	22	1			405	3	2			26	West Point, N.Y. area
1st Mass.	1st Mass.	Joseph Vose	13	36	4	271	324	30	11	35				400	2				10	West Point, N.Y. area
	4th Mass.	William Shepard	14	47	5 [F]	262	328	34	11	34	1	1		409		3			16	West Point, N.Y. area
	7th Mass.	Lt. Col. John Brooks	13	40	5	281	339	29	7	32				407	2	1			9	West Point, N.Y. area
2nd Mass.	2nd Mass.	Lt. Col. Ebenezer Sprout	15	32	3	274	324	19	15	38	1			397		7			14	West Point, N.Y. area
	5th Mass.	Rufus Putnam	20	36	4 [G]	267	327	20	16	34	4			401	1	1			8	West Point, N.Y. area
	8th Mass.	Michael Jackson	16	37	6	258	317	30	24	31				402	3	1			14	West Point, N.Y. area
3rd Mass.	3rd Mass.	John Greaton	13	39	3	296	351	22	14	14				401	1	2	1		11	West Point, N.Y. area
	6th Mass.	Lt. Col. Calvin Smith	15	43	5	291	354	24	10	18				406	2	2			4	West Point, N.Y. area
	9th Mass.	Henry Jackson	16	38	4	293	350	24	8	20				402	2	1		1	9	West Point, N.Y. area
	10th Mass.	Benjamin Tupper	14	47	5	297	364	25	7	10				406	1	1			13	West Point, N.Y. area
N.H.	1st N.H.[A]	Lt. Col. Henry Dearborn	9	34	5	217	265	16	2	68	9			360	1	6		1	11	Albany, N.Y. area
	2nd N.H.[A]	Lt. Col. George Reid	11	19	3	40	73	1	97	137	23			331	2		1		2	Albany, N.Y. area
N.Y.	1st N.Y.	Goose Van Schaick	21	48	4 [H]	343	416	37	13	51		2		519		2			5	Pompton, N.J.
	2nd N.Y.	Philip Van Cortlandt	21	55	5	371	452	38	10	51	2	1		554		3			8	Pompton, N.J.
N.J.	1st N.J.	Matthias Ogden	19	45	4 [I]	286	354	18	6	60		4		442	4	5			12	near Morristown, N.J.
	2nd N.J.	Elias Dayton	20	41	5	284	350	27	19	43		3		442		4			9	near Morristown, N.J.
	R.I.[B]	Lt. Col. Jeremiah Olney	17	42	5	390	454	64	36	16		6		576	1	2			104	
	Canadian[B]	Brevet Brig. Gen. Moses Hazen																		Lancaster, Pa.
	Officers present on duty		50	81	1		132							132						
	TOTAL OF INFANTRY		393	992	98	6103	7586	620	351	805	41	17		9420	29	55	3	6	415	
	CAVALRY																			
	2nd cont'l.	Elisha Sheldon	17	39	3	222	281	15	10	11		1		318					1	Connecticut
	ARTILLERY[C]																			
	3rd cont'l.	John Crane	24	92	3	197	316	14	13	79	1		1	456	1	2		1	7	West Point, N.Y. area
	Det. 2nd cont'l.	Capt. Andrew Moodie	4	9		19	32									1			4	West Point, N.Y. area
	2nd cont'l.[B]	John Lamb																		Burlington, N.J.
	Present on duty			6		17	23							23						
	TOTAL OF ARTILLERY		28	107	3	233	371	14	13	79	1		1	479	1	3		1	11	
	SAPPERS AND MINERS																			
	3 cos.	Maj. Villefranche, Chevalier de[C]	5	5		62	72	4	2	2				80	1	2				West Point, N.Y.
	INVALIDS[C]																			
	Invalid corps	Lewis Nicola	6	25	3	168	202	24	16	27				269	1	2			3	
	TOTAL OF WASHINGTON'S ARMY		449	1168	107	6788	8512	677	392	924	42	18	1	10566	32	62	3	7	430	

MAY 1782
(continued)

BRIGADE	UNIT	COMMANDING OFFICER	PRESENT FIT FOR DUTY & ON DUTY: COMMISSIONED OFFICERS	NONCOMMISSIONED OFFICERS	STAFF OFFICERS	RANK & FILE	TOTAL	RANK & FILE SICK, ON FURLOUGH, ETC.: SICK PRESENT	SICK ABSENT	ON COMMAND & EXTRA SERVICE	ON FURLOUGH	CONFINED	PRISONERS OF WAR	GRAND TOTAL	ALTERATIONS: DEATHS	DESERTED	TAKEN PRISONER	DISCHARGED	JOINED, ENLISTED, RECRUITED	LOCATION
	SOUTHERN DEPARTMENT UNDER MAJOR GENERAL NATHANAEL GREENE																			
N.C.	1st N.C.[D]	Lt. Col. Hardy Murfree	8	23	3	205	239	41	16	84	4			384		6		116	26	Ashley River, S.C.
	2nd N.C.[D]	Lt. Col. Henry Dixon	9	24	5	217	255	14	17	69	2			357		2		70	2	Ashley River, S.C.
Md.	1st Md.[D]	Lt. Col. Peter Adams	16	48	4	250	318	22	63	102	1			506	1	8		1	5	Ashley River, S.C.
	2nd Md.[D]	Lt. Col. John Stewart	13	45	5	267	330	27	35	110	29			531		2			5	Ashley River, S.C.
	Del.	Capt. William McKennan	3	20	2	113	138	9	10	11				168	2	1				Ashley River, S.C.
Pa.	1st Pa.[D]	Thomas Craig	16	44	5	290	355	33	10	91	1			490		7		2	7	Ashley River, S.C.
	2nd Pa.[D]	Lt. Col. Josiah Harmar	19	46	4	288	357	34	12	79	1			483		11			3	Ashley River, S.C.
	Officers present on duty		1	15			16							16						
	TOTAL OF INFANTRY		85	265	28	1630	2008	180	163	546	38			2935	3	37		189	48	
	CAVALRY AND LEGIONARY CORPS																			
	Partizan corps cavalry	Lt. Col. Henry Lee	5	10	3	87	105	2	3	6	5			121	1		1		12	Ashley River, S.C.
	Partizan corps infantry	Lt. Col. Henry Lee	6	14		123	143	1	10	18	2			174				10	3	Ashley River, S.C.
	3rd cont'l. cavalry	Maj. Richard Call	5	9	4	48	66	15	18	16				115					3	Ashley River, S.C.
	4th cont'l. cavalry	Capt. Erasmus Gill	3	4		40	47							47						Ashley River, S.C.
	Officers present on duty		2				2							2						
	TOTAL OF CAVALRY AND LEGIONARY CORPS		21	37	7	298	363	18	31	40	7			459	1		1	10	18	
	ARTILLERY																			
	Va. co., 1st cont'l.	Capt. Anthony Singleton	6	13		35	54	2	1	12				69	1		2			Ashley River, S.C.
	Md. co., 1st cont'l.	Capt. William Brown	1	13		20	34		2	6				42						Ashley River, S.C.
	Md. co., 1st cont'l.	Capt. James Smith	1	10		14	25		2	7				34					1	Ashley River, S.C.
	Pa. co., 4th cont'l.	Capt. William Ferguson	3	13		27	43	1	1	4				49					5	Camden, S.C.
	Pa. co., 4th cont'l.	Capt. John Brice	3	10		25	38							38						Georgia
	Pa. co., 4th cont'l.	Capt. James McClure	2	11		19	32							32						Georgetown, S.C.
	TOTAL OF ARTILLERY		16	70		140	226	3	6[J]	29				264	1		2		6	
	TOTAL OF GREENE'S ARMY		122	372	35	2068	2597	201	200[J]	615	45[J]			3658	5	37	3	199	72	
	GRAND TOTAL		571	1540	142	8856	11109	878	592	1539	87	18	1	14224	37	99	6	206[K]	502	

MAY 1782
(continued)

OFFICERS SICK, ON FURLOUGH, ETC.	WASHINGTON'S ARMY[L]				SOUTHERN DEPARTMENT				GRAND TOTAL
	COMMISSIONED	NONCOMMISSIONED	STAFF	TOTAL	COMMISSIONED	NONCOMMISSIONED	STAFF	TOTAL	
Sick Present	22	56	1	79	10	15		25	104
Sick Absent	24	38		62	12	18	1	31	93
On Command	69	116	13	198	30	36	2	68	266
On Extra Service	7	8		15	2	24		26	41
On Furlough	21	6	7	34	24	17	3	44	78
Furlough Expired	15	16	1	32					32
Absent without Leave	1			1					1
Recruiting	16	8		24	2			2	26
On the Staff	101			101	24			24	125
Prisoners of War	3	2		5	1			1	6
In Arrest	2	1	1	4					4
TOTAL	281	251	23	555	105	110	6	221	776

SOURCES OF THIS REPORT

1. MONTHLY RETURN OF THE CONTINENTAL ARMY UNDER THE IMMEDIATE COMMAND OF HIS EXCELLENCY GEORGE WASHINGTON... FOR THE MONTH OF MAY 1782, ELEPHANT FOLIO OF WASHINGTON RETURNS, WILLIAM L. CLEMENTS LIBRARY. [TWO SECTIONS OF THIS RETURN APPEAR ON THE FOLLOWING PAGE OF THE FOLIO.]

1a. Monthly Return of the Continental Army under... Washington... May, 1782, Record Group 93, National Archives. [The same return, but only to the brigade level.]

2. MONTHLY RETURN OF THE INFANTRY OF THE SOUTHERN ARMY COMMANDED BY THE HONORABLE MAJOR GENERAL GREENE... MAY 25, 1782, RECORD GROUP 93, NATIONAL ARCHIVES. [ALSO CONTAINS SECTIONS FOR THE ARTILLERY AND CAVALRY AND LEGIONARY CORPS.]

A. The National Archives manuscript notes, "The 1st & 2d New Hampshire regiments are entered from Returns of the 9th May being the latest that have reached the office."
B. The line for this regiment is blank on the manuscript.
C. The sections for the artillery and for the invalids of the May monthly return in the Clements folio are not dated, but from their position on the manuscript and by comparison with the National Archives manuscript there is no question of their correct identification.
D. These units are recent consolidations of these Continental lines; see our March and April 1782 reports.
E. Four staff officers in Lieutenant Colonel Isaac Sherman's 5th Connecticut regiment plus one chaplain for the entire brigade.
F. Four staff officers in Lieutenant Colonel John Brooks' 7th Massachusetts regiment plus one chaplain for the entire brigade.
G. Five staff officers in Michael Jackson's 8th Massachusetts regiment plus one chaplain for the entire brigade.
H. Four staff officers in Philip Van Cortlandt's 2nd New York regiment plus one chaplain for the entire brigade.
I. Four staff officers in Elias Dayton's 2nd New Jersey regiment plus one chaplain for the entire brigade.
J. The manuscript notes that a general order of May 17 had directed that the men who were sick absent or on furlough in their home states of Virginia and Maryland be omitted in the returns of the Southern Department. These men were to be kept track of by the recruiting officers in those states, and 242 men of the Maryland line had already been removed from this report. The manuscript goes on to note, "The 29 men who are now returned Sick absent in Virginia and a few furloughed men will be omitted in the next return."
K. Including three men in Washington's infantry discharged for inability.
L. Both manuscripts include this section for all of the parts of the return. However, a discrepancy exists for the sappers and miners. The Clements folio indicates that all the officers were present fit for duty and that none were on command. The National Archives manuscript includes an additional two commissioned and two noncommissioned officers of the sappers and miners as "on command," but then does not add them into the total line below. Apparently the National Archives manuscript is in error; we have followed the Clements folio.

Major General Nathanael Greene developed into perhaps the best American officer next to Washington. After he disbanded his Southern Department at the war's close, Greene received a triumphant welcome in Philadelphia in early October 1783. At that time (before Greene joined Washington for the honors of Continental Congress in Princeton), Charles Willson Peale painted this portrait for his museum. (Courtesy of the Independence National Historical Park Collection, Philadelphia)

JUNE 1782

BRIGADE	UNIT	COMMANDING OFFICER	PRESENT FIT FOR DUTY & ON DUTY: COMMISSIONED OFFICERS	NONCOMMISSIONED OFFICERS	STAFF OFFICERS	RANK & FILE	TOTAL	RANK & FILE SICK, ON FURLOUGH, ETC.: SICK PRESENT	SICK ABSENT	ON COMMAND & EXTRA SERVICE	ON FURLOUGH	CONFINED	PRISONERS OF WAR	GRAND TOTAL	ALTERATIONS: DEATHS	DESERTED	TAKEN PRISONER	DISCHARGED	JOINED, ENLISTED, RECRUITED	LOCATION
	FORCES UNDER COMMANDER-IN-CHIEF GENERAL GEORGE WASHINGTON																			
1st Conn.	1st Conn.	Lt. Col. Thomas Grosvenor	12	38	6	257	313	28	10	64	4			419		6		1	54	West Point, N.Y. area
1st Conn.	3rd Conn.	Samuel Blatchley Webb	15	43	4	294	356	49	19	13	3			440		4			42	West Point, N.Y. area
1st Conn.	5th Conn.	Lt. Col. Isaac Sherman	18	45	5	284	352	53	5	19	12			441	2	5		7	46	West Point, N.Y. area
2nd Conn.	2nd Conn.	Heman Swift	3	6	2	53	64	4	40	262	7			377		5		2	10	West Point, N.Y. area
2nd Conn.	4th Conn.	Zebulon Butler	17	58	4	274	353	25	24	22	8			432		2	2	5	36	West Point, N.Y. area
2nd Conn.	R.I.	Lt. Col. Jeremiah Olney	14	35	4	408	461	34	78	14		2		589	1			1	25	West Point, N.Y. area
1st Mass.	1st Mass.	Joseph Vose	12	38	5	317	372	30	8	12				422	2	3		5	35	West Point, N.Y. area
1st Mass.	4th Mass.	William Shepard	17	43	4 A	307	371	33	10	16	1	2		433	1	6		1	39	West Point, N.Y. area
1st Mass.	7th Mass.	Lt. Col. John Brooks	4	15	6	331	356	31	5	12	1			405	1	1		4	43	West Point, N.Y. area
2nd Mass.	2nd Mass.	Lt. Col. Ebenezer Sprout	16	43	5	310	374	29	18	15		1		437	3			6	37	West Point, N.Y. area
2nd Mass.	5th Mass.	Rufus Putnam	23	44	5 B	313	385	24	13	13	1	1		437	1	4		1	35	West Point, N.Y. area
2nd Mass.	8th Mass.	Michael Jackson	22	48	6	295	371	40	19	12				442	2	4			37	West Point, N.Y. area
3rd Mass.	3rd Mass.	John Greaton			1	76	77	27	12	263		3		382				1	38	West Point, N.Y. area
3rd Mass.	6th Mass.	Lt. Col. Calvin Smith	19	43	5	330	397	28	4	7		1		437	2	8	1	1	47	West Point, N.Y. area
3rd Mass.	9th Mass.	Henry Jackson	13	39	5	314	371	26	4	14	1	1		417		10		1	38	West Point, N.Y. area
	10th Mass.	Benjamin Tupper	17	46	4	304	371	35	10	7				423	2	10		1	41	West Point, N.Y. area
N.H.	1st N.H.	Lt. Col. Henry Dearborn	13	37	5	252	307	16	1	36	2	3		365		7		2	9	Albany, N.Y. area
N.H.	2nd N.H.	Lt. Col. George Reid	10	23	3	114	150	5	15	159	10			339				2	7	Albany, N.Y. area
N.Y.	1st N.Y.	Goose Van Schaick	24	53	4	413	494	48	13	25	1	1		582		2		1	60	Pompton, N.J.
N.Y.	2nd N.Y.	Philip Van Cortlandt	17	51	3	398	469	44	8	74				595		4			54	Pompton, N.J.
N.J.	1st N.J.	Matthias Ogden	21	45	6	279	351	16	6	72				445		5			3	near Morristown, N.J.
N.J.	2nd N.J.	Elias Dayton	20	44	4	267	335	19	14	69		3		440		5			1	near Morristown, N.J.
	Canadian	Brevet Brig. Gen. Moses Hazen	15	30	3	213	261	20	13	141	8	3		446	1	10		2	18	Lancaster, Pa.
	Officers present on duty		51	95	2		148							148						
	TOTAL OF INFANTRY		393	962	101	6403	7859	664	349	1341	59	21		10293	18	101	3	44	755	
	CAVALRY																			
	2nd cont'l.	Elisha Sheldon	15	42	4	216	277	18	5	11		1		312		5			5	Connecticut
	ARTILLERY																			
	3rd cont'l.	John Crane	24	99	3	192	318	20	15	97		2	1	551		6			12	West Point, N.Y. area
	Det. 2nd cont'l.	Capt. Andrew Moodie	4	11		83	98									8			84	West Point, N.Y. area
	Present on duty		1	3		10	14							14						
	TOTAL OF ARTILLERY		29	113	3	285	430	20	15	97		2	1	565		14			96	
	SAPPERS AND MINERS																			
	3 cos.		3	5		51	59	4	6	3		6		78					1	West Point, N.Y. area
	INVALIDS																			
	Invalid corps	Lewis Nicola	10	29	3	263	305	50	47	30	1			433		1		1	110	
	TOTAL OF WASHINGTON'S ARMY		450	1151	111	7218	8930	756	422	1482	60	30	1	11681	18	121	3	45 C	967	

OFFICERS SICK, ON FURLOUGH, ETC.	WASHINGTON'S ARMY			
	COMMISSIONED	NONCOMMISSIONED	STAFF	TOTAL
Sick Present	20	75		95
Sick Absent	29	47	1	77
On Command	106	214	19	339
On Extra Service	7	6		13
On Furlough	17	6	2	25
Furlough Expired	7	6		13
Absent without Leave	3			3
Recruiting	14	5		19
On the Staff	106			106
Prisoners of War	3	1		4
In Arrest	5	1	1	7
TOTAL	317	361	23	701

SOURCE OF THIS REPORT

1. MONTHLY RETURN OF THE CONTINENTAL ARMY UNDER THE COMMAND OF HIS EXCELLENCY GEORGE WASHINGTON...FOR THE MONTH OF JUNE 1782, ELEPHANT FOLIO OF WASHINGTON RETURNS, WILLIAM L. CLEMENTS LIBRARY.

1a. Monthly Return of the Continental Army under...Washington...June 1782, Record Group 93, National Archives. [Contains the same figures, but only to the brigade level.]

A. Five staff officers in Lieutenant Colonel John Brooks' 7th Massachusetts regiment plus one chaplain for the entire brigade.
B. Five staff officers in Michael Jackson's 8th Massachusetts regiment plus one chaplain for the entire brigade.
C. Including sixteen men in Washington's infantry and one man in the Invalid Corps discharged for inability.

JULY 1782

BRIGADE: 1st Conn. | 1st Mass. \ 3rd Mass. N.H. | N.J. — 2nd Conn. 2nd Mass. N.Y.

UNIT	COMMANDING OFFICER	PRESENT FIT FOR DUTY & ON DUTY: COMMISSIONED OFFICERS	NONCOMMISSIONED OFFICERS	STAFF OFFICERS	RANK & FILE	TOTAL	RANK & FILE SICK, ON FURLOUGH, ETC.: SICK PRESENT	SICK ABSENT	ON COMMAND & EXTRA SERVICE	ON FURLOUGH	CONFINED	RECRUITING	PRISONERS OF WAR	GRAND TOTAL	ALTERATIONS: DEATHS	DESERTED	TAKEN PRISONER	DISCHARGED	JOINED, ENLISTED, RECRUITED	LOCATION
FORCES UNDER COMMANDER-IN-CHIEF GENERAL GEORGE WASHINGTON																				
1st Conn.	Lt. Col. Thomas Grosvenor	15	38	5	304	362	37	16	17					432		7			18	West Point, N.Y. area
3rd Conn.	Samuel Blatchley Webb	14 A	37	4	286	341	53	20	13	2				429		4		14	14	West Point, N.Y. area
5th Conn.	Lt. Col. Isaac Sherman	18	43	5	262	328	67	10	16	3				424		12		14	11	West Point, N.Y. area
2nd Conn.	Heman Swift	17	46	6	304	373	36	5	20	2				436		9			15	West Point, N.Y. area
4th Conn.	Zebulon Butler	12	51	4	287	354	39	21	21	3				438	1	2		1	22	West Point, N.Y. area
R.I.	Lt. Col. Jeremiah Olney	9	37	5	435	486	69	17	13		2			587	3	5			8	West Point, N.Y. area
1st Mass.	Joseph Vose	11	40	5	342	398	29	7	10		1			445	4	2			27	West Point, N.Y. area
4th Mass.	William Shepard	13	44	5	326	388	33	7	14					442	1	5			18	West Point, N.Y. area
7th Mass.	Lt. Col. John Brooks	4	14	4	344	366	33	3	11					413	1	2			15	West Point, N.Y. area
2nd Mass.	Lt. Col. Ebenezer Sprout	15	35	5	320	375	32	18	17					442	1	5			22	West Point, N.Y. area
5th Mass.	Rufus Putnam	20	43	4	326	393	27	15	12	2	1			450	3	4			26	West Point, N.Y. area
8th Mass.	Michael Jackson	18	49	5	323	395	36	17	11					459	1	3			24	West Point, N.Y. area
3rd Mass.	John Greaton	17	44	5	322	388	39	11	11					449		7			16	West Point, N.Y. area
6th Mass.	Lt. Col. Calvin Smith	23	47	5	344	419	23	10	7	1				460		4	1		20	West Point, N.Y. area
9th Mass.	Henry Jackson	1		1	363	365		12	13	1				391	1	4			35	West Point, N.Y. area
10th Mass.	Benjamin Tupper	19	48	5	327	399	42	3	7		1			452	1	7			35	West Point, N.Y. area
1st N.H.	Lt. Col. Henry Dearborn	12	39	5	272	328	21	2	38		1			390	2	1		1	29	Albany, N.Y. area
2nd N.H.	Lt. Col. George Reid	11	38	3	198	250	12	12	98	7				379	1	1	7	1	34	Albany, N.Y. area
1st N.Y.	Goose Van Schaick	21	43	5	346	415	55	14	100		1			585	1	4			17	Pompton, N.J.
2nd N.Y.	Philip Van Cortlandt	17	53	4	389	463	52	7	93					615	1	5			20	Pompton, N.J.
1st N.J.	Matthias Ogden	24	48	6	312	390	10	12	45					457		3			9	near Morristown, N.J.
2nd N.J.	Elias Dayton	22	44	5	287	358	26	15	40		1			440		3		1	2	near Morristown, N.J.
Canadian	Brevet Brig. Gen. Moses Hazen	14	32	2	219	267	23	14	140	9	3			456		1			6	Lancaster, Pa.
Officers present on duty		94	158	8		260								260						
TOTAL OF INFANTRY		441	1071	111	7238	8861	794	268	767	30	11			10731	22	100	8	32	443	
CAVALRY																				
2nd cont'l.	Elisha Sheldon	15	37	4	221	277	14	4	12		1			308		2		1	10	Connecticut
ARTILLERY																				
2nd cont'l.	John Lamb	28	80	3	129	240													1	Burlington, N.J.
3rd cont'l.	John Crane	24	97	3	178	302	32	19	103		2	3	1	827	2	12			1	West Point, N.Y. area
Det. 2nd cont'l.	Capt. Andrew Moodie	3	11		111	125										2			27	West Point, N.Y. area
Present on duty		1	3		21	25								25						
TOTAL OF ARTILLERY		56	191	6	439	692	32	19	103		2	3	1	852	2	14			29	
SAPPERS AND MINERS																				
3 cos.		3	6		58	67	5	5	1		1			79					1	West Point, N.Y. area
INVALIDS																				
Invalid corps	Lewis Nicola	7	25	5	174	211	58	44	108		1			422	1	8			3	West Point, N.Y. area
TOTAL OF WASHINGTON'S ARMY		522	1330	126	8130	10108	903	340	991	30	16	3	1	12392	25	124	8	B 33	486	

OFFICERS SICK, ON FURLOUGH, ETC.	WASHINGTON'S ARMY			
	COMMISSIONED	NONCOMMISSIONED	STAFF	TOTAL
Sick Present	29	85	1	115
Sick Absent	31	48	1	80
On Command	57	113	8	178
On Extra Service	6	11		17
On Furlough	16	4	1	21
Furlough Expired	7	3	1	11
Absent without Leave	3			3
Recruiting	16	6		22
On the Staff	113			113
Prisoners of War	4	1		5
In Arrest	10			10
TOTAL	292	271	12	575

SOURCE OF THIS REPORT

1. MONTHLY RETURN OF THE CONTINENTAL ARMY UNDER THE COMMAND OF HIS EXCELLENCY GEORGE WASHINGTON... FOR THE MONTH OF JULY 1782, ELEPHANT FOLIO OF WASHINGTON RETURNS, WILLIAM L. CLEMENTS LIBRARY.

A. Seventeen commissioned officers in Lieutenant Colonel Isaac Sherman's 5th Connecticut regiment plus one brigadier general for the entire brigade.
B. Including two men in Washington's infantry discharged for inability.

AUGUST 1782

BRIGADE	UNIT	COMMANDING OFFICER	PRESENT FIT FOR DUTY & ON DUTY: COMMISSIONED OFFICERS	NONCOMMISSIONED OFFICERS	STAFF OFFICERS	RANK & FILE	TOTAL	RANK & FILE SICK, ON FURLOUGH, ETC.: SICK PRESENT	SICK ABSENT	ON COMMAND & EXTRA SERVICE	ON FURLOUGH	CONFINED	RECRUITING	PRISONERS OF WAR	GRAND TOTAL	ALTERATIONS: DEATHS	DESERTED	TAKEN PRISONER	DISCHARGED	JOINED, ENLISTED, RECRUITED	LOCATION
	FORCES UNDER COMMANDER-IN-CHIEF GENERAL GEORGE WASHINGTON																				
N.J.	1st N.J.	Matthias Ogden	21	45	5 C	312	383	16	10	43					452					4	Verplancks Point, N.Y. H
N.J.	2nd N.J.	Elias Dayton	22	39	6	288	355	22	13	39		1			430		3		3		Verplancks Point, N.Y.
N.Y.	1st N.Y.	Goose Van Schaick	19	49	3	368	439	55	14	80		2			590		2			5	Verplancks Point, N.Y.
N.Y.	2nd N.Y.	Philip Van Cortlandt	20	57	4	406	487	51	5	77		2			622		1		1	5	Verplancks Point, N.Y.
1st Conn.	1st Conn.	Lt. Col. Thomas Grosvenor	14	40	5	302	361	28	29	17					435	1	3			6	Verplancks Point, N.Y.
1st Conn.	3rd Conn.	Samuel Blatchley Webb	10	35	3	277	325	50	29	12	2				418		6			2	Verplancks Point, N.Y.
1st Conn.	5th Conn.	Lt. Col. Isaac Sherman	12 A	37	5 D	276	330	56	19	16	1	1			423		5		1	16	Verplancks Point, N.Y.
2nd Conn.	2nd Conn.	Heman Swift	11	36	5	294	346	46	9	17	1	1			420	1	1			2	Verplancks Point, N.Y.
2nd Conn.	4th Conn.	Zebulon Butler	11	49	4	275	339	31	36	20	2				428	2	11			7	Verplancks Point, N.Y.
2nd Conn.	R.I.	Lt. Col. Jeremiah Olney				48	48		88	391					527	2	3			1	Verplancks Point, etc. I
1st Mass.	1st Mass.	Joseph Vose	17	46	5	347	415	17	11	14		1			458	1	4			18	Verplancks Point, N.Y.
1st Mass.	4th Mass.	William Shepard	17	51	4 E	339	411	28	10	14		2			465	1	3			17	Verplancks Point, N.Y.
1st Mass.	7th Mass.	Lt. Col. John Brooks	15	43	6	343	407	38	4	11		1			461		5			15	Verplancks Point, N.Y.
2nd Mass.	2nd Mass.	Lt. Col. Ebenezer Sprout	15	40	4	333	392	40	13	15					460		3			16	Verplancks Point, N.Y.
2nd Mass.	5th Mass.	Rufus Putnam	17 B	44	5 F	333	399	25	16	13	1				454		5		1	15	Verplancks Point, N.Y.
2nd Mass.	8th Mass.	Michael Jackson	12	45	6	342	405	28	13	11		1			458		2			12	Verplancks Point, N.Y.
3rd Mass.	3rd Mass.	John Greaton	16	37	4	339	396	30	15	10					451	1	5			18	Verplancks Point, N.Y.
3rd Mass.	6th Mass.	Lt. Col. Calvin Smith	16	42	4	351	413	18	21	6	1				459	1	6			19	Verplancks Point, N.Y.
3rd Mass.	9th Mass.	Henry Jackson	17	39	5	340	401	35	9	13		2			460		2			13	Verplancks Point, N.Y.
	10th Mass.	Benjamin Tupper	18	41	5	335	399	36	5	9		1			450		8			18	West Point & dependencies
N.H.	1st N.H.	Lt. Col. Henry Dearborn	15	40	5	279	339	23	2	33		1			398		4			13	Albany, N.Y. area
N.H.	2nd N.H.	Lt. Col. George Reid	8	32	4	141	185	15	13	153	5				371	5	2	1		9	Albany, N.Y. area
	Canadian	Brevet Brig. Gen. Moses Hazen	13	28	2	227	270	25	14	150	9	2			470					19	Lancaster, Pa.
	Officers present on duty		77	118	3		198								198						
	TOTAL OF INFANTRY		413	1033	102	6895	8443	713	398	1164	22	18			10758	15	84	1	6	250	
	CAVALRY																				
	2nd cont'l.	Elisha Sheldon	15	38	3	182	238	14	5	43		1			301		7		1	4	New York state
	Marechaussie	Capt. Bartholomew Von Heer	3	11		39	53			12					65						Verplancks Point, N.Y.
	TOTAL OF CAVALRY		18	49	3	221	291	14	5	55		1			366		7		1	4	
	ARTILLERY																				
	2nd cont'l.	John Lamb	23	78	4	116	221										4		2	1	
	3rd cont'l.	John Crane	27	110	3	214	354	40	16	84		2	3	1	866		1		2	6	West Point & dependencies J
	Det. 2nd cont'l.	(John Lamb)	3	16		126	145										3				West Point & dependencies
	Present on duty		1	3		42	46								46						
	TOTAL OF ARTILLERY		54	207	7	498	766	40	16	84		2	3	1	912		8		4	7	
	SAPPERS AND MINERS																				
	3 cos.		2	5		61	68	2	6	2					78					1	West Point & dependencies
	INVALIDS																				
	Invalid corps	Lewis Nicola	2	18	3	99	122	23	78	180	2				405	1	4		1	4	West Point & dependencies
	TOTAL OF WASHINGTON'S ARMY		489	1312	115	7774	9690	792	503	1485	24	21	3	1	12519	16	103	1	12 G	266	

OFFICERS SICK, ON FURLOUGH, ETC.	WASHINGTON'S ARMY			
	COMMISSIONED	NONCOMMISSIONED	STAFF	TOTAL
Sick Present	21	71	2	94
Sick Absent	30	63	3	96
On Command	84	166	15	265
On Extra Service	6	11		17
On Furlough	20	6	2	28
Furlough Expired	7	2		9
Absent without Leave	1			1
Recruiting	10	6		16
On the Staff	108			108
Prisoners of War	4			4
In Arrest	10			10
TOTAL	301	325	22	648

SOURCE OF THIS REPORT

1. MONTHLY RETURN OF THE CONTINENTAL ARMY UNDER THE COMMAND OF HIS EXCELLENCY GEORGE WASHINGTON... FOR THE MONTH OF AUGUST 1782, ELEPHANT FOLIO OF WASHINGTON RETURNS, WILLIAM L. CLEMENTS LIBRARY.

1a. Monthly Return of the Continental Army under...Washington...August 1782, Record Group 93, National Archives. [Contains the same figures, but only to the brigade level.]

A. Eleven commissioned officers in Lieutenant Colonel Isaac Sherman's 5th Connecticut regiment plus one brigadier general for the entire brigade.
B. Eleven commissioned officers in Michael Jackson's 8th Massachusetts regiment plus one brigadier general for the entire brigade.
C. Five staff officers in Elias Dayton's 2nd New Jersey regiment plus one chaplain for the entire brigade.
D. Four staff officers in Lieutenant Colonel Isaac Sherman's 5th Connecticut regiment plus one chaplain for the entire brigade.
E. Five staff officers in Lieutenant Colonel John Brooks' 7th Massachusetts regiment plus one chaplain for the entire brigade.
F. Five staff officers in Michael Jackson's 8th Massachusetts regiment plus one chaplain for the entire brigade.
G. Including four men in Washington's infantry discharged for inability.
H. On August 31, in a combined land and water movement, Washington moved his army into the field at Verplancks Point. Doubtless, most or all of these figures were collected before that movement.
I. On August 22 (before the army moved to Verplancks Point), the bulk of the Rhode Island regiment had marched to relieve the posts at Dobbs Ferry, Stony Point, and Verplancks Point. Earlier, about one hundred men from the regiment had been ordered to Fishkill to help with removing the barracks there.
J. Although some artillery pieces were attached to the light infantry and to the brigades, the bulk of the artillery was to remain at West Point. It is not clear when that part of the 2nd Continental artillery which had been at Burlington, New Jersey, joined the detachment of that regiment which had been at West Point. This must have occurred after these artillery figures were compiled and before the next month's return was made out.

SEPTEMBER 1782

BRIGADE	UNIT	COMMANDING OFFICER	PRESENT FIT FOR DUTY & ON DUTY: COMMISSIONED OFFICERS	NONCOMMISSIONED OFFICERS	STAFF OFFICERS	RANK & FILE	TOTAL	RANK & FILE SICK, ON FURLOUGH, ETC.: SICK PRESENT	SICK ABSENT	ON COMMAND & EXTRA SERVICE	ON FURLOUGH	CONFINED	RECRUITING	PRISONERS OF WAR	GRAND TOTAL	ALTERATIONS: DEATHS	DESERTED	TAKEN PRISONER	DISCHARGED	JOINED, ENLISTED, RECRUITED	LOCATION
	FORCES UNDER COMMANDER-IN-CHIEF GENERAL GEORGE WASHINGTON																				
N.J.	1st N.J. A	Matthias Ogden	15	41	4	303	363	14	11	55					443	2				4	Verplancks Point, N.Y.
N.J.	2nd N.J. A	Elias Dayton			2	54	56	17	20	272		1			366		1			3	Verplancks Point, N.Y.
N.Y.	1st N.Y.	Goose Van Schaick	19	48	3	406	476	46	16	48		2			588		1			6	Stony Point & Kakiat, N.Y. J
N.Y.	2nd N.Y.	Philip Van Cortlandt	17	54	5	429	505	40	5	67		2			619	2	3			6	Verplancks Point, N.Y.
1st Conn.	1st Conn.	Lt. Col. Thomas Grosvenor	14	41	3	268	326	31	24	50	1				432	4			1	3	Verplancks Point, N.Y.
1st Conn.	3rd Conn.	Samuel Blatchley Webb	13	39	3	264	319	34	28	38					419	2	1		1	3	Verplancks Point, N.Y.
1st Conn.	5th Conn.	Lt. Col. Isaac Sherman	12	35	4	229	280	54	25	51	1				411	1	3		3	2	Verplancks Point, N.Y.
2nd Conn.	2nd Conn.	Heman Swift	14	40	5	269	328	31	18	48	1				426		1		2	3	Verplancks Point, N.Y.
2nd Conn.	4th Conn.	Zebulon Butler	14	50	3 D	232	299	32	28	57	2				418		5		2	1	Verplancks Point, N.Y.
2nd Conn.	R.I.	Lt. Col. Jeremiah Olney	14	36	6	309	365	48	19	126		2			560	5	4		9		Verplancks Point, N.Y.
1st Mass.	1st Mass.	Joseph Vose	15	41	5	328	389	24	17	21		1			452	2			5	8	Verplancks Point, N.Y.
1st Mass.	4th Mass.	William Shepard	13	44	3	332	392	21	7	29		2			451	1			1	6	Verplancks Point, N.Y.
1st Mass.	7th Mass.	Lt. Col. John Brooks	13	38	5 E	321	377	44	9	20					450		1		4	6	West Point, N.Y. K
2nd Mass.	2nd Mass.	Lt. Col. Ebenezer Sprout	13	39	4	325	381	26	23	21	1	1			453		1		7	7	Verplancks Point, N.Y.
2nd Mass.	5th Mass.	Rufus Putnam	18 C	45	5 F	320	388	22	18	25	1				454	1	3		4	10	Verplancks Point, N.Y.
2nd Mass.	8th Mass.	Michael Jackson	10	46	6	336	398	26	13	16		1			454	2	2		5	10	Verplancks Point, N.Y.
3rd Mass.	3rd Mass.	John Greaton	16	38	3	327	384	36	11	22					453	1	1		3	11	Verplancks Point, N.Y.
3rd Mass.	6th Mass.	Lt. Col. Calvin Smith	16	40	5 G	330	391	23	16	21					451	1	2		7	8	Verplancks Point, N.Y.
3rd Mass.	9th Mass.	Henry Jackson	13	38	6	327	384	42	8	23		1			458		2		1	10	Verplancks Point, N.Y.
	10th Mass.	Benjamin Tupper	22	46	5	337	410	34	8	9					461	2	2		2	8	West Point & dependencies
N.H.	1st N.H. B	Lt. Col. Henry Dearborn																			Albany, N.Y. area
N.H.	2nd N.H. B	Lt. Col. George Reid																			Albany, N.Y. area
	Canadian	Brevet Brig. Gen. Moses Hazen	11	24	1	260	296	23	17	152	6	2			496	2	2			36	Lancaster, Pa.
	Officers present on duty		86	132	5		223								223						
	TOTAL OF INFANTRY		378	955	91	6306	7730	668	341	1171	13	15			9938	28	35		57	151	
	CAVALRY																				
	2nd cont'l.	Elisha Sheldon	16	42	3	202	263	3	6	37		1			310		1			6	New York state
	Marechaussie	Capt. Bartholomew Von Heer	3	12		41	56	1	2	7					66					1	Verplancks Point, N.Y.
	TOTAL OF CAVALRY		19	54	3	243	319	4	8	44		1			376		1			7	
	ARTILLERY																				
	2nd cont'l.	John Lamb	23	68	3	191	285	25	18	75		2	2	1	808	1				118 I	West Point & dependencies
	3rd cont'l.	John Crane	28	130	2	240	400												9	5	West Point & dependencies
	Present on duty		4	20		36	60								60						
	TOTAL OF ARTILLERY		55	218	5	467	745	25	18	75		2	2	1	868	1			9	123	
	SAPPERS AND MINERS																				
	3 cos.	Maj. Villefranche, Chevalier de	3	6		60	69	3	5	3					80						West Point & dependencies
	INVALIDS																				
	Invalid corps	Lewis Nicola	5	18	5	96	124	25	73	153	1	2			378	1	6		97 H	76	West Point & dependencies
	TOTAL OF WASHINGTON'S ARMY		460	1251	104	7172	8987	725	445	1446	14	20	2	1	11640	30	42		163	357	

OFFICERS SICK, ON FURLOUGH, ETC.	WASHINGTON'S ARMY			
	COMMISSIONED	NONCOMMISSIONED	STAFF	TOTAL
Sick Present	13	61	1	75
Sick Absent	37	56	2	95
On Command	80	135	13	228
On Extra Service	3	11		14
On Furlough	21	3	5	29
Furlough Expired	3			3
Absent without Leave	2			2
Recruiting	5	5		10
On the Staff	103			103
Prisoners of War	3			3
In Arrest	5	1		6
TOTAL	275	272	21	568

SOURCE OF THIS REPORT

1. MONTHLY RETURN OF THE CONTINENTAL ARMY UNDER THE COMMAND OF HIS EXCELLENCY GEORGE WASHINGTON...FOR THE MONTH OF SEPTEMBER 1782, ELEPHANT FOLIO OF WASHINGTON RETURNS, WILLIAM L. CLEMENTS LIBRARY.

1a. Monthly Return of the Continental Army under...Washington...September 1782, Record Group 93, National Archives. [Contains the same figures, but only to the brigade level.]

A. The figures for this regiment obviously date from before September 29, when the bulk of the regiment returned from a tour of duty doing construction work at West Point.
B. The lines for these units are blank on the manuscript. The National Archives copy of the return notes, "No Return from the New Hampshire Line this month."
C. Nine commissioned officers in Michael Jackson's 8th Massachusetts regiment plus one brigadier general for the entire brigade.
D. Five staff officers in Lieutenant Colonel Jeremiah Olney's Rhode Island regiment plus one chaplain for the entire brigade.
E. Four staff officers in Lieutenant Colonel John Brooks' 7th Massachusetts regiment plus one chaplain for the entire brigade.
F. Five staff officers in Michael Jackson's 8th Massachusetts regiment plus one chaplain for the entire brigade.
G. Five staff officers in Henry Jackson's 9th Massachusetts regiment plus one chaplain for the entire brigade.
H. Including fifty-three men in Washington's infantry and ninety-seven men in the Invalid Corps discharged for inability.
I. This figure mainly represents the joining of the two portions of this regiment, not a large addition of new soldiers.
J. On September 29 the 1st New York regiment began a short tour of duty as a garrison at these places.
K. On September 29 the 7th Massachusetts regiment replaced the 2nd New Jersey for a week's construction work at West Point. The figures for the regiment must have been collected before that date.

OCTOBER 1782

BRIGADE	UNIT	COMMANDING OFFICER	PRESENT FIT FOR DUTY & ON DUTY: COMMISSIONED OFFICERS	NONCOMMISSIONED OFFICERS	STAFF OFFICERS	RANK & FILE	TOTAL	RANK & FILE SICK, ON FURLOUGH, ETC.: SICK PRESENT	SICK ABSENT	ON COMMAND & EXTRA SERVICE	ON FURLOUGH	CONFINED	RECRUITING	PRISONERS OF WAR	GRAND TOTAL	ALTERATIONS: DEATHS	DESERTED	TAKEN PRISONER	DISCHARGED	JOINED, ENLISTED, RECRUITED	LOCATION
	FORCES UNDER COMMANDER-IN-CHIEF GENERAL GEORGE WASHINGTON																				
N.J.	1st N.J.	Matthias Ogden	16	39	6	300	361	5	11	69					446	1				1	near Newburgh, N.Y.
N.J.	2nd N.J.	Elias Dayton	17	36	5	272	330	21	13	56		1			421		1		1		near Newburgh, N.Y.
N.Y.	1st N.Y.	Goose Van Schaick	17	41	3	400	461	36	16	64		4			581		1		1	3	near Newburgh, N.Y. H
N.Y.	2nd N.Y.	Philip Van Cortlandt				66	66			475					541		2			2	near Newburgh, N.Y. H
1st Conn.	1st Conn.	Lt. Col. Thomas Grosvenor	13	42	4	264	323	25	23	58	1				430	1	4				West Point, N.Y.
1st Conn.	3rd Conn.	Samuel Blatchley Webb	12 B	39	4 D	248	303	36	27	45	2				413		6			1	West Point, N.Y.
1st Conn.	5th Conn.	Lt. Col. Isaac Sherman	14	37	4	203	258	48	24	82	1				413	1	1				West Point, N.Y.
2nd Conn.	2nd Conn.	Heman Swift	15	44	6	262	327	26	9	67	2				431	3				3	West Point, N.Y.
2nd Conn.	4th Conn.	Zebulon Butler	13	52	4	217	286	28	26	75	3				418		2				West Point, N.Y.
2nd Conn.	R.I.	Lt. Col. Jeremiah Olney	15	44	5	275	339	32	19	171		4			565		5			2	near Newburgh, N.Y.
1st Mass.	1st Mass.	Joseph Vose	14	40	5	319	378	37	20	20					455		3			9	near Newburgh, N.Y.
1st Mass.	4th Mass.	William Shepard	13	45	3 E	331	392	29	7	25					453		3			4	near Newburgh, N.Y.
1st Mass.	7th Mass.	Lt. Col. John Brooks	13	39	6	330	388	40	9	20		1			458	1	1			8	near Newburgh, N.Y.
2nd Mass.	2nd Mass.	Lt. Col. Ebenezer Sprout	14	39	4	330	387	27	22	22	1				459	1	1			7	near Newburgh, N.Y.
2nd Mass.	5th Mass.	Rufus Putnam	15 C	41	5 F	320	381	20	23	25	2	1			452	1	6		1	14	near Newburgh, N.Y.
2nd Mass.	8th Mass.	Michael Jackson	12	42	6	340	400	24	11	24					459	1	1		1	8	near Newburgh, N.Y.
3rd Mass.	3rd Mass.	John Greaton	15	35	4	325	379	40	10	23		1			453		6			9	near Newburgh, N.Y.
3rd Mass.	6th Mass.	Lt. Col. Calvin Smith	17	40	3	334	394	28	14	23					459	1				10	near Newburgh, N.Y.
3rd Mass.	9th Mass.	Henry Jackson	13	38	5	315	371	46	14	22					453		2		2		near Newburgh, N.Y.
	10th Mass.	Benjamin Tupper	19	48	5	337	409	36	12	9		1			467		7			14	near Newburgh, N.Y.
N.H.	1st N.H.	Lt. Col. Henry Dearborn	8	39	5	221	273	51	2	119		3			448		1			16	Albany, N.Y. area
N.H.	2nd N.H. A	Lt. Col. George Reid	16	54	3	281	354	26	11	61					452	3	2			26	Albany, N.Y. area
	Canadian A	Brevet Brig. Gen. Moses Hazen																			
	Officers present on duty		77	128	5		210								210						
	TOTAL OF INFANTRY		378	1002	100	6290	7770	661	323	1555	12	16			10337	14	55		6	137	
	CAVALRY																				
	2nd cont'l.	Elisha Sheldon	14	42	3	195	254	8	5	40	1				308		1		1	1	"on the Lines," N.Y.
	Marechaussie	Capt. Bartholomew Von Heer	2	10		44	56	1		6		1			64						
	TOTAL OF CAVALRY		16	52	3	239	310	9	5	46	1	1			372		1		1	1	
	ARTILLERY																				
	2nd cont'l.	John Lamb	17	62	3	169	251	21	14	93	1	2	1	1	751		2		1	6	West Point, N.Y.
	3rd cont'l.	John Crane	27	119	2	219	367									1	5			2	West Point, N.Y.
	Present on duty		3	27		70	100								100						
	TOTAL OF ARTILLERY		47	208	5	458	718	21	14	93	1	2	1	1	851	1	7		1	8	
	SAPPERS AND MINERS																				
	3 cos.	Maj. Villefranche, Chevalier de	2	6		58	66	4	5	2	1				78				1		West Point, N.Y.
	INVALIDS																				
	Invalid corps	Lewis Nicola	3	19	5	112	139	27	64	143					363	1			10 G	7	West Point, N.Y.
	TOTAL OF WASHINGTON'S ARMY		446	1287	113	7157	9003	722	411	1839	15	19	1	1	12011	16	63		19	153	

OFFICERS SICK, ON FURLOUGH, ETC.	WASHINGTON'S ARMY			
	COMMISSIONED	NONCOMMISSIONED	STAFF	TOTAL
Sick Present	18	52	1	71
Sick Absent	38	45	2	85
On Command	96	163	11	270
On Extra Service	2	7		9
On Furlough	28	10	6	44
Furlough Expired	3			3
Absent without Leave	1	1		2
Recruiting	1	5		6
On the Staff	107			107
Prisoners of War	3			3
In Arrest	4	1		5
TOTAL	301	284	20	605

SOURCE OF THIS REPORT

1. MONTHLY RETURN OF THE CONTINENTAL ARMY UNDER THE COMMAND OF HIS EXCELLENCY GEORGE WASHINGTON...FOR THE MONTH OF OCTOBER 1782, ELEPHANT FOLIO OF WASHINGTON RETURNS, WILLIAM L. CLEMENTS LIBRARY.

1a. Monthly Return of the Continental Army under...Washington...October 1782, Record Group 93, National Archives. [Contains the same figures, but only to the brigade level.]

A. The line for this regiment is blank on the manuscript. The National Archives copy of the return notes, "The Return of Hazen's regiment lies at the Post office, but not having money to redeem it, it is of necessity excluded in this."
B. Thirteen commissioned officers in Lieutenant Colonel Isaac Sherman's 5th Connecticut regiment plus one brigadier general for the entire brigade.
C. Eleven commissioned officers in Michael Jackson's 8th Massachusetts regiment plus one brigadier general for the entire brigade.
D. Three staff officers in Lieutenant Colonel Isaac Sherman's 5th Connecticut regiment plus one chaplain for the entire brigade.
E. Five staff officers in Lieutenant Colonel John Brooks' 7th Massachusetts regiment plus one chaplain for the entire brigade.
F. Five staff officers in Michael Jackson's 8th Massachusetts regiment plus one chaplain for the entire brigade.
G. Including two men in Washington's infantry, one in Washington's cavalry, one in the sappers and miners, and nine in the invalids discharged for inability.
H. The 2nd New York regiment left the main encampment at Verplancks Point on October 20 and began a tour of duty on the construction work at West Point. When the army moved into winter quarters at the very end of the month, the regiment left West Point and went to the winter camp in the area of New Windsor and Newburgh. Most or all of the figures on this return must have been collected shortly before the end of the month, before the move to winter quarters. Thus most of the men in the 2nd New York regiment were entered to reflect their detached condition at that time, although they were not detached by October 31.

NOVEMBER 1782

BRIGADE	UNIT	COMMANDING OFFICER	PRESENT FIT FOR DUTY & ON DUTY: COMMISSIONED OFFICERS	NONCOMMISSIONED OFFICERS	STAFF OFFICERS	RANK & FILE	TOTAL	RANK & FILE SICK, ON FURLOUGH, ETC.: SICK PRESENT	SICK ABSENT	ON COMMAND & EXTRA SERVICE	ON FURLOUGH	CONFINED	RECRUITING	PRISONERS OF WAR	GRAND TOTAL	ALTERATIONS: DEATHS	DESERTED	TAKEN PRISONER	DISCHARGED	JOINED, ENLISTED, RECRUITED	LOCATION
	FORCES UNDER COMMANDER-IN-CHIEF GENERAL GEORGE WASHINGTON																				
	Det. 3rd Md.	Maj. Thomas Lansdale	9	26	5	186	226	18	20	3		3			270		25				near Newburgh, N.Y.
N.J.	1st N.J.	Matthias Ogden	17	44	4	297	362	13	10	55		2			442	1	5			1	near Newburgh, N.Y.
N.J.	2nd N.J.	Elias Dayton	16	38	4	287	345	11	17	41	2	1			417		8			3	near Newburgh, N.Y.
N.Y.	1st N.Y.	Goose Van Schaick	18	40	3	400	461	45	17	47	1	1			572		2		8	1	near Newburgh, N.Y.
N.Y.	2nd N.Y. A	Philip Van Cortlandt	20	54	5	434	513	39	9	46	4	1			612	2 G	1		5		near Newburgh, N.Y.
Conn.	1st Conn. A	Zebulon Butler	7 C	58	4	429	498	38	17	101	13	1			668						West Point, N.Y.
Conn.	3rd Conn. A	Samuel Blatchley Webb	8	68	4	440	520	40	26	113	11	2			712						West Point, N.Y.
	2nd Conn.	Heman Swift	13	65	5	458	541	31	12	28	10				622						West Point, N.Y.
1st Mass.	1st Mass.	Joseph Vose	14	42	4	357	417	19	15	13					464		1			9	near Newburgh, N.Y.
1st Mass.	4th Mass.	William Shepard	13	44	3 E	350	410	23	10	11					454	3	3			8	near Newburgh, N.Y.
1st Mass.	7th Mass.	Lt. Col. John Brooks	13	39	6	347	405	31	11	13					460	1	3			6	near Newburgh, N.Y.
2nd Mass.	2nd Mass.	Lt. Col. Ebenezer Sprout	11	36	4	356	407	16	13	18	2				456	1	3			7	near Newburgh, N.Y.
2nd Mass.	5th Mass.	Rufus Putnam	13 D	43	4 F	336	396	21	20	13	1	4			455		4		1	8	near Newburgh, N.Y.
2nd Mass.	8th Mass.	Michael Jackson	15	43	5	353	416	30	8	11	2				467				1	6	near Newburgh, N.Y.
3rd Mass.	3rd Mass.	John Greaton	17	36	2	336	391	44	9	14		1			459		2			7	near Newburgh, N.Y.
3rd Mass.	6th Mass.	Lt. Col. Calvin Smith	13	41	3	348	405	28	15	10		1			459		4			7	near Newburgh, N.Y.
3rd Mass.	9th Mass.	Henry Jackson	12	40	5	328	385	34	15	15					449		3		1		near Newburgh, N.Y.
	10th Mass.	Benjamin Tupper	14	43	3	339	399	5	37	9					450	2	5			2	Verplancks Point, N.Y. I
	R.I. B	Lt. Col. Jeremiah Olney																			Albany, N.Y. area
N.H.	1st N.H.	Lt. Col. Henry Dearborn	12	43	4	321	380	21	26	16	2				445		5		8	3	near Newburgh, N.Y.
N.H.	2nd N.H.	Lt. Col. George Reid	13	49	4	294	360	50	20	16	1				447		2				near Newburgh, N.Y.
	Canadian	Brevet Brig. Gen. Moses Hazen	13	39	3	427	482	14	29	67	20	4			616		1			17	Pompton, N.J.
	Officers present on duty		81	120	7		208								208						
	TOTAL OF INFANTRY		362	1051	91	7423	8927	571	356	660	69	21			10604	10	77		24	85	
	CAVALRY																				
	2nd cont'l. B	Elisha Sheldon	14	41	4	181	240	14	5	44					303		3				
	Marechaussie	Capt. Bartholomew Von Heer																			
	TOTAL OF CAVALRY		14	41	4	181	240	14	5	44					303		3				
	ARTILLERY																				
	2nd cont'l.	John Lamb	12	44	3	106	165	32	20	54	6	4	2	1	497		5			9	West Point, N.Y.
	3rd cont'l.	John Crane	16	76	3	118	213									1	1		2	8	West Point, N.Y.
	Present on duty		25	103		255	383								383						
	TOTAL OF ARTILLERY		53	223	6	479	761	32	20	54	6	4	2	1	880	1	6		2	17	
	SAPPERS AND MINERS																				
	3 cos.		3	6		52	61	9	7	2					79						West Point, N.Y.
	INVALIDS																				
	Invalid corps	Lewis Nicola	1	21	5	114	141	30	54	146	3				374	3				4	West Point, N.Y.
	TOTAL OF WASHINGTON'S ARMY		433	1335	106	8249	10130	656	442	906	78	25	2	1	12240	14	86		26 H	106	

OFFICERS SICK, ON FURLOUGH, ETC.	WASHINGTON'S ARMY			
	COMMISSIONED	NONCOMMISSIONED	STAFF	TOTAL
Sick Present	17	43	2	62
Sick Absent	23	42	1	66
On Command	42	69	6	117
On Extra Service	2	10		12
On Furlough	51	16	12	79
Furlough Expired	3	2		5
Absent without Leave	1			1
Recruiting	1	4		5
On the Staff	110			110
Prisoners of War	3	1		4
In Arrest	3	1		4
TOTAL	256	188	21	465

SOURCE OF THIS REPORT

1. MONTHLY RETURN OF THE CONTINENTAL ARMY UNDER THE COMMAND OF HIS EXCELLENCY GEORGE WASHINGTON... FOR THE MONTH OF NOVEMBER 1782, ELEPHANT FOLIO OF WASHINGTON RETURNS, WILLIAM L. CLEMENTS LIBRARY.

1a. Monthly Return of the Continental Army under... Washington... November 1782, Record Group 93, National Archives. [Contains the same figures, but only to the brigade level.]

A. By orders of October 30, 1782, the five Connecticut Continental regiments had been consolidated into three; the new regiments, indicated here, include the men from the old 4th and 5th Connecticut.
B. No figures are supplied on the manuscript for these units.
C. Seven commissioned officers in Samuel Blatchley Webb's 3rd Connecticut regiment plus one brigadier general for the entire brigade.
D. Fourteen commissioned officers in Michael Jackson's 8th Massachusetts regiment plus one brigadier general for the entire brigade.
E. Five staff officers in Lieutenant Colonel John Brooks' 7th Massachusetts regiment plus one chaplain for the entire brigade.
F. Four staff officers in Michael Jackson's 8th Massachusetts regiment plus one chaplain for the entire brigade.
G. It will be noted that the manuscript makes no attempt to provide alterations for the Connecticut regiments which had been reduced in number and consolidated during this month. In contrast, the next month's report does provide alterations for the consolidated Massachusetts regiments, but in that case it must be kept in mind that the men listed in the joined, enlisted, recruited column were mostly men from the old discontinued regiments (men already in the army), not new soldiers.
H. Including twenty-three men in Washington's infantry discharged for inability.
I. On November 28 the 10th Massachusetts regiment marched to Verplancks Point in order to repair the fortifications there. The figures for this regiment must have been collected before that move.

DECEMBER 1782

BRIGADE	UNIT	COMMANDING OFFICER	PRESENT FIT FOR DUTY & ON DUTY: COMMISSIONED OFFICERS	NONCOMMISSIONED OFFICERS	STAFF OFFICERS	RANK & FILE	TOTAL	RANK & FILE SICK, ON FURLOUGH, ETC.: SICK PRESENT	SICK ABSENT	ON COMMAND & EXTRA SERVICE	ON FURLOUGH	CONFINED	RECRUITING	WANTING ARMS	GRAND TOTAL	ALTERATIONS: DEATHS	DESERTED	TAKEN PRISONER	DISCHARGED	JOINED, ENLISTED, RECRUITED	LOCATION
	FORCES UNDER COMMANDER-IN-CHIEF GENERAL GEORGE WASHINGTON																				
	Det 3rd Md.	Maj. Thomas Lansdale	7	23	5	175	210	27	14	8	1				260		6		1	2	near Newburgh, N.Y.
N.J.	1st N.J.	Matthias Ogden	14	43	4	279	340	18	8	50	19	2			437		1				near Newburgh, N.Y.
N.J.	2nd N.J.	Elias Dayton	11	40	3	258	312	22	9	45	17	4			409		1		1		near Newburgh, N.Y.
N.Y.	1st N.Y.	Goose Van Schaick	21	48	2	358	429	50	17	19	20	2			537	1	3		37		near Newburgh, N.Y.
N.Y.	2nd N.Y.	Philip Van Cortlandt	20	51	4	395	470	37	12	15	21	1			556		4		52	5	near Newburgh, N.Y.
Conn.	1st Conn.	Zebulon Butler	8	56	5	381	450	64	20	39	24				597	2	6		71	7	West Point, N.Y.
Conn.	3rd Conn.	Samuel Blatchley Webb	9	64	3	402	478	60	29	39	21				627		6		81	5	West Point, N.Y.
Conn.	2nd Conn. A	Heman Swift	8	61	3	427	499	28	10	26	29				592		2		21	4 F	West Point, N.Y.
1st Mass.	1st Mass.	Joseph Vose	2	8	3	412	425	30	19	12	18	11			515					111	"on the Lines," N.Y. G
1st Mass.	4th Mass.	Henry Jackson	13 B	44	4 C	410	471	34	15	17	22				559		3			116	near Newburgh, N.Y.
1st Mass.	7th Mass.	Lt. Col. John Brooks	13	49	6	412	480	38	12	14	19	2			565	2	2			113	near Newburgh, N.Y.
2nd Mass.	2nd Mass.	Lt. Col. Ebenezer Sprout	14	44	4	415	477	29	14	21	19				560		4			111	near Newburgh, N.Y.
2nd Mass.	5th Mass.	Rufus Putnam	15	51	5	422	493	23	18	13	20	1			568		1			115	near Newburgh, N.Y.
2nd Mass.	8th Mass.	Michael Jackson	17	49	4	436	506	19	15	13	20				573		1			112	near Newburgh, N.Y.
3rd Mass.	3rd Mass.	John Greaton	19	47	3	394	463	43	15	20	21	2			564	3	1			110	near Newburgh, N.Y.
3rd Mass.	6th Mass.	Benjamin Tupper	16	54	4	426	500	28	13	9	21	1			572		1			110	near Newburgh, N.Y.
N.H.	1st N.H.	Lt. Col. Henry Dearborn	9	39	4	321	373	15	10	12	21	3			434		3		2	1	near Newburgh, N.Y.
N.H.	2nd N.H.	Lt. Col. George Reid	6	39	5 D	274	324	27	24	19	21				415	12	4		1	1	near Newburgh, N.Y.
	R.I.	Lt. Col. Jeremiah Olney	12	32	4	311	359	43	10	138		1			551				1	1	Albany, N.Y. area
	Canadian	Brevet Brig. Gen. Moses Hazen	12	28	2	355	397	15	28	126	33	5			604		11			11	Pompton, N.J.
	Officers present on duty		39	72	2		113								113						
	TOTAL OF INFANTRY		285	942	79	7263	8569	650	312	655	387	35			10608	20	60		268	935	
	CAVALRY																				
	2nd cont'l.	Elisha Sheldon	13	43	4	196	256	6	5	39					306		7			1	Connecticut
	Marechaussie	Capt. Bartholomew Von Heer	3	14		38	55			3	9				67		1		2		
	TOTAL OF CAVALRY		16	57	4	234	311	6	5	42	9				373		8		2	1	
	ARTILLERY																				
	2nd cont'l.	John Lamb	13	36	2	88	139	33	19	61	31	6	3		483	3	4		35	10	West Point, N.Y.
	3rd cont'l.	John Crane	14	62	3	112	191										2			1	West Point, N.Y.
	Present on duty		18	84		216	318								318						
	TOTAL OF ARTILLERY		45	182	5	416	648	33	19	61	31	6	3		801	3	6		35	11	
	SAPPERS AND MINERS																				
	3 cos.		3	5		51	59	4	12	2	1				78						West Point, N.Y.
	INVALIDS																				
	Invalid corps	Lewis Nicola	1	20	5	117	143	22	56	139	4				364						West Point, N.Y.
	TOTAL OF WASHINGTON'S ARMY		350	1206	93	8081	9730	715	404	899	432	41	3		12224	23	74		305 E	947	
	SOUTHERN DEPARTMENT UNDER MAJOR GENERAL NATHANAEL GREENE (To Brigade Level Only)																				
	1st brig.	Lt. Col. Archibald Lytle	27	75	12	497	611	95							706						Ashley River, S.C. H
	2nd brig.	Lt. Col. Josiah Harmar	30	103	8	616	757	183						9	949						Ashley River, S.C.
	TOTAL OF INFANTRY		57	178	20	1113	1368	278						9	1655						
	ARTILLERY																				
	1st cont'l.	Charles Harrison	3	35		56	94								94						Ashley River, S.C.
	TOTAL OF GREENE'S ARMY		60	213	20	1169	1462	278						9	1749						
	GRAND TOTAL		410	1419	113	9250	11192	993	404	899	432	41	3	9	13973						

OFFICERS SICK, ON FURLOUGH, ETC.	WASHINGTON'S ARMY			
	COMMISSIONED	NONCOMMISSIONED	STAFF	TOTAL
Sick Present	19	83		102
Sick Absent	25	42	2	69
On Command I	44	89	5	138
On Extra Service	2	9		11
On Furlough I	134	180	24	338
Absent without Leave	6			6
Recruiting	3	4		7
On the Staff	106			106
Prisoners of War	3	1		4
In Arrest	3			3
TOTAL	345	408	31	784

SOURCES OF THIS REPORT

1. MONTHLY RETURN OF THE CONTINENTAL ARMY UNDER THE COMMAND OF HIS EXCELLENCY GEORGE WASHINGTON. . . FOR THE MONTH OF DECEMBER 1782, ELEPHANT FOLIO OF WASHINGTON RETURNS, WILLIAM L. CLEMENTS LIBRARY.

   1a. Monthly Return of the Continental Army under. . . Washington. . . December 28, 1782, Record Group 93, National Archives. [Contains the same figures, but only to the brigade level.]

2. FIELD RETURN OF THE SOUTHERN ARMY COMMANDED BY THE HONORABLE MAJOR GENERAL GREENE, DECEMBER 24, 1782, GREENE PAPERS, WILLIAM L. CLEMENTS LIBRARY.

A. The ten Massachusetts Continental regiments had been consolidated into eight since the last return.
B. Twelve commissioned officers in Lieutenant Colonel John Brooks' 7th Massachusetts regiment plus one brigadier general for the entire brigade.
C. Five staff officers in Lieutenant Colonel John Brooks' 7th Massachusetts regiment plus one chaplain for the entire brigade.
D. Four staff officers in Lieutenant Colonel George Reid's 2nd New Hampshire regiment plus one chaplain for the entire brigade.
E. Including sixteen men in Washington's infantry and one man in Washington's cavalry discharged for inability.
F. Clearly, the figures in this column for these new consolidated Massachusetts regiments mainly represent only those men who were reassigned from those Massachusetts regiments that had been disbanded, not new soldiers.
G. When the army fell back from Verplancks Point to winter quarters, the light infantry companies of the various regiments remained serving at the various posts on the lines. In early December the light infantry corps was relieved, and these companies rejoined their regiments. Their place was taken by various regiments that served a tour of duty on the lines. The 1st Massachusetts regiment did this from December 18 through January 2.
H. In July Greene moved his army further down the Ashley River to within twelve miles of Charleston. On December 14 the British evacuated Charleston, but at the time of this return Greene had not yet moved his camp to James Island in Charleston harbor, as he was soon to do.
I. The section for officers who were sick, on furlough, etc., for the cavalry includes three commissioned officers and two noncommissioned officers in a combined "On Command & On Furlough" column. We have entered these men in the on command column here. The National Archives manuscript differs in having separate columns for the men who were on command and for those who were on furlough, but because it also differs by only reporting on Sheldon's 2nd Continental cavalry regiment and not including the Marechaussie, the existence of this other manuscript does not allow an absolute determination of how many of the five men we have entered in the on command column here were really on furlough. Probably there should be one less man in the on command column and one more in the on furlough column.

JANUARY 1783

BRIGADE	UNIT	COMMANDING OFFICER	PRESENT FIT FOR DUTY & ON DUTY: COMMISSIONED OFFICERS	NONCOMMISSIONED OFFICERS	STAFF OFFICERS	RANK & FILE	TOTAL	RANK & FILE SICK, ON FURLOUGH, ETC.: SICK PRESENT	SICK ABSENT	ON COMMAND & EXTRA SERVICE	ON FURLOUGH	CONFINED	RECRUITING	GRAND TOTAL	ALTERATIONS: DEATHS	DESERTED	TAKEN PRISONER	DISCHARGED	JOINED, ENLISTED, RECRUITED	LOCATION
		FORCES UNDER COMMANDER-IN-CHIEF GENERAL GEORGE WASHINGTON																		
	Det. 3rd Md.	Maj. Thomas Lansdale	9	24	5	183	221	23	13	4				261	1			4	5	near Newburgh, N.Y.
N.J.	1st N.J.	Matthias Ogden	10	42	2	280	334	20	6	47	19	2		428				3	1	near Newburgh, N.Y.
N.J.	2nd N.J.	Francis Barber	12	44	3	258	317	19	5	44	23	2		410		5		6	7	near Newburgh, N.Y. G
N.Y.	1st N.Y.	Goose Van Schaick	15	46	1 D	340	402	59	16	19	26	1		523		2		4	2	"on the Lines," N.Y.
N.Y.	2nd N.Y.	Philip Van Cortlandt	11	53	5	388	457	33	9	14	29			542		2		10	6	near Newburgh, N.Y.
Conn.	1st Conn.	Zebulon Butler	6 A	53	5	370	434	48	17	32	35	2		568		12		20	8	West Point, N.Y.
Conn.	3rd Conn.	Samuel Blatchley Webb	8	61	2	364	435	68	21	30	34			588		2		32	1	West Point, N.Y.
Conn.	2nd Conn.	Heman Swift	9	66	3	410	488	35	12	25	31	1		592		4		5	5	West Point, N.Y.
1st Mass.	1st Mass.	Joseph Vose	13	47	4	407	471	31	18	13	21	10		564		3		4	3	near Newburgh, N.Y.
1st Mass.	4th Mass.	Henry Jackson	12	39	3	380	434	45	14	31	22			546	1	2		6	4	near Newburgh, N.Y.
1st Mass.	7th Mass.	Lt. Col. John Brooks		7	3	410	420	39	9	16	20			504				6	4	near Newburgh, N.Y.
2nd Mass.	2nd Mass.	Lt. Col. Ebenezer Sprout	14	42	4	428	488	18	10	20	21			557		1		5	4	near Newburgh, N.Y.
2nd Mass.	5th Mass.	Lt. Col. David Cobb	10	54	5 E	411	480	34	12	14	23	1		564	2	1		4	5	near Newburgh, N.Y.
2nd Mass.	8th Mass.	Michael Jackson	10	48	5	424	487	31	9	15	21			563		3		2	2	near Newburgh, N.Y.
3rd Mass.	3rd Mass.	Lt. Col. James Mellen	11 B	50	2	383	446	56	12	21	23	3		561		4			8	near Newburgh, N.Y.
3rd Mass.	6th Mass.	Benjamin Tupper	11	55	4	416	486	37	9	12	20	1		565	1	2		2	2	near Newburgh, N.Y.
N.H.	1st N.H.	Lt. Col. Henry Dearborn	8	39	3	314	364	27	6	10	21			428				4	1	near Newburgh, N.Y.
N.H.	2nd N.H.	Lt. Col. George Reid	7	45	3	284	339	28	10	13	22			412	3	3		2		near Newburgh, N.Y.
	R.I.	Lt. Col. Jeremiah Olney	11	35	2	215	263	19	11	46	45	1		385		1		135	7	Albany, N.Y. area
	Canadian	Brevet Brig. Gen. Moses Hazen	17	39	2	433	491	1	26	65	30	8		621	1	4		3	8	Pompton, N.J.
	Officers present on duty		50	67	2		119							119						
	TOTAL OF INFANTRY		254	956	68	7098	8376	671	245	491	486	32		10301	9	51		257	83	
	CAVALRY																			
	2nd cont'l.	Elisha Sheldon	11	36	4	194	245	3	3	30	10			291					1	Connecticut
	Marechaussie	Capt. Bartholomew Von Heer	4	8	1	32	45		2	4	8			59		2		2		
	TOTAL OF CAVALRY		15	44	5	226	290	3	5	34	18			350		2		2	1	
	ARTILLERY																			
	2nd cont'l.	John Lamb	15	36	2	83	136	24	14	59	31	7	3	485	2	10		33	7	West Point, N.Y.
	3rd cont'l.	John Crane	12	65	4	130	211												3	West Point, N.Y.
	Present on duty		14	76		182	272							272						
	TOTAL OF ARTILLERY		41	177	6	395	619	24	14	59	31	7	3	757	2	10		33	10	
	SAPPERS AND MINERS																			
	3 cos.			5		44	49	5	9	2	6	4		75						West Point, N.Y.
	INVALIDS																			
	Invalid corps	Lewis Nicola	1	17	5	145	168	23	39	71	12			313						West Point, N.Y.
	TOTAL OF WASHINGTON'S ARMY		311	1199	84	7908	9502	726	312	657	553	43	3	11796	11	63		292	94	
	ARTILLERY OF THE SOUTHERN DEPARTMENT UNDER MAJOR GENERAL NATHANAEL GREENE																			
	Va. co., 1st cont'l.	(late) Capt. Anthony Singleton	5		1	26		3	1	18	2				1					James Island, S.C.
	Md. co., 1st cont'l.	Capt. William Brown		46 C		21	126	1	1	5										James Island, S.C.
	Md. co., 1st cont'l.	Capt. James Smith	1			16				7				166						James Island, S.C.
	Pa. co., 4th cont'l.	Capt. William Ferguson	1			9		1		11					2					James Island, S.C.
	Pa. co., 4th cont'l.	Capt. John Brice	1	9		8	18	1		5				24				6		James Island, S.C.
	Pa. co., 4th cont'l.	Capt. James McClure	1	9		18	38	2		4	1			45		1				James Island, S.C.
	TOTAL OF GREENE'S ARTILLERY		9	64	1	98	172	8	2	50	3			235	3	1		6		
	GRAND TOTAL		320	1263	85	8006	9674	734	314	707	556	43	3	12031	14	64		298 F	94	

OFFICERS SICK, ON FURLOUGH, ETC.	WASHINGTON'S ARMY				ARTILLERY OF SOUTHERN DEPARTMENT				GRAND TOTAL
	COMMISSIONED	NONCOMMISSIONED	STAFF	TOTAL	COMMISSIONED	NONCOMMISSIONED	STAFF	TOTAL	
Sick Present	18	79	2	99	1	3		4	103
Sick Absent	19	39	1	59					59
On Command	34	64	5	103	3	4		7	110
On Extra Service		7		7		6		6	13
On Furlough	190	194	30	414	7	1		8	422
Absent without Leave	2	1	1	4					4
Recruiting	2	4		6					6
On the Staff	104			104					104
Prisoners of War	3			3					3
In Arrest	8	1		9					9
Not Assigned H						4		4	4
TOTAL	380	389	39	808	11	18		29	837

A. Seven commissioned officers in Samuel Blatchley Webb's 3rd Connecticut regiment plus one brigadier general for the entire brigade.
B. Ten commissioned officers in Benjamin Tupper's 6th Massachusetts regiment plus one brigadier general for the entire brigade.
C. Because the column for corporals on this manuscript is so badly creased that it is largely illegible, it is not possible to tell how many were in each of these four companies, and, therefore, a combined figure must be given for noncommissioned officers.
D. Four staff officers in Philip Van Cortlandt's 2nd New York regiment plus one chaplain for the entire brigade.
E. Four staff officers in Michael Jackson's 8th Massachusetts regiment plus one chaplain for the entire brigade.
F. Including seventy-nine men in Washington's infantry and fifty-one men in the Invalid Corps discharged for inability.
G. On January 30, the 1st New York regiment marched to relieve the 7th Massachusetts regiment on the lines. By the next day (the last day of the month, the day for which we supply locations), they may have been still in transit, and the 7th Massachusetts still on detached duty.
H. Because of a crease in the manuscript it is not possible to determine exactly why these four officers were not present fit for duty or on duty.

SOURCES OF THIS REPORT

1. MONTHLY RETURN OF THE CONTINENTAL ARMY UNDER THE COMMAND OF HIS EXCELLENCY GEORGE WASHINGTON...JANUARY 1783, ELEPHANT FOLIO OF WASHINGTON RETURNS, WILLIAM L. CLEMENTS LIBRARY. [SOME SECTIONS OF THIS RETURN APPEAR ON THE FOLLOWING PAGE OF THE FOLIO.]
   1a. Monthly Return of the Continental Army under...Washington...January 1783, Record Group 93, National Archives. [Contains the same figures, but only to the brigade level.]

2. MONTHLY RETURN OF THE CORPS OF ARTILLERY SOUTHERN ARMY COMMANDED BY THE HONBLE. MAJOR GENERAL GREENE...JANUARY 31, 1783, RECORD GROUP 93, NATIONAL ARCHIVES.

FEBRUARY 1783

BRIGADE	UNIT	COMMANDING OFFICER	PRESENT FIT FOR DUTY & ON DUTY: COMMISSIONED OFFICERS	NONCOMMISSIONED OFFICERS	STAFF OFFICERS	RANK & FILE	TOTAL	RANK & FILE SICK, ON FURLOUGH, ETC.: SICK PRESENT	SICK ABSENT	ON COMMAND & EXTRA SERVICE	ON FURLOUGH	CONFINED	RECRUITING		GRAND TOTAL	ALTERATIONS: DEATHS	DESERTED	TAKEN PRISONER	DISCHARGED	JOINED, ENLISTED, RECRUITED	LOCATION
	FORCES UNDER COMMANDER-IN-CHIEF GENERAL GEORGE WASHINGTON																				
	Det. 3rd Md.	Maj. Thomas Lansdale	6	25	5	185	221	22	6	5					254		8			4	near Newburgh, N.Y.
N.J.	1st N.J.	Matthias Ogden	13 A	40	1	277	331	20	10	44	23	2			430					2	near Newburgh, N.Y.
N.J.	2nd N.J.	(late) Francis Barber	12	38	3	259	312	22	6	40	22	1			403		5		1	6	near Newburgh, N.Y.
N.Y.	1st N.Y.	Goose Van Schaick	15	53	2 D	353	423	45	14	19	25				526	1	8			4	near Newburgh, N.Y. H
N.Y.	2nd N.Y.	Philip Van Cortlandt	1	18	2	70	91	40	8	330	22	1			492		7			6	"on the Lines," N.Y.
Conn.	1st Conn.	Zebulon Butler	10 B	57	2	371	440	53	15	30	29	1			568		10		6	12	West Point, N.Y.
Conn.	3rd Conn.	Samuel Blatchley Webb	10	53	3	361	427	67	20	25	33				572		16		2	10	West Point, N.Y.
	2nd Conn.	Heman Swift	11	68	3	397	479	47	9	26	32				593		8		2	9	West Point, N.Y.
1st Mass.	1st Mass.	Joseph Vose	14	53	4	440	511	12	16	13	14				566		5			1	near Newburgh, N.Y.
1st Mass.	4th Mass.	Henry Jackson	2	12	2	394	410	50	14	14	18				506	1	5			5	near Newburgh, N.Y.
1st Mass.	7th Mass.	Lt. Col. John Brooks	11	54	5	411	481	38	5	15	17				556	1	7		1	1	near Newburgh, N.Y.
2nd Mass.	2nd Mass.	Lt. Col. Ebenezer Sprout	13	45	4	421	483	20	9	19	24	1			556		7			4	near Newburgh, N.Y.
2nd Mass.	5th Mass.	Lt. Col. David Cobb	12	47	4 E	396	459	36	14	14	28	1			552	1	7		3	6	near Newburgh, N.Y.
2nd Mass.	8th Mass.	Michael Jackson	10	56	5	404	475	47	6	13	23				564	1	11			5	near Newburgh, N.Y.
3rd Mass.	3rd Mass.	Lt. Col. James Mellen	10 C	44	2	415	471	37	9	18	18	1			554		4			2	near Newburgh, N.Y.
3rd Mass.	6th Mass.	Benjamin Tupper	12	56	5	417	490	35	5	11	19	1			561	1	10		1	6	near Newburgh, N.Y.
N.H.	1st N.H.	Lt. Col. Henry Dearborn	9	36	3 F	317	365	24	9	8	18	3			427		6			5	near Newburgh, N.Y.
N.H.	2nd N.H.	Lt. Col. George Reid	7	40	5	278	330	26	10	14	22	2			404		10			5	near Newburgh, N.Y.
	R.I.	Lt. Col. Jeremiah Olney	11	43	2	183	239	57	49	15	26	2			388	6	1		2	4	Albany, N.Y. area
	Canadian	Brevet Brig. Gen. Moses Hazen	18	36	2	386	442	25	21	81	45	5			619		4				Pompton, N.J.
	Officers present on duty		41	58	1		100								100						
	TOTAL OF INFANTRY		248	932	65	6735	7980	723	255	754	458	21			10191	12	139		18	97	
	CAVALRY																				
	2nd cont'l.	Elisha Sheldon	12	38	4	192	246	5	2	35	11				299		1			7	Connecticut
	Marechaussie	Capt. Bartholomew Von Heer	4	10		33	47		5	3	4				59	1				6	
	TOTAL OF CAVALRY		16	48	4	225	293	5	7	38	15				358	1	1			13	
	ARTILLERY																				
	2nd cont'l.	John Lamb	12	36	2	87	137	29	14	60	25	4	4		487		9		2	24	West Point, N.Y.
	3rd cont'l.	John Crane	11	65	3	135	214										1			1	West Point, N.Y.
	Present on duty		14	74		188	276								276						
	TOTAL OF ARTILLERY		37	175	5	410	627	29	14	60	25	4	4		763		10		2	25	
	SAPPERS AND MINERS																				
	3 cos.		1	6		42	49	4	3	15	4				75		1			1	West Point, N.Y.
	INVALIDS																				
	Invalid corps	Lewis Nicola	1	20	5	132	158	26	44	69	12	1			310	2	1		1 G	1	West Point, N.Y.
	TOTAL OF WASHINGTON'S ARMY		303	1181	79	7544	9107	787	323	936	514	26	4		11697	15	152		21	137	

OFFICERS SICK, ON FURLOUGH, ETC.	WASHINGTON'S ARMY			
	COMMISSIONED	NONCOMMISSIONED	STAFF	TOTAL
Sick Present	20	61	1	82
Sick Absent	21	41		62
On Command	41	95	6	142
On Extra Service		10		10
On Furlough	197	180	37	414
Recruiting	1	4		5
On the Staff	102			102
Prisoners of War	3	1		4
In Arrest	6			6
Absent without Leave	1	6	1	8
TOTAL	392	398	45	835

SOURCE OF THIS REPORT

1. MONTHLY RETURN OF THE CONTINENTAL ARMY UNDER THE COMMAND OF HIS EXCELLENCY GEORGE WASHINGTON...FEBRUARY 1783, ELEPHANT FOLIO OF WASHINGTON RETURNS, WILLIAM L. CLEMENTS LIBRARY.

1a. Abstract of the Monthly Return of the Continental Army under...Washington...February 1783, Record Group 93, National Archives. [Contains the same figures, but only to the brigade level.]

A. Eleven commissioned officers in the 2nd New Jersey regiment, of which Francis Barber had been colonel, plus one brigadier general for the entire brigade.
B. Nine commissioned officers in Samuel Blatchley Webb's 3rd Connecticut regiment plus one brigadier general for the entire brigade.
C. Eleven commissioned officers in Benjamin Tupper's 6th Massachusetts regiment plus one brigadier general for the entire brigade.
D. One staff officer in Philip Van Cortlandt's 2nd New York regiment plus one chaplain for the entire brigade.
E. Four staff officers in Michael Jackson's 8th Massachusetts regiment plus one chaplain for the entire brigade.
F. Four staff officers in Lieutenant Colonel George Reid's 2nd New Hampshire regiment plus one chaplain for the entire brigade.
G. Including six men in Washington's infantry and one man in the Invalid Corps discharged for inability.
H. On February 27 the bulk of the 2nd New York regiment marched for a tour of duty on the lines. This return must have been made out after that date.

MARCH 1783

BRIGADE	UNIT	COMMANDING OFFICER	PRESENT FIT FOR DUTY & ON DUTY: COMMISSIONED OFFICERS	NONCOMMISSIONED OFFICERS	STAFF OFFICERS	RANK & FILE	TOTAL	RANK & FILE SICK, ON FURLOUGH, ETC.: SICK PRESENT	SICK ABSENT	ON COMMAND & EXTRA SERVICE	ON FURLOUGH	CONFINED	RECRUITING	GRAND TOTAL	ALTERATIONS: DEATHS	DESERTED	TAKEN PRISONER	DISCHARGED	JOINED, ENLISTED, RECRUITED	LOCATION
	FORCES UNDER COMMANDER-IN-CHIEF GENERAL GEORGE WASHINGTON																			
	Det. 3rd Md.	Maj. Thomas Lansdale	9	25	5	185	224	24	6	4				258	1			1	3	near Newburgh, N.Y.
N.J.	N.J. regt. A	Matthias Ogden	13 D	54	4	404	475	28	11	26	37	1		578	5	6			3	near Newburgh, N.Y.
N.J.	N.J. bn. A	Lt. Col. John Noble Cumming	6	25		157	188	29	4	4	12			237	3	3		2	1	near Newburgh, N.Y.
N.Y.	1st N.Y.	Goose Van Schaick	13	46	4 J	347	410	58	15	20	21			524	1	1			8	near Newburgh, N.Y.
N.Y.	2nd N.Y.	Philip Van Cortlandt	15	52	5	384	456	46	2	15	19	1		539	1	7			5	near Newburgh, N.Y.
Conn.	1st Conn.	Zebulon Butler	9 E	53	1	353	416	48	14	24	34			536		6		22	5	West Point, N.Y.
Conn.	3rd Conn.	Samuel Blatchley Webb	12	58	3	358	431	60	20	24	36			571		10		12	11	West Point, N.Y.
	2nd Conn.	Heman Swift	11	61	3	399	474	45	9	29	31			588		3		8	5	West Point, N.Y.
1st Mass.	1st Mass.	Joseph Vose	12	53	4	420	489	26	16	14	15	4		564		2			3	near Newburgh, N.Y.
1st Mass.	4th Mass.	Henry Jackson	14 F	45	3	390	452	48	13	13	25			551		6			5	near Newburgh, N.Y.
1st Mass.	7th Mass.	Lt. Col. John Brooks	16	47	3	432	498	18	5	15	20			556		4			7	near Newburgh, N.Y.
2nd Mass.	2nd Mass.	Lt. Col. Ebenezer Sprout	12	47	3	405	467	32	9	20	26	1		555		3			3	near Newburgh, N.Y.
2nd Mass.	5th Mass.	Lt. Col. David Cobb	15	54	4 K	407	480	29	12	14	28			563	1				3	near Newburgh, N.Y.
2nd Mass.	8th Mass.	Michael Jackson	12	53	6	410	481	43	8	13	24			569		1			6	near Newburgh, N.Y.
3rd Mass.	3rd Mass.	Lt. Col. James Mellen	G	1		416	417	36	8	17	23			501					2	near Newburgh, N.Y.
3rd Mass.	6th Mass. A	Benjamin Tupper	11	54	5	410	480	43	2	11	24			560		5			7	near Newburgh, N.Y.
N.H.	N.H. regt. A	Lt. Col. George Reid	1	6	1 L	452	460	39	9	15	25	2		550	1	5			15	"on the Lines," N.Y. O
N.H.	N.H. bn. A	Maj. William Scott	5	23	4	163	195	17	2	6	12			232		2			2	near Newburgh, N.Y.
	R.I.	Lt. Col. Jeremiah Olney	6	33	1	173	213	29	46	40	23	1		352	1	2		18	1	Albany, N.Y. area
	Canadian	Brevet Brig. Gen. Moses Hazen	18	34	3	383	438	19	20	115	18	3		613		10			6	Pompton, N.J.
	Officers present on duty		47	110	5		162							162						
	TOTAL OF INFANTRY		257	934	67	7048	8306	717	231	439	453	13		10159	14	76		63	101	
	CAVALRY																			
	2nd cont'l. B	Elisha Sheldon	10	34	5	186	235	8	2	39	12			296					2	Connecticut
	Marechaussie	Capt. Bartholomew Von Heer																		
	TOTAL OF CAVALRY		10	34	5	186	235	8	2	39	12			296					2	
	ARTILLERY																			
	2nd cont'l.	John Lamb	14	52	4	130	200	34	9	64	28	1	3	585	1	10		1	49	West Point, N.Y.
	3rd cont'l.	John Crane	13	76	3	154	246									3			42	West Point, N.Y.
	Present on duty		14	66		197	277							277						
	TOTAL OF ARTILLERY		41	194	7	481	723	34	9	64	28	1	3	862	1	13		1	91	
	SAPPERS AND MINERS																			
	3 cos.		1	5		49	55	3	3	8	5			74						West Point, N.Y.
	INVALIDS																			
	Invalid corps	Lewis Nicola	2	18	4	127	151	32	40	66	14			303		4		2	1	West Point, N.Y.
	TOTAL OF WASHINGTON'S ARMY		311	1185	83	7891	9470	794	285	616	512	14	3	11694	15	93		66	195	

MARCH 1783 (continued)

BRIGADE

UNIT	COMMANDING OFFICER	Present Fit for Duty & on Duty: COMMISSIONED OFFICERS	NONCOMMISSIONED OFFICERS	STAFF OFFICERS	RANK & FILE	TOTAL	Rank & File Sick, on Furlough, etc.: SICK PRESENT	SICK ABSENT	ON COMMAND & EXTRA SERVICE	ON FURLOUGH	CONFINED	RECRUITING	GRAND TOTAL	Alterations: DEATHS	DESERTED	TAKEN PRISONER	DISCHARGED	JOINED, ENLISTED, RECRUITED	LOCATION
SOUTHERN DEPARTMENT UNDER MAJOR GENERAL NATHANAEL GREENE																			
S.C. [C]	Maj. Edmund Hyrne	9	14	3	86	112	11		16	1	3		143		6		1	6	James Island, S.C.
N.C.	Lt. Col. Archibald Lytle	19	51	4	415	489	93	16	90	4	4		696	3	7			6	James Island, S.C.
Md.	John Gunby	16 [H]	48	3	426	493	48	9	104				654	7	1			6	James Island, S.C.
Pa.	Daniel Brodhead	10	53	3	380	446	96	7	85	1	3		638	1	4			5	James Island, S.C.
Officers present on duty		3	14			17							17						
TOTAL OF INFANTRY		57	180	13	1307	1557	248	32	295	6	10		2148	11	18		1	23	
CAVALRY AND LEGIONARY CORPS																			
Baylor's dragoons (Va.)	George Baylor	8	22	4	107	141	31	6	128	6			312		1				Beaufort, S.C. area
Partizan corps cavalry	Lt. Col. Henry Lee	4	11	4	76	95	10	1	5	3			114						Georgetown, S.C. area
Partizan corps infantry	Lt. Col. Henry Lee	2	7		65	74	7	2	3	1	2		89		1			1	Georgetown, S.C. area
Officers present on duty			1			1							1						
TOTAL OF CAVALRY AND LEGIONARY CORPS		14	41	8	248	311	48	9	136	10	2		516		2			1	
ARTILLERY [B]																			
Va. co., 1st cont'l.	(late) Capt. Anthony Singleton																		Georgia
Md. co., 1st cont'l.	Capt. William Brown	1	13		24			1	3										James Island, S.C.
Md. co., 1st cont'l.	Capt. James Smith	1	14	1	14	135	2		6				169						James Island, S.C.
Pa. co., 4th cont'l.	Capt. William Ferguson	2 [I]	14		19		3		6						1				James Island, S.C.
Pa. co., 4th cont'l.	Capt. John Brice	4	13		15		3		9	1				1	1				James Island, S.C.
TOTAL OF ARTILLERY		8	54	1	72	135	8	1	24	1			169 [M]	1	2				
TOTAL OF GREENE'S ARMY		79	275	22	1627	2003	304	42	455	17	12		2833	12	22		1	24	
GRAND TOTAL		390	1460	105	9518	11473	1098	327	1071	529	26	3	14527	27	115		67 [N]	219	

MARCH 1783
(continued)

OFFICERS SICK, ON FURLOUGH, ETC.	WASHINGTON'S ARMY				SOUTHERN DEPARTMENT				GRAND TOTAL
	COMMISSIONED	NONCOMMISSIONED	STAFF	TOTAL	COMMISSIONED	NONCOMMISSIONED	STAFF	TOTAL	
Sick Present	14	65	2	81	16	31	2	49	130
Sick Absent	21	33		54	1	3		4	58
On Command	27	65	3	95	7	14		21	116
On Extra Service		9		9	1	14		15	24
On Furlough	192	179	33	404	31	8	3	42	446
Absent without Leave	3	2	2	7	1			1	8
Recruiting	1	1		2					2
On the Staff	97			97	17			17	114
Prisoners of War	3	1		4	2			2	6
In Arrest or Confined	5	1		6					6
TOTAL	363	356	40	759	76	70	5	151	910

SOURCES OF THIS REPORT

1. MONTHLY RETURN OF THE CONTINENTAL ARMY UNDER THE COMMAND OF HIS EXCELLENCY GEORGE WASHINGTON...MARCH 1783, ELEPHANT FOLIO OF WASHINGTON RETURNS, WILLIAM L. CLEMENTS LIBRARY.

1a. Abstract of the Monthly Return of the Continental Army under...Washington... March 1783, Record Group 93, National Archives. [Contains the same figures, but only to the brigade level.]

2. MONTHLY RETURN OF THE INFANTRY SOUTHERN ARMY...COMMANDED BY THE HONBLE. MAJ. GENL. GREENE, MARCH 31, 1783, RECORD GROUP 93, NATIONAL ARCHIVES AND RETURNS FOR THE ARTILLERY AND CAVALRY AND LEGIONARY CORPS BEARING THE SAME DATE AND IN THE SAME PLACE.

A. By orders of February 18, 1783, the New Jersey Continental line was reformed on March 1 into a battalion of four companies of fifty rank and file each and a regiment consisting of the remainder of the troops. The same was done with the New Hampshire line.
B. The line for this unit is blank on the manuscript. The manuscript for the artillery of the Southern Department notes that no return was received for Singleton's company in Georgia.
C. Late in 1782, with the British evacuation of Charleston imminent, Greene reduced the Southern Department. In the North Carolina, Maryland, and Pennsylvania lines, one complete regiment was formed from the men of each of these states and the remainder were sent home to be furloughed. At this time the 1st and 3rd cavalry regiments were consolidated into one unit, thereafter usually known as Baylor's Dragoons.
D. Five commissioned officers in Lieutenant Colonel John Noble Cumming's New Jersey battalion plus one brigadier general for the entire brigade.
E. Eleven commissioned officers in Samuel Blatchley Webb's 3rd Connecticut regiment plus one brigadier general for the entire brigade.
F. Fifteen commissioned officers in Lieutenant Colonel John Brooks' 7th Massachusetts regiment plus one brigadier general for the entire brigade.
G. Ten commissioned officers in Benjamin Tupper's 6th Massachusetts regiment plus one brigadier general for the entire brigade.
H. Eight commissioned officers in Daniel Brodhead's Pennsylvania regiment plus two brigadier generals for the Southern Department.
I. Three commissioned officers in Captain John Brice's Pennsylvania company of the 4th Continental artillery plus one colonel for all of the artillery.
J. Four staff officers in Philip Van Cortlandt's 2nd New York regiment plus one chaplain for the entire brigade.
K. Five staff officers in Michael Jackson's 8th Massachusetts regiment plus one chaplain for the entire brigade.
L. Three staff officers in Major William Scott's New Hampshire battalion plus one chaplain for the entire brigade.
M. The manuscript for the infantry notes that no returns had been received from Georgia even though they had been particularly requested. The Virginia troops had been marched to Georgia.
N. Including one man in Washington's infantry and two men in the Invalid Corps discharged for inability.
O. On March 27 the New Hampshire regiment marched to replace the 3rd Massachusetts regiment for a tour of duty on the lines.

Monthly Return of the Continental Army under the Command of His Excellency George Washington Esquire General and Commander in Chief of the Armies of the United States of America.

Part of the April 1783 monthly return from the Clements folio manuscript.

APRIL 1783

BRIGADE	UNIT	COMMANDING OFFICER	PRESENT FIT FOR DUTY & ON DUTY: COMMISSIONED OFFICERS	NONCOMMISSIONED OFFICERS	STAFF OFFICERS	RANK & FILE	TOTAL	RANK & FILE SICK, ON FURLOUGH, ETC.: SICK PRESENT	SICK ABSENT	ON COMMAND & EXTRA SERVICE	ON FURLOUGH	CONFINED	RECRUITING	GRAND TOTAL	ALTERATIONS: DEATHS	DESERTED	TAKEN PRISONER	DISCHARGED	JOINED, ENLISTED, RECRUITED	LOCATION
	FORCES UNDER COMMANDER-IN-CHIEF GENERAL GEORGE WASHINGTON																			
	Det. 3rd Md.	Maj. Thomas Lansdale	7	22	5	189	223	17	7	4				251				2		"on the Lines," N.Y. O
N.J.	N.J. regt.	Matthias Ogden	22 B	65	4 H	451	542	21	13	17		1		594		5			1	near Newburgh, N.Y.
N.J.	N.J. bn.	Lt. Col. John Noble Cumming	12	28	5	188	233	9	4	4				250		5			5	near Newburgh, N.Y.
N.Y.	1st N.Y.	Goose Van Schaick	25	49	5 I	355	434	60	17	22	1			534	1	7			1	near Newburgh, N.Y.
N.Y.	2nd N.Y.	Philip Van Cortlandt	23	60	5	393	481	52	3	16		2		554		3		1	3	near Newburgh, N.Y.
Conn.	1st Conn.	Zebulon Butler	16 C	64	4 J	373	457	59	12	22				550	1	7		5	6	West Point, N.Y.
Conn.	3rd Conn.	Samuel Blatchley Webb	21	62	6	383	472	74	16	19				581	1	5		6	5	West Point, N.Y.
	2nd Conn.	Heman Swift	23	69	5	414	511	48	8	25	4			596	1	4		12	3	West Point, N.Y.
1st Mass.	1st Mass.	Joseph Vose	18	58	4	436	516	34	10	13	1	3		577		3			3	near Newburgh, N.Y.
1st Mass.	4th Mass.	Henry Jackson	17 D	55	5 K	419	496	40	15	14	1			566		3			5	near Newburgh, N.Y.
1st Mass.	7th Mass.	Lt. Col. John Brooks	19	55	4	441	519	21	5	18		4		567	1	8			8	near Newburgh, N.Y.
2nd Mass.	2nd Mass.	Lt. Col. Ebenezer Sprout	20	58	4	434	516	33	8	22				579	1	5			11	near Newburgh, N.Y.
2nd Mass.	5th Mass.	Lt. Col. David Cobb	19 E	56	5 L	421	501	39	10	17	1			568	3	6			8	near Newburgh, N.Y.
2nd Mass.	8th Mass.	Michael Jackson	24	60	6	427	517	44	8	15		1		585		6			8	near Newburgh, N.Y.
3rd Mass.	3rd Mass.	Lt. Col. James Mellen	18 F	50	5	429	502	44	8	16	4	1		575	1	3		1	7	near Newburgh, N.Y.
3rd Mass.	6th Mass.	Benjamin Tupper	2	7	2	420	431	62	2	8	1			504		5			8	near Newburgh, N.Y.
N.H.	N.H. regt.	Lt. Col. George Reid	17 G	60	5 M	470	552	54	7	18	1	3		635		6			19	near Newburgh, N.Y. O
N.H.	N.H. bn.	Maj. William Scott	6	29	5	176	216	14	2	5				237		3				"on the Lines," N.Y.
	R.I. A	Lt. Col. Jeremiah Olney																		Albany, N.Y. area
	Canadian	Brevet Brig. Gen. Moses Hazen	12	37	3	383	435	13	16	118	5	4		591		20		1	1	Pompton, N.J.
	Officers present on duty		40	71	3		114							114						
	TOTAL OF INFANTRY		361	1015	90	7202	8668	738	171	393	19	19		10008	10	104		28	102	
	CAVALRY																			
	2nd cont'l.	Elisha Sheldon	13	53	5	200	271	8	2	28				309		1				Connecticut
	Marechaussie	Capt. Bartholomew Von Heer	5	11		37	53		3	4				60				2	6	
	TOTAL OF CAVALRY		18	64	5	237	324	8	5	32				369		1		2	6	
	ARTILLERY																			
	2nd cont'l.	John Lamb	19	56	4	141	220	31	10	68		1	1	602		2			12	West Point, N.Y.
	3rd cont'l.	John Crane	18	77	4	172	271									2			5	West Point, N.Y.
	Present on duty		23	89		203	315							315						
	TOTAL OF ARTILLERY		60	222	8	516	806	31	10	68		1	1	917		4			17	
	SAPPERS AND MINERS																			
	3 cos.		2	6		49	57	7	5	7				76	1				1	West Point, N.Y.
	INVALIDS																			
	Invalid corps	Lewis Nicola	6	22	4	134	166	29	47	72		6		320			5	2	19	
	TOTAL OF WASHINGTON'S ARMY		447	1329	107	8138	10021	813	238	572	19	26	1	11690	11	109	5	32 N	145	

OFFICERS SICK, ON FURLOUGH, ETC.	WASHINGTON'S ARMY			
	COMMISSIONED	NONCOMMISSIONED	STAFF	TOTAL
Sick Present	26	94	1	121
Sick Absent	19	29	2	50
On Command	28	37	1	66
On Extra Service		8		8
On Furlough	20	6	6	32
Absent without Leave	9	3	2	14
Recruiting	1	1		2
On the Staff	105			105
Prisoners of War		1		1
In Arrest or Confined	3	2		5
TOTAL	211	181	12	404

SOURCE OF THIS REPORT

1. MONTHLY RETURN OF THE CONTINENTAL ARMY UNDER THE COMMAND OF HIS EXCELLENCY GEORGE WASHINGTON. . . FOR THE MONTH OF APRIL 1783, ELEPHANT FOLIO OF WASHINGTON RETURNS, WILLIAM L. CLEMENTS LIBRARY.

1a. Abstract of the Monthly Return of the Continental Army under. . . Washington. . . April 1783, Record Group 93, National Archives. [Contains the same figures, but only to the brigade level.]

A. The line for this unit is blank on the manuscript. The National Archives manuscript notes that no return was received for the regiment, which was doing duty "to the Northward."
B. Eleven commissioned officers in Lieutenant Colonel John Noble Cumming's New Jersey battalion plus a brigadier general for the entire brigade.
C. Twenty commissioned officers in Samuel Blatchley Webb's 3rd Connecticut regiment plus a brigadier general for the entire brigade.
D. Eighteen commissioned officers in Lieutenant Colonel John Brooks' 7th Massachusetts regiment plus a brigadier general for the entire brigade.
E. Twenty-three commissioned officers in Michael Jackson's 8th Massachusetts regiment plus a brigadier general for the entire brigade.
F. One commissioned officer in Benjamin Tupper's 6th Massachusetts regiment plus a brigadier general for the entire brigade.
G. Five commissioned officers in Major William Scott's New Hampshire battalion plus a brigadier general for the entire brigade.
H. Four staff officers in Lieutenant Colonel John Noble Cumming's New Jersey battalion plus a chaplain for the entire brigade.
I. Four staff officers in Philip Van Cortlandt's 2nd New York regiment plus a chaplain for the entire brigade.
J. Five staff officers in Samuel Blatchley Webb's 3rd Connecticut regiment plus a chaplain for the entire brigade.
K. Three staff officers in Lieutenant Colonel John Brooks' 7th Massachusetts regiment plus a chaplain for the entire brigade.
L. Five staff officers in Michael Jackson's 8th Massachusetts regiment plus a chaplain for the entire brigade.
M. Four staff officers in Major William Scott's New Hampshire battalion plus a chaplain for the entire brigade.
N. Including three men in Washington's infantry, one man in Washington's cavalry, and one man in the Invalid Corps discharged for inability.
O. On April 29 the New Hampshire battalion and the detachment of the 3rd Maryland marched to relieve the 6th Massachusetts regiment for a tour of duty on the lines.

MAY 1783

UNIT	COMMANDING OFFICER	PRESENT FIT FOR DUTY & ON DUTY: COMMISSIONED OFFICERS	NONCOMMISSIONED OFFICERS	STAFF OFFICERS	RANK & FILE	TOTAL	RANK & FILE SICK, ON FURLOUGH, ETC.: SICK PRESENT	SICK ABSENT	ON COMMAND & EXTRA SERVICE	ON FURLOUGH	CONFINED	GRAND TOTAL	ALTERATIONS: DEATHS	DESERTED	TAKEN PRISONER	DISCHARGED	JOINED, ENLISTED, RECRUITED	LOCATION
FORCES UNDER COMMANDER-IN-CHIEF GENERAL GEORGE WASHINGTON																		
Det 3rd Md.	Maj. Thomas Lansdale	8	24	5	193	230	13	3	3			249	1	1		3		near Newburgh, N.Y.
N.J. regt.	Matthias Ogden	22 B	68	3	453	546	18	6	17	1		588	1	2		5		near Newburgh, N.Y.
N.J. bn.	Lt. Col. John Noble Cumming	12	29	4	174	219	13	6	5	1		244		1		6	1	near Newburgh, N.Y.
1st N.Y.	Goose Van Schaick	23	51	5 H	365	444	46	16	23		3	532		1		4	3	near Newburgh, N.Y.
2nd N.Y.	Philip Van Cortlandt	20	56	6	389	471	49	3	20			543		4		4	2	near Newburgh, N.Y.
1st Conn.	Zebulon Butler	15 C	59	5 I	343	422	62	10	24	14		532		4		13	3	West Point, N.Y.
3rd Conn.	Samuel Blatchley Webb	21	56	6	336	419	100	25	19	8		571		4		4	4	West Point, N.Y.
2nd Conn.	Heman Swift	19	59	5	402	485	56	8	23	2	2	576		7		2	2	West Point, N.Y.
1st Mass.	Joseph Vose	19	58	5	430	512	36	6	13		2	569		1		8	1	near Newburgh, N.Y.
4th Mass.	Henry Jackson	21 D	55	5 J	408	489	36	11	19	1		556		7		9	2	near Newburgh, N.Y.
7th Mass.	Lt. Col. John Brooks	21	51	6	438	516	27	6	17	1	1	568		2		2	6	near Newburgh, N.Y.
2nd Mass.	Lt. Col. Ebenezer Sprout	21	57	5	442	525	14	4	21			564	2	8		8	3	near Newburgh, N.Y.
5th Mass.	Lt. Col. David Cobb	18 E	56	5 K	428	507	32	7	16	3		565	2			5	5	near Newburgh, N.Y. O
8th Mass.	Michael Jackson	2	4	3	409	418	43	6	16	4		487	1			17	2	"on the Lines," N.Y.
3rd Mass.	Lt. Col. James Mellen	19 F	56	5 L	434	514	41	6	18			579				3	1	near Newburgh, N.Y.
6th Mass.	Benjamin Tupper	19	59	6	441	525	37	2	12			576		1		6	7	near Newburgh, N.Y.
N.H. regt.	Lt. Col. George Reid	16 G	57	5 M	429	507	73	9	22		2	613		17		2	2	near Newburgh, N.Y.
N.H. bn.	Maj. William Scott	6	24	5	160	195	15	3	7		3	223		10			1	near Newburgh, N.Y.
R.I.	Lt. Col. Jeremiah Olney	13	46	4	233	296	21	37	13		1	368		1		1		Albany, N.Y. area
Canadian	Brevet Brig. Gen. Moses Hazen	21	46	4	433	504	6	11	52	6	4	583	2	22				Pompton, N.J.
Officers present on duty		39	77	3		119						119						
TOTAL OF INFANTRY		375	1048	100	7340	8863	738	185	360	41	18	10205	9	93		102	45	
CAVALRY																		
2nd cont'l. A	Elisha Sheldon	6	51	3	192	252	6	1	34			293	1	3			1	Connecticut
Marechaussie	Capt. Bartholomew Von Heer																	
TOTAL OF CAVALRY		6	51	3	192	252	6	1	34			293	1	3			1	
ARTILLERY																		
2nd cont'l.	John Lamb	20	58	5	144	227	29	6	70		1	610		5		2	2	West Point, N.Y.
3rd cont'l.	John Crane	18	83	5	171	277												West Point, N.Y.
Present on duty		22	84		200	306						306						
TOTAL OF ARTILLERY		60	225	10	515	810	29	6	70		1	916		5		2	2	
SAPPERS AND MINERS																		
3 cos.		3	6		51	60	3	5	8			76				1		West Point, N.Y.
INVALIDS																		
Invalid corps	Lewis Nicola	5	26	5	134	170	22	37	78			307		3		15 N	1	West Point, N.Y.
TOTAL OF WASHINGTON'S ARMY		449	1356	118	8232	10155	798	234	550	41	19	11797	10	104		120	49	

BRIGADE: N.J. | N.Y. | Conn. | 1st Mass. | 2nd Mass. | 3rd Mass. | N.H.

OFFICERS SICK, ON FURLOUGH, ETC.	WASHINGTON'S ARMY			
	COMMISSIONED	NONCOMMISSIONED	STAFF	TOTAL
Sick Present	21	98	2	121
Sick Absent	25	21		46
On Command	39	43	2	84
On Extra Service		6		6
On Furlough	31	14	1	46
Absent without Leave	6			6
On the Staff	105			105
In Arrest or Confined	2	1		3
TOTAL	229	183	5	417

SOURCE OF THIS REPORT

1. MONTHLY RETURN OF THE CONTINENTAL ARMY UNDER THE COMMAND OF HIS EXCELLENCY GEORGE WASHINGTON... FOR THE MONTH OF MAY 1783, ELEPHANT FOLIO OF WASHINGTON RETURNS, WILLIAM L. CLEMENTS LIBRARY. [SOME SECTIONS OF THIS RETURN ARE ON THE FOLLOWING PAGE OF THE FOLIO.]

1a. Abstract of the Monthly Return of the Continental Army under... Washington... May 1783, Record Group 93, National Archives. [Contains the same figures, but only to the brigade level.]

A. The line for this unit is blank on the manuscript. The National Archives manuscript notes that no return for this unit had "come to hand."
B. Eleven commissioned officers in Lieutenant Colonel John Noble Cumming's New Jersey battalion plus one brigadier general for the entire brigade.
C. Twenty commissioned officers in Samuel Blatchley Webb's 3rd Connecticut regiment plus one brigadier general for the entire brigade.
D. Twenty commissioned officers in Lieutenant Colonel John Brooks' 7th Massachusetts regiment plus one brigadier general for the entire brigade.
E. One commissioned officer in Michael Jackson's 8th Massachusetts regiment plus one brigadier general for the entire brigade.
F. Eighteen commissioned officers in Benjamin Tupper's 6th Massachusetts regiment plus one brigadier general for the entire brigade.
G. Five commissioned officers in Major William Scott's New Hampshire battalion plus one brigadier general for the entire brigade.
H. Five staff officers in Philip Van Cortlandt's 2nd New York regiment plus one chaplain for the entire brigade.
I. Five staff officers in Samuel Blatchley Webb's 3rd Connecticut regiment plus one chaplain for the entire brigade.
J. Five staff officers in Lieutenant Colonel John Brooks' 7th Massachusetts regiment plus one chaplain for the entire brigade.
K. Two staff officers in Michael Jackson's 8th Massachusetts regiment plus one chaplain for the entire brigade.
L. Five staff officers in Benjamin Tupper's 6th Massachusetts regiment plus one chaplain for the entire brigade.
M. Four staff officers in Major William Scott's New Hampshire battalion plus one chaplain for the entire brigade.
N. Including eighty-seven men in Washington's infantry, one man in the sappers and miners, and fifteen men in the Invalid Corps discharged for inability.
O. On May 27 the 8th Massachusetts regiment marched to relieve the 2nd Massachusetts regiment for duty on the lines.

BRIGADE

JUNE 1783

UNIT	COMMANDING OFFICER	PRESENT FIT FOR DUTY & ON DUTY: COMMISSIONED OFFICERS	NONCOMMISSIONED OFFICERS	STAFF OFFICERS	RANK & FILE	TOTAL	RANK & FILE SICK, ON FURLOUGH, ETC.: SICK PRESENT	SICK ABSENT	ON COMMAND & EXTRA SERVICE	ON FURLOUGH	CONFINED			GRAND TOTAL	ALTERATIONS: DEATHS	DESERTED	TAKEN PRISONER	DISCHARGED	JOINED, ENLISTED, RECRUITED	LOCATION
FORCES UNDER COMMANDER-IN-CHIEF GENERAL GEORGE WASHINGTON [A]																				
Conn. regt.	Heman Swift	15	17	4	407	443	79	14	27	2	1			566		2		4	1	West Point, N.Y.
1st Mass. brig. [B]																				
2nd Mass. brig. [B]		16	32	5	505	558	29	95	675					1357					2	West Point, N.Y.
N.H. (5 cos.)	Lt. Col. George Reid	9	16	4	282	311	47	7	11					376		2		1		West Point, N.Y.
R.I. (2 cos.)	Lt. Col. Jeremiah Olney	5	8	2	79	94	8	13	3		1			119		1				Saratoga, N.Y.
Canadian [C]	Brevet Brig. Gen. Moses Hazen																			
Officers present on duty		17	33	1		51								51						
TOTAL OF INFANTRY		62	106	16	1273	1457	163	129	716	2	2			2469		5		5	3	
ARTILLERY																				
2nd cont'l. (2 cos.)	John Lamb	5	9	4	41	59	17	2	54		1			238		2		1		West Point, N.Y.
3rd cont'l. (3 cos.)	John Crane	7	19	4	75	105														West Point, N.Y.
Present on duty		10	20		84	114								114						
TOTAL OF ARTILLERY		22	48	8	200	278	17	2	54		1			352		2		1		
SAPPERS AND MINERS																				
Sapper and miner cos.	Capt. David Bushnell	1	1		16	18	1		1					20						West Point, N.Y.
TOTAL OF WASHINGTON'S ARMY		85	155	24	1489	1753	181	131	771	2	3			2760		7		6	3	

OFFICERS SICK, ON FURLOUGH, ETC.	WASHINGTON'S ARMY: COMMISSIONED	NONCOMMISSIONED	STAFF	TOTAL
Sick Present		9		9
Sick Absent	1	5		6
On Command	34	58	6	98
On Furlough	16	45	1	62
On the Staff	29			29
TOTAL	80	117	7	204

SOURCE OF THIS REPORT

1. ABSTRACT OF THE MONTHLY RETURN OF THE CONTINENTAL ARMY UNDER THE COMMAND OF HIS EXCELLENCY GEORGE WASHINGTON... FOR THE MONTH OF JUNE 1783, RECORD GROUP 93, NATIONAL ARCHIVES.

A. After the preliminary treaty of peace was ratified, the army became far smaller than on the previous return. The chief method of reducing the army was to send home all of the men who had enlisted for the war (with an appropriate proportion of officers) and to keep on those men who had enlisted for three years. Those sent home were not officially discharged, but were given certificates granting them a furlough which stated they would be discharged when the final treaty of peace was ratified. The men who were sent home, however, were no longer to be carried on returns and musters. Sheldon's cavalry was totally dissolved; those men in it who were enlisted for three years were given special personal furloughs by Washington. An option, which was little used, was offered to those who had enlisted for the war but did not want to be furloughed; they were allowed to stay on if they wished and their furloughs taken by three-year men.

B. In the reduction, the Massachusetts men were consolidated into four regiments. The 1st and 3rd of these reorganized Massachusetts regiments formed the first brigade and marched to Pennsylvania in response to mutinous activities in Philadelphia by some Pennsylvania soldiers. The manuscript notes this as an explanation of why no return was available. One of the Massachusetts regiments in the 2nd Massachusetts brigade and a detachment of artillery had also marched to Pennsylvania; this accounts for the large on command and extra service figures for those units on this report and on the July report. At this time there were also temporary detachments doing duty in the Newburgh area and in Westchester County, but these detachments were apparently not entered as "on Command" on the returns.

C. The line for this unit is blank on the manuscript.

JULY 1783

BRIGADE / UNIT	COMMANDING OFFICER	PRESENT FIT FOR DUTY & ON DUTY: COMMISSIONED OFFICERS	NONCOMMISSIONED OFFICERS	STAFF OFFICERS	RANK & FILE	TOTAL	RANK & FILE SICK, ON FURLOUGH, ETC.: SICK PRESENT	SICK ABSENT	ON COMMAND & EXTRA SERVICE	ON FURLOUGH	CONFINED			GRAND TOTAL	ALTERATIONS: DEATHS	DESERTED	TAKEN PRISONER	DISCHARGED	JOINED, ENLISTED, RECRUITED	LOCATION
FORCES UNDER COMMANDER-IN-CHIEF GENERAL GEORGE WASHINGTON																				
Conn. regt. A	Heman Swift	9	26	5	394	434	46	13	20		1			514		14		40	1	West Point, N.Y.
1st Mass. brig.																				Pennsylvania
2nd Mass. brig.		17	38	3	592	650	97	28	530					1305	1	4		47	1	West Point, N.Y.
N.H. (5 cos.) A	Lt. Col. George Reid	8	10	4	255	277	48	11	12		2			350	3	3		13	1	West Point, N.Y.
R.I. (2 cos.)	Lt. Col. Jeremiah Olney																			Saratoga, N.Y.
Officers present on duty		20	40	2		62								62						
TOTAL OF INFANTRY		54	114	14	1241	1423	191	52	562		3			2231	4	21		100	3	
ARTILLERY																				
2nd cont'l. (2 cos.)	John Lamb	6	12	4	51	73	10	2	53		2			242		1		1		West Point, N.Y.
3rd cont'l. (3 cos.)	John Crane	6	18	4	74	102										1		8		West Point, N.Y.
Present on duty		8	17		72	97								97						
TOTAL OF ARTILLERY		20	47	8	197	272	10	2	53		2			339		2		9		
SAPPERS AND MINERS																				
Sapper and miner cos.	Capt. David Bushnell	1	1		10	12	2		2		1			17		1		2		West Point, N.Y.
TOTAL OF WASHINGTON'S ARMY		75	162	22	1448	1707	203	54	617		6			2587	4	24		111 B	3	

OFFICERS SICK, ON FURLOUGH, ETC.	WASHINGTON'S ARMY (EXCEPT SAPPERS AND MINERS): COMMISSIONED	NONCOMMISSIONED	STAFF	TOTAL
Sick Present	4	8	1	13
Sick Absent		2		2
On Command	30	48	4	82
On Extra Service		1		1
On Furlough	5		1	6
On the Staff	28			28
TOTAL	67	59	6	132

SOURCE OF THIS REPORT

1. ABSTRACT OF THE MONTHLY RETURN OF THE CONTINENTAL ARMY UNDER THE COMMAND OF HIS EXCELLENCY GEORGE WASHINGTON. . . FOR THE MONTH OF JULY 1783, RECORD GROUP 93, NATIONAL ARCHIVES.

A. The manuscript notes that no returns were received for these units.
B. Including seventy-six men in Washington's infantry discharged for inability.

BIBLIOGRAPHY

Sources of Manuscript Strength Returns

Library of Congress
Peter Force Transcripts of Continental Army Returns
Nathanael Greene Papers

National Archives
Record Group 93 (War Department Collection of Revolutionary War Records)

Record Group 360 (Papers of the Continental Congress)

Archives Division, Commonwealth of Massachusetts
Massachusetts Archives

Massachusetts Historical Society
Benjamin Lincoln Papers

Timothy Pickering Papers

William Heath Papers

William L. Clements Library, University of Michigan
Adjutants General's Elephant Folio of Returns, 1778-1783

Sir Henry Clinton Papers

New-York Historical Society
Horatio Gates Papers

New York Public Library, Astor, Lenox, and Tilden Foundations
Philip Schuyler Papers
Emmet Collection

North Carolina Department of Archives and History
Military Collection

Bureau of Archives and History, Pennsylvania Historical and Museum Commission
Record Group 27 (Records of the Supreme Executive Council)

Historical Society of Pennsylvania
William Irvine Papers

Virginia State Library
James Wood Manuscripts

Printed Works

Although shelf upon shelf of published regimental histories exist for the American Civil War, very few such volumes are available for the War for Independence. Indeed, when Frederic Kidder published his *History of the First New Hampshire Regiment in the War of the Revolution* (Albany: Joel Munsell, 1868), he thought that he might have been writing the first history of a Revolutionary regiment. In the late 1920s Frank A. Gardner did a series of articles on individual Massachusetts regiments for the *Massachusetts Magazine* (Salem); earlier, Nathan Goold had written histories of a few other units (contained in the Maine Historical Society *Collections and Proceedings*, 2d ser., vols. 7-10). Although scattered efforts like these were of some assistance, we had to look elsewhere in our research to establish the complete, correct designations for regiments and their commanders and to find their locations at various monthly intervals. Much of the time we worked in primary materials; the Nathanael Greene Papers in the Clements Library and the Benjamin Lincoln Papers of the Massachusetts Historical Society (on microfilm) were our most frequent recourses among materials as yet unpublished. The Fitzpatrick edition of the letters of Washington will remain an indispensable resource (occasionally supplemented by the microfilm of the original manuscripts) until the new edition now in progress begins to appear. Many of the books that are useful in this kind of research have previously been utilized chiefly by genealogists. The next volume in our series will be a guide to the voluminous sources of biographical information on Revolutionary soldiers and sailors. Until that is complete, Appendix D in Gilbert H. Doane, *Searching for Your Ancestors*, 3d ed. (Minneapolis: University of Minnesota Press, 1960) is perhaps the best list of such materials. We found the following works of the greatest assistance in preparing this volume.

Berg, Fred Anderson. *Encyclopedia of Continental Army Units; Battalions, Regiments, and Independent Corps*. Harrisburg, Pa.: Stackpole Books, 1972.

Boatner, Mark Mayo, III. *Encyclopedia of the American Revolution*. New York: David McKay Co., 1966.

Burgess, Louis A., ed. *Virginia Soldiers of 1776, Compiled from Documents on File in the Virginia Land Office; Together with Material Found in the Archives Department of the Virginia State Library and Other Reliable Sources*. 3 vols. Richmond: Richmond Press, 1927-29; reprint ed., Baltimore: Genealogical Publishing Co., 1973.

Clark, Walter, ed. "Roster of the Continental Line from North Carolina, 1783." *State Records of North Carolina* 16: 1002-1197. Raleigh, 1899.

Clinton, George. *Public Papers of George Clinton, First Governor of New York*. Compiled by Hugh Hastings. War of the Revolution Series. 10 vols. Albany, 1899-1914.

Connecticut Historical Society. *Rolls and Lists of Connecticut Men in the Revolution, 1775-1783. Lists and Returns of Connecticut Men in the Revolution, 1775-1783*. Collections of the Connecticut Historical Society; vols. 8, 12. Hartford, 1901, 1909.

Cowell, Benjamin. *Spirit of '76 in Rhode Island: Or, Sketches of the Efforts of the Government and People in the War of the Revolution Together with the Names of Those Who Belonged to Rhode Island Regiments in the Army. With Biographical Notices, Reminiscences, &c., &c.* Boston: A.J. Wright, 1850; reprint ed., Baltimore: Genealogical Publishing Co., 1973.

Daughters of the American Revolution. *Lineage Book.* 170+ vols. Washington, D.C., 1890–.

Daughters of the American Revolution, North Carolina. *Roster of Soldiers from North Carolina in the American Revolution.* Durham: Daughters of the American Revolution, 1932.

Davis, Sallie Joyner. "North Carolina's Part in the Revolution." *South Atlantic Quarterly* 2: 314–24; 3: 27–38, 154–65.

Delaware. Public Archives Commission. *Delaware Archives.* Vols. 1–3. Wilmington, 1911–19.

Deutrich, Mabel E. *Struggle for Supremacy; The Career of General Fred C. Ainsworth.* Washington, D.C.: Public Affairs Press, 1962.

Deutrich, Mabel E., and Wehmann, Howard H. *Preliminary Inventory of the War Department Collection of Revolutionary War Records.* Washington: National Archives, 1970.

Fernow, Berthold, ed. *New York State Archives; New York in the Revolution.* Documents Relating to the Colonial History of the State of New York, vol. 15. Albany, 1887.

Fitzpatrick, John C., ed. *The Writings of George Washington.* 39 vols. Washington: Government Printing Office, 1931–44.

Flagg, C. A., and Waters, W. O. "Virginia's Soldiers in the Revolution; A Bibliography of Muster and Pay Rolls, Regimental Histories, etc. with Introductory and Explanatory Notes." *Virginia Magazine of History and Biography* 19: 402–14; 20: 52–68, 181–94, 267–81; 21: 337–46; 22: 57–67, 177–86.

Force, Peter, comp. *American Archives: Consisting of a Collection of Authentick Records, State Papers, Debates, and Letters and Other Notices of Publick Affairs. . . .* 9 vols. Washington: Peter Force, 1837–53.

France, Ministère des Affaires Étrangères. *Les Combattants Français de la Guerre Américaine, 1778–1783.* Paris: Ancienne Maison Quantin, 1903.

Gardner, Asa Bird. "The New York Continental Line in the Army of the Revolution." *Magazine of American History* 7: 401–19.

Gardner, Asa Bird. *The Rhode Island Line in the Continental Army, and Its Society of Cincinnati; A Paper Read before the Rhode Island Historical Society, April 30, 1878.* Providence: Providence Press Co., 1878.

Goodrich, John E. *Rolls of Soldiers in the Revolutionary War, 1775–1783.* Rutland, Vt.: Tuttle, Co., 1904.

Gwathmey, John Hastings. *Historical Register of Virginians in the Revolution; Soldiers, Sailors, Marines; 1775–1783.* Richmond: Deitz Press, 1938.

Hammond, Isaac W., ed. *Rolls and Documents Relating to the Soldiers in the Revolutionary War.* Provincial and State Papers of New Hampshire, vols. 14–17, 30. Concord, 1885–89, 1910.

Hatch, Louis Clinton. *The Administration of the American Revolutionary Army.* New York: Longmans, Green, and Co., 1904.

Heitman, Francis B. *Historical Register of Officers of the Continental Army during the War of the Revolution, April, 1775 to December, 1783*. 1893; reprint ed., with revisions and supplements of 1914 and 1932, Baltimore: Genealogical Publishing Co., 1973.

Johnston, Henry Phelps, ed. *The Record of Connecticut Men in the Military and Naval Service during the War of the Revolution, 1775-1783*. In Connecticut, Adjutant General's Office, *Record of Service of Connecticut Men in the I.—War of the Revolution, II.—War of 1812, III.—Mexican War*. Hartford: Case, Lockwood & Brainard Co., 1889.

Kapp, Friedrich. *The Life of Frederick William Von Steuben*. New York: Mason Bros., 1859.

Kellogg, Louise Phelps, ed. *Frontier Advance on the Upper Ohio, 1778-1779*. Publications of the State Historical Society of Wisconsin; Collections, vol. 23; Draper Series, vol. 4. Madison, 1916.

———. *Frontier Retreat on the Upper Ohio, 1779-1781*. Publications of the State Historical Society of Wisconsin; Collections, vol. 24; Draper Series, vol. 5, Madison, 1917.

Knight, Lucian Lamar, comp. *Georgia's Roster of the Revolution: Containing a List of the State's Defenders, Officers and Men, Soldiers and Sailors, Partisans and Regulars, Whether Enlisted from Georgia or Settled in Georgia after the Close of Hostilities*. Atlanta: Index Printing Co., 1920.

Lowrie, Walter, and Clarke, Matthew St. Clair, eds. *American State Papers: Military Affairs*. 7 vols. Washington: Gales and Seaton, 1832-61.

McCall, Mrs. Ettie (Tidwell). *Roster of Revolutionary Soldiers in Georgia*. Atlanta: G. T. Hancock for the Georgia Society, Daughters of the American Revolution, 1941; 3 vols., Baltimore: Genealogical Publishing Co., 1968-69. [Vol. 1, reprint; vols. 2-3 new.]

McCrady, Edward. *The History of South Carolina in the Revolution, 1775-1783*. 2 vols. New York: Macmillan Co., 1901-2; reprint ed., New York: Russell & Russell, 1969.

McIlwaine, Henry Read, gen. ed. *Official Letters of the Governors of the State of Virginia*. 3 vols. Richmond: Virginia State Library, 1926-29.

Maryland Historical Records Survey. *Calendar of the General Otho Holland Williams Papers in the Maryland Historical Society*. Baltimore: Maryland Historical Records Survey Project, 1940.

Maryland Historical Society. *Muster Rolls and Other Records of Service of Maryland Troops in the American Revolution, 1775-1783*. Archives of Maryland, vol. 18. Baltimore, 1900.

Massachusetts, Secretary of the Commonwealth. *Massachusetts Soldiers and Sailors of the Revolutionary War; A Compilation from the Archives*. 17 vols. Boston: Wright & Potter, 1896-1908.

New-York Historical Society. *Revolutionary Muster Rolls*. 2 vols. *Minutes of the Council of Appointment, 1778-1779*. Collections of the New-York Historical Society, Publication Fund Series; vols. 47-48, 58. New York; 1914-15, 1925.

New York (State), Secretary of State. *Calendar of Historical Manuscripts*

Relating to the War of the Revolution in the Office of the Secretary of State, Albany, N.Y. 2 vols. Albany: Weed, Parsons and Co., 1868.

Palmer, William P., ed. *Calendar of Virginia State Papers and Other Manuscripts Preserved in the Capitol at Richmond.* Vols. 1-3. Richmond, 1875-83.

Peckham, Howard H. *The War for Independence; A Military History.* Chicago and London: University of Chicago Press, 1958.

Pennsylvania Archives. Philadelphia, 1852-56; Harrisburg, 1874-; especially ser. 2, 5, 6, and 7.

Rankin, Hugh F. *The North Carolina Continentals.* Chapel Hill: University of North Carolina Press, 1971.

Reed, William B. *Life and Correspondence of Joseph Reed.* 2 vols. Philadelphia: Lindsay and Blackiston, 1847.

Roberts, James A., comp. *New York in the Revolution as Colony and State.* 2d ed. Albany: Brandow Printing Co., 1898.

Simes, Thomas. *The Military Guide for Young Officers.* 2 vols. Philadelphia: J. Humphreys, R. Bell, and R. Aitken, 1776.

Smith, Justin H. *Our Struggle for the Fourteenth Colony; Canada and the American Revolution.* 2 vols. New York and London: G. P. Putnam's Sons, 1907.

Steuart, Reiman. *A History of the Maryland Line in the Revolutionary War, 1775-1783.* Society of the Cincinnati of Maryland, 1969.

Stryker, William S., comp. *Official Register of the Officers and Men of New Jersey in the Revolutionary War.* Trenton: Wm. T. Nicholson & Co., 1872. (Also, New Jersey Historical Records Survey Program. *Index of the Official Register of the Officers and Men of New Jersey in the Revolutionary War.* Newark, 1941; reprint ed., Baltimore: Genealogical Publishing Co., 1965.)

Thwaites, Reuben Gold and Kellogg, Louise Phelps, eds. *Frontier Defense on the Upper Ohio, 1777-1778.* Draper Series, vol. 3. Madison: Wisconsin Historical Society, 1912.

———, eds. *The Revolution on the Upper Ohio, 1775-1777.* Draper Series, vol. 2. Madison: Wisconsin Historical Society, 1908.

U.S. Continental Congress. *Journals of the Continental Congress, 1774-1789.* Washington: Government Printing Office, 1904-37.

———. *Rules and Articles for the Better Government of the Troops Raised, or to be raised, and kept in pay by and at the joint Expence of the Twelve United English Colonies of North America.* Philadelphia: William and Thomas Bradford, 1775.

———. *Rules and Articles for the Better Government of the Troops Raised or to be Raised and kept in Pay by and at the Expense of the United States of America.* Philadelphia: John Dunlap, 1776.

U.S. Register of the Treasury. *Statements of the Receipts and Expenditures of Public Monies, During the Administration of the Finances by Robert Morris, Esquire, Late Superintendent of Finances; with Other Extracts and Accounts from the Public Records....* Philadelphia: Francis Childs and John Swaine, 1791.

Ward, Christopher L. *The Delaware Continentals, 1776–1783.* Wilmington: Historical Society of Delaware, 1941.

——. *The War of the Revolution.* Edited by John R. Alden. 2 vols. New York: Macmillan Co., 1952.

Young, Gordon R., ed. *The Army Almanac: A Book of Facts Concerning the Army of the United States.* 2d ed. Harrisburg, Pa.: Stackpole Co., 1952.